Avizandum Legislation on

The Scots Law of Obligations

Seventh edition

Editor

Laura J Macgregor LLB, LLM, DipLP
Professor of Commercial Contract Law,
University of Edinburgh

Avizandum Publishing Ltd
Edinburgh
2015

Published by
Avizandum Publishing Ltd
58 Candlemaker Row
Edinburgh EH1 2QE

First published 2003
2nd edition   2005
3rd edition   2007
4th edition   2009
5th edition   2011
Reprinted   2013
6th edition   2013
7th edition   2015

ISBN 1-904968-71-9

British Library Cataloguing in Publication Data
A catalogue record for this book is available from the British Library

Typeset by AFS Image Setters Ltd, Glasgow
Printed and bound by Bell & Bain Ltd, Glasgow

EDITOR'S PREFACE

The aim in producing this seventh edition of *Legislation on the Scots Law of Obligations* remains unchanged: in making her selection, the editor hopes to produce a comprehensive set of materials to support the study of the law of obligations whilst at the same time keeping the purchase price at a reasonable level.

From edition to edition, new content often concerns either the law of sale or the law of unfair contract terms. The approach to the teaching of both these subjects varies amongst the Scottish Law Schools. They may be taught either as part of a course on the law of obligations or as part of a course on commercial law. Bearing in mind this difference of approach, each successive edition of *Legislation on the Scots Law of Obligations* has included all such material.

The most significant new Act contained in this edition impacts on the law of sale of goods and unfair terms in so far as they affect consumers. This is the Consumer Rights Act 2015. With most of its provisions due to come into force on 1 October 2015, this Act implements certain of the provisions of the Consumer Rights Directive (2011/83/EU) and replaces the Unfair Terms in Consumer Contracts Regulations 1999. According to the Act's Explanatory Notes (para 3) it 'sets out a framework that consolidates in one place key consumer rights concerning contracts for goods, services, digital content and the law relating to unfair terms in consumer contracts'.

Also relevant (and included in this edition) are the Consumer Contracts (Information Cancellation and Additional Charges) Regulations 2013. These regulations contain important consumer protection measures such as traders' obligations to provide information to consumers in relation to goods or services purchased, the passing of risk, and cancellation rights. Finally, the Consumer Protection (Amendment) Regulations 2014 have amended the Consumer Protection from Unfair Trading Regulations 2008 by inserting a new part 4A, entitled Consumer's Rights to Redress. Now, the consumer will have much stronger remedies in relation to unfair commercial practices, including for example misleading advertising, high pressure selling and misleading and dishonest mailings to consumers. Clearly, although the Consumer Rights Act 2015 has simplified the law applying to consumers, it has not consolidated all consumer legislation into one statutory source. This complexity of sources has led some commentators to explore the idea of a statutory restatement.[1]

For *non-consumer* issues the Sale of Goods Act 1979 and Unfair Contract Terms Act 1977 remain the most important statutory sources. Certain provisions of the Sale of Goods Act 1979 will continue to apply to all sales contracts, regardless of whether they are consumer or non-consumer, for example, the provisions relating to the passing of property in goods.

Turning to Scottish rather than UK legislation, this edition includes the new Legal Writings (Counterparts and Delivery) (Scotland) Act 2015. This legislation is likely to be of significant practical use to Scottish solicitors, simplifying the process of conclusion of contracts.

I welcome suggestions on what to include in successive editions of this work. (Please send any suggestions to l.macgregor@ed.ac.uk.) Several of my friends from my own and other Scottish universities have provided helpful suggestions as to the content of this edition. I would therefore like to express my sincere

---

[1] See, eg, C Twigg-Flesner, 'Some Thoughts on Consumer Law Reform: Consolidation, Codification or a Restatement?' in L Gullifer and S Vogenauer (eds) *English and European Perspectives on Contract and Commercial Law* (2014, Hart Publishing) 66 at 79.

thanks to Gordon Cameron, Fraser Davidson, Martin Hogg, Hector MacQueen, Elspeth Reid, Dot Reid, and Tikus Little in this respect. Sincere thanks are also due to Mary Jane Bennett and Margaret Cherry of Avizandum for their hard work in the production process.

Laura Macgregor
Edinburgh
August 2015

CONTENTS

PART I

STATUTES

LAWBURROWS ACT 1429
(1429, c 20)

Item It is statute ande ordanit that gif ony of the kingis liegis haf ony doute of his life outhir be dede or manance or violent presumpcioun ande he ask souerte of thaim that he doutis the schiref sal tak souerte of the party that the complante is maid apoun sa that the party playntife mak prufe of the dede or of manance or of the violent presumpcioun maid or done till hym [. . .].

LAWBURROWS ACT 1581
(1581, c 22)

Oure souerane lord with aduise of his thre estatis in this present parliament Ordanis that all letteris of lawborrowis salbe direct in tyme cuming at the instance of the pairteis complenand chargeing the personis complenit vpoun to find sicker souertie and lawborrowis that the complenaris thair wyffis bairnis tenentis and seruandis salbe harmeles and skaithles in thair bodeis landis takkis possessionis guidis and geir and on na wayis to be molestit or trublit thairin be the personis complenit vpoun nor na vtheris of thair causing sending hunding out resetting command assistance and ratihabitioun quhome thai may stop or let direclie or indireclie vthirwayis nor be the ordoure of law and justice vnder greit panes to be modifeit be the [. . .] ordinar Judges Be quhome in caise the said lawborrowis salbe dewlie tryit to be brokin the ane half of the pane sall pertene to oure souerane lord and the vthair half to the pairte grevit according to the effect and meaning of the said act maid to that effect of befoir.

COMPENSATION ACT 1592
(1592, c 61)

Oure Sourane Lord and estaitis of parliament statutis and Ordanis that ony debt de liquido ad liquidum instantlie verifiet be wreit or aith of the partie befoir the geving of decreit be admittit be all Jugis within this realme be way of exceptioun Bot nocht eftir the geving thairof In the suspensioun or in reductioun of the same decreit.

PARLIAMENTARY PAPERS ACT 1840
(3 & 4 Vict, c 9)

1 Proceedings, criminal or civil, against persons for publication of papers printed by order of Parliament, to be stayed upon delivery of a certificate and affidavit to the effect that such publication is by order of either House of Parliament
It shall and may be lawful for any person or persons who now is or are, or here-after shall be, a defendant or defendants in any civil or criminal proceeding com-

menced or prosecuted in any manner soever, for or on account or in respect of the publication of any such report, paper, votes, or proceedings by such person or persons, or by his, her, or their servant or servants, by or under the authority of either House of Parliament, to bring before the court in which such proceeding shall have been or shall be so commenced or prosecuted, or before any judge of the same (if one of the superior courts at Westminster), first giving twenty-four hours notice of his intention so to do to the prosecutor or plaintiff in such proceeding, a certificate under the hand of [the Speaker of the House of Lords], or of the clerk of the Parliaments, or of the speaker of the House of Commons, or of the clerk of the same house, stating that the report, paper, votes, or proceedings, as the case may be, in respect whereof such civil or criminal proceeding shall have been commenced or prosecuted, was published by such person or persons, or by his, her, or their servant or servants, by order or under the authority of the House of Lords or of the House of Commons, as the case may be, together with an affidavit verifying such certificate; and such court or judge shall thereupon immediately stay such civil or criminal proceeding; and the same, and every writ or process issued therein, shall be and shall be deemed and taken to be finally put an end to, determined, and superseded by virtue of this Act.

2 Proceedings to be stayed when commenced in respect of a copy of an authenticated report, &c

And be it enacted, that in case of any civil or criminal proceeding hereafter to be commenced or prosecuted for or on account or in respect of the publication of any copy of such report, paper, votes, or proceedings, it shall be lawful for the defendant or defendants at any stage of the proceedings to lay before the court or judge such report, paper, votes, or proceedings, and such copy, with an affidavit verifying such report, paper, votes, or proceedings, and the correctness of such copy, and the court or judge shall immediately stay such civil or criminal proceeding; and the same, and every writ or process issued therein, shall be and shall be deemed and taken to be finally put an end to, determined, and superseded by virtue of this Act.

3 In proceedings for printing any extract or abstract of a paper, it may be shewn that such extract was bonâ fide made

And be it enacted, that it shall be lawful in any civil or criminal proceeding to be commenced or prosecuted for printing any extract from or abstract of such report, paper, votes, or proceedings, to give in evidence [. . .] such report, paper, votes, or proceedings, and to show that such extract or abstract was published bonâ fide and without malice; and if such shall be the opinion of the jury, a verdict of not guilty shall be entered for the defendant or defendants.

4 Act not to affect the privileges of Parliament

Provided always, and it is hereby expressly declared and enacted, that nothing herein contained shall be deemed or taken, or held or construed, directly or indirectly, by implication or otherwise, to affect the privileges of Parliament in any manner whatsoever.

TRESPASS (SCOTLAND) ACT 1865
(1865, c lvi)

1 Short Title
This Act may be cited for all Purposes as 'The Trespass (Scotland) Act, 1865.'

2 Interpretation of Terms
In this Act the following Words shall have the Meanings hereby assigned to them:

'Premises' shall mean and include any House, Barn, Stable, Shed, Loft, Granary, Outhouse, Garden, Stackyard, Court, Close, or inclosed Place:

'Magistrate' shall mean and include the [sheriff principal and sheriff], or any One or more Justice or Justices of the Peace, or any One or more Magistrate or Magistrates, having Jurisdiction respectively in the County or Burgh where any Offence against the Provisions of this Act is committed, or where any Person charged with such Offence is found or brought to Trial:

'Procurator Fiscal' shall mean and include the Procurator Fiscal of the Court having such Jurisdiction.

['Road' shall mean and include any way, other than—
  (a) a waterway; or
  (b) without prejudice to section 100(c) (damage to roads by fire) or 129(4) (camping in a road) of the Roads (Scotland) Act 1984, a road within the meaning of that Act.]

3 Parties lodging in Premises or encamping on Land, without Permission, guilty of an Offence
[(1)] Every Person who lodges in any Premises, or occupies or encamps on any Land, being private Property, without the Consent and Permission of the Owner or legal Occupier of such Premises or Land, and every Person who encamps or lights a Fire on or near any [. . .] Road or inclosed or cultivated Land, or in or near any Plantation, without the Consent and Permission of the Owner or Legal Occupier of such Road, Land, or Plantation, [. . .] shall be guilty of an Offence punishable as herein-after provided.

[(2) Subsection (1) above does not extend to anything done by a person in the exercise of the access rights created by the Land Reform (Scotland) Act 2003 (asp 2).]

4 Apprehension and Punishment of Offenders
Every Person who commits any Offence against the Provisions of this Act may, if found in the Act of committing the same by any Officer of Police or Constable, be apprehended by such Officer or Constable, and detained in any Prison, Police Station, Lock-up, or other Place of safe Custody, and not later than in the course of the next lawful Day after he shall have been so taken into Custody shall be brought before a Magistrate; and every Person charged with the Commission of any such Offence may, if not so taken into Custody, or if he shall have been liberated on Bail or Pledge, be summoned to appear before a Magistrate [; and every person committing an offence against the provisions of this Act shall be liable, on summary conviction, to a fine not exceeding level 1 on the standard scale.]

5 As to Prosecutions under Act
Every Prosecution for an Offence against the Provisions of this Act shall be raised and proceeded in at the Instance of the Procurator Fiscal, and shall be heard and determined by One or more Magistrate or Magistrates in a summary Form; and every such Prosecution shall be commenced within One Month after the Offence has been committed.

BILLS OF EXCHANGE ACT 1882
(1882, c 61)

3 Bill of exchange defined

(1) A bill of exchange is an unconditional order in writing, addressed by one person to another, signed by the person giving it, requiring the person to whom it is addressed to pay on demand or at a fixed or determinable future time a sum certain in money to or to the order of a specified person, or to bearer.

(2) An instrument which does not comply with these conditions, or which orders any act to be done in addition to the payment of money, is not a bill of exchange.

(3) An order to pay out of a particular fund is not unconditional within the meaning of this section; but an unqualified order to pay, coupled with (a) an indication of a particular fund out of which the drawee is to re-imburse himself or a particular account to be debited with the amount, or (b) a statement of the transaction which gives rise to the bill, is unconditional.

(4) A bill is not invalid by reason—

(a) That it is not dated;

(b) That it does not specify the value given, or that any value has been given therefor;

(c) That it does not specify the place where it is drawn or the place where it is payable.

73 Cheque defined

A cheque is a bill of exchange drawn on a banker payable on demand. Except as otherwise provided in this Part, the provisions of this Act applicable to a bill of exchange payable on demand apply to a cheque.

83 Promissory note defined

(1) A promissory note is an unconditional promise in writing made by one person to another signed by the maker, engaging to pay, on demand, or at a fixed or determinable future time, a sum certain in money, to, or to the order of, a specified person or to bearer.

(2) An instrument in the form of a note payable to maker's order is not a note within the meaning of this section unless and until it is indorsed by the maker.

(3) A note is not invalid by reason only that it contains also a pledge of collateral security with authority to sell or dispose thereof.

(4) A note which is, or on the face of it purports to be, both made and payable within the British Islands is an inland note. Any other note is a foreign note.

FACTORS ACT 1889
(1889, c 45)

Preliminary

1 Definitions

For the purposes of this Act—

(1) The expression 'mercantile agent' shall mean a mercantile agent having in the customary course of his business as such agent authority either to sell goods or to consign goods for the purpose of sale, or to buy goods, or to raise money on the security of goods:

(2) A person shall be deemed to be in possession of goods or of the documents of title to goods, where the goods or documents are in his actual custody or are held by any other person subject to his control or for him or on his behalf:

(3) The expression 'goods' shall include wares and merchandise:

(4) The expression 'document of title' shall include any bill of lading, dock warrant, warehouse-keeper's certificate, and warrant or order for the delivery of

goods, and any other document used in the ordinary course of business as proof of the possession or control of goods, or authorising or purporting to authorise, either by endorsement or by delivery, the possessor of the document to transfer or receive goods thereby represented:

(5)   The expression 'pledge' shall include any contract pledging, or giving a lien or security on, goods, whether in consideration of an original advance or of any further or continuing advance or of any pecuniary liability:

(6)   The expression 'person' shall include any body of persons corporate or unincorporate.

Dispositions by mercantile agents

2   Powers of mercantile agent with respect to disposition of goods

(1)   Where a mercantile agent is, with the consent of the owner, in possession of goods or of the documents of title to goods, any sale, pledge, or other disposition of the goods, made by him when acting in the ordinary course of business of a mercantile agent, shall, subject to the provisions of this Act, be as valid as if he were expressly authorised by the owner of the goods to make the same; provided that the person taking under the disposition acts in good faith, and has not at the time of the disposition notice that the person making the disposition has not authority to make the same.

(2)   Where a mercantile agent has, with the consent of the owner, been in possession of goods or of the documents of title to goods, any sale, pledge, or other disposition, which would have been valid if the consent had continued, shall be valid notwithstanding the determination of the consent; provided that the person taking under the disposition has not at the time thereof notice that the consent has been determined.

(3)   Where a mercantile agent has obtained possession of any documents of title to goods by reason of his being or having been, with the consent of the owner, in possession of the goods represented thereby, or of any other documents of title to the goods, his possession of the first-mentioned documents shall, for the purposes of this Act, be deemed to be with the consent of the owner.

(4)   For the purposes of this Act the consent of the owner shall be presumed in the absence of evidence to the contrary.

3   Effect of pledges of documents of title

A pledge of the documents of title to goods shall be deemed to be a pledge of the goods.

4   Pledge for antecedent debt

Where a mercantile agent pledges goods as security for a debt or liability due from the pledgor to the pledgee before the time of the pledge, the pledgee shall acquire no further right to the goods than could have been enforced by the pledgor at the time of the pledge.

5   Rights acquired by exchange of goods or documents

The consideration necessary for the validity of a sale, pledge, or other disposition of goods, in pursuance of this Act, may be either a payment in cash, or the delivery or transfer of other goods, or of a document of title to goods, or of a negotiable security, or any other valuable consideration; but where goods are pledged by a mercantile agent in consideration of the delivery or transfer of other goods, or of a document of title to goods, or of a negotiable security, the pledgee shall acquire no right or interest in the goods so pledged in excess of the value of the goods, documents, or security when so delivered or transferred in exchange.

6   Agreements through clerks, &c

For the purposes of this Act an agreement made with a mercantile agent through a clerk or other person authorised in the ordinary course of business to make contracts of sale or pledge on his behalf shall be deemed to be an agreement with the agent.

7 Provisions as to consignors and consignees

(1) Where the owner of goods has given possession of the goods to another person for the purpose of consignment or sale, or has shipped the goods in the name of another person, and the consignee of the goods has not had notice that such person is not the owner of the goods, the consignee shall, in respect of advances made to or for the use of such person, have the same lien on the goods as if such person were the owner of the goods, and may transfer any such lien to another person.

(2) Nothing in this section shall limit or affect the validity of any sale, pledge, or disposition, by a mercantile agent.

Dispositions by sellers and buyers of goods

8 Disposition by seller remaining in possession

Where a person, having sold goods, continues, or is, in possession of the goods or of the documents of title to the goods, the delivery or transfer by that person, or by a mercantile agent acting for him, of the goods or documents of title under any sale, pledge, or other disposition thereof, or under any agreement for sale, pledge, or other disposition thereof, to any person receiving the same in good faith and without notice of the previous sale, shall have the same effect as if the person making the delivery or transfer were expressly authorised by the owner of the goods to make the same.

9 Disposition by buyer obtaining possession

Where a person, having bought or agreed to buy goods, obtains with the consent of the seller possession of the goods or the documents of title to the goods, the delivery or transfer, by that person or by a mercantile agent acting for him, of the goods or documents of title under any sale, pledge, or other disposition thereof, or under any agreement for sale, pledge, or other disposition thereof, to any person receiving the same in good faith and without notice of any lien or other right of the original seller in respect of the goods, shall have the same effect as if the person making the delivery or transfer were a mercantile agent in possession of the goods or documents of title with the consent of the owner.

[For the purposes of this section—

(i) the buyer under a conditional sale agreement shall be deemed not to be a person who has bought or agreed to buy goods, and

(ii) 'conditional sale agreement' means an agreement for the sale of goods which is a consumer credit agreement within the meaning of the Consumer Credit Act 1974 under which the purchase price or part of it is payable in instalments, and the property in the goods is to remain in the seller (notwithstanding that the buyer is to be in possession of the goods) until such conditions as to the payment of instalments or otherwise as may be specified in the agreement are fulfilled.]

10 Effect of transfer of documents on vendor's lien or right of stoppage in transitu

Where a document of title to goods has been lawfully transferred to a person as a buyer or owner of the goods, and that person transfers the document to a person who takes the document in good faith and for valuable consideration, the last-mentioned transfer shall have the same effect for defeating any vendor's lien or right of stoppage in transitu as the transfer of a bill of lading has for defeating the right of stoppage in transitu.

Supplemental

11 Mode of transferring documents

For the purposes of this Act, the transfer of a document may be by endorsement, or, where the document is by custom or by its express terms transferable by delivery or makes the goods deliverable to the bearer, then by delivery.

12 Saving for rights of true owner

(1) Nothing in this Act shall authorise an agent to exceed or depart from his authority as between himself and his principal, or exempt him from any liability, civil or criminal, for so doing.

(2) Nothing in this Act shall prevent the owner of goods from recovering the goods from any agent or his trustee in bankruptcy at any time before the sale or pledge thereof, or shall prevent the owner of goods pledged by an agent from having the right to redeem the goods at any time before the sale thereof, on satisfying the claim for which the goods were pledged, and paying to the agent, if by him required, any money in respect of which the agent would by law be entitled to retain the goods or the documents of title thereto, or any of them, by way of lien as against the owner, or from recovering from any person with whom the goods have been pledged any balance of money remaining in his hands as the produce of the sale of the goods after deducting the amount of his lien.

(3) Nothing in this Act shall prevent the owner of goods sold by an agent from recovering from the buyer the price agreed to be paid for the same, or any part of that price, subject to any right of set off on the part of the buyer against the agent.

13 Saving for common law powers of agent

The provisions of this Act shall be construed in amplification and not in derogation of the powers exercisable by an agent independently of this Act.

[. . .]

16 Extent of Act

This Act shall not extend to Scotland.

17 Short title

This Act may be cited as the Factors Act, 1889.

FACTORS (SCOTLAND) ACT 1890
(1890, c 40)

1 Application of 52 & 53 Vict c 45 to Scotland

Subject to the following provisions, the Factors Act, 1889, shall apply to Scotland:—

(1) The expression 'lien' shall mean and include right of retention; the expression 'vendor's lien' shall mean and include any right of retention competent to the original owner or vendor; and the expression 'set off' shall mean and include compensation.

(2) In the application of section five of the recited Act, a sale, pledge, or other disposition of goods shall not be valid unless made for valuable consideration.

2 Short title

This Act may be cited as the Factors (Scotland) Act, 1890.

LAW REFORM (MISCELLANEOUS PROVISIONS) (SCOTLAND) ACT 1940
(1940, c 42)

1 Amendment of the law as to enforcement of decrees ad factum praestandum

(1) No person shall be apprehended or imprisoned on account of his failure to

comply with a decree ad factum praestandum except in accordance with the following provisions—

    (i) On an application by the person in right of such a decree (hereinafter referred to as the applicant) to the court by which the decree was granted, the court may, if it is satisfied that the person against whom such decree was granted (hereinafter referred to as the respondent) is wilfully refusing to comply with the decree, grant warrant for his imprisonment for any period not exceeding six months;

    (ii) Where the court is satisfied that a person undergoing imprisonment in pursuance of a warrant granted under this section has complied, or is no longer wilfully refusing to comply, with the decree, the court shall, notwithstanding any period specified in the warrant, order the immediate liberation of such person, and it shall be the duty of the applicant, as soon as he is satisfied that the decree has been complied with, forthwith to inform the clerk of the court of such compliance;

    (iii) Imprisonment under a warrant granted under this subsection shall not operate to extinguish the obligation imposed by the decree on which the application proceeds;

    (iv) The person on whose application a warrant for imprisonment has been granted under this subsection shall not be liable to aliment, or to contribute to the aliment of, the respondent while in prison.

(2) On any application in pursuance of the foregoing subsection, the court may, in lieu of granting warrant for imprisonment, recall the decree on which the application proceeds and make an order for the payment by the respondent to the applicant of a specified sum or make such other order as appears to the court to be just and equitable in the circumstances, including, in the case where the decree on which the application proceeds is a decree for delivery of corporeal moveables, a warrant to officers of court to search any premises in the occupation of the respondent or of such other person as may be named in the warrant, and to take possession of, and deliver to the applicant, any such moveables which may be found in such premises.

(3) Any warrant granted under the last foregoing subsection shall be deemed to include authority to open shut and lockfast places for the purpose of carrying the warrant into lawful execution.

3 Contribution among joint wrongdoers

(1) Where in any action of damages in respect of loss or damage arising from any wrongful acts or negligent acts or omissions two or more persons are, in pursuance of the verdict of a jury or the judgment of a court found jointly and severally liable in damages or expenses, they shall be liable *inter se* to contribute to such damages or expenses in such proportions as the jury or the court, as the case may be, may deem just: Provided that nothing in this subsection shall affect the right of the person to whom such damages or expenses have been awarded to obtain a joint and several decree therefor against the persons so found liable.

(2) Where any person has paid any damages or expenses in which he has been found liable in any such action as aforesaid, he shall be entitled to recover from any other person who, if sued, might also have been held liable in respect of the loss or damage on which the action was founded, such contribution, if any, as the court may deem just.

(3) Nothing in this section shall—

    (a) apply to any action in respect of loss or damage suffered before the commencement of this Act; or

    (b) affect any contractual or other right of relief or indemnity or render enforceable any agreement for indemnity which could not have been enforced if this section had not been enacted.

LAW REFORM (CONTRIBUTORY NEGLIGENCE) ACT 1945
(1945, c 28)

1 Apportionment of liability in case of contributory negligence

(1) Where any person suffers damage as the result partly of his own fault and partly of the fault of any other person or persons, a claim in respect of that damage shall not be defeated by reason of the fault of the person suffering the damage, but the damages recoverable in respect thereof shall be reduced to such extent as the court thinks just and equitable having regard to the claimant's share in the responsibility for the damage:

Provided that—

(a) this subsection shall not operate to defeat any defence arising under a contract;

(b) where any contract or enactment providing for the limitation of liability is applicable to the claim, the amount of damages recoverable by the claimant by virtue of this subsection shall not exceed the maximum limit so applicable.

(2) Where damages are recoverable by any person by virtue of the foregoing subsection subject to such reduction as is therein mentioned, the court shall find and record the total damages which would have been recoverable if the claimant had not been at fault.

[. . .]

(4) Where any person dies as the result partly of his own fault and partly of the fault of any other person or persons, a claim by any dependant of the first mentioned person for damages or solatium in respect of that person's death shall not be defeated by reason of his fault, but the damages or solatium recoverable shall be reduced to such extent as the court thinks just and equitable having regard to the share of the said person in the responsibility for his death.

(5) Where, in any case to which subsection (1) of this section applies, one of the persons at fault avoids liability to any other such person or his personal representative by pleading the Limitation Act, 1939, or any other enactment limiting the time within which proceedings may be taken, he shall not be entitled to recover any damages [or contributions] from that other person or representative by virtue of the said subsection.

(6) Where any case to which subsection (1) of this section applies is tried with a jury, the jury shall determine the total damages which would have been recoverable if the claimant had not been at fault and the extent to which those damages are to be reduced.

[. . .]

3 Saving for Maritime Conventions Act, 1911, and past cases

(1) This Act shall not apply to any claim to which section one of the Maritime Conventions Act, 1911, applies and that Act shall have effect as if this Act had not passed.

(2) This Act shall not apply to any case where the acts or omissions giving rise to the claim occurred before the passing of this Act.

4 Interpretation

The following expressions have the meanings hereby respectively assigned to them, that is to say—

'court' means, in relation to any claim, the court or arbitrator by or before whom the claim falls to be determined;

'damage' includes loss of life and personal injury;

[. . .]

'fault' means negligence, breach of statutory duty or other act or omission which gives rise to a liability in tort or would, apart from this Act, give rise to the defence of contributory negligence.

5 Application to Scotland

In the application of this Act to Scotland—

(a) the expression 'dependant' means, in relation to any person, any person who would in the event of such first mentioned person's death through the fault of a third party be entitled to sue that third party for damages or solatium; and the expression 'fault' means wrongful act, breach of statutory duty or negligent act or omission which gives rise to liability in damages, or would apart from this Act, give rise to the defence of contributory negligence;

[(b) section 3 of the Law Reform (Miscellaneous Provisions) (Scotland) Act 1940 (contribution among joint wrongdoers) shall apply in any case where two or more persons are liable, or would if they had all been sued be liable, by virtue of section 1(1) of this Act in respect of the damage suffered by any person;]

(c) [substitutes s 1(4) above]

6 [Northern Ireland provisions]

7 Short title and extent

This Act may be cited as the Law Reform (Contributory Negligence) Act, 1945.

DEFAMATION ACT 1952
(1952, c 66)

3 Actions for verbal injury

In any action for verbal injury it shall not be necessary for the pursuer to aver or prove special damage if the words on which the action is founded are calculated to cause pecuniary damage to the pursuer.

[. . .]

5 Justification

In an action for libel or slander in respect of words containing two or more distinct charges against the plaintiff, a defence of justification shall not fail by reason only that the truth of every charge is not proved if the words not proved to be true do not materially injure the plaintiff's reputation having regard to the truth of the remaining charges.

6 Fair comment

In an action for libel or slander in respect of words consisting partly of allegations of fact and partly of expression of opinion, a defence of fair comment shall not fail by reason only that the truth of every allegation or fact is not proved if the expression of opinion is fair comment having regard to such of the facts alleged or referred to in the words complained of as are proved.

[. . .]

9 Extension of certain defences to broadcasting

(1) Section three of the Parliamentary Papers Act, 1840 (which confers protection in respect of proceedings for printing extracts from or abstracts of parliamentary papers) shall have effect as if the reference to printing included a reference to broadcasting by means of wireless telegraphy.

[. . .]

10 Limitation on privilege at elections

A defamatory statement published by or on behalf of a candidate in any election to a local government authority [, to the National Assembly for Wales, to the Scottish Parliament] or to Parliament shall not be deemed to be published on a privileged occasion on the ground that it is material to a question in issue in the election, whether or not the person by whom it is published is qualified to vote at the election.

11 Agreements for indemnity
An agreement for indemnifying any person against civil liability for libel in respect of the publication of any matter shall not be unlawful unless at the time of the publication that person knows that the matter is defamatory, and does not reasonably believe that there is a good defence to any action brought upon it.

12 Evidence of other damages recovered by plaintiff
In any action for libel or slander the defendant may give evidence in mitigation of damages that the plaintiff has recovered damages, or has brought actions for damages, for libel or slander in respect of the publication of words to the same effect as the words on which the action is founded, or has received or agreed to receive compensation in respect of any such publication.

14 Application of Act to Scotland
This Act shall apply to Scotland subject to the following modifications, that is to say—
(a)   sections one, two, eight and thirteen shall be omitted;
(b)   [*substitute s 3 for Scotland*]
[. . .]
(d)   for any reference to libel, or to libel or slander, there shall be substituted a reference to defamation; the expression 'plaintiff' means pursuer; the expression 'defendant' means defender; for any reference to an affidavit made by any person there shall be substituted a reference to a written declaration signed by that person; for any reference to the High Court there shall be substituted a reference to the Court of Session or, if an action of defamation is depending in the sheriff court in respect of the publication in question, the sheriff; the expression 'costs' means expenses; and for any reference to a defence of justification there shall be substituted a reference to a defence of veritas.

16 Interpretation
(1)   Any reference in this Act to words shall be construed as including a reference to pictures, visual images, gestures and other methods of signifying meaning.
[. . .]

INTEREST ON DAMAGES (SCOTLAND) ACT 1958
(1958, c 61)

1 Power of courts to grant interest on damages
(1)   [Where a court pronounces an interlocutor decerning for payment by any person of a sum of money as damages, the interlocutor may include decree for payment by that person of interest, at such rate or rates as may be specified in the interlocutor, on the whole or any part of that sum for the whole or any part of the period between the date when the right of action arose and the date of the interlocutor.]
[(1A)   Where a court pronounces an interlocutor decerning for payment of a sum which consists of or includes damages or solatium in respect of personal injuries sustained by the pursuer or any other person, then (without prejudice to the exercise of the power conferred by subsection (1) of this section in relation to any part of that sum which does not represent such damages or solatium) the court shall exercise that power so as to include in that sum interest on those damages and on that solatium or on such part of each as the court considers appropriate, unless the court is satisfied that there are reasons special to the case why no interest should be given in respect thereof.
(1B)   For the avoidance of doubt, it is hereby declared that where, in any action in which it is competent for the court to award interest under this Act, a tender is made in the course of the action, the tender shall, unless otherwise stated therein,

be in full satisfaction of any claim to interest thereunder by any person in whose favour the tender is made; and in considering in any such action whether an award is equal to or greater than an amount tendered in the action, the court shall take account of the amount of any interest awarded under this Act, or such part of that interest as the court considers appropriate.]

(2)   Nothing in this section shall—

(a)   authorise the granting of interest upon interest, or

(b)   prejudice any other power of the court as to the granting of interest, or

(c)   affect the running of any interest which apart from this section would run by virtue of any enactment or rule of law.

[. . .]

3   Citation, interpretation, extent and commencement

(1)   This Act may be cited as the Interest on Damages (Scotland) Act, 1958.

(2)   [In this Act, 'personal injuries' includes any disease and any impairment of a person's physical or mental condition.]

(3)   This Act shall extend to Scotland only, and shall not apply to any action commenced against any person before the passing of this Act.

OCCUPIERS' LIABILITY (SCOTLAND) ACT 1960
(1960, c 30)

1   Variation of rules of common law as to duty of care owed by occupiers

(1)   The provisions of the next following section of this Act shall have effect, in place of the rules of the common law, for the purpose of determining the care which a person occupying or having control of land or other premises (in this Act referred to as an 'occupier of premises') is required, by reason of such occupation or control, to show towards persons entering on the premises in respect of dangers which are due to the state of the premises or to anything done or omitted to be done on them and for which he is in law responsible.

(2)   Nothing in those provisions shall be taken to alter the rules of the common law which determine the person on whom in relation to any premises a duty to show care as aforesaid towards persons entering thereon is incumbent.

(3)   Those provisions shall apply, in like manner and to the same extent as they do in relation to an occupier of premises and to persons entering thereon,—

(a)   in relation to a person occupying or having control of any fixed or moveable structure, including any vessel, vehicle or aircraft, and to persons entering thereon; and

(b)   in relation to an occupier of premises or a person occupying or having control of any such structure and to property thereon, including the property of persons who have not themselves entered on the premises or structure.

2   Extent of occupier's duty to show care

(1)   The care which an occupier of premises is required, by reason of his occupation or control of the premises, to show towards a person entering thereon in respect of dangers which are due to the state of the premises or to anything done or omitted to be done on them and for which the occupier is in law responsible shall, except in so far as he is entitled to and does extend, restrict, modify or exclude by agreement his obligations towards that person, be such care as in all the circumstances of the case is reasonable to see that that person will not suffer injury or damage by reason of any such danger.

(2)   Nothing in the foregoing subsection shall relieve an occupier of premises of any duty to show in any particular case any higher standard of care which in that case is incumbent on him by virtue of any enactment or rule of law imposing special standards of care on particular classes of persons.

(3)　Nothing in the foregoing provisions of this Act shall be held to impose on an occupier any obligation to a person entering on his premises in respect of risks which that person has willingly accepted as his; and any question whether a risk was so accepted shall be decided on the same principles as in other cases in which one person owes to another a duty to show care.

3　Landlord's liability by virtue of responsibility for repairs

(1)　Where premises are occupied or used by virtue of a tenancy under which the landlord is responsible for the maintenance or repair of the premises, it shall be the duty of the landlord to show towards any persons who or whose property may from time to time be on the premises the same care in respect of dangers arising from any failure on his part in carrying out his responsibility aforesaid as is required by virtue of the foregoing provisions of this Act to be shown by an occupier of premises towards persons entering on them.

(2)　Where premises are occupied or used by virtue of a subtenancy, the foregoing subsection shall apply to any landlord who is responsible for the maintenance or repair of the premises comprised in the sub-tenancy.

(3)　Nothing in this section shall relieve a landlord of any duty which he is under apart from this section.

(4)　For the purposes of this section, any obligation imposed on a landlord by any enactment by reason of the premises being subject to a tenancy shall be treated as if it were an obligation imposed on him by the tenancy, 'tenancy' includes a statutory tenancy which does not in law amount to a tenancy and includes also any contract conferring a right of occupation, and 'landlord' shall be construed accordingly.

(5)　This section shall apply to tenancies created before the commencement of this Act as well as to tenancies created after its commencement.

4　Application to Crown

This Act shall bind the Crown, but as regards the liability of the Crown for any wrongful or negligent act or omission giving rise to liability in reparation shall not bind the Crown any further than the Crown is made liable in respect of such acts or omissions by the Crown Proceedings Act, 1947, and that Act and in particular section two thereof shall apply in relation to duties under section two or section three of this Act as statutory duties.

5　Short title, extent and commencement

(1)　This Act may be cited as the Occupiers' Liability (Scotland) Act 1960, and shall extend to Scotland only.

(2)　This Act shall come into operation at the end of the period of three months beginning with the day on which it is passed.

HIRE-PURCHASE ACT 1964
(1964, c 53)

[PART III
TITLE TO MOTOR VEHICLES ON HIRE-PURCHASE OR CONDITIONAL SALE

27　Protection of purchasers of motor vehicles

(1)　This section applies where a motor vehicle has been bailed or (in Scotland) hired under a hire-purchase agreement, or has been agreed to be sold under a conditional sale agreement, and, before the property in the vehicle has become vested in the debtor, he disposes of the vehicle to another person.

(2)　Where the disposition referred to in subsection (1) above is to a private purchaser, and he is a purchaser of the motor vehicle in good faith without notice of the hire-purchase or conditional sale agreement (the 'relevant agreement') that disposition shall have effect as if the creditor's title to the vehicle has been vested in the debtor immediately before that disposition.

(3)   Where the person to whom the disposition referred to in subsection (1) above is made (the 'original purchaser') is a trade or finance purchaser, then if the person who is the first private purchaser of the motor vehicle after that disposition (the 'first private purchaser') is a purchaser of the vehicle in good faith without notice of the relevant agreement, the disposition of the vehicle to the first private purchaser shall have effect as if the title of the creditor to the vehicle had been vested in the debtor immediately before he disposed of it to the original purchaser.

(4)   Where, in a case within subsection (3) above—

(a)   the disposition by which the first private purchaser becomes a purchaser of the motor vehicle in good faith without notice of the relevant agreement is itself a bailment or hiring under a hire-purchase agreement, and

(b)   the person who is the creditor in relation to that agreement disposes of the vehicle to the first private purchaser, or a person claiming under him, by transferring to him the property in the vehicle in pursuance of a provision in the agreement in that behalf, the disposition referred to in paragraph (b) above (whether or not the person to whom it is made is a purchaser in good faith without notice of the relevant agreement) shall as well as the disposition referred to in paragraph (a) above, have effect as mentioned in subsection (3) above.

(5)   The preceding provisions of this section apply—

(a)   notwithstanding anything in [section 21 of the Sale of Goods Act 1979] (sale of goods by a person not the owner), but

(b)   without prejudice to the provisions of the Factors Acts (as defined by [section 61(1) of the said Act of 1979]) or any other enactment enabling the apparent owner of goods to dispose of them as if he were the true owner.

(6)   Nothing in this section shall exonerate the debtor from any liability (whether criminal or civil) to which he would be subject apart from this section; and, in a case where the debtor disposes of the motor vehicle to a trade or finance purchaser, nothing in this section shall exonerate—

(a)   that trade or finance purchaser, or

(b)   any other trade or finance purchaser who becomes a purchaser of the vehicle and is not a person claiming under the first private purchaser,

from any liability (whether criminal or civil) to which he would be subject apart from this section.

28   Presumptions relating to dealings with motor vehicles

(1)   Where in any proceedings (whether criminal or civil) relating to a motor vehicle it is proved—

(a)   that the vehicle was bailed or (in Scotland) hired under a hire-purchase agreement, or was agreed to be sold under a conditional sale agreement, and

(b)   that a person (whether a party to the proceedings or not) became a private purchaser of the vehicle in good faith without notice of the hire-purchase or conditional sale agreement (the 'relevant agreement'), this section shall have effect for the purposes of the operation of section 27 of this Act in relation to those proceedings.

(2)   It shall be presumed for those purposes unless the contrary is proved, that the disposition of the vehicle to the person referred to in subsection (1)(b) above (the 'relevant purchaser') was made by the debtor.

(3)   If it is proved that that disposition was not made by the debtor, then it shall be presumed for those purposes, unless the contrary is proved—

(a)   that the debtor disposed of the vehicle to a private purchaser purchasing in good faith without notice of the relevant agreement, and

(b)   that the relevant purchaser is or was a person claiming under the person to whom the debtor so disposed of the vehicle.

(4)   If it is proved that the disposition of the vehicle to the relevant purchaser was not made by the debtor, and that the person to whom the debtor disposed of

the vehicle (the 'original purchaser') was a trade or finance purchaser, then it shall be presumed for those purposes, unless the contrary is proved—

(a)   that the person who, after the disposition of the vehicle to the original purchaser, first became a private purchaser of the vehicle was a purchaser in good faith without notice of the relevant agreement, and

(b)   that the relevant purchaser is or was a person claiming under the original purchaser.

(5)   Without prejudice to any other method of proof, where in any proceedings a party thereto admits a fact, that fact shall, for the purposes of this section, be taken as against him to be proved in relation to those proceedings.

29   Interpretation of Part III

(1)   In this Part of this Act—

'conditional sale agreement' means an agreement for the sale of goods under which the purchase price or part of it is payable by instalments, and the property in the goods is to remain in the seller (notwithstanding that the buyer is to be in possession of the goods) until such conditions as to the payment of instalments or otherwise as may be specified in the agreement are fulfilled;

'creditor' means the person by whom goods are bailed or (in Scotland) hired under a hire-purchase agreement or as the case may be, the seller under a conditional sale agreement, or the person to whom his rights and duties have passed by assignment or operation of law;

'disposition' means any sale or contract of sale (including a conditional sale agreement), any bailment or (in Scotland) hiring under a hire-purchase agreement and any transfer of the property of goods in pursuance of a provision in that behalf contained in a hire-purchase agreement, and includes any transaction purporting to be a disposition (as so defined), and 'dispose of' shall be construed accordingly;

'hire-purchase agreement' means an agreement, other than a conditional sale agreement, under which—

(a)   goods are bailed or (in Scotland) hired in return for periodical payments by the person to whom they are bailed or hired, and

(b)   the property in the goods will pass to that person if the terms of the agreement are complied with and one or more of the following occurs—

(i)   the exercise of an option to purchase by that person,

(ii)   the doing of any other specified act by any party to the agreement,

(iii)   the happening of any other specified events; and

'motor vehicle' means a mechanically propelled vehicle intended or adapted for use on roads to which the public has access.

(2)   In this Part of this Act 'trade or finance purchaser' means a purchaser who, at the time of the disposition made to him, carries on a business which consists, wholly or partly—

(a)   of purchasing motor vehicles for the purpose of offering or exposing them for sale, or

(b)   of providing finance by purchasing motor vehicles for the purpose of bailing or (in Scotland) hiring them under hire-purchase agreements or agreeing to sell them under conditional sale agreements,

and 'private purchaser' means a purchaser who, at the time of the disposition made to him, does not carry on any such business.

(3)   For the purposes of this Part of this Act a person becomes a purchaser of a motor vehicle if, and at the time when, a disposition of the vehicle is made to him; and a person shall be taken to be a purchaser of a motor vehicle without notice of a hire-purchase agreement or conditional sale agreement if, at the time of the disposition made to him, he has no actual notice that the vehicle is or was the subject of any such agreement.

(4)   In this Part of this Act the 'debtor' in relation to a motor vehicle which has

been bailed or hired under a hire-purchase agreement, or, as the case may be, agreed to be sold under a conditional sale agreement, means the person who at the material time (whether the agreement has before that time been terminated or not) either—

(a)   is the person to whom the vehicle is bailed or hired under that agreement, or

(b)   is, in relation to the agreement, the buyer,

including a person who at that time is, by virtue of section 130(4) of the Consumer Credit Act 1974 treated as a bailee or (in Scotland) a custodier of the vehicle.

(5)   In this Part of this Act any reference to the title of the creditor to a motor vehicle which has been bailed or (in Scotland) hired under a hire-purchase agreement or agreed to be sold under a conditional sale agreement, and is disposed of by the debtor, is a reference to such title (if any) to the vehicle as, immediately before that disposition, was vested in the person who then was the creditor in relation to the agreement.]

EMPLOYER'S LIABILITY (DEFECTIVE EQUIPMENT) ACT 1969
(1969, c 37)

1   Extension of employer's liability for defective equipment

(1)   Where after the commencement of this Act—

(a)   an employee suffers personal injury in the course of his employment in consequence of a defect in equipment provided by his employer for the purposes of the employer's business; and

(b)   the defect is attributable wholly or partly to the fault of a third party (whether identified or not),

the injury shall be deemed to be also attributable to negligence on the part of the employer (whether or not he is liable in respect of the injury apart from this subsection), but without prejudice to the law relating to contributory negligence and to any remedy by way of contribution or in contract or otherwise which is available to the employer in respect of the injury.

(2)   In so far as any agreement purports to exclude or limit any liability of an employer arising under subsection (1) of this section, the agreement shall be void.

(3)   In this section—

'business' includes the activities carried on by any public body;

'employee' means a person who is employed by another person under a contract of service or apprenticeship and is so employed for the purposes of a business carried on by that other person, and 'employer' shall be construed accordingly;

'equipment' includes any plant and machinery, vehicle, aircraft and clothing;

'fault' means negligence, breach of statutory duty or other act or omission which gives rise to liability in tort in England and Wales or which is wrongful and gives rise to liability in damages in Scotland; and

'personal injury' includes loss of life, any impairment of a person's physical or mental condition and any disease.

(4)   This section binds the Crown, and persons in the service of the Crown shall accordingly be treated for the purposes of this section as employees of the Crown if they would not be so treated apart from this subsection.

EMPLOYER'S LIABILITY (COMPULSORY INSURANCE) ACT 1969
(1969, c 57)

1   Insurance against liability for employees

(1)   Except as otherwise provided by this Act, every employer [. . .] shall insure, and maintain insurance, under one or more approved policies with an authorised insurer or insurers against liability for bodily injury or disease sustained by [those of his relevant employees who are employed by him for work on or from an off-

shore installation, or on or from an associated structure in the course of an activity undertaken on or in connection with an offshore installation, and arising out of and in the course of their employment for that work.]

(2) Regulations may provide that the amount for which an employer is required by this Act to insure and maintain insurance shall, either generally or in such cases or classes of case as may be prescribed by the regulations, be limited in such manner as may be so prescribed.

2 Employees to be covered

(1) For the purposes of this Act the term 'employee' means an individual who has entered into or works under a contract of service or apprenticeship with an employer whether by way of manual labour, clerical work or otherwise, whether such contract is expressed or implied, oral or in writing.

(2) This Act shall not require an employer to insure—

(a) in respect of an employee of whom the employer is the husband, wife, [civil partner,] father, mother, grandfather, grandmother, step-father, step-mother, son, daughter, grandson, granddaughter, stepson, stepdaughter, brother, sister, half-brother, half-sister.

SUPPLY OF GOODS (IMPLIED TERMS) ACT 1973
(1973, c 13)

8 Implied terms as to title

[(1) In every [relevant hire-purchase agreement], other than one to which sub-section (2) below applies, there is—

(a) an implied term on the part of the creditor that he will have a right to sell the goods at the time when the property is to pass; and

(b) an implied term that—

(i) the goods are free, and will remain free until the time when the property is to pass, from any charge or encumbrance not disclosed or known to the person to whom the goods are bailed or (in Scotland) hired before the agreement is made, and

(ii) that person will enjoy quiet possession of the goods except so far as it may be disturbed by any person entitled to the benefit of any charge or encumbrance so disclosed or known.

(2) In a [relevant hire-purchase agreement], in the case of which there appears from the agreement or is to be inferred from the circumstances of the agreement an intention that the creditor should transfer only such title as he or a third person may have, there is—

(a) an implied term that all charges or encumbrances known to the creditor and not known to the person to whom the goods are bailed or hired have been disclosed to that person before the agreement is made; and

(b) an implied term that neither—

(i) the creditor; nor

(ii) in a case where the parties to the agreement intend that any title which may be transferred shall be only such title as a third person may have, that person; nor

(iii) anyone claiming through or under the creditor or that third person not otherwise than under a charge or encumbrance disclosed or known to the person to whom the goods are bailed or hired, before the agreement is made; will disturb the quiet possession of the person to whom the goods are bailed or hired.

(3) As regards England and Wales and Northern Ireland, the term implied by subsection (1)(a) above is a condition and the terms implied by subsections (1)(b), (2)(a) and (2)(b) above are warranties.]

9 Bailing or hiring by description

(1) [Where under a [relevant hire-purchase agreement] goods are bailed or (in Scotland) hired by description, there is an implied term that the goods will correspond with the description, and if under the agreement the goods are bailed or hired by reference to a sample as well as a description, it is not sufficient that the bulk of the goods corresponds with the sample if the goods do not also correspond with the description.]

[(1A) As regards England and Wales and Northern Ireland, the term implied by subsection (1) above is a condition.]

(2) [Goods shall not be prevented from being bailed or hired by description by reason only that, being exposed for sale, bailment or hire, they are selected by the person to whom they are bailed or hired.]

10 Implied undertakings as to quality or fitness

(1) [Except as provided by this section and section 11 below and subject to the provisions of any other enactment, including any enactment of the Parliament of Northern Ireland or the Northern Ireland Assembly, there is no implied term as to the quality or fitness for any particular purpose of goods bailed or (in Scotland) hired under a [relevant hire-purchase agreement].]

(2) [Where the creditor bails or hires goods under a [relevant hire-purchase agreement] in the course of a business, there is an implied term that the goods supplied under the agreement are of satisfactory quality.]

[(2A) For the purposes of this Act, goods are of satisfactory quality if they meet the standard that a reasonable person would regard as satisfactory, taking account of any description of the goods, the price (if relevant) and all the other relevant circumstances.

(2B) For the purposes of this Act, the quality of goods includes their state and condition and the following (among others) are in appropriate cases aspects of the quality of goods—

(a) fitness for all the purposes for which goods of the kind in question are commonly supplied,

(b) appearance and finish,

(c) freedom from minor defects,

(d) safety, and

(e) durability.

(2C) The term implied by subsection (2) above does not extend to any matter making the quality of goods unsatisfactory—

(a) which is specifically drawn to the attention of the person to whom the goods are bailed or hired before the agreement is made,

(b) where that person examines the goods before the agreement is made, which that examination ought to reveal, or

(c) where the goods are bailed or hired by reference to a sample, which would have been apparent on a reasonable examination of the sample.

[. . .]

(3) Where the creditor bails or hires goods under a [relevant hire-purchase agreement] in the course of a business and the person to whom the goods are bailed or hired, expressly or by implication, makes known—

(a) to the creditor in the course of negotiations conducted by the creditor in relation to the making of the [relevant hire-purchase agreement], or

(b) to a credit-broker in the course of negotiations conducted by that broker in relation to goods sold by him to the creditor before forming the subject matter of the [relevant hire-purchase agreement],

any particular purpose for which the goods are being bailed or hired, there is an implied term that the goods supplied under the agreement are reasonably fit for that purpose, whether or not that is a purpose for which such goods are commonly supplied, except where the circumstances show that the person to whom the goods are bailed or hired does not rely, or that it is unreasonable for him to rely, on the skill or judgment of the creditor or credit-broker.

(4)   An implied term as to quality or fitness for a particular purpose may be annexed to a [relevant hire-purchase agreement] by usage.

(5)   The preceding provisions of this section apply to a [relevant hire-purchase agreement] made by a person who in the course of a business is acting as agent for the creditor as they apply to an agreement made by the creditor in the course of a business, except where the creditor is not bailing or hiring in the course of a business and either the person to whom the goods are bailed or hired knows that fact or reasonable steps are taken to bring it to the notice of that person before the agreement is made.

(6)   In subsection (3) above and this subsection—

(a)   'credit-broker' means a person acting in the course of a business of credit brokerage;

(b)   'credit brokerage' means the effecting of introductions of individuals desiring to obtain credit—

(i)   to persons carrying on any business so far as it relates to the provision of credit, or

(ii)   to other persons engaged in credit brokerage.

(7)   As regards England and Wales and Northern Ireland, the terms implied by subsections (2) and (3) above are conditions.

[. . .]

11   Samples

[(1)   Where under a [relevant hire-purchase agreement] goods are bailed or (in Scotland) hired by reference to a sample, there is an implied term—

(a)   that the bulk will correspond with the sample in quality; and

(b)   that the person to whom the goods are bailed or hired will have a reasonable opportunity of comparing the bulk with the sample; and

(c)   that the goods will be free from any defect, making their quality unsatisfactory, which would not be apparent on reasonable examination of the sample.

(2)   As regards England and Wales and Northern Ireland, the term implied by subsection (1) above is a condition.]

[12   Exclusion of implied terms

An express term does not negative a term implied by this Act unless inconsistent with it.]

[12A   Remedies for breach of [relevant hire-purchase agreement] as respects Scotland

(1)   Where in a [relevant hire-purchase agreement] the creditor is in breach of any term of the agreement (express or implied), the person to whom the goods are hired shall be entitled—

(a)   to claim damages, and

(b)   if the breach is material, to reject any goods delivered under the agreement and treat it as repudiated.

[. . .]

(4)   This section applies to Scotland only.]

[. . .]

15   Supplementary

[(1)   In sections 8 to 14 above and this section—

'business' includes a profession and the activities of any government department (including a Northern Ireland department), [or local or public authority];

'buyer' and 'seller' includes a person to whom rights and duties under a conditional sale agreement have passed by assignment or operation of law;

'conditional sale agreement' means an agreement for the sale of goods under which the purchase price or part of it is payable by instalments, and the property in the goods is to remain in the seller (notwithstanding that the buyer is to be in possession of the goods) until such conditions as to the payment of instalments or otherwise as may be specified in the agreement are fulfilled;

['consumer sale' has the same meaning as in section 55 of the Sale of Goods Act 1979 (as set out in paragraph 11 of Schedule 1 to that Act)];

'creditor' means the person by whom the goods are bailed or (in Scotland) hired under a hire-purchase agreement or the person to whom his rights and duties under the agreement have passed by assignment or operation of law; and

'hire-purchase agreement' means an agreement, other than conditional sale agreement, under which—

(a) goods are bailed or (in Scotland) hired in return for periodical payments by the person to whom they are bailed or hired, and

(b) the property in the goods will pass to that person if the terms of the agreement are complied with and one or more of the following occurs—

(i) the exercise of an option to purchase by that person,

(ii) the doing of any other specified act by any party to the agreement,

(iii) the happening of any other specified event.

[and a hire-purchase agreement is relevant if it is not a contract to which Chapter 2 of Part I of the Consumer Rights Act 2015 applies;]

[. . .]

(4) Nothing in sections 8 to 13 above shall prejudice the operation of any other enactment including any enactment of the Parliament of Northern Ireland or the Northern Ireland Assembly or any rule of law whereby any term, other than one relating to quality or fitness, is to be implied in any [relevant hire-purchase agreement].]

PRESCRIPTION AND LIMITATION (SCOTLAND) ACT 1973
(1973 c 52)

PART I
PRESCRIPTION

Positive prescription

[1   Validity of right

(1) If land has been possessed by any person, or by any person and his successors, for a continuous period of ten years openly, peaceably and without any judicial interruption and the possession was founded on, and followed—

(a) the recording of a deed which is sufficient in respect of its terms to constitute in favour of that person a real right in—

(i) that land; or

(ii) land of a description *habile* to include that land; or

[(b) the registration of a deed which is sufficient in respect of its terms to constitute in favour of that person a real right in—

(i) that land; or

(ii) land of a description habile to include that land;]

then, as from the expiry of that period, the real right so far as relating to that land shall be exempt from challenge.

(2) Subsection (1) above shall not apply where—

(a) possession was founded on the recording of a deed which is invalid *ex facie* or was forged; or

(b) possession was founded on registration in the Land Register of Scotland proceeding on a forged deed and the person appearing from the Register to have the real right in question was aware of the forgery at the time of registration in his favour.

(3)   In subsection (1) above, the reference to a real right is to a real right which is registrable in the Land Register of Scotland or a deed relating to which can competently be recorded; but this section does not apply to [real burdens,] servitudes or public rights of way.

[. . .]

(5)   Where, in any question involving any foreshore or any salmon fishings, this section is pled against the Crown as owner of the regalia, subsection (1) above shall have effect as if for the words 'ten years' there were substituted 'twenty years'.

(6)   This section is without prejudice to section 2 of this Act.]

[2   Special cases

(1)   If—

(a)   land has been possessed by any person, or by any person and his successors, for a continuous period of twenty years openly, peaceably and without any judicial interruption; and

(b)   the possession was founded on, and followed the execution of, a deed (whether [or not registered or recorded]) which is sufficient in respect of its terms to constitute in favour of that person a real right in that land, or in land of a description *habile* to include that land, then, as from the expiry of that period, the real right so far as relating to that land shall be exempt from challenge except on the ground that the deed is invalid *ex facie* or was forged.

(2)   This section applies—

(a)   to the real right of the lessee under a lease; and

(b)   to any other real right in land, being a real right of a kind which, under the law in force immediately before the commencement of this Part of this Act, was sufficient to form a foundation for positive prescription without the deed constituting the title to the real right having been [registered or] recorded, but does not apply to servitudes or public rights of way.

(3)   This section is without prejudice to section 1 of this Act or to [section 20B or 20C of the Registration of Leases (Scotland) Act 1857 (c 26)].]

3   Positive servitudes and public rights of way

(1)   If in the case of a positive servitude over land—

(a)   the servitude has been possessed for a continuous period of twenty years openly, peaceably and without any judicial interruption, and

(b)   the possession was founded on, and followed the execution of, a deed which is sufficient in respect of its terms (whether expressly or by implication) to constitute the servitude,

then, as from the expiration of the said period, the validity of the servitude as so constituted shall be exempt from challenge except on the ground that the deed is invalid *ex facie* or was forged.

(2)   If a positive servitude over land has been possessed for a continuous period of twenty years openly, peaceably and without judicial interruption, then, as from the expiration of that period, the existence of the servitude as so possessed shall be exempt from challenge.

(3)   If a public right of way over land has been possessed by the public for a continuous period of twenty years openly, peaceably and without judicial interruption, then, as from the expiration of that period, the existence of the right of way as so possessed shall be exempt from challenge.

(4)   References in subsections (1) and (2) of this section to possession of a servitude are references to possession of the servitude by any person in possession of the relative dominant tenement.

(5)   This section is without prejudice to the operation of section 7 of this Act.

4   Judicial interruption of periods of possession for purposes of sections 1, 2 and 3

(1)   In sections 1, 2 and 3 of this Act references to a judicial interruption, in relation to possession, are references to the making in appropriate proceedings, by any person having a proper interest to do so, of a claim which challenges the possession in question.

(2)   In this section 'appropriate proceedings' means—

(a)   any proceedings in a court of competent jurisdiction in Scotland or elsewhere, except proceedings in the Court of Session initiated by a summons which is not subsequently called;

(b)   any arbitration in Scotland [in respect of which an arbitrator (or panel of arbitrators) has been appointed];

(c)   any arbitration in a country other than Scotland, being an arbitration an award in which would be enforceable in Scotland.

(3)   The date of a judicial interruption shall be taken to be—

(a)   where the claim has been made in an arbitration [the date when the arbitration begins];

(b)   in any other case, the date when the claim was made.

[(4)   An arbitration begins for the purposes of this section—

(a)   when the parties to the arbitration agree that it begins, or

(b)   in the absence of such agreement, in accordance with rule 1 of the Scottish Arbitration Rules (see section 7 of, and schedule 1 to, the Arbitration (Scotland) Act 2010.]

5   Further provisions supplementary to sections 1, 2 and 3

(1)   In sections 1, 2 and 3 of this Act 'deed' includes a judicial decree; and for the purposes of the said sections any of the following, namely an instrument of sasine, a notarial instrument and a notice of title, which narrates or declares that a person has a [right in land shall be treated as a deed sufficient to constitute that right].

[(1A)   Any reference in those sections to a real right's being exempt from challenge as from the expiration of some continuous period is to be construed, if the real right of the possessor was void immediately before that expiration, as including reference to acquisition of the real right by the possessor.]

[. . .]

Negative prescription

6   Extinction of obligations by prescriptive periods of five years

(1)   If, after the appropriate date, an obligation to which this section applies has subsisted for a continuous period of five years—

(a)   without any relevant claim having been made in relation to the obligation, and

(b)   without the subsistence of the obligation having been relevantly acknowledged,

then as from the expiration of that period the obligation shall be extinguished:

Provided that in its application to an obligation under a bill of exchange or a promissory note this subsection shall have effect as if paragraph (b) thereof were omitted.

(2)   Schedule 1 to this Act shall have effect for defining the obligations to which this section applies.

(3)   In subsection (1) above the reference to the appropriate date, in relation to an obligation of any kind specified in Schedule 2 to this Act is a reference to the date specified in that Schedule in relation to obligations of that kind, and in relation to an obligation of any other kind is a reference to the date when the obligation became enforceable.

(4)   In the computation of a prescriptive period in relation to any obligation for the purposes of this section—

(a)   any period during which by reason of—

(i)   fraud on the part of the debtor or any person acting on his behalf, or

(ii)   error induced by words or conduct of the debtor or any person acting on his behalf,

the creditor was induced to refrain from making a relevant claim in relation to the obligation, and

(b)   any period during which the original creditor (while he is the creditor) was under legal disability,

shall not be reckoned as, or as part of, the prescriptive period:

Provided that any period such as is mentioned in paragraph (a) of this subsection shall not include any time occurring after the creditor could with reasonable diligence have discovered the fraud or error, as the case may be, referred to in that paragraph.

(5)   Any period such as is mentioned in paragraph (a) or (b) of subsection (4) of this section shall not be regarded as separating the time immediately before it from the time immediately after it.

7   Extinction of obligations by prescriptive periods of twenty years

(1)   If, after the date when any obligation to which this section applies has become enforceable, the obligation has subsisted for a continuous period of twenty years—

(a)   without any relevant claim having been made in relation to the obligation, and

(b)   without the subsistence of the obligation having been relevantly acknowledged,

then as from the expiration of that period the obligation shall be extinguished:

Provided that in its application to an obligation under a bill of exchange or a promissory note this subsection shall have effect as if paragraph (b) thereof were omitted.

(2)   This section applies to an obligation of any kind (including an obligation to which section 6 of this Act applies), not being an obligation [to which section 22A of this Act applies or an obligation] specified in Schedule 3 to this Act as an imprescriptible obligation [or an obligation to make reparation in respect of personal injuries within the meaning of Part II of this Act or in respect of the death of any person as a result of such injuries.]

8   Extinction of other rights relating to property by prescriptive periods of twenty years

(1)   If, after the date when any right to which this section applies has become exercisable or enforceable, the right has subsisted for a continuous period of twenty years unexercised by or unenforced, and without any relevant claim in relation to it having been made, then as from the expiration of that period the right shall be extinguished.

(2)   This section applies to any right relating to property, whether heritable or moveable, not being a right specified in Schedule 3 to this Act as an imprescriptible right or falling within section 6 or 7 of this Act as being a right correlative to an obligation to which either of those sections applies.

[8A   Extinction of obligations to make contribution between wrongdoers

(1)   If any obligation to make a contribution by virtue of section 3(2) of the Law Reform (Miscellaneous Provisions) (Scotland) Act 1940 in respect of any damages or expenses has subsisted for a continuous period of 2 years after the date on which the right to recover the contribution became enforceable by the creditor in the obligation—

(a)   without any relevant claim having been made in relation to the obligation; and

(b)   without the subsistence of the obligation having been relevantly acknowledged;

then as from the expiration of that period the obligation shall be extinguished.

(2)   Subsections (4) and (5) of section 6 of this Act shall apply for the purposes of this section as they apply for the purposes of that section.]

9   Definition of 'relevant claim' for purposes of sections 6, 7 and 8

(1)   In sections 6 [, 7 and 8A] of this Act the expression 'relevant claim', in relation to an obligation, means a claim made by or on behalf of the creditor for implement or part-implement of the obligation, being a claim made—

(a)   in appropriate proceedings, or

[(b)   by the presentation of, or the concurring in, a petition for sequestration or by the submission of a claim under section 22 or 48 of the Bankruptcy (Scotland) Act 1985 [. . .]; or

(c)   by a creditor to the trustee acting under a trust deed as defined in section 5(2)(c) of the Bankruptcy (Scotland) Act 1985; or

(d)   by the presentation of, or the concurring in, a petition for the winding up of a company or by the submission of a claim in a liquidation in accordance with rules made under section 411 of the Insolvency Act 1986;]

and for the purposes of the said sections 6 [, 7 and 8A] the execution by or on behalf of the creditor in an obligation of any form of diligence directed to the enforcement of the obligation shall be deemed to be a relevant claim in relation to the obligation.

(2)   In section 8 of this Act the expression 'relevant claim', in relation to a right, means a claim made in appropriate proceedings by or on behalf of the creditor to establish the right or to contest any claim to a right inconsistent therewith.

(3)   Where a claim which, in accordance with the foregoing provisions of this section, is a relevant claim for the purposes of section 6, 7[, 8 or 8A] of this Act is made in an arbitration, [the date when the arbitration begins] shall be taken for those purposes to be the date of the making of the claim.

(4)   In this section the expression 'appropriate proceedings' and, in relation to an arbitration, the expression ['the date when the arbitration begins'] have the same meanings as in section 4 of this Act.

10   Relevant acknowledgement for purposes of sections 6 and 7

(1)   The subsistence of an obligation shall be regarded for the purposes of sections 6 [, 7 and 8A] of this Act as having been relevantly acknowledged if, and only if, either of the following conditions is satisfied, namely—

(a)   that there has been such performance by or on behalf of the debtor towards implement of the obligation as clearly indicates that the obligation still subsists;

(b)   that there has been made by or on behalf of the debtor to the creditor or his agent an unequivocal written admission clearly acknowledging that the obligation still subsists.

(2)   Subject to subsection (3) below, where two or more persons are bound jointly by an obligation so that each is liable for the whole, and the subsistence of the obligation has been relevantly acknowledged by or on behalf of one of those persons then—

(a)   if the acknowledgment is made in the manner specified in paragraph (a) of the foregoing subsection it shall have effect for the purposes of the said sections 6 [, 7 and 8A] as respects the liability of each of those persons, and

(b)   if it is made in the manner specified in paragraph (b) of that subsection it shall have effect for those purposes only as respects the liability of the person who makes it.

(3)   Where the subsistence of an obligation affecting a trust has been relevantly

acknowledged by or on behalf of one two or more co-trustees in the manner specified in paragraph (a) or (b) of subsection (1) of this section, the acknowledgment
shall have effect for the purposes of the said sections 6 [, 7 and 8A] as respects the
liability of the trust estate and any liability of each of the trustees.

(4) In this section references to performance in relation to an obligation include,
where the nature of the obligation so requires, references to refraining from doing
something and to permitting or suffering something to be done or maintained.

11 Obligations to make reparation

(1) Subject to subsections (2) and (3) below, any obligation (whether arising
from any enactment, or from any rule of law or from, or by reason of any breach
of, a contract or promise) to make reparation for loss, injury or damage caused by
an act, neglect or default shall be regarded for the purposes of section 6 of this
Act as having become enforceable on the date when the loss, injury or damage
occurred.

(2) Where as a result of a continuing act, neglect or default loss, injury or
damage has occurred before the cessation of the act, neglect or default the loss,
injury or damage shall be deemed for the purposes of subsection (1) above to have
occurred on the date when the act, neglect or default ceased.

(3) In relation to a case where on the date referred to in subsection (1) above
(or, as the case may be, that subsection as modified by subsection (2) above) the
creditor was not aware, and could not with reasonable diligence have been aware,
that loss, injury or damage caused as aforesaid had occurred, the said subsection
(1) shall have effect as if for the reference therein to that date there were substituted a reference to the date when the creditor first became, or could with
reasonable diligence have become, so aware.

(4) Subsections (1) and (2) above (with the omission of any reference therein to
subsection (3) above) shall have effect for the purposes of section 7 of this Act as
they have effect for the purposes of section 6 of this Act.

12 Savings

(1) Where by virtue of any enactment passed or made before the passing of
this Act a claim to establish a right or enforce implement of an obligation may be
made only within a period of limitation specified in or determined under the
enactment, and, by the expiration of a prescriptive period determined under section 6, 7 or 8 of this Act the right or obligation would, apart from this subsection,
be extinguished before the expiration of the period of limitation, the said section
shall have effect as if the relevant prescriptive period were extended so that it
expires—
    (a)   on the date when the period of limitation expires, or
    (b)   if on that date any such claim made within that period has not been
finally disposed of, on the date when the claim is so disposed of.

(2) Nothing in section 6, 7 or 8 of this Act shall be construed so as to exempt
any deed from challenge at any time on the ground that it is invalid *ex facie* or was
forged.

13 Prohibition of contracting out

Any provision in any agreement purporting to provide in relation to any right
or obligation that section 6, 7 [, 8 or 8A] of this Act shall not have effect shall
be null.

General

14 Computation of prescriptive periods

(1) In the computation of a prescriptive period for the purposes of any provision of this Part of this Act—
    (a)   time occurring before the commencement of this Part of this Act shall be
    reckonable towards the prescriptive period in like manner as time occurring

thereafter, but subject to the restriction that any time reckoned under this paragraph shall be less than the prescriptive period;

(b)   any time during which any person against whom the provision is pled was under legal disability shall (except so far as otherwise provided by [subsection (4) of section 6 of this Act including that subsection as applied by section 8A of this Act] be reckoned as if the person were free from that disability;

(c)   if the commencement of the prescriptive period would, apart from this paragraph, fall at a time in any day other than the beginning of the day, the period shall be deemed to have commenced at the beginning of the next following day;

(d)   if the last day of the prescriptive period would, apart from this paragraph, be a holiday, the period shall, notwithstanding anything in the said provision, be extended to include any immediately succeeding day which is a holiday, any further immediately succeeding days which are holidays, and the next succeeding day which is not a holiday;

(e)   save as otherwise provided in this Part of this Act regard shall be had to the like principles as immediately before the commencement of this Part of this Act were applicable to the computation of periods of prescription for the purposes of the Prescription Act 1617.

[(1A)   The prescriptive period calculated in relation to a relevant cross-border dispute for the purposes of any provision of this Part of this Act is extended where the last day of the period would, apart from this subsection, fall—

(a)   in the 8 weeks after the date that a mediation in relation to the dispute ends;

(b)   on the date that a mediation in relation to the dispute ends; or

(c)   after the date when all of the parties to the dispute agree to participate in a mediation in relation to the dispute but before the date that such mediation ends.

(1B)   Where subsection (1A) applies, the prescriptive period is extended so that it expires on the date falling 8 weeks after the date on which the mediation ends.

(1C)   For the purposes of subsections (1A) and (1B), a mediation ends on the date that any of the following occurs—

(a)   all of the parties reach an agreement in resolution of the dispute;

(b)   all of the parties agree to end the mediation;

(c)   a party withdraws from the mediation, which is the date on which—

(i)   a party informs all of the other parties of that party's withdrawal,

(ii)   in the case of a mediation involving 2 parties, 14 days expire after a request made by one party to the other party for confirmation of whether the other party has withdrawn, if the other party does not respond in that period, or

(iii)   in the case of a mediation involving more than 2 parties, a party informs all of the remaining parties that the party received no response in the 14 days after a request to another party for confirmation of whether the other party had withdrawn; or

(d)   a period of 14 days expires after the date on which the mediator's tenure ends (by reason of death, resignation or otherwise), if a replacement mediator has not been appointed.]

(2)   In this section [—

'the Directive' means Directive 2008/52/EC of the European Parliament and of the Council of 21st May 2008 on certain aspects of mediation in civil and commercial matters;]

'holiday' means a day of any of the following descriptions, namely, a Saturday, a Sunday and a day which, in Scotland, is a bank holiday under the Banking and Financial Dealings Act 1971 [;

'mediation' and 'mediator' have the meanings given by Article 3 of the Directive; and 'relevant cross-border dispute' means a cross-border dispute within the meaning given by Article 2 of the Directive—

(a)   which is about a right or obligation to which a prescriptive period applies by virtue of this Part of this Act; and

(b)   to which the Directive applies.]

15   Interpretation of Part I

(1)   In this Part of this Act, unless the context otherwise requires, the following expressions have the meanings hereby assigned to them, namely—

'bill of exchange' has the same meaning as it has for the purposes of the Bills of Exchange Act 1882;

'date of execution', in relation to a deed executed on several dates, means the last of those dates;

'enactment' includes an order, regulation, rule or other instrument having effect by virtue of an Act;

'holiday' has the meaning assigned to it by section 14 of this Act;

'land' includes heritable property of any description;

'lease' includes a sub-lease;

'legal disability' means legal disability by reason of nonage or unsoundness of mind;

'possession' includes civil possession, and 'possessed' shall be construed accordingly;

'prescriptive period' means a period required for the operation of section 1, 2, 3, 6, 7 [, 8 or 8A] of this Act;

'promissory note' has the same meaning as it has for the purposes of the Bills of Exchange Act 1882;

'trustee' includes any person holding property in fiduciary capacity for another and, without prejudice to that generality, includes a trustee within the meaning of the Trusts (Scotland) Act 1921; and 'trust' shall be construed accordingly;

and references to the recording of a deed are references to the recording thereof in the General Register of Sasines [and to the registering of a deed are to the registering thereof in the Land Register of Scotland].

(2)   In this Part of this Act, unless the context otherwise requires, any reference to an obligation or to a right includes a reference to the right or, as the case may be, to the obligation (if any), correlative thereto.

(3)   In this Part of this Act any reference to an enactment shall, unless the context otherwise requires, be construed as a reference to that enactment as amended or extended, and as including a reference thereto as applied, by or under any other enactment.

16   Amendments and repeals related to Part I

(1)   The enactment specified in Part I of Schedule 4 to this Act shall have effect subject to the amendment there specified, being an amendment related to this Part of this Act.

(2)   Subject to the next following subsection, the enactments specified in Part I of Schedule 5 to this Act (which includes certain enactments relating to the limitation of proof) are hereby repealed to the extent specified in column 3 of that Schedule.

(3)   Where by virtue of any Act repealed by this section the subsistence of an obligation in force at the date of the commencement of this Part of this Act was immediately before that date, by reason of the passage of time, provable only by the writ or oath of the debtor the subsistence of the obligation shall [(notwithstanding anything in sections 16(1) and 17(2)(a) of the Interpretation Act 1978, which relates to the effect of repeals)] as from that date be provable as if the said repealed Act had not passed.

PART II

LIMITATION OF ACTIONS

[16A   Part II not to extend to product liability

This Part of this Act does not apply to any action to which section 22B or 22C of this Act applies.]

[17   Actions in respect of personal injuries not resulting in death

(1)   This section applies to an action of damages where the damages claimed consist of or include damages in respect of personal injuries, being an action (other than an action to which section 18 of this Act applies) brought by the person who sustained the injuries or any other person.

(2)   Subject to subsection (3) below and section 19A of this Act, no action to which this section applies shall be brought unless it is commenced within a period of 3 years after—

    (a)   the date on which the injuries were sustained or, where the act or omission to which the injuries were attributable was a continuing one, that date or the date on which the act or omission ceased, whichever is the later; or

    (b)   the date (if later than any date mentioned in paragraph (a) above) on which the pursuer in the action became, or on which, in the opinion of the court, it would have been reasonably practicable for him in all the circumstances to become, aware of all the following facts—

        (i)   that the injuries in question were sufficiently serious to justify his bringing an action of damages on the assumption that the person against whom the action was brought did not dispute liability and was able to satisfy a decree;

        (ii)   that the injuries were attributable in whole or in part to an act or omission; and

        (iii)   that the defender was a person to whose act or omission the injuries were attributable in whole or in part or the employer or principal of such a person.

(3)   In the computation of the period specified in subsection (2) above there shall be disregarded any time during which the person who sustained the injuries was under legal disability by reason of nonage or unsoundness of mind.

18   Actions where death has resulted from personal injuries

(1)   This section applies to any action in which, following the death of any person from personal injuries, damages are claimed in respect of the injuries or the death.

(2)   Subject to subsections (3) and (4) below and section 19A of this Act, no action to which this section applies shall be brought unless it is commenced within a period of 3 years after—

    (a)   the date of death of the deceased; or

    (b)   the date (if later than the date of death) on which the pursuer in the action became, or on which, in the opinion of the court, it would have been reasonably practicable for him in all the circumstances to become, aware of both of the following facts—

        (i)   that the injuries of the deceased were attributable in whole or in part to an act or omission; and

        (ii)   that the defender was a person to whose act or omission the injuries were attributable in whole or in part or the employer or principal of such a person.

(3)   Where the pursuer is a relative of the deceased, there shall be disregarded in the computation of the period specified in subsection (2) above any time during which the relative was under legal disability by reason of nonage or unsoundness of mind.

(4)   Subject to section 19A of this Act, where an action of damages has not been

brought by or on behalf of a person who has sustained personal injuries within the period specified in section 17(2) of this Act and that person subsequently dies in consequence of those injuries, no action to which this section applies shall be brought in respect of those injuries or the death from those injuries.

(5)   In this section 'relative' has the same meaning as in [the Damages (Scotland) Act 2011].

[18A   **Limitation of defamation and other actions**

(1)   Subject to subsections (2) and (3) below and section 19A of this Act, no action for defamation shall be brought unless it is commenced within a period of 3 years after the date when the right of action accrued.

(2)   In the computation of the period specified in subsection (1) above there shall be disregarded any time during which the person alleged to have been defamed was under legal disability by reason of nonage or unsoundness of mind.

(3)   Nothing in this section shall affect any right of action which accrued before the commencement of this section.

(4)   In this section—

(a)   'defamation' includes *convicium* and malicious falsehood, and 'defamed' shall be construed accordingly; and

(b)   references to the date when a right of action accrued shall be construed as references to the date when the publication or communication in respect of which the action for defamation is to be brought first came to the notice of the pursuer.]

[18B   **Actions of harassment**

(1)   This section applies to actions of harassment (within the meaning of section 8 [or section 8A] of the Protection from Harassment Act 1997) which include a claim for damages.

(2)   Subject to subsection (3) below and to section 19A of this Act, no action to which this section applies shall be brought unless it is commenced within a period of 3 years after—

(a)   the date on which the alleged harassment ceased; or

(b)   the date (if later than the date mentioned in paragraph (a) above) on which the pursuer in the action became, or on which, in the opinion of the court, it would have been reasonably practicable for him in all the circumstances to have become, aware, that the defender was a person responsible for the alleged harassment or the employer or principal of such a person.

(3)   In the computation of the period specified in subsection (2) above there shall be disregarded any time during which the person who is alleged to have suffered the harassment was under legal disability by reason of nonage or unsoundness of mind.]

[. . .]

[19A   **Power of court to override time-limits etc**

(1)   Where a person would be entitled, but for any of the provisions of sections 17, [18, 18A or 18B] of this Act, to bring an action, the court may, if it seems to it equitable to do so, allow him to bring the action notwithstanding that provision.

(2)   The provisions of subsection (1) above shall have effect not only as regards rights of action accruing after the commencement of this section but also as regards those, in respect of which a final judgment has not been pronounced, accruing before such commencement.

(3)   In subsection (2) above, the expression 'final judgment' means an interlocutor of a court of first instance which, by itself, or taken along with previous interlocutors, disposes of the subject matter of a cause notwithstanding that judgment may not have been pronounced on every question raised or that the expenses found due may not have been modified, taxed or decerned for; but the expression

does not include an interlocutor dismissing a cause by reason only of a provision mentioned in subsection (1) above.

(4)   An action which would not be entertained but for this section shall not be tried by jury.]

. . .

[19D   Interruption of limitation period: arbitration

(1)   Any period during which an arbitration is ongoing in relation to a matter is to be disregarded in any computation of the period specified in section 17(2), 18(2), 18A(1) or 18B(2) of this Act in relation to that matter.

(2)   In this section, 'arbitration' means—

    (a)   any arbitration in Scotland,

    (b)   any arbitration in a country other than Scotland, being an arbitration an award in which would be enforceable in Scotland.]

[19F   Extension of limitation periods: cross-border mediation

(1)   The limitation period calculated in relation to a relevant cross-border dispute for the purposes of sections 17, 18, 18A or 18B of this Act is extended where the last day of the period would, apart from this subsection, fall—

    (a)   in the 8 weeks after the date that a mediation in relation to the dispute ends;

    (b)   on the date that a mediation in relation to the dispute ends; or

    (c)   after the date when all of the parties to the dispute agree to participate in a mediation in relation to the dispute but before the date that such mediation ends.

(2)   Where subsection (1) applies, the limitation period is extended so that it expires on the date falling 8 weeks after the date on which the mediation ends.

(3)   For the purpose of this section, mediation in relation to a relevant cross-border dispute ends when any of the following occurs—

    (a)   all of the parties reach an agreement in resolution of the dispute;

    (b)   all of the parties agree to end the mediation;

    (c)   a party withdraws from the mediation, which is the date on which—

        (i)   a party informs all of the other parties of that party's withdrawal,

        (ii)   in the case of a mediation involving 2 parties, 14 days expire after a request made by one party to the other party for confirmation of whether the other party has withdrawn, if the other party does not respond in that period, or

        (iii)   in the case of a mediation involving more than 2 parties, a party informs all of the remaining parties that the party received no response in the 14 days after a request to another party for confirmation of whether the other party had withdrawn; or

    (d)   a period of 14 days expires after the date on which the mediator's tenure ends (by reason of death, resignation or otherwise), if a replacement mediator has not been appointed.

(4)   In this section—

'the Directive' means Directive 2008/52/EC of the European Parliament and of the Council of 21st May 2008 on certain aspects of mediation in civil and commercial matters;

'mediation' and 'mediator' have the meanings given by Article 3 of the Directive; and

'relevant cross-border dispute' means a cross-border dispute within the meaning given by Article 2 of the Directive—

    (a)   which is about a matter to which a limitation period applies by virtue of sections 17 to 18B; and

    (b)   to which the Directive applies.]

[. . .]

[22 Interpretation of Part II and supplementary provisions

(1) In this Part of this Act—

'the court' means the Court of Session or the sheriff court; and

'personal injuries' includes any disease and any impairment of a person's physical or mental condition.

(2) Where the pursuer in an action to which section 17, 18 [or 18A] of this Act applies is pursuing the action by virtue of the assignation of a right of action, the reference in subsection (2)(b) of the said section 17 or, [of the said section, or, as the case may be, subsection (4)(b) of the said section 18A] to the pursuer in the action shall be construed as a reference to the assignor of the right of action.

(3) For the purposes of the said subsection (2)(b) knowledge that any act or omission was or was not, as a matter of law, actionable, is irrelevant.

(4) An action which would not be entertained but for the said subsection (2)(b) shall not be tried by jury.]

[PART IIA
PRESCRIPTION OF OBLIGATIONS AND LIMITATION OF ACTIONS UNDER PART I OF THE CONSUMER PROTECTION ACT 1987

Prescription of obligations

[22A Ten years' prescription of obligations

(1) An obligation arising from liability under section 2 of the 1987 Act (to make reparation for damage caused wholly or partly by a defect in a product) shall be extinguished if a period of 10 years has expired from the relevant time, unless a relevant claim was made within that period and has not been finally disposed of, and no such obligation shall come into existence after the expiration of the said period.

(2) If, at the expiration of the period of 10 years mentioned in subsection (1) above, a relevant claim has been made but has not been finally disposed of, the obligation to which the claim relates shall be extinguished when the claim is finally disposed of.

(3) In this section a claim is finally disposed of when—

(a) a decision disposing of the claim has been made against which no appeal is competent;

(b) an appeal against such a decision is competent with leave, and the time limit for leave has expired and no application has been made or leave has been refused;

(c) leave to appeal against such a decision is granted or is not required, and no appeal is made within the time limit for appeal; or

(d) the claim is abandoned;

'relevant claim' in relation to an obligation means a claim made by or on behalf of the creditor for implement or part implement of the obligation, being a claim made—

(a) in appropriate proceedings within the meaning of section 4(2) of this Act; or

(b) by the presentation of, or the concurring in, a petition for sequestration or by the submission of a claim under section 22 or 48 of the Bankruptcy (Scotland) Act 1985; or

(c) by the presentation of, or the concurring in, a petition for the winding up of a company or by the submission of a claim in a liquidation in accordance with the rules made under section 411 of the Insolvency Act 1986;

'relevant time' has the meaning given in section 4(2) of the 1987 Act.

(4) Where a relevant claim is made in an arbitration, [the date when the arbi-

tration begins (within the meaning of section 4(4) of this Act)] shall be taken for those purposes to be the date of the making of the claim.]

[(5)   The prescriptive period calculated in relation to a relevant cross-border dispute for the purposes of this section is extended where the last day of the period would, apart from this subsection, fall—

(a)   in the eight weeks after the date that a mediation in relation to the dispute ends;

(b)   on the date that a mediation in relation to the dispute ends, or

(c)   after the date when all of the parties to the dispute agree to participate in a mediation in relation to the dispute but before the date that such mediation ends.

(6)   Where subsection (5) applies, the prescriptive period is extended so that it expires on the date falling 8 weeks after the date on which the mediation ends.

(7)   For the purposes of subsections (5) and (6), a mediation ends on the date that any of the following occurs—

(a)   all of the parties reach an agreement in resolution of the dispute;

(b)   all of the parties agree to end the mediation;

(c)   a party withdraws from the mediation, which is the date on which—

(i)   a party informs all of the other parties of that party's withdrawal,

(ii)   in the case of a mediation involving 2 parties, 14 days expire after a request made by one party to the other party seeking confirmation of whether the other party has withdrawn, if the other party does not respond in that period, or

(iii)   in the case of a mediation involving more than 2 parties, a party informs all of the remaining parties that the party received no response in the 14 days after that party's request to another party seeking confirmation of whether the other party had withdrawn; or

(d)   a period of 14 days expires after the date on which the mediator's tenure ends (whether by reason of death, resignation or otherwise), if a replacement mediator has not been appointed.

(8)   In this section—

'the Directive' means Directive 2008/52/EC of the European Parliament and of the Council of 21st May 2008 on certain aspects of mediation in civil and commercial matters;

'mediation' and 'mediator' have the meanings given by Article 3 of the Directive; and

'relevant cross-border dispute' means a cross-border dispute within the meaning given by Article 2 of the Directive—

(a)   which is about an obligation to which a prescriptive period applies by virtue of this section, and

(b)   to which the Directive applies.]

Limitation of actions

[22B   3 year limitation of actions

(1)   This section shall apply to an action to enforce an obligation arising from liability under section 2 of the 1987 Act (to make reparation for damage caused wholly or partly by a defect in a product), except where section 22C of this Act applies.

(2)   Subject to subsection (4) below, an action to which this section applies shall not be competent unless it is commenced within the period of 3 years after the earliest date on which the person seeking to bring (or a person who could at an earlier date have brought) the action was aware, or on which, in the opinion of the court, it was reasonably practicable for him in all the circumstances to become aware, of all the facts mentioned in subsection (3) below.

(3)   The facts referred to in subsection (2) above are—

    (a)   that there was a defect in a product;

    (b)   that the damage was caused or partly caused by the defect;

    (c)   that the damage was sufficiently serious to justify the pursuer (or other person referred to in subsection (2) above) in bringing an action to which this section applies on the assumption that the defender did not dispute liability and was able to satisfy a decree;

    (d)   that the defender was a person liable for the damage under the said section 2.

(4)   In the computation of the period of 3 years mentioned in subsection (2) above, there shall be disregarded any period during which the person seeking to bring the action was under legal disability by reason of nonage or unsoundness of mind.

(5)   The facts mentioned in subsection (3) above do not include knowledge of whether particular facts and circumstances would or would not, as a matter of law, result in liability for damage under the said section 2.

(6)   Where a person would be entitled, but for this section, to bring an action for reparation other than one in which the damages claimed are confined to damages for loss of or damage to property, the court may, if it seems to it equitable to do so, allow him to bring the action notwithstanding this section.]

[22C Actions under the 1987 Act where death has resulted from personal injuries

(1)   This section shall apply to an action to enforce an obligation arising from liability under section 2 of the 1987 Act (to make reparation for damage caused wholly or partly by a defect in a product) where a person has died from personal injuries and the damages claimed include damages for those personal injuries or that death.

(2)   Subject to subsection (4) below, an action to which this section applies shall not be competent unless it is commenced within the period of 3 years after the later of—

    (a)   the date of death of the injured person;

    (b)   the earliest date on which the person seeking to make (or a person who could at an earlier date have made) the claim was aware, or on which, in the opinion of the court, it was reasonably practicable for him in all the circumstances to become aware—

      (i)   that there was a defect in the product;

      (ii)   that the injuries of the deceased were caused (or partly caused) by the defect; and

      (iii)   that the defender was a person liable for the damage under the said section 2.

(3)   Where the person seeking to make the claim is a relative of the deceased, there shall be disregarded in the computation of the period mentioned in subsection (2) above any period during which that relative was under legal disability by reason of nonage or unsoundness of mind.

(4)   Where an action to which section 22B of this Act applies has not been brought within the period mentioned in subsection (2) of that section and the person subsequently dies in consequence of his injuries, an action to which this section applies shall not be competent in respect of those injuries or that death.

(5)   Where a person would be entitled, but for this section, to bring an action for reparation other than one in which the damages claimed are confined to damages for loss of or damage to property, the court may, if it seems to it equitable to do so, allow him to bring the action notwithstanding this section.

(6)   In this section 'relative' has the same meaning as in the [Damages (Scotland) Act 2011].

(7)   For the purposes of subsection (2)(b) above there shall be disregarded

knowledge of whether particular facts and circumstances would or would not, as a matter of law, result in liability for damage under the said section 2.]

[22CA   Interruption of limitation period for 1987 Act actions: arbitration

(1)   Any period during which an arbitration is ongoing in relation to a matter is to be disregarded in any computation of the period specified in section 22B(2) or 22C(2) of this Act in relation to that matter.

(2)   In this section, 'arbitration' means—

   (a)   any arbitration in Scotland,

   (b)   any arbitration in a country, other than Scotland, being an arbitration an award in which would be enforceable in Scotland.]

[22CB   Extension of limitation periods for 1987 Act actions: mediation

(1)   The limitation period calculated in relation to a relevant cross-border dispute for the purposes of section 22B(2) or 22C(2) is extended where the last day of the period would, apart from this subsection, fall—

   (a)   in the 8 weeks after the date that a mediation in relation to the dispute ends;

   (b)   on the date that a mediation in relation to the dispute ends; or

   (c)   after the date when all of the parties to the dispute agree to participate in a mediation in relation to the dispute but before the date that such mediation ends.

(2)   Where subsection (1) applies, the limitation period is extended so that it expires on the date falling 8 weeks after the date on which the mediation ends.

(3)   For the purposes of this section, a mediation ends on the date that any of the following occurs—

   (a)   all of the parties reach an agreement in resolution of the dispute;

   (b)   all of the parties agree to end the mediation;

   (c)   a party withdraws from the mediation, which is the date on which—

      (i)   a party informs all of the other parties of that party's withdrawal,

      (ii)   in the case of a mediation involving 2 parties, 14 days expire after a request made by one party to the other party seeking confirmation of whether the other party has withdrawn, if the other party does not respond in that period, or

      (iii)   in the case of a mediation involving more than 2 parties, a party informs all of the remaining parties that the party received no response in the 14 days after that party's request to another party seeking confirmation of whether the other party had withdrawn; or

   (d)   a period of 14 days expires after the date on which the mediator's tenure ends (whether by reason of death, resignation or otherwise), if a replacement mediator has not been appointed.

(4)   In this section—

'the Directive' means Directive 2008/52/EC of the European Parliament and of the Council of 21st May 2008 on certain aspects of mediation in civil and commercial matters;

'mediation' and 'mediator' have the meanings given by Article 3 of the Directive; and

'relevant cross-border dispute' means a cross-border dispute within the meaning given by Article 2 of the Directive—

   (a)   which is about a matter to which a limitation period applies by virtue of section 22B or 22C, and

   (b)   to which the Directive applies.]

Supplementary

[22D Interpretation of this Part

(1)   Expressions used in this Part and in Part I of the 1987 Act shall have the same meanings in this Part as in the said Part I.

(2)   For the purposes of section 1(1) of the 1987 Act, this Part shall have effect and be construed as if it were contained in Part I of that Act.

(3)   In this Part, 'the 1987 Act' means the Consumer Protection Act 1987.]

[. . .]

[23A   Private international law application

(1)   Where the substantive law of a country other than Scotland falls to be applied by a Scottish court as the law governing an obligation, the court shall apply the relevant rules of law of that country relating to the extinction of the obligations or the limitation of time within which proceedings may be brought to enforce the obligation to the exclusion of any corresponding rule of Scots law.

(2)   This section shall not apply where it appears to the court that the application of the relevant foreign rule of law would be incompatible with the principles of public policy applied by the court.

(3)   This section shall not apply in any case where the application of the corresponding rule of Scots law has extinguished the obligation, or barred the bringing of proceedings prior to the coming into force of the Prescription and Limitation (Scotland) Act 1984.]

[(4)   This section shall not apply in any case where the law of a country other than Scotland falls to be applied by virtue of any choice of law rule contained in [the Rome I Regulation or] the Rome II Regulation.

(5)   In subsection (4)—

[(a)   'the Rome I Regulation' means Regulation (EC) No 593/2008 of the European Parliament and of the Council on the law applicable to contractual obligations (Rome I), including that Regulation as applied by regulation 4 of the Law Applicable to Contractual Obligations (Scotland) Regulations 2009 (conflicts falling within Article 22(2) of Regulation (EC) No 593/2008), and

(b)]   'the Rome II Regulation' means Regulation (EC) No 864/2007 of the European Parliament and of the Council on the law applicable to non-contractual obligations (Rome II), including that Regulation as applied by regulation 4 of the Law Applicable to Non-Contractual Obligations (Scotland) Regulations 2008 (conflicts falling within Article 25(2) of Regulation (EC) No 864/2007).]

24   The Crown

This Act binds the Crown.

25   Short title, commencement and extent

(1)   This Act may be cited as the Prescription and Limitation (Scotland) Act 1973.

(2)   This Act shall come into operation as follows—

(a)   Parts II and III of this Act, Part II of Schedule 4 to this Act and Part II of Schedule 5 to this Act shall come into operation on the date on which this Act is passed;

(b)   except as aforesaid this Act shall come into operation on the expiration of three years from the said date.

   [. . .]

(4)   This Act extends to Scotland only.

SCHEDULES

Section 6   SCHEDULE 1
OBLIGATIONS AFFECTED BY PRESCRIPTIVE PERIODS OF FIVE YEARS
UNDER SECTION 6

1.   Subject to paragraph 2 below, section 6 of this Act applies—
   (a)   to any obligation to pay a sum of money due in respect of a particular
period—
      (i)   by way of interest;
      (ii)   by way of an instalment of an annuity;
      [. . .]
      (v)   by way of rent or other periodical payment under a lease;
      (vi)   by way of a periodical payment in respect of the occupancy or use of
land, not being an obligation falling within any other provision of this sub-
paragraph;
      (vii)   by way of a periodical payment under a [title condition], not being an
obligation falling within any other provision of this sub-paragraph;
   (aa)   to any obligation to pay compensation by virtue of section 2 of the
Leasehold Casualties (Scotland) Act 2001 (asp 5);
   (ab)   to any obligation arising by virtue of a right—
      (i)   of reversion under the third proviso to section 2 of the School Sites Act
1841 (4 & 5 Vict c 38) (or of reversion under that proviso as applied by virtue
of any other enactment);
      (ii)   to petition for a declaration of forfeiture under section 7 of the Entail
Sites Act 1840 (3 & 4 Vict c 48);
   (ac)   to any obligation to pay a sum of money by way of costs to which
section 12 of the Tenements (Scotland) Act 2004 (asp 11) applies;]
   [(aca)   to any obligation to make a payment under section 46, 53(2) or 54(5) of
the Long Leases (Scotland) Act 2012 (asp 9),]
   [(ad)   to any obligation of the Keeper of the Registers of Scotland to pay
compensation by virtue of section 84 of the Land Registration etc (Scotland) Act
2012 (asp 5);
   (ae)   to any obligation to pay compensation by virtue of section 111 of that
Act;]
   [(af)   to any obligation arising by virtue of a right to redress under Part 4A of
the Consumer Protection from Unfair Trading Regulations 2008 (SI 2008/1277);]
   (b)   to any obligation based on redress of unjustified enrichment, including
without prejudice to that generality any obligation of restitution, repetition or
recompense;
   (c)   to any obligation arising from *negotiorum gestio*;
   (d)   to any obligation arising from liability (whether arising from any enactment or from any rule of law) to make reparation;
   [(dd)   to any obligation arising by virtue of section 7A(1) of the Criminal
Injuries Compensation Act 1995 (recovery of compensation from offenders:
general);]
   (e)   to any obligation under a bill of exchange or a promissory note;
   (f)   to any obligation of accounting, other than accounting for trust funds;
   (g)   to any obligation arising from, or by reason of any breach of, a contract
or promise, not being an obligation falling within any other provision of this
paragraph.
2.   Notwithstanding anything in the foregoing paragraph, section 6 of this Act
does not apply—
   (a)   to any obligation to recognise or obtemper a decree of court, an arbitration award or an order of a tribunal or authority exercising jurisdiction under
any enactment;

(b)   to any obligation arising from the issue of a bank note;

[. . .]

(d)   to any obligation under a contract of partnership or of agency, not being an obligation remaining, or becoming prestable on or after the termination of the relationship between the parties under the contract;

(e)   except as provided in paragraph 1(a) [to (ae)] of this Schedule, to any obligation relating to land (including an obligation to recognise a servitude) [and any obligation of the Keeper of the Registers of Scotland to pay compensation by virtue of section 77 or 94 of the Land Registration etc (Scotland) Act 2012 (asp 5)];

[(ee)   so as to extinguish, before the expiry of the continuous period of five years which immediately follows the coming into force of section 88 of the Title Conditions (Scotland) Act 2003 (asp 9) (prescriptive period for obligations arising by virtue of 1841 Act or 1840 Act), an obligation mentioned in sub-paragraph (ab) of paragraph 1 of this Schedule;]

(f)   to any obligation to satisfy any claim to [. . .] legitim, jus relicti or jus relictae, or to any prior right of a surviving spouse under section 8 or 9 of the Succession (Scotland) Act 1964;

(g)   to any obligation to make reparation in respect of personal injuries within the meaning of Part II of this Act or in respect of the death of any person as a result of such injuries;

[(gg)   to any obligation to make reparation or otherwise make good in respect of defamation within the meaning of section 18A of this Act;

(ggg)   to any obligation arising from liability under section 2 of the Consumer Protection Act 1987 (to make reparation for damage caused wholly or partly by a defect in a product);]

(h)   to any obligation specified in Schedule 3 to this Act as an imprescriptible obligation.

[. . .]

[4.   In this Schedule, 'title condition' shall be construed in accordance with section 122(1) of the Title Conditions (Scotland) Act 2003 (asp 9).]

Section 6   SCHEDULE 2
APPROPRIATE DATES FOR CERTAIN OBLIGATIONS FOR PURPOSES OF
                                           SECTION 6

1—(1)   This paragraph applies to any obligation, not being part of a banking transaction, to pay money in respect of—

(a)   goods supplied on sale or hire, or

(b)   services rendered,

in a series of transactions between the same parties (whether under a single contract or under several contracts) and charged on continuing account.

(2)   In the foregoing sub-paragraph—

(a)   any reference to the supply of goods on sale includes a reference to the supply of goods under a hire-purchase agreement, a credit-sale agreement or a conditional sale agreement as defined (in each case) by section 1 of the Hire-Purchase (Scotland) Act 1965; and

(b)   any reference to services rendered does not include the work of keeping the account in question.

(3)   Where there is a series of transactions between a partnership and another party, the series shall be regarded for the purposes of this paragraph as terminated (without prejudice to any other mode of termination) if the partnership (in the further provisions of this sub-paragraph referred to as 'the old partnership') is dissolved and is replaced by a single new partnership having among its partners any person who was a partner in the old partnership, then, for the purposes of this

paragraph, the new partnership shall be regarded as if it were identical with the old partnership.

(4)   The appropriate date in relation to an obligation to which this paragraph applies is the date on which payment for the goods last supplied, or, as the case may be, the services last rendered, became due.

2—(1)   This paragraph applies to any obligation to repay the whole, or any part of, a sum of money lent to, or deposited with, the debtor under a contract of loan or, as the case may be, deposit.

(2)   The appropriate date in relation to an obligation to which this paragraph applies is—

(a)   if the contract contains a stipulation which makes provision with respect to the date on or before which repayment of the sum or, as the case may be, the part thereof is to be made, the date on or before which, in terms of that stipulation, the sum or part thereof is to be repaid; and

(b)   if the contract contains no such stipulation, but a written demand for repayment of the sum, or, as the case may be, the part thereof, is made by or on behalf of the creditor to the debtor, the date when such demand is made or first made.

3—(1)   This paragraph applies to any obligation under a contract of partnership or of agency, being an obligation remaining, or becoming, prestable on or after the termination of the relationship between the parties under the contract.

(2)   The appropriate date in relation to an obligation to which this paragraph applies is—

(a)   if the contract contains a stipulation which makes provision with respect to the date on or before which performance on the obligation is to be due, the date on or before which, in terms of that stipulation, the obligation is to be performed; and

(b)   in any other case the date when the said relationship terminated.

4—(1)   This paragraph applies to any obligation—

(a)   to pay an instalment of a sum of money payable by instalments,

(b)   to execute any instalment of work due to be executed by instalments, not being an obligation to which any of the foregoing paragraphs applies.

(2)   The appropriate date in relation to an obligation to which this paragraph applies is the date on which the last of the instalments is due to be paid or, as the case may be, to be executed.

Sections 7 & 8: Schedule 1   SCHEDULE 3
RIGHTS AND OBLIGATIONS WHICH ARE IMPRESCRIPTIBLE FOR THE
PURPOSES OF SECTIONS 7 AND 8 AND SCHEDULE 1

The following are imprescriptible rights and obligations for the purposes of sections 7(2) and 8(2) of, and paragraph 2(h) of Schedule 1 to, this Act, namely—

(a)   any real right of ownership in land;

(b)   the right in land of the lessee under a recorded lease;

(c)   any right exercisable as a *res merae facultatis*;

(d)   any right to recover property *extra commercium*;

(e)   any obligation of a trustee—

(i)   to produce accounts of the trustee's intromissions with any property of the trust;

(ii)   to make reparation or restitution in respect of any fraudulent breach of trust to which the trustee was a party or was privy;

(iii)   to make furthcoming to any person entitled thereto any trust property, or the proceeds of any such property, in the possession of the trustee, or to make good the value of any such property previously received by the trustee and appropriated to his own use;

(f)   any obligation of a third party to make furthcoming to any person entitled thereto any trust property received by the third party otherwise then in good faith and in his possession;

(g)   any right to recover stolen property from the person by whom it was stolen or from any person privy to the stealing thereof;

(h)   any right to be served as heir to an ancestor or to take any steps necessary for making up or completing title to any [real right] in land;

[(i)   any obligation of the Keeper of the Registers of Scotland to rectify an inaccuracy in the Land Register of Scotland].

HEALTH AND SAFETY AT WORK ETC ACT 1974
(1974, c 37)

47   Civil liability

(1)   Nothing in this Part shall be construed—

(a)   as conferring a right of action in any civil proceedings in respect of any failure to comply with any duty imposed by sections 2 to 7 or any contravention of section 8; or

[. . .]

(c)   as affecting the operation of section 12 of the Nuclear Installations Act 1965 (right to compensation by virtue of certain provisions of that Act).

[(2)   Breach of a duty imposed by a statutory instrument containing (whether alone or with other provision) health and safety regulations shall not be actionable except to the extent that regulations under this section so provide.]

[(2A)   Breach of a duty imposed by an existing statutory provision shall not be actionable except to the extent that regulations under this section so provide (including by modifying any of the existing statutory provisions).]

[(2B)   Regulations under this section may include provision for—

(a)   a defence to be available in any action for breach of the duty mentioned in subsection (2) or (2A);

(b)   any term of an agreement which purports to exclude or restrict any liability for such a breach to be void.]

(3)   No provision made by virtue of section 15(6)(b) shall afford a defence in any civil proceedings [. . .].

(4)   Subsections (1)(a) [, (2) and (2A)] above are without prejudice to any right of action which exists apart from the provisions of this Act, and subsection [(2B)(a)] above is without prejudice to any defence which may be available apart from the provisions of the regulations there mentioned.

[. . .]

[(7)   The power to make regulations under this section shall be exercisable by the Secretary of State.]

GUARD DOGS ACT 1975
(1975, c 50)

1   Control of guard dogs

(1)   A person shall not use or permit the use of a guard dog at any premises unless a person ('the handler') who is capable of controlling the dog is present on the premises and the dog is under the control of the handler at all times while it is being so used except while it is secured so that it is not at liberty to go freely about the premises.

(2)   The handler of a guard dog shall keep the dog under his control at all times while it is being used as a guard dog at any premises except—

(a)   while another handler has control over the dog; or

(b)   while the dog is secured so that it is not at liberty to go freely about the premises.

(3)   A person shall not use or permit the use of a guard dog at any premises unless a notice containing a warning that a guard dog is present is clearly exhibited at each entrance to the premises.

DANGEROUS WILD ANIMALS ACT 1976
(1976, c 38)

7   Interpretation

(1)   Subject to subsection (2) of this section, for the purposes of this Act a person is a keeper of an animal if he has it in his possession; and if at any time an animal ceases to be in the possession of a person, any person who immediately before that time was a keeper thereof by virtue of the preceding provisions of this subsection continues to be a keeper of the animal until another person becomes a keeper thereof by virtue of those provisions.

(2)   Where an animal is in the possession of any person for the purpose of—

   (a)   preventing it from causing damage,
   (b)   restoring it to its owner,
   (c)   undergoing veterinary treatment, or
   (d)   being transported on behalf of another person,

the person having such possession shall not by virtue only of that possession be treated for the purposes of this Act as a keeper of the animal.

(3)   In this Act expressions cognate with 'keeper' shall be construed in accordance with subsections (1) and (2) of this section.

(4)   In this Act, unless the context otherwise requires, the following expressions have the meanings hereby respectively assigned to them, that is to say—

'circus' includes any place where animals are kept or introduced wholly or mainly for the purpose of performing tricks or manoeuvres;

'damage' includes the death of, or injury to, any person;

'dangerous wild animal' means any animal of a kind for the time being specified in the first column of the Schedule to this Act;

'local authority' means in relation to England [. . .] a district council, a London borough council or the Common Council of the City of London [, in relation to Wales, a county council or county borough council] and, in relation to Scotland, [a council constituted under section 2 of the Local Government etc (Scotland) Act 1994];

'premises' includes any place;

'veterinary practitioner' means a person who is for the time being registered in the supplementary veterinary register;

'veterinary surgeon' means a person who is for the time being registered in the register of veterinary surgeons;

[. . .]

(5)   The second column of the Schedule to this Act is included by way of explanation only; in the event of any dispute or proceedings, only the first column is to be taken into account.

SCHEDULE* Section 7
KINDS OF DANGEROUS WILD ANIMALS

NOTE: See section 7(5) of this Act for the effect of the second column of this Schedule.

Scientific name of kind	Common name or names
MAMMALS	
Marsupials	
Family *Dasyuridae*: The species *Sarcophilus laniarius*.	The Tasmanian devil.
Family *Macropodidae*: The species *Macropus fuliginosus, Macropus giganteus, Macropus robustus* and *Macropus rufus*.	The western and eastern grey kangaroos, the wallaroo and the red kangaroo
Primates	
Family *Cebidae*: All species except those of the genera *Aotus, Callicebus* and *Saimiri*.	New-world monkeys (including capuchin, howler, saki, uacari, spider and woolly monkeys). *Exceptions*: Night monkeys (also known as owl monkeys), titi monkeys and squirrel monkeys.
Family *Cercopithecidae*.	Old-world monkeys (including baboons, the drill, colobus monkeys, the gelada, guenons, langurs, leaf monkeys, macaques, the mandrill, mangabeys, the patas monkey, the proboscis monkey and the talapoin).
Family *Hominidae*: All species except those of the genus *Homo*	Anthropoid apes (including the chimpanzee, the bonobo, the orang-utan and gorillas). *Exception*: Man.
Family *Hylobatidae*: All species.	Gibbons and Siamangs.
Family *Indriidae*: All species except those of the genus *Avahi*.	Leaping lemurs (including the indri and sifakas). *Exception*: Woolly lemurs.
Family *Lemuridae*: All species except those of the genus *Hapalemur*.	Large lemurs. *Exceptions*: Bamboo lemurs (also known as gentle lemurs).
Edentates	
Family *Dasypodidae*: The species *Priodontes maximus*.	The giant armadillo.
Family *Myrmecophagidae*: The species *Myrmecophaga tridactyla*.	The giant anteater.
Carnivores	
Family *Canidae*: All species except— (a) those of the genera *Alopex, Cerdocyon, Dusicyon, Otocyon, Pseudalopex, Urocyon, Vulpes* and *Nyctereutes* (b) *Canis familiaris*, other than the subspecies *Canis familiaris dingo*.	Canids (including wild dogs, wolves, jackals, the maned wolf, the dhole, the bush dog, and the dingo) other than the excepted species. Exceptions: (a) foxes, culpeo, grey zorro, raccoon dogs (b) domestic dogs.

Schedule substituted by the Dangerous Wild Animals Act 1976 (Modification) (Scotland) Order 2008 (SSI 2008/302)

Scientific name of kind	Common name or names

Family *Felidae*: All species except—
(a) *Felis silvestris* (including the subspecies *Felis silvestris catus*), *Felis margarita*, *Felis nigripes*, *Otocolobus manul*, *Leopardus tigrinus*, *Leopardus geoffroyi* (also known as *Oncifelis geoffroyi*), *Leopardus guigna* (also known as *Oncifelis guigna*), *Catopuma badia* (also known as *Pardofelis badia*) and *Prionailurus rubiginosus*
(b) a hybrid descended exclusively from two or more of the species described in paragraph (a)
(c) a hybrid of which—
  (i) one parent is *Felis silvestris catus*, and
  (ii) the other parent is a first generation hybrid of *Felis silvestris catus* and any species not described in paragraph (a)
(d) a hybrid descended exclusively from hybrid cats as described in paragraph (c) (ignoring, for the purpose of determining exclusivity of descent, the parents and remoter ancestors of any hybrid within that paragraph)
(e) a hybrid descended exclusively from *Felis silvestris catus* and any one or more hybrid cat as described in paragraph (c) (ignoring, for the purpose of determining exclusivity of descent, the parents and remoter ancestors of any hybrid within that paragraph).
	Cats (including the bobcat, caracal, cheetah, jaguar, leopard, lion, lynx, ocelot, puma, serval and tiger) other than the excepted species.
	Exceptions:
	(a) the wild cat (including the domestic cat), the sand cat, the black-footed cat, the pallas cat (also known as the manul), the little spotted cat (also known as the oncilla or tiger cat), the Geoffroy's cat, the kodkod (also known as the guina), the bay cat (also known as the Borneo cat), and the rusty-spotted cat
	(b) a cat descended exclusively from two or more of the species described in paragraph (a)
	(c) a cat of which one parent is a domestic cat and the other parent is a first generation hybrid of a domestic cat and a cat that is a dangerous wild animal
	(d) a cat descended exclusively from hybrid cats described in paragraph (c)
	(e) a cat descended exclusively from the domestic cat and hybrid cats described in paragraph (c).

Family *Hyaenidae*: All species except *Proteles cristatus*.	Hyenas. *Exception*: Aardwolf.
Family *Mustelidae*: (a) all species of the genera *Arctonyx*, *Melogale*, *Mydaus*, *Taxidea*, *Pteronura*, *Aonyx*, *Enhydra* and *Lontra* (b) the genus *Lutra* except the species *Lutra lutra* (c) the species *Eira barbara*, *Gulo gulo*, *Martes pennanti* and *Mellivora capensis*.	(a) the hog badger, the ferret badger, the stink badger, the American badger, the giant otter, the African clawless otter, the oriental small-clawed otter, the sea otter, the river otters, and the marine otter; (b) the hairy-nosed otter (c) the tayra, the wolverine, the fisher (also known as the peken or fisher cat) and the honey badger. *Exception*: European otter.
Family *Ursidae*: All species including the species *Ailuropoda melanoleuca* and *Ailurus fulgens*.	All bears including the giant panda and the red panda.
Family *Viverridae*: (a) all species of the genera *Civettictis* and *Viverra* (b) the species *Cryptoprocta ferox*.	(a) civets (including the African civet, the large-spotted civets, the Malayan civet and the Indian civets) (b) the fossa.

Scientific name of kind	Common name or names
Pinnipedes	
Family *Odobenidae*: All species.	The walrus.
Family *Otariidae*: All species.	Eared seals.
Family *Phocidae*: All species except *Phoca vitulina* and *Halichoerus grypus*.	True seals (also known as earless seals) other than the excepted species. *Exceptions*: Common seal (also known as the harbour seal). Grey seal.
Elephants	
Family *Elephantidae*: All species.	Elephants.
Aardvark	
Family *Orycteropodidae*: The species *Orycteropus afer*.	The aardvark.
Odd-toed ungulates	
Family *Equidae*: All species except *Equus asinus* and *Equus caballus*.	Horses, wild asses, zebras. *Exceptions*: Donkey (also known as the ass), domestic horse.
Family *Rhinocerotidae*: All species.	Rhinoceroses.
Family *Tapiridae*: All species.	Tapirs.
Even-toed ungulates	
Family *Antilocapridae*: The species *Antilocapra Americana*.	The pronghorn.
Family *Bovidae*: All species except domestic forms of the genera *Bos*, *Bubalus*, *Capra* and *Ovis*.	Antelopes, bison, buffalo, gazelles, goats and sheep. *Exceptions*: Domestic cattle, domestic buffalo, domestic goats, domestic sheep.
Family *Camelidae*: All species of the genera *Camelus*.	Camels.
Family *Cervidae*: All species of the genera *Alces* and *Rangifer*, except domestic forms of the species *Rangifer tarandus*.	Moose (also known as the elk) Caribou (also known as the reindeer). *Exception*: Domestic reindeer.
Family *Giraffidae*: All species.	The giraffe and the okapi.
Family *Hippopotamidae*: All species.	The hippopotamus and the pygmy hippopotamus.
Family *Suidae*: All species, except domestic forms of the species *Sus scrofa* other than farmed wild boar.	Old-world pigs other than animals of the excepted kind. *Exception*: Domestic pig, other than farmed wild boar.
Family *Tayassuidae*: All species.	New-world pigs (otherwise known as peccaries).

Scientific name of kind	*Common name or names*
Hybrids	
A hybrid of a mammal specified in the first column of this Schedule where one parent is, or both parents are, of a kind so specified, but not including an excepted hybrid of the Family *Felidae*.	A hybrid animal with a dangerous wild animal as a parent. *Exception*: A cat hybrid that is not a dangerous wild animal.
BIRDS	
Cassowaries	
Family *Casuariidae*: All species.	Cassowaries
Ostrich	
Family *Struthionidae*: All species.	The ostrich.
REPTILES	
Crocodilians	
Family *Alligatoridae*: All species.	Alligators and caimans.
Family *Crocodylidae*: All species.	Crocodiles and the false gharial.
Family *Gavialidae*: All species.	The gharial (also known as the gavial).
Lizards and snakes	
Family *Atractaspididae*: All species of the genera *Atractaspis*.	Burrowing asps (also known as mole vipers, or burrowing vipers). Stiletto snakes.
Family *Colubridae*: (a) all species of the genera *Malpolon* and *Thelotornis* (b) the species *Dispholidus typus, Rhabdophis subminiatus, Rhabdophis tigrinus, Elapomorphus lemniscatus, Philodryas olfersii, Tachymenis peruviana, Xenodon severus*.	(a) all rear-fanged venomous colubrid snakes of the specified genera (including montpellier snakes, the false cobra, and twig or bird snakes) (b) the boomslang, the red-necked keelback, the tiger keelback (also known as the yamakagashi or the Japanese tiger-snake), the Argentine black-headed snake, the South American green racer, the Peruvian racer (also known as the Peru slender snake), the Amazon false viper (also known as the false fer-de-lance).
Family *Elapidae*: All species.	Front-fanged venomous snakes of the specified family (including cobras, coral snakes, kraits, mambas, whipsnakes, death adders and all other Australian poisonous snakes).
Family *Hydrophiidae*: All species.	Sea snakes.
Family *Helodermatidae*: All species.	The gila monster and the Mexican beaded lizard.
Family *Viperidae*: All species.	Front-fanged venomous snakes of the specified family (including adders, the barba amarilla, the bushmaster, the fer-de-lance, moccasins, rattlesnakes and vipers).

Scientific name of kind	Common name or names
INVERTEBRATES	
Spiders	
Family *Ctenidae*: All species of the genus *Phoneutria*.	Wandering spiders.
Family *Hexathelidae*: All species of the genus *Atrax*.	The Sydney funnel-web spider and its close relatives.
Family *Sicariidae*: All species of the genus *Loxosceles*.	Brown recluse spiders (also known as violin spiders).
Family *Theridiidae*: All species of the genus *Latrodectus*.	The widow spiders and close relatives.
Scorpions	
Family *Buthidae*: All species.	Buthid scorpions.
Family *Hemioscorpiidae*: The species *Hemiscorpius lepturus*.	Middle Eastern thin-tailed scorpion.

DIVORCE (SCOTLAND) ACT 1976
(1976, c 39)

10   Right of husband to cite paramour as a co-defender and to sue for damages abolished

(1)   After the commencement of this Act the following rights of a husband shall be abolished, that is to say—

(a)   the right to cite a paramour of his wife as a co-defender in an action for divorce, and

(b)   the right to claim or to obtain damages (including solatium) from a paramour by way of reparation.

(2)   Nothing in the provisions of the foregoing subsection shall preclude the court from awarding the expenses of the action for or against the paramour or alleged paramour in accordance with the practice of the court.

[. . .]

UNFAIR CONTRACT TERMS ACT 1977
(1977, c 50)

PART II
AMENDMENT OF LAW FOR SCOTLAND

15 Scope of Part II

(1)   This Part of this Act [. . .] is subject to Part III of this Act and does not affect
the validity of any discharge or indemnity given by a person in consideration of
the receipt by him of compensation in settlement of any claim which he has.

(2)   Subject to subsection (3) below, sections 16 [and 17] of this Act apply to any
contract only to the extent that the contract—

(a)   relates to the transfer of the ownership or possession of goods from one
person to another (with or without work having been done on them);

(b)   constitutes a contract of service or apprenticeship;

(c)   relates to services of whatever kind, including (without prejudice to the
foregoing generality) carriage, deposit and pledge, care and custody, mandate,
agency, loan and services relating to the use of land;

(d)   relates to the liability of an occupier of land to persons entering upon or
using that land;

(e)   relates to a grant of any right or permission to enter upon or use land not
amounting to an estate or interest in the land.

(3)   Notwithstanding anything in subsection (2) above, sections 16 [and 17]—

(a)   do not apply to any contract to the extent that the contract—

(i)   is a contract of insurance (including a contract to pay an annuity on
human life);

(ii)   relates to the formation, constitution or dissolution of any body
corporate or unincorporated association or partnership;

(b)   apply to—

a contract of marine salvage or towage;

a charter party of a ship or hovercraft;

a contract for the carriage of goods by ship or hovercraft; or

a contract to which subsection (4) below relates,

only to the extent that—

(i)   both parties deal or hold themselves out as dealing in the course of
a business (and then only in so far as the contract purports to exclude or
restrict liability for breach of duty in respect of death or personal injury).
[. . .]

(4)   This subsection relates to a contract in pursuance of which goods are
carried by ship or hovercraft and which either—

(a)   specifies ship or hovercraft as the means of carriage over part of the jour-
ney to be covered; or

(b)   makes no provision as to the means of carriage and does not exclude
ship or hovercraft as that means,

in so far as the contract operates for and in relation to the carriage of the goods by
that means.

16 Liability for breach of duty

(1)   [Subject to subsection (1A) below,] where a term of a contract [, or a provision of a notice given to persons generally or to particular persons,] purports to
exclude or restrict liability for breach of duty arising in the course of any business
or from the occupation of any premises used for business purposes of the occupier, that term [or provision]—

(a)   shall be void in any case where such exclusion or restriction is in respect
of death or personal injury;

(b)   shall, in any other case, have no effect if it was not fair and reasonable to incorporate the term in the contract [or, as the case may be, if it is not fair and reasonable to allow reliance on the provision].

[(1A)   Nothing in paragraph (b) of subsection (1) above shall be taken as implying that a provision of a notice has effect in circumstances where, apart from that paragraph, it would not have effect.]

(2)   Subsection (1)(a) above does not affect the validity of any discharge and indemnity given by a person, on or in connection with an award to him of compensation for pneumoconiosis attributable to employment in the coal industry, in respect of any further claim arising from his contracting that disease.

(3)   Where under subsection (1) above a term of a contract [or a provision of a notice] is void or has no effect, the fact that a person agreed to, or was aware of, the term [or provision] shall not of itself be sufficient evidence that he knowingly and voluntarily assumed any risk.

[(4)   This section does not apply to—
(a)   a term in a consumer contract, or
(b)   a notice to the extent that it is a consumer notice,
(but see the provision made about such contracts and notices in sections 62 and 65 of the Consumer Rights Act 2015).]

17   Control of unreasonable exemptions in [. . .] standard form contracts

(1)   Any term of a contract which is [. . .] a standard form contract shall have no effect for the purpose of enabling a party to the contract—
(a)   who is in breach of a contractual obligation, to exclude or restrict any liability of his to the [. . .] customer in respect of the breach;
(b)   in respect of a contractual obligation, to render no performance, or to render a performance substantially different from that which the [. . .] customer reasonably expected from the contract;
if it was not fair and reasonable to incorporate the term in the contract.

(2)   In this section 'customer' means a party to a standard form contract who deals on the basis of written standard terms of business of the other party to the contract who himself deals in the course of a business.

[(3)   This section does not apply to a term in a consumer contract (but see the provision made about such contracts in section 62 of the Consumer Rights Act 2015).]

[. . .]

20   Obligations implied by law in sale and hire-purchase contracts

(1)   Any term of a contract which purports to exclude or restrict liability for breach of the obligations arising from—
(a)   section 12 of the Sale of Goods Act [1979] (seller's implied undertakings as to title etc);
(b)   section 8 of the Supply of Goods (Implied Terms) Act 1973 (implied terms as to title in hire-purchase agreements),
shall be void.

[(1A)   Any term of a contract which purports to exclude or restrict liability for breach of the obligations arising from—
(a)   section 13, 14 or 15 of the 1979 Act (seller's implied undertakings as to conformity of goods with description or sample, or as to their quality or fitness for a particular purpose);
(b)   section 9, 10 or 11 of the 1973 Act (the corresponding things in relation to hire purchase),
shall have effect only if it was fair and reasonable to incorporate the term in the contract.

(1B)   This section does not apply to a consumer contract (but see the provision made about such contracts in section 31 of the Consumer Rights Act 2015).]

[. . .]

21   Obligations implied by law in other contracts for the supply of goods

(1)   Any term of a contract to which this section applies purporting to exclude or restrict liability for breach of an obligation [such as is referred to in subsection (3) below shall have no effect if it was not fair and reasonable to incorporate the term in the contract.]

(2)   This section applies to any contract to the extent that it relates to any such matter as is referred to in section 15(2)(a) of this Act, but does not apply to—

(a)   a contract of sale of goods or a hire-purchase agreement; or

(b)   a charterparty of a ship or hovercraft [. . .].

(3)   An obligation referred to in this subsection is an obligation incurred under a contract in the course of a business and arising by implication of law from the nature of the contract which relates—

(a)   to the correspondence of goods with description or sample, or to the quality or fitness of goods for any particular purpose; or

(b)   to any right to transfer ownership or possession of goods, or to the enjoyment of quiet possession of goods.

[(3A)   Notwithstanding anything in the foregoing provisions of this section, any term of a contract which purports to exclude or restrict liability for breach of the obligations arising under section 11B of the Supply of Goods and Services Act 1982 (implied terms about title, freedom from encumbrances and quiet possession in certain contracts for the transfer of property in goods) shall be void.]

[(3B)   This section does not apply to a consumer contract (but see the provision made about such contracts in section 31 of the Consumer Rights Act 2015).]

[. . .]

[. . .]

23   Evasion by means of secondary contract

Any term of any contract shall be void which purports to exclude or restrict, or has the effect of excluding or restricting—

(a)   the exercise, by a party to any other contract, of any right or remedy which arises in respect of that other contract in consequence of breach of duty, or of obligation, liability for which could not by virtue of the provisions of this Part of this Act be excluded or restricted by a term of that other contract;

(b)   the application of the provisions of this Part of this Act in respect of that or any other contract.

24   The 'reasonableness' test

(1)   In determining for the purposes of this Part of this Act whether it was fair and reasonable to incorporate a term in a contract, regard shall be had only to the circumstances which were, or ought reasonably to have been, known to or in the contemplation of the parties to the contract at the time the contract was made.

(2)   In determining for the purposes of section 20 or 21 of this Act whether it was fair and reasonable to incorporate a term in a contract, regard shall be had in particular to the matters specified in Schedule 2 to this Act; but this sub-section shall not prevent a court or arbiter from holding in accordance with any rule of law, that a term which purports to exclude or restrict any relevant liability is not a term of the contract.

[(2A)   In determining for the purposes of this Part of this Act whether it is fair and reasonable to allow reliance on a provision of a notice (not being a notice having contractual effect), regard shall be had to all the circumstances obtaining when the liability arose or (but for the provision) would have arisen.]

(3)   Where a term in a contract [or a provision of a notice] purports to restrict liability to a specified sum of money, and the question arises for the purposes of this Part of this Act whether it was fair and reasonable to incorporate the term in the contract [or whether it is fair and reasonable to allow reliance on the pro-

vision], then, without prejudice to subsection (2) above [in the case of a term in a contract], regard shall be had in particular to—

(a) the resources which the party seeking to rely on that term [or provision] could expect to be available to him for the purpose of meeting the liability should it arise;

(b) how far it was open to that party to cover himself by insurance.

(4) The onus of proving that it was fair and reasonable to incorporate a term in a contract [or that it is fair and reasonable to allow reliance on a provision of a notice] shall lie on the party so contending.

25 Interpretation of Part II

(1) In this Part of this Act—

'breach of duty' means the breach—

(a) of any obligation, arising from the express or implied terms of a contract, to take reasonable care or exercise reasonable skill in the performance of the contract;

(b) of any common law duty to take reasonable care or exercise reasonable skill;

(c) of the duty of reasonable care imposed by section 2(1) of the Occupiers' Liability (Scotland) Act 1960;

'business' includes a profession and the activities of any government department or local or public authority;

[. . .]

['consumer contract' has the same meaning as in the Consumer Rights Act 2015 (see section 61);

'consumer notice' has the same meaning as in the Consumer Rights Act 2015 (see section 61);]

'goods' has the same meaning as in the Sale of Goods Act [1979];

'hire-purchase agreement' has the same meaning as in section 189(1) of the Consumer Credit Act 1974;

['notice' includes an announcement, whether or not in writing, and any other communication or pretended communication;]

'personal injury' includes any disease and any impairment of physical or mental condition.

[. . .]

(2) In relation to any breach of duty or obligation, it is immaterial for any purpose of this Part of this Act whether the act or omission giving rise to that breach was inadvertent or intentional or whether liability for it arises directly or vicariously.

(3) In this Part of this Act, any reference to excluding or restricting any liability includes—

(a) making the liability or its enforcement subject to any restrictive or onerous conditions;

(b) excluding or restricting any right or remedy in respect of the liability, or subjecting a person to any prejudice in consequence of his pursuing any such right or remedy;

(c) excluding or restricting any rule of evidence or procedure;

[. . .]

but does not include an agreement to submit any question to arbitration.

(5) In section 15 [, 16, 20 and] 21 of this Act, any reference to excluding or restricting liability for breach of any obligation or duty shall include a reference to excluding or restricting the obligation or duty itself.

PART III
PROVISIONS APPLYING TO WHOLE OF UNITED KINGDOM

26 International supply contracts

(1) The limits imposed by this Act on the extent to which a person may

exclude or restrict liability by reference to a contract term do not apply to liability arising under such a contract as is described in subsection (3) below.

(2) The terms of such a contract are not subject to any requirement of reasonableness under section 3 [. . .]: and nothing in Part II of this Act should require the incorporation of the terms of such a contract to be fair and reasonable for them to have effect.

(3) Subject to subsection (4), that description of contract is one whose characteristics are the following—

(a) either it is a contract of sale of goods or it is one under or in pursuance of which the possession of ownership of goods passes, and

(b) it is made by parties whose places of business (or, if they have none, habitual residences) are in the territories of different States (the Channel Islands and the Isle of Man being treated for this purpose as different States from the United Kingdom).

(4) A contract falls within subsection (3) above only if either—

(a) the goods in question are, at the time of the conclusion of the contract, in the course of carriage, or will be carried, from the territory of one State to the territory of another; or

(b) the acts constituting the offer and acceptance have been done in the territories of different States; or

(c) the contract provides for the goods to be delivered to the territory of a state other than that within whose territory those acts were done.

27 Choice of law clauses

(1) Where the [law applicable to] a contract is the law of any part of the United Kingdom only by choice of the parties (and apart from that choice would be the law of some country outside the United Kingdom) sections 2 to 7 and 16 to 21 of this Act do not operate as part [of the law applicable to the contract].

(2) This Act has effect notwithstanding any contract term which applies or purports to apply the law of some country outside the United Kingdom, where [. . .]—

(a) the term appears to the court, or arbitrator or arbiter to have been imposed wholly or mainly for the purpose of enabling the party imposing it to evade the operation of this Act; [. . .]

29 Saving for other relevant legislation

(1) Nothing in this Act removes or restricts the effect of, or prevents reliance upon, any contractual provision which—

(a) is authorised or required by the express terms or necessary implication of an enactment; or

(b) being made with a view to compliance with an international agreement to which the United Kingdom is a party, does not operate more restrictively than is contemplated by the agreement.

(2) A contract term is to be taken—

(a) for the purposes of Part I of this Act, as satisfying the requirement of reasonableness; and

(b) for those of Part II, to have been fair and reasonable to incorporate,

if it is incorporated or approved by, or incorporated pursuant to a decision or ruling of, a competent authority acting in the exercise of any statutory jurisdiction or function and is not a term in a contract to which the competent authority is itself a party.

(3) In this section—

'competent authority' means any court, arbitrator or arbiter, government department or public authority;

'enactment' means any legislation (including subordinate legislation) of the United Kingdom or Northern Ireland and any instrument having effect by virtue of such legislation; and

'statutory' means conferred by an enactment.

. . .

SCHEDULE 2
'GUIDELINES' FOR APPLICATION OF REASONABLENESS TEST

Sections 11(2) and 24(2)

The matters to which regard is to be had in particular for the purposes of sections [6(1A), 7(1A) and (4),], 20 and 21 are any of the following which appear to be relevant—

(a)   the strength of the bargaining positions of the parties relative to each other, taking into account (among other things) alternative means by which the customer's requirements could have been met;

(b)   whether the customer received an inducement to agree to the terms, or in accepting it had an opportunity of entering into a similar contract with other persons, but without having to accept similar terms;

(c)   whether the customer knew or ought reasonably to have known of the existence and extent of the term (having regard, among other things, to any customs of the trade and any previous course of dealing between the parties);

(d)   where the term excludes or restricts any relevant liability if some condition is not complied with, whether it was reasonable at the time of the contract to expect that compliance with that condition would be practicable;

(e)   whether the goods were manufactured, processed or adapted to the special order of the customer.

SALE OF GOODS ACT 1979
(1979, c 54)

PART I
CONTRACTS TO WHICH ACT APPLIES

1   Contracts to which Act applies

(1)   This Act applies to contracts of sale of goods made on or after (but not to those made before) 1 January 1894.

(2)   In relation to contracts made on certain dates, this Act applies subject to the modification of certain of its sections as mentioned in Schedule 1 below.

(3)   Any such modification is indicated in the section concerned by a reference to Schedule 1 below.

(4)   Accordingly, where a section does not contain such a reference, this Act applies in relation to the contract concerned without such modification of the section.

[(5)   Certain sections or subsections of this Act do not apply to a contract to which Chapter 2 of Part 1 of the Consumer Rights Act 2015 applies.

(6)   Where that is the case it is indicated in the section concerned.]

PART II
FORMATION OF THE CONTRACT

Contract of sale

2   Contract of sale

(1)   A contract of sale of goods is a contract by which the seller transfers or agrees to transfer the property in goods to the buyer for a money consideration, called the price.

(2)   There may be a contract of sale between one part owner and another.

(3)   A contract of sale may be absolute or conditional.

(4)   Where under a contract of sale the property in the goods is transferred from the seller to the buyer the contract is called a sale.

(5)   Where under a contract of sale the transfer of the property in the goods is to take place at a future time or subject to some condition later to be fulfilled the contract is called an agreement to sell.

(6)   An agreement to sell becomes a sale when the time elapses or the conditions are fulfilled subject to which the property in the goods is to be transferred.

3   Capacity to buy and sell

(1)   Capacity to buy and sell is regulated by the general law concerning capacity to contract and to transfer and acquire property.

(2)   Where necessaries are sold and delivered [. . .] to a person who by reason of mental incapacity or drunkenness is incompetent to contract, he must pay a reasonable price for them.

(3)   In subsection (2) above 'necessaries' means goods suitable to the condition in life of the [. . .] person concerned and to his actual requirements at the time of the sale and delivery.

Formalities of contract

4   How contract of sale is made

(1)   Subject to this and any other Act, a contract of sale may be made in writing (either with or without seal), or by word of mouth, or partly in writing and partly by word of mouth, or may be implied from the conduct of the parties.

(2)   Nothing in this section affects the law relating to corporations.

Subject matter of contract

5   Existing or future goods

(1)   The goods which form the subject of a contract of sale may be either existing goods, owned or possessed by the seller, or goods to be manufactured or acquired by him after the making of the contract of sale, in this Act called future goods.

(2)   There may be a contract for the sale of goods the acquisition of which by the seller depends on a contingency which may or may not happen.

(3)   Where by a contract of sale the seller purports to effect a present sale of future goods, the contract operates as an agreement to sell the goods.

6   Goods which have perished

Where there is a contract for the sale of specific goods, and the goods without the knowledge of the seller have perished at the time when a contract is made, the contract is void.

7   Goods perishing before sale but after agreement to sell

Where there is an agreement to sell specific goods and subsequently the goods, without any fault on the part of the seller or buyer, perish before the risk passes to the buyer, the agreement is avoided.

The price

8   Ascertainment of price

(1)   The price in a contract of sale may be fixed by the contract, or may be left to be fixed in a manner agreed by the contract, or may be determined by the course of dealing between the parties.

(2)   Where the price is not determined as mentioned in subsection (1) above the buyer must pay a reasonable price.

(3)   What is a reasonable price is a question of fact dependent on the circumstances of each particular case.

9   Agreement to sell at valuation

(1)   Where there is an agreement to sell goods on the terms that the price is to be fixed by the valuation of a third party, and he cannot or does not make the valuation, the agreement is avoided; but if the goods or any part of them have been delivered to and appropriated by the buyer he must pay a reasonable price for them.

(2)   Where the third party is prevented from making the valuation by the fault of the seller or buyer, the party not at fault may maintain an action for damages against the party at fault.

[Implied terms etc]

10   Stipulations about time

(1)   Unless a different intention appears from the terms of the contract, stipulations as to time of payment are not of the essence of a contract of sale.

(2)   Whether any other stipulation as to time is or is not of the essence of the contract depends on the terms of the contract.

(3)   In a contract of sale 'month' prima facie means calendar month.

11   [*Does not apply to Scotland.*]

12   Implied terms about title, etc

(1)   In a contract of sale, other than one to which subsection (3) below applies, there is an implied [term] on the part of the seller that in the case of a sale he has a right to sell the goods, and in the case of an agreement to sell he will have such a right at the time when the property is to pass.

(2)   In a contract of sale, other than one to which subsection (3) below applies, there is also an implied [term] that—

  (a)   the goods are free, and will remain free until the time when the property is to pass, from any charge or encumbrance not disclosed or known to the buyer before the contract is made, and

  (b)   the buyer will enjoy quiet possession of the goods except so far as it may be disturbed by the owner or other person entitled to the benefit of any charge or encumbrance so disclosed or known.

(3)   This subsection applies to a contract of sale in the case of which there appears from the contract or is to be inferred from its circumstances an intention that the seller should transfer only such title as he or a third person may have.

(4)   In a contract to which subsection (3) above applies there is an implied [term] that all charges or encumbrances known to the seller and not known to the buyer have been disclosed to the buyer before the contract is made.

(5)   In a contract to which subsection (3) above applies there is also an implied [term] that none of the following will disturb the buyer's quiet possession of the goods, namely—

  (a)   the seller;

  (b)   in a case where the parties to the contract intend that the seller should transfer only such title as a third person may have, that person;

  (c)   anyone claiming through or under the seller or that third person otherwise than under a charge or encumbrance disclosed or known to the buyer before the contract is made.

[(5A)   As regards England and Wales and Northern Ireland, the term implied by subsection (1) above is a condition and the terms implied by subsections (2), (4) and (5) above are warranties.]

(6)   Paragraph 3 of Schedule 1 below applies in relation to a contract made before 18 May 1973.

[(7)   This section does not apply to a contract to which Chapter 2 of Part 1 of the Consumer Rights Act 2015 applies (but see the provision made about such contracts in section 17 of that Act).]

13 Sale by description

(1) Where there is a contract for the sale of goods by description, there is an implied [term] that the goods will correspond with the description.

[(1A) As regards England and Wales and Northern Ireland, the term implied by subsection (1) above is a condition.]

(2) If the sale is by sample as well as by description it is not sufficient that the bulk of the goods corresponds with the sample if the goods do not also correspond with the description.

(3) A sale of goods is not prevented from being a sale by description by reason only that, being exposed for sale or hire, they are selected by the buyer.

(4) Paragraph 4 of Schedule 1 below applies in relation to a contract made before 18 May 1973.

[(5) This section does not apply to a contract to which Chapter 2 of Part 1 of the Consumer Rights Act 2015 applies (but see the provision made about such contracts in section 11 of that Act).]

14 Implied terms about quality or fitness

(1) Except as provided by this section and section 15 below and subject to any other enactment, there is no implied [term] about the quality or fitness for any particular purpose of goods supplied under a contract of sale.

[(2) Where the seller sells goods in the course of a business, there is an implied term that the goods supplied under the contract are of satisfactory quality.

(2A) For the purposes of this Act, goods are of satisfactory quality if they meet the standard that a reasonable person would regard as satisfactory, taking account of any description of the goods, the price (if relevant) and all the other relevant circumstances.

(2B) For the purposes of this Act, the quality of goods includes their state and condition and the following (among others) are in appropriate cases aspects of the quality of goods—

(a) fitness for all the purposes for which goods of the kind in question are commonly supplied,

(b) appearance and finish,

(c) freedom from minor defects,

(d) safety, and

(e) durability.

(2C) The term implied by subsection (2) above does not extend to any matter making the quality of goods unsatisfactory—

(a) which is specifically drawn to the buyer's attention before the contract is made,

(b) where the buyer examines the goods before the contract is made, which that examination ought to reveal, or

(c) in the case of a contract for sale by sample, which would have been apparent on a reasonable examination of the sample.]

[. . .]

(3) Where the seller sells goods in the course of a business and the buyer, expressly or by implication, makes known—

(a) to the seller, or

(b) where the purchase price or part of it is payable by instalments and the goods were previously sold by a credit-broker to the seller, to that credit-broker,

any particular purpose for which the goods are being bought,

there is an implied [term] that the goods supplied under the contract are reasonably fit for that purpose, whether or not that is a purpose for which such goods are commonly supplied, except where the circumstances show that the buyer does not rely, or that it is unreasonable for him to rely, on the skill or judgment of the seller or credit-broker.

(4) An implied [term] about quality or fitness for a particular purpose may be annexed to a contract of sale by usage.

(5) The preceding provisions of this section apply to a sale by a person who in the course of a business is acting as agent for another as they apply to a sale by a principal in the course of a business, except where that other is not selling in the course of a business and either the buyer knows that fact or reasonable steps are taken to bring it to the notice of the buyer before the contract is made.

[(6) As regards England and Wales and Northern Ireland, the terms implied by subsections (2) and (3) above are conditions.]

(7) Paragraph 5 of Schedule 1 below applies in relation to a contract made on or after 18 May 1973 and before the appointed day, and paragraph 6 in relation to one made before 18 May 1973.

(8) In subsection (7) above and paragraph 5 of Schedule 1 below references to the appointed day are to the day appointed for the purposes of those provisions by an order of the Secretary of State made by statutory instrument.

[(9) This section does not apply to a contract to which Chapter 2 of Part 1 of the Consumer Rights Act 2015 applies (but see the provision made about such contracts in sections 9, 10 and 18 of that Act).]

Sale by sample

15 Sale by sample

(1) A contract of sale is a contract for sale by sample where there is an express or implied term to that effect in the contract.

(2) In the case of a contract for sale by sample there is an implied [term]—

(a) that the bulk will correspond with the sample in quality;

[. . .]

(c) that the goods will be free from any defect, making their quality unsatisfactory, which would not be apparent on reasonable examination of the sample.

[(3) As regards England and Wales and Northern Ireland, the term implied by subsection (2) above is a condition.]

(4) Paragraph 7 of Schedule 1 below applies in relation to a contract made before 18 May 1973.

[(5) This section does not apply to a contract to which Chapter 2 of Part 1 of the Consumer Rights Act 2015 applies (but see the provision made about such contracts in sections 13 and 18 of that Act).]

Miscellaneous

15A [*Does not apply to Scotland.*]

[15B Remedies for breach of contract as respects Scotland

(1) Where in a contract of sale the seller is in breach of any term of the contract (express or implied), the buyer shall be entitled—

(a) to claim damages, and

(b) if the breach is material, to reject any goods delivered under the contract and treat it as repudiated.

[(1A) Subsection (1) does not apply to a contract to which Chapter 2 of Part 1 of the Consumer Rights Act 2015 applies (but see the provision made about such contracts in sections 19 to 22 of that Act).]

[. . .]

(3) This section applies to Scotland only.]

PART III
EFFECTS OF THE CONTRACT

Transfer of property as between seller and buyer

16   Goods must be ascertained
[Subject to section 20A below] where there is a contract for the sale of unascertained goods no property in the goods is transferred to the buyer unless and until the goods are ascertained.

17   Property passes when intended to pass
(1)   Where there is a contract for the sale of specific or ascertained goods the property in them is transferred to the buyer at such time as the parties to the contract intend it to be transferred.

(2)   For the purpose of ascertaining the intention of the parties regard shall be had to the terms of the contract, the conduct of the parties and the circumstances of the case.

18   Rules for ascertaining intention
Unless a different intention appears, the following are rules for ascertaining the intention of the parties as to the time at which the property in the goods is to pass to the buyer.

Rule 1.—Where there is an unconditional contract for the sale of specific goods in a deliverable state the property in the goods passes to the buyer when the contract is made, and it is immaterial whether the time of payment or the time of delivery, or both, be postponed.

Rule 2.—Where there is a contract for the sale of specific goods and the seller is bound to do something to the goods for the purpose of putting them into a deliverable state, the property does not pass until the thing is done and the buyer has notice that it has been done.

Rule 3.—Where there is a contract for the sale of specific goods in a deliverable state but the seller is bound to weigh, measure, test, or do some other act or thing with reference to the goods for the purpose of ascertaining the price, the property does not pass until the act or thing is done and the buyer has notice that it has been done.

Rule 4.—When goods are delivered to the buyer on approval or on sale or return or other similar terms the property in the goods passes to the buyer:—

   (a)   when he signifies his approval or acceptance to the seller or does any other act adopting the transaction;

   (b)   if he does not signify his approval or acceptance to the seller but retains the goods without giving notice of rejection, then, if a time has been fixed for the return of the goods, on the expiration of that time, and, if no time has been fixed, on the expiration of a reasonable time.

Rule 5.—(1)   Where there is a contract for the sale of unascertained or future goods by description, and goods of that description and in a deliverable state are unconditionally appropriated to the contract, either by the seller with the assent of the buyer or by the buyer with the assent of the seller, the property in the goods then passes to the buyer; and the assent may be express or implied, and may be given either before or after the appropriation is made.

(2)   Where, in pursuance of the contract, the seller delivers the goods to the buyer or to a carrier or other bailee or custodier (whether named by the buyer or not) for the purpose of transmission to the buyer, and does not reserve the right of disposal, he is to be taken to have unconditionally appropriated the goods to the contract.

[(3)   Where there is a contract for the sale of a specified quantity of unascertained goods in a deliverable state forming part of a bulk which is identified either in the contract or by subsequent agreement between the parties and the bulk is reduced to (or to less than) that quantity, then, if the buyer under that contract is the only buyer to whom goods are then due out of the bulk—

(a)   the remaining goods are to be taken as appropriated to that contract at the time when the bulk is so reduced; and

(b)   the property in those goods then passes to that buyer.

(4)   Paragraph (3) above applies also (with the necessary modifications) where a bulk is reduced to (or to less than) the aggregate of the quantities due to a single buyer under separate contracts relating to that bulk and he is the only buyer to whom goods are then due out of that bulk.]

19   Reservation of right of disposal

(1)   Where there is a contract for the sale of specific goods or where goods are subsequently appropriated to the contract, the seller may, by the terms of the contract or appropriation, reserve the right of disposal of the goods until certain conditions are fulfilled; and in such a case, notwithstanding the delivery of the goods to the buyer, or to a carrier or other bailee or custodier for the purpose of transmission to the buyer, the property in the goods does not pass to the buyer until the conditions imposed by the seller are fulfilled.

(2)   Where goods are shipped, and by the bill of lading the goods are deliverable to the order of the seller or his agent, the seller is prima facie to be taken to reserve the right of disposal.

(3)   Where the seller of goods draws on the buyer for the price, and transmits the bill of exchange and bill of lading to the buyer together to secure acceptance or payment of the bill of exchange, the buyer is bound to return the bill of lading if he does not honour the bill of exchange, and if he wrongfully retains the bill of lading the property in the goods does not pass to him.

20   [Passing of risk]

(1)   Unless otherwise agreed, the goods remain at the seller's risk until the property in them is transferred to the buyer, but when the property in them is transferred to the buyer the goods are at the buyer's risk whether delivery has been made or not.

(2)   But where delivery has been delayed through the fault of either buyer or seller the goods are at the risk of the party at fault as regards any loss which might not have occurred but for such fault.

(3)   Nothing in this section affects the duties or liabilities of either seller or buyer as a bailee or custodier of the goods of the other party.

[(4)   This section does not apply to a contract to which Chapter 2 of Part 1 of the Consumer Rights Act 2015 applies (but see the provision made about such contracts in section 29 of that Act).]

[20A   Undivided shares in goods forming part of a bulk

(1)   This section applies to a contract for the sale of a specified quantity of un-ascertained goods if the following conditions are met—

(a)   the goods or some of them form part of a bulk which is identified either in the contract or by subsequent agreement between the parties; and

(b)   the buyer has paid the price for some or all of the goods which are the subject of the contract and which form part of the bulk.

(2)   Where this section applies, then (unless the parties agree otherwise), as soon as the conditions specified in paragraphs (a) and (b) of subsection (1) above are met or at such later time as the parties may agree—

(a)   property in an undivided share in the bulk is transferred to the buyer; and

(b)   the buyer becomes an owner in common of the bulk.

(3)   Subject to subsection (4) below, for the purposes of this section, the undivided share of a buyer in a bulk at any time shall be such share as the quantity

of goods paid for and due to the buyer out of the bulk bears to the quantity of goods in the bulk at that time.

(4) Where the aggregate of the undivided shares of buyers in a bulk determined under subsection (3) above would at any time exceed the whole of the bulk at that time, the undivided share in the bulk of each buyer shall be reduced proportionately so that the aggregate of the undivided shares is equal to the whole bulk.

(5) Where a buyer has paid the price for only some of the goods due to him out of a bulk, any delivery to the buyer out of the bulk shall, for the purposes of this section, be ascribed in the first place to the goods in respect of which payment has been made.

(6) For the purpose of this section payment of part of the price for any goods shall be treated as payment for a corresponding part of the goods.]

[20B Deemed consent by co-owner to dealings in bulk goods

(1) A person who has become an owner in common of a bulk by virtue of section 20A above shall be deemed to have consented to—

(a) any delivery of goods out of the bulk to any other owner in common of the bulk, being goods which are due to him under his contract;

(b) any dealing with or removal, delivery or disposal of goods in the bulk by any other person who is an owner in common of the bulk in so far as the goods fall within that co-owner's undivided share in the bulk at the time of the removal, dealing, delivery or disposal.

(2) No cause of action shall accrue to anyone against a person by reason of that person having acted in accordance with paragraph (a) or (b) of subsection (1) above in reliance on any consent deemed to have been given under that subsection.

(3) Nothing in this section or section 20A above shall—

(a) impose an obligation on a buyer of goods out of a bulk to compensate any other buyer of goods out of that bulk for any shortfall in the goods received by that other buyer;

(b) affects any contractual arrangement between buyers of goods out of a bulk for adjustments between themselves; or

(c) affect the rights of any buyer under his contract.]

Transfer of title

21 Sale by person not the owner

(1) Subject to this Act, where goods are sold by a person who is not their owner, and who does not sell them under the authority or with the consent of the owner, the buyer acquires no better title to the goods than the seller had, unless the owner of the goods is by his conduct precluded from denying the seller's authority to sell.

(2) Nothing in this Act affects—

(a) the provisions of the Factors Acts or any enactment enabling the apparent owner of goods to dispose of them as if he were their true owner;

(b) the validity of any contract of sale under any special common law or statutory power of sale or under the order of a court of competent jurisdiction.

22 [*Does not apply to Scotland.*]

23 Sale under voidable title

When the seller of goods has a voidable title to them, but his title has not been avoided at the time of the sale, the buyer acquires a good title to the goods, provided he buys them in good faith and without notice of the seller's defect of title.

24 Seller in possession after sale

Where a person having sold goods continues or is in possession of the goods, or of the documents of title to the goods, the delivery or transfer by that person, or by a mercantile agent acting for him, of the goods or documents of title under any sale, pledge, or other disposition thereof, to any person receiving the same in good faith and without notice of the previous sale, has the same effect as if the person making the delivery or transfer were expressly authorised by the owner of the goods to make the same.

25 Buyer in possession after sale

(1) Where a person having bought or agreed to buy goods obtains, with the consent of the seller, possession of the goods or the documents of title to the goods, the delivery or transfer by that person, or by a mercantile agent acting for him, of the goods or documents of title, under any sale, pledge, or other disposition thereof, to any person receiving the same in good faith and without notice of any lien or other right of the original seller in respect of the goods, has the same effect as if the person making the delivery or transfer were a mercantile agent in possession of the goods or documents of title with the consent of the owner.

(2) For the purposes of subsection (1) above—

(a) the buyer under a conditional sale agreement is to be taken not to be a person who has bought or agreed to buy goods, and

(b) 'conditional sale agreement' means an agreement for the sale of goods which is a consumer credit agreement within the meaning of the Consumer Credit Act 1974 under which the purchase price or part of it is payable by instalments, and the property in the goods is to remain in the seller (notwithstanding that the buyer is to be in possession of the goods) until such conditions as to the payment of instalments or otherwise as may be specified in the agreement are fulfilled.

(3) Paragraph 9 of Schedule 1 below applies in relation to a contract under which a person buys or agrees to buy goods and which is made before the appointed day.

(4) In subsection (3) above and paragraph 9 of Schedule 1 below references to the appointed day are to the day appointed for the purposes of those provisions by an order of the Secretary of State made by statutory instrument.

26 Supplementary to sections 24 and 25

In sections 24 and 25 above 'mercantile agent' means a mercantile agent having in the customary course of his business as such agent authority either—

(a) to sell goods, or

(b) to consign goods for the purpose of sale, or

(c) to buy goods, or

(d) to raise money on the security of goods.

PART IV
PERFORMANCE OF THE CONTRACT

27 Duties of seller and buyer

It is the duty of the seller to deliver the goods, and of the buyer to accept and pay for them, in accordance with the terms of the contract of sale.

28 Payment and delivery are concurrent conditions

Unless otherwise agreed, delivery of the goods and payment of the price are concurrent conditions, that is to say, the seller must be ready and willing to give possession of the goods to the buyer in exchange for the price and the buyer must be ready and willing to pay the price in exchange for possession of the goods.

29 Rules about delivery

(1) Whether it is for the buyer to take possession of the goods or for the seller to send them to the buyer is a question depending in each case on the contract, express or implied, between the parties.

(2)   Apart from any such contract, express or implied, the place of delivery is the seller's place of business if he has one, and if not, his residence; except that, if the contract is for the sale of specific goods, which to the knowledge of the parties when the contract is made are in some other place, then that place is the place of delivery.

(3)   Where under the contract of sale the seller is bound to send the goods to the buyer, but no time for sending them is fixed, the seller is bound to send them within a reasonable time.

[(3A)   Subsection (3) does not apply to a contract to which Chapter 2 of Part 1 of the Consumer Rights Act 2015 applies (but see the provision made about such contracts in section 28 of that Act).]

(4)   Where the goods at the time of sale are in the possession of a third person, there is no delivery by seller to buyer unless and until the third person acknowledges to the buyer that he holds the goods on his behalf; but nothing in this section affects the operation of the issue or transfer of any document of title to goods.

(5)   Demand or tender of delivery may be treated as ineffectual unless made at a reasonable hour, and what is a reasonable hour is a question of fact.

(6)   Unless otherwise agreed, the expenses of and incidental to putting the goods into a deliverable state must be borne by the seller.

30   Delivery of wrong quantity

(1)   Where the seller delivers to the buyer a quantity of goods less than he contracted to sell, the buyer may reject them, but if the buyer accepts the goods so delivered he must pay for them at the contract rate.

(2)   Where the seller delivers to the buyer a quantity of goods larger than he contracted to sell, the buyer may accept the goods included in the contract and reject the rest, or he may reject the whole.

. . .

[(2C)   Subsections (2A) and (2B) above do not apply to Scotland.

(2D)   Where the seller delivers a quantity of goods—

   (a)   less than he contracted to sell, the buyer shall not be entitled to reject the goods under subsection (1) above,

   (b)   larger than he contracted to sell, the buyer shall not be entitled to reject the whole under subsection (2) above,

unless the shortfall or excess is material.

(2E)   Subsection (2D) above applies to Scotland only.]

(3)   Where the seller delivers to the buyer a quantity of goods larger than he contracted to sell and the buyer accepts the whole of the goods so delivered he must pay for them at the contract rate.

[. . .]

(5)   This section is subject to any usage of trade, special agreement, or course of dealing between the parties.

[(6)   This section does not apply to a contract to which Chapter 2 of Part 1 of the Consumer Rights Act 2015 applies (but see the provision made about such contracts in section 25 of that Act).]

31   Instalment deliveries

(1)   Unless otherwise agreed, the buyer of goods is not bound to accept delivery of them by instalments.

(2)   Where there is a contract for the sale of goods to be delivered by stated instalments, which are to be separately paid for, and the seller makes defective deliveries in respect of one or more instalments, or the buyer neglects or refuses to take delivery of or pay for one or more instalments, it is a question in each case depending on the terms of the contract and the circumstances of the case whether the breach of contract is a repudiation of the whole contract or whether it is a

severable breach giving rise to a claim for compensation but not to a right to treat the whole contract as repudiated.

[(3) This section does not apply to a contract to which Chapter 2 of Part 1 of the Consumer Rights Act 2015 applies (but see the provision made about such contracts in section 26 of that Act).]

32 Delivery to carrier

(1) Where, in pursuance of a contract of sale, the seller is authorised or required to send the goods to the buyer, delivery of the goods to a carrier (whether named by the buyer or not) for the purpose of transmission to the buyer is prima facie deemed to be delivery of the goods to the buyer.

(2) Unless otherwise authorised by the buyer, the seller must make such contact with the carrier on behalf of the buyer as may be reasonable having regard to the nature of the goods and the other circumstances of the case; and if the seller omits to do so, and the goods are lost or damaged in course of transit, the buyer may decline to treat the delivery to the carrier as a delivery to himself or may hold the seller responsible in damages.

(3) Unless otherwise agreed, where goods are sent by the seller to the buyer by a route involving sea transit, under circumstances in which it is usual to insure, the seller must give such notice to the buyer as may enable him to insure them during their sea transit, and if the seller fails to do so, the goods are at his risk during such sea transit.

[(4) This section does not apply to a contract to which Chapter 2 of Part 1 of the Consumer Rights Act 2015 applies (but see the provision made about such contracts in section 29 of that Act).]

33 Risk where goods are delivered at distant place

[(1)] Where the seller of goods agrees to deliver them at his own risk at a place other than that where they are when sold, the buyer must nevertheless (unless otherwise agreed) take any risk of deterioration in the goods necessarily incident to the course of transit.

[(2) This section does not apply to a contract to which Chapter 2 of Part 1 of the Consumer Rights Act 2015 applies (but see the provision made about such contracts in section 29 of that Act).]

34 Buyer's right of examining the goods

[(1)] [Unless otherwise agreed, when the seller tenders delivery of goods to the buyer, he is bound on request to afford the buyer a reasonable opportunity of examining the goods for the purpose of ascertaining whether they are in conformity with the contract and, in the case of a contract for sale by sample, of comparing the bulk with the sample.]

(2) Nothing in this section affects the operation of section 22 (time limit for short-term right to reject) of the Consumer Rights Act 2015.]

35 Acceptance

(1) The buyer is deemed to have accepted the goods [subject to subsection (2) below—

(a) when he intimates to the seller that he has accepted them, or

(b) when the goods have been delivered to him and he does any act in relation to them which is inconsistent with the ownership of the seller.

(2) Where goods are delivered to the buyer, and he has not previously examined them, he is not deemed to have accepted them under subsection (1) above until he has had a reasonable opportunity of examining them for the purpose—

(a) of ascertaining whether they are in conformity with the contract, and

(b) in the case of a contract for sale by sample, of comparing the bulk with the sample.

[. . .]

(4) The buyer is also deemed to have accepted the goods when after the lapse

of a reasonable time he retains the goods without intimating to the seller that he has rejected them.

(5)   The questions that are material in determining for the purposes of subsection (4) above whether a reasonable time has elapsed include whether the buyer has had a reasonable opportunity of examining the goods for the purpose mentioned in subsection (2) above.

(6)   The buyer is not by virtue of this section deemed to have accepted the goods merely because—

(a)   he asks for, or agrees to, their repair by or under an arrangement with the seller, or

(b)   the goods are delivered to another under a sub-sale or other disposition.

(7)   Where the contract is for the sale of goods making one or more commercial units, a buyer accepting any goods included in a unit is deemed to have accepted all the goods making the unit; and in this subsection 'commercial unit' means a unit division of which would materially impair the value of the goods or the character of the unit.

(8)]   Paragraph 10 of Schedule 1 below applies in relation to a contract made before 22 April 1967 or (in the application of this Act to Northern Ireland) 28 July 1967.

[(9)   This section does not apply to a contract to which Chapter 2 of Part 1 of the Consumer Rights Act 2015 applies (but see the provision made about such contracts in section 21 of that Act).]

[35A   Right of partial rejection

(1)   If the buyer—

(a)   has the right to reject the goods by reason of a breach on the part of the seller that affects some or all of them, but

(b)   accepts some of the goods, including, where there are any goods unaffected by the breach, all such goods,

he does not by accepting them lose his right to reject the rest.

(2)   In the case of a buyer having the right to reject an instalment of goods, subsection (1) above applies as if references to the goods were references to the goods comprised in the instalment.

(3)   For the purposes of subsection (1) above, goods are affected by a breach if by reason of the breach they are not in conformity with the contract.

(4)   This section applies unless a contrary intention appears in, or is to be implied from, the contract.]

[(5)   This section does not apply to a contract to which Chapter 2 of Part 1 of the Consumer Rights Act 2015 applies (but see the provision made about such contracts in section 21 of that Act).]

36   Buyer not bound to return rejected goods

[(1)]   Unless otherwise agreed, where goods are delivered to the buyer, and he refuses to accept them, having the right to do so, he is not bound to return them to the seller, but it is sufficient if he intimates to the seller that he refuses to accept them.

[(2)   This section does not apply to a contract to which Chapter 2 of Part 1 of the Consumer Rights Act 2015 applies (but see the provision made about such contracts in section 20 of that Act).]

37   Buyer's liability for not taking delivery of goods

(1)   When the seller is ready and willing to deliver the goods, and requests the buyer to take delivery, and the buyer does not within a reasonable time after such request take delivery of the goods, he is liable to the seller for any loss occasioned by his neglect or refusal to take delivery, and also for a reasonable charge for the care and custody of the goods.

(2)   Nothing in this section affects the rights of the seller where the neglect or refusal of the buyer to take delivery amounts to a repudiation of the contract.

PART V
RIGHTS OF UNPAID SELLER AGAINST THE GOODS

Preliminary

38   Unpaid seller defined

(1)   The seller of goods is an unpaid seller within the meaning of this Act—

(a)   when the whole of the price has not been paid or tendered;

(b)   when a bill of exchange or other negotiable instrument has been received as conditional payment, and the condition on which it was received has not been fulfilled by reason of the dishonour of the instrument or otherwise.

(2)   In this Part of this Act 'seller' includes any person who is in the position of a seller, as, for instance, an agent of the seller to whom the bill of lading has been indorsed, or a consignor or agent who has himself paid (or is directly responsible for) the price.

39   Unpaid seller's rights

(1)   Subject to this and any other Act, notwithstanding that the property in the goods may have passed to the buyer, the unpaid seller of goods, as such, has by implication of law—

(a)   a lien on the goods or right to retain them for the price while he is in possession of them;

(b)   in the case of the insolvency of the buyer, a right of stopping the goods in transit after he has parted with the possession of them;

(c)   a right of re-sale as limited by this Act.

(2)   Where the property in goods has not passed to the buyer, the unpaid seller has (in addition to his other remedies) a right of withholding delivery similar to and coextensive with his rights of lien or retention and stoppage in transit where the property has passed to the buyer.

[. . .]

Unpaid seller's lien

41   Seller's lien

(1)   Subject to this Act, the unpaid seller of goods who is in possession of them is entitled to retain possession of them until payment or tender of the price in the following cases:—

(a)   where the goods have been sold without any stipulation as to credit;

(b)   where the goods have been sold on credit but the term of credit has expired;

(c)   where the buyer becomes insolvent.

(2)   The seller may exercise his lien or right of retention notwithstanding that he is in possession of the goods as agent or bailee or custodier for the buyer.

42   Part delivery

Where an unpaid seller has made part delivery of the goods, he may exercise his lien or right of retention on the remainder, unless such part delivery has been made under such circumstances as to show an agreement to waive the lien or right of retention.

43   Termination of lien

(1)   The unpaid seller of goods loses his lien or right of retention in respect of them—

(a)   when he delivers the goods to a carrier or other bailee or custodier for the purpose of transmission to the buyer without reserving the right of disposal of the goods;

(b)   when the buyer or his agent lawfully obtains possession of the goods;

(c)   by waiver of the lien or right of retention.

(2)   An unpaid seller of goods who has a lien or right of retention in respect of them does not lose his lien or right of retention by reason only that he has obtained judgment or decree for the price of the goods.

Stoppage in transit

44   Right of stoppage in transit

Subject to this Act, when the buyer of goods becomes insolvent the unpaid seller who has parted with the possession of the goods has the right of stopping them in transit, that is to say, he may resume possession of the goods as long as they are in course of transit, and may retain them until payment or tender of the price.

45   Duration of transit

(1)   Goods are deemed to be in course of transit from the time when they are delivered to a carrier or other bailee or custodier for the purpose of transmission to the buyer, until the buyer or his agent in that behalf takes delivery of them from the carrier or other bailee or custodier.

(2)   If the buyer or his agent in that behalf obtains delivery of the goods before their arrival at the appointed destination, the transit is at an end.

(3)   If, after the arrival of the goods at the appointed destination, the carrier or other bailee or custodier acknowledges to the buyer or his agent that he holds the goods on his behalf and continues in possession of them as bailee or custodier for the buyer or his agent, the transit is at an end, and it is immaterial that a further destination for the goods may have been indicated by the buyer.

(4)   If the goods are rejected by the buyer, and the carrier or other bailee or custodier continues in possession of them, the transit is not deemed to be at an end, even if the seller has refused to receive them back.

(5)   When goods are delivered to a ship chartered by the buyer it is a question depending on the circumstances of the particular case whether they are in the possession of the master as a carrier or as agent to the buyer.

(6)   Where the carrier or other bailee or custodier wrongfully refuses to deliver the goods to the buyer or his agent in that behalf, the transit is deemed to be at an end.

(7)   Where part delivery of the goods has been made to the buyer or his agent in that behalf, the remainder of the goods may be stopped in transit, unless such part delivery has been made under such circumstances as to show an agreement to give up possession of the whole of the goods.

46   How stoppage in transit is effected

(1)   The unpaid seller may exercise his right of stoppage in transit either by taking actual possession of the goods or by giving notice of his claim to the carrier or other bailee or custodier in whose possession the goods are.

(2)   The notice may be given either to the person in actual possession of the goods or to his principal.

(3)   If given to the principal, the notice is ineffective unless given at such time and under such circumstances that the principal, by the exercise of reasonable diligence, may communicate it to his servant or agent in time to prevent a delivery to the buyer.

(4)   When notice of stoppage in transit is given by the seller to the carrier or other bailee or custodier in possession of the goods, he must re-deliver the goods to, or according to the directions of, the seller; and the expenses of the re-delivery must be borne by the seller.

Re-sale etc by buyer

47 Effect of sub-sale etc by buyer

(1) Subject to this Act, the unpaid seller's right of lien or retention or stoppage in transit is not affected by any sale or other disposition of the goods which the buyer may have made, unless the seller has assented to it.

(2) Where a document of title to goods has been lawfully transferred to any person as buyer or owner of the goods, and that person transfers the document to a person who takes it in good faith and for valuable consideration, then—

(a) if the last-mentioned transfer was by way of sale the unpaid seller's right of lien or retention or stoppage in transit is defeated; and

(b) if the last-mentioned transfer was made by way of pledge or other disposition for value, the unpaid seller's right of lien or retention of stoppage in transit can only be exercised subject to the rights of the transferee.

Rescission: and re-sale by seller

48 Rescission: and re-sale by seller

(1) Subject to this section, a contract of sale is not rescinded by the mere exercise by an unpaid seller of his right of lien or retention or stoppage in transit.

(2) Where an unpaid seller who has exercised his right of lien or retention or stoppage in transit re-sells the goods, the buyer acquires a good title to them as against the original buyer.

(3) Where the goods are of a perishable nature, or where the unpaid seller gives notice to the buyer of his intention to re-sell, and the buyer does not within a reasonable time pay or tender the price, the unpaid seller may re-sell the goods and recover from the original buyer damages for any loss occasioned by his breach of contract.

(4) Where the seller expressly reserves the right of re-sale in case the buyer should make default, and on the buyer making default re-sells the goods, the original contract of sale is rescinded but without prejudice to any claim the seller may have for damages.

[. . .]

PART VI
ACTIONS FOR BREACH OF THE CONTRACT

Seller's remedies

49 Action for price

(1) Where, under a contract of sale, the property in the goods has passed to the buyer and he wrongfully neglects or refuses to pay for the goods according to the terms of the contract, the seller may maintain an action against him for the price of the goods.

(2) Where, under a contract of sale, the price is payable on a day certain irrespective of delivery and the buyer wrongfully neglects or refuses to pay such price, the seller may maintain an action for the price, although the property in goods has not passed and the goods have not been appropriated to the contract.

(3) Nothing in this section prejudices the right of the seller in Scotland to recover interest on the price from the date of tender of the goods, or from the date on which the price was payable, as the case may be.

50 Damages for non-acceptance

(1) Where the buyer wrongfully neglects or refuses to accept and pay for the goods, the seller may maintain an action against him for damages for non-acceptance.

(2)   The measure of damages is the estimated loss directly and naturally result-ing in the ordinary course of events, from the buyer's breach of contract.

(3)   Where there is an available market for the goods in question the measure of damages is prima facie to be ascertained by the difference between the contract price and the market or current price at the time or times when the goods ought to have been accepted or (if no time was fixed for acceptance) at the time of the refusal to accept.

Buyer's remedies

51   Damages for non-delivery

(1)   Where the seller wrongfully neglects or refuses to deliver the goods to the buyer, the buyer may maintain an action against the seller for damages for non-delivery.

(2)   The measure of damages is the estimated loss directly and naturally result-ing, in the ordinary course of events, from the seller's breach of contract.

(3)   Where there is an available market for the goods in question the measure of damages is prima facie to be ascertained by the difference between the contract price and the market or current price of the goods at the time or times when they ought to have been delivered or (if no time was fixed) at the time of the refusal to deliver.

[(4)   This section does not apply to a contract to which Chapter 2 of Part 1 of the Consumer Rights Act 2015 applies (but see the provision made about such contracts in section 19 of that Act).]

52   Specific performance

(1)   If any action for breach of contract to deliver specific or ascertained goods the court may, if it thinks fit, on the plaintiff's application, by its judgment or decree direct that the contract shall be performed specifically, without giving the defendant the option of retaining the goods on payment of damages.

(2)   The plaintiff's application may be made at any time before judgment or decree.

(3)   The judgment or decree may be unconditional, or on such terms and con-ditions as to damages, payment of the price and otherwise as seem just to the court.

(4)   The provisions of this section shall be deemed to be supplementary to, and not in derogation of, the right of specific implement in Scotland.

[(5)   This section does not apply to a contract to which Chapter 2 of Part 1 of the Consumer Rights Act 2015 applies (but see the provision made about such contracts in section 19 of that Act).]

53   [*Does not apply to Scotland.*]

[53A   Measure of damages as respects Scotland

(1)   The measure of damages for the seller's breach of contract is the estimated loss directly and naturally resulting, in the ordinary course of events, from the breach.

(2)   Where the seller's breach consists of the delivery of goods which are not of the quality required by the contract and the buyer retains the goods, such loss as aforesaid is prima facie the difference between the value of the goods at the time of delivery to the buyer and the value they would have had if they had fulfilled the contract.

[(2A)   This section does not apply to a contract to which Chapter 2 of Part 1 of the Consumer Rights Act 2015 applies (but see the provision made about such contracts in section 19 of that Act).]

(3)   This section applies to Scotland only.]

Interest, etc

54   Interest, etc

[(1)]   Nothing in this Act affects the right of the buyer or the seller to recover interest or special damages in any case where by law interest or special damages may be recoverable, or to recover money paid where the consideration for the payment of it has failed.

[(2)   This section does not apply to a contract to which Chapter 2 of Part 1 of the Consumer Rights Act 2015 applies (but see the provision made about such contracts in section 19 of that Act).]

PART VII
SUPPLEMENTARY

55   Exclusion of implied terms

(1)   Where a right, duty or liability would arise under a contract of sale of goods by implication of law, it may (subject to the Unfair Contract Terms Act 1977) be negatived or varied by express agreement, or by the course of dealing between the parties, or by such usage as binds both parties to the contract.

[(1A)   Subsection (1) does not apply to a contract to which Chapter 2 of Part 1 of the Consumer Rights Act 2015 applies (but see the provision made about such contracts in section 31 of that Act).]

(2)   An express [term] does not negative a [term] implied by this Act unless inconsistent with it.

(3)   Paragraph 11 of Schedule 1 below applies in relation to a contract made on or after 18 May 1973 and before 1 February 1978, and paragraph 12 in relation to one made before 18 May 1973.

56   Conflict of laws

Paragraph 13 of Schedule 1 below applies in relation to a contract made on or after 18 May 1973 and before 1 February 1978, so as to make provision about conflict of laws in relation to such a contract.

57   Auction sales

(1)   Where goods are put up for sale by auction in lots, each lot is prima facie deemed to be the subject of a separate contract of sale.

(2)   A sale by auction is complete when the auctioneer announces its completion by the fall of the hammer, or in other customary manner; and until the announcement is made any bidder may retract his bid.

(3)   A sale by auction may be notified to be subject to a reserve or upset price, and a right to bid may also be reserved expressly by or on behalf of the seller.

(4)   Where a sale by auction is not notified to be subject to a right to bid by or on behalf of the seller, it is not lawful for the seller to bid himself or to employ any person to bid at the sale, or for the auctioneer knowingly to take any bid from the seller or any such person.

(5)   A sale contravening subsection (4) above may be treated as fraudulent by the buyer.

(6)   Where, in respect of a sale by auction, a right to bid is expressly reserved (but not otherwise) the seller or any one person on his behalf may bid at the auction.

58   Payment into court in Scotland

[(1)]   In Scotland where a buyer has elected to accept goods which he might have rejected, and to treat a breach of contract as only giving rise to a claim for damages, he may, in an action by the seller for the price, be required, in the discretion of the court before which the action depends, to consign or pay into court the price of the goods, or part of the price, or to give other reasonable security for its due payment.

[(2) This section does not apply to a contract to which Chapter 2 of Part 1 of the Consumer Rights Act 2015 applies (but see the provision made about such contracts in section 27 of that Act).]

59   Reasonable time a question of fact
Where a reference is made in this Act to a reasonable time the question what is a reasonable time is a question of fact.

60   Rights etc enforceable by action
Where a right, duty or liability is declared by this Act, it may (unless otherwise provided by this Act) be enforced by action.

61   Interpretation
(1)   In this Act, unless the context or subject matter otherwise requires,—
'action' includes counterclaim and set-off, and in Scotland condescendence and claim and compensation;
['bulk' means a mass or collection of goods of the same kind which—
   (a)   is contained in a defined space or area; and
   (b)   is such that any goods in the bulk are interchangeable with any other goods therein of the same number or quantity;]
'business' includes a profession and the activities of any government department (including a Northern Ireland department) or local or public authority;
'buyer' means a person who buys or agrees to buy goods;
[. . .]
'contract of sale' includes an agreement to sell as well as a sale;
'credit-broker' means a person acting in the course of a business of credit brokerage carried on by him, that is a business of effecting introductions of individuals desiring to obtain credit—
   (a)   to persons carrying on any business so far as it relates to the provision of credit, or
   (b)   to other persons engaged in credit brokerage;
'defendant' includes in Scotland defender, respondent, and claimant in a multiplepoinding;
'delivery' means voluntary transfer of possession from one person to another; [except that in relation to sections 20A and 20B above it includes such appropriation of goods to the contract as results in property in the goods being transferred to the buyer;]
'document of title to goods' has the same meaning as it has in the Factors Acts;
'Factors Acts' means the Factors Act 1889, the Factors (Scotland) Act 1890, and any enactment amending or substituted for the same;
'fault' means wrongful act or default;
'future goods' means goods to be manufactured or acquired by the seller after the making of the contract of sale;
'goods' includes all personal chattels other than things in action and money, and in Scotland all corporeal moveables except money; and in particular 'goods' includes emblements, industrial growing crops, and things attached to or forming part of the land which are agreed to be severed before sale or under the contract of sale; [and includes an undivided share in goods;]
'plaintiff' includes pursuer, complainer, claimant in a multiplepoinding and defendant or defender counter-claiming;
[. . .]
'property' means the general property in goods, and not merely a special property;
[. . .]
'sale' includes a bargain and sale as well as a sale and delivery;

'seller' means a person who sells or agrees to sell goods;

'specific goods' means goods identified and agreed on at the time a contract of sale is made; [and includes an undivided share, specified as a fraction or percentage, of goods identified and agreed on as aforesaid;]

'warranty' (as regards England and Wales and Northern Ireland) means an agreement with reference to goods which are the subject of a contract of sale, but collateral to the main purpose of such contract, the breach of which gives rise to a claim for damages, but not to a right to reject the goods and treat the contract as repudiated.

[. . .]

(3)   A thing is deemed to be done in good faith within the meaning of this Act when it is in fact done honestly, whether it is done negligently or not.

(4)   A person is deemed to be insolvent within the meaning of this Act if he has either ceased to pay his debts in the ordinary course of business or he cannot pay his debts as they become due, [. . .]

(5)   Goods are in a deliverable state within the meaning of this Act when they are in such a state that the buyer would under the contract be bound to take delivery of them.

[. . .]

(6)   As regards the definition of 'business' in subsection (1) above, paragraph 14 of Schedule 1 below applies in relation to a contract made on or after 18 May 1973 and before 1 February 1978, and paragraph 15 in relation to one made before 18 May 1973,

62   Savings: rules of law etc

(1)   The rules in bankruptcy relating to contracts of sale apply to those contracts, notwithstanding anything in this Act.

(2)   The rules of the common law, including the law merchant, except in so far as they are inconsistent with the provisions of [legislation including this Act and the Consumer Rights Act 2015], and in particular the rules relating to the law of principal and agent and the effect of fraud, misrepresentation, duress or coercion, mistake, or other invalidating cause, apply to contracts for the sale of goods.

(3)   Nothing in this Act or the Sale of Goods Act 1893 affects the enactments relating to bills of sale, or any enactment relating to the sale of goods which is not expressly repealed or amended by this Act or that.

(4)   The provisions of this Act about contracts of sale do not apply to a transaction in the form of a contract of sale which is intended to operate by way of mortgage, pledge, charge, or other security.

(5)   Nothing in this Act prejudices or affects the landlord's right of hypothec [. . .] in Scotland.

64   Short title and commencement

(1)   This Act may be cited as the Sale of Goods Act 1979.

(2)   This Act comes into force on 1 January 1980.

CIVIL AVIATION ACT 1982
(1982, c 16)

Trespass by aircraft and aircraft nuisance, noise, etc

76   Liability of aircraft in respect of trespass, nuisance and surface damage

(1)   No action shall lie in respect of trespass or in respect of nuisance, by reason only of the flight of an aircraft over any property at a height above the ground which, having regard to wind, weather and all the circumstances of the case is reasonable, or the ordinary incidents of such flight, so long as the provisions of any Air Navigation Order and of any orders under section 62 above have been duly complied with [. . .].

(2)   Subject to subsection (3) below, where material loss or damage is caused to
any person or property on land or water by, or by a person in, or an article, animal
or person falling from, an aircraft while in flight, taking off or landing, then unless
the loss or damage was caused or contributed to by the negligence of the person
by whom it was suffered, damages in respect of the loss or damage shall be recoverable without proof of negligence or intention or other cause of action, as if
the loss or damage had been caused by the wilful act, neglect, or default of the
owner of the aircraft.

(3)   Where material loss or damage is caused as aforesaid in circumstances in
which—

(a)   damages are recoverable in respect of the said loss or damage by virtue
only of subsection (2) above, and

(b)   a legal liability is created in some person other than the owner to pay
damages in respect of the said loss or damage,

the owner shall be entitled to be indemnified by that other person against any
claim in respect of the said loss or damage.

Rights etc in relation to aircraft

86   Power to provide for the mortgaging of aircraft

(1)   Her Majesty may by Order in Council make provision for the mortgaging
of aircraft registered in the United Kingdom or capable of being so registered.

(2)   Without prejudice to the generality of the powers conferred by subsection
(1) above, an Order in Council under this section may, in particular—

(a)   include provisions which correspond (subject to such modifications as
appear to Her Majesty in Council to be necessary or expedient) to any of the
provisions of the Merchant Shipping Act [1995] relating to the mortgaging of
ships;

(b)   make provision as respects the rights and liabilities of mortgagors and
mortgagees of such aircraft as are mentioned in subsection (1) above, and as
respects the priority inter se of such rights and the relationship of such rights to
other rights in or over such aircraft, including possessory liens for work done to
such aircraft and rights under section 88 below or under regulations made by
virtue of [section 83 of the Transport Act 2000 (detention and sale of aircraft)];

(c)   make provision as respects the operation, in relation to such aircraft as
aforesaid, of any of the enactments in force in any part of the United Kingdom
relating to bills of sale or the registration of charges on the property or undertaking of companies;

(d)   provide for the rights of mortgagees of such aircraft to be exercisable, in
such circumstances as may be specified in the Order, in relation to payments for
the use of the aircraft;

(e)   confer on courts in the United Kingdom powers in respect of any register
maintained in pursuance of the Order and in respect of transactions affecting
aircraft registered therein;

(f)   make provision for enabling the mortgage of an aircraft to extend to any
store of spare parts for that aircraft and for applying, for that purpose, to any
such spare parts provisions such as are mentioned in the preceding paragraphs
of this subsection;

(g)   make provision specifying, subject to the consent of the Treasury, the
fees to be paid in respect of the making or deletion of entries in any such register as aforesaid and in respect of any other matters in respect of which it
appears to Her Majesty in Council to be expedient for the purposes of the Order
to charge fees;

(h)   provide for the imposition of penalties in respect of the making of false
statements in connection with matters dealt with in the Order and in respect of
the forgery of documents relating to such matters.

SUPPLY OF GOODS AND SERVICES ACT 1982
(1982, c 29)

[PART IA
SUPPLY OF GOODS AS RESPECTS SCOTLAND

Contracts for the transfer of property in goods

11A The contracts concerned

(1) In this Act in its application to Scotland a ['*relevant* contract for the transfer of goods'] means a contract under which one person transfers or agrees to transfer to another the property in goods, other than an excepted contract [, and other than a contract to which Chapter 2 of Part 1 of the Consumer Rights Act 2015 applies].

(2) For the purposes of this section an excepted contract means any of the following—

(a)   a contract of sale of goods;

(b)   a hire-purchase agreement;

[. . .]

(d)   a transfer or agreement to transfer for which there is no consideration;

(e)   a contract intended to operate by way of mortgage, pledge, charge or other security.

(3) For the purposes of this Act in its application to Scotland a contract is a [relevant contract for the transfer of goods] whether or not services are also provided or to be provided under the contract, and (subject to subsection (2) above) whatever is the nature of the consideration for the transfer or agreement to transfer.

11B Implied terms about title, etc

(1) In a [relevant contract for the transfer of goods], other than one to which subsection (3) below applies, there is an implied term on the part of the transferor that in the case of a transfer of the property in the goods he has a right to transfer the property and in the case of an agreement to transfer the property in the goods he will have such a right at the time when the property is to be transferred.

(2) In a [relevant contract for the transfer of goods], other than one to which subsection (3) below applies, there is also an implied term that—

(a)   the goods are free, and will remain free until the time when the property is to be transferred, from any charge or encumbrance not disclosed or known to the transferee before the contract is made, and

(b)   the transferee will enjoy quiet possession of the goods except so far as it may be disturbed by the owner or other person entitled to the benefit of any charge or encumbrance so disclosed or known.

(3) This subsection applies to a [relevant contract for the transfer of goods] in the case of which there appears from the contract or is to be inferred from its circumstances an intention that the transferor should transfer only such title as he or a third person may have.

(4) In a contract to which subsection (3) above applies there is an implied term that all charges or encumbrances known to the transferor and not known to the transferee have been disclosed to the transferee before the contract is made.

(5) In a contract to which subsection (3) above applies there is also an implied term that none of the following will disturb the transferee's quiet possession of the goods, namely—

(a)   the transferor;

(b)   in a case where the parties to the contract intend that the transferor should transfer only such title as a third person may have, that person;

(c)   anyone claiming through or under the transferor or that third person otherwise than under a charge or encumbrance disclosed or known to the transferee before the contract is made.

(6) [*amends Unfair Contract Terms Act 1977*]

11C Implied terms where transfer is by description

(1) This section applies where, under a [relevant contract for the transfer of goods], the transferor transfers or agrees to transfer the property in the goods by description.

(2) In such a case there is an implied term that the goods will correspond with the description.

(3) If the transferor transfers or agrees to transfer the property in the goods by reference to a sample as well as by description it is not sufficient that the bulk of the goods corresponds with the sample if the goods do not also correspond with the description.

(4) A contract is not prevented from falling within subsection (1) above by reason only that, being exposed for supply, the goods are selected by the transferee.

11D Implied terms about quality or fitness

(1) Except as provided by this section and section 11E below and subject to the provisions of any other enactment, there is no implied term about the quality or fitness for any particular purpose of goods supplied under a [relevant contract for the transfer of goods].

(2) Where, under such a contract, the transferor transfers the property in goods in the course of a business, there is an implied term that the goods supplied under the contract are of satisfactory quality.

(3) For the purposes of this section and section 11E below, goods are of satisfactory quality if they meet the standard that a reasonable person would regard as satisfactory, taking account of any description of the goods, the price (if relevant) and all the other relevant circumstances.

[. . .]

(4) The term implied by subsection (2) above does not extend to any matter making the quality of goods unsatisfactory—

(a) which is specifically drawn to the transferee's attention before the contract is made,

(b) where the transferee examines the goods before the contract is made, which that examination ought to reveal, or

(c) where the property in the goods is, or is to be, transferred by reference to a sample, which would have been apparent on a reasonable examination of the sample.

(5) Subsection (6) below applies where, under a [relevant contract for the transfer of goods], the transferor transfers the property in goods in the course of a business and the transferee, expressly or by implication, makes known—

(a) to the transferor, or

(b) where the consideration or part of the consideration for the transfer is a sum payable by instalments and the goods were previously sold by a credit-broker to the transferor, to that credit-broker,

any particular purpose for which the goods are being acquired.

(6) In that case there is (subject to subsection (7) below) an implied term that the goods supplied under the contract are reasonably fit for the purpose, whether or not that is a purpose for which such goods are commonly supplied.

(7) Subsection (6) above does not apply where the circumstances show that the transferee does not rely, or that it is unreasonable for him to rely, on the skill or judgment of the transferor or credit-broker.

(8) An implied term about quality or fitness for a particular purpose may be annexed by usage to a [relevant contract for the transfer of goods].

(9) The preceding provisions of this section apply to a transfer by a person who in the course of a business is acting as agent for another as they apply to a transfer by a principal in the course of a business, except where that other is not

transferring in the course of a business and either the transferee knows that fact or reasonable steps are taken to bring it to the transferee's notice before the contract concerned is made.

[. . .]

11E Implied terms where transfer is by sample

(1) This section applies where, under a [relevant contract for the transfer of goods], the transferor transfers or agrees to transfer the property in the goods by reference to a sample.

(2) In such a case there is an implied term—

(a) that the bulk will correspond with the sample in quality;

(b) that the transferee will have a reasonable opportunity of comparing the bulk with the sample; and

(c) that the goods will be free from any defect, making their quality unsatisfactory, which would not be apparent on reasonable examination of the sample.

(3) For the purposes of this section a transferor transfers or agrees to transfer the property in goods by reference to a sample where there is an express or implied term to that effect in the contract concerned.

11F Remedies for breach of contract

(1) Where in a [relevant contract for the transfer of goods] a transferor is in breach of any term of the contract (express or implied), the other party to the contract (in this section referred to as 'the transferee') shall be entitled—

(a) to claim damages; and

(b) if the breach is material, to reject any goods delivered under the contract and treat it as repudiated.

[. . .]

Contracts for the hire of goods

11G The contracts concerned

(1) In this Act in its application to Scotland a '[relevant contract for the hire of goods'] means a contract under which one person ('the supplier') hires or agrees to hire goods to another, other than [a hire-purchase agreement] [and other than a contract to which Chapter 2 of Part 1 of the Consumer Rights Act 2015 applies].

[. . .]

(3) For the purposes of this Act in its application to Scotland a contract is a [relevant contract for the hire of goods] whether or not services are also provided or to be provided under the contract, and [. . .] whatever is the nature of the consideration for the hire or agreement to hire.

11H Implied terms about right to transfer possession etc

(1) In a [relevant contract for the hire of goods] there is an implied term on the part of the supplier that—

(a) in the case of a hire, he has a right to transfer possession of the goods by way of hire for the period of the hire; and

(b) in the case of an agreement to hire, he will have such a right at the time of commencement of the period of the hire.

(2) In a [relevant contract for the hire of goods] there is also an implied term that the person to whom the goods are hired will enjoy quiet possession of the goods for the period of the hire except so far as the possession may be disturbed by the owner or other person entitled to the benefit of any charge or encumbrance disclosed or known to the person to whom the goods are hired before the contract is made.

(3) The preceding provisions of this section do not affect the right of the supplier to repossess the goods under an express or implied term of the contract.

11I Implied terms where hire is by description
(1)   This section applies where, under a [relevant contract for the hire of goods], the supplier hires or agrees to hire the goods by description.
(2)   In such a case there is an implied term that the goods will correspond with the description.
(3)   If under the contract the supplier hires or agrees to hire the goods by reference to a sample as well as by description it is not sufficient that the bulk of the goods corresponds with the sample if the goods do not also correspond with the description.
(4)   A contract is not prevented from falling within subsection (1) above by reason only that, being exposed for supply, the goods are selected by the person to whom the goods are hired.

11J Implied terms about quality or fitness
(1)   Except as provided by this section and section 11K below and subject to the provisions of any other enactment, there is no implied term about the quality or fitness for any particular purpose of goods hired under a [relevant contract for the hire of goods].
(2)   Where, under such a contract, the supplier hires goods in the course of a business, there is an implied term that the goods supplied under the contract are of satisfactory quality.
(3)   For the purposes of this section and section 11K below, goods are of satisfactory quality if they meet the standard that a reasonable person would regard as satisfactory, taking account of any description of the goods, the consideration for the hire (if relevant) and all the other relevant circumstances.
[. . .]
(4)   The term implied by subsection (2) above does not extend to any matter making the quality of goods unsatisfactory—
    (a)   which is specifically drawn to the attention of the person to whom the goods are hired before the contract is made, or
    (b)   where that person examines the goods before the contract is made, which that examination ought to reveal; or
    (c)   where the goods are hired by reference to a sample, which would have been apparent on reasonable examination of the sample.
(5)   Subsection (6) below applies where, under a [relevant contract for the hire of goods], the supplier hires goods in the course of a business and the person to whom the goods are hired, expressly or by implication, makes known—
    (a)   to the supplier in the course of negotiations conducted by him in relation to the making of the contract; or
    (b)   to a credit-broker in the course of negotiations conducted by that broker in relation to goods sold by him to the supplier before forming the subject matter of the contract,
any particular purpose for which the goods are being hired.
(6)   In that case there is (subject to subsection (7) below) an implied term that the goods supplied under the contract are reasonably fit for that purpose, whether or not that is a purpose for which such goods are commonly supplied.
(7)   Subsection (6) above does not apply where the circumstances show that the person to whom the goods are hired does not rely, or that it is unreasonable for him to rely, on the skill or judgment of the hirer or credit-broker.
(8)   An implied term about quality or fitness for a particular purpose may be annexed by usage to a contract for the hire of goods.
(9)   The preceding provisions of this section apply to a hire by a person who in the course of a business is acting as agent for another as they apply to a hire by a principal in the course of a business, except where that other is not hiring in the course of a business and either the person to whom the goods are hired knows

that fact or reasonable steps are taken to bring it to that person's notice before the contract concerned is made.

[. . .]

11K Implied terms where hire is by sample

(1) This section applies where, under a [relevant contract for the hire of goods], the supplier hires or agrees to hire the goods by reference to a sample.

(2) In such a case there is an implied term—

    (a) that the bulk will correspond with the sample in quality; and

    (b) that the person to whom the goods are hired will have a reasonable opportunity of comparing the bulk with the sample; and

    (c) that the goods will be free from any defect, making their quality unsatisfactory, which would not be apparent on reasonable examination of the sample.

(3) For the purposes of this section a supplier hires or agrees to hire goods by reference to a sample where there is an express or implied term to that effect in the contract concerned.

Exclusion of implied terms, etc

11L Exclusion of implied terms etc

(1) Where a right, duty or liability would arise under a [relevant contract for the transfer of goods] or a [relevant contract for the hire of goods] by implication of law, it may (subject to subsection (2) below and the 1977 Act) be negatived or varied by express agreement, or by the course of dealing between the parties, or by such usage as binds both parties to the contract.

(2) An express term does not negative a term implied by the preceding provisions of this Part of this Act unless inconsistent with it.

(3) Nothing in the preceding provisions of this Part of this Act prejudices the operation of any other enactment or any rule of law whereby any term (other than one relating to quality or fitness) is to be implied in a [relevant contract for the transfer of goods] or a [relevant contract for the hire of goods].]

ADMINISTRATION OF JUSTICE ACT 1982
(1982, c 53)

8 Services rendered to injured person

(1) Where necessary services have been rendered to the injured person by a relative in consequence of the injuries in question, then, unless the relative has expressly agreed in the knowledge that an action for damages has been raised or is in contemplation that no payment should be made in respect of those services, the responsible person shall be liable to pay to the injured person by way of damages such sum as represents reasonable remuneration for those services and repayment of reasonable expenses incurred in connection therewith.

[(2) The injured person shall be under an obligation to account to the relative for any damages recovered from the responsible person under subsection (1) above.

(3) Where, at the date of an award of damages in favour of the injured person, it is likely that necessary services will, after that date, be rendered to him by a relative in consequence of the injuries in question, then, unless the relative has expressly agreed that no payment shall be made in respect of those services, the

responsible person shall be liable to pay to the injured person by way of damages such sum as represents—

(a)   reasonable remuneration for those services; and

(b)   reasonable expenses which are likely to be incurred in connection there-with.

(4)   The relative shall have no direct right of action in delict against the responsible person in respect of any services or expenses referred to in this section.]

9   Services to injured person's relative

(1)   The responsible person shall be liable to pay to the injured person a reasonable sum by way of damages in respect of the inability of the injured person to render the personal services referred to in subsection (3) below.

[(1A)   In assessing the amount of damages payable by virtue of subsection (1) above to an injured person whose date of death is expected to be earlier than had the injuries not been sustained, the court is to assume that the person will live until the date when death would have been expected had the injuries not been sustained.]

[. . .]

(3)   The personal services referred to in [subsection 1] above are personal services—

(a)   which were or might have been expected to have been rendered by the injured person before the occurrence of the act or omission giving rise to liability,

(b)   of a kind which, when rendered by a person other than a relative, would ordinarily be obtainable on payment, and

(c)   which the injured person but for the injuries in question might have been expected to render gratuitously to a relative.

(4)   Subject to [section 6(1) of the Damages (Scotland) Act 2011 (asp 7) (relative's loss of personal services)], the relative shall have no direct right of action in delict against the responsible person in respect of the personal services mentioned in subsection (3) above.

10   Assessment of damages for personal injuries

Subject to any agreement to the contrary, in assessing the amount of damages payable to the injured person in respect of personal injuries there shall not be taken into account so as to reduce that amount—

(a)   any contractual pension or benefit (including any payment by a friendly society or trade union);

(b)   any pension or retirement benefit payable from public funds other than any pension or benefit to which section 2(1) of the Law Reform (Personal Injuries) Act 1948 applies;

(c)   any benefit payable from public funds, in respect of any period after the date of the award of damages, designed to secure to the injured person or any relative of his a minimum level of subsistence;

(d)   any redundancy payment under the [Employment Rights Act 1996], or any payment made in circumstances corresponding to those in which a right to a redundancy payment would have accrued if section 135 of that Act had applied;

(e)   any payment made to the injured person or to any relative of his by the injured person's employer following upon the injuries in question where the recipient is under an obligation to reimburse the employer in the event of damages being recovered in respect of those injuries;

(f)   subject to paragraph (iv) below, any payment of a benevolent character made to the injured person or to any relative of his by any person following upon the injuries in question;

but there shall be taken into account—

(i)   any remuneration or earnings from employment;

(ii)   any [contribution-based jobseeker's allowance (payable under the Jobseekers Act 1995)];

(iii)   any benefit referred to in paragraph (c) above payable in respect of any period prior to the date of the award of damages;

(iv)   any payment of a benevolent character made to the injured person or to any relative of his by the responsible person following on the injuries in question, where such a payment is made directly and not through a trust or other fund from which the injured person or his relatives have benefited or may benefit.

11   Maintenance at public expense to be taken into account in assessment of damages: Scotland

In an action for damages for personal injuries (including any such action arising out of a contract) any saving to the injured person which is attributable to his maintenance wholly or partly at public expense in—

(a)   a hospital [. . .] or other institution

[(b)   accommodation provided by a care home service (as defined by section 2(3) of the Regulation of Care (Scotland) Act 2001 (asp 8)).]

shall be set off against any income lost by him as a result of the injuries.

12   Award of provisional damages for personal injuries: Scotland

(1)   This section applies to an action for damages for personal injuries in which—

(a)   there is proved or admitted to be a risk that at some definite or indefinite time in the future the injured person will, as a result of the act or omission which gave rise to the cause of the action, develop some serious disease or suffer some serious deterioration in his physical or mental condition; and

(b)   the responsible person was, at the time of the act or omission giving rise to the cause of the action,

(i)   a public authority or public corporation; or

(ii)   insured or otherwise indemnified in respect of the claim.

(2)   In any case to which this section applies, the court may, on the application of the injured person, order—

(a)   that the damages referred to in subsection (4)(a) below be awarded to the injured person; and

(b)   that the injured person may apply for the further award of damages referred to in subsection (4)(b) below,

and the court may, if it considers it appropriate, order that an application under paragraph (b) above may be made only within a specified period.

(3)   Where an injured person in respect of whom an award has been made under subsection (2)(a) above applies to the court for an award under subsection (2)(b) above, the court may award to the injured person the further damages referred to in subsection (4)(b) below.

(4)   The damages referred to in subsections (2) and (3) above are—

(a)   damages assessed on the assumption that the injured person will not develop the disease or suffer the deterioration in his condition; and

(b)   further damages if he develops the disease or suffers the deterioration.

(5)   Nothing in this section shall be construed—

(a)   as affecting the exercise of any power relating to expenses including a power to make rules of court relating to expenses; or

(b)   as prejudicing any duty of the court under any enactment or rule of law to reduce or limit the total damages which would have been recoverable apart from any such duty.

(6)   The Secretary of State may, by order, provide that categories of defenders shall, for the purposes of paragraph (b) of subsection (1) above, become or cease to

be responsible persons, and may make such modifications of that paragraph as appear to him to be necessary for the purpose.

And an order under this subsection shall be made by statutory instrument subject to annulment in pursuance of a resolution of either House of Parliament.

13 Supplementary

(1)   In this Part of this Act, unless the context otherwise requires—

['personal injuries' means—

    (a)   any disease, and

    (b)   any impairment of a person's physical or mental condition;]

'relative', in relation to the injured person, means—

    (a)   the spouse or divorced spouse;

    [(aa)   the civil partner or former civil partner,]

    (b)   any person, not being the spouse of the injured person, who was, at the time of the act or omission giving rise to liability in the responsible person, living with the injured person as husband or wife;

    [(ba)   any person, not being the civil partner of the injured person, who was, at the time of the act or omission giving rise to liability in the responsible person, living with the injured person as the civil partner of the injured person.]

    (c)   any ascendant or descendant;

    (d)   any brother, sister, uncle or aunt; or any issue of any such person;

    (e)   any person accepted by the injured person as a child of his family.

In deducing any relationship for the purposes of the foregoing definition—

    (a)   any relationship by affinity shall be treated as a relationship by consanguinity; any relationship of the half blood shall be treated as a relationship of the whole blood; and the stepchild of any person shall be treated as his child; and

    (b)   [section 1(1) of the Law Reform (Parent and Child) (Scotland) Act 1986 shall apply; and any reference (however expressed) in this Part of this Act to a relative shall be construed accordingly.]

(2)   Any reference in this Part of this Act to a payment, benefit or pension shall be construed as a reference to any such payment, benefit or pension whether in cash or in kind.

(3)   This Part of this Act binds the Crown.

LAW REFORM (HUSBAND AND WIFE) (SCOTLAND) ACT 1984
(1984, c 15)

Abolition of actions of breach of promise of marriage, adherence and enticement

1 Promise of marriage not an enforceable obligation

(1)   No promise of marriage or agreement between two persons to marry one another shall have effect under the law of Scotland to create any rights or obligations; and no action for breach of any such promise or agreement may be brought in any court in Scotland, whatever the law applicable to the promise or agreement.

(2)   This section shall have effect in relation to any promise made or agreement entered into before it comes into force, but shall not affect any action commenced before it comes into force.

2 Actions of adherence and enticement abolished

(1)   No spouse shall be entitled to apply for a decree from any court in Scotland ordaining the other spouse to adhere.

(2)   No person shall be liable in delict to any person by reason only of having induced the spouse of that person to leave or remain apart from that person.

(3)   This section shall not affect any action commenced before this Act comes into force.

LAW REFORM (MISCELLANEOUS PROVISIONS) (SCOTLAND) ACT 1985
(1985, c 73)

Provisions relating to leases

. . .

4 Irritancy clauses etc relating to monetary breaches of lease

(1) A landlord shall not, for the purpose of treating a lease as terminated or terminating it, be entitled to rely—

(a) on a provision in the lease which purports to terminate it, or to enable him to terminate it, in the event of a failure of the tenant to pay rent, or to make any other payment, on or before the due date therefor or such later date or within such period as may be provided for in the lease; or

(b) on the fact that such a failure is, or is deemed by a provision of the lease to be, a material breach of contract,

unless subsection (2) or (5) below applies.

(2) This subsection applies if—

(a) the landlord has, at any time after the payment of rent or other payment mentioned in subsection (1) above has become due, served a notice on the tenant—

(i) requiring the tenant to make payment of the sum which he has failed to pay together with any interest thereon in terms of the lease within the period specified in the notice; and

(ii) stating that, if the tenant does not comply with the requirement mentioned in sub-paragraph (i) above, the lease may be terminated; and

(b) the tenant has not complied with that requirement.

(3) The period to be specified in any such notice shall be not less than—

(a) a period of 14 days immediately following the service of the notice; or

(b) if any period remaining between the service of the notice and the expiry of any time provided for in the lease or otherwise for the late payment of the sum which the tenant has failed to pay is greater than 14 days, that greater period.

(4) Any notice served under subsection (2) above shall be sent by recorded delivery and shall be sufficiently served if it is sent to the tenant's last business or residential address in the United Kingdom known to the landlord or to the last address in the United Kingdom provided to the landlord by the tenant for the purpose of such service.

(5) This subsection applies if the tenant does not have an address in the United Kingdom known to the landlord and has not provided an address in the United Kingdom to the landlord for the purpose of service.

5 Irritancy clauses etc not relating to monetary breaches of leases

(1) Subject to subsection (2) below, a landlord shall not, for the purpose of treating a lease as terminated or terminating it, be entitled to rely—

(a) on a provision in the lease which purports to terminate it, or to enable the landlord to terminate it, in the event of an act or omission by the tenant (other than such a failure as is mentioned in section 4(1)(a) of this Act) or of a change in the tenant's circumstances; or

(b) on the fact that such act or omission or change is, or is deemed by a provision of the lease to be, a material breach of contract,

if in all the circumstances of the case a fair and reasonable landlord would not seek so to rely.

(2) No provision of a lease shall of itself, irrespective of the particular circumstances of the case, be held to be unenforceable by virtue of subsection (1) above.

(3) In the consideration, for the purposes of subsection (1)(a) or (b) above, of the circumstances of a case where—

(a)   an act, omission or change is alleged to constitute a breach of a provision of the lease or a breach of contract; and

(b)   the breach is capable of being remedied in reasonable time,

regard shall be had to whether a reasonable opportunity has been afforded to the tenant to enable the breach to be remedied.

6   Supplementary and transitional provisions relating to sections 4 and 5

(1)   The parties to a lease shall not be entitled to disapply any provision of section 4 or 5 of this Act from it.

(2)   Where circumstances have occurred before the commencement of sections 4 and 5 of this Act which would have entitled a landlord to terminate a lease in reliance on a provision in the lease or on the ground that the circumstances constituted a material breach of contract, but the landlord has not before such commencement given written notice to the tenant of his intention to terminate the lease in respect of those circumstances, he shall, after such commencement, be entitled to terminate the lease in respect of those circumstances only in accordance with the provisions of section 4 or 5 (as the case may be) of this Act.

(3)   Nothing in section 4 or 5 of this Act shall apply in relation to any payment which has to be made, or any other condition which has to be fulfilled, before a tenant is entitled to entry under a lease.

7   Interpretation of sections 4 to 6

(1)   In sections 4 to 6 of this Act 'lease' means a lease of land, whether entered into before or after the commencement of those sections, but does not include a lease of land—

(a)   used wholly or mainly for residential purposes;

(b)   comprising [. . .] a croft, the subject of a cottar or the holding of a landholder or a statutory small tenant [; or

(c)   where the lease is an agricultural lease.]

(2)   In subsection (1) above—

['agricultural lease' means a lease constituting a 1991 Act tenancy within the meaning of the Agricultural Holdings (Scotland) Act 2003 (asp 11) or a lease constituting a short limited duration tenancy or a limited duration tenancy (within the meaning of that Act);]

'cottar' has the same meaning as in section 28(4) of the Crofters (Scotland) Act 1955;

'croft' has the same meaning as in section 3 of the Crofters (Scotland) Act 1955; and

'holding' (in relation to a landholder or statutory small tenant), 'landholder' and 'statutory small tenant' have the same meanings as in the Small Landholders (Scotland) Acts 1886 to 1931.

Provisions relating to other contracts and obligations

8   Rectification of defectively expressed documents

(1)   Subject to section 9 of this Act, where the court is satisfied, on an application made to it, that—

(a)   a document intended to express or to give effect to an agreement fails to express accurately the common intention of the parties to the agreement at the date when it was made; or

(b)   a document intended to create, transfer, vary or renounce a right, not being a document falling within paragraph (a) above, fails to express accurately the intention of the grantor of the document at the date when it was executed,

it may order the document to be rectified in any manner that it may specify in order to give effect to that intention.

(2)   For the purposes of subsection (1) above, the court shall be entitled to have regard to all relevant evidence, whether written or oral.

(3)   Subject to section 9 of this Act, in ordering the rectification of a document

under subsection (1) above (in this subsection referred to as 'the original document'), the court may, at its own instance or on an application made to it [and in either case after calling all parties who appear to it to have an interest], order the rectification of any other document intended for any of the purposes mentioned in paragraph (a) or (b) of subsection (1) above which is defectively expressed by reason of the defect in the original document.

[(3A)   If a document is registered in the Land Register of Scotland in favour of a person acting in good faith then, unless the person consents to rectification of the document, it is not competent to order its rectification under subsection (3) above.]

(4)   Subject to [sections 8A and 9(4)] of this Act, a document ordered to be rectified under this section shall have effect as if it had always been so rectified.

(5)   Subject to section 9(5) of this Act, where a document recorded in the Register of Sasines is ordered to be rectified under this section and the order is likewise recorded, the document shall be treated as having been always so recorded as rectified.

[(5A)   *Subsection (5) above applies in relation to documents registered in the Register of Floating Charges as it applies in relation to a document recorded in the Register of Sasines (and the references to recording are to be read accordingly).*]

(6)   Nothing in this section shall apply to a document of a testamentary nature.

(7)   It shall be competent to register in the Register of Inhibitions [. . .] a notice of an application under this section for the rectification of a deed relating to land, being an application in respect of which authority for service or citation has been granted; and the land to which the application relates shall be rendered litigious as from the date of registration of such a notice [except that this subsection is subject to subsection (8A) below].

(8)   A notice under subsection (7) above shall specify the names and designations of the parties to the application and the date when authority for service or citation was granted and contain a description of the land to which the application relates.

[(8A)   A notice under subsection (7) above registered on or after the date on which section 67 of the Land Registration etc (Scotland) Act 2012 (asp 5) (warrant to place a caveat) comes into force shall not have any effect in rendering litigious any land for which there is a title sheet in the Land Register of Scotland or in placing in bad faith any person acquiring such land.]

(9)   In this section and section 9 of this Act 'the court' means the Court of Session or the sheriff court.

[8A   Registration of order for rectification
An order for rectification made under section 8 of this Act in respect of a document which has been registered in the Land Register of Scotland—
   (a)   may be registered in that register, and
   (b)   does not have real effect until so registered.]

9   Provisions supplementary to section 8: protection of other interest
(1)   The court shall order a document to be rectified under section 8 of this Act only where it is satisfied—
   (a)   that the interests of a person to whom this section applies would not be adversely affected to a material extent by the rectification; or
   (b)   that that person has consented to the proposed rectification.
(2)   Subject to [subsections (2A) and (3)] below, this section applies to a person (other than a party to the agreement or the grantor of the document) who has acted or refrained from acting in reliance on the terms of the document [. . .], with the result that his position has been affected to a material extent.

[(2A)   This section does not apply where the document to be rectified is a deed registered in the Land Register of Scotland.]

(3)   This section does not apply to a person—

(a)   who, at the time when he acted or refrained from acting as mentioned in subsection (2) above, knew, or ought in the circumstances known to him at that time to have been aware, that the document [. . .] failed accurately to express the common intention of the parties to the agreement or, as the case may be, the intention of the grantor of the document; or

(b)   whose reliance on the terms of the document [. . .] was otherwise unreasonable.

(4)   Notwithstanding subsection (4) of section 8 of this Act and without prejudice to subsection (5) below, the court may, for the purpose of protecting the interests of a person to whom this section applies, order that the rectification of a document shall have effect as at such date as it may specify, being a date later than that as at which it would have effect by virtue of the said subsection (4).

(5)   Notwithstanding subsection (5) of section 8 of this Act and without prejudice to subsection (4) above, the court may, for the purpose of protecting the interests of a person to whom this section applies, order that a document as rectified shall be treated as having been recorded as mentioned in the said subsection (5) at such date as it may specify, being a date later than that as at which it would be treated by virtue of that subsection as having been so recorded.

[. . .]

(7)   Where a person to whom this section applies was unaware, before a document was ordered to be rectified under section 8 of this Act, that an application had been made under that section for the rectification of the document, the Court of Session, on an application made by that person within the time specified in subsection (8) below, may—

(a)   reduce the rectifying order; or

(b)   order the applicant for the rectifying order to pay such compensation to that person as it thinks fit in respect of his reliance on the terms of the document or on the title sheet.

(8)   The time referred to in subsection (7) above is whichever is the earlier of the following—

(a)   the expiry of 5 years after the making of the rectifying order;

(b)   the expiry of 2 years after the making of that order first came to the notice of the person referred to in that subsection.

10   Negligent misrepresentation

(1)   A party to a contract who has been induced to enter into it by negligent misrepresentation made by or on behalf of another party to the contract shall not be disentitled, by reason only that the misrepresentation is not fraudulent, from recovering damages from the other party in respect of any loss or damage he has suffered as a result of the misrepresentation; and any rule of law that such damages cannot be recovered unless fraud is proved shall cease to have effect.

(2)   Subsection (1) applies to any proceedings commenced on or after the date on which it comes into force, whether or not the negligent misrepresentation was made before or after that date, but does not apply to any proceedings commenced before that date.

[(3)   This section does not entitle a person to be paid damages in respect of a misrepresentation if the person has a right to redress under Part 4A of the Consumer Protection from Unfair Trading Regulations 2008 (SI 2008/1277) in respect of the conduct constituting the misrepresentation.

(4)   Subsection (3) does not prevent a debtor from bringing a claim under section 75(1) of the Consumer Credit Act 1974 against a creditor under a debtor-creditor-supplier agreement in a case where, but for subsection (4), the debtor would have a claim against the supplier in respect of a misrepresentation (and, where section 75 of that Act would otherwise apply, it accordingly applies as if the debtor had a claim against the supplier).]

ANIMALS (SCOTLAND) ACT 1987
(1987, c 9)

1 New provisions as to strict liability for injury or damage caused by animals

(1) Subject to subsection (4) and (5) below and section 2 of this Act, a person shall be liable for any injury or damage caused by an animal if—

(a) at the time of the injury or damage complained of, he was a keeper of the animal;

(b) the animal belongs to a species whose members generally are by virtue of their physical attributes or habits likely (unless controlled or restrained) to injure severely or kill persons or animals, or damage property to a material extent; and

(c) the injury or damage complained of is directly referable to such physical attributes or habits.

(2) In this section 'species' includes—

(a) a form or variety of the species or a sub-division of the species, or the form or variety, identifiable by age, sex or such other criteria as are relevant to the behaviour of animals; and

(b) a kind which is the product of hybridisation.

(3) For the purposes of subsection (1)(b) above—

(a) dogs, and dangerous wild animals within the meaning of section 7(4) of the Dangerous Wild Animals Act 1976, shall be deemed to be likely (unless controlled or restrained) to injure severely or kill persons or animals by biting or otherwise savaging, attacking or harrying; and

(b) any of the following animals in the course of foraging, namely—

cattle, horses, asses, mules, hinnies, sheep, pigs, goats and deer,

shall be deemed to be likely (unless controlled or restrained) to damage to a material extent land or the produce of land, whether harvested or not.

(4) Subsection (1) above shall not apply to any injury caused by an animal where the injury consists of disease transmitted by means which are unlikely to cause severe injury other than disease.

(5) Subsection (1) above shall not apply to injury or damage caused by the mere fact that an animal is present on a road or in any other place.

(6) For the purposes of the Law Reform (Contributory Negligence) Act 1945, any injury or damage for which a person is liable under this section shall be treated as due to his fault as defined in that Act.

(7) Subsections (1) and (2) of section 3 of the Law Reform (Miscellaneous Provisions) (Scotland) Act 1940 (contribution among joint wrongdoers) shall, subject to any necessary modifications, apply in relation to an action of damages in respect of injury or damage which is brought in pursuance of this section as they apply in relation to an action of damages in respect of loss or damage arising from any wrongful acts or omissions; but nothing in this subsection shall affect any contractual, or (except as aforesaid) any other, right of relief or indemnity.

(8) The foregoing provisions of this section and section 2 of this Act replace—

(a) any rule of law which imposes liability, without proof of a negligent act or omission, on the owner or possessor of an animal for injury or damage caused by that animal on the ground that the animal is *ferae naturae* or is otherwise known to be dangerous or harmful;

(b) the Winter Herding Act 1686;

(c) section 1(1) and (2) of the Dogs Act 1906 (injury to cattle or poultry).

2 Exceptions from liability under section 1

(1) A person shall not be liable under section 1(1) of this Act if—

(a) the injury or damage was due wholly to the fault of—

(i) the person sustaining it; or

(ii) in the case of injury sustained by an animal, a keeper of the animal;

(b)   the person sustaining the injury or damage or a keeper of the animal sustaining the injury willingly accepted the risk of it as his; or

(c)   subject to subsection (2) below, the injury or damage was sustained on, or in consequence of the person or animal sustaining the injury or damage coming on to, land which was occupied by a person who was a keeper, or by another person who authorised the presence on the land, of the animal which caused the injury or damage; and, either—

(i)   the person sustaining the injury or damage was not authorised or entitled to be on that land; or (as the case may be)

(ii)   no keeper of the animal sustaining the injury was authorised or entitled to have the animal present on that land.

(2)   A person shall not be exempt from liability by virtue of subsection (1)(c) above if the animal causing the injury or damage was kept on the land wholly or partly for the purpose of protecting persons or property, unless the keeping of the animal there, and the use made of the animal, for that purpose was reasonable, and, if the animal was a guard dog within the meaning of the Guard Dogs Act 1975, unless there was compliance with section 1 of that Act.

(3)   In subsection (1) above—

(a)   in paragraph (a) 'fault' has the same meaning as in the Law Reform (Contributory Negligence) Act 1945;

(b)   in paragraph (c) 'authorised' means expressly or impliedly authorised.

3   Detention of straying animals

(1)   Without prejudice to section 98 of the Roads (Scotland) Act 1984, where an animal strays on to any land and is not then under the control of any person, the occupier of the land may detain the animal for the purpose of preventing injury or damage by it.

(2)   Part VI of the Civic Government (Scotland) Act 1982 (lost and abandoned property) shall apply in relation to an animal, other than a stray dog, detained under subsection (1) above as it applies in relation to any property taken possession of under section 67 of that Act subject to the omission from section 74 of the words from 'or livestock' to '129 of this Act' and to any other necessary modifications; and section 4 of the Dogs Act 1906 shall, subject to any necessary modifications, apply to a stray dog detained under subsection (1) above as it applies to a stray dog taken possession of under that section.

4   Killing of, or injury to, animals attacking or harrying persons or livestock

(1)   Subject to subsection (2) below, in any civil proceedings against a person for killing or causing injury to an animal, it shall be a defence for him to prove—

(a)   that he acted—

(i)   in self-defence;

(ii)   for the protection of any other person; or

(iii)   for the protection of any livestock and was one of the persons mentioned in subsection (3) below; and

(b)   that within 48 hours after the killing or injury notice thereof was given by him or on his behalf at a police station or to a constable.

(2)   There shall be no defence available under subsection (1) above to a person killing or causing injury to an animal where the killing or injury—

(a)   occurred at or near a place where the person was present for the purpose of engaging in a criminal activity; and

(b)   was in furtherance of that activity.

(3)   The persons referred to in subsection (1)(a)(iii) above are—

(a)   a person who, at the time of the injury or killing complained of, was a keeper of the livestock concerned;

(b)   the owner or occupier of the land where the livestock was present; and

(c)   a person authorised (either expressly or impliedly) to act for the protection of the livestock by such a keeper of the livestock or by the owner or occupier of the land where the livestock was present.

(4) A person killing or causing injury to an animal ('the defender') shall be regarded, for the purposes of this section, as acting in self defence or for the protection of another person or any livestock if, and only if—

(a) the animal is attacking him or that other person or that livestock and (whether or not the animal is under the control of anyone) the defender has reasonable grounds for believing that there are no other practicable means of ending the attack; or

(b) the defender has reasonable grounds for believing—

(i) that the animal is about to attack him, such person or livestock and that (whether or not the animal is under the control of anyone) there are no other practicable means of preventing the attack; or

(ii) that the animal has been attacking a person or livestock, is not under the control of anyone and has not left the vicinity where the attack took place, and that there are no other practicable means of preventing a further attack by the animal while it is still in that vicinity.

(5) In subsection (4) above 'attack' or 'attacking' includes 'harry' or 'harrying'.

(6) In this section—

'livestock' means any animal of a domestic variety (including in particular sheep, cattle and horses) and, while they are in captivity, any other animals.

5 Meaning of a keeper of an animal

(1) Subject to subsection (2) below, for the purposes of this Act a person is a keeper of an animal if—

(a) he owns the animal or has possession of it; or

(b) he has actual care and control of a child under the age of 16 who owns the animal or has possession of it.

(2) For the purposes of this section—

(a) a person shall not be regarded as having possession of an animal by reason only that he is detaining it under section 3 of this Act or is otherwise temporarily detaining it for the purpose of protecting it or any person or other animal or of restoring it as soon as is reasonably practicable to its owner or a possessor of it;

(b) if an animal has been abandoned or has escaped, a person who at the time of the abandonment or escape was the owner of it or had it in his possession shall remain its owner or shall be regarded as continuing to have possession of it until another person acquires its ownership or (as the case may be) comes into possession of it; and

(c) the Crown shall not acquire ownership of an animal on its abandonment.

6 Application to Crown

This Act binds the Crown, but this section shall not authorise proceedings to be brought against Her Majesty in her private capacity.

7 Interpretation

In this Act, unless the context otherwise requires—

'animal' does not include viruses, bacteria, algae, fungi or protozoa;

'harry' includes chase in such a way as may be likely to cause injury or suffering; and 'harrying' shall be construed accordingly;

'injury' includes death, any abortion or other impairment of physical or mental condition and any loss of or diminution in the produce of an animal and, subject to section 1(4) of this Act, disease.

8 Transitional provision and repeals

(1) This Act shall apply only in relation to injury or damage caused after the commencement of the Act.

(2)   The enactments mentioned in the Schedule to this Act are hereby repealed
to the extent specified in the third column of that Schedule.

9   Short title, commencement and extent

(1)   This Act may be cited as the Animals (Scotland) Act 1987.

(2)   This Act shall come into force at the end of a period of 2 months beginning
with the date on which it is passed.

(3)   This Act extends to Scotland only.

CONSUMER PROTECTION ACT 1987
(1987, c 43)

PART I
PRODUCT LIABILITY

1   Purpose and construction of Part I

(1)   This Part shall have effect for the purpose of making such provision as is
necessary in order to comply with the product liability Directive and shall be construed accordingly.

(2)   In this Part, except in so far as the context otherwise requires—

[. . .]

'dependant' and 'relative' have the same meaning as they have in, respectively, the Fatal Accidents Act 1976 and the [Damages (Scotland) Act 2011];

'producer', in relation to a product, means—

(a)   the person who manufactured it;

(b)   in the case of a substance which has not been manufactured but has been
won or abstracted, the person who won or abstracted it;

(c)   in the case of a product which has not been manufactured, won or
abstracted but essential characteristics of which are attributable to an industrial
or other process having been carried out (for example, in relation to agricultural
produce), the person who carried out that process;

'product' means any goods or electricity and (subject to subsection (3) below)
includes a product which is comprised in another product, whether by virtue of
being a component part or raw material or otherwise; and

'the product liability Directive' means the Directive of the Council of the European Communities, dated 25th July 1985, (No 85/374/EEC) on the approximation
of the laws, regulations and administrative provisions of the member States concerning liability for defective products.

(3)   For the purposes of this Part a person who supplies any product in which
products are comprised, whether by virtue of being component parts or raw materials or otherwise, shall not be treated by reason only of his supply of that product as supplying any of the products so comprised.

2   Liability for defective products

(1)   Subject to the following provisions of this Part, where any damage is
caused wholly or partly by a defect in a product, every person to whom subsection
(2) below applies shall be liable for the damage.

(2)   This subsection applies to—

(a)   the producer of the product;

(b)   any person who, by putting his name on the product or using a trade
mark or other distinguishing mark in relation to the product, has held himself
out to be the producer of the product;

(c)   any person who has imported the product into a member State from a
place outside the member States in order, in the course of any business of his, to
supply it to another.

(3)   Subject as aforesaid, where any damage is caused wholly or partly by a

defect in a product, any person who supplied the product (whether to the person who suffered the damage, to the producer of any product in which the product in question is comprised or to any other person) shall be liable for the damage if—

(a) the person who suffered the damage requests the supplier to identify one or more of the persons (whether still in existence or not) to whom subsection (2) above applies in relation to the product;

(b) that request is made within a reasonable period after the damage occurs and at a time when it is not reasonably practicable for the person making the request to identify all those persons; and

(c) the supplier fails, within a reasonable period after receiving the request, either to comply with the request or to identify the person who supplied the product to him.

[. . .]

(5) Where two or more persons are liable by virtue of this Part for the same damage, their liability shall be joint and several.

(6) This section shall be without prejudice to any liability arising otherwise than by virtue of this Part.

3 Meaning of 'defect'

(1) Subject to the following provisions of the section, there is a defect in a product for the purposes of this Part if the safety of the product is not such as persons generally are entitled to expect; and for those purposes 'safety', in relation to a product, shall include safety with respect to products comprised in that product and safety in the context of risks of damage to property, as well as in the context of risks of death or personal injury.

(2) In determining for the purposes of subsection (1) above what persons generally are entitled to expect in relation to a product all the circumstances shall be taken into account, including—

(a) the manner in which, and purposes for which, the product has been marketed, its get-up, the use of any mark in relation to the product and any instructions for, or warnings with respect to, doing or refraining from doing anything with or in relation to the product;

(b) what might reasonably be expected to be done with or in relation to the product; and

(c) the time when the product was supplied by its producer to another;

and nothing in this section shall require a defect to be inferred from the fact alone that the safety of a product which is supplied after that time is greater than the safety of the product in question.

4 Defences

(1) In any civil proceedings by virtue of this Part against any person ('the person proceeded against') in respect of a defect in a product it shall be a defence for him to show—

(a) that the defect is attributable to compliance with any requirement imposed by or under any enactment or with any [EU] obligation; or

(b) that the person proceeded against did not at any time supply the product to another; or

(c) that the following conditions are satisfied, that is to say—

(i) that the only supply of the product to another by the person proceeded against was otherwise than in the course of a business of that person's; and

(ii) that section 2(2) above does not apply to that person or applies to him by virtue only of things done otherwise than with a view to profit; or

(d) that the defect did not exist in the product at the relevant time; or

(e) that the state of scientific and technical knowledge at the relevant time was not such that a producer of products of the same description as the product in question might be expected to have discovered the defect if it had existed in his products while they were under his control; or

(f)   that the defect—

(i)   constituted a defect in a product ('the subsequent product') in which the product in question had been comprised; and

(ii)   was wholly attributable to the design of the subsequent product or to compliance by the producer of the product in question with instructions given by the producer of the subsequent product.

(2)   In this section 'the relevant time', in relation to electricity, means the time at which it was generated, being a time before it was transmitted or distributed, and in relation to any other product, means—

(a)   if the person proceeded against is a person to whom subsection (2) of section 2 above applies in relation to the product, the time when he supplied the product to another;

(b)   if that subsection does not apply to that person in relation to the product, the time when the product was last supplied by a person to whom that subsection does apply in relation to the product.

5   Damage giving rise to liability

(1)   Subject to the following provisions of this section, in this Part 'damages' means death or personal injury or any loss of or damage to any property (including land).

(2)   A person shall not be liable under section 2 above in respect of any defect in a product for the loss of or any damage to the product itself or for the loss of or any damage to the whole or any part of any product which has been supplied with the product in question comprised in it.

(3)   A person shall not be liable under section 2 above for any loss of or damage to any property which, at the time it is lost or damaged, is not—

(a)   of a description of property ordinarily intended for private use, occupation or consumption; and

(b)   intended by the person suffering the loss or damage mainly for his own private use, occupation or consumption.

(4)   No damages shall be awarded to any person by virtue of this Part in respect of any loss of or damage to any property if the amount which would fall to be so awarded to that person, apart from this subsection and any liability for interest, does not exceed £275.

. . .

(8)   Subsections (5) to (7) above shall not extend to Scotland.

6   Application of certain enactments etc

(1)   Any damage for which a person is liable under section 2 above shall be deemed to have been caused—

(a)   for the purposes of the Fatal Accidents Act 1976, by that person's wrongful act, neglect or default;

(b)   for the purposes of section 3 of the Law Reform (Miscellaneous Provisions) (Scotland) Act 1940 (contribution among joint wrongdoers), by that person's wrongful act or negligent act or omission;

(c)   for the purposes of [sections 3 to 6 of the Damages (Scotland) Act 2011] (rights of relatives of a deceased), by that person's act or omission, and

(d)   for the purposes of Part II of the Administration of Justice Act 1982 (damages for personal injuries, etc—Scotland), by an act or omission giving rise to liability in that person to pay damages.

(2)   Where—

(a)   a person's death is caused wholly or partly by a defect in a product, or a person dies after suffering damage which has been so caused;

(b)   a request such as mentioned in paragraph (a) of subsection (3) of section 2 above is made to a supplier of the product by that person's personal representatives or, in the case of a person whose death is caused wholly or partly by the defect, by any dependant or relative of that person; and

(c)   the conditions specified in paragraphs (b) and (c) of that subsection are satisfied in relation to that request,

this Part shall have effect for the purposes of the Law Reform (Miscellaneous Provisions) Act 1934, the Fatal Accidents Acts 1976 and the [Damages (Scotland) Act 2011] as if liability of the supplier to that person under that subsection did not depend on that person having requested the supplier to identify certain persons or on the said conditions having been satisfied in relation to a request made by that person.

(3)   Section 1 of the Congenital Disabilities (Civil Liability) Act 1976 shall have effect for the purposes of this Part as if—

(a)   a person were answerable to a child in respect of an occurrence caused wholly or partly by a defect in a product if he is or has been liable under section 2 above in respect of any effect of the occurrence on a parent of the child, or would be so liable if the occurrence caused a parent of the child to suffer damage;

(b)   the provisions of this Part relating to liability under section 2 above applied in relation to liability by virtue of paragraph (a) above under the said section 1; and

(c)   subsection (6) of the said section 1 (exclusion of liability) were omitted.

(4)   Where any damage is caused partly by a defect in a product and partly by the fault of the person suffering the damage, the Law Reform (Contributory Negligence) Act 1945 and section 5 of the Fatal Accidents Act 1976 (contributory negligence) shall have effect as if the defect were the fault of every person liable by virtue of this Part for the damage caused by the defect.

(5)   In subsection (4) above 'fault' has the same meaning as in the said Act of 1945.

(6)   Schedule 1 to this Act shall have effect for the purpose of amending the Limitation Act 1980 and the Prescription and Limitation (Scotland) Act 1973 in their application in relation to the bringing of actions by virtue of this Part.

(7)   It is hereby declared that liability by virtue of this Part is to be treated as liability in tort for the purposes of any enactment conferring jurisdiction on any court with respect to any matter.

(8)   Nothing in this Part shall prejudice the operation of section 12 of the Nuclear Installations Act 1965 (rights to compensation for certain breaches of duties confined to rights under that Act).

7   Prohibition on exclusions from liability

The liability of a person by virtue of this Part to a person who has suffered damage caused wholly or partly by a defect in a product, or to a dependant or relative of such a person, shall not be limited or excluded by any contract term, by any notice or by any other provision.

8   Power to modify Part I

(1)   Her Majesty may by Order in Council make such modifications of this Part and of any other enactment (including an enactment contained in the following Parts of this Act, or in an Act passed after this Act) as appear to Her Majesty in Council to be necessary or expedient in consequence of any modification of the product liability Directive which is made at any time after the passing of this Act.

(2)   An Order in Council under subsection (1) above shall not be submitted to Her Majesty in Council unless a draft of the Order has been laid before, and approved by a resolution of, each House of Parliament.

9   Application of Part I to Crown

(1)   Subject to subsection (2) below, this Part shall bind the Crown.

(2)   The Crown shall not, as regards the Crown's liability by virtue of this Part,

be bound by this Part further than the Crown is made liable in tort or in reparation under the Crown Proceedings Act 1947, as that Act has effect from time to time.

45 Interpretation

(1) In this Act, except in so far as the context otherwise requires—

'aircraft' includes gliders, balloons and hovercraft;

'business' includes a trade or profession and the activities of a professional or trade association or of a local authority or other public authority;

'conditional sale agreement', 'credit-sale agreement' and 'hire-purchase agreement' have the same meanings as in the Consumer Credit Act 1974 but as if in the definitions in that Act 'goods' had the same meaning as in this Act;

'contravention' includes a failure to comply and cognate expressions shall be construed accordingly;

'enforcement authority' means the Secretary of State, any other Minister of the Crown in charge of a Government department, any such department and any authority, council or other person on whom functions under this Act are conferred by or under section 27 above;

'gas' has the same meaning as in Part I of the Gas Act 1986;

'goods' includes substances, growing crops and things comprised in land by virtue of being attached to it and any ship, aircraft or vehicle;

'information' includes accounts, estimates and returns;

'magistrates' court', in relation to Northern Ireland, means a court of summary jurisdiction;

'modifications' includes additions, alterations and omissions, and cognate expressions shall be construed accordingly;

'motor vehicle' has the same meaning as in the Road Traffic Act [1988];

'notice' means a notice in writing;

'notice to warn' means a notice under section 13(1)(b) above;

'officer', in relation to an enforcement authority, means a person authorised in writing to assist the authority in carrying out its functions under or for the purposes of the enforcement of any of the safety provisions or of any of the provisions made by or under Part III of this Act;

'personal injury' includes any disease and any other impairment of a person's physical or mental condition;

'premises' includes any place and any ship, aircraft or vehicle;

'prohibition notice' means a notice under section 13(1)(a) above;

'records' includes any books or documents and any records in non-documentary form;

'safety provision' means [. . .] any provision of safety regulations, a prohibition notice or a suspension notice;

'safety regulations' means regulations under section 11 above;

'ship' includes any boat and any other description of vessel used in navigation;

'subordinate legislation' has the same meaning as in the Interpretation Act 1978;

'substance' means any natural or artificial substance, whether in solid, liquid or gaseous form or in the form of a vapour, and includes substances that are comprised in or mixed with other goods;

'supply' and cognate expressions shall be construed in accordance with section 46 below;

'suspension notice' means a notice under section 14 above.

(2) Except in so far as the context otherwise requires, references in this Act to a contravention of a safety provision shall, in relation to any goods, include references to anything which would constitute such a contravention if the goods were supplied to any person.

(3) References in this Act to any goods in relation to which any safety provision has been or may have been contravened shall include references to any goods which it is not reasonably practicable to separate from any such goods.

[. . .]

(5)   In Scotland, any reference in this Act to things comprised in land by virtue of being attached to it is a reference to moveables which have become heritable by accession to heritable property.

COURT OF SESSION ACT 1988
(1988, c 36)

46   Specific relief may be granted in interdict proceedings

Where a respondent in any application or proceedings in the Court, whether before or after the institution of such proceedings or application, has done any act which the Court might have prohibited by interdict, the Court may ordain the respondent to perform any act which may be necessary for reinstating the petitioner in his possessory right, or for granting specific relief against the illegal act complained of.

47   Interim interdict and other interim orders

(1)   In any cause containing a conclusion or a crave for interdict or liberation, the Division of the Inner House or the Lord Ordinary (as the case may be) may, on the motion of any party to the cause, grant interim interdict or liberation; and it shall be competent for the Division of the Inner House or the Lord Ordinary before whom any cause in which interim interdict has been granted is pending to deal with any breach of the interim interdict without the presentation of a petition and complaint.

(2)   In any cause in dependence before the Court, the Court may, on the motion of any party to the cause, make such order regarding the interim possession of any property to which the cause relates, or regarding the subject matter of the cause, as the Court may think fit.

[(2A)   The power under subsection (2) to make an order includes, in particular, power to make an order ad factum praestandum (including an interim order).]

(3)   Every interim act, warrant and decree granted during the dependence of a cause in the Court shall, unless the Court otherwise directs, be extractible *ad interim.*

ENVIRONMENTAL PROTECTION ACT 1990
(1990, c 43)

79   Statutory nuisances and inspections therefor

(1)   [Subject to subsections [(1ZA)] to (6A) below], the following matters constitute 'statutory nuisances' for the purposes of this Part, that is to say—

(a)   any premises in such a state as to be prejudicial to health or a nuisance;

(b)   smoke emitted from premises so as to be prejudicial to health or a nuisance;

(c)   fumes or gases emitted from premises so as to be prejudicial to health or a nuisance;

(d)   any dust, steam, smell or other effluvia arising on industrial, trade or business premises and being prejudicial to health or a nuisance;

(e)   any accumulation or deposit which is prejudicial to health or a nuisance;

[(ea)   any water covering land or land covered with water which is in such a state as to be prejudicial to health or a nuisance;]

(f)   any animal kept in such a place or manner as to be prejudicial to health or a nuisance;

[(faa)   any insects emanating from premises and being prejudicial to health or a nuisance;]

[(fba)   artificial light emitted from—

    (i)   premises;

    (ii)   any stationary object,

so as to be prejudicial to health or a nuisance;]

    (g)   noise emitted from premises so as to be prejudicial to health or a nuisance;

    [(ga)   noise that is prejudicial to health or a nuisance and is emitted from or caused by a vehicle, machinery or equipment in a street [or in Scotland, road];]

    (h)   any other matter declared by any enactment to be a statutory nuisance;

and it shall be the duty of every local authority to cause its area to be inspected from time to time to detect any statutory nuisances which ought to be dealt with under section 80 below [or sections 80 and 80A below] and, where a complaint of a statutory nuisance is made to it by a person living within its area, to take such steps as are reasonably practicable to investigate the complaint.

[(1ZA)   The Scottish Ministers may by regulations—

    (a)   amend this section so as to—

       (i)   prescribe additional matters which constitute statutory nuisances for the purposes of this Part;

       (ii)   vary the description of any matter which constitutes a statutory nuisance;

    (b)   in relation to an amendment under paragraph (a), amend this Act and any other enactment to make such incidental, supplementary, consequential, transitory, transitional or saving provision as the Scottish Ministers consider appropriate.]

[(1ZB)   Before making regulations under subsection (1ZA) above, the Scottish Ministers must consult, in so far as it is reasonably practicable to do so, the persons mentioned in subsection (1ZC) below.]

[(1ZC)   Those persons are—

    (a)   such associations of local authorities; and

    (b)   such other persons,

as the Scottish Ministers consider appropriate.]

[(1A)   No matter shall constitute a statutory nuisance to the extent that it consists of, or is caused by, any land being in a contaminated state.]

[(1B)   Land is in a 'contaminated state' for the purposes of subsection (1A) above if, and only if, it is in such a condition, by reason of substances in, on or under the land, that—

    (a)   significant harm is being caused or there is a significant possibility of such harm being caused; or

    (b)   significant pollution of the water environment is being caused or there is a significant possibility of such pollution being caused;

and in this subsection 'harm', 'pollution' in relation to the water environment, 'substance' and 'the water environment' have the same meanings as in Part IIA of this Act.]

    (2)   Subsection (1)(b) [, (fba)] and (g) above do not apply in relation to premises [(or, in respect of paragraph (fba)(ii) above, a stationary object located on premises)]—

    (a)   occupied on behalf of the Crown for naval, military or air force purposes or for the purposes of the department of the Secretary of State having responsibility for defence, or

    (b)   occupied by or for the purposes of a visiting force;

and 'visiting force' means any such body, contingent or detachment of the forces of any country as is a visiting force for the purposes of any of the provisions of the Visiting Forces Act 1952.

    (3)   Subsection (1)(b) above does not apply to—

       (i)   smoke emitted from a chimney of a private dwelling within a smoke control area,

       (ii)   dark smoke emitted from a chimney of a building or a chimney serving the furnace of a boiler or industrial plant attached to a building or for the time being fixed to or installed on any land,

(iii) smoke emitted from a railway locomotive steam engine, or

(iv) dark smoke emitted otherwise than as mentioned above from industrial or trade premises.

(4) Subsection (1)(c) above does not apply in relation to premises other than private dwellings.

(5) Subsection (1)(d) above does not apply to steam emitted from a railway locomotive engine.

[(5ZA) For the purposes of subsection (1)(ea) above, 'land'—

(a) includes structures (other than buildings) in, on or over land;

(b) does not include—

(i) mains or other pipes used for carrying a water supply;

(ii) any part of the public sewerage system;

(iii) any other sewers, drains or other pipes used for carrying sewage;

(iv) the foreshore, that is to say, the land between the high and low water marks of ordinary spring tides;

(v) the seabed.

[(5ZB) In subsection (5ZA) above—

'drain', 'sewage' and 'sewer' have the meanings given by section 59 of the Sewerage (Scotland) Act 1968;

'main' has the meaning given by section 109(1) of the Water (Scotland) Act 1980;

'pipe' includes a service pipe within the meaning of that section of that Act;

'public sewerage system' has the meaning given by section 29 of the Water Services etc (Scotland) Act 2005.]

[(5AA) Subsection (1)(faa) above does not apply to insects that are wild animals included in Schedule 5 to the Wildlife and Countryside Act 1981.]

[(5AB) For the purposes of subsection (1)(faa) above, 'premises' does not include—

(a) a site of special scientific interest (within the meaning of section 3(6) of the Nature Conservation (Scotland) Act 2004);

(b) such other place (or type of place) as may be prescribed in regulations made by the Scottish Ministers.]

[(5AC) Before making regulations under subsection (5AB)(b) above, the Scottish Ministers must consult, in so far as it is reasonably practicable to do so, the persons mentioned in subsection (5AD) below.]

[(5AD) Those persons are—

(a) such associations of local authorities; and

(b) such other persons,

as the Scottish Ministers consider appropriate.]

[(5BA) Subsection (1)(fba) above does not apply to artificial light emitted from a lighthouse (within the meaning of Part 8 of the Merchant Shipping Act 1995.]

(6) Subsection (1)(g) above does not apply to noise caused by aircraft other than model aircraft.

[(6A) Subsection (1)(ga) above does not apply to noise made—

(a) by traffic,

(b) by any naval, military or air force of the Crown or by a visiting force (as defined in subsection (2) above), or

(c) by a political demonstration or a demonstration supporting or opposing a cause or campaign.]

(7) In this Part—

'chimney' includes structures and openings of any kind from or through which smoke may be emitted;

'dust' does not include dust emitted from a chimney as an ingredient of smoke;

['equipment' includes a musical instrument;]

'fumes' means any airborne solid matter smaller than dust;

'gas' includes vapour and moisture precipitated from vapour;

'industrial, trade or business premises' means premises used for any industrial, trade or business purposes or premises not so used on which matter is burnt in connection with any industrial, trade or business process, and premises are used for industrial purposes where they are used for the purposes of any treatment or process as well as where they are used for the purposes of manufacturing;

'local authority' means [. . .]—

(a)   in Greater London, a London borough council, the Common Council of the City of London and, as respects the Temples, the Sub-Treasurer of the Inner Temple and the Under-Treasurer of the Middle Temple respectively;

(b)   [in England and Wales] outside Greater London, a district council; . . .

[(bb)   in Wales, a county council or county borough council;]

(c)   the Council of the Isles of Scilly; [and

(d)   in Scotland, a district or islands council or a council constituted under section 2 of the Local Government etc (Scotland) Act 1994;]

'noise' includes vibration;

['person responsible'—

(a)   in relation to a statutory nuisance, means the person to whose act, default or sufferance the nuisance is attributable;

(b)   in relation to a vehicle, includes the person in whose name the vehicle is for the time being registered under [the Vehicle Excise and Registration Act 1994] and any other person who is for the time being the driver of the vehicle;

(c)   in relation to machinery or equipment, includes any person who is for the time being the operator of the machinery or equipment;]

'prejudicial to health' means injurious, or likely to cause injury, to health;

'premises' includes land [(subject to subsection (5AB) above)] and, subject to subsection (12) [and [, in relation to England and Wales,] section 81A(9)] below, any vessel;

'private dwelling' means any building, or part of a building, used or intended to be used, as a dwelling;

['road' has the same meaning as in Part IV of the New Roads and Street Works Act 1991;]

'smoke' includes soot, ash, grit and gritty particles emitted in smoke;

['street' means a highway and any other road, footway, square or court that is for the time being open to the public;]

and any expressions used in this section and in [the Clean Air Act 1993] have the same meaning in this section as in that Act and [section 3 of the Clean Air Act 1993] shall apply for the interpretation of the expression 'dark smoke' and the operation of this Part in relation to it.

(8)   Where, by an order under section 2 of the Public Health (Control of Disease) Act 1984, a port health authority has been constituted for any port health district, [. . .] the port health authority [. . .] shall have by virtue of this subsection, as respects its district, the functions conferred or imposed by this Part in relation to statutory nuisances other than a nuisance falling within paragraph (g) [or (ga)] of subsection (1) above and no such order shall be made assigning those functions; and 'local authority' and 'area' shall be construed accordingly.

(9)   In this Part 'best practicable means' is to be interpreted by reference to the following provisions—

(a)   'practicable' means reasonably practicable having regard among other things to local conditions and circumstances, to the current state of technical knowledge and to the financial implications;

(b)   the means to be employed include the design, installation, maintenance and manner and periods of operation of plant and machinery, and the design, construction and maintenance of buildings and structures;

(c)   the test is to apply only so far as compatible with any duty imposed by law;

(d)   the test is to apply only so far as compatible with safety and safe working conditions, and with the exigencies of any emergency or unforeseeable circumstances;

and, in circumstances where a code of practice under section 71 of the Control of Pollution Act 1974 (noise minimisation) is applicable, regard shall also be had to guidance given in it.

(10)   A local authority shall not without the consent of the Secretary of State institute summary proceedings under this Part in respect of a nuisance falling within paragraph (b), (d) [, (e) or (g) and, in relation to Scotland, [paragraph (ga)],] of subsection (1) above if proceedings in respect thereof might be instituted under Part I [of the Alkali &c Works Regulation Act 1906 or section 5 of the Health and Safety at Work etc Act 1974 or under regulations under section 2 of the Pollution Prevention and Control Act 1999.]

(11)   The area of a local authority which includes part of the seashore shall also include for the purposes of this Part the territorial sea lying seawards from that part of the shore; and subject to subsection (12) [and [, in relation to England and Wales,] section 81A(9)] below, this Part shall have effect, in relation to any area included in the area of a local authority by virtue of this subsection—

(a)   as if references to premises and the occupier of premises included respectively a vessel and the master of a vessel; and

(b)   with such other modifications, if any, as are prescribed in regulations made by the Secretary of State.

(12)   A vessel powered by steam reciprocating machinery is not a vessel to which this Part of this Act applies.

AGE OF LEGAL CAPACITY (SCOTLAND) ACT 1991
(1991, c 50)

1   Age of legal capacity

(1)   As from the commencement of this Act—

(a)   a person under the age of 16 years shall, subject to section 2 below, have no legal capacity to enter into any transaction;

(b)   a person of or over the age of 16 years shall have legal capacity to enter into any transaction.

(2)   Subject to section 8 below, any reference in any enactment to a pupil (other than in the context of education or training) or to a person under legal disability or incapacity by reason of nonage shall, insofar as it relates to any time after the commencement of this Act, be construed as a reference to a person under the age of 16 years.

(3)   Nothing in this Act shall—

(a)   apply to any transaction entered into before the commencement of this Act;

(b)   confer any legal capacity on any person who is under legal disability or incapacity other than by reason of nonage;

(c)   affect the delictual or criminal responsibility of any person;

(d)   affect any enactment which lays down an age limit expressed in years for any particular purpose;

(e)   prevent any person under the age of 16 years from receiving or holding any right, title or interest;

(f)   affect any existing rule of law or practice whereby—

(i) any civil proceedings may be brought or defended, or any step in civil proceedings may be taken, in the name of a person under the age of 16 years [in relation to whom there is no person entitled to act as his legal representative (within the meaning of Part I of the Children (Scotland) Act 1995), or where there is such a person,] is unable (whether by reason of conflict of interest or otherwise) or refuses to bring or defend such proceedings or take such step;

　　(ii)　the court may, in any civil proceedings, appoint a curator ad litem to a person under the age of 16 years;

　　(iii)　the court may, in relation to the approval of an arrangement under section 1 of the Trusts (Scotland) Act 1961, appoint a curator ad litem to a person of or over the age of 16 years but under the age of 18 years;

　　(iv)　the court may appoint a curator bonis to any person;

　(g)　prevent any person under the age of 16 years from [exercising parental responsibilities and parental rights (within the meaning of sections 1(3) and 2(4) respectively of the Children (Scotland) Act 1995) in relation to any child of his.]

(4)　Any existing rule of law relating to the legal capacity of minors and pupils which is inconsistent with the provisions of this Act shall cease to have effect.

(5)　Any existing rule of law relating to reduction of a transaction on the ground of minority and lesion shall cease to have effect.

2　Exceptions to general rule

(1)　A person under the age of 16 years shall have legal capacity to enter into a transaction—

　(a)　of a kind commonly entered into by persons of his age and circumstances, and

　(b)　on terms which are not unreasonable.

(2)　A person of or over the age of 12 years shall have testamentary capacity, including legal capacity to exercise by testamentary writing any power of appointment.

(3)　A person of or over the age of 12 years shall have legal capacity to consent to the making of an adoption order in relation to him. [. . .]

(4)　A person under the age of 16 years shall have legal capacity to consent on his own behalf to any surgical, medical or dental procedure or treatment where, in the opinion of a qualified medical practitioner attending him, he is capable of understanding the nature and possible consequences of the procedure or treatment.

[(4ZA)　For the purposes of subsection (4), the storage of gametes in accordance with the Human Fertilisation and Embryology Act 1990 is to be treated as a medical procedure.

(4ZB)　A person under the age of 16 years shall have legal capacity to consent to the use of the person's human cells in accordance with Schedule 3 to the Human Fertilisation and Embryology Act 1990 for the purposes of a project of research where the person is capable of understanding the nature of the research; and in this subsection 'human cells' has the same meaning as in that Schedule.]

[(4A)　A person under the age of sixteen years shall have legal capacity to instruct a solicitor, in connection with any civil matter, where that person has a general understanding of what it means to do so; and without prejudice to the generality of this subsection a person twelve years of age or more shall be presumed to be of sufficient age and maturity to have such understanding.

(4B)　A person who by virtue of subsection (4A) above has legal capacity to instruct a solicitor shall also have legal capacity to sue, or to defend, in any civil proceedings.

(4C)　Subsections (4A) and (4B) above are without prejudice to any question of legal capacity arising in connection with any criminal matter.]

(5)　Any transaction—

　(a)　which a person under the age of 16 years purports to enter into after the commencement of this Act, and

(b)   in relation to which that person does not have legal capacity by virtue of this section,
shall be void.

3   Setting aside of transactions
(1)   A person under the age of 21 years ('the applicant') may make application to the court to set aside a transaction which he entered into while he was of or over the age of 16 years but under the age of 18 years and which is a prejudicial transaction.
(2)   In this section 'prejudicial transaction' means a transaction which—
(a)   an adult, exercising reasonable prudence, would not have entered into in the circumstances of the applicant at the time of entering into the transaction, and
(b)   has caused or is likely to cause substantial prejudice to the applicant.
(3)   Subsection (1) above shall not apply to—
(a)   the exercise of testamentary capacity;
(b)   the exercise by testamentary writing of any power of appointment;
(c)   the giving of consent to the making of an adoption order;
(d)   the bringing or defending of, or the taking of any step in, civil proceedings;
(e)   the giving of consent to any surgical, medical or dental procedure or treatment;
(f)   a transaction in the course of the applicant's trade, business or profession;
(g)   a transaction into which any other party was induced to enter by virtue of any fraudulent misrepresentation by the applicant as to age or other material fact;
(h)   a transaction ratified by the applicant after he attained the age of 18 years and in the knowledge that it could be the subject of an application to the court under this section to set it aside; or
(j)   a transaction ratified by the court under section 4 below.
(4)   Where an application to set aside a transaction can be made or could have been made under this section by the person referred to in subsection (1) above, such application may instead be made by that person's executor, trustee in bankruptcy, trustee acting under a trust deed for creditors or curator bonis at any time prior to the date on which that person attains or would have attained the age of 21 years.
(5)   An application under this section to set aside a transaction may be made—
(a)   by an action in the Court of Session or the sheriff court, or
(b)   by an incidental application in other proceedings in such court,
and the court may make an order setting aside the transaction and such further order, if any, as seems appropriate to the court in order to give effect to the rights of the parties.

4   Ratification by court of proposed transaction
(1)   Where a person of or over the age of 16 years but under the age of 18 years proposes to enter into a transaction which, if completed, could be the subject of an application to the court under section 3 above to set aside, all parties to the proposed transaction may make a joint application to have it ratified by the court.
(2)   The court shall not grant an application under this section if it appears to the court that an adult, exercising reasonable prudence and in the circumstances of the person referred to in subsection (1) above, would not enter into the transaction.
(3)   An application under this section shall be made by means of a summary application—
(a)   to the sheriff of the sheriffdom in which any of the parties to the proposed transaction resides, or

(b) where none of the said parties resides in Scotland, to the sheriff at Edinburgh,
and the decision of the sheriff on such application shall be final.

5 Guardians of persons under 16

(1) Except insofar as otherwise provided in Schedule 1 to this Act, as from the commencement of this Act any reference in any rule of law, enactment or document to the tutor [. . .] of a pupil child shall be construed as a reference to [a person entitled to act as a child's legal representative (within the meaning of Part I of the Children (Scotland) Act 1995) and any reference to the tutory of such a child shall be construed as a reference to the entitlement to act as a child's legal representative enjoyed by a person, by, under or by virtue of the said Part I.]

(2) Subject to section 1(3)(f) above, as from the commencement of this Act no guardian of a person under the age of 16 years shall be appointed as such except under [section 7 of the Children (Scotland) Act 1995.]

(3) As from the commencement of this Act, no person shall, by reason of age alone, be subject to the curatory of another person.

(4) As from the commencement of this Act, no person shall be appointed as factor loco tutoris.

6 Attainment of age

(1) The time at which a person attains a particular age expressed in years shall be taken to be the beginning of the relevant anniversary of the date of his birth.

(2) Where a person has been born on 29th February in a leap year, the relevant anniversary in any year other than a leap year shall be taken to be 1st March.

(3) The provisions of this section shall apply only to a relevant anniversary which occurs after the commencement of this Act.

[. . .]

8 Transitional provision

Where any person referred to in section 6(4)(b), 17(3), 18(3) or 18A(2) of the Prescription and Limitation (Scotland) Act 1973 as having been under legal disability by reason of nonage was of or over the age of 16 years but under the age of 18 years immediately before the commencement of this Act, any period prior to such commencement shall not be reckoned as, or as part of, the period of 5 years, or (as the case may be) 3 years, specified respectively in section 6, 17, 18 or 18A of that Act.

9 Interpretation

In this Act, unless the context otherwise requires—
    'existing' means existing immediately before the commencement of this Act;
    [. . .]
    'transaction' means a transaction having legal effect, and includes—
        (a) any unilateral transaction;
        (b) the exercise of testamentary capacity;
        (c) the exercise of any power of appointment;
        (d) the giving by a person of any consent having legal effect;
        (e) the bringing or defending of, or the taking of any step in, civil proceedings;
        (f) acting as arbiter or trustee;
        (g) acting as an instrumentary witness.

10 Amendments and repeals

(1) The enactments mentioned in Schedule 1 to this Act shall have effect subject to the amendments therein specified.

(2) The enactments specified in Schedule 2 to this Act are repealed to the extent specified in the third column of that Schedule.

11   Short title, commencement and extent

(1)   This Act may be cited as the Age of Legal Capacity (Scotland) Act 1991.

(2)   This Act shall come into force at the end of the period of two months beginning with the date on which it is passed.

(3)   This Act shall extend to Scotland only.

CARRIAGE OF GOODS BY SEA ACT 1992
(1992, c 50)

1   Shipping documents etc to which Act applies

(1)   This Act applies to the following documents, that is to say—

(a)   any bill of lading;

(b)   any sea waybill; and

(c)   any ship's delivery order.

(2)   References in this Act to a bill of lading—

(a)   do not include references to a document which is incapable of transfer either by indorsement or, as a bearer bill, by delivery without indorsement; but

(b)   subject to that, do include references to a received for shipment bill of lading.

(3)   References in this Act to a sea waybill are references to any document which is not a bill of lading but—

(a)   is such a receipt for goods as contains or evidences a contract for the carriage of goods by sea; and

(b)   identifies the person to whom delivery of the goods is to be made by the carrier in accordance with that contract.

(4)   References in this Act to a ship's delivery order are references to any document which is neither a bill of lading nor a sea waybill but contains an undertaking which—

(a)   is given under or for the purposes of a contract for the carriage by sea of the goods to which the document relates, or of goods which include those goods; and

(b)   is an undertaking by the carrier to a person identified in the document to deliver the goods to which the document relates to that person.

(5)   The Secretary of State may by regulations make provision for the application of this Act to cases where an electronic communications network or any other information technology is used for effecting transactions corresponding to—

(a)   the issue of a document to which this Act applies;

(b)   the indorsement, delivery or other transfer of such a document; or

(c)   the doing of anything else in relation to such a document.

(6)   Regulations under subsection (5) above may—

(a)   make such modifications of the following provisions of this Act as the Secretary of State considers appropriate in connection with the application of this Act to any case mentioned in that subsection; and

(b)   contain supplemental, incidental, consequential and transitional provision;

and the power to make regulations under that subsection shall be exercisable by statutory instrument subject to annulment in pursuance of a resolution of either House of Parliament.

2   Rights under shipping documents

(1)   Subject to the following provisions of this section, a person who becomes—

(a)   the lawful holder of a bill of lading;

(b)   the person who (without being an original party to the contract of carriage) is the person to whom delivery of the goods to which a sea waybill relates is to be made by the carrier in accordance with that contract; or

(c)   the person to whom delivery of the goods to which a ship's delivery order relates is to be made in accordance with the undertaking contained in the order,

shall (by virtue of becoming the holder of the bill or, as the case may be, the person to whom delivery is to be made) have transferred to and vested in him all rights of suit under the contract of carriage as if he had been a party to that contract.

(2)   Where, when a person becomes the lawful holder of a bill of lading, possession of the bill no longer gives a right (as against the carrier) to possession of the goods to which the bill relates, that person shall not have any rights transferred to him by virtue of subsection (1) above unless he becomes the holder of the bill—

(a)   by virtue of a transaction effected in pursuance of any contractual or other arrangements made before the time when such a right to possession ceased to attach to possession of the bill; or

(b)   as a result of the rejection to that person by another person of goods or documents delivered to the other person in pursuance of any such arrangements.

(3)   The rights vested in any person by virtue of the operation of subsection (1) above in relation to a ship's delivery order—

(a)   shall be so vested subject to the terms of the order; and

(b)   where the goods to which the order relates form a part only of the goods to which the contract of carriage relates, shall be confined to rights in respect of the goods to which the order relates.

(4)   Where, in the case of any document to which this Act applies—

(a)   a person with any interest or right in or in relation to goods to which the document relates sustains loss or damage in consequence of a breach of the contract of carriage; but

(b)   subsection (1) above operates in relation to that document so that rights of suit in respect of that breach are vested in another person,

the other person shall be entitled to exercise those rights for the benefit of the person who sustained the loss or damage to the same extent as they could have been exercised if they had been vested in the person for whose benefit they are exercised.

(5)   Where rights are transferred by virtue of the operation of subsection (1) above in relation to any document, the transfer for which that subsection provides shall extinguish any entitlement to those rights which derives—

(a)   where that document is a bill of lading, from a person's having been an original party to the contract of carriage; or

(b)   in the case of any document to which this Act applies, from the previous operation of that subsection in relation to that document;

but the operation of that subsection shall be without prejudice to any rights which derive from a person's having been an original party to the contract contained in, or evidenced by, a sea waybill and, in relation to a ship's delivery order, shall be without prejudice to any rights deriving otherwise than from the previous operation of that subsection in relation to that order.

3   Liabilities under shipping documents

(1)   Where subsection (1) of section 2 of this Act operates in relation to any document to which this Act applies and the person in whom rights are vested by virtue of that subsection—

(a)   takes or demands delivery from the carrier of any of the goods to which the document relates;

(b) makes a claim under the contract of carriage against the carrier in respect of any of those goods; or

(c) is a person who, at a time before those rights were vested in him, took or demanded delivery from the carrier of any of those goods,

that person shall (by virtue of taking or demanding delivery or making the claim or, in a case falling within paragraph (c) above, of having the rights vested in him) become subject to the same liabilities under that contract as if he had been a party to that contract.

(2) Where the goods to which a ship's delivery order relates form a part only of the goods to which the contract of carriage relates, the liabilities to which any person is subject by virtue of the operation of this section in relation to that order shall exclude liabilities in respect of any goods to which the order does not relate.

(3) This section, so far as it imposes liabilities under any contract on any person, shall be without prejudice to the liabilities under the contract of any person as an original party to the contract.

4 Representations in bills of lading

A bill of lading which—

(a) represents goods to have been shipped on board a vessel or to have been received for shipment on board a vessel; and

(b) has been signed by the master of the vessel or by a person who was not the master but had the express, implied or apparent authority of the carrier to sign bills of lading,

shall, in favour of a person who has become the lawful holder of the bill, be conclusive evidence against the carrier of the shipment of the goods or, as the case may be, of their receipt for shipment.

5 Interpretation etc

(1) In this Act—

'bill of lading', 'sea waybill' and 'ship's delivery order' shall be construed in accordance with section 1 above;

'the contract of carriage'—

(a) in relation to a bill of lading or sea waybill, means the contract contained in or evidenced by that bill or waybill; and

(b) in relation to a ship's delivery order, means the contract under or for the purposes of which the undertaking contained in the order is given;

'holder', in relation to a bill of lading, shall be construed in accordance with subsection (2) below;

'information technology' includes any computer or other technology by means of which information or other matter may be recorded or communicated without being reduced to documentary form; [. . .]

(2) References in this Act to the holder of a bill of lading are references to any of the following persons, that is to say—

(a) a person with possession of the bill who, by virtue of being the person identified in the bill, is the consignee of the goods to which the bill relates;

(b) a person with possession of the bill as a result of the completion, by delivery of the bill, of any indorsement of the bill or, in the case of a bearer bill, of any other transfer of the bill;

(c) a person with possession of the bill as a result of any transaction by virtue of which he would have become a holder falling within paragraph (a) or (b) above had not the transaction been effected at a time when possession of the bill no longer gave a right (as against the carrier) to possession of the goods to which the bill relates;

and a person shall be regarded for the purposes of this Act as having become the lawful holder of a bill of lading wherever he has become the holder of the bill in good faith.

(3) References in this Act to a person's being identified in a document include

references to his being identified by a description which allows for the identity of
the person in question to be varied, in accordance with the terms of the document,
after its issue; and the reference in section 1(3)(b) of this Act to a document's identifying a person shall be construed accordingly.

(4)   Without prejudice to sections 2(2) and 4 above, nothing in this Act shall
preclude its operation in relation to a case where the goods to which a document
relates—

(a)   cease to exist after the issue of the document; or

(b)   cannot be identified (whether because they are mixed with other goods
or for any other reason);

and references in this Act to the goods to which a document relates shall be construed accordingly.

(5)   The preceding provisions of this Act shall have effect without prejudice to
the application, in relation to any case, of the rules (the Hague-Visby Rules) which
for the time being have the force of law by virtue of section 1 of the Carriage of
Goods by Sea Act 1971.

6   Short title, repeal, commencement and extent

(1)   This Act may be cited as the Carriage of Goods by Sea Act 1992.

(2)   The Bills of Lading Act 1855 is hereby repealed.

(3)   This Act shall come into force at the end of the period of two months beginning with the day on which it is passed; but nothing in this Act shall have effect in
relation to any document issued before the coming into force of this Act.

(4)   This Act extends to Northern Ireland.

REQUIREMENTS OF WRITING (SCOTLAND) ACT 1995
(1995, c 7)

[PART 1
WHEN WRITING IS REQUIRED]

1   Writing required for certain contracts, obligations, trusts, conveyances and wills

(1)   Subject to subsection (2) below and any other enactment, writing shall not
be required for the constitution of a contract, unilateral obligation or trust.

(2)   Subject to [subsection (3)] below, a written document [which is a traditional
document] complying with section 2 [or an electronic document complying with
section 9B] of this Act shall be required for—

(a)   the constitution of—

(i)   a contract or unilateral obligation for the creation, transfer, variation or
extinction of [a real right] in land;

(ii)   a gratuitous unilateral obligation except an obligation undertaken in
the course of business; and

(iii)   a trust whereby a person declares himself to be sole trustee of his own
property or any property which he may acquire;

(b)   the creation, transfer, variation or extinction of [a real right] in land
otherwise than by the operation of a court decree, enactment or rule of law; and

[(ba)   the constitution of an agreement under section 66(1) of the Land Registration etc (Scotland) Act 2002 (asp 5),]

(c)   the making of any will, testamentary trust disposition and settlement or
codicil.

(3)   Where a contract, obligation or trust mentioned in [subsection (2)(a)] above
is not constituted in a [. . .] document complying with section 2 [or, as the case
may be, section 9B], of this Act but one of the parties to the contract, a creditor in
the obligation or a beneficiary under the trust ('the first person') has acted or

refrained from acting in reliance on the contract, obligation or trust with the knowledge and acquiescence of the other party to the contract, the debtor in the obligation or the truster ('the second person')—

(a)   the second person shall not be entitled to withdraw from the contract, obligation or trust; and

(b)   the contract, obligation or trust shall not be regarded as invalid, on the ground that it is not so constituted, if the condition set out in subsection (4) below is satisfied.

(4)   The condition referred to in subsection (3) above is that the position of the first person—

(a)   as a result of acting or refraining from acting as mentioned in that subsection has been affected to a material extent; and

(b)   as a result of such a withdrawal as is mentioned in that subsection would be adversely affected to a material extent.

(5)   In relation to the constitution of any contract, obligation or trust mentioned in [subsection (2)(a)] above, subsections (3) and (4) above replace the rules of law known as *rei interventus* and homologation.

(6)   This section shall apply to the variation of a contract, obligation or trust as it applies to the constitution thereof but as if in subsections (3) and (4) for the references to acting or refraining from acting in reliance on the contract, obligation or trust and withdrawing therefrom there were substituted respectively references to acting or refraining from acting in reliance on the variation of the contract, obligation or trust and withdrawing from the variation.

(7)   In this section ['real right in land' means any real] right in or over land, including any right to occupy or to use land or to restrict the occupation or use of land, but does not include—

(a)   a tenancy;

(b)   a right to occupy or use land; or

(c)   a right to restrict the occupation or use of land,

if the tenancy or right is not granted for more than one year, unless the tenancy or right is for a recurring period or recurring periods and there is a gap of more than one year between the beginning of the first, and the end of the last, such period.

(8)   For the purposes of subsection (7) above 'land' does not include—

(a)   growing crops; or

(b)   a moveable building or other moveable structure.

[PART 2
TRADITIONAL DOCUMENTS]

[1A   Application of Part 2
This Part of this Act applies to documents written on paper, parchment or some similar tangible surface ('traditional documents').]

2   Type of writing required for formal validity of certain [traditional] documents

(1)   No [traditional document] required by section 1(2) of this Act shall be valid in respect of the formalities of execution unless it is subscribed by the granter of it or, if there is more than one granter, by each granter, but nothing apart from such subscription shall be required for the document to be valid as aforesaid.

(2)   A contract mentioned in section 1(2)(a)(i) of this Act may be regarded as constituted or varied (as the case may be) if the offer is contained in one or more [traditional documents] and the acceptance is contained in another [traditional document] or other [traditional documents], and each [such] document is subscribed by the granter or granters thereof.

(3)   Nothing in this section shall prevent a [traditional document] which has not

been subscribed by the granter or granters of it from being used as evidence in relation to any right or obligation to which the document relates.

(4)   This section is without prejudice to any other enactment which makes different provision in respect of the formalities of execution of a document to which this section applies.

[. . .]

3   Presumption as to granter's subscription or date or place of subscription

(1)   Subject to subsections (2) to (7) below, where—

   (a)   a [traditional document] bears to have been subscribed by a granter of it;

   (b)   the document bears to have been signed by a person as a witness of that granter's subscription and the document, or the testing clause or its equivalent, bears to state the name and address of the witness; and

   (c)   nothing in the document, or in the testing clause or its equivalent, indicates—

      (i)   that it was not subscribed by that granter as it bears to have been so subscribed; or

      (ii)   that it was not validly witnessed for any reason specified in paragraphs (a) to (e) of subsection (4) below,

the document shall be presumed to have been subscribed by that granter.

(2)   Where a [traditional document is a testamentary document consisting] of more than one sheet, it shall not be presumed to have been subscribed by a granter as mentioned in subsection (1) above unless, in addition to it bearing to have been subscribed by him and otherwise complying with that subsection, it bears to have been signed by him on every sheet.

(3)   For the purposes of subsection (1)(b) above—

   (a)   the name and address of a witness may be added at any time before the document is—

      (i)   founded on in legal proceedings; or

      (ii)   registered for preservation in the Books of Council and Session or in sheriff court books; and

   (b)   the name and address of a witness need not be written by the witness himself.

(4)   Where, in any proceedings relating to a [traditional document] in which a question arises as to a granter's subscription, it is established—

   (a)   that a signature bearing to be the signature of the witness of that granter's subscription is not such a signature, whether by reason of forgery or otherwise;

   (b)   that the person who signed the document as the witness of that granter's subscription is a person who is named in the document as a granter of it;

   (c)   that the person who signed the document as the witness of that granter's subscription, at the time of signing—

      (i)   did not know the granter;

      (ii)   was under the age of 16 years; or

      (iii)   was mentally incapable of acting as a witness;

   (d)   that the person who signed the document, purporting to be the witness of that granter's subscription, did not witness such subscription;

   (e)   that the person who signed the document as the witness of that granter's subscription did not sign the document after him or that the granter's subscription or, as the case may be, acknowledgement of his subscription and the person's signature as witness of that subscription were not one continuous process;

   (f)   that the name or address of the witness of that granter's subscription was added after the document was founded on or registered as mentioned in subsection (3)(a) above or is erroneous in any material respect; or

   (g)   in the case of a testamentary document consisting of more than one sheet, that a signature on any sheet bearing to be the signature of the granter is not such a signature, whether by reason of forgery or otherwise,

then, for the purposes of those proceedings, there shall be no presumption that the document has been subscribed by that granter.

(5) For the purposes of subsection (4)(c)(i) above, the witness shall be regarded as having known the person whose subscription he has witnessed at the time of witnessing if he had credible information at that time of his identity.

(6) For the purposes of subsection (4)(e) above, where—

(a) a document is granted by more than one granter; and

(b) a person is the witness to the subscription of more than one granter,

the subscription or acknowledgement of any such granter and the signature of the person witnessing that granter's subscription shall not be regarded as not being one continuous process by reason only that, between the time of that subscription or acknowledgement and that signature, another granter has subscribed the document or acknowledged his subscription.

(7) For the purposes of the foregoing provisions of this section a person witnesses a granter's subscription of a document—

(a) if he sees the granter subscribe it; or

(b) if the granter acknowledges his subscription to that person.

(8) Where—

(a) by virtue of subsection (1) above a document to which this subsection applies is presumed to have been subscribed by a granter of it;

(b) the document, or the testing clause or its equivalent, bears to state the date or place of subscription of the document by that granter; and

(c) nothing in the document, or in the testing clause or its equivalent, indicates that that statement as to date or place is incorrect,

there shall be a presumption that the document was subscribed by that granter on the date or at the place as stated.

(9) Subsection (8) above applies to any [traditional document] other than a testamentary document.

(10) Where—

(a) a [traditional document is a testamentary document bearing] to have been subscribed and the document, or the testing clause or its equivalent, bears to state the date or place of subscription (whether or not it is presumed under subsections (1) to (7) above to have been subscribed by a granter of it); and

(b) nothing in the document, or in the testing clause or its equivalent, indicates that that statement as to date or place is incorrect,

there shall be a presumption that the statement as to date or place is correct.

[. . .]

4 Presumption as to granter's subscription or date or place of subscription when established in court proceedings

(1) Where a [traditional document] bears to have been subscribed by a granter of it, but there is no presumption under section 3 of this Act that the document has been subscribed by that granter, then, if the court, on an application being made to it by any person who has an interest in the document, is satisfied that the document was subscribed by that granter, it shall—

(a) cause the document to be endorsed with a certificate to that effect; or

(b) where the document has already been registered in the Books of Council and Session or in sheriff court books, grant decree to that effect.

(2) Where a [traditional document] bears to have been subscribed by a granter of it, but there is no presumption under section 3 of this Act as to the date or place of subscription, then, if the court, on an application being made to it by any person who has an interest in the document, is satisfied as to the date or place of subscription, it shall—

(a) cause the document to be endorsed with a certificate to that effect; or

(b)   where the document has already been registered in the Books of Council and Session or in sheriff court books, grant decree to that effect.

(3)   On an application under subsection (1) or (2) above evidence shall, unless the court otherwise directs, be given by affidavit.

(4)   An application under subsection (1) or (2) above may be made either as a summary application or as incidental to and in the course of other proceedings.

(5)   The effect of a certificate or decree—

(a)   under subsection (1) above shall be to establish a presumption that the document has been subscribed by the granter concerned;

(b)   under subsection (2) above shall be to establish a presumption that the statement in the certificate or decree as to date or place is correct.

(6)   In this section 'the court' means—

(a)   in the case of a summary application—

(i)   the sheriff in whose sheriffdom the applicant resides; or

(ii)   if the applicant does not reside in Scotland, the sheriff at Edinburgh; and

(b)   in the case of an application made in the course of other proceedings, the court before which those proceedings are pending.

5   Alterations to [traditional documents]: formal validity and presumptions

(1)   An alteration made to a [traditional document] required by section 1(2) of this Act—

(a)   before the document is subscribed by the granter or, if there is more than one granter, by the granter first subscribing it, shall form part of the document as so subscribed;

(b)   after the document is so subscribed shall, if the alteration has been signed by the granter or (as the case may be) by all the granters, have effect as a formally valid alteration of the document as so subscribed,

but an alteration made to such a document otherwise than as mentioned in paragraphs (a) and (b) above shall not be formally valid.

(2)   Subsection (1) above is without prejudice to—

(a)   any rule of law enabling any provision in a testamentary document to be revoked by deletion or erasure without authentication of the deletion or erasure by the testator;

(b)   the Erasures in Deeds (Scotland) Act 1836 and section 54 of the Conveyancing (Scotland) Act 1874.

(3)   The fact that an alteration to a [traditional document] was made before the document was subscribed by the granter of it, or by the granter first subscribing it, may be established by all relevant evidence, whether written or oral.

(4)   Where a [traditional document] bears to have been subscribed by the granter or, if there is more than one granter, by all the granters of it, then, if subsection (5) or (6) below applies, an alteration made to the document shall be presumed to have been made before the document was subscribed by the granter or, if there is more than one granter, by the granter first subscribing it, and to form part of the document as so subscribed.

(5)   This subsection applies where—

(a)   the document is presumed under section 3 of this Act to have been subscribed by the granter or granters (as the case may be);

(b)   it is stated in the document, or in the testing clause or its equivalent, that the alteration was made before the document was subscribed; and

(c)   nothing in the document, or in the testing clause or its equivalent, indicates that the alteration was made after the document was subscribed.

(6)   This subsection applies where subsection (5) above does not apply, but the court is satisfied, on an application being made to it, that the alteration was made before the document was subscribed by the granter or, if there is more than one granter, by the granter first subscribing it, and causes the document to be endorsed

with a certificate to that effect or, where the document has already been registered in the Books of Council and Session or in sheriff court books, grants decree to that effect.

(7) Subsections (3), (4) and (6) of section 4 of this Act shall apply in relation to an application under subsection (6) above as they apply in relation to an application under subsection (1) of that section.

(8) Where an alteration is made to a [traditional document] after the document has been subscribed by a granter, Schedule 1 to this Act (presumptions as to granter's signature and date and place of signing in relation to such alterations) shall have effect.

6 Registration of [traditional documents]

(1) Subject to subsection (3) below, it shall not be competent—

(a) to record a [traditional document] in the Register of Sasines; or

(b) to register a [traditional document] for execution or preservation in the Books of Council and Session or in sheriff court books,

[(ba) to register a traditional document in the Land Register of Scotland,]
unless subsection (2) below applies in relation to the document.

(2) This subsection applies where—

(a) the document is presumed under section 3 or 4 of this Act to have been subscribed by the granter; or

(b) if there is more than one granter, the document is presumed under section 3 or 4 or partly under the one section and partly under the other to have been subscribed by at least one of the granters.

(3) Subsection (1) above shall not apply in relation to—

[(a) a document's—

(i) being recorded in the Register of Sasines, or

(ii) being registered in the Land Register of Scotland, in the Books of Council and Session or in sheriff court books,

if an enactment requires or expressly permits such recording or registration notwithstanding that the document is not presumed to have been subscribed by the granter or by at least one of the granters,]

(b) the recording of a court decree in the Register of Sasines [or the registering of such a decree in the Land Register of Scotland];

(c) the registration in the Books of Council and Session or in sheriff court books of—

(i) a testamentary document;

(ii) a document which is directed by the Court of Session or (as the case may be) the sheriff to be so registered;

(iii) a document whose formal validity is governed by a law other than Scots law, if the Keeper of the Registers of Scotland or (as the case may be) the sheriff clerk is satisfied that the document is formally valid according to the law governing such validity;

(iv) a court decree granted under section 4 or 5 of this Act in relation to a document already registered in the Books of Council and Session or in sheriff court books (as the case may be); or

(d) the registration of a court decree in a separate register maintained for that purpose.

(4) A [traditional document] may be registered for preservation in the Books of Council and Session or in sheriff court books without a clause of consent to registration.

[. . .]

7 Subscription and signing

(1) Except where an enactment expressly provides otherwise, a [traditional document] is subscribed by a granter of it if it is signed by him at the end of the

last page (excluding any annexation, whether or not incorporated in the document as provided for in section 8 of this Act).

(2)   Subject to paragraph 2(2) of Schedule 2 to this Act, a [traditional document], or an alteration to [such a document], is signed by an individual natural person as a granter or on behalf of a granter of it if it is signed by him—

(a)   with the full name by which he is identified in the document or in any testing clause or its equivalent; or

(b)   with his surname, preceded by at least one forename (or an initial or abbreviation or familiar form of a forename); or

(c)   except for the purposes of section 3(1) to (7) of this Act, with a name (not in accordance with paragraph (a) or (b) above) or description or an initial or mark if it is established that the name, description, initial or mark—

(i)   was his usual method of signing, or his usual method of signing documents or alterations of the type in question; or

(ii)   was intended by him as his signature of the document or alteration.

(3)   Where there is more than one granter, the requirement under subsection (1) above of signing at the end of the last page of a document shall be regarded as complied with if at least one granter signs at the end of the last page and any other granter signs on an additional page.

(4)   Where a person grants a [traditional document] in more than one capacity, one subscription of the document by him shall be sufficient to bind him in all such capacities.

(5)   A [traditional document], or an alteration to [such a document], is signed by a witness if it is signed by him—

(a)   with the full name by which he is identified in the document or in any testing clause or its equivalent; or

(b)   with his surname, preceded by at least one forename (or an initial or abbreviation or familiar form of a forename),

and if the witness is witnessing the signature of more than one granter, it shall be unnecessary for him to sign the document or alteration more than once.

(6)   This section is without prejudice to any rule of law relating to the subscription or signing of documents by members of the Royal Family, by peers or by the wives or the eldest sons of peers.

(7)   Schedule 2 to this Act (special rules relating to subscription and signing of [traditional documents] etc by partnerships, companies, [limited liability partnerships,] local authorities, other bodies corporate and Ministers) shall have effect.

8   Annexations to [traditional documents]

(1)   Subject to subsection (2) below and except where an enactment expressly otherwise provides, any annexation to a [traditional document] shall be regarded as incorporated in the document if it is—

(a)   referred to in the document; and

(b)   identified on its face as being the annexation referred to in the document, without the annexation having to be signed or subscribed.

(2)   Where a document relates to land and an annexation to it describes or shows all or any part of the land to which the document relates, the annexation shall be regarded as incorporated in the document if and only if—

(a)   it is referred to in the document; and

(b)   it is identified on its face as being the annexation referred to in the document; and

(c)   it is signed on—

(i)   each page, where it is a plan, drawing, photograph or other representation; or

(ii)   the last page, where it is an inventory, appendix, schedule or other writing.

(3) Any annexation referred to in subsection (2) above which bears to have been signed by a granter of the document shall be presumed to have been signed by the person who subscribed the document as that granter.

(4) Section 7(2) of this Act shall apply in relation to any annexation referred to in subsection (2) above as it applies in relation to a [traditional document] as if for any reference to a document (except the reference in paragraph (a)) there were substituted a reference to an annexation.

(5) It shall be competent to sign any annexation to a [traditional document] at any time before the document is—

(a) founded on in legal proceedings;

(b) registered for preservation in the Books of Council and Session or in sheriff court books;

(c) recorded in the Register of Sasines;

(d) registered in the Land Register of Scotland.

(6) Where there is more than one granter, the requirement under subsection (2)(c)(ii) above of signing on the last page shall be regarded as complied with (provided that at least one granter signs at the end of the last page) if any other granter signs on an additional page.

9 Subscription on behalf of blind granter or granter unable to write

(1) Where a granter of a [traditional document] makes a declaration to a relevant person that he is blind or unable to write, the relevant person—

(a) having read the document to that granter; or

(b) if the granter makes a declaration that he does not wish him to do so, without having read it to the granter,

shall, if authorised by the granter, be entitled to subscribe it and, if it is a testamentary document, sign it as mentioned in section 3(2) of this Act, on the granter's behalf.

(2) Subscription or signing by a relevant person under subsection (1) above shall take place in the presence of the granter.

(3) This Act shall have effect in relation to subscription or signing by a relevant person under subsection (1) above subject to the modifications set out in Schedule 3 to this Act.

(4) A document subscribed by a relevant person under subsection (1) above which confers on the relevant person or his spouse, son or daughter a benefit in money or money's worth (whether directly or indirectly) shall be invalid to the extent, but only to the extent, that it confers such benefit.

(5) This section and Schedule 3 to this Act apply in relation to the signing of—

(a) an annexation to a [traditional document] as mentioned in section 8(2) of this Act;

(b) an alteration made to a [traditional document as mentioned in section 5(1)] or to any such annexation to a document, as they apply in relation to the subscription of a document; and for that purpose, any reference to reading a document includes a reference to describing a plan, drawing, photograph or other representation in such an annexation or in an alteration to such an annexation.

(6) In this Act 'relevant person' means a solicitor who has in force a practising certificate as defined in section 4(c) of the Solicitors (Scotland) Act 1980, an advocate, a justice of the peace or a sheriff clerk and, in relation to the execution of documents outwith Scotland, includes a notary public or any other person with official authority under the law of the place of execution to execute documents on behalf of persons who are blind or unable to write.

(7) Nothing in this section shall prevent the granter of a document who is blind from subscribing or signing the document as mentioned in section 7 of this Act.

[PART 3
ELECTRONIC DOCUMENTS

[9A　Application of Part 3
This Part applies to documents which, rather than being written on paper, parchment or some similar tangible surface are created in electronic form ('electronic documents').]

[9B　Validity of electronic documents
(1)　No electronic document required by section 1(2) is valid in respect of the formalities of execution unless—
　　(a)　it is authenticated by the granter, or if there is more than one granter by each granter, in accordance with subsection (2), and
　　(b)　it meets such other requirements (if any) as may be prescribed by the Scottish Ministers in regulations.
(2)　An electronic document is authenticated by a person if the electronic signature of that person—
　　(a)　is incorporated into, or logically associated with, the electronic document,
　　(b)　was created by the person by whom it purports to have been created, and
　　(c)　is of such type, and satisfies such requirements (if any), as may be prescribed by the Scottish Ministers in regulations.
(3)　A contract mentioned in section 1(2)(a) may be regarded as constituted or varied (as the case may be) if—
　　(a)　the offer is contained in one or more electronic documents,
　　(b)　the acceptance is contained in another electronic document or in other such documents, and
　　(c)　each of the documents is authenticated by its granter or granters.
(4)　Where a person grants an electronic document in more than one capacity, authentication by the person of the document, in accordance with subsection (3), is sufficient to bind the person in all such capacities.
(5)　Nothing in this section prevents an electronic document which has not been authenticated by the granter or granters of it from being used as evidence in relation to any right or obligation to which the document relates.
(6)　Regulations under subsection (1)(b) or (2)(c) are subject to the negative procedure.]

[9C　Presumption as to authentication of electronic documents
(1)　Where—
　　(a)　an electronic document bears to have been authenticated by the granter,
　　(b)　nothing in the document or in the authentication indicates that it was not so authenticated, and
　　(c)　the conditions set out in subsection (2) are satisfied,
the document is to be presumed to have been authenticated by the granter.
(2)　The conditions are that the electronic signature incorporated into, or logically associated with, the document—
　　(a)　is of such type and satisfies such requirements as may be prescribed by the Scottish Ministers in regulations, and
　　(b)　(either or both)—
　　　　(i)　is used in such circumstances as may be so prescribed,
　　　　(ii)　bears to be certified,
and that if the electronic signature bears to be certified (and does not conform with paragraph (b)(i)) the certification is of such type and satisfies such requirements as may be so prescribed.
(3)　Regulations under subsection (2) are subject to the negative procedure.]

[9D   Presumptions as to granter's authentication etc when established in court proceedings

(1)   Where—

(a)   an electronic document bears to have been authenticated by a granter of it, and

(b)   there is no presumption under section 9C that the document has been authenticated by that granter,

the court must, on an application being made to it by any person who has an interest in the document, if satisfied that the document was authenticated by that granter, grant decree to that effect.

(2)   Where—

(a)   an electronic document bears to have been authenticated by a granter of it, and

(b)   there is no presumption by virtue of section 9E(1) as to the time, date or place of authentication,

the court must, on an application being made to it by any person who has an interest in the document, if satisfied as to that time, date or place, grant decree to that effect.

(3)   On an application under subsection (1) or (2), evidence is, unless the court otherwise directs, to be given by affidavit.

(4)   An application under subsection (1) or (2) may be made either as a summary application or as incidental to, and in the course of, other proceedings.

(5)   The effect of a decree—

(a)   under subsection (1), is to establish a presumption that the document has been authenticated by the granter concerned, or

(b)   under subsection (2), is to establish a presumption that the statement in the decree as to time, date or place is correct.

(6)   In this section, 'the court' means—

(a)   in the case of a summary application—

(i)   the sheriff in whose sheriffdom the applicant resides, or

(ii)   if the applicant does not reside in Scotland, the sheriff at Edinburgh, or

(b)   in the case of an application made in the course of other proceedings, the court before which those proceedings are pending.]

[9E   Further provision by Scottish Ministers about electronic documents

(1)   The Scottish Ministers may, in regulations, make provision as to the effectiveness or formal validity of, or presumptions to be made with regard to—

(a)   any alteration made, whether before or after authentication, to an electronic document,

(b)   the authentication, by or on behalf of the granter, of such a document,

(c)   the authentication, by or on behalf of a person with a disability, of such a document, or

(d)   any annexation to such a document,

(including, without prejudice to the generality of this subsection, presumptions to be made with regard to the time, date and place of authentication of such a document).

(2)   Regulations under subsection (1) may make such incidental, supplemental, consequential, transitional, transitory or saving provision as the Scottish Ministers consider necessary or expedient for the purposes of, or in consequence of, the regulations.

(3)   Subject to subsection (4), regulations under subsection (1) are subject to the negative procedure.

(4)   Regulations which—

(a)   make provision of the kind mentioned in subsection (1)(b), or

(b)   add to, replace or omit any part of an Act (including this Act),

are subject to the affirmative procedure.]

[9F   Delivery of electronic documents

(1) An electronic document may be delivered electronically or by such other means as are reasonably practicable.

(2) But such a document must be in a form, and such delivery must be by a means—

    (a) the intended recipient has agreed to accept, or

    (b) which it is reasonable in all the circumstances for the intended recipient to accept.]

[9G   Registration and recording of electronic documents

(1) Subject to subsection (6), it is not competent—

    (a) to record an electronic document in the Register of Sasines,

    (b) to register such a document in the Land Register of Scotland,

    (c) to register such a document for execution or preservation in the Books of Council and Session, or

    (d) to record or register such a document in any other register under the management and control of the Keeper of the Registers of Scotland,

unless both subsection (2) and subsection (3) apply in relation to the document.

(2) This subsection applies where—

    (a) the document is presumed under section 9C or 9D or by virtue of section 9E(1) to have been authenticated by the granter, or

    (b) if there is more than one granter, the document is presumed by virtue of any of those provisions to have been authenticated by at least one of the granters.

(3) This subsection applies where—

    (a) the document,

    (b) the electronic signature authenticating it, and

    (c) if the document bears to be certified, the certification,

are in such form and of such type as are prescribed by the Scottish Ministers in regulations.

(4) Before making regulations under subsection (3), the Scottish Ministers must consult with—

    (a) the Keeper of the Registers of Scotland,

    (b) the Keeper of the Records of Scotland, and

    (c) the Lord President of the Court of Session.

(5) Regulations under subsection (3)—

    (a) may make different provision for different cases or classes of case, and

    (b) are subject to the negative procedure.

(6) Subsection (1) above does not apply in relation to—

    (a) a document's—

       (i) being recorded in the Register of Sasines,

       (ii) being registered in the Land Register of Scotland or in the Books of Council and Session, or

       (iii) being recorded or registered in any other register under the management and control of the Keeper of the Registers of Scotland,

if an enactment requires or expressly permits such recording or registration notwithstanding that the document is not presumed to have been authenticated by the granter or by at least one of the granters,

    (b) the recording of a court decree in the Register of Sasines or the registering of such a decree in the Land Register of Scotland,

    (c) the registering in the Books of Council and Session of—

       (i) a document registration of which is directed by the Court of Session,

       (ii) a document the formal validity of which is governed by a law other than Scots law, provided that the Keeper of the Registers of Scotland is satisfied that the document is formally valid according to that other law,

       (iii) a court decree granted under section 9D, or by virtue of section 9E(1), of this Act in relation to a document already registered in the Books of Council and Session, or

(d)   the registration of a court decree in a separate register maintained for that purpose.

(7)   An electronic document may be registered for preservation in the Books of Council and Session without a clause of consent to registration.]]

[PART 4
GENERAL PROVISIONS]

10   Forms of testing clause

(1)   Without prejudice to the effectiveness of any other means of providing information relating to the execution of a document, this information may be provided in such form of testing clause as may be prescribed in regulations made by the Secretary of State.

(2)   Regulations under subsection (1) above shall be made by statutory instrument which shall be subject to annulment in pursuance of a resolution of either House of Parliament and may prescribe different forms for different cases or classes of case.

[. . .]

12   Interpretation

(1)   In this Act, except where the context otherwise requires—

'alteration' includes interlineation, marginal addition, deletion, substitution, erasure or anything written on erasure;

'annexation' includes any inventory, appendix, schedule, other writing, plan, drawing, photograph or other representation annexed to a document;

[. . .]

'authorised' means expressly or impliedly authorised and any reference to a person authorised to sign includes a reference to a person authorised to sign generally or in relation to a particular document;

['certification', in relation to an electronic signature incorporated into or logically associated with an electronic document, means confirming in a statement that—

(a)   the electronic signature,

(b)   a means of producing, communicating or verifying that signature, or

(c)   a procedure applied to that signature,

is, either alone or combined with other factors, a valid means of establishing the authenticity of the electronic document, its integrity or both its authenticity and its integrity (it being immaterial, in construing this definition, whether the statement is made before or after the authentication of an electronic document to which the statement relates),]

'company' has the same meaning as in [section 1(1) of the Companies Act 2006];

[. . .]

'decree' includes a judgment or order, or an official certified copy, abbreviate or extract of a decree;

[. . .]

'director' includes any person occupying the position of director, by whatever name he is called;

'document' includes [, in the case of a traditional document,] any annexation which is incorporated in it under section 8 of this Act and any reference, however expressed, to the signing of a document includes a reference to the signing of an annexation;

[. . .]

['electronic document' has the meaning given by section 9A,]

['electronic signature' means so much of anything in electronic form as—

(a)   is incorporated into, or logically associated with, an electronic document, and

(b)   purports to be so incorporated or associated for the purpose of being used in establishing the authenticity of the electronic document, its integrity or both its authenticity and its integrity,]

'enactment' includes an enactment contained in a statutory instrument [and an enactment comprised in, or in an instrument made under, an Act of the Scottish Parliament];

'governing board', in relation to a body corporate to which paragraph 5 of Schedule 2 to this Act applies, means any governing body, however described;

'local authority' means a local authority within the meaning of section 235(1) of the Local Government (Scotland) Act 1973 and a council constituted under section 2 of the Local Government etc. (Scotland) Act 1994;

'Minister' has the same meaning as 'Minister of the Crown' has in section 8 of the Ministers of the Crown Act 1975 [and also includes a Member of the Scottish Government];

'office-holder' does not include a Minister but, subject to that, means—

(a)   the holder of an office created or continued in existence by a public general Act of Parliament;

(b)   the holder of an office the remuneration in respect of which is paid out of money provided by Parliament [or out of the Scottish Consolidated Fund];

(c)   the registrar of companies [. . .];

'officer'—

(a)   in relation to a Minister, means any person in the civil service of the Crown who is serving in his Department [or as the case may be, as a member of the staff of the Scottish Ministers or the Lord Advocate];

(b)   in relation to an office-holder, means any member of his staff, or any person in the civil service of the Crown who has been assigned or appointed to assist him in the exercise of his functions;

'proper officer', in relation to a local authority, has the same meaning as in section 235(3) of the Local Government (Scotland) Act 1973; and

'secretary' means, if there are two or more joint secretaries, any one of them.

[. . .]

['traditional document' has the meaning given by section 1A].

(2)   Any reference in this Act to subscription or signing by a granter of a document or an alteration made to a document, in a case where a person is subscribing or signing under a power of attorney on behalf of the granter, shall be construed as a reference to subscription or signing by that person of the document or alteration.

[(3)   In a case where a person is authenticating an electronic document on behalf of a granter, any reference in this Act to authentication by a granter of an electronic document shall be construed as a reference to authentication by that person.]

[(4)   In relation to an electronic document—

(a)   references to authenticity—

(i)   are references to whether the document has been electronically signed by a particular person, and

(ii)   may include references to whether the document is accurately timed or dated, and

(b)   references to integrity are references as to whether there has been any tampering with, or other modification of, the document.]

13   Application of Act to Crown

(1)   Nothing in this Act shall—

(a)   prevent Her Majesty from authenticating—

(i)   a document by superscription; or

(ii)   a document relating to her private estates situated or arising in Scotland in accordance with section 6 of the Crown Private Estates Act 1862;

(b)   prevent authentication under the Writs Act 1672 of a document passing the seal appointed by the Treaty of Union to be kept and used in Scotland in place of the Great Seal of Scotland formerly in use; or

(c)   prevent any document mentioned in paragraph (a) or (b) above authenticated as aforesaid from being recorded in the Register of Sasines [, registered in the Land Register of Scotland] or registered for execution or preservation in the Books of Council and Session or in sheriff court books.

(2)   [. . .]

(3)   Subject to subsections (1) and (2) above, this Act binds the Crown.

14   Minor and consequential amendments, repeals, transitional provisions and savings

(1)   The enactments mentioned in Schedule 4 to this Act shall have effect subject to the minor and consequential amendments specified in that Schedule.

(2)   The enactments mentioned in Schedule 5 to this Act are hereby repealed to the extent specified in the third column of that Schedule.

(3)   Subject to subsection (4) below and without prejudice to subsection (5) below and section 11(4) of this Act, nothing in this Act shall—

(a)   apply to any document executed or anything done before the commencement of this Act; or

(b)   affect the operation, in relation to any document executed before such commencement, of any procedure for establishing the authenticity of such a document.

(4)   In the repeal of the Blank Bonds and Trusts Act 1696 (provided for in Schedule 5 to this Act), the repeal of the words from 'And farder' to the end—

(a)   shall have effect in relation to a deed of trust, whether executed before or after the commencement of this Act; but

(b)   notwithstanding paragraph (a) above, shall not have effect in relation to proceedings commenced before the commencement of this Act in which a question arises as to the deed of trust.

(5)   The repeal of certain provisions of the Lyon King of Arms Act 1672 (provided for in Schedule 5 to this Act) shall not affect any right of a person to add a territorial designation to his signature or the jurisdiction of the Lord Lyon King of Arms in relation to any such designation.

(6)   For the purposes of this Act, if it cannot be ascertained whether a document was executed before or after the commencement of this Act, there shall be a presumption that it was executed after such commencement.

15   Short title, commencement and extent

(1)   This Act may be cited as the Requirements of Writing (Scotland) Act 1995.

(2)   This Act shall come into force at the end of the period of three months beginning with the date on which it is passed.

(3)   This Act extends to Scotland only.

SCHEDULES

Section 5(8)   SCHEDULE 1
ALTERATIONS MADE TO A [TRADITIONAL DOCUMENT] AFTER IT HAS
BEEN SUBSCRIBED

Presumption as to granter's signature or date or place of signing

1.—(1)   Subject to sub-paragraphs (2) to (7) below, where—
   (a)   an alteration to a [traditional document] bears to have been signed by a
granter of the document;
   (b)   the alteration bears to have been signed by a person as a witness of that
granter's signature and the alteration, or the testing clause or its equivalent,
bears to state the name and address of the witness; and
   (c)   nothing in the document or alteration, or in the testing clause or its
equivalent, indicates—
      (i)   that the alteration was not signed by that granter as it bears to have
   been so signed; or
      (ii)   that it was not validly witnessed for any reason specified in
   paragraphs (a) to (e) of sub-paragraph (4) below,
the alteration shall be presumed to have been signed by that granter.
   (2)   Where an alteration to a testamentary document consists of more than one
sheet, the alteration shall not be presumed to have been signed by a granter as
mentioned in sub-paragraph (1) above unless, in addition to it bearing to have
been signed by him on the last sheet and otherwise complying with that sub-
paragraph, it bears to have been signed by him on every other sheet.
   (3)   For the purposes of sub-paragraph (1)(b) above—
   (a)   the name and address of a witness may be added at any time before the
alteration is—
      (i)   founded on in legal proceedings; or
      (ii)   registered for preservation in the Books of Council and Session or in
   sheriff court books; and
   (b)   the name and address of a witness need not be written by the witness
himself.
   (4)   Where, in any proceedings relating to an alteration to a document in which
a question arises as to a granter's signature, it is established—
   (a)   that a signature bearing to be the signature of the witness of that granter's signature is not such a signature, whether by reason of forgery or otherwise;
   (b)   that the person who signed the alteration as the witness of that granter's
signature is a person who is named in the document as a granter of the document;
   (c)   that the person who signed the alteration as the witness of that granter's
signature, at the time of signing—
      (i)   did not know the granter;
      (ii)   was under the age of 16 years; or
      (iii)   was mentally incapable of acting as a witness;
   (d)   that the person who signed the alteration, purporting to be the witness of
that granter's signature, did not witness such signature;
   (e)   that the person who signed the alteration as the witness of that granter's
signature did not sign the alteration after him or that the signing of the alteration by the granter or, as the case may be, the granter's acknowledgement of his
signature and the signing by the person as witness were not one continuous process;
   (f)   that the name or address of the witness of that granter's signature was

added after the alteration was founded on or registered as mentioned in sub-paragraph (3)(a) above or is erroneous in any material respect; or

(g)   in the case of an alteration to a testamentary document consisting of more than one sheet, that a signature on any sheet of the alteration bearing to be the signature of the granter is not such a signature, whether by reason of forgery or otherwise,

then, for the purposes of those proceedings, there shall be no presumption that the alteration has been signed by that granter.

(5)   For the purposes of sub-paragraph (4)(c)(i) above, the witness shall be regarded as having known the person whose signature he has witnessed at the time of witnessing if he had credible information at that time of his identity.

(6)   For the purposes of sub-paragraph (4)(e) above, where—

(a)   an alteration to a document is made by more than one granter; and

(b)   a person is the witness to the signature of more than one granter,

the signing of the alteration by any such granter or the acknowledgement of his signature and the signing by the person witnessing that granter's signature shall not be regarded as not being one continuous process by reason only that, between the time of signing or acknowledgement by that granter and of signing by that witness, another granter has signed the alteration or acknowledged his signature.

(7)   For the purposes of the foregoing provisions of this paragraph a person witnesses a granter's signature of an alteration—

(a)   if he sees the granter sign it; or

(b)   if the granter acknowledges his signature to that person.

(8)   Where—

(a)   by virtue of sub-paragraph (1) above an alteration to a document to which this sub-paragraph applies is presumed to have been signed by a granter of the document;

(b)   the alteration, or the testing clause or its equivalent, bears to state the date or place of signing of the alteration by that granter; and

(c)   nothing in the document or alteration, or in the testing clause or its equivalent, indicates that that statement as to date or place is incorrect,

there shall be a presumption that the alteration was signed by that granter on the date or at the place as stated.

(9)   Sub-paragraph (8) above applies to any document other than a testamentary document.

(10)   Where—

(a)   an alteration to a testamentary document bears to have been signed and the alteration, or the testing clause or its equivalent, bears to state the date or place of signing (whether or not it is presumed under sub-paragraphs (1) to (7) above to have been signed by a granter of the document); and

(b)   nothing in the document or alteration, or in the testing clause or its equivalent, indicates that that statement as to date or place is incorrect,

there shall be a presumption that the statement as to date or place is correct.

Presumption as to granter's signature or date or place of signing when established in court proceedings

2.—(1)   Where an alteration to a [traditional document] bears to have been signed by a granter of the document, but there is no presumption under paragraph 1 above that the alteration has been signed by that granter, then, if the court, on an application being made to it by any person having an interest in the document, is satisfied that the alteration was signed by that granter, it shall—

(a)   cause the document to be endorsed with a certificate to that effect; or

(b)   where the document has already been registered in the Books of Council and Session or in sheriff court books, grant decree to that effect.

(2)   Where an alteration to a [traditional document] bears to have been signed

by a granter of the document, but there is no presumption under paragraph 1 above as to the date or place of signing, then, if the court, on an application being made to it by any person having an interest in the document, is satisfied as to the date or place of signing, it shall—

(a)   cause the document to be endorsed with a certificate to that effect; or

(b)   where the document has already been registered in the Books of Council and Session or in sheriff court books, grant decree to that effect.

(3)   In relation to an application under sub-paragraph (1) or (2) above evidence shall, unless the court otherwise directs, be given by affidavit.

(4)   An application under sub-paragraph (1) or (2) above may be made either as a summary application or as incidental to and in the course of other proceedings.

(5)   The effect of a certificate or decree—

(a)   under sub-paragraph (1) above shall be to establish a presumption that the alteration has been signed by the granter concerned;

(b)   under sub-paragraph (2) above shall be to establish a presumption that the statement in the certificate or decree as to date or place is correct.

(6)   In this paragraph 'the court' means—

(a)   in the case of a summary application—

(i)   the sheriff in whose sheriffdom the applicant resides; or

(ii)   if the applicant does not reside in Scotland, the sheriff at Edinburgh; and

(b)   in the case of an application made in the course of other proceedings, the court before which those proceedings are pending.

Section 7(7)   SCHEDULE 2
                      SUBSCRIPTION AND SIGNING: SPECIAL CASES

General

1.   Any reference in this Act to subscription or signing by a granter of a [traditional document] or an alteration to a document, in a case where the granter is a person to whom any of paragraphs 2 to 6 of this Schedule applies shall, unless the context otherwise requires, be construed as a reference to subscription or, as the case may be, signing of the document or alteration by a person in accordance with that paragraph.

Partnerships

2.—(1)   Except where an enactment expressly provides otherwise, where a granter of a [traditional document] is a partnership, the document is signed by the partnership if it is signed on its behalf by a partner or by a person authorised to sign the document on its behalf.

(2)   A person signing on behalf of a partnership under this paragraph may use his own name or the firm name.

(3)   Sub-paragraphs (1) and (2) of this paragraph apply in relation to the signing of an alteration made to a document as they apply in relation to the signing of a document.

(4)   In this paragraph 'partnership' has the same meaning as in section 1 of the Partnership Act 1890.

Companies

3.—(1)   Except where an enactment expressly provides otherwise, where a granter of a [traditional document] is a company, the document is signed by the company if it is signed on its behalf by a director, or by the secretary, of the company or by a person authorised to sign the document on its behalf.

(2)   This Act is without prejudice to—
  (a)   [sections 270(3) and 274 of the Companies Act 2006; and]
  (b)   paragraph 9 of Schedule 1, paragraph 9 of Schedule 2, and paragraph 7 of Schedule 4, to the Insolvency Act 1986.

(3)   Sub-paragraphs (1) and (2) of this paragraph apply in relation to the signing of an alteration made to a document as they apply in relation to the signing of a document.

(4)   Where a granter of a [traditional document] is a company, section 3 of and Schedule 1 to this Act shall have effect subject to the modifications set out in sub-paragraphs (5) and (6) below.

(5)   In section 3—
  (a)   for subsection (1) there shall be substituted the following subsections—
    '(1)   Subject to subsections (1A) to (7) below, where—
      (a)   a [traditional document] bears to have been subscribed on behalf of a company by a director, or by the secretary, of the company or by a person bearing to have been authorised to subscribe the document on its behalf;
      (b)   the document bears to have been signed by a person as a witness of the subscription of the director, secretary or other person subscribing on behalf of the company and to state the name and address of the witness; and
      (c)   nothing in the document, or in the testing clause or its equivalent, indicates—
        (i)   that it was not subscribed on behalf of the company as it bears to have been so subscribed; or
        (ii)   that it was not validly witnessed for any reason specified in paragraphs (a) to (e) of subsection (4) below,
    the document shall be presumed to have been subscribed by the company.
    (1A)   Where a document does not bear to have been signed by a person as a witness of the subscription of the director, secretary or other person subscribing on behalf of the company it shall be presumed to have been subscribed by the company if it bears to have been subscribed on behalf of the company by—
      (a)   two directors of the company; or
      (b)   a director and secretary of the company; or
      (c)   two persons bearing to have been authorised to subscribe the document on its behalf.
    (1B)   For the purposes of subsection (1)(b) above, the name and address of the witness may bear to be stated in the document itself or in the testing clause or its equivalent.
    (1C)   A presumption under subsection (1) or (1A) above as to subscription of a document does not include a presumption—
      (a)   that a person bearing to subscribe the document as a director or the secretary of the company was such director or secretary; or
      (b)   that a person subscribing the document on behalf of the company bearing to have been authorised to do so was authorised to do so.';
  (b)   in subsection (4) after paragraph (g) there shall be inserted the following paragraph—
    '(h)   if the document does not bear to have been witnessed, but bears to have been subscribed on behalf of the company by two of the directors of the company, or by a director and secretary of the company, or by two authorised persons, that a signature bearing to be the signature of a director, secretary or authorised person is not such a signature, whether by reason of forgery or otherwise;'.

(6)   In paragraph 1 of Schedule 1—

(a)   for sub-paragraph (1) there shall be substituted the following sub-paragraphs—

'(1)   Subject to sub-paragraphs (1A) to (7) below, where—

(a)   an alteration to a [traditional document] bears to have been signed on behalf of a company by a director, or by the secretary, of the company or by a person bearing to have been authorised to sign the alteration on its behalf;

(b)   the alteration bears to have been signed by a person as a witness of the signature of the director, secretary or other person signing on behalf of the company and to state the name and address of the witness; and

(c)   nothing in the document or alteration, or in the testing clause or its equivalent, indicates—

(i)   that the alteration was not signed on behalf of the company as it bears to have been so signed; or

(ii)   that the alteration was not validly witnessed for any reason specified in paragraphs (a) to (e) of sub-paragraph (4) below,

the alteration shall be presumed to have been signed by the company.

(1A)   Where an alteration does not bear to have been signed by a person as a witness of the signature of the director, secretary or other person signing on behalf of the company it shall be presumed to have been signed by the company if it bears to have been signed on behalf of the company by—

(a)   two directors of the company; or

(b)   a director and secretary of the company; or

(c)   two persons bearing to have been authorised to sign the alteration on its behalf.

(1B)   For the purposes of sub-paragraph (1)(b) above, the name and address of the witness may bear to be stated in the alteration itself or in the testing clause or its equivalent.

(1C)   A presumption under sub-paragraph (1) or (1A) above as to signing of an alteration to a document does not include a presumption—

(a)   that a person bearing to sign the alteration as a director or the secretary of the company was such director or secretary; or

(b)   that a person signing the alteration on behalf of the company bearing to have been authorised to do so was authorised to do so.';

(b)   in sub-paragraph (4) after paragraph (g) there shall be inserted the following paragraph—

'(h)   if the alteration does not bear to have been witnessed, but bears to have been signed on behalf of the company by two of the directors of the company, or by a director and secretary of the company, or by two authorised persons, that a signature bearing to be the signature of a director, secretary or authorised person is not such a signature, whether by reason of forgery or otherwise;'.

[Limited liability partnerships

3A.   (1)   Except where an enactment expressly provides otherwise, where a granter of a [traditional document] is a limited liability partnership, the document is signed by the limited liability partnership if it is signed on its behalf by a member of the limited liability partnership.

(2)   This Act is without prejudice to paragraph 9 of Schedule 1, paragraph 9 of Schedule 2, and paragraph 7 of Schedule 4, to the Insolvency Act 1986.

(3)   Sub-paragraphs (1) and (2) of this paragraph apply in relation to the signing of an alteration made to a document as they apply in relation to the signing of a document.

(4)   Where a granter of a [traditional document] is a limited liability partnership, section 3 of and Schedule 1 to this Act shall have effect subject to the modifications set out in sub-paragraphs (5) and (6) below.

(5)   In section 3—

(a)   for subsection (1) there shall be substituted the following subsections—

'(1)   Subject to subsections (1A) to (7) below, where—

(a)   a [traditional document] bears to have been subscribed on behalf of a limited liability partnership by a member of the limited liability partnership;

(b)   the document bears to have been signed by a person as a witness of the subscription of the member of the limited liability partnership and to state the name and address of the witness; and

(c)   nothing in the document, or in the testing clause or its equivalent, indicates—

(i)   that it was not subscribed on behalf of the limited liability partnership as it bears to have been so subscribed; or

(ii)   that it was not validly witnessed for any reason specified in paragraphs (a) to (e) of subsection (4) below,

the document shall be presumed to have been subscribed by the limited liability partnership.

(1A)   Where a document does not bear to have been signed by a person as a witness of the subscription of the member of the limited liability partnership it shall be presumed to have been subscribed by the limited liability partnership if it bears to have been subscribed on behalf of the limited liability partnership by two members of the limited liability partnership.

(1B)   A presumption under subsection (1) or (1A) above as to subscription of a document does not include a presumption that a person bearing to subscribe the document as a member of the limited liability partnership was such member.'

(b)   in subsection (4) after paragraph (g) there shall be inserted the following paragraph—

'(h)   if the document does not bear to have been witnessed, but bears to have been subscribed on behalf of the limited liability partnership by two of the members of the limited liability partnership, that a signature bearing to be the signature of a member is not such a signature, whether by reason of forgery or otherwise;'

(6)   In paragraph 1 of Schedule 1—

(a)   for sub-paragraph (1) there shall be substituted the following subparagraphs—

'(1)   Subject to sub-paragraphs (1A) to (7) below, where—

(a)   an alteration to a [traditional document] bears to have been signed on behalf of a limited liability partnership by a member of the limited liability partnership;

(b)   the alteration bears to have been signed by a person as a witness of the signature of the member of the limited liability partnership and to state the name and address of the witness; and

(c)   nothing in the document or alteration, or in the testing clause or its equivalent, indicates—

(i)   that the alteration was not signed on behalf of the limited liability partnership as it bears to have been so signed; or

(ii)   that the alteration was not validly witnessed for any reason specified in paragraphs (a) to (e) of sub-paragraph (4) below,

the alteration shall be presumed to have been signed by the limited liability partnership.

(1A)   Where an alteration does not bear to have been signed by a person as a witness of the signature of the member of the limited liability partnership it shall be presumed to have been signed by the limited liability partnership if it bears to have been signed on behalf of the limited liability partnership by two members of the limited liability partnership.

(1B)   For the purposes of sub-paragraph (1)(b) above, the name and address of the witness may bear to be stated in the alteration itself or in the testing clause or its equivalent.

(1C)   A presumption under sub-paragraph (1) or (1A) above as to signing of an alteration to a document does not include a presumption that a person bearing to sign the alteration as a member of the limited liability partnership was such member';

(b)   in sub-paragraph (4) after paragraph (g) there shall be inserted the following—

'; or

(h)   if the alteration does not bear to have been witnessed, but bears to have been signed on behalf of the limited liability partnership by two of the members of the limited liability partnership, that a signature bearing to be the signature of a member is not such a signature, whether by reason of forgery or otherwise;']

Local authorities

4.—(1)   Except where an enactment expressly provides otherwise, where a granter of a [traditional document] is a local authority, the document is signed by the authority if it is signed on their behalf by the proper officer of the authority.

(2)   For the purposes of the signing of a document under this paragraph, a person purporting to sign on behalf of a local authority as an officer of the authority shall be presumed to be the proper officer of the authority.

(3)   Sub-paragraphs (1) and (2) of this paragraph apply in relation to the signing of an alteration made to a document as they apply in relation to the signing of a document.

(4)   Where a granter of a [traditional document] is a local authority, section 3 of and Schedule 1 to this Act shall have effect subject to the modifications set out in sub-paragraphs (5) to (8) below.

(5)   For section 3(1) there shall be substituted the following subsections—

'(1)   Subject to subsections (1A) to (7) below, where—

(a)   a [traditional document] bears to have been subscribed on behalf of a local authority by the proper officer of the authority;

(b)   the document bears—

(i)   to have been signed by a person as a witness of the proper officer's subscription and to state the name and address of the witness; or

(ii)   (if the subscription is not so witnessed), to have been sealed with the common seal of the authority; and

(c)   nothing in the document, or in the testing clause or its equivalent, indicates—

(i)   that it was not subscribed on behalf of the authority as it bears to have been so subscribed; or

(ii)   that it was not validly witnessed for any reason specified in paragraphs (a) to (e) of subsection (4) below or that it was not sealed as it bears to have been sealed or that it was not validly sealed for the reason specified in subsection (4)(h) below,

the document shall be presumed to have been subscribed by the proper officer and by the authority.

(1A)   For the purposes of subsection (1)(b)(i) above, the name and address of the witness may bear to be stated in the document itself or in the testing clause or its equivalent.'.

(6) In section 3(4) after paragraph (g) there shall be inserted the following paragraph—

'(h) if the document does not bear to have been witnessed, but bears to have been sealed with the common seal of the authority, that it was sealed by a person without authority to do so or was not sealed on the date on which it was subscribed on behalf of the authority;'.

(7) For paragraph 1(1) of Schedule 1 there shall be substituted the following sub-paragraphs—

'(1) Subject to sub-paragraphs (1A) to (7) below, where—

(a) an alteration to a [traditional document] bears to have been signed on behalf of a local authority by the proper officer of the authority;

(b) the alteration bears—

(i) to have been signed by a person as a witness of the proper officer's signature and to state the name and address of the witness; or

(ii) (if the signature is not so witnessed), to have been sealed with the common seal of the authority; and

(c) nothing in the document or alteration, or in the testing clause or its equivalent, indicates—

(i) that the alteration was not signed on behalf of the authority as it bears to have been so signed; or

(ii) that the alteration was not validly witnessed for any reason specified in paragraphs (a) to (e) of sub-paragraph (4) below or that it was not sealed as it bears to have been sealed or that it was not validly sealed for the reason specified in sub-paragraph (4)(h) below,

the alteration shall be presumed to have been signed by the proper officer and by the authority.

(1A) For the purposes of sub-paragraph (1)(b)(i) above, the name and address of the witness may bear to be stated in the alteration itself or in the testing clause or its equivalent.'.

(8) In paragraph 1(4) of Schedule 1 after paragraph (g) there shall be inserted the following paragraph—

'(h) if the alteration does not bear to have been witnessed, but bears to have been sealed with the common seal of the authority, that it was sealed by a person without authority to do so or was not sealed on the date on which it was signed on behalf of the authority;'.

Other bodies corporate

5.—(1) This paragraph applies to any body corporate other than a company or a local authority.

(2) Except where an enactment expressly provides otherwise, where a granter of a [traditional document] is a body corporate to which this paragraph applies, the document is signed by the body if it is signed on its behalf by—

(a) a member of the body's governing board or, if there is no governing board, a member of the body;

(b) the secretary of the body by whatever name he is called; or

(c) a person authorised to sign the document on behalf of the body.

(3) Sub-paragraphs (1) and (2) of this paragraph apply in relation to the signing of an alteration made to a document as they apply in relation to the signing of a document.

(4) Where a granter of a [traditional document] is a body corporate to which this paragraph applies, section 3 of and Schedule 1 to this Act shall have effect subject to the modifications set out in sub-paragraphs (5) to (8) below.

(5) For section 3(1) there shall be substituted the following subsections—

'(1)   Subject to subsections (1A) to (7) below, where—

(a)   a [traditional document] bears to have been subscribed on behalf of a body corporate to which paragraph 5 of Schedule 2 to this Act applies by—

(i)   a member of the body's governing board or, if there is no governing board, a member of the body;

(ii)   the secretary of the body; or

(iii)   a person bearing to have been authorised to subscribe the document on its behalf;

(b)   the document bears—

(i)   to have been signed by a person as a witness of the subscription of the member, secretary or other person signing on behalf of the body and to state the name and address of the witness; or

(ii)   (if the subscription is not so witnessed), to have been sealed with the common seal of the body; and

(c)   nothing in the document, or in the testing clause or its equivalent, indicates—

(i)   that it was not subscribed on behalf of the body as it bears to have been so subscribed; or

(ii)   that it was not validly witnessed for any reason specified in paragraphs (a) to (e) of subsection (4) below or that it was not sealed as it bears to have been sealed or that it was not validly sealed for the reason specified in subsection (4)(h) below,

the document shall be presumed to have been subscribed by the member, secretary or authorised person (as the case may be) and by the body.

(1A)   For the purposes of subsection (1)(b)(i) above, the name and address of the witness may bear to be stated in the document itself or in the testing clause or its equivalent.

(1B)   A presumption under subsection (1) above as to subscription of a document does not include a presumption—

(a)   that a person bearing to subscribe the document as a member of the body's governing board, a member of the body or the secretary of the body was such member or secretary; or

(b)   that a person subscribing the document on behalf of the body bearing to have been authorised to do so was authorised to do so.'.

(6)   In section 3(4) after paragraph (g) there shall be inserted the following paragraph—

'(h)   if the document does not bear to have been witnessed, but bears to have been sealed with the common seal of the body, that it was sealed by a person without authority to do so or was not sealed on the date on which it was subscribed on behalf of the body;'.

(7)   For paragraph 1(1) of Schedule 1 there shall be substituted the following sub-paragraphs—

'(1) Subject to sub-paragraphs (1A) to (7) below, where—

(a)   an alteration to a [traditional document] bears to have been signed on behalf of a body corporate to which paragraph 5 of Schedule 2 to this Act applies by—

(i)   a member of the body's governing board or, if there is no governing board, a member of the body;

(ii)   the secretary of the body; or

(iii)   a person bearing to have been authorised to sign the alteration on its behalf,

(b)   the alteration bears—

(i)   to have been signed by a person as a witness of the signature of the member, secretary or other person signing on behalf of the body and to state the name and address of the witness; or

(ii)   (if the signature is not so witnessed), to have been sealed with the common seal of the body; and

(c)   nothing in the document or alteration, or in the testing clause or its equivalent, indicates—

(i)   that the alteration was not signed on behalf of the body as it bears to have been so signed; or

(ii)   that the alteration was not validly witnessed for any reason specified in paragraphs (a) to (e) of sub-paragraph (4) below or that it was not sealed as it bears to have been sealed or that it was not validly sealed for the reason specified in sub-paragraph (4)(h) below,

the alteration shall be presumed to have been signed by the member, secretary or authorised person (as the case may be) and by the body.

(1A)   For the purposes of sub-paragraph (1)(b)(i) above, the name and address of the witness may bear to be stated in the alteration itself or in the testing clause or its equivalent.

(1B)   A presumption under sub-paragraph (1) above as to signing of an alteration to a document does not include a presumption—

(a)   that a person bearing to sign the alteration as a member of the body's governing board, a member of the body or the secretary of the body was such member or secretary; or

(b)   that a person signing the alteration on behalf of the body bearing to have been authorised to do so was authorised to do so.'.

(8)   In paragraph 1(4) of Schedule 1 after paragraph (g) there shall be inserted the following paragraph—

'(h)   if the alteration does not bear to have been witnessed, but bears to have been sealed with the common seal of the body, that it was sealed by a person without authority to do so or was not sealed on the date on which it was signed on behalf of the body;'.

Ministers of the Crown and office-holders

6.—(1)   Except where an enactment expressly provides otherwise, where a granter of a [traditional document] is a Minister or an office-holder, the document is signed by the Minister or office-holder if it is signed—

(a)   by him personally; or

(b)   in a case where by virtue of any enactment or rule of law a document by a Minister may be signed by an officer of his or by any other Minister, by that officer or by that other Minister as the case may be; or

(c)   in a case where by virtue of any enactment or rule of law a document by an office-holder may be signed by an officer of his, by that officer; or

(d)   by any other person authorised to sign the document on his behalf.

(2)   For the purposes of the signing of a document under this paragraph, a person purporting to sign—

(a)   as an officer as mentioned in sub-paragraph (1)(b) or (1)(c) above;

(b)   as another Minister as mentioned in sub-paragraph (1)(b) above;

(c)   as a person authorised as mentioned in sub-paragraph (1)(d) above,

shall be presumed to be the officer, other Minister or authorised person, as the case may be.

(3)   Sub-paragraphs (1) and (2) of this paragraph are without prejudice to section 3 of and Schedule 1 to the Ministers of the Crown Act 1975.

(4)   Sub-paragraphs (1) to (3) of this paragraph apply in relation to the signing of an alteration made to a document as they apply in relation to the signing of a document.

(5)   Where a granter of a [traditional document] is a Minister or office-holder, section 3 of and Schedule 1 to this Act shall have effect subject to the modifications set out in sub-paragraphs (6) and (7) below.

(6)   For section 3(1) there shall be substituted the following subsections—
     '(1)   Subject to subsections (1A) to (7) below, where—
          (a)   a [traditional document] bears to have been subscribed—
               (i)   by a Minister or, in a case where by virtue of any enactment
          or rule of law a document by a Minister may be signed by an officer
          of his or by any other Minister, by that officer or by that other
          Minister; or
               (ii)   by an office-holder or, in a case where by virtue of any enact-
          ment or rule of law a document by an office-holder may be signed by an
          officer of his, by that officer; or
               (iii)   by any other person bearing to have been authorised to
          subscribe the document on behalf of the Minister or office-holder;
          (b)   the document bears to have been signed by a person as a witness
     of the subscription mentioned in paragraph (a) above and to state the
     name and address of the witness; and
          (c)   nothing in the document, or in the testing clause or its equivalent,
     indicates—
               (i)   that it was not subscribed as it bears to have been subscribed;
          or
               (ii)   that it was not validly witnessed for any reason specified in
          paragraphs (a) to (e) of subsection (4) below,
     the document shall be presumed to have been subscribed by the officer,
     other Minister or authorised person and by the Minister or office-holder,
     as the case may be.
          (1A)   For the purposes of subsection (1)(b) above, the name and address
     of the witness may bear to be stated in the document itself or in the testing
     clause or its equivalent.'.
     (7)   For paragraph 1(1) of Schedule 1 there shall be substituted the following
sub-paragraphs—
     '(1)   Subject to sub-paragraphs (1A) to (7) below, where—
          (a)   an alteration to a [traditional document] bears to have been signed
     by—
               (i)   a Minister or, in a case where by virtue of any enactment or
          rule of law a document by a Minister may be signed by an officer of
          his or by any other Minister, by that officer or by that other Minister;
          or
               (ii)   an office-holder or, in a case where by virtue of any enactment
          or rule of law a document by an office-holder may be signed by an
          officer of his, by that officer; or
               (iii)   any other person bearing to have been authorised to sign the
          alteration on behalf of the Minister or office-holder;
          (b)   the alteration bears to have been signed by a person as a witness of
     the signature mentioned in paragraph (a) above and to state the name and
     address of the witness; and
          (c)   nothing in the document or alteration, or in the testing clause or its
     equivalent, indicates—
               (i)   that the alteration was not signed as it bears to have been
          signed; or
               (ii)   that the alteration was not validly witnessed for any reason
          specified in paragraphs (a) to (e) of sub-paragraph (4) below,
     the alteration shall be presumed to have been signed by the officer, other
     Minister or authorised person and by the Minister or office-holder, as the
     case may be.
          (1A)   For the purposes of sub-paragraph (1)(b) above, the name and
     address of the witness may bear to be stated in the alteration itself or in the
     testing clause or its equivalent.'.

SCHEDULE 3 Section 9(3)
MODIFICATIONS OF THIS ACT IN RELATION TO SUBSCRIPTION OR
SIGNING BY RELEVANT PERSON UNDER SECTION 9

1. For any reference to the subscription or signing of a document by a granter there shall be substituted a reference to such subscription or signing by a relevant person under section 9(1).

2. For section 3(1) there shall be substituted the following subsection—
'(1) Subject to subsections (2) to (6) below, where—
(a) a [traditional document] bears to have been subscribed by a relevant person with the authority of a granter of it;
(b) the document, or the testing clause or its equivalent, states that the document was read to that granter by the relevant person before such subscription or states that it was not so read because the granter made a declaration that he did not wish him to do so;
(c) the document bears to have been signed by a person as a witness of the relevant person's subscription and the document, or the testing clause or its equivalent, bears to state the name and address of the witness; and
(d) nothing in the document, or in the testing clause or its equivalent, indicates—
(i) that it was not subscribed by the relevant person as it bears to have been so subscribed;
(ii) that the statement mentioned in paragraph (b) above is incorrect; or
(iii) that it was not validly witnessed for any reason specified in paragraphs (a) to (e) of subsection (4) below (as modified by paragraph 4 of Schedule 3 to this Act),
the document shall be presumed to have been subscribed by the relevant person and the statement so mentioned shall be presumed to be correct.'.

3. In section 3(3) for the words 'subsection (1)(b)' there shall be substituted the words 'subsection (1)(c)'.

4. For section 3(4) there shall be substituted the following subsection—
'(4) Where, in any proceedings relating to a [traditional document] in which a question arises as to a relevant person's subscription on behalf of a granter under section 9(1) of this Act, it is established—
(a) that a signature bearing to be the signature of the witness of the relevant person's subscription is not such a signature, whether by reason of forgery or otherwise;
(b) that the person who signed the document as the witness of the relevant person's subscription is a person who is named in the document as a granter of it;
(c) that the person who signed the document as the witness of the relevant person's subscription, at the time of signing—
(i) did not know the granter on whose behalf the relevant person had so subscribed;
(ii) was under the age of 16 years; or
(iii) was mentally incapable of acting as a witness;
(d) that the person who signed the document, purporting to be the witness of the relevant person's subscription, did not see him subscribe it;
(dd) that the person who signed the document as the witness of the relevant person's subscription did not witness the granting of authority by the granter concerned to the relevant person to subscribe the document on

his behalf or did not witness the reading of the document to the granter by the relevant person or the declaration that the granter did not wish him to do so;

(e)   that the person who signed the document as the witness of the relevant person's subscription did not sign the document after him or that such subscription and signature were not one continuous process;

(f)   that the name or address of such a witness was added after the document was founded on or registered as mentioned in subsection (3)(a) above or is erroneous in any material respect; or

(g)   in the case of a testamentary document consisting of more than one sheet, that a signature on any sheet bearing to be the signature of the relevant person is not such a signature, whether by reason of forgery or otherwise,

then, for the purposes of those proceedings, there shall be no presumption that the document has been subscribed by the relevant person on behalf of the granter concerned.'.

5.   In section 3(6) the words 'or acknowledgement' in both places where they occur shall be omitted.

6.   Section 3(7) shall be omitted.

7.   For section 4(1) there shall be substituted the following subsection—

'(1)   Where—

(a)   a [traditional document] bears to have been subscribed by a relevant person under section 9(1) of this Act on behalf of a granter of it; but

(b)   there is no presumption under section 3 of this Act (as modified by paragraph 2 of Schedule 3 to this Act) that the document has been subscribed by that person or that the procedure referred to section 3(1)(b) of this Act as so modified was followed,

then, if the court, on an application being made to it by any person who has an interest in the document, is satisfied that the document was so subscribed by the relevant person with the authority of the granter and that the relevant person read the document to the granter before subscription or did not so read it because the granter declared that he did not wish him to do so, it shall—

(i)   cause the document to be endorsed with a certificate to that effect; or

(ii)   where the document has already been registered in the Books of Council and Session or in sheriff court books, grant decree to that effect.'.

8.   At the end of section 4(5)(a) there shall be added the following words—
'and that the procedure referred to in section 3(1)(b) of this Act as modified by paragraph 2 of Schedule 3 to this Act was followed.'.

9.   For paragraph 1(1) of Schedule 1 there shall be substituted the following sub-paragraph—

'(1)   Subject to sub-paragraphs (2) to (6) below, where—

(a)   an alteration to a [traditional document] bears to have been signed by a relevant person with the authority of a granter of the document;

(b)   the document or alteration, or the testing clause or its equivalent, states that the alteration was read to that granter by the relevant person before such signature or states that the alteration was not so read because the granter made a declaration that he did not wish him to do so;

(c)   the alteration bears to have been signed by a person as a witness of the relevant person's signature and the alteration, or the testing clause or its equivalent, bears to state the name and address of the witness; and

(d)   nothing in the document or alteration, or in the testing clause or its equivalent, indicates—

(i)   that the alteration was not signed by the relevant person as it bears to have been so signed;

(ii)   that the statement mentioned in paragraph (b) above is incorrect; or

(iii)   that the alteration was not validly witnessed for any reason specified in paragraphs (a) to (e) of sub-paragraph (4) below (as modified by paragraph 11 of Schedule 3 to this Act),

the alteration shall be presumed to have been signed by the relevant person and the statement so mentioned shall be presumed to be correct.'.

10.   In paragraph 1(3) of Schedule 1 for the words 'sub-paragraph (1)(b)' there shall be substituted the words 'sub-paragraph (1)(c)'.

11.   For paragraph 1(4) of Schedule 1 there shall be substituted the following subparagraph—

'(4)   Where, in any proceedings relating to an alteration to a document in which a question arises as to a relevant person's signature on behalf of a granter under section 9(1) of this Act, it is established—

(a)   that a signature bearing to be the signature of the witness of the relevant person's signature is not such a signature, whether by reason of forgery or otherwise;

(b)   that the person who signed the alteration as the witness of the relevant person's signature is a person who is named in the document as a granter of it;

(c)   that the person who signed the alteration as the witness of the relevant person's signature, at the time of signing—

(i)   did not know the granter on whose behalf the relevant person had so signed;

(ii)   was under the age of 16 years; or

(iii)   was mentally incapable of acting as a witness;

(d)   that the person who signed the alteration, purporting to be the witness of the relevant person's signature, did not see him sign it;

(dd) that the person who signed the alteration as the witness of the relevant person's signature did not witness the granting of authority by the granter concerned to the relevant person to sign the alteration on his behalf or did not witness the reading of the alteration to the granter by the relevant person or the declaration that the granter did not wish him to do so;

(e)   that the person who signed the alteration as the witness of the relevant person's signature did not sign the alteration after him or that the signing of the alteration by the granter and the witness was not one continuous process;

(f)   that the name or address of such a witness was added after the alteration was founded on or registered as mentioned in sub-paragraph (3)(a) above or is erroneous in any material respect; or

(g)   in the case of an alteration to a testamentary document consisting of more than one sheet, that a signature on any sheet of the alteration bearing to be the signature of the relevant person is not such a signature, whether by reason of forgery or otherwise,

then, for the purposes of those proceedings, there shall be no presumption that the alteration has been signed by the relevant person on behalf of the granter concerned.'.

12.   In paragraph 1(6) of Schedule 1 the words 'or the acknowledgement of his signature' and the words 'or acknowledgement' shall be omitted.

13. Paragraph 1(7) of Schedule 1 shall be omitted.

14. For paragraph 2(1) of Schedule 1 there shall be substituted the following sub-paragraph—

'(1) Where—

(a) an alteration to a [traditional document] bears to have been signed by a relevant person under section 9(1) of this Act on behalf of a granter of the document; but

(b) there is no presumption under paragraph 1 of Schedule 1 to this Act (as modified by paragraph 9 of Schedule 3 to this Act) that the alteration has been signed by that person or that the procedure referred to in paragraph 1(1)(b) of Schedule 1 to this Act as so modified was followed,

then, if the court, on an application being made to it by any person who has an interest in the document, is satisfied that the alteration was so signed by the relevant person with the authority of the granter and that the relevant person read the alteration to the granter before signing or did not so read it because the granter declared that he did not wish him to do so, it shall—

(i) cause the document to be endorsed with a certificate to that effect; or

(ii) where the document has already been registered in the Books of Council and Session or in sheriff court books, grant decree to that effect.'.

15. At the end of paragraph 2(5)(a) of Schedule 1 there shall be added the following words—

'and that the procedure referred to in paragraph 1(1)(b) of Schedule 1 to this Act as modified by paragraph 9 of Schedule 3 to this Act was followed.'.

CHILDREN (SCOTLAND) ACT 1995
(1995, c 36)

PART I
PARENTS, CHILDREN AND GUARDIANS

Parental responsibilities and parental rights

1 Parental responsibilities

(1) Subject to section 3(1)(b) [, and (d)] and (3) of this Act, a parent has in relation to his child the responsibility—

(a) to safeguard and promote the child's health, development and welfare;

(b) to provide, in a manner appropriate to the stage of development of the child—

(i) direction;

(ii) guidance,

to the child;

(c) if the child is not living with the parent, to maintain personal relations and direct contact with the child on a regular basis; and

(d) to act as the child's legal representative,

but only in so far as compliance with this section is practicable and in the interests of the child.

(2) 'Child' means for the purposes of—

(a) paragraphs (a), (b)(i), (c) and (d) of subsection (1) above, a person under the age of sixteen years;

(b) paragraph (b)(ii) of that subsection, a person under the age of eighteen years.

(3) The responsibilities mentioned in paragraphs (a) to (d) of subsection (1)

above are in this Act referred to as 'parental responsibilities'; and the child, or any person acting on his behalf, shall have title to sue, or to defend, in any proceedings as respects those responsibilities.

(4)   The parental responsibilities supersede any analogous duties imposed on a parent at common law; but this section is without prejudice to any other duty so imposed on him or to any duty imposed on him by, under or by virtue of any other provision of this Act or of any other enactment.

6 Views of children

(1)   A person shall, in reaching any major decision which involves—

(a)   his fulfilling a parental responsibility or the responsibility mentioned in section 5(1) of this Act; or

(b)   his exercising a parental right or giving consent by virtue of that section, have regard so far as practicable to the views (if he wishes to express them) of the child concerned, taking account of the child's age and maturity, and to those of any other person who has parental responsibilities or parental rights in relation to the child (and wishes to express those views); and without prejudice to the generality of this subsection a child twelve years of age or more shall be presumed to be of sufficient age and maturity to form a view.

(2)   A transaction entered into in good faith by a third party and a person acting as legal representative of a child shall not be challengeable on the ground only that the child, or a person with parental responsibilities or parental rights in relation to the child, was not consulted or that due regard was not given to his views before the transaction was entered into.

Guardianship

. . .

10 Obligations and rights of person administering child's property

(1)   A person acting as a child's legal representative in relation to the administration of the child's property—

(a)   shall be required to act as a reasonable and prudent person would act on his own behalf; and

(b)   subject to any order made under section 11 of this Act, shall be entitled to do anything which the child, if of full age and capacity, could do in relation to that property;

and subject to subsection (2) below, on ceasing to act as legal representative, shall be liable to account to the child for his intromissions with the child's property.

(2)   No liability shall be incurred by virtue of subsection (1) above in respect of funds which have been used in the proper discharge of the person's responsibility to safeguard and promote the child's health, development and welfare.

CRIMINAL PROCEDURE (SCOTLAND) ACT 1995
(1995, c 46)

170 Damages in respect of summary proceedings

(1)   No judge, clerk of court or prosecutor in the public interest shall be found liable by any court in damages for or in respect of any proceedings taken, act done, or judgment, decree or sentence pronounced in any summary proceedings under this Act, unless—

(a)   the person suing has suffered imprisonment in consequence thereof; and

(b)   such proceedings, act, judgment, decree or sentence has been quashed; and

(c)   the person suing specifically avers and proves that such proceeding, act, judgment, decree or sentence was taken, done or pronounced maliciously and without probable cause.

(2)   No such liability as aforesaid shall be incurred or found where such judge, clerk of court or prosecutor establishes that the person suing was guilty of the offence in respect whereof he had been convicted, or on account of which he had been apprehended or had otherwise suffered, and that he had undergone no greater punishment than was assigned by law to such offence.

(3)   No action to enforce such liability as aforesaid shall lie unless it is commenced within two months after the proceeding, act, judgment, decree or sentence founded on, or in the case where the Act under which the action is brought fixes a shorter period, within that shorter period.

(4)   In this section 'judge' shall not include 'sheriff', and the provisions of this section shall be without prejudice to the privileges and immunities possessed by sheriffs.

DEFAMATION ACT 1996
(1996, c 31)

1   Responsibility for publication

(1)   In defamation proceedings a person has a defence if he shows that—

(a)   he was not the author, editor or publisher of the statement complained of,

(b)   he took reasonable care in relation to its publication, and

(c)   he did not know, and had no reason to believe, that what he did caused or contributed to the publication of a defamatory statement.

(2)   For this purpose 'author', 'editor' and 'publisher' have the following meanings, which are further explained in subsection (3)—

'author' means the originator of the statement, but does not include a person who did not intend that his statement be published at all;

'editor' means a person having editorial or equivalent responsibility for the content of the statement or the decision to publish it; and

'publisher' means a commercial publisher, that is, a person whose business is issuing material to the public, or a section of the public, who issues material containing the statement in the course of that business.

(3)   A person shall not be considered the author, editor or publisher of a statement if he is only involved—

(a)   in printing, producing, distributing or selling printed material containing the statement;

(b)   in processing, making copies of, distributing, exhibiting or selling a film or sound recording (as defined in Part I of the Copyright, Designs and Patents Act 1988) containing the statement;

(c)   in processing, making copies of, distributing or selling any electronic medium in or on which the statement is recorded, or in operating or providing any equipment, system or service by means of which the statement is retrieved, copied, distributed or made available in electronic form;

(d)   as the broadcaster of a live programme containing the statement in circumstances in which he has no effective control over the maker of the statement;

(e)   as the operator of or provider of access to a communications system by means of which the statement is transmitted, or made available, by a person over whom he has no effective control.

In a case not within paragraphs (a) to (e) the court may have regard to those provisions by way of analogy in deciding whether a person is to be considered the author, editor or publisher of a statement.

(4)   Employees or agents of an author, editor or publisher are in the same position as their employer or principal to the extent that they are responsible for the content of the statement or the decision to publish it.

(5) In determining for the purposes of this section whether a person took reasonable care, or had reason to believe that what he did caused or contributed to the publication of a defamatory statement, regard shall be had to—

    (a)   the extent of his responsibility for the content of the statement or the decision to publish it,

    (b)   the nature or circumstances of the publication, and

    (c)   the previous conduct or character of the author, editor or publisher.

(6)   This section does not apply to any cause of action which arose before the section came into force.

2 Offer to make amends

(1)   A person who has published a statement alleged to be defamatory of another may offer to make amends under this section.

(2)   The offer may be in relation to the statement generally or in relation to a specific defamatory meaning which the person making the offer accepts that the statement conveys ('a qualified offer').

(3)   An offer to make amends—

    (a)   must be in writing

    (b)   must be expressed to be an offer to make amends under section 2 of the Defamation Act 1996, and

    (c)   must state whether it is a qualified offer and, if so, set out the defamatory meaning in relation to which it is made.

(4)   An offer to make amends under this section is an offer—

    (a)   to make a suitable correction of the statement complained of and a sufficient apology to the aggrieved party;

    (b)   to publish the correction and apology in a manner that is reasonable and practicable in the circumstances, and

    (c)   to pay to the aggrieved party such compensation (if any), and such costs, as may be agreed or determined to be payable.

The fact that the offer is accompanied by an offer to take specific steps does not affect the fact that an offer to make amends under this section is an offer to do all the things mentioned in paragraphs (a) to (c).

(5)   An offer to make amends under this section may not be made by a person after serving a defence in defamation proceedings brought against him by the aggrieved party in respect of the publication in question.

(6)   An offer to make amends under this section may be withdrawn before it is accepted; and a renewal of an offer which has been withdrawn shall be treated as a new offer.

3 Accepting an offer to make amends

(1)   If an offer to make amends under section 2 is accepted by the aggrieved party, the following provisions apply.

(2)   The party accepting the offer may not bring or continue defamation proceedings in respect of the publication concerned against the person making the offer, but he is entitled to enforce the offer to make amends, as follows.

(3)   If the parties agree on the steps to be taken in fulfilment of the offer, the aggrieved party may apply to the court for an order that the other party fulfil his offer by taking the steps agreed.

(4)   If the parties do not agree on the steps to be taken by way of correction, apology and publication, the party who made the offer may take such steps as he thinks appropriate, and may in particular—

    (a)   make the correction and apology by a statement in open court in terms approved by the court, and

    (b)   give an undertaking to the court as to the manner of their publication.

(5)   If the parties do not agree on the amount to be paid by way of compensation, it shall be determined by the court on the same principles as damages in defamation proceedings.

The court shall take account of any steps taken in fulfilment of the offer and (so far as not agreed between the parties) of the suitability of the correction, the sufficiency of the apology and whether the manner of their publication was reasonable in the circumstances, and may reduce or increase the amount of compensation accordingly.

(6)   If the parties do not agree on the amount to be paid by way of costs, it shall be determined by the court on the same principles as costs awarded in court proceedings.

(7)   The acceptance of an offer by one person to make amends does not affect any cause of action against another person in respect of the same publication, subject as follows.

(8)   [*applies to England and Wales only*]

(9)   In Scotland—

   (a)   subsection (2) of section 3 of the Law Reform (Miscellaneous Provisions) (Scotland) Act 1940 (right of one joint wrongdoer as respects another to recover contribution towards damages) applies in relation to compensation paid under an offer to make amends as it applies in relation to damages in an action to which that section applies; and

   (b)   where another person is liable in respect of the same damage (whether jointly or otherwise), the person whose offer to make amends was accepted is not required to pay by virtue of any contribution under section 3(2) of that Act a greater amount than the amount of compensation payable in pursuance of the offer.

(10)   Proceedings under this section shall be heard and determined without a jury.

4   Failure to accept offer to make amends

(1)   If an offer to make amends under section 2, duly made and not withdrawn, is not accepted by the aggrieved party, the following provisions apply.

(2)   The fact that the offer was made is a defence (subject to subsection (3)) to defamation proceedings in respect of the publication in question by that party against the person making the offer.

A qualified offer is only a defence in respect of the meaning to which the offer related.

(3)   There is no such defence if the person by whom the offer was made knew or had reason to believe that the statement complained of—

   (a)   referred to the aggrieved party or was likely to be understood as referring to him, and

   (b)   was both false and defamatory of that party;

but it shall be presumed until the contrary is shown that he did not know and had no reason to believe that was the case.

(4)   The person who made the offer need not rely on it by way of defence, but if he does he may not rely on any other defence.

If the offer was a qualified offer, this applies only in respect of the meaning to which the offer related.

(5)   The offer may be relied on in mitigation of damages whether or not it was relied on as a defence.

. . .

The meaning of a statement

7   Ruling on the meaning of a statement

In defamation proceedings the court shall not be asked to rule whether a statement is arguably capable, as opposed to capable, of bearing a particular meaning or meanings attributed to it.

. . .

Evidence of convictions

12 Evidence of convictions
(1) [*applies to England and Wales only*]
(2) In section 12 of the Law Reform (Miscellaneous Provisions) (Scotland) Act 1968 (conclusiveness of convictions for purposes of defamation actions), in subsections (1) and (2) for 'a person' substitute 'the pursuer' and for 'that person' substitute 'he'; and after subsection (2) insert—

'(2A) In the case of an action for defamation in which there is more than one pursuer—
(a) the references in subsections (1) and (2) above to the pursuer shall be construed as references to any of the pursuers, and
(b) proof that any of the pursuers stands convicted of an offence shall be conclusive evidence that he committed that offence so far as that fact is relevant to any issue arising in relation to his cause of action or that of any other pursuer.'.

The amendments made by this subsection apply only for the purposes of an action begun after this section comes into force, whenever the cause of action arose.
(3) [*applies to Northern Ireland only*]

Evidence concerning proceedings in Parliament

13 Evidence concerning proceedings in Parliament
(1) Where the conduct of a person in or in relation to proceedings in Parliament is in issue in defamation proceedings, he may waive for the purposes of those proceedings, so far as concerns him, the protection of any enactment or rule of law which prevents proceedings in Parliament being impeached or questioned in any court or place out of Parliament.
(2) Where a person waives that protection—
(a) any such enactment or rule of law shall not apply to prevent evidence being given, questions being asked or statements, submissions, comments or findings being made about his conduct, and
(b) none of those things shall be regarded as infringing the privilege of either House of Parliament.
(3) The waiver by one person of that protection does not affect its operation in relation to another person who has not waived it.
(4) Nothing in this section affects any enactment or rule of law so far as it protects a person (including a person who has waived the protection referred to above) from legal liability for words spoken or things done in the course of, or for the purposes of or incidental to, any proceedings in Parliament.
(5) Without prejudice to the generality of subsection (4), that subsection applies to—
(a) the giving of evidence before either House or a committee;
(b) the presentation or submission of a document to either House or a committee;
(c) the preparation of a document for the purposes of or incidental to the transacting of any such business;
(d) the formulation, making or publication of a document, including a report, by or pursuant to an order of either House or a committee; and
(e) any communication with the Parliamentary Commissioner for Standards or any person having functions in connection with the registration of members' interests.

In this subsection 'a committee' means a committee of either House or a joint committee of both Houses of Parliament.

Statutory privilege

14 Reports of court proceedings absolutely privileged

(1) A fair and accurate report of proceedings in public before a court to which this section applies, if published contemporaneously with the proceedings, is absolutely privileged.

(2) A report of proceedings which by an order of the court, or as a consequence of any statutory provision, is required to be postponed shall be treated as published contemporaneously if it is published as soon as practicable after publication is permitted.

[(3) This section applies to—
  (a) any court in the United Kingdom;
  (b) any court established under the law of a country or territory outside the United Kingdom;
  (c) any international court or tribunal established by the Security Council of the United Nations or by an international agreement;
and in paragraphs (a) and (b) 'court' includes any tribunal or body exercising the judicial power of the State.]

(4) In section 8(6) of the Rehabilitation of Offenders Act 1974 and in Article 9(6) of the Rehabilitation of Offenders (Northern Ireland) Order 1978 (defamation actions: reports of court proceedings), for 'section 3 of the Law of Libel Amendment Act 1888' substitute 'section 14 of the Defamation Act 1996'.

15 Reports, etc protected by qualified privilege

(1) The publication of any report or other statement mentioned in Schedule 1 to this Act is privileged unless the publication is shown to be made with malice, subject as follows.

(2) In defamation proceedings in respect of the publication of a report or other statement mentioned in Part II of that Schedule, there is no defence under this section if the plaintiff shows that the defendant—
  (a) was requested by him to publish in a suitable manner a reasonable letter or statement by way of explanation or contradiction, and
  (b) refused or neglected to do so.
For this purpose 'in a suitable manner' means in the same manner as the publication complained of or in a manner that is adequate and reasonable in the circumstances.

(3) This section does not apply to the publication to the public, or a section of the public, of matter which is not of [public interest] and the publication of which is not for the public benefit.

(4) Nothing in this section shall be construed—
  (a) as protecting the publication of matter the publication of which is prohibited by law, or
  (b) as limiting or abridging any privilege subsisting apart from this section.

Supplementary provisions

. . .

17 Interpretation

(1) In this Act—
  'publication' and 'publish', in relation to a statement, have the meaning they have for the purposes of the law of defamation generally, but 'publisher' is specially defined for the purposes of section 1;

'statement' means words, pictures, visual images, gestures or any other method of signifying meaning; and

'statutory provision' means—

(a)   a provision contained in an Act or in subordinate legislation within the meaning of the Interpretation Act 1978,

[(aa)   a provision contained in an Act of the Scottish Parliament or in an instrument made under such an Act], or

(b)   a statutory provision within the meaning given by section 1(f) of the Interpretation Act (Northern Ireland) 1954.

(2)   In this Act as it applies to proceedings in Scotland—

'costs' means expenses; and

'plaintiff' and 'defendant' mean pursuer and defender.

General provisions

18   Extent

. . .

(2)   The following provisions of this Act extend to Scotland—

section 1 (responsibility for publication),

sections 2 to 4 (offer to make amends), except section 3(8),

section 12(2) (evidence of convictions),

section 13 (evidence concerning proceedings in Parliament),

sections 14 and 15 and Schedule 1 (statutory privilege),

section 16 and Schedule 2 (repeals) so far as relating to enactments extending to Scotland,

section 17 (interpretation),

this subsection,

section 19 (commencement) so far as relating to provisions which extend to Scotland, and

section 20 (short title and saving).

. . .

20   Short title and saving

(1)   This Act may be cited as the Defamation Act 1996.

[. . .]

SCHEDULES

SCHEDULE 1
QUALIFIED PRIVILEGE

PART I
STATEMENTS HAVING QUALIFIED PRIVILEGE WITHOUT EXPLANATION OR CONTRADICTION

1.   A fair and accurate report of proceedings in public of a legislature anywhere in the world.

2.   A fair and accurate report of proceedings in public before a court anywhere in the world.

3.   A fair and accurate report of proceedings in public of a person appointed to hold a public inquiry by a government or legislature anywhere in the world.

4.   A fair and accurate report of proceedings in public anywhere in the world of an international organisation or an international conference.

5.   A fair and accurate copy of or extract from any register or other document required by law to be open to public inspection.

6. A notice or advertisement published by or on the authority of a court, or of a judge or officer of a court, anywhere in the world.

7. A fair and accurate copy of or extract from matter published by or on the authority of a government or legislature anywhere in the world.

8. A fair and accurate copy of or extract from matter published anywhere in the world by an international organisation or an international conference.

PART II
STATEMENTS PRIVILEGED SUBJECT TO EXPLANATION OR CONTRADICTION

[9. (1) A fair and accurate copy of, extract from or summary of a notice or other matter issued for the information of the public by or on behalf of—

    (a)   a legislature or government anywhere in the world;

    (b)   an authority anywhere in the world performing governmental functions;

    (c)   an international organisation or international conference.

(2) In this paragraph 'governmental functions' includes police functions.

10. A fair and accurate copy of, extract from or summary of a document made available by a court anywhere in the world, or by a judge or officer of such a court.]

11. (1) A fair and accurate report of proceedings at any public meeting or sitting in the United Kingdom of—

    (a)   a local authority [, local authority committee or in the case of a local authority which are operating executive arrangements the executive of that authority or a committee of that executive];

    (b)   a justice or justices of the peace acting otherwise than as a court exercising judicial authority;

    (c)   a commission, tribunal, committee or person appointed for the purposes of any inquiry by any statutory provision, by Her Majesty or by a Minister of the Crown [, a member of the Scottish Government], [the Welsh Ministers or the Counsel General to the Welsh Assembly Government] or a Northern Ireland Department;

    (d)   a person appointed by a local authority to hold a local inquiry in pursuance of any statutory provision;

    (e)   any other tribunal, board, committee or body constituted by or under, and exercising functions under, any statutory provision.

[(1A) In the case of a local authority which are operating executive arrangements, a fair and accurate record of any decision made by any member of the executive where that record is required to be made and available for public inspection by virtue of section 22 of the Local Government Act 2000 or of any provision in regulations made under that section.]

(2) [In sub-paragraphs (1)(a) and (1A)]—

['executive' and 'executive arrangements' have the same meaning as in Part II of the Local Government Act 2000;]

'local authority' means—

    (a)   in relation to England and Wales, a principal council within the meaning of the Local Government Act 1972, any body falling within any paragraph of section 100J(1) of that Act or an authority or body to which the Public Bodies (Admission to Meetings) Act 1960 applies,

    (b)   in relation to Scotland, a council constituted under section 2 of the Local Government etc (Scotland) Act 1994 or an authority or body to which the Public Bodies (Admission to Meetings) Act 1960 applies,

    (c)   in relation to Northern Ireland, any authority or body to which sections 23 to 27 of the Local Government Act (Northern Ireland) 1972 apply; and

'local authority committee' means any committee of a local authority or of local authorities, and includes—

(a)   any committee or sub-committee in relation to which sections 100A to
100D of the Local Government Act 1972 apply by virtue of section 100E of that
Act (whether or not also by virtue of section 100J of that Act), and

(b)   any committee or sub-committee in relation to which sections 50A to
50D of the Local Government (Scotland) Act 1973 apply by virtue of section
50E of that Act.

(3)   A fair and accurate report of any corresponding proceedings in any of the
Channel Islands or the Isle of Man or in another member State.

[11A.   A fair and accurate report of proceedings at a press conference held anywhere in the world for the discussion of a matter of public interest.]

12.   (1)   A fair and accurate report of proceedings at any public meeting held
[anywhere in the world].

(2)   In this paragraph a 'public meeting' means a meeting bona fide and
lawfully held for a lawful purpose and for the furtherance or discussion of a
matter of [public interest], whether admission to the meeting is general or
restricted.

13.   (1)   A fair and accurate report of proceedings at a general meeting of a
[listed company].

[(2)   A fair and accurate copy of, extract from or summary of any document
circulated to members of a listed company—

(a)   by or with the authority of the board of directors of the company,

(b)   by the auditors of the company, or

(c)   by any member of the company in pursuance of a right conferred by any
statutory provision.

(3)   A fair and accurate copy of, extract from or summary of any document
circulated to members of a listed company which relates to the appointment, resignation, retirement or dismissal of directors of the company or its auditors.

(4)   In this paragraph 'listed company' has the same meaning as in Part 12 of
the Corporation Tax Act 2009 (see section 1005 of that Act).]

14.   A fair and accurate report of any finding or decision of any of the following
descriptions of association, formed [anywhere in the world], or of any committee
or governing body of such an association—

(a)   an association formed for the purpose of promoting or encouraging the
exercise of or interest in any art, science, religion or learning, and empowered by
its constitution to exercise control over or adjudicate on matters of interest or
concern to the association, or the actions or conduct of any person subject to
such control or adjudication;

(b)   an association formed for the purpose of promoting or safeguarding the
interests of any trade, business, industry or profession, or of the persons carrying on or engaged in any trade, business, industry or profession, and empowered by its constitution to exercise control over or adjudicate upon matters
connected with that trade, business, industry or profession, or the actions or
conduct of those persons;

(c)   an association formed for the purpose of promoting or safeguarding the
interests of a game, sport or pastime to the playing or exercise of which members of the public are invited or admitted, and empowered by its constitution to
exercise control over or adjudicate upon persons connected with or taking part
in the game, sport or pastime;

(d)   an association formed for the purpose of promoting charitable objects or
other objects beneficial to the community and empowered by its constitution to
exercise control over or to adjudicate on matters of interest or concern to the
association, or the actions or conduct of any person subject to such control or
adjudication.

[14A.   A fair and accurate—

(a)   report of proceedings of a scientific or academic conference held anywhere in the world, or

(b) copy of, extract from or summary or matter published by such a conference.]

[15. (1) A fair and accurate report or summary of, copy of or extract from, any adjudication, report, statement or notice issued by a body, officer or other person designated for the purposes of this paragraph by order of the Lord Chancellor.

(2) An order under this paragraph shall be made by statutory instrument which shall be subject to annulment in pursuance of a resolution of either House of Parliament.]

PART III
SUPPLEMENTARY PROVISIONS

[16. In this Schedule—
'court' includes—
(a) any tribunal or body established under the law of any country or territory exercising the judicial power of the State;
(b) any international tribunal established by the Security Council of the United Nations or by an international agreement;
(c) any international tribunal deciding matters in dispute between States;
'international conference' means a conference attended by representatives of two or more governments;
'international organisation' means an organisation of which two or more governments are members, and includes any committee or other subordinate body of such an organisation;
'legislature' includes a local legislature; and
'member State' includes any European dependent territory of a member State.]

DAMAGES ACT 1996
(1996, c 48)

1 Assumed rate of return on investment of damages

(1) In determining the return to be expected from the investment of a sum awarded as damages for future pecuniary loss in an action for personal injury the court shall, subject to and in accordance with rules of court made for the purposes of this section, take into account such rate of return (if any) as may from time to time be prescribed by an order made by the Lord Chancellor.

(2) Subsection (1) above shall not however prevent the court taking a different rate of return into account if any party to the proceedings shows that it is more appropriate in the case in question.

(3) An order under subsection (1) above may prescribe different rates of return for different classes of case.

(4) Before making an order under subsection (1) above the Lord Chancellor shall consult the Government Actuary and the Treasury; and any order under that subsection shall be made by statutory instrument subject to annulment in pursuance of a resolution of either House of Parliament.

(5) In the application of this section to Scotland—
(a) for the reference to the Lord Chancellor in subsections (1) and (4) there is substituted a reference to the Scottish Ministers; and
(b) in subsection (4)—
(i) 'and the Treasury' is omitted; and
(ii) for 'either House of Parliament' there is substituted 'the Scottish Parliament'.

HOUSING GRANTS, CONSTRUCTION AND REGENERATION ACT 1996
(1996, c 53)

113 Prohibition of conditional payment provisions

(1) A provision making payment under a construction contract conditional on the payer receiving payment from a third person is ineffective, unless that third person, or any other person payment by whom is under the contract (directly or indirectly) a condition of payment by that third person, is insolvent.

(2) For the purposes of this section a company becomes insolvent—

[(a) when it enters administration within the meaning of Schedule B1 to the Insolvency Act 1986,]

(b) on the appointment of an administrative receiver or a receiver or manager of its property under Chapter I of Part III of that Act, or the appointment of a receiver under Chapter II of that Part,

(c) on the passing of a resolution for voluntary winding-up without a declaration of solvency under section 89 of that Act, or

(d) on the making of a winding-up order under Part IV or V of that Act.

(3) For the purposes of this section a partnership becomes insolvent—

(a) on the making of a winding-up order against it under any provision of the Insolvency Act 1986 as applied by an order under section 420 of that Act, or

(b) when sequestration is awarded on the estate of the partnership under section 12 of the Bankruptcy (Scotland) Act 1985 or the partnership grants a trust deed for its creditors.

(4) For the purposes of this section an individual becomes insolvent—

(a) on the making of a bankruptcy order against him under Part IX of the Insolvency Act 1986, or

(b) on the sequestration of his estate under the Bankruptcy (Scotland) Act 1985 or when he grants a trust deed for his creditors.

(5) A company, partnership or individual shall also be treated as insolvent on the occurrence of any event corresponding to those specified in subsection (2), (3) or (4) under the law of Northern Ireland or of a country outside the United Kingdom.

(6) Where a provision is rendered ineffective by subsection (1), the parties are free to agree other terms for payment.

In the absence of such agreement, the relevant provisions of the Scheme for Construction Contracts apply.

SOCIAL SECURITY (RECOVERY OF BENEFITS) ACT 1997
(1997, c 27)

3 'The relevant period'

(1)   In relation to a person ('the claimant') who has suffered any accident, injury or disease, 'the relevant period' has the meaning given by the following subsections.

(2)   Subject to subsection (4), if it is a case of accident or injury, the relevant period is the period of five years immediately following the day on which the accident or injury in question occurred.

(3)   Subject to subsection (4), if it is a case of disease, the relevant period is the period of five years beginning with the date on which the claimant first claims a listed benefit in consequence of the disease.

(4)   If at any time before the end of the period referred to in subsection (2) or (3)—

(a)   a person makes a compensation payment in final discharge of any claim made by or in respect of the claimant and arising out of the accident, injury or disease, or

(b)   an agreement is made under which an earlier compensation payment is treated as having been made in final discharge of any such claim,

the relevant period ends at that time.

6 Liability to pay Secretary of State amount of benefits

(1)   A person who makes a compensation payment in any case is liable to pay to the Secretary of State an amount equal to the total amount of the recoverable benefits.

(2)   The liability referred to in subsection (1) arises immediately before the compensation payment or, if there is more than one, the first of them is made.

(3)   No amount becomes payable under this section before the end of the period of 14 days following the day on which the liability arises.

7 Recovery of payments due under section 6

(1)   This section applies where a person has made a compensation payment but—

(a)   has not applied for a certificate of recoverable benefits, or

(b)   has not made a payment to the Secretary of State under section 6 before the end of the period allowed under that section.

(2)   The Secretary of State may—

(a)   issue the person who made the compensation payment with a certificate of recoverable benefits, if none has been issued, or

(b)   issue him with a copy of the certificate of recoverable benefits or (if more than one has been issued) the most recent one,

and (in either case) issue him with a demand that payment of any amount due under section 6 be made immediately.

(3)   The Secretary of State may, in accordance with subsections (4) and (5), recover the amount for which a demand for payment is made under subsection (2) from the person who made the compensation payment.

(4)   If the person who made the compensation payment resides or carries on business in England and Wales and a county court so orders, any amount recoverable under subsection (3) is recoverable [under section 85 of the County Courts Act 1984] or otherwise as if it were payable under an order of that court.

(5)   If the person who made the payment resides or carries on business in Scotland, any amount recoverable under subsection (3) may be enforced in like manner as an extract registered decree arbitral bearing a warrant for execution issued by the sheriff court of any sheriffdom in Scotland.

(6)   A document bearing a certificate which—

(a)   is signed by a person authorised to do so by the Secretary of State, and

(b)   states that the document, apart from the certificate, is a record of the amount recoverable under subsection (3),

is conclusive evidence that that amount is so recoverable.

(7)   A certificate under subsection (6) purporting to be signed by a person authorised to do so by the Secretary of State is to be treated as so signed unless the contrary is proved.

SCHEDULES

SCHEDULE 1
COMPENSATION PAYMENTS

PART I
EXEMPTED PAYMENTS

1.   Any small payment (defined in Part II of this Schedule).

2.   Any payment made to or for the injured person under section [130 of the Powers of Criminal Courts (Sentencing) Act 2000 or section 175 of the Armed Forces Act 2006] or section 249 of the Criminal Procedure (Scotland) Act 1995 (compensation orders against convicted persons).

3.   Any payment made in the exercise of a discretion out of property held subject to a trust in a case where no more than 50 per cent. by value of the capital contributed to the trust was directly or indirectly provided by persons who are, or are alleged to be, liable in respect of—

(a)   the accident, injury or disease suffered by the injured person, or

(b)   the same or any connected accident, injury or disease suffered by another.

4.   Any payment made out of property held for the purposes of any prescribed trust (whether the payment also falls within paragraph 3 or not).

5.   (1)   Any payment made to the injured person by an [insurer] under the terms of any contract of insurance entered into between the injured person and the [insurer] before—

(a)   the date on which the injured person first claims a listed benefit in consequence of the disease in question, or

(b)   the occurrence of the accident or injury in question.

[(2)   'Insurer' means—

(a)   a person who has permission under [Part 4A of the Financial Services and Markets Act 2000] to effect or carry out contracts of insurance; or

(b)   an EEA firm of the kind mentioned in paragraph 5(d) of Schedule 3 to that Act which has permission under paragraph 15 of that Schedule (as a result of qualifying for authorisation under paragraph 12 of that Schedule) to effect or carry out contracts of insurance.

(3)   Sub-paragraph (2) must be read with—

(a)   section 22 of the Financial Services and Markets Act 2000;

(b)   any relevant order under that section; and

(c)   Schedule 2 to that Act.]

6.   Any redundancy payment falling to be taken into account in the assessment of damages in respect of an accident, injury or disease.

7.   So much of any payment as is referable to costs.

8.   Any prescribed payment.

PART II
POWER TO DISREGARD SMALL PAYMENTS

9.—(1) Regulations may make provision for compensation payments to be disregarded for the purposes of sections 6 and 8 in prescribed cases where the amount of the compensation payment, or the aggregate amount of two or more connected compensation payments, does not exceed the prescribed sum.

(2) A compensation payment disregarded by virtue of this paragraph is referred to in paragraph 1 as a 'small payment'.

(3) For the purposes of this paragraph—

 (a) two or more compensation payments are 'connected' if each is made to or in respect of the same injured person and in respect of the same accident, injury or disease, and

 (b) any reference to a compensation payment is a reference to a payment which would be such a payment apart from paragraph 1.

SCHEDULE 2
CALCULATION OF COMPENSATION PAYMENT

(1) *Head of compensation*	(2) *Benefit*
1. Compensation for earnings lost during the relevant period	. . . Disablement pension payable under section 103 of the 1992 Act [Employment and support allowance] Incapacity benefit Income support Invalidity pension and allowance Jobseeker's allowance Reduced earnings allowance Severe disablement allowance Sickness benefit Statutory sick pay Unemployability supplement Unemployment benefit
2. Compensation for cost of care incurred during the relevant period	Attendance allowance Care component of disability living allowance Disablement pension increase payable under section 104 or 105 of the 1992 Act
3. Compensation for loss of mobility during the relevant period	Mobility allowance Mobility component of disability living allowance

CONTRACT (SCOTLAND) ACT 1997
(1997, c 34)

1 Extrinsic evidence of additional contract term etc

(1) Where a document appears (or two or more documents appear) to comprise all the express terms of a contract or unilateral voluntary obligation, it shall be presumed, unless the contrary is proved, that the document does (or the documents do) comprise all the express terms of the contract or unilateral voluntary obligation.

(2) Extrinsic oral or documentary evidence shall be admissible to prove, for the purposes of subsection (1) above, that the contract or unilateral voluntary obligation includes additional express terms (whether or not written terms).

(3) Notwithstanding the foregoing provisions of this section, where one of the terms in the document (or in the documents) is to the effect that the document does (or the documents do) comprise all the express terms of the contract or unilateral voluntary obligation, that term shall be conclusive in the matter.

(4) This section is without prejudice to any enactment which makes provision as respects the constitution, or formalities of execution, of a contract or unilateral voluntary obligation.

2 Supersession

(1) Where a deed is executed in implement, or purportedly in implement, of a contract, an unimplemented, or otherwise unfulfilled, term of the contract shall not be taken to be superseded by virtue only of that execution or of the delivery and acceptance of the deed.

(2) Subsection (1) above is without prejudice to any agreement which the parties to a contract may reach (whether or not an agreement incorporated into the contract) as to supersession of the contract.

3 Damages for breach of contract of sale

Any rule of law which precludes the buyer in a contract of sale of property from obtaining damages for breach of that contract by the seller unless the buyer rejects the property and rescinds the contract shall cease to have effect.

4 Short title, extent etc

(1) This Act may be cited as the Contract (Scotland) Act 1997.

(2) This Act shall come into force at the end of that period of three months which begins with the day on which the Act is passed.

(3) Section 1 of this Act applies only for the purposes of proceedings commenced on or after, and sections 2 and 3 only as respects contracts entered into on or after, the date on which this Act comes into force.

(4) This Act extends to Scotland only.

PROTECTION FROM HARASSMENT ACT 1997
(1997, c 40)

Scotland

8 Harassment

(1) Every individual has a right to be free from harassment and, accordingly, a person must not pursue a course of conduct which amounts to harassment of another and—

(a) is intended to amount to harassment of that person; or

(b) occurs in circumstances where it would appear to a reasonable person that it would amount to harassment of that person.

[1A Subsection (1) is subject to section 8A.]

(2) An actual or apprehended breach of subsection (1) may be the subject of a claim in civil proceedings by the person who is or may be the victim of the course

of conduct in question; and any such claim shall be known as an action of harassment.

(3) For the purposes of this section—

'conduct' includes speech;

'harassment' of a person includes causing the person alarm or distress; and

a course of conduct must involve conduct on at least two occasions.

(4) It shall be a defence to any action of harassment to show that the course of conduct complained of—

    (a) was authorised by, under or by virtue of any enactment or rule of law;

    (b) was [engaged in] for the purpose of preventing or detecting crime; or

    (c) was, in the particular circumstances, reasonable.

(5) In an action of harassment the court may, without prejudice to any other remedies which it may grant—

    (a) award damages;

    (b) grant—

        (i) interdict or interim interdict;

        (ii) if it is satisfied that it is appropriate for it to do so in order to protect the person from further harassment, an order, to be known as a 'non-harassment order', requiring the defender to refrain from such conduct in relation to the pursuer as may be specified in the order for such period (which includes an indeterminate period) as may be so specified,

but a person may not be subjected to the same prohibitions in an interdict or interim interdict and a non-harassment order at the same time.

(6) The damages which may be awarded in an action of harassment include damages for any anxiety caused by the harassment and any financial loss resulting from it.

(7) Without prejudice to any right to seek review of any interlocutor, a person against whom a non-harassment order has been made, or the person for whose protection the order was made, may apply to the court by which the order was made for revocation of or a variation of the order and, on any such application, the court may revoke the order or vary it in such manner as it considers appropriate.

    [. . .]

[8A Harassment amounting to domestic abuse

(1) Every individual has a right to be free from harassment and, accordingly, a person must not engage in conduct which amounts to harassment of another and—

    (a) is intended to amount to harassment of that person; or

    (b) occurs in circumstances where it would appear to a reasonable person that it would amount to harassment of that person.

(2) Subsection (1) only applies where the conduct referred to amounts to domestic abuse.

(3) Subsections (2) to (7) of section 8 apply in relation to subsection (1) as they apply in relation to subsection (1) of that section but with the following modifications—

    (a) in subsections (2) and (4), the words 'course of' are omitted;

    (b) for subsection (3) there is substituted—

      '(3) For the purposes of this section—

      "conduct"—

        (a) may involve behaviour on one or more than one occasion; and

        (b) includes—

          (i) speech; and

          (ii) presence in any place or area; and

      "harassment" of a person includes causing the person alarm or distress.';

and

    (c) in subsection (4)(b) for 'pursued' substitute 'engaged in'.

9 Breach of non-harassment order

(1)   Any person who is [. . .] in breach of a non-harassment order made under section 8 [or section 8A] is guilty of an offence and liable—

(a)   on conviction on indictment, to imprisonment for a term not exceeding five years or to a fine, or to both such imprisonment and such fine; and

(b)   on summary conviction, to imprisonment for a period not exceeding six months or to a fine not exceeding the statutory maximum, or to both such imprisonment and such fine.

(2)   A breach of a non-harassment order shall not be punishable other than in accordance with subsection (1).

[(3)   A constable may arrest without warrant any person he reasonably believes is committing or has committed an offence under subsection (1).

(4)   Subsection (3) is without prejudice to any power of arrest conferred by law apart from that subsection.]

LATE PAYMENT OF COMMERCIAL DEBTS (INTEREST) ACT 1998
(1998, c 20)

PART I
STATUTORY INTEREST ON QUALIFYING DEBTS

1 Statutory interest

(1)   It is an implied term in a contract to which this Act applies that any qualifying debt created by the contract carries simple interest subject to and in accordance with this Part.

(2)   Interest carried under that implied term (in this Act referred to as 'statutory interest') shall be treated, for the purposes of any rule of law or enactment (other than this Act) relating to interest on debts, in the same way as interest carried under an express contract term.

(3)   This Part has effect subject to Part II (which in certain circumstances permits contract terms to oust or vary the right to statutory interest that would otherwise be conferred by virtue of the term implied by subsection (1)).

2 Contracts to which Act applies

(1)   This Act applies to a contract for the supply of goods or services where the purchaser and the supplier are each acting in the course of a business, other than an excepted contract.

(2)   In this Act 'contract for the supply of goods or services' means—

(a)   a contract of sale of goods; or

(b)   a contract (other than a contract of sale of goods) by which a person does any, or any combination, of the things mentioned in subsection (3) for a consideration that is (or includes) a money consideration.

(3)   Those things are—

(a)   transferring or agreeing to transfer to another the property in goods;

(b)   bailing or agreeing to bail goods to another by way of hire or, in Scotland, hiring or agreeing to hire goods to another; and

(c)   agreeing to carry out a service.

(4)   For the avoidance of doubt a contract of service or apprenticeship is not a contract for the supply of goods or services.

(5)   The following are excepted contracts—

(a)   a consumer credit agreement;

(b)   a contract intended to operate by way of mortgage, pledge, charge or other security.

[. . .]

(7) In this section—

'business' includes a profession and the activities of any government department or local or public authority;

'consumer credit agreement' has the same meaning as in the Consumer Credit Act 1974;

'contract of sale of goods' and 'goods' have the same meaning as in the Sale of Goods Act 1979;

['government department' includes any part of the Scottish Administration].

'property in goods' means the general property in them and not merely a special property.

[2A Application of the Act to advocates

The provisions of this Act apply to a transaction in respect of which fees are paid for professional services to a member of the Faculty of Advocates as they apply to a contract for the supply of services for the purpose of this Act.]

3 Qualifying debts

(1) A debt created by virtue of an obligation under a contract to which this Act applies to pay the whole or any part of the contract price is a 'qualifying debt' for the purposes of this Act, unless (when created) the whole of the debt is prevented from carrying statutory interest by this section.

(2) A debt does not carry statutory interest if or to the extent that it consists of a sum to which a right to interest or to charge interest applies by virtue of any enactment (other than section 1 of this Act).

This subsection does not prevent a sum from carrying statutory interest by reason of the fact that a court, arbitrator or arbiter would, apart from this Act, have power to award interest on it.

(3) A debt does not carry (and shall be treated as never having carried) statutory interest if or to the extent that a right to demand interest on it, which exists by virtue of any rule of law, is exercised.

[. . .]

4 Period for which statutory interest runs

(1) Statutory interest runs in relation to a qualifying debt in accordance with this section (unless section 5 applies).

(2) Statutory interest starts to run on the day after the relevant day for the debt, at the rate prevailing under section 6 at the end of the relevant day.

[(2A) The relevant day for a debt is—

(a) where there is an agreed payment day, that day, unless a different day is given by subsection (2D), (2E) or (2G);

(b) where there is not an agreed payment day, the last day of the relevant 30-day period.

(2B) An 'agreed payment day' is a date agreed between the supplier and the purchaser for payment of the debt (that is, the day on which the debt is to be created by the contract).

(2C) A date agreed for payment of a debt may be a fixed date or may depend on the happening of an event or the failure of an event to happen.

(2D) Where—

(a) the purchaser is a public authority; and

(b) the last day of the relevant 30-day period falls earlier than the agreed payment day,

the relevant day is the last day of the relevant 30-day period, unless subsection (2G) applies.

(2E) Where—

(a) the purchaser is not a public authority; and

(b) the last day of the relevant 60-day period falls earlier than the agreed payment day, the relevant day is the last day of the relevant 60-day period, unless subsection (2G) applies.

(2F)   But subsection (2E) does not apply (and so the relevant day is the agreed payment day, unless subsection (2G) applies) if the agreed payment day is not grossly unfair to the supplier (see subsection (7A)).

(2G)   Where the debt relates to an obligation to make an advance payment, the relevant day is the day on which the debt is treated by section 11 as having been created (instead of the agreed payment day or the day given by subsection (2D) or (2E)).

(2H)   'The relevant 30-day period' is the period of 30 days beginning with the later or latest of—

(a)   the day on which the obligation of the supplier to which the debt relates is performed;

(b)   the day on which the purchaser has notice of the amount of the debt or (where that amount is unascertained) the sum which the supplier claims is the amount of the debt;

(c)   where subsection (5A) applies, the day determined under subsection (5B).

(2I)   'The relevant 60-day period' is the period of 60 days beginning with the later or latest of—

(a)   the day on which the obligation of the supplier to which the debt relates is performed;

(b)   the day on which the purchaser has notice of the amount of the debt or (where that amount is unascertained) the sum which the supplier claims is the amount of the debt;

(c)   where subsection (5A) applies, the day determined under subsection (5B).]

[. . .]

[(5A)   This subsection applies where—

(a)   there is a procedure of acceptance or verification (whether provided for by an enactment or by the contract), under which the conforming of goods or services with the contract is to be ascertained; and

(b)   the purchaser has notice of the amount of the debt on or before the day on which the procedure is completed.

(5B)   For the purposes of [subsections (2H)(c) and (2I)(c)], the day in question is the day [. . .] after the day on which the procedure is completed.

(5C)   Where, in a case where subsection (5A) applies, the procedure in question is completed after the end of the period of 30 days beginning with the day on which the obligation of the supplier to which the debt relates is performed, the procedure is to be treated for the purposes of subsection (5B) as being completed immediately after the end of that period.

(5D)   Subsection (5C) does not apply if—

(a)   the supplier and the purchaser expressly agree in the contract a period for completing the procedure in question that is longer than the period mentioned in that subsection; and

(b)   that longer period is not grossly unfair to the supplier (see subsection (7A)).]

(6)   Where the debt is created by virtue of an obligation to pay a sum due in respect of a period of hire of goods, [subsections (2H)(a) and (2I)(a) have effect as if they] referred to the last day of that period.

(7)   Statutory interest ceases to run when the interest would cease to run if it were carried under an express contract term.

(7A)   In determining for the purposes of subsection [(2F)] or (5D) whether something is grossly unfair, all circumstances of the case shall be considered; and for that purpose, the circumstances of the case include in particular—

(a)   anything that is a gross deviation from good commercial practice and contrary to good faith and fair dealing;

(b)   the nature of the goods or services in question; and

(c)   whether the purchaser has any objective reason to deviate from the result which is provided for by subsection [(2E)] or (5C).]

[(8)   In this section—

'advance payment' has the same meaning as in section 11;

'enactment' has the same meaning as in section 126(1) of the Scotland Act 1998;

'public authority' means a contracting authority (within the meaning of regulation 3 of the Public Contracts (Scotland) Regulations 2012).]

5   Remission of statutory interest

(1)   This section applies where, by reason of any conduct of the supplier, the interests of justice require that statutory interest should be remitted in whole or part in respect of a period for which it would otherwise run in relation to a qualifying debt.

(2)   If the interests of justice require that the supplier should receive no statutory interest for a period, statutory interest shall not run for that period.

(3)   If the interests of justice require that the supplier should receive statutory interest at a reduced rate for a period, statutory interest shall run at such rate as meets the justice of the case for that period.

(4)   Remission of statutory interest under this section may be required—

(a)   by reason of conduct at any time (whether before or after the time at which the debt is created); and

(b)   for the whole period for which statutory interest would otherwise run or for one or more parts of that period.

(5)   In this section 'conduct' includes any act or omission.

[5A   Compensation arising out of late payment

(1)   Once statutory interest begins to run in relation to a qualifying debt, the supplier shall be entitled to a fixed sum (in addition to the statutory interest on the debt).

(2)   That sum shall be—

(a)   for a debt less than £1,000, the sum of £40;

(b)   for a debt of £1,000 or more, but less than £10,000, the sum of £70;

(c)   for a debt of £10,000 or more, the sum of £100.

[(2A)   If the reasonable costs of the supplier in recovering the debt are not met by the fixed sum, the supplier shall also be entitled to a sum equivalent to the difference between the fixed sum and those costs.]

(3)   The obligation to pay [a sum] under this section in respect of a qualifying debt shall be treated as part of the term implied by section 1(1) in the contract creating the debt.]

[(4)   Section 17(1)(b) of the Unfair Contract Terms Act 1977 (no reliance to be placed on certain contract terms) shall apply in cases where a contract term is not contained in written standard terms of the purchaser as well as in cases where the term is contained in such standard terms.

(5)   In this section 'contract term' means a term of the contract relating to a sum due to the supplier under this section.]

6   Rate of statutory interest

(1)   The Secretary of State shall by order made with the consent of the Treasury set the rate of statutory interest by prescribing—

(a)   a formula for calculating the rate of statutory interest; or

(b)   the rate of statutory interest.

(2)   Before making such an order the Secretary of State shall, among other things, consider the extent to which it may be desirable to set the rate so as to—

(a)   protect suppliers whose financial position makes them particularly vulnerable if their qualifying debts are paid late; and

(b)   deter generally the late payment of qualifying debts.

PART II
CONTRACT TERMS RELATING TO LATE PAYMENT OF QUALIFYING DEBTS

7 Purpose of Part II

(1)   This Part deals with the extent to which the parties to a contract to which this Act applies may by reference to contract terms oust or vary the right to statutory interest that would otherwise apply when a qualifying debt created by the contract (in this Part referred to as 'the debt') is not paid.

(2)   This Part applies to contract terms agreed before the debt is created; after that time the parties are free to agree terms dealing with the debt.

(3)   This Part has effect without prejudice to any other ground which may affect the validity of a contract term.

8 Circumstances where statutory interest may be ousted or varied

(1)   Any contract terms are void to the extent that they purport to exclude the right to statutory interest in relation to the debt, unless there is a substantial contractual remedy for late payment of the debt.

(2)   Where the parties agree a contractual remedy for late payment of the debt that is a substantial remedy, statutory interest is not carried by the debt (unless they agree otherwise).

(3)   The parties may not agree to vary the right to statutory interest in relation to the debt unless either the right to statutory interest as varied or the overall remedy for late payment of the debt is a substantial remedy.

(4)   Any contract terms are void to the extent that they purport to—

(a)   confer a contractual right to interest that is not a substantial remedy for late payment of the debt, or

(b)   vary the right to statutory interest so as to provide for a right to statutory interest that is not a substantial remedy for late payment of the debt,

unless the overall remedy for late payment of the debt is a substantial remedy.

(5)   Subject to this section, the parties are free to agree contract terms which deal with the consequences of late payment of the debt.

9 Meaning of 'substantial remedy'

(1)   A remedy for the late payment of the debt shall be regarded as a substantial remedy unless—

(a)   the remedy is insufficient either for the purpose of compensating the supplier for late payment or for deterring late payment; and

(b)   it would not be fair or reasonable to allow the remedy to be relied on to oust or (as the case may be) to vary the right to statutory interest that would otherwise apply in relation to the debt.

(2)   In determining whether a remedy is not a substantial remedy, regard shall be had to all the relevant circumstances at the time the terms in question are agreed.

(3)   In determining whether subsection (1)(b) applies, regard shall be had (without prejudice to the generality of subsection (2)) to the following matters—

(a)   the benefits of commercial certainty;

(b)   the strength of the bargaining positions of the parties relative to each other;

(c)   whether the term was imposed by one party to the detriment of the other (whether by the use of standard terms or otherwise); and

(d)   whether the supplier received an inducement to agree to the term.

10 Interpretation of Part II

In this Part—

'contract term' means a term of the contract creating the debt or any other contract term binding the parties (or either of them);

'contractual remedy' means a contractual right to interest or any contractual remedy other than interest;

'contractual right to interest' includes a reference to a contractual right to charge interest;

'overall remedy', in relation to the late payment of the debt, means any combination of a contractual right to interest, a varied right to statutory interest or a contractual remedy other than interest;

'substantial remedy' shall be construed in accordance with section 9.

(2)   In this Part a reference (however worded) to contract terms which vary the right to statutory interest is a reference to terms altering in any way the effect of Part I in relation to the debt (for example by postponing the time at which interest starts to run or by imposing conditions on the right to interest).

(3)   In this Part a reference to late payment of the debt is a reference to late payment of the sum due when the debt is created (excluding any part of that sum which is prevented from carrying statutory interest by section 3).

PART III
GENERAL AND SUPPLEMENTARY

11   Treatment of advance payments of the contract price

(1)   A qualifying debt created by virtue of an obligation to make an advance payment shall be treated for the purposes of this Act as if it was created on the day mentioned in subsection (3), (4) or (5) (as the case may be).

(2)   In this section 'advance payment' means a payment falling due before the obligation of the supplier to which the whole contract price relates ('the supplier's obligation') is performed, other than a payment of a part of the contract price that is due in respect of any part performance of that obligation and payable on or after the day on which that part performance is completed.

(3)   Where the advance payment is the whole contract price, the debt shall be treated as created on the day on which the supplier's obligation is performed.

(4)   Where the advance payment is a part of the contract price, but the sum is not due in respect of any part performance of the supplier's obligation, the debt shall be treated as created on the day on which the supplier's obligation is performed.

(5)   Where the advance payment is a part of the contract price due in respect of any part performance of the supplier's obligation, but is payable before that part performance is completed, the debt shall be treated as created on the day on which the relevant part performance is completed.

(6)   Where the debt is created by virtue of an obligation to pay a sum due in respect of a period of hire of goods, this section has effect as if—

(a)   references to the day on which the supplier's obligation is performed were references to the last day of that period; and

(b)   references to part performance of that obligation were references to part of that period.

(7)   For the purposes of this section an obligation to pay the whole outstanding balance of the contract price shall be regarded as an obligation to pay the whole contract price and not as an obligation to pay a part of the contract price.

12   Conflict of laws

(1)   This Act does not have effect in relation to a contract governed by the law of a part of the United Kingdom by choice of the parties if—

(a)   there is no significant connection between the contract and that part of the United Kingdom; and

(b)   but for that choice, the applicable law would be a foreign law.

(2)   This Act has effect in relation to a contract governed by a foreign law by choice of the parties if—

(a)   but for that choice, the applicable law would be the law of a part of the United Kingdom; and

(b)   there is no significant connection between the contract and any country other than that part of the United Kingdom.

(3)   In this section—

'contract' means a contract falling within section 2(1); and

'foreign law' means the law of a country outside the United Kingdom.

13   Assignments, etc

(1)   The operation of this Act in relation to a qualifying debt is not affected by—

   (a)   any change in the identity of the parties to the contract creating the debt; or

   (b)   the passing of the right to be paid the debt, or the duty to pay it (in whole or in part) to a person other than the person who is the original creditor or the original debtor when the debt is created.

(2)   Any reference in this Act to the supplier or the purchaser is a reference to the person who is for the time being the supplier or the purchaser or, in relation to a time after the debt in question has been created, the person who is for the time being the creditor or the debtor, as the case may be.

(3)   Where the right to be paid part of a debt passes to a person other than the person who is the original creditor when the debt is created, any reference in this Act to a debt shall be construed as (or, if the context so requires, as including) a reference to part of a debt.

(4)   A reference in this section to the identity of the parties to a contract changing, or to a right or duty passing, is a reference to it changing or passing by assignment or assignation, by operation of law or otherwise.

14   Contract terms relating to the date for payment of the contract price

(1)   This section applies to any contract term which purports to have the effect of postponing the time at which a qualifying debt would otherwise be created by a contract to which this Act applies.

(2)   Sections 3(2)(b) and 17(1)(b) of the Unfair Contract Terms Act 1977 (no reliance to be placed on certain contract terms) shall apply in cases where such a contract term is not contained in written standard terms of the purchaser as well as in cases where the term is contained in such standard terms.

(3)   In this section 'contract term' has the same meaning as in section 10(1).

15   Orders and regulations

(1)   Any power to make an order or regulations under this Act is exercisable by statutory instrument.

(2)   Any statutory instrument containing an order or regulations under this Act, other than an order under section 17(2), shall be subject to annulment in pursuance of a resolution of either House of Parliament.

16   Interpretation

(1)   In this Act—

'contract for the supply of goods or services' has the meaning given in section 2(2);

'contract price' means the price in a contract of sale of goods or the money consideration referred to in section 2(2)(b) in any other contract for the supply of goods or services;

'purchaser' means (subject to section 13(2)) the buyer in a contract of sale or the person who contracts with the supplier in any other contract for the supply of goods or services;

'qualifying debt' means a debt falling within section 3(1);

'statutory interest' means interest carried by virtue of the term implied by section 1(1); and

'supplier' means (subject to section 13(2)) the seller in a contract of sale of goods or the person who does one or more of the things mentioned in section 2(3) in any other contract for the supply of goods or services.

(2)   In this Act any reference (however worded) to an agreement or to contract

terms includes a reference to both express and implied terms (including terms established by a course of dealing or by such usage as binds the parties).

17 Short title, commencement and extent

(1) This Act may be cited as the Late Payment of Commercial Debts (Interest) Act 1998.

(2) This Act (apart from this section) shall come into force on such day as the Secretary of State may by order appoint; and different days may be appointed for different descriptions of contract or for other different purposes.

An order under this subsection may specify a description of contract by reference to any feature of the contract (including the parties).

(3) The Secretary of State may by regulations make such transitional, supplemental or incidental provision (including provision modifying any provision of this Act) as the Secretary of State may consider necessary or expedient in connection with the operation of this Act while it is not fully in force.

(4) This Act does not affect contracts of any description made before this Act comes into force for contracts of that description.

(5) This Act extends to Northern Ireland.

HUMAN RIGHTS ACT 1998
(1998, c 42)

Introduction

1 The Convention Rights

(1) In this Act 'the Convention rights' means the rights and fundamental freedoms set out in—

  (a)   Articles 2 to 12 and 14 of the Convention,

  (b)   Articles 1 to 3 of the First Protocol, and

  (c)   [Article 1 of the Thirteenth Protocol],

as read with Articles 16 to 18 of the Convention.

(2) Those Articles are to have effect for the purposes of this Act subject to any designated derogation or reservation (as to which see sections 14 and 15).

(3) The Articles are set out in Schedule 1.

(4) The [Secretary of State] may by order make such amendments to this Act as he considers appropriate to reflect the effect, in relation to the United Kingdom, of a protocol.

(5) In subsection (4) 'protocol' means a protocol to the Convention—

  (a)   which the United Kingdom has ratified; or

  (b)   which the United Kingdom has signed with a view to ratification.

(6) No amendment may be made by an order under subsection (4) so as to come into force before the protocol concerned is in force in relation to the United Kingdom.

2 Interpretation of Convention rights

(1) A court or tribunal determining a question which has arisen in connection with a Convention right must take into account any—

  (a)   judgment, decision, declaration or advisory opinion of the European Court of Human Rights,

  (b)   opinion of the Commission given in a report adopted under Article 31 of the Convention,

  (c)   decision of the Commission in connection with Article 26 or 27(2) of the Convention, or

  (d)   decision of the Committee of Ministers taken under Article 46 of the Convention,

whenever made or given, so far as, in the opinion of the court or tribunal, it is relevant to the proceedings in which that question has arisen.

(2) Evidence of any judgment, decision, declaration or opinion of which account may have to be taken under this section is to be given in proceedings before any court or tribunal in such manner as may be provided by rules.

(3) In this section 'rules' means rules of court or, in the case of proceedings before a tribunal, rules made for the purposes of this section—

(a) by [the Lord Chancellor or] the Secretary of State, in relation to any proceedings outside Scotland;

(b) by the Secretary of State, in relation to proceedings in Scotland; or

(c) by a Northern Ireland department, in relation to proceedings before a tribunal in Northern Ireland—

(i) which deals with transferred matters; and

(ii) for which no rules made under paragraph (a) are in force.

Legislation

3 Interpretation of legislation

(1) So far as it is possible to do so, primary legislation and subordinate legislation must be read and given effect in a way which is compatible with the Convention rights.

(2) This section—

(a) applies to primary legislation and subordinate legislation whenever enacted;

(b) does not affect the validity, continuing operation or enforcement of any incompatible primary legislation; and

(c) does not affect the validity, continuing operation or enforcement of any incompatible subordinate legislation if (disregarding any possibility of revocation) primary legislation prevents removal of the incompatibility.

4 Declaration of incompatibility

(1) Subsection (2) applies in any proceedings in which a court determines whether a provision of primary legislation is compatible with a Convention right.

(2) If the court is satisfied that the provision is incompatible with a Convention right, it may make a declaration of that incompatibility.

(3) Subsection (4) applies in any proceedings in which a court determines whether a provision of subordinate legislation, made in the exercise of a power conferred by primary legislation, is compatible with a Convention right.

(4) If the court is satisfied—

(a) that the provision is incompatible with a Convention right, and

(b) that (disregarding any possibility of revocation) the primary legislation concerned prevents removal of the incompatibility,

it may make a declaration of that incompatibility.

(5) In this section 'court' means—

(a) [the Supreme Court;]

(b) the Judicial Committee of the Privy Council;

(c) [the Court Martial Appeal Court];

(d) in Scotland, the High Court of Justiciary sitting otherwise than as a trial court or the Court of Session;

(e) in England and Wales or Northern Ireland, the High Court or the Court of Appeal;

[(f) the Court of Protection, in any matter being dealt with by the President of the Family Division, the Vice-Chancellor or a puisne judge of the High Court.]

(6) A declaration under this section ('a declaration of incompatibility')—

(a) does not affect the validity, continuing operation or enforcement of the provision in respect of which it is given; and

(b) is not binding on the parties to the proceedings in which it is made.

5 Right of Crown to intervene

(1) Where a court is considering whether to make a declaration of incompatibility, the Crown is entitled to notice in accordance with rules of court.

(2) In any case to which subsection (1) applies—

   (a)   a Minister of the Crown (or a person nominated by him),
   (b)   a member of the Scottish Executive,
   (c)   a Northern Ireland Minister,
   (d)   a Northern Ireland department,

is entitled, on giving notice in accordance with rules of court, to be joined as a party to the proceedings.

(3) Notice under subsection (2) may be given at any time during the proceedings.

(4) A person who has been made a party to criminal proceedings (other than in Scotland) as the result of a notice under subsection (2) may, with leave, appeal to the [Supreme Court] against any declaration of incompatibility made in the proceedings.

(5) In subsection (4)—

'criminal proceedings' includes all proceedings before the Courts-Martial Appeal Court; and

'leave' means leave granted by the court making the declaration of incompatibility or by the [Supreme Court].

Remedial action

10 Power to take remedial action

(1) This section applies if—

   (a)   a provision of legislation has been declared under section 4 to be incompatible with a Convention right and, if an appeal lies—

      (i)   all persons who may appeal have stated in writing that they do not intend to do so;
      (ii) the time for bringing an appeal has expired and no appeal has been brought within that time; or
      (iii) an appeal brought within that time has been determined or abandoned; or

   (b)   it appears to a Minister of the Crown or Her Majesty in Council that, having regard to a finding of the European Court of Human Rights made after the coming into force of this section in proceedings against the United Kingdom, a provision of legislation is incompatible with an obligation of the United Kingdom arising from the Convention.

(2) If a Minister of the Crown considers that there are compelling reasons for proceeding under this section, he may by order make such amendments to the legislation as he considers necessary to remove the incompatibility.

(3) If, in the case of subordinate legislation, a Minister of the Crown considers—

   (a)   that it is necessary to amend the primary legislation under which the subordinate legislation in question was made, in order to enable the incompatibility to be removed, and
   (b)   that there are compelling reasons for proceeding under this section,

he may by order make such amendments to the primary legislation as he considers necessary.

(4) This section also applies where the provision in question is in subordinate legislation and has been quashed, or declared invalid, by reason of incompatibility with a Convention right and the Minister proposes to proceed under paragraph 2(b) of Schedule 2.

(5) If the legislation is an Order in Council, the power conferred by subsection (2) or (3) is exercisable by Her Majesty in Council.

(6)   In this section 'legislation' does not include a Measure of the Church Assembly or of the General Synod of the Church of England.

(7)   Schedule 2 makes further provision about remedial orders.

21   Interpretation, etc

(1)   In this Act—

'amend' includes repeal and apply (with or without modifications);

'the appropriate Minister' means the Minister of the Crown having charge of the appropriate authorised government department (within the meaning of the Crown Proceedings Act 1947);

'the Commission' means the European Commission of Human Rights;

'the Convention' means the Convention for the Protection of Human Rights and Fundamental Freedoms, agreed by the Council of Europe at Rome on 4th November 1950 as it has effect for the time being in relation to the United Kingdom;

'declaration of incompatibility' means a declaration under section 4;

'Minister of the Crown' has the same meaning as in the Ministers of the Crown Act 1975;

'Northern Ireland Minister' includes the First Minister and the deputy First Minister in Northern Ireland;

'primary legislation' means any—

   (a)   public general Act;
   (b)   local and personal Act;
   (c)   private Act;
   (d)   Measure of the Church Assembly;
   (e)   Measure of the General Synod of the Church of England;
   (f)   Order in Council—
        (i)   made in exercise of Her Majesty's Royal Prerogative;
        (ii)   made under section 38(1)(a) of the Northern Ireland Constitution Act 1973 or the corresponding provision of the Northern Ireland Act 1998; or
        (iii)   amending an Act of a kind mentioned in paragraph (a), (b) or (c);

and includes an order or other instrument made under primary legislation (otherwise than by the [Welsh Ministers, the First Minister for Wales, the Counsel General to the Welsh Assembly Government], a member of the Scottish Executive, a Northern Ireland Minister or a Northern Ireland department) to the extent to which it operates to bring one or more provisions of that legislation into force or amends any primary legislation;

'the First Protocol' means the protocol to the Convention agreed at Paris on 20th March 1952;

[. . .]

'the Eleventh Protocol' means the protocol to the Convention (restructuring the control machinery established by the Convention) agreed at Strasbourg on 11th May 1994;

['the Thirteenth Protocol' means the protocol to the Convention (concerning the abolition of the death penalty in all circumstances) agreed at Vilnius on 3rd May 2002;]

'remedial order' means an order under section 10;

'subordinate legislation' means any—

   (a)   Order in Council other than one—
        (i)   made in exercise of Her Majesty's Royal Prerogative;
        (ii)   made under section 38(1)(a) of the Northern Ireland Constitution Act 1973 or the corresponding provision of the Northern Ireland Act 1998; or
        (iii)   amending an Act of a kind mentioned in the definition of primary legislation;
   (b)   Act of the Scottish Parliament;
   [(ba)   Measure of the National Assembly for Wales;]

(bb)   Act of the National Assembly for Wales;]

(c)   Act of the Parliament of Northern Ireland;

(d)   Measure of the Assembly established under section 1 of the Northern Ireland Assembly Act 1973;

(e)   Act of the Northern Ireland Assembly;

(f)   order, rules, regulations, scheme, warrant, byelaw or other instrument made under primary legislation (except to the extent to which it operates to bring one or more provisions of that legislation into force or amends any primary legislation);

(g)   order, rules, regulations, scheme, warrant, byelaw or other instrument made under legislation mentioned in paragraph (b), (c), (d) or (e) or made under an Order in Council applying only to Northern Ireland;

(h)   order, rules, regulations, scheme, warrant, byelaw or other instrument made by a member of the Scottish Executive, [Welsh Ministers, the First Minister for Wales, the Counsel General to the Welsh Assembly Government,] a Northern Ireland Minister or a Northern Ireland department in exercise of prerogative or other executive functions of Her Majesty which are exercisable by such a person on behalf of Her Majesty;

'transferred matters' has the same meaning as in the Northern Ireland Act 1998; and

'tribunal' means any tribunal in which legal proceedings may be brought.

(2)   The references in paragraphs (b) and (c) of section 2(1) to Articles are to Articles of the Convention as they had effect immediately before the coming into force of the Eleventh Protocol.

(3)   The reference in paragraph (d) of section 2(1) to Article 46 includes a reference to Articles 32 and 54 of the Convention as they had effect immediately before the coming into force of the Eleventh Protocol.

(4)   The references in section 2(1) to a report or decision of the Commission or a decision of the Committee of Ministers include references to a report or decision made as provided by paragraphs 3, 4 and 6 of Article 5 of the Eleventh Protocol (transitional provisions).

[. . .]

22   Short title, commencement, application and extent

(1)   This Act may be cited as the Human Rights Act 1998.

. . .

SCHEDULES

SCHEDULE 1
THE ARTICLES

PART I
THE CONVENTION

Rights and Freedoms

Article 2. Right to Life

1.   Everyone's right to life shall be protected by law. No one shall be deprived of his life intentionally save in the execution of a sentence of a court following his conviction of a crime for which this penalty is provided by law.

2.   Deprivation of life shall not be regarded as inflicted in contravention of this Article when it results from the use of force which is no more than absolutely necessary:

(a)   in defence of any person from unlawful violence;

(b)   in order to effect a lawful arrest or to prevent the escape of a person lawfully detained;

(c)   in action lawfully taken for the purpose of quelling a riot or insurrection.

Article 3. Prohibition of Torture
No one shall be subjected to torture or to inhuman or degrading treatment or punishment.

Article 4. Prohibition of Slavery and Forced Labour
1.   No one shall be held in slavery or servitude.
2.   No one shall be required to perform forced or compulsory labour.
3.   For the purpose of this Article the term 'forced or compulsory labour' shall not include:
(a)   any work required to be done in the ordinary course of detention imposed according to the provisions of Article 5 of this Convention or during conditional release from such detention;
(b)   any service of a military character or, in case of conscientious objectors in countries where they are recognised, service exacted instead of compulsory military service;
(c)   any service exacted in case of an emergency or calamity threatening the life or well-being of the community;
(d)   any work or service which forms part of normal civic obligations.

Article 5. Right to Liberty and Security
1.   Everyone has the right to liberty and security of person. No one shall be deprived of his liberty save in the following cases and in accordance with a procedure prescribed by law:
(a)   the lawful detention of a person after conviction by a competent court;
(b)   the lawful arrest or detention of a person for non-compliance with the lawful order of a court or in order to secure the fulfilment of any obligation prescribed by law;
(c)   the lawful arrest or detention of a person effected for the purpose of bringing him before the competent legal authority on reasonable suspicion of having committed an offence or when it is reasonably considered necessary to prevent his committing an offence or fleeing after having done so;
(d)   the detention of a minor by lawful order for the purpose of educational supervision or his lawful detention for the purpose of bringing him before the competent legal authority;
(e)   the lawful detention of persons for the prevention of the spreading of infectious diseases, of persons of unsound mind, alcoholics or drug addicts or vagrants;
(f)   the lawful arrest or detention of a person to prevent his effecting an unauthorised entry into the country or of a person against whom action is being taken with a view to deportation or extradition.
2.   Everyone who is arrested shall be informed promptly, in a language which he understands, of the reasons for his arrest and of any charge against him.
3.   Everyone arrested or detained in accordance with the provisions of paragraph 1(c) of this Article shall be brought promptly before a judge or other officer authorised by law to exercise judicial power and shall be entitled to trial within a reasonable time or to release pending trial. Release may be conditioned by guarantees to appear for trial.
4.   Everyone who is deprived of his liberty by arrest or detention shall be entitled to take proceedings by which the lawfulness of his detention shall be decided speedily by a court and his release ordered if the detention is not lawful.
5.   Everyone who has been the victim of arrest or detention in contravention of the provisions of this Article shall have an enforceable right to compensation.

Article 6. Right to a Fair Trial
1.   In the determination of his civil rights and obligations or of any criminal charge against him, everyone is entitled to a fair and public hearing within a

reasonable time by an independent and impartial tribunal established by law. Judgment shall be pronounced publicly but the press and public may be excluded from all or part of the trial in the interest of morals, public order or national security in a democratic society, where the interests of juveniles or the protection of the private life of the parties so require, or to the extent strictly necessary in the opinion of the court in special circumstances where publicity would prejudice the interests of justice.

2. Everyone charged with a criminal offence shall be presumed innocent until proved guilty according to law.

3. Everyone charged with a criminal offence has the following minimum rights:

(a)   to be informed promptly, in a language which he understands and in detail, of the nature and cause of the accusation against him;

(b)   to have adequate time and facilities for the preparation of his defence;

(c)   to defend himself in person or through legal assistance of his own choosing or, if he has not sufficient means to pay for legal assistance, to be given it free when the interests of justice so require;

(d)   to examine or have examined witnesses against him and to obtain the attendance and examination of witnesses on his behalf under the same conditions as witnesses against him;

(e)   to have the free assistance of an interpreter if he cannot understand or speak the language used in court.

Article 7. No Punishment Without Law

1. No one shall be held guilty of any criminal offence on account of any act or omission which did not constitute a criminal offence under national or international law at the time when it was committed. Nor shall a heavier penalty be imposed than the one that was applicable at the time the criminal offence was committed.

2. This Article shall not prejudice the trial and punishment of any person for any act or omission which, at the time when it was committed, was criminal according to the general principles of law recognised by civilised nations.

Article 8. Right to Respect for Private and Family Life

1. Everyone has the right to respect for his private and family life, his home and his correspondence.

2. There shall be no interference by a public authority with the exercise of this right except such as is in accordance with the law and is necessary in a democratic society in the interests of national security, public safety or the economic well-being of the country, for the prevention of disorder or crime, for the protection of health or morals, or for the protection of the rights and freedoms of others.

Article 9. Freedom of Thought, Conscience and Religion

1. Everyone has the right to freedom of thought, conscience and religion; this right includes freedom to change his religion or belief and freedom, either alone or in community with others and in public or private, to manifest his religion or belief, in worship, teaching, practice and observance.

2. Freedom to manifest one's religion or beliefs shall be subject only to such limitations as are prescribed by law and are necessary in a democratic society in the interests of public safety, for the protection of public order, health or morals, or for the protection of the rights and freedoms of others.

Article 10. Freedom of Expression

1. Everyone has the right to freedom of expression. This right shall include freedom to hold opinions and to receive and impart information and ideas without interference by public authority and regardless of frontiers. This Article shall not prevent States from requiring the licensing of broadcasting, television or cinema enterprises.

2. The exercise of these freedoms, since it carries with it duties and responsi-

bilities, may be subject to such formalities, conditions, restrictions or penalties as are prescribed by law and are necessary in a democratic society, in the interests of national security, territorial integrity or public safety, for the prevention of disorder or crime, for the protection of health or morals, for the protection of the reputation or rights of others, for preventing the disclosure of information received in confidence, or for maintaining the authority and impartiality of the judiciary.

Article 11. Freedom of Assembly and Association

1. Everyone has the right to freedom of peaceful assembly and to freedom of association with others, including the right to form and to join trade unions for the protection of his interests.

2. No restrictions shall be placed on the exercise of these rights other than such as are prescribed by law and are necessary in a democratic society in the interests of national security or public safety, for the prevention of disorder or crime, for the protection of health or morals or for the protection of the rights and freedoms of others. This Article shall not prevent the imposition of lawful restrictions on the exercise of these rights by members of the armed forces, of the police or of the administration of the State.

Article 12. Right to Marry

Men and women of marriageable age have the right to marry and to found a family, according to the national laws governing the exercise of this right.

Article 14. Prohibition of Discrimination

The enjoyment of the rights and freedoms set forth in this Convention shall be secured without discrimination on any ground such as sex, race, colour, language, religion, political or other opinion, national or social origin, association with a national minority, property, birth or other status.

Article 16. Restrictions on Political Activity of Aliens

Nothing in Articles 10, 11 and 14 shall be regarded as preventing the High Contracting Parties from imposing restrictions on the political activity of aliens.

Article 17. Prohibition of Abuse of Rights

Nothing in this Convention may be interpreted as implying for any State, group or person any right to engage in any activity or perform any act aimed at the destruction of any of the rights and freedoms set forth herein or at their limitation to a greater extent than is provided for in the Convention.

Article 18. Limitation on Use of Restrictions on Rights

The restrictions permitted under this Convention to the said rights and freedoms shall not be applied for any purpose other than those for which they have been prescribed.

PART II
THE FIRST PROTOCOL

Article 1. Protection of Property

Every natural or legal person is entitled to the peaceful enjoyment of his possessions. No one shall be deprived of his possessions except in the public interest and subject to the conditions provided for by law and by the general principles of international law.

The preceding provisions shall not, however, in any way impair the right of a State to enforce such laws as it deems necessary to control the use of property in accordance with the general interest or to secure the payment of taxes or other contributions or penalties.

Article 2. Right to Education

No person shall be denied the right to education. In the exercise of any functions which it assumes in relation to education and to teaching, the State shall respect the right of parents to ensure such education and teaching in conformity with their own religious and philosophical convictions.

Article 3. Right to Free Elections
The High Contracting Parties undertake to hold free elections at reasonable intervals by secret ballot, under conditions which will ensure the free expression of the opinion of the people in the choice of the legislature.

[PART III
ARTICLE 1 OF THE THIRTEENTH PROTOCOL

Abolition of the Death Penalty
The death penalty shall be abolished. No one shall be condemned to such penalty or executed.]

SCHEDULE 2
REMEDIAL ORDERS

1 Orders
(1)   A remedial order may—

(a)   contain such incidental, supplemental, consequential or transitional provision as the person making it considers appropriate;

(b)   be made so as to have effect from a date earlier than that on which it is made;

(c)   make provision for the delegation of specific functions;

(d)   make different provision for different cases.

(2)   The power conferred by sub-paragraph (1)(a) includes—

(a)   power to amend primary legislation (including primary legislation other than that which contains the incompatible provision); and

(b)   power to amend or revoke subordinate legislation (including subordinate legislation other than that which contains the incompatible provision).

(3)   A remedial order may be made so as to have the same extent as the legislation which it affects.

(4)   No person is to be guilty of an offence solely as a result of the retrospective effect of a remedial order.

2 Procedure
No remedial order may be made unless—

(a)   a draft of the order has been approved by a resolution of each House of Parliament made after the end of the period of 60 days beginning with the day on which the draft was laid; or

(b)   it is declared in the order that it appears to the person making it that, because of the urgency of the matter, it is necessary to make the order without a draft being so approved.

3 Orders laid in draft
(1)   No draft may be laid under paragraph 2(a) unless—

(a)   the person proposing to make the order has laid before Parliament a document which contains a draft of the proposed order and the required information; and

(b)   the period of 60 days, beginning with the day on which the document required by this sub-paragraph was laid, has ended.

(2)   If representations have been made during that period, the draft laid under paragraph 2(a) must be accompanied by a statement containing—

(a)   a summary of the representations; and

(b)   if, as a result of the representations, the proposed order has been changed, details of the changes.

4   Urgent cases

(1)   If a remedial order ('the original order') is made without being approved in draft, the person making it must lay it before Parliament, accompanied by the required information, after it is made.

(2)   If representations have been made during the period of 60 days beginning with the day on which the original order was made, the person making it must (after the end of that period) lay before Parliament a statement containing—

(a)   a summary of the representations; and

(b)   if, as a result of the representations, he considers it appropriate to make changes to the original order, details of the changes.

(3)   If sub-paragraph (2)(b) applies, the person making the statement must—

(a)   make a further remedial order replacing the original order; and

(b)   lay the replacement order before Parliament.

(4)   If, at the end of the period of 120 days beginning with the day on which the original order was made, a resolution has not been passed by each House approving the original or replacement order, the order ceases to have effect (but without that affecting anything previously done under either order or the power to make a fresh remedial order).

5   Definitions

In this Schedule—

'representations' means representations about a remedial order (or proposed remedial order) made to the person making (or proposing to make) it and includes any relevant Parliamentary report or resolution; and

'required information' means—

(a)   an explanation of the incompatibility which the order (or proposed order) seeks to remove, including particulars of the relevant declaration, finding or order; and

(b)   a statement of the reasons for proceeding under section 10 and for making an order in those terms.

6   Calculating periods

In calculating any period for the purposes of this Schedule, no account is to be taken of any time during which—

(a)   Parliament is dissolved or prorogued; or

(b)   both Houses are adjourned for more than four days.

[7   (1)   This paragraph applies in relation to—

(a)   any remedial order made, and any draft of such an order proposed to be made,—

(i)   by the Scottish Ministers; or

(ii)   within devolved competence (within the meaning of the Scotland Act 1998) by Her Majesty in Council; and

(b)   any document or statement to be laid in connection with such an order (or proposed order).

(2)   This Schedule has effect in relation to any such order (or proposed order), document or statement subject to the following modifications.

(3)   Any reference to Parliament, each House of Parliament or both Houses of Parliament shall be construed as a reference to the Scottish Parliament.

(4)   Paragraph 6 does not apply and instead, in calculating any period for the purposes of this Schedule, no account is to be taken of any time during which the Scottish Parliament is dissolved or is in recess for more than four days.]

SCOTLAND ACT 1998
(1998, c 46)

41 Defamatory statements

(1) For the purposes of the law of defamation—

(a) any statement made in proceedings of the Parliament, and

(b) the publication under the authority of the Parliament of any statement, shall be absolutely privileged.

(2) In subsection (1), 'statement' has the same meaning as in the Defamation Act 1996.

126 Interpretation

(1) In this Act—

'body' includes unincorporated association,

'constituencies' and 'regions', in relation to the Parliament, mean the constituencies and regions provided for by Schedule 1,

'constituency member' means a member of the Parliament for a constituency,

'the Convention rights' has the same meaning as in the Human Rights Act 1998,

'document' means anything in which information is recorded in any form (and references to producing a document are to be read accordingly),

'enactment' includes an Act of the Scottish Parliament, Northern Ireland legislation (within the meaning of the Northern Ireland Act 1998) and an enactment comprised in subordinate legislation, and includes an enactment comprised in, or in subordinate legislation under, an Act of Parliament, whenever passed or made,

'financial year' means a year ending with 31st March,

'functions' includes powers and duties, and 'confer', in relation to functions, includes impose,

'government department' means any department of the Government of the United Kingdom,

'the Human Rights Convention' means—

(a) the Convention for the Protection of Human Rights and Fundamental Freedoms, agreed by the Council of Europe at Rome on 4th November 1950, and

(b) the Protocols to the Convention,

as they have effect for the time being in relation to the United Kingdom,

'Minister of the Crown' includes the Treasury,

'modify' includes amend or repeal,

'occupational pension scheme', 'personal pension scheme' and 'public service pension scheme' have the meanings given by section 1 of the Pension Schemes Act 1993, . . .

'the Parliament' means the Scottish Parliament,

'parliamentary', in relation to constituencies, elections and electors, is to be taken to refer to the Parliament of the United Kingdom,

'prerogative instrument' means an Order in Council, warrant, charter or other instrument made under the prerogative,

'the principal appointed day' means the day appointed by an order under section 130 which is designated by the order as the principal appointed day,

'proceedings', in relation to the Parliament, includes proceedings of any committee or sub-committee,

'property' includes rights and interests of any description,

'regional member' means a member of the Parliament for a region,

'Scotland' includes so much of the internal waters and territorial sea of the United Kingdom as are adjacent to Scotland,

'Scottish public authority' means any public body (except the Parliamentary corporation), public office or holder of such an office whose functions (in each case) are exercisable only in or as regards Scotland, 'the Scottish zone' means the sea within British fishery limits (that is, the limits set by or under section 1 of the Fishery Limits Act 1976) which is adjacent to Scotland,

'standing orders' means standing orders of the Parliament,

'subordinate legislation' has the same meaning as in the Interpretation Act 1978 and also includes an instrument made under an Act of the Scottish Parliament,

'tribunal' means any tribunal in which legal proceedings may be brought.

(2) Her Majesty may by Order in Council determine, or make provision for determining, for the purposes of this Act any boundary between waters which are to be treated as internal waters or territorial sea of the United Kingdom, or sea within British fishery limits, adjacent to Scotland and those which are not.

(3) For the purposes of this Act—

(a) the question whether any function of a body, government department, office or office-holder relates to reserved matters is to be determined by reference to the purpose for which the function is exercisable, having regard (among other things) to the likely effects in all the circumstances of any exercise of the function, but

(b) bodies to which paragraph 3 of Part III of Schedule 5 applies are to be treated as if all their functions were functions which relate to reserved matters.

(4) References in this Act to Scots private law are to the following areas of the civil law of Scotland—

(a) the general principles of private law (including private international law),

(b) the law of persons (including natural persons, legal persons and unincorporated bodies),

(c) the law of obligations (including obligations arising from contract, unilateral promise, delict, unjustified enrichment and negotiorum gestio),

(d) the law of property (including heritable and moveable property, trusts and succession), and

(e) the law of actions (including jurisdiction, remedies, evidence, procedure, diligence, recognition and enforcement of court orders, limitation of actions and arbitration),

and include references to judicial review of administrative action.

(5) References in this Act to Scots criminal law include criminal offences, jurisdiction, evidence, procedure and penalties and the treatment of offenders.

(6) References in this Act and in any other enactment to the Scottish Administration are to the office-holders in the Scottish Administration and the members of the staff of the Scottish Administration.

(7) For the purposes of this Act—

(a) references to office-holders in the Scottish Administration are to—

(i) members of the [Scottish Government] and junior Scottish Ministers, and

(ii) the holders of offices in the Scottish Administration which are not ministerial offices, and

(b) references to members of the staff of the Scottish Administration are to the staff of the persons referred to in paragraph (a).

(8) For the purposes of this Act, the offices in the Scottish Administration which are not ministerial offices are—

(a) the Registrar General of Births, Deaths and Marriages for Scotland, the Keeper of the Registers of Scotland and the Keeper of the Records of Scotland, and

(b) any other office of a description specified in an Order in Council made by Her Majesty under this subsection.

(9) In this Act—

(a) all those rights, powers, liabilities, obligations and restrictions from time to time created or arising by or under the [EU] Treaties, and

(b) all those remedies and procedures from time to time provided for by or under the [EU] Treaties,

are referred to as '[EU] law'.

(10)   In this Act, 'international obligations' means any international obligations of the United Kingdom other than obligations to observe and implement [EU] law or the Convention rights.

(11)   In this Act, 'by virtue of' includes 'by' and 'under'.

CONTRACTS (RIGHTS OF THIRD PARTIES) ACT 1999
(1999 c 31)

This Act does not apply to Scotland (see s 10), but is included in this volume for comparative purposes.

1   Right of third parties to enforce contractual claim

(1)   Subject to the provisions of this Act, a person who is not a party to a contract (a 'third party') may in his own right enforce a term of the contract if—

(a)   the contract expressly provides that he may, or

(b)   subject to subsection (2), the term purports to confer a benefit on him.

(2)   Subsection (1)(b) does not apply if on a proper construction of the contract it appears that the parties did not intend the term to be enforceable by the third party.

(3)   The third party must be expressly identified in the contract by name, as a member of a class or as answering a particular description but need not be in existence when the contract is entered into.

(4)   This section does not confer a right on a third party to enforce a term of a contract otherwise than subject to and in accordance with any other relevant terms of the contract.

(5)   For the purpose of exercising his right to enforce a term of the contract, there shall be available to the third party any remedy that would have been available to him in an action for breach of contract if he had been a party to the contract (and the rules relating to damages, injunctions, specific performance and other relief shall apply accordingly).

(6)   Where a term of a contract excludes or limits liability in relation to any matter references in this Act to the third party enforcing the term shall be construed as references to his availing himself of the exclusion or limitation.

(7)   In this Act, in relation to a term of a contract which is enforceable by a third party—

'the promisor' means the party to the contract against whom the term is enforceable by the third party, and

'the promisee' means the party to the contract by whom the term is enforceable against the promisor.

2   Variation and rescission of contract

(1)   Subject to the provisions of this section, where a third party has a right under section 1 to enforce a term of the contract, the parties to the contract may not, by agreement, rescind the contract, or vary it in such a way as to extinguish or alter his entitlement under that right, without his consent if—

(a)   the third party has communicated his assent to the term to the promisor,

(b)   the promisor is aware that the third party has relied on the term, or

(c)   the promisor can reasonably be expected to have foreseen that the third party would rely on the term and the third party has in fact relied on it.

(2)   The assent referred to in subsection (1)(a)—

(a)   may be by words or conduct, and

(b)   if sent to the promisor by post or other means, shall not be regarded as communicated to the promisor until received by him.

(3)   Subsection (1) is subject to any express term of the contract under which—

(a)   the parties to the contract may by agreement rescind or vary the contract without the consent of the third party, or

(b) the consent of the third party is required in circumstances specified in the contract instead of those set out in subsection (1)(a) to (c).

(4) Where the consent of a third party is required under subsection (1) or (3), the court or arbitral tribunal may, on the application of the parties to the contract, dispense with his consent if satisfied—

(a) that his consent cannot be obtained because his whereabouts cannot reasonably be ascertained, or

(b) that he is mentally incapable of giving his consent.

(5) The court or arbitral tribunal may, on the application of the parties to a contract, dispense with any consent that may be required under subsection (1)(c) if satisfied that it cannot reasonably be ascertained whether or not the third party has in fact relied on the term.

(6) If the court or arbitral tribunal dispenses with a third party's consent, it may impose such conditions as it thinks fit, including a condition requiring the payment of compensation to the third party.

(7) The jurisdiction conferred on the court by subsections (4) to (6) is exercisable by both the High Court and a county court.

3 Defences etc available to promisor

(1) Subsections (2) to (5) apply where, in reliance on section 1, proceedings for the enforcement of a term of a contract are brought by a third party.

(2) The promisor shall have available to him by way of defence or set-off any matter that—

(a) arises from or in connection with the contract and is relevant to the term, and

(b) would have been available to him by way of defence or set-off if the proceedings had been brought by the promisee.

(3) The promisor shall also have available to him by way of defence or set-off any matter if—

(a) an express term of the contract provides for it to be available to him in proceedings brought by the third party, and

(b) it would have been available to him by way of defence or set-off if the proceedings had been brought by the promisee.

(4) The promisor shall also have available to him—

(a) by way of defence or set-off any matter, and

(b) by way of counterclaim any matter not arising from the contract,

that would have been available to him by way of defence or set-off or, as the case may be, by way of counterclaim against the third party if the third party had been a party to the contract.

(5) Subsections (2) and (4) are subject to any express term of the contract as to the matters that are not to be available to the promisor by way of defence, set-off or counterclaim.

(6) Where in any proceedings brought against him a third party seeks in reliance on section 1 to enforce a term of a contract (including, in particular, a term purporting to exclude or limit liability), he may not do so if he could not have done so (whether by reason of any particular circumstances relating to him or otherwise) had he been a party to the contract.

4 Enforcement of contract by promisee

Section 1 does not affect any right of the promisee to enforce any term of the contract.

5 Protection of promisor from double liability

Where under section 1 a term of a contract is enforceable by a third party, and the promisee has recovered from the promisor a sum in respect of—

(a) the third party's loss in respect of the term, or

(b)   the expense to the promisee of making good to the third party the default of the promisor,

then, in any proceedings brought in reliance on that section by the third party, the court or arbitral tribunal shall reduce any award to the third party to such extent as it thinks appropriate to take account of the sum recovered by the promisee.

6   Exceptions

(1)   Section 1 confers no rights on a third party in the case of a contract on a bill of exchange, promissory note or other negotiable instrument.

(2)   Section 1 confers no rights on a third party in the case of any contract binding on a company and its members under [section 33 of the Companies Act 2006 (effect of company's constitution)].

[(2A)   Section 1 confers no rights on a third party in the case of any incorporation document of a limited liability partnership [or any agreement (express or implied) between the members of a limited liability partnership, or between a limited liability partnership and its members, that determines the mutual rights and duties of the members and their rights and duties in relation to the limited liability partnership].]

(3)   Section 1 confers no right on a third party to enforce—

(a)   any term of a contract of employment against an employee,

(b)   any term of a worker's contract against a worker (including a home worker), or

(c)   any term of a relevant contract against an agency worker.

(4)   In subsection (3)—

(a)   'contract of employment', 'employee', 'worker's contract', and 'worker' have the meaning given by section 54 of the National Minimum Wage Act 1998,

(b)   'home worker' has the meaning given by section 35(2) of that Act,

(c)   'agency worker' has the same meaning as in section 34(1) of that Act, and

(d)   'relevant contract' means a contract entered into, in a case where section 34 of that Act applies, by the agency worker as respects work falling within subsection (1)(a) of that section.

(5)   Section 1 confers no rights on a third party in the case of—

(a)   a contract for the carriage of goods by sea, or

(b)   a contract for the carriage of goods by rail or road, or for the carriage of cargo by air, which is subject to the rules of the appropriate international transport convention,

except that a third party may in reliance on that section avail himself of an exclusion or limitation of liability in such a contract.

(6)   In subsection (5) 'contract for the carriage of goods by sea' means a contract of carriage—

(a)   contained in or evidenced by a bill of lading, sea waybill or a corresponding electronic transaction, or

(b)   under or for the purposes of which there is given an undertaking which is contained in a ship's delivery order or a corresponding electronic transaction.

(7)   For the purposes of subsection (6)—

(a)   'bill of lading', 'sea waybill' and 'ship's delivery order' have the same meaning as in the Carriage of Goods by Sea Act 1992, and

(b)   a corresponding electronic transaction is a transaction within section 1(5) of that Act which corresponds to the issue, indorsement, delivery or transfer of a bill of lading, sea waybill or ship's delivery order.

(8)   In subsection (5) 'the appropriate international transport convention' means—

(a)   in relation to a contract for the carriage of goods by rail, the Convention which has the force of law in the United Kingdom under section 1 of the International Transport Conventions Act 1983,

(b)   in relation to a contract for the carriage of goods by road, the Convention which has the force of law in the United Kingdom under section 1 of the Carriage of Goods by Road Act 1965, and

(c)   in relation to a contract for the carriage of cargo by air—

(i) the Convention which has the force of law in the United Kingdom under section 1 of the Carriage by Air Act 1961, or

(ii) the Convention which has the force of law under section 1 of the Carriage by Air (Supplementary Provisions) Act 1962, or

(iii) either of the amended Conventions set out in Part B of Schedule 2 or 3 to the Carriage by Air Acts (Application of Provisions) Order 1967.

7   Supplementary provisions relating to third party

(1)   Section 1 does not affect any right or remedy of a third party that exists or is available apart from this Act.

(2)   Section 2(2) of the Unfair Contract Terms Act 1977 (restriction on exclusion etc. of liability for negligence) shall not apply where the negligence consists of the breach of an obligation arising from a term of a contract and the person seeking to enforce it is a third party acting in reliance on section 1.

(3)   In sections 5 and 8 of the Limitation Act 1980 the references to an action founded on a simple contract and an action upon a specialty shall respectively include references to an action brought in reliance on section 1 relating to a simple contract and an action brought in reliance on that section relating to a specialty.

(4)   A third party shall not, by virtue of section 1(5) or 3(4) or (6), be treated as a party to the contract for the purposes of any other Act (or any instrument made under any other Act).

8   Arbitration provisions

(1)   Where—

(a)   a right under section 1 to enforce a term ('the substantive term') is subject to a term providing for the submission of disputes to arbitration ('the arbitration agreement'), and

(b)   the arbitration agreement is an agreement in writing for the purposes of Part I of the Arbitration Act 1996,

the third party shall be treated for the purposes of that Act as a party to the arbitration agreement as regards disputes between himself and the promisor relating to the enforcement of the substantive term by the third party.

(2)   Where—

(a)   a third party has a right under section 1 to enforce a term providing for one or more descriptions of dispute between the third party and the promisor to be submitted to arbitration ('the arbitration agreement'),

(b)   the arbitration agreement is an agreement in writing for the purposes of Part I of the Arbitration Act 1996, and

(c)   the third party does not fall to be treated under subsection (1) as a party to the arbitration agreement,

the third party shall, if he exercises the right, be treated for the purposes of that Act as a party to the arbitration agreement in relation to the matter with respect to which the right is exercised, and be treated as having been so immediately before the exercise of the right.

9   [Amends Northern Irish statutes.]

10   Short title, commencement and extent

(1)   This Act may be cited as the Contracts (Rights of Third Parties) Act 1999.

(2)   This Act comes into force on the day on which it is passed but, subject to subsection (3), does not apply in relation to a contract entered into before the end of the period of six months beginning with that day.

(3)   The restriction in subsection (2) does not apply in relation to a contract which—

(a)   is entered into on or after the day on which this Act is passed, and

(b)   expressly provides for the application of this Act.

(4)   This Act extends as follows—

(a)   section 9 extends to Northern Ireland only;

(b)   the remaining provisions extend to England and Wales and Northern Ireland only.

ADULTS WITH INCAPACITY (SCOTLAND) ACT 2000
(2000, asp 4)

PART 5
MEDICAL TREATMENT AND RESEARCH

47   Authority of persons responsible for medical treatment

(1)   This section applies where [any of the persons mentioned in subsection (1A)]—

(a)   is of the opinion that [an adult] is incapable in relation to a decision about the medical treatment in question; and

(b)   has certified in accordance with subsection (5) that he is of this opinion.

[(1A)   The persons are—

(a)   the medical practitioner primarily responsible for the medical treatment of the adult;

(b)   a person who is—

(i)   a dental practitioner;

(ii)   an ophthalmic optician;

(iii)   a registered nurse; or

(iv)   an individual who falls within such description of persons as may be prescribed by the Scottish Ministers,

who satisfies such requirements as may be so prescribed and who is primarily responsible for medical treatment of the kind in question.]

(2)   [. . .] [T]he [person who by virtue of subsection (1) has issued a certificate for the purposes of that subsection] shall have, during the period specified in the certificate, authority to do what is reasonable in the circumstances, in relation to [the medical treatment in question], to safeguard or promote the physical or mental health of the adult.

[(2A)   Subsection (2)—

(a)   does not affect any authority conferred by any other enactment or rule of law; and

(b)   is subject to—

(i)   the following provisions of this section;

(ii)   sections 49 and 50; and

(iii)   sections 234, 237, 240, 242, 243 and 244 of the 2003 Act.]

(3)   The authority conferred by subsection (2) shall be exercisable also by any other person who is authorised by the [person on whom that authority is conferred] to carry out [the medical treatment in question] and who is acting—

(a)   on his behalf under his instructions; or

(b)   with his approval or agreement.

(4)   In this Part 'medical treatment' includes any procedure or treatment designed to safeguard or promote physical or mental health.

(5)   A certificate for the purposes of subsection (1) shall be in the prescribed form and shall specify the period during which the authority conferred by subsection (2) shall subsist, being a period which—

(a)   the [person who issues the certificate] considers appropriate to the condition or circumstances of the adult; but

(b)   [does not exceed—

(i)   one year; or

(ii)   if, in the opinion of that person any of the conditions or circumstances prescribed by the Scottish Ministers applies as respects the adult, 3 years, from] the date of the examination on which the certificate is based.

(6)   If after issuing a certificate, the [person who issued it] is of the opinion that the condition or circumstances of the adult have changed he may—

(a)   revoke the certificate;

(b)   issue a new certificate specifying such period [not exceeding—

(i)   one year; or

(ii)   if, in the opinion of that person any of the conditions or circumstances prescribed by the Scottish Ministers applies as respects the adult, 3 years, from] the date of revocation of the old certificate as he considers appropriate to the new condition or circumstances of the adult.

(7)   The authority conferred by subsection (2) shall not authorise—

(a)   the use of force or detention, unless it is immediately necessary and only for so long as is necessary in the circumstances;

(b)   action which would be inconsistent with any decision by a competent court;

(c)   placing an adult in a hospital for the treatment of mental disorder against his will.

[. . .]

(9)   Subject to subsection (10), where any question as to the authority of any person to provide medical treatment in pursuance of subsection (2)—

(a)   is the subject of proceedings in any court (other than for the purposes of any application to the court made under regulations made under section 48); and

(b)   has not been determined,

medical treatment authorised by subsection (2) shall not be given unless it is authorised by any other enactment or rule of law for the preservation of the life of the adult or the prevention of serious deterioration in his medical condition.

(10)   Nothing in subsection (9) shall authorise the provision of any medical treatment where an interdict has been granted and continues to have effect prohibiting the provision of such medical treatment.

[(11)   In subsection (1A)—

'dental practitioner' has the same meaning as in section 108(1) of the National Health Service (Scotland) Act 1978 (c 29);

'ophthalmic optician' means a person registered in either of the registers kept under section 7 of the Opticians Act 1989 (c 44) of ophthalmic opticians.]

ELECTRONIC COMMUNICATIONS ACT 2000
(2000, c 7)

PART II
FACILITATION OF ELECTRONIC COMMERCE, DATA STORAGE, ETC

7   Electronic signatures and related certificates

(1)   In any legal proceedings—

(a)   an electronic signature incorporated into or logically associated with a particular electronic communication or particular electronic data, and

(b)   the certification by any person of such a signature,

shall each be admissible in evidence in relation to any question as to the authenticity of the communication or data or as to the integrity of the communication or data.

(2)   For the purposes of this section an electronic signature is so much of anything in electronic form as—

(a)   is incorporated into or otherwise logically associated with any electronic communication or electronic data; and

(b)   purports to be so incorporated or associated for the purpose of being used in establishing the authenticity of the communication or data, the integrity of the communication or data, or both.

(3)   For the purposes of this section an electronic signature incorporated into or associated with a particular electronic communication or particular electronic data is certified by any person if that person (whether before or after the making of the communication) has made a statement confirming that—

(a)   the signature,

(b)   a means of producing, communicating or verifying the signature, or

(c)   a procedure applied to the signature,

is (either alone or in combination with other factors) a valid means of establishing the authenticity of the communication or data, the integrity of the communication or data, or both.

8   Power to modify legislation

(1)   Subject to subsection (3), the appropriate Minister may by order made by statutory instrument modify the provisions of—

(a)   any enactment or subordinate legislation, or

(b)   any scheme, licence, authorisation or approval issued, granted or given by or under any enactment or subordinate legislation,

in such manner as he may think fit for the purpose of authorising or facilitating the use of electronic communications or electronic storage (instead of other forms of communication or storage) for any purpose mentioned in subsection (2).

(2)   Those purposes are—

(a)   the doing of anything which under any such provisions is required to be or may be done or evidenced in writing or otherwise using a document, notice or instrument;

(b)   the doing of anything which under any such provisions is required to be or may be done by post or other specified means of delivery;

(c)   the doing of anything which under any such provisions is required to be or may be authorised by a person's signature or seal, or is required to be delivered as a deed or witnessed;

(d)   the making of any statement or declaration which under any such provisions is required to be made under oath or to be contained in a statutory declaration;

(e)   the keeping, maintenance or preservation, for the purposes or in pursuance of any such provisions, of any account, record, notice, instrument or other document;

(f)   the provision, production or publication under any such provisions of any information or other matter;

(g)   the making of any payment that is required to be or may be made under any such provisions.

(3)   The appropriate Minister shall not make an order under this section authorising the use of electronic communications or electronic storage for any purpose, unless he considers that the authorisation is such that the extent (if any) to which records of things done for that purpose will be available will be no less satisfactory in cases where use is made of electronic communications or electronic storage than in other cases.

(4)   Without prejudice to the generality of subsection (1), the power to make an order under this section shall include power to make an order containing any of the following provisions—

(a)   provision as to the electronic form to be taken by any electronic communications or electronic storage the use of which is authorised by an order under this section;

(b)   provision imposing conditions subject to which the use of electronic communications or electronic storage is so authorised;

(c)   provision, in relation to cases in which any such conditions are not satisfied, for treating anything for the purposes of which the use of such communications or storage is so authorised as not having been done;

(d)   provision, in connection with anything so authorised, for a person to be able to refuse to accept receipt of something in electronic form except in such circumstances as may be specified in or determined under the order;

(e)   provision, in connection with any use of electronic communications so authorised, for intermediaries to be used, or to be capable of being used, for the transmission of any data or for establishing the authenticity or integrity of any data;

(f)   provision, in connection with any use of electronic storage so authorised, for persons satisfying such conditions as may be specified in or determined under the regulations to carry out functions in relation to the storage;

(g)   provision, in relation to cases in which the use of electronic communications or electronic storage is so authorised, for the determination of any of the matters mentioned in subsection (5), or as to the manner in which they may be proved in legal proceedings;

(h)   provision, in relation to cases in which fees or charges are or may be imposed in connection with anything for the purposes of which the use of electronic communications or electronic storage is so authorised, for different fees or charges to apply where use is made of such communications or storage;

(i)   provision, in relation to any criminal or other liabilities that may arise (in respect of the making of false or misleading statements or otherwise) in connection with anything for the purposes of which the use of electronic communications or electronic storage is so authorised, for corresponding liabilities to arise in corresponding circumstances where use is made of such communications or storage;

(j)   provision requiring persons to prepare and keep records in connection with any use of electronic communications or electronic storage which is so authorised;

(k)   provision requiring the production of the contents of any records kept in accordance with an order under this section;

(l)   provision for a requirement imposed by virtue of paragraph (j) or (k) to be enforceable at the suit or instance of such person as may be specified in or determined in accordance with the order;

(m)   any such provision, in relation to electronic communications or electronic storage the use of which is authorised otherwise than by an order under this section, as corresponds to any provision falling within any of the preceding paragraphs that may be made where it is such an order that authorises the use of the communications or storage.

(5)   The matters referred to in subsection (4)(g) are—

(a)   whether a thing has been done using an electronic communication or electronic storage;

(b)   the time at which, or date on which, a thing done using any such communication or storage was done;

(c)   the place where a thing done using such communication or storage was done;

(d)   the person by whom such a thing was done; and

(e)   the contents, authenticity or integrity of any electronic data.

(6)   An order under this section—

(a)   shall not (subject to paragraph (b)) require the use of electronic communications or electronic storage for any purpose; but

(b)   may make provision that a period of notice specified in the order must expire before effect is given to a variation or withdrawal of an election or other decision which—

(i) has been made for the purposes of such an order; and

(ii) is an election or decision to make use of electronic communications or electronic storage.

(7) The matters in relation to which provision may be made by an order under this section do not include any matter under the care and management of the Commissioners of Inland Revenue or any matter under the care and management of the Commissioners of Customs and Excise.

(8) In this section references to doing anything under the provisions of any enactment include references to doing it under the provisions of any subordinate legislation the power to make which is conferred by that enactment.

9 Section 8 orders

(1) In this Part 'the appropriate Minister' means (subject to subsections (2) and (7) and section 10(1))—

(a) in relation to any matter with which a department of the Secretary of State is concerned, the Secretary of State;

(b) in relation to any matter with which the Treasury is concerned, the Treasury; and

(c) in relation to any matter with which any Government department other than a department of the Secretary of State or the Treasury is concerned, the Minister in charge of the other department.

(2) Where in the case of any matter—

(a) that matter falls within more than one paragraph of subsection (1),

(b) there is more than one such department as is mentioned in paragraph (c) of that subsection that is concerned with that matter, or

(c) both paragraphs (a) and (b) of this subsection apply,

references, in relation to that matter, to the appropriate Minister are references to any one or more of the appropriate Ministers acting (in the case of more than one) jointly.

(3) Subject to subsection (4) and section 10(6), a statutory instrument containing an order under section 8 shall be subject to annulment in pursuance of a resolution of either House of Parliament.

(4) Subsection (3) does not apply in the case of an order a draft of which has been laid before Parliament and approved by a resolution of each House.

(5) An order under section 8 may—

(a) provide for any conditions or requirements imposed by such an order to be framed by reference to the directions of such persons as may be specified in or determined in accordance with the order;

(b) provide that any such condition or requirement is to be satisfied only where a person so specified or determined is satisfied as to specified matters.

(6) The provision made by such an order may include—

(a) different provision for different cases;

(b) such exceptions and exclusions as the person making the order may think fit; and

(c) any such incidental, supplemental, consequential and transitional provision as he may think fit;

and the provision that may be made by virtue of paragraph (c) includes provision modifying any enactment or subordinate legislation or any scheme, licence, authorisation or approval issued, granted or given by or under any enactment or subordinate legislation.

(7) In the case of any matter which is not one of the reserved matters within the meaning of the Scotland Act 1998 or in respect of which functions are, by virtue of section 63 of that Act, exercisable by the Scottish Ministers instead of by or concurrently with a Minister of the Crown, this section and section 8 shall apply to Scotland subject to the following modifications—

(a) subsections (1) and (2) of this section are omitted;

(b)   any reference to the appropriate Minister is to be read as a reference to the Secretary of State;

(c)   any power of the Secretary of State, by virtue of paragraph (b), to make an order under section 8 may also be exercised by the Scottish Ministers with the consent of the Secretary of State; and

(d)   where the Scottish Ministers make an order under section 8—

(i)   any reference to the Secretary of State (other than a reference in this subsection) shall be construed as a reference to the Scottish Ministers; and

(ii)   any reference to Parliament or to a House of Parliament shall be construed as a reference to the Scottish Parliament.

[10   *Modifications in relation to Welsh matters*]

PART III
MISCELLANEOUS AND SUPPLEMENTAL

[. . .]

Supplemental

13   Ministerial expenditure etc
There shall be paid out of money provided by Parliament—

(a)   any expenditure incurred by the Secretary of State for or in connection with the carrying out of his functions under this Act; and

(b)   any increase attributable to this Act in the sums which are payable out of money so provided under any other Act.

14   Prohibition on key escrow requirements
(1)   Subject to subsection (2), nothing in this Act shall confer any power on any Minister of the Crown, on the Scottish Ministers, on the National Assembly for Wales or on any person appointed under section 3—

(a)   by conditions of an approval under Part I, or

(b)   by any regulations or order under this Act,

to impose a requirement on any person to deposit a key for electronic data with another person.

(2)   Subsection (1) shall not prohibit the imposition by an order under section 8 of—

(a)   a requirement to deposit a key for electronic data with the intended recipient of electronic communications comprising the data; or

(b)   a requirement for arrangements to be made, in cases where a key for data is not deposited with another person, which otherwise secure that the loss of a key, or its becoming unusable, does not have the effect that the information contained in a record kept in pursuance of any provision made by or under any enactment or subordinate legislation becomes inaccessible or incapable of being put into an intelligible form.

(3)   In this section 'key', in relation to electronic data, means any code, password, algorithm, key or other data the use of which (with or without other keys)—

(a)   allows access to the electronic data, or

(b)   facilitates the putting of the electronic data into an intelligible form;

and references in this section to depositing a key for electronic data with a person include references to doing anything that has the effect of making the key available to that person.

15   General interpretation
(1)   In this Act, except in so far as the context otherwise requires—

'document' includes a map, plan, design, drawing, picture or other image;

'communication' includes a communication comprising sounds or images or both and a communication effecting a payment;

'electronic communication' means a communication transmitted (whether from one person to another, from one device to another or from a person to a device or vice versa)—

    (a)   by means of [an electronic communications network]; or

    (b)   by other means but while in an electronic form;

'enactment' includes—

    (a)   an enactment passed after the passing of this Act,

    (b)   an enactment comprised in an Act of the Scottish Parliament, and

    (c)   an enactment contained in Northern Ireland legislation,

but does not include an enactment contained in Part I or II of this Act;

'modification' includes any alteration, addition or omission, and cognate expressions shall be construed accordingly;

'record' includes an electronic record; and

'subordinate legislation' means—

    (a)   any subordinate legislation (within the meaning of the Interpretation Act 1978);

    (b)   any instrument made under an Act of the Scottish Parliament; or

    (c)   any statutory rules (within the meaning of the Statutory Rules (Northern Ireland) Order 1979).

(2)   In this Act—

    (a)   references to the authenticity of any communication or data are references to any one or more of the following—

        (i)   whether the communication or data comes from a particular person or other source;

        (ii)   whether it is accurately timed and dated;

        (iii)   whether it is intended to have legal effect; and

    (b)   references to the integrity of any communication or data are references to whether there has been any tampering with or other modification of the communication or data.

(3)   References in this Act to something's being put into an intelligible form include references to its being restored to the condition in which it was before any encryption or similar process was applied to it.

16 Short title, commencement, extent

(1)   This Act may be cited as the Electronic Communications Act 2000.

(2)   Part I of this Act and sections 7, 11 and 12 shall come into force on such day as the Secretary of State may by order made by statutory instrument appoint; and different days may be appointed under this subsection for different purposes.

(3)   An order shall not be made for bringing any of Part I of this Act into force for any purpose unless a draft of the order has been laid before Parliament and approved by a resolution of each House.

(4)   If no order for bringing Part I of this Act into force has been made under subsection (2) by the end of the period of five years beginning with the day on which this Act is passed, that Part shall, by virtue of this subsection, be repealed at the end of that period.

(5)   This Act extends to Northern Ireland.

ANTISOCIAL BEHAVIOUR ETC (SCOTLAND) ACT 2004
(2004, asp 8)

4 Antisocial behaviour orders

(1) On the application of a relevant authority, the sheriff may, if satisfied that the conditions mentioned in subsection (2) are met as respects the person to whom the application relates (the 'specified person'), make an antisocial behaviour order.

(2) Those conditions are—

(a) that the specified person is at least 12 years of age;

(b) that the specified person has engaged in antisocial behaviour towards a relevant person; and

(c) that an antisocial behaviour order is necessary for the purpose of protecting relevant persons from further antisocial behaviour by the specified person.

(3) For the purpose of determining whether the condition mentioned in subsection (2)(b) is met, the sheriff shall disregard any act or conduct of the specified person which that person shows was reasonable in the circumstances.

(4) Where the specified person is a child, the sheriff shall, before determining the application, require the Principal Reporter to arrange a children's hearing for the purpose of obtaining their advice as to whether the condition mentioned in subsection (2)(c) is met; and the sheriff shall, in determining whether that condition is met, have regard to that advice.

(5) Subject to subsections (6) and (7), an antisocial behaviour order is an order which prohibits, indefinitely or for such period as may be specified in the order, the specified person from doing anything described in the order.

(6) The prohibitions that may be imposed by an antisocial behaviour order are those necessary for the purpose of protecting relevant persons from further antisocial behaviour by the specified person.

(7) If an antisocial behaviour order is made on the application of a local authority the order may, in addition to imposing prohibitions that are necessary for the purpose mentioned in subsection (6), impose such prohibitions as are necessary for the purpose of protecting other persons ('affected persons') from further antisocial behaviour by the specified person.

(8) Before making an antisocial behaviour order, the sheriff shall, where the specified person is present in court, explain in ordinary language—

(a) the effect of the order and the prohibitions proposed to be included in it;

(b) the consequences of failing to comply with the order;

(c) the powers the sheriff has under sections 5 and 6; and

(d) the entitlement of the specified person to appeal against the making of the order.

(9) Failure to comply with subsection (8) shall not affect the validity of the order.

(10) An application for an antisocial behaviour order shall be made by summary application to the sheriff within whose sheriffdom the specified person is alleged to have engaged in antisocial behaviour.

(11) Before making an application under this section—

(a) a relevant authority shall consult the relevant consultees; and

(b) a registered social landlord shall—

(i) in the case where the specified person is a child, consult the local authority within whose area the specified person resides or appears to reside about the proposed application;

(ii) in the case where the specified person is not a child, notify that local authority of the proposed application.

(12) Nothing in this section shall prevent a relevant authority from instituting any legal proceedings otherwise than under this section against any person in relation to any antisocial behaviour.

(13)   In this section, 'relevant person' means—

(a)   in relation to an application by a local authority, a person within the area of the authority; and

(b)   in relation to an application by a registered social landlord—

(i)   a person residing in, or otherwise in or likely to be in, property provided or managed by that landlord; or

(ii)   a person in, or likely to be in, the vicinity of such property.

9   Breach of orders

(1)   Subject to subsection (3), a person who—

(a)   is subject to an antisocial behaviour order or an interim order; and

(b)   without reasonable excuse, does anything that the order to which the person is subject prohibits the person from doing,

shall be guilty of an offence.

(2)   A person guilty of an offence under subsection (1) shall be liable—

(a)   on summary conviction, to imprisonment for a term not exceeding 6 months or to a fine not exceeding the statutory maximum or to both; or

(b)   on conviction on indictment, to imprisonment for a term not exceeding 5 years or to a fine or to both.

(3)   If—

(a)   otherwise than under subsection (1), the thing done by the person constitutes an offence (a 'separate offence'); and

(b)   the person is charged with the separate offence,

the person shall not be liable to be proceeded against for an offence under subsection (1).

(4)   Subject to subsection (5), if a person is convicted of a separate offence, the court which sentences the person for that offence shall, in determining the appropriate sentence or disposal, have regard to—

(a)   the fact that the separate offence was committed while the person was subject to the antisocial behaviour order or, as the case may be, interim order;

(b)   the number of antisocial behaviour orders and interim orders to which the person was subject at the time of commission of the separate offence;

(c)   any previous conviction of the person for an offence under subsection (1); and

(d)   the extent to which the sentence or disposal in respect of any previous conviction of the person differed, by virtue of this subsection, from that which the court would have imposed but for this section.

(5)   The court shall not, under subsection (4)(a), have regard to the fact that the separate offence was committed while the person was subject to the antisocial behaviour order or, as the case may be, the interim order unless that fact is libelled in the indictment or, as the case may be, specified in the complaint.

(6)   The fact that the separate offence was committed while the person was subject to an antisocial behaviour order or, as the case may be, an interim order, shall, unless challenged—

(a)   in the case of proceedings on indictment, by the giving of notice of a preliminary objection in accordance with section 71(2) or 72(6)(b)(i) of the Criminal Procedure (Scotland) Act 1995; or

(b)   in summary proceedings, by preliminary objection before the person's plea is recorded,

be held as admitted.

143   Interpretation: 'antisocial behaviour' and other expressions

(1)   For the purposes of this Act (other than Parts 7 and 8), a person ('A') engages in antisocial behaviour if A—

(a)   acts in a manner that causes or is likely to cause alarm or distress; or

(b)   pursues a course of conduct that causes or is likely to cause alarm or distress,

to at least one person who is not of the same household as A; and 'antisocial behaviour' shall be construed accordingly.

(2)   In this Act, unless the context otherwise requires—

'conduct' includes speech; and a course of conduct must involve conduct on at
least two occasions;

'local authority' means a council constituted under section 2 of the Local
Government etc (Scotland) Act 1994; and 'area', in relation to a local authority,
means the local government area (within the meaning of that Act) for which the
council is constituted;

'registered social landlord' means a body registered in the register maintained
under [section 20(1) of the Housing (Scotland) Act 2010]; and

'senior police officer' has the meaning given by section 19(1).

CIVIL PARTNERSHIP ACT 2004
(2004, c 33)

128   Promise or agreement to enter into civil partnership

No promise or agreement to enter into civil partnership creates any rights or obligations under the law of Scotland; and no action for breach of such a promise or
agreement may be brought in any court in Scotland, whatever the law applicable
to the promise or agreement.

GAMBLING ACT 2005
(2005, c 19)

PART 1
INTERPRETATION OF KEY CONCEPTS

Principal concepts

3   Gambling

In this Act 'gambling' means—

(a)   gaming (within the meaning of section 6),

(b)   betting (within the meaning of section 9), and

(c)   participating in a lottery (within the meaning of section 14 and subject to
section 15).

Gaming

6   Gaming & game of chance

(1)   In this Act 'gaming' means playing a game of chance for a prize.

(2)   In this Act 'game of chance'—

(a)   includes—

(i) a game that involves both an element of chance and an element of
skill,

(ii) a game that involves an element of chance that can be eliminated by
superlative skill, and

(iii) a game that is presented as involving an element of chance, but

(b)   does not include a sport.

(3)   For the purposes of this Act a person plays a game of chance if he partici-
pates in a game of chance—

(a)   whether or not there are other participants in the game, and

(b)   whether or not a computer generates images or data taken to represent
the actions of other participants in the game.

(4)   For the purposes of this Act a person plays a game of chance for a prize—

(a)   if he plays a game of chance and thereby acquires a chance of winning a prize, and

(b)   whether or not he risks losing anything at the game.

(5)   In this Act 'prize' in relation to gaming (except in the context of a gaming machine)—

(a)   means money or money's worth, and

(b)   includes both a prize provided by a person organising gaming and winnings of money staked.

(6)   The Secretary of State may by regulations provide that a specified activity, or an activity carried on in specified circumstances, is or is not to be treated for the purposes of this Act as—

(a)   a game;

(b)   a game of chance;

(c)   a sport.

Betting

9   Betting: general

(1)   In this Act 'betting' means making or accepting a bet on—

(a)   the outcome of a race, competition or other event or process,

(b)   the likelihood of anything occurring or not occurring, or

(c)   whether anything is or is not true.

(2)   A transaction that relates to the outcome of a race, competition or other event or process may be a bet within the meaning of subsection (1) despite the facts that—

(a)   the race, competition, event or process has already occurred or been completed, and

(b)   one party to the transaction knows the outcome.

(3)   A transaction that relates to the likelihood of anything occurring or not occurring may be a bet within the meaning of subsection (1) despite the facts that—

(a)   the thing has already occurred or failed to occur, and

(b)   one party to the transaction knows that the thing has already occurred or failed to occur.

Lottery

14   Lottery

(1)   For the purposes of this Act an arrangement is a lottery, irrespective of how it is described, if it satisfies one of the descriptions of lottery in subsections (2) and (3).

(2)   An arrangement is a simple lottery if—

(a)   persons are required to pay in order to participate in the arrangement,

(b)   in the course of the arrangement one or more prizes are allocated to one or more members of a class, and

(c)   the prizes are allocated by a process which relies wholly on chance.

(3)   An arrangement is a complex lottery if—

(a)   persons are required to pay in order to participate in the arrangement,

(b)   in the course of the arrangement one or more prizes are allocated to one or more members of a class,

(c)   the prizes are allocated by a series of processes, and

(d)   the first of those processes relies wholly on chance.

(4)   In this Act 'prize' in relation to lotteries includes any money, articles or services—

(a)   whether or not described as a prize, and

(b)   whether or not consisting wholly or partly of money paid, or articles or services provided, by the members of the class among whom the prize is allocated.

(5)   A process which requires persons to exercise skill or judgment or to display knowledge shall be treated for the purposes of this section as relying wholly on chance if—

(a)   the requirement cannot reasonably be expected to prevent a significant proportion of persons who participate in the arrangement of which the process forms part from receiving a prize, and

(b)   the requirement cannot reasonably be expected to prevent a significant proportion of persons who wish to participate in that arrangement from doing so.

(6)   Schedule 2 makes further provision about when an arrangement is to be or not to be treated for the purposes of this section as requiring persons to pay.

(7)   The Secretary of State may by regulations provide that an arrangement of a specified kind is to be or not to be treated as a lottery for the purposes of this Act; and—

(a)   the power in this subsection is not constrained by subsections (1) to (6) or Schedule 2, and

(b)   regulations under this subsection may amend other provisions of this section or Schedule 2.

15   National Lottery

(1)   Participating in a lottery which forms part of the National Lottery is not gambling for the purposes of this Act (despite section 3(c) but subject to subsections (2) and (3) below).

(2)   Participating in a lottery which forms part of the National Lottery is gambling for the purposes of—

(a)   section 42, and

(b)   section 335.

(3)   Where participating in a lottery which forms part of the National Lottery would also constitute gaming within the meaning of section 6, it shall be treated as gaming for the purposes of this Act if and only if a person participating in the lottery is required to participate in, or to be successful in, more than three processes before becoming entitled to a prize.

(4)   Participating in a lottery which forms part of the National Lottery shall not be treated as betting for the purposes of this Act where it would—

(a)   satisfy the definition of pool betting in section 12, or

(b)   satisfy the definition of betting in section 9 by virtue of section 11.

(5)   Schedule 3 shall have effect.

PART 17
LEGALITY AND ENFORCEMENT OF GAMBLING CONTRACTS

. . .

335   Enforceability of gambling contracts

(1)   The fact that a contract relates to gambling shall not prevent its enforcement.

(2)   Subsection (1) is without prejudice to any rule of law preventing the enforcement of a contract on the grounds of unlawfulness (other than a rule relating specifically to gambling).

PART 18
MISCELLANEOUS AND GENERAL

. . .

361   Extent

(1)   The following provisions of this Act extend to England and Wales, Scotland and Northern Ireland—

(a)   section 43,

(b)   section 331, and

(c)   section 340 (and the related entry in Schedule 17).

(2)   The other provisions of this Act shall extend only to—

(a)   England and Wales, and

(b)   Scotland.

(3)   This section is subject to section 356.

COMPENSATION ACT 2006
(2006 c 29)

3   Mesothelioma: damages

(1)   This section applies where—

(a)   a person ('the responsible person') has negligently or in breach of statutory duty caused or permitted another person ('the victim') to be exposed to asbestos,

(b)   the victim has contracted mesothelioma as a result of exposure to asbestos,

(c)   because of the nature of mesothelioma and the state of medical science, it is not possible to determine with certainty whether it was the exposure mentioned in paragraph (a) or another exposure which caused the victim to become ill, and

(d)   the responsible person is liable in tort, by virtue of the exposure mentioned in paragraph (a), in connection with damage caused to the victim by the disease (whether by reason of having materially increased a risk or for any other reason).

(2)   The responsible person shall be liable—

(a)   in respect of the whole of the damage caused to the victim by the disease (irrespective of whether the victim was also exposed to asbestos—

(i)   other than by the responsible person, whether or not in circumstances in which another person has liability in tort, or

(ii)   by the responsible person in circumstances in which he has no liability in tort), and

(b)   jointly and severally with any other responsible person.

(3)   Subsection (2) does not prevent—

(a)   one responsible person from claiming a contribution from another, or

(b)   a finding of contributory negligence.

(4)   In determining the extent of contributions of different responsible persons in accordance with subsection (3)(a), a court shall have regard to the relative lengths of the periods of exposure for which each was responsible; but this subsection shall not apply—

(a)   if or to the extent that responsible persons agree to apportion responsibility amongst themselves on some other basis, or

(b)   if or to the extent that the court thinks that another basis for determining contributions is more appropriate in the circumstances of a particular case.

(5)   In subsection (1) the reference to causing or permitting a person to be exposed to asbestos includes a reference to failing to protect a person from exposure to asbestos.

(6)   In the application of this section to Scotland—

(a)   a reference to tort shall be taken as a reference to delict, and

(b)   a reference to a court shall be taken to include a reference to a jury.

(7)   The Treasury may make regulations about the provision of compensation to a responsible person where—

(a)   he claims, or would claim, a contribution from another responsible person in accordance with subsection (3)(a), but

(b)   he is unable or likely to be unable to obtain the contribution, because an insurer of the other responsible person is unable or likely to be unable to satisfy the claim for a contribution.

(8)   The regulations may, in particular—

[. . .]

(b)   replicate or apply (with or without modification) a transitional compensation provision;

(c)   provide for a specified person to assess and pay compensation;

(d)   provide for expenses incurred (including the payment of compensation) to be met out of levies collected in accordance with section 213(3)(b) of the Financial Services and Markets Act 2000 (c 8) (the Financial Services Compensation Scheme);

(e)   modify the effect of a transitional compensation provision;

(f)   enable the [Financial Conduct Authority or the Prudential Regulation Authority] to amend the Financial Services Compensation Scheme;

(g)   modify the Financial Services and Markets Act 2000 in its application to an amendment pursuant to paragraph (f);

(h)   make, or require the making of, provision for the making of a claim by a responsible person for compensation whether or not he has already satisfied claims in tort against him;

(i)   make, or require the making of, provision which has effect in relation to claims for contributions made on or after the date on which this Act is passed.

[. . .]

(10)   In subsections (7) and (8)—

(a)   a reference to a responsible person includes a reference to an insurer of a responsible person, and

(b)   'transitional compensation provision' means a provision of an enactment which is made under the Financial Services and Markets Act 2000 and—

(i)   preserves the effect of the Policyholders Protection Act 1975 (c 75), or

(ii)   applies the Financial Services Compensation Scheme in relation to matters arising before its establishment.

(11)   Regulations under subsection (7)—

(a)   may include consequential or incidental provision,

(b)   may make provision which has effect generally or only in relation to specified cases or circumstances,

(c)   may make different provision for different cases or circumstances,

(d)   shall be made by statutory instrument, and

(e)   may not be made unless a draft has been laid before and approved by resolution of each House of Parliament.

16   Commencement

(1), (2)   [Do not apply to Scotland.]

(3)   Section 3 shall be treated as having always had effect.

(4)   But the section shall have no effect in relation to—

(a)   a claim which is settled before 3rd May 2006 (whether or not legal proceedings in relation to the claim have been instituted), or

(b)   legal proceedings which are determined before that date.

(5)   Where a claim is settled on or after that date and before the date on which this Act is passed, a party to the settlement may apply to a relevant court to have the settlement varied; and—

(a)   a court is a relevant court for that purpose if it had, or would have had, jurisdiction to determine the claim by way of legal proceedings,

(b)   an application shall be brought as an application in, or by way of, proceedings on the claim, and

(c)   a court to which an application is made shall vary the settlement to such extent (if any) as appears appropriate to reflect the effect of section 3.

(6)   Where legal proceedings are determined on or after that date and before the date on which this Act is passed, a party to the proceedings may apply to the court to vary the determination; and—

(a)   'the court' means the court which determined the proceedings,

(b)   the application shall be treated as an application in the proceedings, and

(c)   the court shall vary the determination to such extent (if any) as appears appropriate to reflect the effect of section 3.

17   Extent

(1)   This Act shall extend to England and Wales only.

(2)   But section 3 (and section 16(3) to (6)) shall extend to—

(a)   England and Wales,

(b)   Scotland, and

(c)   Northern Ireland.

DAMAGES (ASBESTOS-RELATED CONDITIONS) (SCOTLAND) ACT 2009
(2009, asp 4)

1   Pleural plaques

(1)   Asbestos-related pleural plaques are a personal injury which is not negligible.

(2)   Accordingly, they constitute actionable harm for the purposes of an action of damages for personal injuries.

(3)   Any rule of law the effect of which is that asbestos-related pleural plaques do not constitute actionable harm ceases to apply to the extent it has that effect.

(4)   But nothing in this section otherwise affects any enactment or rule of law which determines whether and in what circumstances a person may be liable in damages in respect of personal injuries.

2   Pleural thickening and asbestosis

(1)   For the avoidance of doubt, a condition mentioned in subsection (2) which has not caused and is not causing impairment of a person's physical condition is a personal injury which is not negligible.

(2)   Those conditions are—

(a)   asbestos-related pleural thickening; and

(b)   asbestosis.

(3)   Accordingly, such a condition constitutes actionable harm for the purposes of an action of damages for personal injuries.

(4)   Any rule of law the effect of which is that such a condition does not constitute actionable harm ceases to apply to the extent it has that effect.

(5)   But nothing in this section otherwise affects any enactment or rule of law which determines whether and in what circumstances a person may be liable in damages in respect of personal injuries.

3   Limitation of actions

(1)   This section applies to an action of damages for personal injuries—

(a)   in which the damages claimed consist of or include damages in respect of—

(i)   asbestos-related pleural plaques; or

(ii)   a condition to which section 2 applies; and

(b)   which, in the case of an action commenced before the date this section comes into force, has not been determined by that date.

(2)   For the purposes of sections 17 and 18 of the Prescription and Limitation (Scotland) Act 1973 (limitation in respect of actions for personal injuries), the period beginning with 17 October 2007 and ending with the day on which this section comes into force is to be left out of account.

4   Commencement and retrospective effect

(1)   This Act (other than this subsection and section 5) comes into force on such day as the Scottish Ministers may, by order made by statutory instrument, appoint.

(2)   Sections 1 and 2 are to be treated for all purposes as having always had effect.

(3)   But those sections have no effect in relation to—

(a)   a claim which is settled before the date on which subsection (2) comes into force (whether or not legal proceedings in relation to the claim have been commenced); or

(b)   legal proceedings which are determined before that date.

5   Short title and Crown application

(1)   This Act may be cited as the Damages (Asbestos-related Conditions) (Scotland) Act 2009.

(2)   This Act binds the Crown.

EQUALITY ACT 2010
(2010 c 15)

An Act to make provision to require Ministers of the Crown and others when making strategic decisions about the exercise of their functions to have regard to the desirability of reducing socio-economic inequalities; to reform and harmonise equality law and restate the greater part of the enactments relating to discrimination and harassment related to certain personal characteristics; to enable certain employers to be required to publish information about the differences in pay between male and female employees; to prohibit victimisation in certain circumstances; to require the exercise of certain functions to be with regard to the need to eliminate discrimination and other prohibited conduct; to enable duties to be imposed in relation to the exercise of public procurement functions; to increase equality of opportunity; to amend the law relating to rights and responsibilities in family relationships; and for connected purposes.

PART 10
CONTRACTS ETC

Contracts and other agreements

142   Unenforceable terms

(1)   A term of a contract is unenforceable against a person in so far as it constitutes, promotes or provides for treatment of that or another person that is of a description prohibited by this Act.

(2)   A relevant non-contractual term is unenforceable against a person in so far as it constitutes, promotes or provides for treatment of that or another person that is of a description prohibited by this Act, in so far as this Act relates to disability.

(3)   A relevant non-contractual term is a term which—

(a)   is a term of an agreement that is not a contract, and

(b)   relates to the provision of an employment service within section 56(2)(a) to (e) or to the provision under a group insurance arrangement of facilities by way of insurance.

(4)   A reference in subsection (1) or (2) to treatment of a description prohibited by this Act does not include—

(a)   a reference to the inclusion of a term in a contract referred to in section 70(2)(a) or 76(2), or

(b)   a reference to the failure to include a term in a contract as referred to in section 70(2)(b).

(5)   Subsection (4) does not affect the application of section 148(2) to this section.

143   Removal or modification of unenforceable terms

(1)   A county court or the sheriff may, on an application by a person who has an interest in a contract or other agreement which includes a term that is unenforceable as a result of section 142, make an order for the term to be removed or modified.

(2)   An order under this section must not be made unless every person who would be affected by it—

(a)   has been given notice of the application (except where notice is dispensed with in accordance with rules of court), and

(b)   has been afforded an opportunity to make representations to the county court or sheriff.

(3)   An order under this section may include provision in respect of a period before the making of the order.

144   Contracting out

(1)   A term of a contract is unenforceable by a person in whose favour it would operate in so far as it purports to exclude or limit a provision of or made under this Act.

(2)   A relevant non-contractual term (as defined by section 142) is unenforceable by a person in whose favour it would operate in so far as it purports to exclude or limit a provision of or made under this Act, in so far as the provision relates to disability.

(3)   This section does not apply to a contract which settles a claim within section 114.

(4)   This section does not apply to a contract which settles a complaint within section 120 if the contract—

(a)   is made with the assistance of a conciliation officer, or

(b)   is a qualifying compromise contract.

(5)   A contract within subsection (4) includes a contract which settles a complaint relating to a breach of an equality clause or rule or of a non-discrimination rule.

(6)   A contract within subsection (4) includes an agreement by the parties to a dispute to submit the dispute to arbitration if—

(a)   the dispute is covered by a scheme having effect by virtue of an order under section 212A of the Trade Union and Labour Relations (Consolidation) Act 1992, and

(b)   the agreement is to submit the dispute to arbitration in accordance with the scheme.

Collective agreements and rules of undertakings

145   Void and unenforceable terms

(1)   A term of a collective agreement is void in so far as it constitutes, promotes or provides for treatment of a description prohibited by this Act.

(2)   A rule of an undertaking is unenforceable against a person in so far as it constitutes, promotes or provides for treatment of the person that is of a description prohibited by this Act.

146 Declaration in respect of void term, etc

(1)   A qualifying person (P) may make a complaint to an employment tribunal that a term is void, or that a rule is unenforceable, as a result of section 145.

(2)   But subsection (1) applies only if—

(a)   the term or rule may in the future have effect in relation to P, and

(b)   where the complaint alleges that the term or rule provides for treatment of a description prohibited by this Act, P may in the future be subjected to treatment that would (if P were subjected to it in present circumstances) be of that description.

(3)   If the tribunal finds that the complaint is well-founded, it must make an order declaring that the term is void or the rule is unenforceable.

(4)   An order under this section may include provision in respect of a period before the making of the order.

(5)   In the case of a complaint about a term of a collective agreement, where the term is one made by or on behalf of a person of a description specified in the first column of the table, a qualifying person is a person of a description specified in the second column.

Description of person who made collective agreement	Qualifying person
Employer	A person who is, or is seeking to be, an employee of that employer
Organisation of employers	A person who is, or is seeking to be, an employee of an employer who is a member of that organisation
Association of organisation of employers	A person who is, or is seeking to be, an employee of an employer who is a member of an organisation in that association

(6)   In the case of a complaint about a rule of an undertaking, where the rule is one made by or on behalf of a person of a description specified in the first column of the table, a qualifying person is a person of a description specified in the second column.

Description of person who made rule of undertaking	Qualifying person
Employer	A person who is, or is seeking to be, an employee of that employer
Trade organisation or qualifications body	A person who is, or is seeking to be, a member of the organisation of body
	A person upon whom the body has conferred a relevant qualification
	A person seeking conferment by the body of a relevant qualification

Supplementary

147 Meaning of 'qualifying compromise contract'

(1)   This section applies for the purposes of this Part.

(2)   A qualifying compromise contract is a contract in relation to which each of the conditions in subsection (3) is met.

(3)   Those conditions are that—
    (a)   the contract is in writing,
    (b)   the contract relates to the particular complaint,
    (c)   the complainant has, before entering into the contract, received advice from an independent adviser about its terms and effect (including, in particular, its effect on the complainant's ability to pursue the complaint before an employment tribunal),
    (d)   on the date of the giving of the advice, there is in force a contract of insurance, or an indemnity provided for members of a profession or professional body, covering the risk of a claim by the complainant in respect of loss arising from the advice,
    (e)   the contract identifies the adviser, and
    (f)   the contract states that the conditions in paragraphs (c) and (d) are met.
(4)   Each of the following is an independent adviser—
    (a)   a qualified lawyer;
    (b)   an officer, official, employee or member of an independent trade union certified in writing by the trade union as competent to give advice and as authorised to do so on its behalf;
    (c)   a worker at an advice centre (whether as an employee or a volunteer) certified in writing by the centre as competent to give advice and as authorised to do so on its behalf;
    (d)   a person of such description as may be specified by order.
(5)   Despite subsection (4), none of the following is an independent adviser in relation to a qualifying compromise contract—
    (a)   a person who is a party to the contract or the complaint;
    (b)   a person who is connected to a person within paragraph (a);
    (c)   a person who is employed by a person within paragraph (a) or (b);
    (d)   a person who is acting for a person within paragraph (a) or (b) in relation to the contract or the complaint;
    (e)   a person within subsection (4)(b) or (c), if the trade union or advice centre is a person within paragraph (a) or (b);
    (f)   a person within subsection (4)(c) to whom the complainant makes a payment for the advice.
(6)   A 'qualified lawyer', for the purposes of subsection (4)(a), is—
    (a)   in relation to England and Wales, a person who, for the purposes of the Legal Services Act 2007, is an authorised person in relation to an activity which constitutes the exercise of a right of audience or the conduct of litigation;
    (b)   in relation to Scotland, an advocate (whether in practice as such or employed to give legal advice) or a solicitor who holds a practising certificate.
(7)   'Independent trade union' has the meaning given in section 5 of the Trade Union and Labour Relations (Consolidation) Act 1992.
(8)   Two persons are connected for the purposes of subsection (5) if—
    (a)   one is a company of which the other (directly or indirectly) has control, or
    (b)   both are companies of which a third person (directly or indirectly) has control.
(9)   Two persons are also connected for the purposes of subsection (5) in so far as a connection between them gives rise to a conflict of interest in relation to the contract or the complaint.

148   Interpretation
(1)   This section applies for the purposes of this Part.
(2)   A reference to treatment of a description prohibited by this Act does not include treatment in so far as it is treatment that would contravene—
    (a)   Part 1 (public sector duty regarding socio-economic inequalities), or
    (b)   Chapter 1 of Part 11 (public sector equality duty).

(3) 'Group insurance arrangement' means an arrangement between an employer and another person for the provision by that other person of facilities by way of insurance to the employer's employees (or a class of those employees).

(4) 'Collective agreement' has the meaning given in section 178 of the Trade Union and Labour Relations (Consolidation) Act 1992.

(5) A rule of an undertaking is a rule within subsection (6) or (7).

(6) A rule within this subsection is a rule made by a trade organisation or a qualifications body for application to—

    (a)   its members or prospective members,

    (b)   persons on whom it has conferred a relevant qualification, or

    (c)   persons seeking conferment by it of a relevant qualification.

(7) A rule within this subsection is a rule made by an employer for application to—

    (a)   employees,

    (b)   persons who apply for employment, or

    (c)   persons the employer considers for employment.

(8) 'Trade organisation', 'qualifications body' and 'relevant qualification' each have the meaning given in Part 5 (work).

DAMAGES (SCOTLAND) ACT 2011
(2011, asp 7)

1 Damages to injured person whose expectation of life is diminished

(1) This section applies to an action for damages in respect of personal injuries suffered by a pursuer whose date of death is expected to be earlier than had the injuries not been suffered.

(2) In assessing the amount of damages by way of solatium the court is, if the pursuer—

    (a)   was at any time,

    (b)   is, or

    (c)   is likely to become,

aware of the reduced expectation of life, to have regard to the extent to which the pursuer, in consequence of that awareness, has suffered or is likely to suffer.

(3) Subject to subsection (2), no damages by way of solatium are recoverable by the pursuer in respect of loss of expectation of life.

(4) In making an award of damages by way of solatium, the court is not required to ascribe specifically any part of the award to loss of expectation of life.

(5) In assessing the amount of any patrimonial loss in respect of the period after the date of decree the court is to assume that the pursuer will live until the date when death would have been expected had the injuries not been suffered (the 'notional date of death').

(6) Such part of that amount as is attributable to the period between the expected date of death and the notional date of death (the 'lost period') is to be assessed as follows—

    (a)   the court is to estimate what (if anything) the pursuer would have earned during the lost period through the pursuer's own labour or own gainful activity had the injuries not been suffered,

    (b)   the court may, if it thinks fit, add to the amount so estimated (whether or not that amount is nil) an amount equivalent to all or part of what it estimates the pursuer would have received by way of relevant benefits during the lost period had the injuries not been suffered, and

    (c)   the court is then to deduct, from the total amount obtained by virtue of paragraphs (a) and (b), 25% of that amount (to represent what would have been the pursuer's living expenses during the lost period had the injuries not been suffered).

(7)   But, if satisfied that it is necessary to do so for the purpose of avoiding a manifestly and materially unfair result, the court may apply a different percentage to that specified in subsection (6)(c).

(8)   In paragraph (b) of subsection (6), 'relevant benefits' means benefits in money or money's worth other than benefits—

(a)   derived from the pursuer's own estate, or

(b)   consisting of such earnings as are mentioned in paragraph (a) of that subsection.

2   Transmission of deceased's rights to executor

(1)   There are transmissible to a deceased person's executor ('E') the like rights to damages, including a right to damages for non-patrimonial loss, in respect of injuries suffered by the deceased ('A') and vested in A immediately before A's death, being—

(a)   personal injuries, or

(b)   injuries which, though not personal injuries, are—

(i)   injuries to name or reputation, or

(ii)   injuries resulting from harassment actionable under section 8 [or section 8A] of the Protection from Harassment Act 1997 (c 40).

(2)   The 'like rights' mentioned in subsection (1) do not include any right to damages by way of compensation for patrimonial loss attributable to any period after the date of death; and in determining the amount of damages for non-patrimonial loss payable to E by virtue of this section, the only period to which the court is to have regard is that ending immediately before A's death.

(3)   In so far as a right to damages vested in A comprises a right to damages for non-patrimonial loss in respect of such injuries as are mentioned in sub-paragraph (i) of subsection (1)(b), that right is transmissible to E only if an action to enforce the right is brought by A and is not concluded before A's death.

(4)   For the purposes of subsection (3) an action is not to be taken to be concluded—

(a)   while an appeal is competent, or

(b)   before any appeal taken is disposed of.

3   Application of sections 4 to 6

Sections 4 to 6 apply where a person ('A') dies in consequence of suffering personal injuries as the result of the act or omission of another person ('B') and the act or omission—

(a)   gives rise to liability to pay damages to A (or to A's executor), or

(b)   would have given rise to such liability but for A's death.

4   Sums of damages payable to relatives

(1)   B is liable under this subsection to pay—

(a)   to any relative of A who is a member of A's immediate family, such sums of damages as are mentioned in paragraphs (a) and (b) of subsection (3),

(b)   to any other relative of A, such sum of damages as is mentioned in paragraph (a) of that subsection.

(2)   But, except as provided for in section 5, no such liability arises if the liability to pay damages to A (or to A's executor) in respect of the act or omission—

(a)   is excluded or discharged, whether by antecedent agreement or otherwise, by A before A's death, or

(b)   is excluded by virtue of an enactment.

(3)   The sums of damages are—

(a)   such sum as will compensate for any loss of support which as a result of the act or omission is sustained, or is likely to be sustained, by the relative after the date of A's death together with any reasonable expenses incurred by the relative in connection with A's funeral, and

(b)   such sum, if any, as the court thinks just by way of compensation for all or any of the following—

(i)   distress and anxiety endured by the relative in contemplation of the suffering of A before A's death,

(ii)   grief and sorrow of the relative caused by A's death,

(iii)   the loss of such non-patrimonial benefit as the relative might have been expected to derive from A's society and guidance if A had not died.

(4)   The court, in making an award under paragraph (b) of subsection (3) is not required to ascribe any part of the award specifically to any of the sub-paragraphs of that paragraph.

(5)   For the purpose of subsection (1)(a)—

(a)   a relative of A is a member of A's immediate family if the relative falls within any of paragraphs (a) to (d) of the definition of 'relative' in section 14(1),

(b)   paragraphs (a)(i) and (b) of section 14(2) are to be disregarded.

5   Discharge of liability to pay damages: exception for mesothelioma

(1)   This section applies where—

(a)   the liability to pay damages to A (or to A's executor) is discharged, whether by antecedent agreement or otherwise, by A before A's death,

(b)   the personal injury in consequence of which A died is mesothelioma, and

(c)   the discharge and the death each occurred on or after 20th December 2006.

(2)   Liability arises under section 4(1) but is limited to the payment of such sum of damages as is mentioned in paragraph (b) of section 4(3).

6   Relative's loss of personal services

(1)   A relative entitled to damages under paragraph (a) of section 4(3) is entitled to include, as a head of damages under that paragraph, a reasonable sum in respect of the loss to the relative of A's personal services as a result of the act or omission.

(2)   In subsection (1), 'personal services' has the same meaning as in section 9(1) of the Administration of Justice Act 1982 (damages in respect of inability of injured person to render such services).

7   Assessment of compensation for loss of support

(1)   Such part of an award under paragraph (a) of section 4(3) as consists of a sum in compensation for loss of support is to be assessed applying the following paragraphs—

(a)   the total amount to be available to support A's relatives is an amount equivalent to 75% of A's net income,

(b)   in the case of any other relative than—

(i)   a person described in paragraph (a) of the definition of 'relative' in section 14(1), or

(ii)   a dependent child,

the relative is not to be awarded more in compensation for loss of support than the actual amount of that loss,

(c)   if—

(i)   no such other relative is awarded a sum in compensation for loss of support, the total amount mentioned in paragraph (a) is to be taken to be spent by A in supporting such of A's relatives as are mentioned in sub-paragraphs (i) and (ii) of paragraph (b),

(ii)   any such other relative is awarded a sum in compensation for loss of support, the total amount mentioned in paragraph (a) is, after deduction of the amount of the sum so awarded, to be taken to be spent by A in supporting such of A's relatives as are mentioned in those sub-paragraphs, and

(d)　any multiplier applied by the court—
　　(i)　is to run from the date of the interlocutor awarding damages, and
　　(ii)　is to apply only in respect of future loss of support.

(2)　But, if satisfied that it is necessary to do so for the purpose of avoiding a manifestly and materially unfair result, the court may apply a different percentage to that specified in subsection (1)(a).

(3)　In subsection (1)(b)(ii), 'dependent child' means a child who as at the date of A's death—
　　(a)　has not attained the age of 18 years, and
　　(b)　is owed an obligation of aliment by A.

8　Further provision as regards relative's entitlement to damages

(1)　Subject to subsection (3), in assessing for the purposes of section 4 or 6 the amount of any loss of support sustained by a relative of A no account is to be taken of—
　　(a)　any patrimonial gain or advantage which has accrued or will or may accrue to the relative, by way of succession or settlement, from A or from any other person, or
　　(b)　any insurance money, benefit, pension or gratuity which has been, or will or may be, paid as a result of A's death.

(2)　In subsection (1)—
'benefit' means benefit under the Social Security Contributions and Benefits Act 1992 or the Social Security Contributions and Benefits (Northern Ireland) Act 1992 and any payment by a friendly society or trade union for the relief or maintenance of a member's dependants,
'insurance money' includes a return of premiums, and
'pension' includes a return of contributions and any payment of a lump sum in respect of a person's employment.

(3)　Where A has been awarded a provisional award of damages under section 12(2) of the Administration of Justice Act 1982, the making of that award does not prevent liability from arising under section 4(1); but in assessing for the purposes of section 4 or 6 the amount of any loss of support sustained by a relative the court is to take into account such part of the provisional award relating to future patrimonial loss as was intended to compensate A for a period beyond the date on which A died.

(4)　In order to establish loss of support for the purposes of section 4 or 6, it is not essential for a relative to show that A was, or might have become, subject to a duty in law to provide support for, or contribute to the support of, the relative; but if any such fact is established it may be taken into account in determining whether, and if so to what extent, A would (had A not died) have been likely to provide, or contribute to, such support.

(5)　Except as provided for in this Act or in any other enactment, no person is entitled by reason of relationship to damages in respect of the death of another person.

(6)　In subsection (5), 'damages' includes damages by way of solatium.

9　Transmission of relative's rights to executor

(1)　This section applies where liability to pay damages to a relative ('R') has arisen under section 4 or 6 but R dies.

(2)　If the right to damages is vested in R immediately before R's death that right is transmissible to R's executor ('E'); but in determining the amount of damages payable to E by virtue of this section, the only period to which the court is to have regard is the period ending immediately before R's death.

(3)　In a case where—
　　(a)　section 5 applies, and
　　(b)　R died before 27th April 2007,

any right of R to damages under that section is to be taken, for the purposes of subsection (2), to have vested in R on A's death.

10 Enforcement by executor of rights transmitted under section 2 or 9

(1) Where a right is transmitted by virtue of section 2 or 9, the executor in question is entitled—

(a) to bring an action to enforce it, or

(b) if an action to enforce it was brought by the deceased but not concluded before the date of death, to be sisted as pursuer in that action.

(2) For the purposes of subsection (1)(b) an action is not to be taken to be concluded—

(a) while an appeal is competent, or

(b) before any appeal taken is disposed of.

11 Executor's claim not excluded by relative's claim etc

(1) A claim made by virtue of this Act by a deceased's executor is not excluded by a claim so made by a relative of the deceased (or by such a relative's executor).

(2) Nor is a claim so made by a such a relative (or by such a relative's executor) excluded by a claim so made by the deceased's executor.

12 Limitation of total amount of liability

(1) This section applies to an action directed against a defender ('B') in which, following the death of a person ('A') from personal injuries, damages are claimed—

(a) in respect of those injuries, by A's executor, or

(b) in respect of A's death, by any relative of A or by the executor of any relative of A.

(2) If it is shown that the liability arising in relation to B from the personal injuries in question—

(a) had before A's death, by antecedent agreement or otherwise, been limited to damages of a specified or ascertainable amount, or

(b) is so limited by virtue of an enactment,

nothing in this Act makes B liable to pay damages exceeding that amount.

(3) Accordingly, where there are two or more pursuers, any damages to which they would (but for this section) respectively be entitled under this Act are, if necessary, to be reduced pro rata.

(4) And where two or more actions are conjoined the conjoined actions are to be treated, for the purposes of this section, as if they were a single action.

13 *[Amends Administration of Justice Act 1982 s 9]*

14 Interpretation

(1) In this Act, unless the context otherwise requires—

'personal injuries' means—

(a) any disease, and

(b) any impairment of a person's physical or mental condition, and

'relative', in relation to a person who has died, means a person who—

(a) immediately before the death is the deceased's spouse or civil partner or is living with the deceased as if married to, or in civil partnership with, the deceased,

(b) is a parent or child of the deceased, accepted the deceased as a child of the person's family or was accepted by the deceased as a child of the deceased's family,

(c) is the brother or sister of the deceased or was brought up in the same household as the deceased and accepted as a child of the family in which the deceased was a child,

(d) is a grandparent or grandchild of the deceased, accepted the deceased as a grandchild of the person or was accepted by the deceased as a grandchild of the deceased,

(e)   is an ascendant or descendant of the deceased (other than a parent or grandparent or a child or grandchild of the deceased),

(f)   is an uncle or aunt of the deceased,

(g)   is a child or other issue of—

(i)   a brother or sister of the deceased, or

(ii)   an uncle or aunt of the deceased, or

(h)   is a former spouse or civil partner of the deceased having become so by virtue of divorce or (as the case may be) dissolution of the partnership.

(2)   In deducing a relationship for the purposes of the definition of 'relative' in subsection (1)—

(a)   any relationship—

(i)   by affinity is to be treated as a relationship by consanguinity,

(ii)   of the half blood is to be treated as a relationship of the whole blood,

(b)   a stepchild of a person is to be treated as the person's child.

(3)   In any enactment passed or made before this Act, unless the context otherwise requires, any reference to—

(a)   solatium in respect of the death of any person (however expressed), or

(b)   a loss of society award,

is to be construed as a reference to an award under paragraph (b) of section 4(3).

15–17   *[Amendments, repeals and savings]*

18   Transitional provision etc

(1)   The Scottish Ministers may, by order made by statutory instrument, make such incidental, supplemental, consequential, transitional, transitory or saving provision as they consider necessary or expedient for the purposes of, or in consequence of, this Act.

(2)   Subject to subsection (4), a statutory instrument containing an order under subsection (1) is subject to annulment in pursuance of a resolution of the Parliament.

(3)   An order under subsection (1) may make different provision for different cases or for different classes of case.

(4)   A statutory instrument containing an order under subsection (1) which adds to, replaces or omits any part of the text of an Act (including this Act) is not to be made unless a draft of the instrument has been—

(a)   laid before, and

(b)   approved by resolution of, the Parliament.

19   Short title, Crown application and commencement

(1)   This Act may be cited as the Damages (Scotland) Act 2011.

(2)   This Act binds the Crown.

(3)   The provisions of this Act, except section 18 and this section, come into force on such day as the Scottish Ministers may by order made by statutory instrument appoint.

(4)   An order under subsection (3) may include such transitional, transitory or saving provision as the Scottish Ministers consider necessary or expedient in connection with the commencement of this Act.

DEFAMATION ACT 2013
(2013 c 26)

6   Peer-reviewed statement in scientific or academic journal etc

(1)   The publication of a statement in a scientific or academic journal (whether published in electronic form or otherwise) is privileged if the following conditions are met.

(2)   The first condition is that the statement relates to a scientific or academic matter.

(3)   The second condition is that before the statement was published in the journal an independent review of the statement's scientific or academic merit was carried out by—

(a)   the editor of the journal, and

(b)   one or more persons with expertise in the scientific or academic matter concerned.

(4)   Where the publication of a statement in a scientific or academic journal is privileged by virtue of subsection (1), the publication in the same journal of any assessment of the statement's scientific or academic merit is also privileged if—

(a)   the assessment was written by one or more of the persons who carried out the independent review of the statement; and

(b)   the assessment was written in the course of that review.

(5)   Where the publication of a statement or assessment is privileged by virtue of this section, the publication of a fair and accurate copy of, extract from or summary of the statement or assessment is also privileged.

(6)   A publication is not privileged by virtue of this section if it is shown to be made with malice.

(7)   Nothing in this section is to be construed—

(a)   as protecting the publication of matter the publication of which is prohibited by law;

(b)   as limiting any privilege subsisting apart from this section.

(8)   The reference in subsection (3)(a) to 'the editor of the journal' is to be read, in the case of a journal with more than one editor, as a reference to the editor or editors who were responsible for deciding to publish the statement concerned.

15   Meaning of 'publish' and 'statement'

In this Act—

'publish and 'publication', in relation to a statement, have the meaning they have for the purposes of the law of defamation generally;

'statement' means words, pictures, visual images, gestures or any other method of signifying meaning.

MESOTHELIOMA ACT 2014
(2014, c 1)

Diffuse Mesothelioma Payment Scheme

1   Power to establish the scheme

(1)   The Secretary of State may by regulations establish a scheme called the Diffuse Mesothelioma Payment Scheme for making payments to—

    (a)   eligible people with diffuse mesothelioma, and

    (b)   eligible dependants of those who have died with diffuse mesothelioma.

(2)   Later sections of this Act set out things that must be included in the scheme and some of the things that may be included.

Eligibility

2   Eligible people with diffuse mesothelioma

(1)   A person diagnosed with diffuse mesothelioma is eligible for a payment under the scheme if—

    (a)   a relevant employer has negligently or in breach of statutory duty caused or permitted the person to be exposed to asbestos,

    (b)   the person was first diagnosed with the disease on or after 25 July 2012,

    (c)   the person has not brought an action for damages in respect of the disease against the relevant employer or any insurer with whom the employer maintained employers' liability insurance at the time of the person's exposure to asbestos,

    (d)   the person is unable to bring an action for damages in respect of the disease against any employer of the person or any insurer with whom such an employer maintained employers' liability insurance (because they cannot be found or no longer exist or for any other reason), and

    (e)   the person has not received damages or a specified payment in respect of the disease and is not eligible to receive a specified payment.

(2)   In this section—

'first diagnosed' has the meaning to be given to it by the scheme;

'relevant employer' means an employer who, at the time of the person's exposure to asbestos—

    (a)   was required by the compulsory insurance legislation to maintain insurance covering any liability arising because of the exposure to asbestos, or

    (b)   would have been required by the compulsory insurance legislation to maintain insurance covering any liability arising because of the exposure to asbestos if the legislation had been in force at that time;

'specified payment' has the meaning to be given to it by the scheme.

3   Eligible dependants

(1)   A dependant of a person who has died with diffuse mesothelioma is eligible for a payment under the scheme if —

    (a)   the person with the disease was eligible for a payment under the scheme (see section 2) but did not make an application in accordance with the scheme,

    (b)   no one has brought an action for damages in respect of the disease under the fatal accidents legislation, or on behalf of the estate of the person with the disease, against the relevant employer or any insurer with whom the employer maintained employers' liability insurance at the time of that person's exposure to asbestos,

    (c)   no one is able to bring an action for damages in respect of the disease under the fatal accidents legislation, or on behalf of the estate of the person with the disease, against any employer of that person or any insurer with whom such an employer maintained employers' liability insurance (because they cannot be found or no longer exist or for any other reason), and

(d)   no one has received damages or a specified payment in respect of the disease or is eligible to receive a specified payment.

(2)   Where a person who has died with diffuse mesothelioma is first diagnosed with the disease following his or her death and would have been eligible for a payment under the scheme if the diagnosis had been made immediately before the death, assume for the purposes of subsection (1)(a) that the person was eligible for a payment under the scheme.

(3)   A person ceases to be an eligible dependant if the person gives notice in accordance with the scheme that he or she does not want a payment (and this may increase a payment for other dependants – see section 4(2)(b)).

(4)   Where a person with diffuse mesothelioma died on or after 25 July 2012 but before this Act came into force, assume for the purposes of subsections (1)(a) and (2) that this Act has been in force since immediately before the death.

(5)   In this section—

'first diagnosed' has the meaning to be given to it by the scheme;

'specified payment' has the meaning to be given to it by the scheme.

Payments and procedure

4   Payments

(1)   The amount of a payment under the scheme is to be determined in accordance with the scheme.

(2)   The scheme—

(a)   may provide for the amount of the payment to depend on the age of the person with diffuse mesothelioma, and

(b)   must ensure that where there are two or more eligible dependants, the amount for each of them is the amount for a single eligible dependant divided by the number of eligible dependants in the case in question.

(3)   The scheme may—

(a)   make provision for payments to be made subject to conditions (including conditions as to how a payment may be used), and

(b)   in particular, give the scheme administrator power to decide when to impose conditions or what conditions to impose.

(4)   The scheme may make provision for payments to be repaid (in whole or in part) in specified circumstances.

(5)   An amount that falls to be repaid under subsection (4) is recoverable by the scheme administrator as a debt.

(6)   The scheme must provide that where an eligible person has made an application in accordance with the scheme and has died before the payment is made, the payment must be made to his or her personal representatives.

5   Applications and procedure

(1)   The scheme may deal with the procedure for the making and deciding of applications and, in particular, may—

(a)   impose time limits for making an application or taking other steps;

(b)   enable the scheme administrator to require a person to produce documents;

(c)   make other provision about evidence.

(2)   The scheme may enable a court to order a person to comply with a requirement to produce documents.

6   Reviews and appeals

(1)   The scheme—

(a)   must give an applicant the right to request a review of a decision taken under the scheme, and

(b)   may require or allow reviews in other circumstances.

(2)   The scheme may contain provision about initiating and deciding reviews (including provision imposing time limits).

(3)   The scheme must confer a right of appeal to the First-tier Tribunal against a decision taken on a review.

(4)   In a case where a person makes an application and then dies, the reference in subsection (1)(a) to an applicant is to be read as a reference to his or her personal representatives.

Scheme administration

7   Scheme administration

(1)   The Secretary of State may—
  (a)   administer the scheme, or
  (b)   make arrangements for a body to administer the scheme.

(2)   Arrangements under subsection (1)(b)—
  (a)   may include provision for payments by the Secretary of State;
  (b)   may allow the body to arrange for someone else to administer the scheme or any part of the scheme on behalf of the body;
  (c)   may include provision about bringing the arrangements to an end.

(3)   Arrangements under subsection (1)(b) may be made with—
  (a)   a company formed by the Secretary of State under the Companies Act 2006 for that purpose,
  (b)   a body corporate established by the Secretary of State by regulations under this paragraph for that purpose, or
  (c)   any other body.

(4)   A body administering the scheme in accordance with arrangements under subsection (1)(b) is not to be regarded as exercising functions of the Secretary of State or as acting on behalf of the Secretary of State.

(5)   The Secretary of State may by regulations make transitional provision for when there is a change in the scheme administrator (including provision modifying the application of any enactment).

(6)   For the purposes of this Act, a reference to administering the scheme includes carrying out any functions conferred by or under any enactment on the scheme administrator.

8   Unauthorised disclosure of information: offence

(1)   A person involved in the administration of the scheme must not, without lawful authority, disclose information which—
  (a)   was acquired in connection with the administration of the scheme, and
  (b)   relates to a particular person who is identified in the information or whose identity could be deduced from it.

(2)   A disclosure is made with 'lawful authority' only if—
  (a)   it is made for the purposes of the administration of the scheme,
  (b)   it is made for the purpose of preventing or detecting crime,
  (c)   it is made in accordance with any enactment or an order of a court or tribunal,
  (d)   it is made for the purposes of proceedings before a court or tribunal, or
  (e)   it is made with consent given by or on behalf of the person to whom the information relates or the person's personal representatives.

(3)   A person who breaches subsection (1) commits an offence (for penalties, see section 9).

(4)   It is a defence for a person charged with the offence under subsection (3) to prove that he or she reasonably believed—
  (a)   that the disclosure was made with lawful authority, or
  (b)   that someone had, with lawful authority, previously disclosed the information to the public.

(5)   In this section 'person involved in the administration of the scheme' means a person who is or has been—

(a)   the scheme administrator,

(b)   a person providing services to the scheme administrator, or

(c)   an officer or employee of a person within paragraph (a) or (b).

9   Unauthorised disclosure of information: penalties etc

(1)   A person guilty of an offence under section 8 is liable on conviction on indictment to imprisonment for a term not exceeding two years or a fine or both.

(2)   A person guilty of an offence under section 8 is liable—

(a)   on summary conviction in England and Wales, to imprisonment for a term not exceeding 12 months or a fine;

(b)   on summary conviction in Scotland, to imprisonment for a term not exceeding 12 months or a fine not exceeding the statutory maximum or both;

(c)   on summary conviction in Northern Ireland, to imprisonment for a term not exceeding 6 months or a fine not exceeding the statutory maximum or both.

(3)   The court by or before which a person is convicted of an offence under section 8 may order the destruction of a document containing the information disclosed in breach of that section or, if the information disclosed is held in some other form, may order its erasure.

(4)   Where an offence under section 8 committed by a body corporate—

(a)   is committed with the consent or connivance of an officer, or

(b)   is attributable to neglect on the part of an officer,

the officer as well as the body corporate is guilty of the offence.

(5)   Where an offence under section 8 committed by a Scottish partnership—

(a)   is committed with the consent or connivance of a partner, or

(b)   is attributable to neglect on the part of a partner,

the partner as well as the Scottish partnership is guilty of the offence.

(6)   In this section—

'director', in relation to a body corporate whose affairs are managed by its members, means a member of the body corporate;

'officer', in relation to a body corporate, means—

(a)   a director, manager, secretary or other similar officer of the body corporate, or

(b)   a person purporting to act in any such a capacity;

'partner', in relation to a Scottish partnership, includes any person who was purporting to act as a partner in the partnership.

(7)   In relation to an offence committed in England and Wales before section 154(1) of the Criminal Justice Act 2003 comes into force, the reference in subsection (2)(a) above to '12 months' is to be read as a reference to '6 months'.

(8)   In relation to an offence committed in England and Wales before section 85 of the Legal Aid, Sentencing and Punishment of Offenders Act 2012 comes into force, the reference in subsection (2)(a) above to a fine is to be read as a reference to a fine not exceeding the statutory maximum.

Recovery of payments etc

10   Power of scheme administrator to help people bring proceedings

(1)   Where a payment is made under the scheme, the scheme administrator may help a person to bring relevant proceedings (for example by conducting proceedings or by giving advice or financial help).

(2)   'Relevant proceedings' means—

(a)   proceedings by the person with diffuse mesothelioma against—

(i)   an employer for the negligence or breach of statutory duty mentioned in section 2(1)(a), or

(ii)   an insurer with whom the employer maintained insurance covering that liability,

(b)   proceedings by any other person against the employer or insurer for damages under the fatal accidents legislation in respect of the death of the person with diffuse mesothelioma, or

(c)   any appeal arising out of proceedings within paragraph (a) or (b).

(3)   In subsection (2) a reference to a person includes a reference to his or her personal representatives.

(4)   The scheme may include provision about the scheme administrator's functions under this section, including provision as to the circumstances in which the scheme administrator may help a person to bring proceedings.

(5)   The Secretary of State may by regulations amend subsection (2) to include other proceedings (which may be proceedings against someone other than an employer or insurer).

11   Recovery of benefits etc from payments and recovery of payments

Schedule 1 contains amendments to other legislation. Broadly—

Part 1 allows benefits and other sums to be recovered from scheme payments,

Part 2 allows scheme payments to be recovered from compensation, and

Part 3 contains related amendments to do with information sharing.

Relationship with other legislation

12   Exclusion of payments under other legislation

Schedule 2 contains amendments to other legislation to ensure that where an application is made under the scheme a person does not receive certain other payments.

Levy on insurers

13   The levy

(1)   The Secretary of State must make regulations requiring active insurers to pay a levy with a view to meeting the costs of the Diffuse Mesothelioma Payment Scheme during any given period.

(2)   In deciding the total amount of the levy for a period the Secretary of State—

(a)   may take account of estimated as well as actual costs;

(b)   may deduct the amount of any sums recovered or expected to be recovered under the recovery of benefits legislation during the period in respect of scheme payments made during the period or before it.

(3)   In deciding the total amount of the first levy the Secretary of State may reduce it to reflect any amount of costs to be met by the Secretary of State.

(4)   In deciding the total amount of the levy for each of the first 4 periods, the Secretary of State must have regard to the desirability of the total amount of the levy for each of those periods being the same (or if those periods are not equal, the same pro rata) even if that means the amount for a period does not match the costs for that particular period.

(5)   The regulations may require different active insurers to pay different amounts based on criteria relating to their relative market share in the reference period (and may provide for their relative market share to be determined in whatever way the Secretary of State thinks appropriate).

(6)   The regulations may make provision about—

(a)   information to be published or given to active insurers by the Secretary of State;

(b)   payment of the levy, including the timing of payments;

(c)   recovery of the levy.

(7)   In this section—

'active insurer' means a person who, at any time during the reference period, was an authorised insurer within the meaning of the compulsory insurance legislation;

'the costs of the Diffuse Mesothelioma Payment Scheme' means—

(a)   the cost of payments under the scheme,

(b)   the costs of administering the scheme, and

(c)   any costs incurred by the Secretary of State to establish a body with whom to make arrangements under section 7(1)(b);

'the recovery of benefits legislation' means—

(a)   the Social Security (Recovery of Benefits) Act 1997, or

(b)   the Social Security (Recovery of Benefits) (Northern Ireland) Order 1997 (SI 1997/1183 (NI 12));

'reference period' means a 12-month period determined in accordance with the regulations, and a reference period may be a period before this Act was passed.

14   Collecting information for purposes of levy

(1)   The Secretary of State may require an active insurer to provide information for the purposes of working out how much to require different insurers to pay towards the levy under section 13.

(2)   If the active insurer fails without reasonable excuse to comply with the requirement the relevant court may, on an application made by the Secretary of State, order the active insurer to comply with the requirement.

(3)   The relevant court may also order the active insurer to give the Secretary of State other information that the insurer could be required to provide under subsection (1).

(4)   In this section 'the relevant court' means—

(a)   the High Court in England and Wales or Northern Ireland, or

(b)   the Court of Session in Scotland.

Insurance disputes

15   Technical Committee to decide certain insurance disputes

(1)   The Secretary of State may make arrangements with a body to establish a committee called the Technical Committee which, if established in accordance with the arrangements, has the functions given by this section.

(2)   If a question arises between a potential insurance claimant and an insurer about whether an employer maintained employers' liability insurance with the insurer at a particular time, the Technical Committee has jurisdiction to decide that question.

(3)   The Technical Committee's decision is binding on the insurer and any potential insurance claimant who was given an opportunity to make representations, unless the matter is referred to arbitration under section 16.

(4)   The Technical Committee does not have jurisdiction to decide a question that has already been decided by a court.

(5)   A certificate by the Secretary of State that a specified committee has been established in accordance with arrangements under subsection (1) is conclusive evidence of that fact in relation to the period for which the certificate is in force.

(6)   Arrangements under subsection (1) may, in particular, include requirements about—

(a)   the composition of the Technical Committee or the appointment of its members;

(b)   the Technical Committee's procedure or how its procedure is to be determined (including requirements for its procedures to be approved by the Secretary of State);

(c)   review by the Technical Committee of its own decisions.

(7)   The Technical Committee's procedure may, in particular, include provision imposing time limits for making an application for a decision or the taking of other steps.

(8)   In this section 'potential insurance claimant' means—

(a)   a person with diffuse mesothelioma who alleges that the employer is liable for damages in respect of the disease,

(b)   a person who alleges that the employer is liable for damages under the fatal accidents legislation in respect of the death of a person with diffuse mesothelioma, or

(c)   an employer alleged by a person within paragraph (a) or (b) to be liable for damages in respect of the disease or death.

(9)   In subsection (8) a reference to a person includes a reference to his or her personal representatives.

16   Challenging decisions of the Technical Committee

(1)   If the Technical Committee has decided a question under section 15(2), any person on whom the decision is binding may, if dissatisfied with the decision, refer the question to arbitration.

(2)   But a person may not refer a question to arbitration until any review process has been exhausted.

(3)' For statutory arbitrations, see—

(a)   sections 94 to 98 of the Arbitration Act 1996;

(b)   sections 16 and 17 of the Arbitration (Scotland) Act 2010.

(4)   Until the Arbitration (Scotland) Act 2010 is in force in relation to arbitrations under this section, that Act applies as if it were in force in relation to arbitrations under this section.

(5)   The Secretary of State may by regulations adapt or exclude any provision of the Arbitration (Scotland) Act 2010 in relation to arbitrations under this section (and this power may be used in relation to the 2010 Act during the period when it applies because of subsection (4) of this section or otherwise).

General

17   Regulations under this Act

(1)   Regulations under this Act are to be made by statutory instrument.

(2)   A statutory instrument containing—

(a)   the first regulations under section 1 (the scheme), or

(b)   regulations under section 7(3)(b) or 10,

may not be made unless a draft of the instrument has been laid before and approved by a resolution of each House of Parliament.

(3)   Any other statutory instrument containing regulations under this Act is subject to annulment in pursuance of a resolution of either House of Parliament, unless it contains regulations under section 7(5) only.

(4)   Regulations under this Act may include incidental, supplementary, consequential, transitional, transitory or saving provision.

18   Defined terms used in more than one section of this Act

(1)   In this Act—

'application' means an application for a payment under the scheme;

'active insurer' has the meaning given by section 13;

'the compulsory insurance legislation' means—

(a)   the Employers' Liability (Compulsory Insurance) Act 1969, or

(b)   the Employer's Liability (Defective Equipment and Compulsory Insurance) (Northern Ireland) Order 1972 (SI 1972/963 (NI 6));

'damages' includes a payment in settlement of a claim for damages;

'dependant', in relation to a person who has died with diffuse mesothelioma, has the meaning given by section 3(1) of the Pneumoconiosis etc (Workers' Compensation) Act 1979 (reading the reference to the Secretary of State as a reference to the scheme administrator);

'employers' liability insurance', in relation to an employer and a particular time, means insurance that the employer—

(a)   was required by the compulsory insurance legislation to maintain at that time, or

(b)   would have been required by the compulsory insurance legislation to maintain if that legislation had been in force at that time;

'the fatal accidents legislation' means—

(a)   the Fatal Accidents Act 1976,

(b)   the Fatal Accidents (Northern Ireland) Order 1977 (SI 1977/1251 (NI 18)), or

(c)   section 4 of the Damages (Scotland) Act 2011;

'levy' means a levy under section 13;

'relevant employer' has the meaning given by section 2;

'the scheme' means the Diffuse Mesothelioma Payment Scheme;

'scheme administrator' means the person for the time being administering the scheme (see section 7);

'the Technical Committee' means a committee established in accordance with arrangements under section 15.

(2)   In determining for the purposes of this Act whether an employer would have been required to maintain insurance if the compulsory insurance legislation had been in force at any given time, assume that any exemption that has at any time applied under the following provisions applied at the time in question—

(a)   section 3(1)(a) to (c) of the Employers' Liability (Compulsory Insurance) Act 1969, and

(b)   Article 7(a) to (c) of the Employer's Liability (Defective Equipment and Compulsory Insurance) (Northern Ireland) Order 1972.

(3)   The scheme may specify circumstances in which a person is, or is not, to be treated as able to bring an action for the purposes of section 2(1)(d) or 3(1)(c).

19   Commencement

(1)   This Act comes into force on such day or days as the Secretary of State may by order appoint, subject as follows.

(2)   This section and sections 20 and 21 come into force on the day on which this Act is passed.

(3)   The Secretary of State may by order make transitional, transitory or saving provision in connection with the coming into force of any provision of this Act.

(4)   An order under subsection (1) may appoint different days for different purposes.

(5)   An order under this section is to be made by statutory instrument.

20   Extent

(1)   This Act extends to—

(a)   England and Wales,

(b)   Scotland, and

(c)   Northern Ireland.

(2)   Any amendment or repeal made by this Act has the same extent as the enactment to which it relates.

21   Short title

This Act may be cited as the Mesothelioma Act 2014.

LEGAL WRITINGS (COUNTERPARTS AND DELIVERY) (SCOTLAND) ACT 2015
(2015, asp 4)

Execution of documents in counterpart

1   Execution of documents in counterpart

(1)   A document may be executed in counterpart.

(2)   A document is executed in counterpart if—

(a)   it is executed in two or more duplicate, interchangeable, parts, and

(b)   no part is subscribed by both or all parties.

(3)   On such execution, the counterparts are to be treated as a single document.

(4)   That single document may be made up of—

(a)   both or all the counterparts in their entirety, or

(b)   one of the counterparts in its entirety, collated with the page or pages on which the other counterpart has, or other counterparts have, been subscribed.

(5)   A document executed in counterpart becomes effective when—

(a)   both or all the counterparts have been delivered in accordance with subsection (6) or (7), and

(b)   any other step required by an enactment or rule of law for the document to become effective has been taken.

(6)   Each counterpart is to be delivered to the party or parties who did not subscribe the counterpart in question unless it is a counterpart which falls to be delivered under subsection (7).

(7)   If a party has, under section 2(1), nominated a person to take delivery of one or more counterparts, the counterpart in question is (or counterparts in question are) to be delivered to that person.

(8)   Subsection (5) is subject to subsection (9).

(9)   Where a counterpart is to be held by the recipient as undelivered, the counterpart is not to be treated as delivered for the purposes of subsection (5)(a) until—

(a)   the person from whom the counterpart is received indicates to the recipient that it is to be so treated, or

(b)   if a specified condition is to be satisfied before the counterpart may be so treated, the condition has been satisfied.

2   Nomination of person to take delivery of counterparts

(1)   Parties to a document executed in counterpart may nominate a person to take delivery of one or more of the counterparts.

(2)   Subsection (1) does not prevent one of the parties, or an agent of one or more of the parties, being so nominated.

(3)   A person so nominated must, after taking delivery of a counterpart by virtue of subsection (1), hold and preserve it for the benefit of the parties.

(4)   Subsection (3) does not apply in so far as the parties may agree, or be taken to have agreed, otherwise (whether before or after the document has effect).

(5)   A document's having effect is not dependent on compliance with subsection (3) or (4).

3   Use of counterparts: electronic documents

(1)   Sections 1 and 2 apply to traditional documents and electronic documents.

(2)   In section 1 any reference to subscription is to be read, in the case of an electronic document to which section 1(2) of the Requirements of Writing (Scotland) Act 1995 ('the 1995 Act') applies, as a reference to authentication of the electronic document within the meaning of section 9B of the 1995 Act.

(3)   In this section—

'electronic document' has the meaning given by section 9A of the 1995 Act,

'traditional document' has the meaning given by section 1A of the 1995 Act.

Delivery of traditional documents by electronic means

4   Delivery of traditional documents by electronic means

(1)   This section applies where there is a requirement for delivery of a traditional document (whether or not a document executed in counterpart).

(2)   The requirement may be satisfied by delivery by electronic means of—

(a)   a copy of the document, or

(b)   a part of such a copy.

(3)   But the requirement may be satisfied by delivery of a part of such a copy only if the part—

(a)   is sufficient in all the circumstances to show that it is part of the document, and

(b)   is, or includes, the page on which the sender (or the person on whose behalf the sender has effected the delivery) has subscribed the document.

(4)   Delivery under subsection (2) must be by a means (and what is delivered must be in a form) which the intended recipient has agreed to accept (the 'accepted method'), unless subsection (5) applies.

(5)   If—

(a)   no accepted method has been agreed,

(b)   there is uncertainty about the accepted method, or

(c)   the accepted method is impracticable,

delivery may be by such means (and in such form) as is reasonable in all the circumstances.

(6)   Although delivery by electronic means constitutes effective delivery in relation to a traditional document, what is received by that means is not to be treated as being the traditional document itself.

(7)   A traditional document, in relation to which delivery by electronic means has been effected, is to be held by the sender in accordance with whatever arrangements have been made by the sender and the recipient (or, if there is a number of recipients, have been made by the sender and the recipients as a group).

(8)   Any reference in subsection (7) to a recipient is to be construed, in a case where a person takes delivery by virtue of section 2(1), as a reference to the parties who nominated that person.

(9)   In this section, references to delivery by electronic means are to delivery—

(a)   by means of an electronic communications network (for example as an attachment to an e-mail),

(b)   by fax,

(c)   by means of a device on which the thing delivered is stored electronically (such as a disc, a memory stick or other removable or portable media), or

(d)   by other means but in a form which requires the use of electronic apparatus by the recipient to render the thing delivered intelligible.

(10)   In this section—

'electronic communications network' has the meaning given by section 32 of the Communications Act 2003,

'traditional document' has the meaning given by section 1A of the 1995 Act.

Final provisions

5   Ancillary provision

(1)   The Scottish Ministers may by order make such incidental, supplementary, consequential, transitional, transitory or saving provision as they consider appropriate for the purposes of, in connection with or for giving full effect to this Act.

(2)   An order under subsection (1) may modify any enactment (including this Act).

(3) An order under subsection (1) is subject to the negative procedure, unless subsection (4) applies.

(4) An order under subsection (1) which adds to, replaces or omits the text of an Act is subject to the affirmative procedure.

6 Commencement

(1) Section 5, this section and section 7 come into force on the day after Royal Assent.

(2) The other provisions of this Act come into force on such day as the Scottish Ministers may by order appoint.

(3) An order under subsection (2) may include transitional, transitory or saving provision.

7 Short title

The short title of this Act is the Legal Writings (Counterparts and Delivery) (Scotland) Act 2015.

CONSUMER RIGHTS ACT 2015
(2015, c 15)

PART 1
CONSUMER CONTRACTS FOR GOODS, DIGITAL CONTENT AND SERVICES

CHAPTER 1
Introduction

1 Where Part 1 applies

(1) This Part applies where there is an agreement between a trader and a consumer for the trader to supply goods, digital content or services, if the agreement is a contract.

(2) It applies whether the contract is written or oral or implied from the parties' conduct, or more than one of these combined.

(3) Any of Chapters 2, 3 and 4 may apply to a contract—
  (a) if it is a contract for the trader to supply goods, see Chapter 2;
  (b) if it is a contract for the trader to supply digital content, see Chapter 3 (also, subsection (6));
  (c) if it is a contract for the trader to supply a service, see Chapter 4 (also, subsection (6)).

(4) In each case the Chapter applies even if the contract also covers something covered by another Chapter (a mixed contract).

(5) Two or all three of those Chapters may apply to a mixed contract.

(6) For provisions about particular mixed contracts, see—
  (a) section 15 (goods and installation);
  (b) section 16 (goods and digital content).

(7) For other provision applying to contracts to which this Part applies, see Part 2 (unfair terms).

2 Key definitions

(1) These definitions apply in this Part (as well as the definitions in section 59).

(2) 'Trader' means a person acting for purposes relating to that person's trade, business, craft or profession, whether acting personally or through another person acting in the trader's name or on the trader's behalf.

(3) 'Consumer' means an individual acting for purposes that are wholly or mainly outside that individual's trade, business, craft or profession.

(4) A trader claiming that an individual was not acting for purposes wholly or mainly outside the individual's trade, business, craft or profession must prove it.

(5)   For the purposes of Chapter 2, except to the extent mentioned in subsection (6), a person is not a consumer in relation to a sales contract if—

(a)   the goods are second hand goods sold at public auction, and

(b)   individuals have the opportunity of attending the sale in person.

(6)   A person is a consumer in relation to such a contract for the purposes of—

(a)   sections 11(4) and (5), 12, 28 and 29, and

(b)   the other provisions of Chapter 2 as they apply in relation to those sections.

(7)   'Business' includes the activities of any government department or local or public authority.

(8)   'Goods' means any tangible moveable items, but that includes water, gas and electricity if and only if they are put up for supply in a limited volume or set quantity.

(9)   'Digital content' means data which are produced and supplied in digital form.

CHAPTER 2
Goods

What goods contracts are covered?

3   Contracts covered by this Chapter

(1)   This Chapter applies to a contract for a trader to supply goods to a consumer.

(2)   It applies only if the contract is one of these (defined for the purposes of this Part in sections 5 to 8)—

(a)   a sales contract;

(b)   a contract for the hire of goods;

(c)   a hire-purchase agreement;

(d)   a contract for transfer of goods.

(3)   It does not apply—

(a)   to a contract for a trader to supply coins or notes to a consumer for use as currency;

(b)   to a contract for goods to be sold by way of execution or otherwise by authority of law;

(c)   to a contract intended to operate as a mortgage, pledge, charge or other security;

(d)   in relation to England and Wales or Northern Ireland, to a contract made by deed and for which the only consideration is the presumed consideration imported by the deed;

(e)   in relation to Scotland, to a gratuitous contract.

(4)   A contract to which this Chapter applies is referred to in this Part as a 'contract to supply goods'.

(5)   Contracts to supply goods include—

(a)   contracts entered into between one part owner and another;

(b)   contracts for the transfer of an undivided share in goods;

(c)   contracts that are absolute and contracts that are conditional.

(6)   Subsection (1) is subject to any provision of this Chapter that applies a section or part of a section to only some of the kinds of contracts listed in subsection (2).

(7)   A mixed contract (see section 1(4)) may be a contract of any of those kinds.

4   Ownership of goods

(1)   In this Chapter ownership of goods means the general property in goods, not merely a special property.

(2)   For the time when ownership of goods is transferred, see in particular the

following provisions of the Sale of Goods Act 1979 (which relate to contracts of sale)—

section 16: goods must be ascertained

section 17: property passes when intended to pass

section 18: rules for ascertaining intention

section 19: reservation of right of disposal

section 20A: undivided shares in goods forming part of a bulk

section 20B: deemed consent by co-owner to dealings in bulk goods

5 Sales contracts

(1)   A contract is a sales contract if under it—

(a)   the trader transfers or agrees to transfer ownership of goods to the consumer, and

(b)   the consumer pays or agrees to pay the price.

(2)   A contract is a sales contract (whether or not it would be one under subsection (1)) if under the contract—

(a)   goods are to be manufactured or produced and the trader agrees to supply them to the consumer,

(b)   on being supplied, the goods will be owned by the consumer, and

(c)   the consumer pays or agrees to pay the price.

(3)   A sales contract may be conditional (see section 3(5)), but in this Part 'conditional sales contract' means a sales contract under which—

(a)   the price for the goods or part of it is payable by instalments, and

(b)   the trader retains ownership of the goods until the conditions specified in the contract (for the payment of instalments or otherwise) are met;

and it makes no difference whether or not the consumer possesses the goods.

6 Contracts for the hire of goods

(1)   A contract is for the hire of goods if under it the trader gives or agrees to give the consumer possession of the goods with the right to use them, subject to the terms of the contract, for a period determined in accordance with the contract.

(2)   But a contract is not for the hire of goods if it is a hire-purchase agreement.

7 Hire-purchase agreements

(1)   A contract is a hire-purchase agreement if it meets the two conditions set out below.

(2)   The first condition is that under the contract goods are hired by the trader in return for periodical payments by the consumer (and 'hired' is to be read in accordance with section 6(1)).

(3)   The second condition is that under the contract ownership of the goods will transfer to the consumer if the terms of the contract are complied with and—

(a)   the consumer exercises an option to buy the goods,

(b)   any party to the contract does an act specified in it, or

(c)   an event specified in the contract occurs.

(4)   But a contract is not a hire-purchase agreement if it is a conditional sales contract.

8 Contracts for transfer of goods

A contract to supply goods is a contract for transfer of goods if under it the trader transfers or agrees to transfer ownership of the goods to the consumer and—

(a)   the consumer provides or agrees to provide consideration otherwise than by paying a price, or

(b)   the contract is, for any other reason, not a sales contract or a hire-purchase agreement.

What statutory rights are there under a goods contract?

9 Goods to be of satisfactory quality

(1) Every contract to supply goods is to be treated as including a term that the quality of the goods is satisfactory.

(2) The quality of goods is satisfactory if they meet the standard that a reasonable person would consider satisfactory, taking account of—

(a) any description of the goods,

(b) the price or other consideration for the goods (if relevant), and

(c) all the other relevant circumstances (see subsection (5)).

(3) The quality of goods includes their state and condition; and the following aspects (among others) are in appropriate cases aspects of the quality of goods—

(a) fitness for all the purposes for which goods of that kind are usually supplied;

(b) appearance and finish;

(c) freedom from minor defects;

(d) safety;

(e) durability.

(4) The term mentioned in subsection (1) does not cover anything which makes the quality of the goods unsatisfactory—

(a) which is specifically drawn to the consumer's attention before the contract is made,

(b) where the consumer examines the goods before the contract is made, which that examination ought to reveal, or

(c) in the case of a contract to supply goods by sample, which would have been apparent on a reasonable examination of the sample.

(5) The relevant circumstances mentioned in subsection (2)(c) include any public statement about the specific characteristics of the goods made by the trader, the producer or any representative of the trader or the producer.

(6) That includes, in particular, any public statement made in advertising or labelling.

(7) But a public statement is not a relevant circumstance for the purposes of subsection (2)(c) if the trader shows that—

(a) when the contract was made, the trader was not, and could not reasonably have been, aware of the statement,

(b) before the contract was made, the statement had been publicly withdrawn or, to the extent that it contained anything which was incorrect or misleading, it had been publicly corrected, or

(c) the consumer's decision to contract for the goods could not have been influenced by the statement.

(8) In a contract to supply goods a term about the quality of the goods may be treated as included as a matter of custom.

(9) See section 19 for a consumer's rights if the trader is in breach of a term that this section requires to be treated as included in a contract.

10 Goods to be fit for particular purpose

(1) Subsection (3) applies to a contract to supply goods if before the contract is made the consumer makes known to the trader (expressly or by implication) any particular purpose for which the consumer is contracting for the goods.

(2) Subsection (3) also applies to a contract to supply goods if—

(a) the goods were previously sold by a credit-broker to the trader,

(b) in the case of a sales contract or contract for transfer of goods, the consideration or part of it is a sum payable by instalments, and

(c) before the contract is made, the consumer makes known to the credit-broker (expressly or by implication) any particular purpose for which the consumer is contracting for the goods.

(3) The contract is to be treated as including a term that the goods are reason-

ably fit for that purpose, whether or not that is a purpose for which goods of that kind are usually supplied.

(4)   Subsection (3) does not apply if the circumstances show that the consumer does not rely, or it is unreasonable for the consumer to rely, on the skill or judgment of the trader or credit-broker.

(5)   In a contract to supply goods a term about the fitness of the goods for a particular purpose may be treated as included as a matter of custom.

(6)   See section 19 for a consumer's rights if the trader is in breach of a term that this section requires to be treated as included in a contract.

11   Goods to be as described

(1)   Every contract to supply goods by description is to be treated as including a term that the goods will match the description.

(2)   If the supply is by sample as well as by description, it is not sufficient that the bulk of the goods matches the sample if the goods do not also match the description.

(3)   A supply of goods is not prevented from being a supply by description just because—

(a)   the goods are exposed for supply, and

(b)   they are selected by the consumer.

(4)   Any information that is provided by the trader about the goods and is information mentioned in paragraph (a) of Schedule 1 or 2 to the Consumer Contracts (Information, Cancellation and Additional Charges) Regulations 2013 (SI 2013/3134) (main characteristics of goods) is to be treated as included as a term of the contract.

(5)   A change to any of that information, made before entering into the contract or later, is not effective unless expressly agreed between the consumer and the trader.

(6)   See section 2(5) and (6) for the application of subsections (4) and (5) where goods are sold at public auction.

(7)   See section 19 for a consumer's rights if the trader is in breach of a term that this section requires to be treated as included in a contract.

12   Other pre-contract information included in contract

(1)   This section applies to any contract to supply goods.

(2)   Where regulation 9, 10 or 13 of the Consumer Contracts (Information, Cancellation and Additional Charges) Regulations 2013 (SI 2013/3134) required the trader to provide information to the consumer before the contract became binding, any of that information that was provided by the trader other than information about the goods and mentioned in paragraph (a) of Schedule 1 or 2 to the Regulations (main characteristics of goods) is to be treated as included as a term of the contract.

(3)   A change to any of that information, made before entering into the contract or later, is not effective unless expressly agreed between the consumer and the trader.

(4)   See section 2(5) and (6) for the application of this section where goods are sold at public auction.

(5)   See section 19 for a consumer's rights if the trader is in breach of a term that this section requires to be treated as included in the contract.

13   Goods to match a sample

(1)   This section applies to a contract to supply goods by reference to a sample of the goods that is seen or examined by the consumer before the contract is made.

(2)   Every contract to which this section applies is to be treated as including a term that—

(a)   the goods will match the sample except to the extent that any differences between the sample and the goods are brought to the consumer's attention before the contract is made, and

(b)   the goods will be free from any defect that makes their quality unsatisfactory and that would not be apparent on a reasonable examination of the sample.

(3)   See section 19 for a consumer's rights if the trader is in breach of a term that this section requires to be treated as included in a contract.

14   Goods to match a model seen or examined

(1)   This section applies to a contract to supply goods by reference to a model of the goods that is seen or examined by the consumer before entering into the contract.

(2)   Every contract to which this section applies is to be treated as including a term that the goods will match the model except to the extent that any differences between the model and the goods are brought to the consumer's attention before the consumer enters into the contract.

(3)   See section 19 for a consumer's rights if the trader is in breach of a term that this section requires to be treated as included in a contract.

15   Installation as part of conformity of the goods with the contract

(1)   Goods do not conform to a contract to supply goods if—

(a)   installation of the goods forms part of the contract,

(b)   the goods are installed by the trader or under the trader's responsibility, and

(c)   the goods are installed incorrectly.

(2)   See section 19 for the effect of goods not conforming to the contract.

16   Goods not conforming to contract if digital content does not conform

(1)   Goods (whether or not they conform otherwise to a contract to supply goods) do not conform to it if—

(a)   the goods are an item that includes digital content, and

(b)   the digital content does not conform to the contract to supply that content (for which see section 42(1)).

(2)   See section 19 for the effect of goods not conforming to the contract.

17   Trader to have right to supply the goods etc

(1)   Every contract to supply goods, except one within subsection (4), is to be treated as including a term—

(a)   in the case of a contract for the hire of goods, that at the beginning of the period of hire the trader must have the right to transfer possession of the goods by way of hire for that period,

(b)   in any other case, that the trader must have the right to sell or transfer the goods at the time when ownership of the goods is to be transferred.

(2)   Every contract to supply goods, except a contract for the hire of goods or a contract within subsection (4), is to be treated as including a term that—

(a)   the goods are free from any charge or encumbrance not disclosed or known to the consumer before entering into the contract,

(b)   the goods will remain free from any such charge or encumbrance until ownership of them is to be transferred, and

(c)   the consumer will enjoy quiet possession of the goods except so far as it may be disturbed by the owner or other person entitled to the benefit of any charge or encumbrance so disclosed or known.

(3)   Every contract for the hire of goods is to be treated as including a term that the consumer will enjoy quiet possession of the goods for the period of the hire except so far as the possession may be disturbed by the owner or other person entitled to the benefit of any charge or encumbrance disclosed or known to the consumer before entering into the contract.

(4)   This subsection applies to a contract if the contract shows, or the circum-

stances when they enter into the contract imply, that the trader and the consumer intend the trader to transfer only—

(a)   whatever title the trader has, even if it is limited, or

(b)   whatever title a third person has, even if it is limited.

(5)   Every contract within subsection (4) is to be treated as including a term that all charges or encumbrances known to the trader and not known to the consumer were disclosed to the consumer before entering into the contract.

(6)   Every contract within subsection (4) is to be treated as including a term that the consumer's quiet possession of the goods—

(a)   will not be disturbed by the trader, and

(b)   will not be disturbed by a person claiming through or under the trader, unless that person is claiming under a charge or encumbrance that was disclosed or known to the consumer before entering into the contract.

(7)   If subsection (4)(b) applies (transfer of title that a third person has), the contract is also to be treated as including a term that the consumer's quiet possession of the goods—

(a)   will not be disturbed by the third person, and

(b)   will not be disturbed by a person claiming through or under the third person, unless the claim is under a charge or encumbrance that was disclosed or known to the consumer before entering into the contract.

(8)   In the case of a contract for the hire of goods, this section does not affect the right of the trader to repossess the goods where the contract provides or is to be treated as providing for this.

(9)   See section 19 for a consumer's rights if the trader is in breach of a term that this section requires to be treated as included in a contract.

18   No other requirement to treat term about quality or fitness as included

(1)   Except as provided by sections 9, 10, 13 and 16, a contract to supply goods is not to be treated as including any term about the quality of the goods or their fitness for any particular purpose, unless the term is expressly included in the contract.

(2)   Subsection (1) is subject to provision made by any other enactment (whenever passed or made).

What remedies are there if statutory rights under a goods contract are not met?

19   Consumer's rights to enforce terms about goods

(1)   In this section and sections 22 to 24 references to goods conforming to a contract are references to—

(a)   the goods conforming to the terms described in sections 9, 10, 11, 13 and 14,

(b)   the goods not failing to conform to the contract under section 15 or 16, and

(c)   the goods conforming to requirements that are stated in the contract.

(2)   But, for the purposes of this section and sections 22 to 24, a failure to conform as mentioned in subsection (1)(a) to (c) is not a failure to conform to the contract if it has its origin in materials supplied by the consumer.

(3)   If the goods do not conform to the contract because of a breach of any of the terms described in sections 9, 10, 11, 13 and 14, or if they do not conform to the contract under section 16, the consumer's rights (and the provisions about them and when they are available) are—

(a)   the short-term right to reject (sections 20 and 22);

(b)   the right to repair or replacement (section 23); and

(c)   the right to a price reduction or the final right to reject (sections 20 and 24).

(4)   If the goods do not conform to the contract under section 15 or because of a

breach of requirements that are stated in the contract, the consumer's rights (and the provisions about them and when they are available) are—

    (a)   the right to repair or replacement (section 23); and

    (b)   the right to a price reduction or the final right to reject (sections 20 and 24).

(5)   If the trader is in breach of a term that section 12 requires to be treated as included in the contract, the consumer has the right to recover from the trader the amount of any costs incurred by the consumer as a result of the breach, up to the amount of the price paid or the value of other consideration given for the goods.

(6)   If the trader is in breach of the term that section 17(1) (right to supply etc) requires to be treated as included in the contract, the consumer has a right to reject (see section 20 for provisions about that right and when it is available).

(7)   Subsections (3) to (6) are subject to section 25 and subsections (3)(a) and (6) are subject to section 26.

(8)   Section 28 makes provision about remedies for breach of a term about the time for delivery of goods.

(9)   This Chapter does not prevent the consumer seeking other remedies—

    (a)   for a breach of a term that this Chapter requires to be treated as included in the contract,

    (b)   on the grounds that, under section 15 or 16, goods do not conform to the contract, or

    (c)   for a breach of a requirement stated in the contract.

(10)   Those other remedies may be ones—

    (a)   in addition to a remedy referred to in subsections (3) to (6) (but not so as to recover twice for the same loss), or

    (b)   instead of such a remedy, or

    (c)   where no such remedy is provided for.

(11)   Those other remedies include any of the following that is open to the consumer in the circumstances—

    (a)   claiming damages;

    (b)   seeking specific performance;

    (c)   seeking an order for specific implement;

    (d)   relying on the breach against a claim by the trader for the price;

    (e)   for breach of an express term, exercising a right to treat the contract as at an end.

(12)   It is not open to the consumer to treat the contract as at an end for breach of a term that this Chapter requires to be treated as included in the contract, or on the grounds that, under section 15 or 16, goods do not conform to the contract, except as provided by subsections (3), (4) and (6).

(13)   In this Part, treating a contract as at an end means treating it as repudiated.

(14)   For the purposes of subsections (3)(b) and (c) and (4), goods which do not conform to the contract at any time within the period of six months beginning with the day on which the goods were delivered to the consumer must be taken not to have conformed to it on that day.

(15)   Subsection (14) does not apply if—

    (a)   it is established that the goods did conform to the contract on that day, or

    (b)   its application is incompatible with the nature of the goods or with how they fail to conform to the contract.

20   Right to reject

    (1)   The short-term right to reject is subject to section 22.

    (2)   The final right to reject is subject to section 24.

    (3)   The right to reject under section 19(6) is not limited by those sections.

(4) Each of these rights entitles the consumer to reject the goods and treat the contract as at an end, subject to subsections (20) and (21).

(5) The right is exercised if the consumer indicates to the trader that the consumer is rejecting the goods and treating the contract as at an end.

(6) The indication may be something the consumer says or does, but it must be clear enough to be understood by the trader.

(7) From the time when the right is exercised—

(a) the trader has a duty to give the consumer a refund, subject to subsection (18), and

(b) the consumer has a duty to make the goods available for collection by the trader or (if there is an agreement for the consumer to return rejected goods) to return them as agreed.

(8) Whether or not the consumer has a duty to return the rejected goods, the trader must bear any reasonable costs of returning them, other than any costs incurred by the consumer in returning the goods in person to the place where the consumer took physical possession of them.

(9) The consumer's entitlement to receive a refund works as follows.

(10) To the extent that the consumer paid money under the contract, the consumer is entitled to receive back the same amount of money.

(11) To the extent that the consumer transferred anything else under the contract, the consumer is entitled to receive back the same amount of what the consumer transferred, unless subsection (12) applies.

(12) To the extent that the consumer transferred under the contract something for which the same amount of the same thing cannot be substituted, the consumer is entitled to receive back in its original state whatever the consumer transferred.

(13) If the contract is for the hire of goods, the entitlement to a refund extends only to anything paid or otherwise transferred for a period of hire that the consumer does not get because the contract is treated as at an end.

(14) If the contract is a hire-purchase agreement or a conditional sales contract and the contract is treated as at an end before the whole of the price has been paid, the entitlement to a refund extends only to the part of the price paid.

(15) A refund under this section must be given without undue delay, and in any event within 14 days beginning with the day on which the trader agrees that the consumer is entitled to a refund.

(16) If the consumer paid money under the contract, the trader must give the refund using the same means of payment as the consumer used, unless the consumer expressly agrees otherwise.

(17) The trader must not impose any fee on the consumer in respect of the refund.

(18) There is no entitlement to receive a refund—

(a) if none of subsections (10) to (12) applies,

(b) to the extent that anything to which subsection (12) applies cannot be given back in its original state, or

(c) where subsection (13) applies, to the extent that anything the consumer transferred under the contract cannot be divided so as to give back only the amount, or part of the amount, to which the consumer is entitled.

(19) It may be open to a consumer to claim damages where there is no entitlement to receive a refund, or because of the limits of the entitlement, or instead of a refund.

(20) Subsection (21) qualifies the application in relation to England and Wales and Northern Ireland of the rights mentioned in subsections (1) to (3) where—

(a) the contract is a severable contract,

(b) in relation to the final right to reject, the contract is a contract for the hire of goods, a hire-purchase agreement or a contract for transfer of goods, and

(c) section 26(3) does not apply.

(21)   The consumer is entitled, depending on the terms of the contract and the circumstances of the case—

(a)   to reject the goods to which a severable obligation relates and treat that obligation as at an end (so that the entitlement to a refund relates only to what the consumer paid or transferred in relation to that obligation), or

(b)   to exercise any of the rights mentioned in subsections (1) to (3) in respect of the whole contract.

21   Partial rejection of goods

(1)   If the consumer has any of the rights mentioned in section 20(1) to (3), but does not reject all of the goods and treat the contract as at an end, the consumer—

(a)   may reject some or all of the goods that do not conform to the contract, but

(b)   may not reject any goods that do conform to the contract.

(2)   If the consumer is entitled to reject the goods in an instalment, but does not reject all of those goods, the consumer—

(a)   may reject some or all of the goods in the instalment that do not conform to the contract, but

(b)   may not reject any goods in the instalment that do conform to the contract.

(3)   If any of the goods form a commercial unit, the consumer cannot reject some of those goods without also rejecting the rest of them.

(4)   A unit is a 'commercial unit' if division of the unit would materially impair the value of the goods or the character of the unit.

(5)   The consumer rejects goods under this section by indicating to the trader that the consumer is rejecting the goods.

(6)   The indication may be something the consumer says or does, but it must be clear enough to be understood by the trader.

(7)   From the time when a consumer rejects goods under this section—

(a)   the trader has a duty to give the consumer a refund in respect of those goods (subject to subsection (10)), and

(b)   the consumer has a duty to make those goods available for collection by the trader or (if there is an agreement for the consumer to return rejected goods) to return them as agreed.

(8)   Whether or not the consumer has a duty to return the rejected goods, the trader must bear any reasonable costs of returning them, other than any costs incurred by the consumer in returning those goods in person to the place where the consumer took physical possession of them.

(9)   Section 20(10) to (17) apply to a consumer's right to receive a refund under this section (and in section 20(13) and (14) references to the contract being treated as at an end are to be read as references to goods being rejected).

(10)   That right does not apply—

(a)   if none of section 20(10) to (12) applies,

(b)   to the extent that anything to which section 20(12) applies cannot be given back in its original state, or

(c)   to the extent that anything the consumer transferred under the contract cannot be divided so as to give back only the amount, or part of the amount, to which the consumer is entitled.

(11)   It may be open to a consumer to claim damages where there is no right to receive a refund, or because of the limits of the right, or instead of a refund.

(12)   References in this section to goods conforming to a contract are to be read in accordance with section 19(1) and (2), but they also include the goods conforming to the terms described in section 17.

(13)   Where section 20(21)(a) applies the reference in subsection (1) to the consumer treating the contract as at an end is to be read as a reference to the consumer treating the severable obligation as at an end.

22   Time limit for short-term right to reject

(1)   A consumer who has the short-term right to reject loses it if the time limit for exercising it passes without the consumer exercising it, unless the trader and the consumer agree that it may be exercised later.

(2)   An agreement under which the short-term right to reject would be lost before the time limit passes is not binding on the consumer.

(3)   The time limit for exercising the short-term right to reject (unless subsection (4) applies) is the end of 30 days beginning with the first day after these have all happened—

(a)   ownership or (in the case of a contract for the hire of goods, a hire-purchase agreement or a conditional sales contract) possession of the goods has been transferred to the consumer,

(b)   the goods have been delivered, and

(c)   where the contract requires the trader to install the goods or take other action to enable the consumer to use them, the trader has notified the consumer that the action has been taken.

(4)   If any of the goods are of a kind that can reasonably be expected to perish after a shorter period, the time limit for exercising the short-term right to reject in relation to those goods is the end of that shorter period (but without affecting the time limit in relation to goods that are not of that kind).

(5)   Subsections (3) and (4) do not prevent the consumer exercising the short-term right to reject before something mentioned in subsection (3)(a), (b) or (c) has happened.

(6)   If the consumer requests or agrees to the repair or replacement of goods, the period mentioned in subsection (3) or (4) stops running for the length of the waiting period.

(7)   If goods supplied by the trader in response to that request or agreement do not conform to the contract, the time limit for exercising the short-term right to reject is then either—

(a)   7 days after the waiting period ends, or

(b)   if later, the original time limit for exercising that right, extended by the waiting period.

(8)   The waiting period—

(a)   begins with the day the consumer requests or agrees to the repair or replacement of the goods, and

(b)   ends with the day on which the consumer receives goods supplied by the trader in response to the request or agreement.

23   Right to repair or replacement

(1)   This section applies if the consumer has the right to repair or replacement (see section 19(3) and (4)).

(2)   If the consumer requires the trader to repair or replace the goods, the trader must—

(a)   do so within a reasonable time and without significant inconvenience to the consumer, and

(b)   bear any necessary costs incurred in doing so (including in particular the cost of any labour, materials or postage).

(3)   The consumer cannot require the trader to repair or replace the goods if that remedy (the repair or the replacement)—

(a)   is impossible, or

(b)   is disproportionate compared to the other of those remedies.

(4)   Either of those remedies is disproportionate compared to the other if it imposes costs on the trader which, compared to those imposed by the other, are unreasonable, taking into account—

(a)   the value which the goods would have if they conformed to the contract,

(b)   the significance of the lack of conformity, and

(c)   whether the other remedy could be effected without significant inconvenience to the consumer.

(5)   Any question as to what is a reasonable time or significant inconvenience is to be determined taking account of—

(a)   the nature of the goods, and

(b)   the purpose for which the goods were acquired.

(6)   A consumer who requires or agrees to the repair of goods cannot require the trader to replace them, or exercise the short-term right to reject, without giving the trader a reasonable time to repair them (unless giving the trader that time would cause significant inconvenience to the consumer).

(7)   A consumer who requires or agrees to the replacement of goods cannot require the trader to repair them, or exercise the short-term right to reject, without giving the trader a reasonable time to replace them (unless giving the trader that time would cause significant inconvenience to the consumer).

(8)   In this Chapter, 'repair' in relation to goods that do not conform to a contract, means making them conform.

24   Right to price reduction or final right to reject

(1)   The right to a price reduction is the right—

(a)   to require the trader to reduce by an appropriate amount the price the consumer is required to pay under the contract, or anything else the consumer is required to transfer under the contract, and

(b)   to receive a refund from the trader for anything already paid or otherwise transferred by the consumer above the reduced amount.

(2)   The amount of the reduction may, where appropriate, be the full amount of the price or whatever the consumer is required to transfer.

(3)   Section 20(10) to (17) applies to a consumer's right to receive a refund under subsection (1)(b).

(4)   The right to a price reduction does not apply—

(a)   if what the consumer is (before the reduction) required to transfer under the contract, whether or not already transferred, cannot be divided up so as to enable the trader to receive or retain only the reduced amount, or

(b)   if anything to which section 20(12) applies cannot be given back in its original state.

(5)   A consumer who has the right to a price reduction and the final right to reject may only exercise one (not both), and may only do so in one of these situations—

(a)   after one repair or one replacement, the goods do not conform to the contract;

(b)   because of section 23(3) the consumer can require neither repair nor replacement of the goods; or

(c)   the consumer has required the trader to repair or replace the goods, but the trader is in breach of the requirement of section 23(2)(a) to do so within a reasonable time and without significant inconvenience to the consumer.

(6)   There has been a repair or replacement for the purposes of subsection (5)(a) if—

(a)   the consumer has requested or agreed to repair or replacement of the goods (whether in relation to one fault or more than one), and

(b)   the trader has delivered goods to the consumer, or made goods available to the consumer, in response to the request or agreement.

(7)   For the purposes of subsection (6) goods that the trader arranges to repair at the consumer's premises are made available when the trader indicates that the repairs are finished.

(8)   If the consumer exercises the final right to reject, any refund to the consumer may be reduced by a deduction for use, to take account of the use the

consumer has had of the goods in the period since they were delivered, but this is subject to subsections (9) and (10).

(9)   No deduction may be made to take account of use in any period when the consumer had the goods only because the trader failed to collect them at an agreed time.

(10)   No deduction may be made if the final right to reject is exercised in the first 6 months (see subsection (11)), unless—

   (a)   the goods consist of a motor vehicle, or

   (b)   the goods are of a description specified by order made by the Secretary of State by statutory instrument.

(11)   In subsection (10) the first 6 months means 6 months beginning with the first day after these have all happened—

   (a)   ownership or (in the case of a contract for the hire of goods, a hire-purchase agreement or a conditional sales contract) possession of the goods has been transferred to the consumer,

   (b)   the goods have been delivered, and

   (c)   where the contract requires the trader to install the goods or take other action to enable the consumer to use them, the trader has notified the consumer that the action has been taken.

(12)   In subsection (10)(a) 'motor vehicle'—

   (a)   in relation to Great Britain, has the same meaning as in the Road Traffic Act 1988 (see sections 185 to 194 of that Act);

   (b)   in relation to Northern Ireland, has the same meaning as in the Road Traffic (Northern Ireland) Order 1995 (SI 1995/2994 (NI 18)) (see Parts I and V of that Order).

(13)   But a vehicle is not a motor vehicle for the purposes of subsection (10)(a) if it is constructed or adapted—

   (a)   for the use of a person suffering from some physical defect or disability, and

   (b)   so that it may only be used by one such person at any one time.

(14)   An order under subsection (10)(b)—

   (a)   may be made only if the Secretary of State is satisfied that it is appro-priate to do so because of significant detriment caused to traders as a result of the application of subsection (10) in relation to goods of the description specified by the order; (b) may contain transitional or transitory provision or savings.

(15)   No order may be made under subsection (10)(b) unless a draft of the statu-tory instrument containing it has been laid before, and approved by a resolution of, each House of Parliament.

Other rules about remedies under goods contracts

25   Delivery of wrong quantity

(1)   Where the trader delivers to the consumer a quantity of goods less than the trader contracted to supply, the consumer may reject them, but if the consumer accepts them the consumer must pay for them at the contract rate.

(2)   Where the trader delivers to the consumer a quantity of goods larger than the trader contracted to supply, the consumer may accept the goods included in the contract and reject the rest, or may reject all of the goods.

(3)   Where the trader delivers to the consumer a quantity of goods larger than the trader contracted to supply and the consumer accepts all of the goods deli-vered, the consumer must pay for them at the contract rate.

(4)   Where the consumer is entitled to reject goods under this section, any enti-tlement for the consumer to treat the contract as at an end depends on the terms of the contract and the circumstances of the case.

(5)   The consumer rejects goods under this section by indicating to the trader that the consumer is rejecting the goods.

(6)   The indication may be something the consumer says or does, but it must be clear enough to be understood by the trader.

(7)   Subsections (1) to (3) do not prevent the consumer claiming damages, where it is open to the consumer to do so.

(8)   This section is subject to any usage of trade, special agreement, or course of dealing between the parties.

26   Instalment deliveries

(1)   Under a contract to supply goods, the consumer is not bound to accept delivery of the goods by instalments, unless that has been agreed between the consumer and the trader.

(2)   The following provisions apply if the contract provides for the goods to be delivered by stated instalments, which are to be separately paid for.

(3)   If the trader makes defective deliveries in respect of one or more instalments, the consumer, apart from any entitlement to claim damages, may be (but is not necessarily) entitled—

(a)   to exercise the short-term right to reject or the right to reject under section 19(6) (as applicable) in respect of the whole contract, or

(b)   to reject the goods in an instalment.

(4)   Whether paragraph (a) or (b) of subsection (3) (or neither) applies to a consumer depends on the terms of the contract and the circumstances of the case.

(5)   In subsection (3), making defective deliveries does not include failing to make a delivery in accordance with section 28.

(6)   If the consumer neglects or refuses to take delivery of or pay for one or more instalments, the trader may—

(a)   be entitled to treat the whole contract as at an end, or

(b)   if it is a severable breach, have a claim for damages but not a right to treat the whole contract as at an end.

(7)   Whether paragraph (a) or (b) of subsection (6) (or neither) applies to a trader depends on the terms of the contract and the circumstances of the case.

27   Consignation, or payment into court, in Scotland

(1)   Subsection (2) applies where—

(a)   a consumer has not rejected goods which the consumer could have rejected for breach of a term mentioned in section 19(3) or (6),

(b)   the consumer has chosen to treat the breach as giving rise only to a claim for damages or to a right to rely on the breach against a claim by the trader for the price of the goods, and

(c)   the trader has begun proceedings in court to recover the price or has brought a counter-claim for the price.

(2)   The court may require the consumer—

(a)   to consign, or pay into court, the price of the goods, or part of the price, or

(b)   to provide some other reasonable security for payment of the price.

Other rules about goods contracts.

28   Delivery of goods

(1)   This section applies to any sales contract.

(2)   Unless the trader and the consumer have agreed otherwise, the contract is to be treated as including a term that the trader must deliver the goods to the consumer.

(3)   Unless there is an agreed time or period, the contract is to be treated as including a term that the trader must deliver the goods—

(a)   without undue delay, and

(b)   in any event, not more than 30 days after the day on which the contract is entered into.

(4)   In this section—

    (a)   an 'agreed' time or period means a time or period agreed by the trader and the consumer for delivery of the goods;

    (b)   if there is an obligation to deliver the goods at the time the contract is entered into, that time counts as the 'agreed' time.

(5)   Subsections (6) and (7) apply if the trader does not deliver the goods in accordance with subsection (3) or at the agreed time or within the agreed period.

(6)   If the circumstances are that—

    (a)   the trader has refused to deliver the goods,

    (b)   delivery of the goods at the agreed time or within the agreed period is essential taking into account all the relevant circumstances at the time the contract was entered into, or

    (c)   the consumer told the trader before the contract was entered into that delivery in accordance with subsection (3), or at the agreed time or within the agreed period, was essential,

then the consumer may treat the contract as at an end.

(7)   In any other circumstances, the consumer may specify a period that is appropriate in the circumstances and require the trader to deliver the goods before the end of that period.

(8)   If the consumer specifies a period under subsection (7) but the goods are not delivered within that period, then the consumer may treat the contract as at an end.

(9)   If the consumer treats the contract as at an end under subsection (6) or (8), the trader must without undue delay reimburse all payments made under the contract.

(10)   If subsection (6) or (8) applies but the consumer does not treat the contract as at an end—

    (a)   that does not prevent the consumer from cancelling the order for any of the goods or rejecting goods that have been delivered, and

    (b)   the trader must without undue delay reimburse all payments made under the contract in respect of any goods for which the consumer cancels the order or which the consumer rejects.

(11)   If any of the goods form a commercial unit, the consumer cannot reject or cancel the order for some of those goods without also rejecting or cancelling the order for the rest of them.

(12)   A unit is a 'commercial unit' if division of the unit would materially impair the value of the goods or the character of the unit.

(13)   This section does not prevent the consumer seeking other remedies where it is open to the consumer to do so.

(14)   See section 2(5) and (6) for the application of this section where goods are sold at public auction.

29 Passing of risk

(1)   A sales contract is to be treated as including the following provisions as terms.

(2)   The goods remain at the trader's risk until they come into the physical possession of—

    (a)   the consumer, or

    (b)   a person identified by the consumer to take possession of the goods.

(3)   Subsection (2) does not apply if the goods are delivered to a carrier who—

    (a)   is commissioned by the consumer to deliver the goods, and

    (b)   is not a carrier the trader named as an option for the consumer.

(4)   In that case the goods are at the consumer's risk on and after delivery to the carrier.

(5)   Subsection (4) does not affect any liability of the carrier to the consumer in respect of the goods.

(6)   See section 2(5) and (6) for the application of this section where goods are sold at public auction.

30   Goods under guarantee

(1)   This section applies where—
    (a)   there is a contract to supply goods, and
    (b)   there is a guarantee in relation to the goods.

(2)   'Guarantee' here means an undertaking to the consumer given without extra charge by a person acting in the course of the person's business (the 'guarantor') that, if the goods do not meet the specifications set out in the guarantee statement or in any associated advertising—
    (a)   the consumer will be reimbursed for the price paid for the goods, or
    (b)   the goods will be repaired, replaced or handled in any way.

(3)   The guarantee takes effect, at the time the goods are delivered, as a contractual obligation owed by the guarantor under the conditions set out in the guarantee statement and in any associated advertising.

(4)   The guarantor must ensure that—
    (a)   the guarantee sets out in plain and intelligible language the contents of the guarantee and the essential particulars for making claims under the guarantee,
    (b)   the guarantee states that the consumer has statutory rights in relation to the goods and that those rights are not affected by the guarantee, and
    (c)   where the goods are offered within the territory of the United Kingdom, the guarantee is written in English.

(5)   The contents of the guarantee to be set out in it include, in particular—
    (a)   the name and address of the guarantor, and
    (b)   the duration and territorial scope of the guarantee.

(6)   The guarantor and any other person who offers to supply to consumers the goods which are the subject of the guarantee must, on request by the consumer, make the guarantee available to the consumer within a reasonable time, in writing and in a form accessible to the consumer.

(7)   What is a reasonable time is a question of fact.

(8)   If a person fails to comply with a requirement of this section, the enforcement authority may apply to the court for an injunction or (in Scotland) an order of specific implement against that person requiring that person to comply.

(9)   On an application the court may grant an injunction or (in Scotland) an order of specific implement on such terms as it thinks appropriate.

(10)   In this section—
'court' means—
    (a)   in relation to England and Wales, the High Court or the county court,
    (b)   in relation to Northern Ireland, the High Court or a county court, and
    (c)   in relation to Scotland, the Court of Session or the sheriff;
'enforcement authority' means—
    (a)   the Competition and Markets Authority,
    (b)   a local weights and measures authority in Great Britain, and
    (c)   the Department of Enterprise, Trade and Investment in Northern Ireland.

Can a trader contract out of statutory rights and remedies under a goods contract?

31   Liability that cannot be excluded or restricted

(1)   A term of a contract to supply goods is not binding on the consumer to the extent that it would exclude or restrict the trader's liability arising under any of these provisions—
    (a)   section 9 (goods to be of satisfactory quality);
    (b)   section 10 (goods to be fit for particular purpose);
    (c)   section 11 (goods to be as described);
    (d)   section 12 (other pre-contract information included in contract);

(e)   section 13 (goods to match a sample);

(f)   section 14 (goods to match a model seen or examined);

(g)   section 15 (installation as part of conformity of the goods with the contract);

(h)   section 16 (goods not conforming to contract if digital content does not conform);

(i)   section 17 (trader to have right to supply the goods etc);

(j)   section 28 (delivery of goods);

(k)   section 29 (passing of risk).

(2)   That also means that a term of a contract to supply goods is not binding on the consumer to the extent that it would—

(a)   exclude or restrict a right or remedy in respect of a liability under a provision listed in subsection (1),

(b)   make such a right or remedy or its enforcement subject to a restrictive or onerous condition,

(c)   allow a trader to put a person at a disadvantage as a result of pursuing such a right or remedy, or

(d)   exclude or restrict rules of evidence or procedure.

(3)   The reference in subsection (1) to excluding or restricting a liability also includes preventing an obligation or duty arising or limiting its extent.

(4)   An agreement in writing to submit present or future differences to arbitration is not to be regarded as excluding or restricting any liability for the purposes of this section.

(5)   Subsection (1)(i), and subsection (2) so far as it relates to liability under section 17, do not apply to a term of a contract for the hire of goods.

(6)   But an express term of a contract for the hire of goods is not binding on the consumer to the extent that it would exclude or restrict a term that section 17 requires to be treated as included in the contract, unless it is inconsistent with that term (and see also section 62 (requirement for terms to be fair)).

(7)   See Schedule 3 for provision about the enforcement of this section.

32   Contracts applying law of non-EEA State

(1)   If—

(a)   the law of a country or territory other than an EEA State is chosen by the parties to be applicable to a sales contract, but

(b)   the sales contract has a close connection with the United Kingdom, this Chapter, except the provisions in subsection (2), applies despite that choice.

(2)   The exceptions are—

(a)   sections 11(4) and (5) and 12;

(b)   sections 28 and 29;

(c)   section 31(1)(d), (j) and (k).

(3)   For cases where those provisions apply, or where the law applicable has not been chosen or the law of an EEA State is chosen, see Regulation (EC) No 593/2008 of the European Parliament and of the Council of 17 June 2008 on the law applicable to contractual obligations.

CHAPTER 3

Digital content

What digital content contracts are covered?

33   Contracts covered by this Chapter

(1)   This Chapter applies to a contract for a trader to supply digital content to a consumer, if it is supplied or to be supplied for a price paid by the consumer.

(2)   This Chapter also applies to a contract for a trader to supply digital content to a consumer, if—

(a)   it is supplied free with goods or services or other digital content for which the consumer pays a price, and

(b)   it is not generally available to consumers unless they have paid a price for it or for goods or services or other digital content.

(3)   The references in subsections (1) and (2) to the consumer paying a price include references to the consumer using, by way of payment, any facility for which money has been paid.

(4)   A trader does not supply digital content to a consumer for the purposes of this Part merely because the trader supplies a service by which digital content reaches the consumer.

(5)   The Secretary of State may by order provide for this Chapter to apply to other contracts for a trader to supply digital content to a consumer, if the Secretary of State is satisfied that it is appropriate to do so because of significant detriment caused to consumers under contracts of the kind to which the order relates.

(6)   An order under subsection (5)—

(a)   may, in particular, amend this Act;

(b)   may contain transitional or transitory provision or savings.

(7)   A contract to which this Chapter applies is referred to in this Part as a 'contract to supply digital content'.

(8)   This section, other than subsection (4), does not limit the application of section 46.

(9)   The power to make an order under subsection (5) is exercisable by statutory instrument.

(10)   No order may be made under subsection (5) unless a draft of the statutory instrument containing it has been laid before, and approved by a resolution of, each House of Parliament.

What statutory rights are there under a digital content contract?

34   Digital content to be of satisfactory quality

(1)   Every contract to supply digital content is to be treated as including a term that the quality of the digital content is satisfactory.

(2)   The quality of digital content is satisfactory if it meets the standard that a reasonable person would consider satisfactory, taking account of—

(a)   any description of the digital content,

(b)   the price mentioned in section 33(1) or (2)(b) (if relevant), and

(c)   all the other relevant circumstances (see subsection (5)).

(3)   The quality of digital content includes its state and condition; and the following aspects (among others) are in appropriate cases aspects of the quality of digital content—

(a)   fitness for all the purposes for which digital content of that kind is usually supplied;

(b)   freedom from minor defects;

(c)   safety;

(d)   durability.

(4)   The term mentioned in subsection (1) does not cover anything which makes the quality of the digital content unsatisfactory—

(a)   which is specifically drawn to the consumer's attention before the contract is made,

(b)   where the consumer examines the digital content before the contract is made, which that examination ought to reveal, or

(c)   where the consumer examines a trial version before the contract is made, which would have been apparent on a reasonable examination of the trial version.

(5)   The relevant circumstances mentioned in subsection (2)(c) include any

public statement about the specific characteristics of the digital content made by the trader, the producer or any representative of the trader or the producer.

(6)   That includes, in particular, any public statement made in advertising or labelling.

(7)   But a public statement is not a relevant circumstance for the purposes of subsection (2)(c) if the trader shows that—

(a)   when the contract was made, the trader was not, and could not reasonably have been, aware of the statement,

(b)   before the contract was made, the statement had been publicly withdrawn or, to the extent that it contained anything which was incorrect or misleading, it had been publicly corrected, or

(c)   the consumer's decision to contract for the digital content could not have been influenced by the statement.

(8)   In a contract to supply digital content a term about the quality of the digital content may be treated as included as a matter of custom.

(9)   See section 42 for a consumer's rights if the trader is in breach of a term that this section requires to be treated as included in a contract.

35   Digital content to be fit for particular purpose

(1)   Subsection (3) applies to a contract to supply digital content if before the contract is made the consumer makes known to the trader (expressly or by implication) any particular purpose for which the consumer is contracting for the digital content.

(2)   Subsection (3) also applies to a contract to supply digital content if—

(a)   the digital content was previously sold by a credit-broker to the trader,

(b)   the consideration or part of it is a sum payable by instalments, and

(c)   before the contract is made, the consumer makes known to the credit-broker (expressly or by implication) any particular purpose for which the consumer is contracting for the digital content.

(3)   The contract is to be treated as including a term that the digital content is reasonably fit for that purpose, whether or not that is a purpose for which digital content of that kind is usually supplied.

(4)   Subsection (3) does not apply if the circumstances show that the consumer does not rely, or it is unreasonable for the consumer to rely, on the skill or judgment of the trader or credit-broker.

(5)   A contract to supply digital content may be treated as making provision about the fitness of the digital content for a particular purpose as a matter of custom.

(6)   See section 42 for a consumer's rights if the trader is in breach of a term that this section requires to be treated as included in a contract.

36   Digital content to be as described

(1)   Every contract to supply digital content is to be treated as including a term that the digital content will match any description of it given by the trader to the consumer.

(2)   Where the consumer examines a trial version before the contract is made, it is not sufficient that the digital content matches (or is better than) the trial version if the digital content does not also match any description of it given by the trader to the consumer.

(3)   Any information that is provided by the trader about the digital content that is information mentioned in paragraph (a), (j) or (k) of Schedule 1 or paragraph (a), (v) or (w) of Schedule 2 (main characteristics, functionality and compatibility) to the Consumer Contracts (Information, Cancellation and Additional Charges) Regulations 2013 (SI 2013/3134) is to be treated as included as a term of the contract.

(4)   A change to any of that information, made before entering into the contract

or later, is not effective unless expressly agreed between the consumer and the trader.

(5)   See section 42 for a consumer's rights if the trader is in breach of a term that this section requires to be treated as included in a contract.

37   Other pre-contract information included in contract

(1)   This section applies to any contract to supply digital content.

(2)   Where regulation 9, 10 or 13 of the Consumer Contracts (Information, Cancellation and Additional Charges) Regulations 2013 (SI 2013/3134) required the trader to provide information to the consumer before the contract became binding, any of that information that was provided by the trader other than information about the digital content and mentioned in paragraph (a), (j) or (k) of Schedule 1 or paragraph (a), (v) or (w) of Schedule 2 to the Regulations (main characteristics, functionality and compatibility) is to be treated as included as a term of the contract.

(3)   A change to any of that information, made before entering into the contract or later, is not effective unless expressly agreed between the consumer and the trader.

(4)   See section 42 for a consumer's rights if the trader is in breach of a term that this section requires to be treated as included in a contract.

38   No other requirement to treat term about quality or fitness as included

(1)   Except as provided by sections 34 and 35, a contract to supply digital content is not to be treated as including any term about the quality of the digital content or its fitness for any particular purpose, unless the term is expressly included in the contract.

(2)   Subsection (1) is subject to provision made by any other enactment, whenever passed or made.

39   Supply by transmission and facilities for continued transmission

(1)   Subsection (2) applies where there is a contract to supply digital content and the consumer's access to the content on a device requires its transmission to the device under arrangements initiated by the trader.

(2)   For the purposes of this Chapter, the digital content is supplied—

(a)   when the content reaches the device, or

(b)   if earlier, when the content reaches another trader chosen by the consumer to supply, under a contract with the consumer, a service by which digital content reaches the device.

(3)   Subsections (5) to (7) apply where—

(a)   there is a contract to supply digital content, and

(b)   after the trader (T) has supplied the digital content, the consumer is to have access under the contract to a processing facility under arrangements made by T.

(4)   A processing facility is a facility by which T or another trader will receive digital content from the consumer and transmit digital content to the consumer (whether or not other features are to be included under the contract).

(5)   The contract is to be treated as including a term that the processing facility (with any feature that the facility is to include under the contract) must be available to the consumer for a reasonable time, unless a time is specified in the contract.

(6)   The following provisions apply to all digital content transmitted to the consumer on each occasion under the facility, while it is provided under the contract, as they apply to the digital content first supplied—

(a)   section 34 (quality);

(b)   section 35 (fitness for a particular purpose);

(c)   section 36 (description).

(7)   Breach of a term treated as included under subsection (5) has the same effect as breach of a term treated as included under those sections (see section 42).

40 Quality, fitness and description of content supplied subject to modifications

(1)   Where under a contract a trader supplies digital content to a consumer subject to the right of the trader or a third party to modify the digital content, the following provisions apply in relation to the digital content as modified as they apply in relation to the digital content as supplied under the contract—

    (a)   section 34 (quality);

    (b)   section 35 (fitness for a particular purpose);

    (c)   section 36 (description).

(2)   Subsection (1)(c) does not prevent the trader from improving the features of, or adding new features to, the digital content, as long as—

    (a)   the digital content continues to match the description of it given by the trader to the consumer, and

    (b)   the digital content continues to conform to the information provided by the trader as mentioned in subsection (3) of section 36, subject to any change to that information that has been agreed in accordance with subsection (4) of that section.

(3)   A claim on the grounds that digital content does not conform to a term described in any of the sections listed in subsection (1) as applied by that subsection is to be treated as arising at the time when the digital content was supplied under the contract and not the time when it is modified.

41 Trader's right to supply digital content

(1)   Every contract to supply digital content is to be treated as including a term—

    (a)   in relation to any digital content which is supplied under the contract and which the consumer has paid for, that the trader has the right to supply that content to the consumer;

    (b)   in relation to any digital content which the trader agrees to supply under the contract and which the consumer has paid for, that the trader will have the right to supply it to the consumer at the time when it is to be supplied.

(2)   See section 42 for a consumer's rights if the trader is in breach of a term that this section requires to be treated as included in a contract.

What remedies are there if statutory rights under a digital content contract are not met?

42 Consumer's rights to enforce terms about digital content

(1)   In this section and section 43 references to digital content conforming to a contract are references to the digital content conforming to the terms described in sections 34, 35 and 36.

(2)   If the digital content does not conform to the contract, the consumer's rights (and the provisions about them and when they are available) are—

    (a)   the right to repair or replacement (see section 43);

    (b)   the right to a price reduction (see section 44).

(3)   Section 16 also applies if an item including the digital content is supplied.

(4)   If the trader is in breach of a term that section 37 requires to be treated as included in the contract, the consumer has the right to recover from the trader the amount of any costs incurred by the consumer as a result of the breach, up to the amount of the price paid for the digital content or for any facility within section 33(3) used by the consumer.

(5)   If the trader is in breach of the term that section 41(1) (right to supply the content) requires to be treated as included in the contract, the consumer has the right to a refund (see section 45 for provisions about that right and when it is available).

(6)   This Chapter does not prevent the consumer seeking other remedies for a breach of a term to which any of subsections (2), (4) or (5) applies, instead of or in addition to a remedy referred to there (but not so as to recover twice for the same loss).

(7)   Those other remedies include any of the following that is open to the consumer in the circumstances—

(a)   claiming damages;

(b)   seeking to recover money paid where the consideration for payment of the money has failed;

(c)   seeking specific performance;

(d)   seeking an order for specific implement;

(e)   relying on the breach against a claim by the trader for the price.

(8)   It is not open to the consumer to treat the contract as at an end for breach of a term to which any of subsections (2), (4) or (5) applies.

(9)   For the purposes of subsection (2), digital content which does not conform to the contract at any time within the period of six months beginning with the day on which it was supplied must be taken not to have conformed to the contract when it was supplied.

(10)   Subsection (9) does not apply if—

(a)   it is established that the digital content did conform to the contract when it was supplied, or

(b)   its application is incompatible with the nature of the digital content or with how it fails to conform to the contract.

43   Right to repair or replacement

(1)   This section applies if the consumer has the right to repair or replacement.

(2)   If the consumer requires the trader to repair or replace the digital content, the trader must—

(a)   do so within a reasonable time and without significant inconvenience to the consumer; and

(b)   bear any necessary costs incurred in doing so (including in particular the cost of any labour, materials or postage).

(3)   The consumer cannot require the trader to repair or replace the digital content if that remedy (the repair or the replacement)—

(a)   is impossible, or

(b)   is disproportionate compared to the other of those remedies.

(4)   Either of those remedies is disproportionate compared to the other if it imposes costs on the trader which, compared to those imposed by the other, are unreasonable, taking into account—

(a)   the value which the digital content would have if it conformed to the contract,

(b)   the significance of the lack of conformity, and

(c)   whether the other remedy could be effected without significant inconvenience to the consumer.

(5)   Any question as to what is a reasonable time or significant inconvenience is to be determined taking account of—

(a)   the nature of the digital content, and

(b)   the purpose for which the digital content was obtained or accessed.

(6)   A consumer who requires or agrees to the repair of digital content cannot require the trader to replace it without giving the trader a reasonable time to repair it (unless giving the trader that time would cause significant inconvenience to the consumer).

(7)   A consumer who requires or agrees to the replacement of digital content cannot require the trader to repair it without giving the trader a reasonable time to replace it (unless giving the trader that time would cause significant inconvenience to the consumer).

(8)   In this Chapter, 'repair' in relation to digital content that does not conform to a contract, means making it conform.

44   Right to price reduction

(1)   The right to a price reduction is the right to require the trader to reduce the price to the consumer by an appropriate amount (including the right to receive a refund for anything already paid above the reduced amount).

(2)   The amount of the reduction may, where appropriate, be the full amount of the price.

(3)   A consumer who has that right may only exercise it in one of these situations—

(a)   because of section 43(3)(a) the consumer can require neither repair nor replacement of the digital content, or

(b)   the consumer has required the trader to repair or replace the digital content, but the trader is in breach of the requirement of section 43(2)(a) to do so within a reasonable time and without significant inconvenience to the consumer.

(4)   A refund under this section must be given without undue delay, and in any event within 14 days beginning with the day on which the trader agrees that the consumer is entitled to a refund.

(5)   The trader must give the refund using the same means of payment as the consumer used to pay for the digital content, unless the consumer expressly agrees otherwise.

(6)   The trader must not impose any fee on the consumer in respect of the refund.

45   Right to a refund

(1)   The right to a refund gives the consumer the right to receive a refund from the trader of all money paid by the consumer for the digital content (subject to subsection (2)).

(2)   If the breach giving the consumer the right to a refund affects only some of the digital content supplied under the contract, the right to a refund does not extend to any part of the price attributable to digital content that is not affected by the breach.

(3)   A refund must be given without undue delay, and in any event within 14 days beginning with the day on which the trader agrees that the consumer is entitled to a refund.

(4)   The trader must give the refund using the same means of payment as the consumer used to pay for the digital content, unless the consumer expressly agrees otherwise.

(5)   The trader must not impose any fee on the consumer in respect of the refund.

Compensation for damage to device or to other digital content

46   Remedy for damage to device or to other digital content

(1)   This section applies if—

(a)   a trader supplies digital content to a consumer under a contract,

(b)   the digital content causes damage to a device or to other digital content,

(c)   the device or digital content that is damaged belongs to the consumer, and

(d)   the damage is of a kind that would not have occurred if the trader had exercised reasonable care and skill.

(2)   If the consumer requires the trader to provide a remedy under this section, the trader must either—

(a)   repair the damage in accordance with subsection (3), or

(b)   compensate the consumer for the damage with an appropriate payment.

(3)   To repair the damage in accordance with this subsection, the trader must—

(a)   repair the damage within a reasonable time and without significant inconvenience to the consumer, and

(b)   bear any necessary costs incurred in repairing the damage (including in particular the cost of any labour, materials or postage).

(4)   Any question as to what is a reasonable time or significant inconvenience is to be determined taking account of—

(a)   the nature of the device or digital content that is damaged, and

(b)   the purpose for which it is used by the consumer.

(5)   A compensation payment under this section must be made without undue delay, and in any event within 14 days beginning with the day on which the trader agrees that the consumer is entitled to the payment.

(6)   The trader must not impose any fee on the consumer in respect of the payment.

(7)   A consumer with a right to a remedy under this section may bring a claim in civil proceedings to enforce that right.

(8)   The Limitation Act 1980 and the Limitation (Northern Ireland) Order 1989 (SI 1989/1339 (NI 11)) apply to a claim under this section as if it were an action founded on simple contract.

(9)   The Prescription and Limitation (Scotland) Act 1973 applies to a right to a remedy under this section as if it were an obligation to which section 6 of that Act applies.

Can a trader contract out of statutory rights and remedies under a digital content contract?

47 Liability that cannot be excluded or restricted

(1)   A term of a contract to supply digital content is not binding on the consumer to the extent that it would exclude or restrict the trader's liability arising under any of these provisions—

(a)   section 34 (digital content to be of satisfactory quality),

(b)   section 35 (digital content to be fit for particular purpose),

(c)   section 36 (digital content to be as described),

(d)   section 37 (other pre-contract information included in contract), or

(e)   section 41 (trader's right to supply digital content).

(2)   That also means that a term of a contract to supply digital content is not binding on the consumer to the extent that it would—

(a)   exclude or restrict a right or remedy in respect of a liability under a provision listed in subsection (1),

(b)   make such a right or remedy or its enforcement subject to a restrictive or onerous condition,

(c)   allow a trader to put a person at a disadvantage as a result of pursuing such a right or remedy, or

(d)   exclude or restrict rules of evidence or procedure.

(3)   The reference in subsection (1) to excluding or restricting a liability also includes preventing an obligation or duty arising or limiting its extent.

(4)   An agreement in writing to submit present or future differences to arbitration is not to be regarded as excluding or restricting any liability for the purposes of this section.

(5)   See Schedule 3 for provision about the enforcement of this section.

(6)   For provision limiting the ability of a trader under a contract within section 46 to exclude or restrict the trader's liability under that section, see section 62.

CHAPTER 4
Services

What services contracts are covered?

48 Contracts covered by this Chapter

(1) This Chapter applies to a contract for a trader to supply a service to a consumer.

(2) That does not include a contract of employment or apprenticeship.

(3) In relation to Scotland, this Chapter does not apply to a gratuitous contract.

(4) A contract to which this Chapter applies is referred to in this Part as a 'contract to supply a service'.

(5) The Secretary of State may by order made by statutory instrument provide that a provision of this Chapter does not apply in relation to a service of a description specified in the order.

(6) The power in subsection (5) includes power to provide that a provision of this Chapter does not apply in relation to a service of a description specified in the order in the circumstances so specified.

(7) An order under subsection (5) may contain transitional or transitory provision or savings.

(8) No order may be made under subsection (5) unless a draft of the statutory instrument containing it has been laid before, and approved by a resolution of, each House of Parliament.

What statutory rights are there under a services contract?

49 Service to be performed with reasonable care and skill

(1) Every contract to supply a service is to be treated as including a term that the trader must perform the service with reasonable care and skill.

(2) See section 54 for a consumer's rights if the trader is in breach of a term that this section requires to be treated as included in a contract.

50 Information about the trader or service to be binding

(1) Every contract to supply a service is to be treated as including as a term of the contract anything that is said or written to the consumer, by or on behalf of the trader, about the trader or the service, if—

(a) it is taken into account by the consumer when deciding to enter into the contract, or

(b) it is taken into account by the consumer when making any decision about the service after entering into the contract.

(2) Anything taken into account by the consumer as mentioned in subsection (1)(a) or (b) is subject to—

(a) anything that qualified it and was said or written to the consumer by the trader on the same occasion, and

(b) any change to it that has been expressly agreed between the consumer and the trader (before entering into the contract or later).

(3) Without prejudice to subsection (1), any information provided by the trader in accordance with regulation 9, 10 or 13 of the Consumer Contracts (Information, Cancellation and Additional Charges) Regulations 2013 (SI 2013/3134) is to be treated as included as a term of the contract.

(4) A change to any of the information mentioned in subsection (3), made before entering into the contract or later, is not effective unless expressly agreed between the consumer and the trader.

(5) See section 54 for a consumer's rights if the trader is in breach of a term that this section requires to be treated as included in a contract.

51 Reasonable price to be paid for a service

(1) This section applies to a contract to supply a service if—

(a) the consumer has not paid a price or other consideration for the service,

(b) the contract does not expressly fix a price or other consideration, and does not say how it is to be fixed, and

(c) anything that is to be treated under section 50 as included in the contract does not fix a price or other consideration either.

(2) In that case the contract is to be treated as including a term that the consumer must pay a reasonable price for the service, and no more.

(3) What is a reasonable price is a question of fact.

52 Service to be performed within a reasonable time

(1) This section applies to a contract to supply a service, if—

(a) the contract does not expressly fix the time for the service to be performed, and does not say how it is to be fixed, and

(b) information that is to be treated under section 50 as included in the contract does not fix the time either.

(2) In that case the contract is to be treated as including a term that the trader must perform the service within a reasonable time.

(3) What is a reasonable time is a question of fact.

(4) See section 54 for a consumer's rights if the trader is in breach of a term that this section requires to be treated as included in a contract.

53 Relation to other law on contract terms

(1) Nothing in this Chapter affects any enactment or rule of law that imposes a stricter duty on the trader.

(2) This Chapter is subject to any other enactment which defines or restricts the rights, duties or liabilities arising in connection with a service of any description.

What remedies are there if statutory rights under a services contract are not met?

54 Consumer's rights to enforce terms about services

(1) The consumer's rights under this section and sections 55 and 56 do not affect any rights that the contract provides for, if those are not inconsistent.

(2) In this section and section 55 a reference to a service conforming to a contract is a reference to—

(a) the service being performed in accordance with section 49, or

(b) the service conforming to a term that section 50 requires to be treated as included in the contract and that relates to the performance of the service.

(3) If the service does not conform to the contract, the consumer's rights (and the provisions about them and when they are available) are—

(a) the right to require repeat performance (see section 55);

(b) the right to a price reduction (see section 56).

(4) If the trader is in breach of a term that section 50 requires to be treated as included in the contract but that does not relate to the service, the consumer has the right to a price reduction (see section 56 for provisions about that right and when it is available).

(5) If the trader is in breach of what the contract requires under section 52 (performance within a reasonable time), the consumer has the right to a price reduction (see section 56 for provisions about that right and when it is available).

(6) This section and sections 55 and 56 do not prevent the consumer seeking other remedies for a breach of a term to which any of subsections (3) to (5) applies, instead of or in addition to a remedy referred to there (but not so as to recover twice for the same loss).

(7) Those other remedies include any of the following that is open to the consumer in the circumstances—

(a) claiming damages;

(b) seeking to recover money paid where the consideration for payment of the money has failed;

   (c)   seeking specific performance;

   (d)   seeking an order for specific implement;

   (e)   relying on the breach against a claim by the trader under the contract;

   (f)   exercising a right to treat the contract as at an end.

55 Right to repeat performance

(1)   The right to require repeat performance is a right to require the trader to perform the service again, to the extent necessary to complete its performance in conformity with the contract.

(2)   If the consumer requires such repeat performance, the trader—

   (a)   must provide it within a reasonable time and without significant inconvenience to the consumer; and

   (b)   must bear any necessary costs incurred in doing so (including in particular the cost of any labour or materials).

(3)   The consumer cannot require repeat performance if completing performance of the service in conformity with the contract is impossible.

(4)   Any question as to what is a reasonable time or significant inconvenience is to be determined taking account of—

   (a)   the nature of the service, and

   (b)   the purpose for which the service was to be performed.

56 Right to price reduction

(1)   The right to a price reduction is the right to require the trader to reduce the price to the consumer by an appropriate amount (including the right to receive a refund for anything already paid above the reduced amount).

(2)   The amount of the reduction may, where appropriate, be the full amount of the price.

(3)   A consumer who has that right and the right to require repeat performance is only entitled to a price reduction in one of these situations—

   (a)   because of section 55(3) the consumer cannot require repeat performance; or

   (b)   the consumer has required repeat performance, but the trader is in breach of the requirement of section 55(2)(a) to do it within a reasonable time and without significant inconvenience to the consumer.

(4)   A refund under this section must be given without undue delay, and in any event within 14 days beginning with the day on which the trader agrees that the consumer is entitled to a refund.

(5)   The trader must give the refund using the same means of payment as the consumer used to pay for the service, unless the consumer expressly agrees otherwise.

(6)   The trader must not impose any fee on the consumer in respect of the refund.

Can a trader contract out of statutory rights and remedies under a services contract?

57 Liability that cannot be excluded or restricted

(1)   A term of a contract to supply services is not binding on the consumer to the extent that it would exclude the trader's liability arising under section 49 (service to be performed with reasonable care and skill).

(2)   Subject to section 50(2), a term of a contract to supply services is not binding on the consumer to the extent that it would exclude the trader's liability arising under section 50 (information about trader or service to be binding).

(3)   A term of a contract to supply services is not binding on the consumer to the extent that it would restrict the trader's liability arising under any of sections 49 and 50 and, where they apply, sections 51 and 52 (reasonable price and reasonable time), if it would prevent the consumer in an appropriate case from recovering the price paid or the value of any other consideration. (If it would not prevent the consumer from doing so, Part 2 (unfair terms) may apply.)

(4)   That also means that a term of a contract to supply services is not binding on the consumer to the extent that it would —

(a)   exclude or restrict a right or remedy in respect of a liability under any of sections 49 to 52,

(b)   make such a right or remedy or its enforcement subject to a restrictive or onerous condition,

(c)   allow a trader to put a person at a disadvantage as a result of pursuing such a right or remedy, or

(d)   exclude or restrict rules of evidence or procedure.

(5)   The references in subsections (1) to (3) to excluding or restricting a liability also include preventing an obligation or duty arising or limiting its extent.

(6)   An agreement in writing to submit present or future differences to arbitration is not to be regarded as excluding or restricting any liability for the purposes of this section.

(7)   See Schedule 3 for provision about the enforcement of this section.

CHAPTER 5
General and supplementary provisions

58   Powers of the court

(1)   In any proceedings in which a remedy is sought by virtue of section 19(3) or (4), 42(2) or 54(3), the court, in addition to any other power it has, may act under this section.

(2)   On the application of the consumer the court may make an order requiring specific performance or, in Scotland, specific implement by the trader of any obligation imposed on the trader by virtue of section 23, 43 or 55.

(3)   Subsection (4) applies if—

(a)   the consumer claims to exercise a right under the relevant remedies provisions, but

(b)   the court decides that those provisions have the effect that exercise of another right is appropriate.

(4)   The court may proceed as if the consumer had exercised that other right.

(5)   If the consumer has claimed to exercise the final right to reject, the court may order that any reimbursement to the consumer is reduced by a deduction for use, to take account of the use the consumer has had of the goods in the period since they were delivered.

(6)   Any deduction for use is limited as set out in section 24(9) and (10).

(7)   The court may make an order under this section unconditionally or on such terms and conditions as to damages, payment of the price and otherwise as it thinks just.

(8)   The 'relevant remedies provisions' are—

(a)   where Chapter 2 applies, sections 23 and 24;

(b)   where Chapter 3 applies, sections 43 and 44;

(c)   where Chapter 4 applies, sections 55 and 56.

59   Interpretation

(1)   These definitions apply in this Part (as well as the key definitions in section 2)—

'conditional sales contract' has the meaning given in section 5(3);

'Consumer Rights Directive' means Directive 2011/83/EU of the European Parliament and of the Council of 25 October 2011 on consumer rights, amending Council Directive 93/13/EEC and Directive 1999/44/EC of the European Parliament and of the Council and repealing Council Directive 85/577/EEC and Directive 97/7/EC of the European Parliament and of the Council;

'credit-broker' means a person acting in the course of a business of credit brokerage carried on by that person;

'credit brokerage' means—

(a)   introducing individuals who want to obtain credit to persons carrying on any business so far as it relates to the provision of credit,

(b)   introducing individuals who want to obtain goods on hire to persons carrying on a business which comprises or relates to supplying goods under a contract for the hire of goods, or

(c)   introducing individuals who want to obtain credit, or to obtain goods on hire, to other persons engaged in credit brokerage;

'delivery' means voluntary transfer of possession from one person to another;

'enactment' includes—

(a)   an enactment contained in subordinate legislation within the meaning of the Interpretation Act 1978,

(b)   an enactment contained in, or in an instrument made under, a Measure or Act of the National Assembly for Wales,

(c)   an enactment contained in, or in an instrument made under, an Act of the Scottish Parliament, and

(d)   an enactment contained in, or in an instrument made under, Northern Ireland legislation;

'producer', in relation to goods or digital content, means—

(a)   the manufacturer,

(b)   the importer into the European Economic Area, or

(c)   any person who purports to be a producer by placing the person's name, trade mark or other distinctive sign on the goods or using it in connection with the digital content.

(2)   References in this Part to treating a contract as at an end are to be read in accordance with section 19(13).

60   Changes to other legislation

Schedule 1 (amendments consequential on this Part) has effect.

PART 2
UNFAIR TERMS

What contracts and notices are covered by this Part?

61   Contracts and notices covered by this Part

(1)   This Part applies to a contract between a trader and a consumer.

(2)   This does not include a contract of employment or apprenticeship.

(3)   A contract to which this Part applies is referred to in this Part as a 'consumer contract'.

(4)   This Part applies to a notice to the extent that it—

(a)   relates to rights or obligations as between a trader and a consumer, or

(b)   purports to exclude or restrict a trader's liability to a consumer.

(5)   This does not include a notice relating to rights, obligations or liabilities as between an employer and an employee.

(6)   It does not matter for the purposes of subsection (4) whether the notice is expressed to apply to a consumer, as long as it is reasonable to assume it is intended to be seen or heard by a consumer.

(7)   A notice to which this Part applies is referred to in this Part as a 'consumer notice'.

(8)   In this section 'notice' includes an announcement, whether or not in writing, and any other communication or purported communication.

What are the general rules about fairness of contract terms and notices?

62   Requirement for contract terms and notices to be fair

(1)   An unfair term of a consumer contract is not binding on the consumer.

(2) An unfair consumer notice is not binding on the consumer.

(3) This does not prevent the consumer from relying on the term or notice if the consumer chooses to do so.

(4) A term is unfair if, contrary to the requirement of good faith, it causes a significant imbalance in the parties' rights and obligations under the contract to the detriment of the consumer.

(5) Whether a term is fair is to be determined—

    (a) taking into account the nature of the subject matter of the contract, and

    (b) by reference to all the circumstances existing when the term was agreed and to all of the other terms of the contract or of any other contract on which it depends.

(6) A notice is unfair if, contrary to the requirement of good faith, it causes a significant imbalance in the parties' rights and obligations to the detriment of the consumer.

(7) Whether a notice is fair is to be determined—

    (a) taking into account the nature of the subject matter of the notice, and

    (b) by reference to all the circumstances existing when the rights or obligations to which it relates arose and to the terms of any contract on which it depends.

(8) This section does not affect the operation of—

    (a) section 31 (exclusion of liability: goods contracts),

    (b) section 47 (exclusion of liability: digital content contracts),

    (c) section 57 (exclusion of liability: services contracts), or

    (d) section 65 (exclusion of negligence liability).

63 Contract terms which may or must be regarded as unfair

(1) Part 1 of Schedule 2 contains an indicative and non-exhaustive list of terms of consumer contracts that may be regarded as unfair for the purposes of this Part.

(2) Part 1 of Schedule 2 is subject to Part 2 of that Schedule; but a term listed in Part 2 of that Schedule may nevertheless be assessed for fairness under section 62 unless section 64 or 73 applies to it.

(3) The Secretary of State may by order made by statutory instrument amend Schedule 2 so as to add, modify or remove an entry in Part 1 or Part 2 of that Schedule.

(4) An order under subsection (3) may contain transitional or transitory provision or savings.

(5) No order may be made under subsection (3) unless a draft of the statutory instrument containing it has been laid before, and approved by a resolution of, each House of Parliament.

(6) A term of a consumer contract must be regarded as unfair if it has the effect that the consumer bears the burden of proof with respect to compliance by a distance supplier or an intermediary with an obligation under any enactment or rule implementing the Distance Marketing Directive.

(7) In subsection (6)—

'the Distance Marketing Directive' means Directive 2002/65/EC of the European Parliament and of the Council of 23 September 2002 concerning the distance marketing of consumer financial services and amending Council Directive 90/619/EEC and Directives 97/7/EC and 98/27/EC;

'distance supplier' means—

    (a) a supplier under a distance contract within the meaning of the Financial Services (Distance Marketing) Regulations 2004 (SI 2004/2095), or

    (b) a supplier of unsolicited financial services within the meaning of regulation 15 of those regulations;

'enactment' includes an enactment contained in subordinate legislation within the meaning of the Interpretation Act 1978;

'intermediary' has the same meaning as in the Financial Services (Distance Marketing) Regulations 2004;

'rule' means a rule made by the Financial Conduct Authority or the Prudential Regulation Authority under the Financial Services and Markets Act 2000 or by a designated professional body within the meaning of section 326(2) of that Act.

64   Exclusion from assessment of fairness

(1)   A term of a consumer contract may not be assessed for fairness under section 62 to the extent that—

(a)   it specifies the main subject matter of the contract, or

(b)   the assessment is of the appropriateness of the price payable under the contract by comparison with the goods, digital content or services supplied under it.

(2)   Subsection (1) excludes a term from an assessment under section 62 only if it is transparent and prominent.

(3)   A term is transparent for the purposes of this Part if it is expressed in plain and intelligible language and (in the case of a written term) is legible.

(4)   A term is prominent for the purposes of this section if it is brought to the consumer's attention in such a way that an average consumer would be aware of the term.

(5)   In subsection (4) 'average consumer' means a consumer who is reasonably well-informed, observant and circumspect.

(6)   This section does not apply to a term of a contract listed in Part 1 of Schedule 2.

65   Bar on exclusion or restriction of negligence liability

(1)   A trader cannot by a term of a consumer contract or by a consumer notice exclude or restrict liability for death or personal injury resulting from negligence.

(2)   Where a term of a consumer contract, or a consumer notice, purports to exclude or restrict a trader's liability for negligence, a person is not to be taken to have voluntarily accepted any risk merely because the person agreed to or knew about the term or notice.

(3)   In this section 'personal injury' includes any disease and any impairment of physical or mental condition.

(4)   In this section 'negligence' means the breach of—

(a)   any obligation to take reasonable care or exercise reasonable skill in the performance of a contract where the obligation arises from an express or implied term of the contract,

(b)   a common law duty to take reasonable care or exercise reasonable skill,

(c)   the common duty of care imposed by the Occupiers' Liability Act 1957 or the Occupiers' Liability Act (Northern Ireland) 1957, or

(d)   the duty of reasonable care imposed by section 2(1) of the Occupiers' Liability (Scotland) Act 1960.

(5)   It is immaterial for the purposes of subsection (4)—

(a)   whether a breach of duty or obligation was inadvertent or intentional, or

(b)   whether liability for it arises directly or vicariously.

(6)   This section is subject to section 66 (which makes provision about the scope of this section).

66   Scope of section 65

(1)   Section 65 does not apply to—

(a)   any contract so far as it is a contract of insurance, including a contract to pay an annuity on human life, or

(b)   any contract so far as it relates to the creation or transfer of an interest in land.

(2)   Section 65 does not affect the validity of any discharge or indemnity given

by a person in consideration of the receipt by that person of compensation in settlement of any claim the person has.

(3) Section 65 does not—

(a) apply to liability which is excluded or discharged as mentioned in section 4(2)(a) (exception to liability to pay damages to relatives) of the Damages (Scotland) Act 2011, or

(b) affect the operation of section 5 (discharge of liability to pay damages: exception for mesothelioma) of that Act.

(4) Section 65 does not apply to the liability of an occupier of premises to a person who obtains access to the premises for recreational purposes if—

(a) the person suffers loss or damage because of the dangerous state of the premises, and

(b) allowing the person access for those purposes is not within the purposes of the occupier's trade, business, craft or profession.

67 Effect of an unfair term on the rest of a contract

Where a term of a consumer contract is not binding on the consumer as a result of this Part, the contract continues, so far as practicable, to have effect in every other respect.

68 Requirement for transparency

(1) A trader must ensure that a written term of a consumer contract, or a consumer notice in writing, is transparent.

(2) A consumer notice is transparent for the purposes of subsection (1) if it is expressed in plain and intelligible language and it is legible.

69 Contract terms that may have different meanings

(1) If a term in a consumer contract, or a consumer notice, could have different meanings, the meaning that is most favourable to the consumer is to prevail.

(2) Subsection (1) does not apply to the construction of a term or a notice in proceedings on an application for an injunction or interdict under paragraph 3 of Schedule 3.

How are the general rules enforced?

70 Enforcement of the law on unfair contract terms

(1) Schedule 3 confers functions on the Competition and Markets Authority and other regulators in relation to the enforcement of this Part.

(2) For provision about the investigatory powers that are available to those regulators for the purposes of that Schedule, see Schedule 5.

Supplementary provisions

71 Duty of court to consider fairness of term

(1) Subsection (2) applies to proceedings before a court which relate to a term of a consumer contract.

(2) The court must consider whether the term is fair even if none of the parties to the proceedings has raised that issue or indicated that it intends to raise it.

(3) But subsection (2) does not apply unless the court considers that it has before it sufficient legal and factual material to enable it to consider the fairness of the term.

72 Application of rules to secondary contracts

(1) This section applies if a term of a contract ('the secondary contract') reduces the rights or remedies or increases the obligations of a person under another contract ('the main contract').

(2) The term is subject to the provisions of this Part that would apply to the term if it were in the main contract.

(3)   It does not matter for the purposes of this section—

(a)   whether the parties to the secondary contract are the same as the parties to the main contract, or

(b)   whether the secondary contract is a consumer contract.

(4)   This section does not apply if the secondary contract is a settlement of a claim arising under the main contract.

73   Disapplication of rules to mandatory terms and notices

(1)   This Part does not apply to a term of a contract, or to a notice, to the extent that it reflects—

(a)   mandatory statutory or regulatory provisions, or

(b)   the provisions or principles of an international convention to which the United Kingdom or the EU is a party.

(2)   In subsection (1) 'mandatory statutory or regulatory provisions' includes rules which, according to law, apply between the parties on the basis that no other arrangements have been established.

74   Contracts applying law of non-EEA State

(1)   If—

(a)   the law of a country or territory other than an EEA State is chosen by the parties to be applicable to a consumer contract, but

(b)   the consumer contract has a close connection with the United Kingdom, this Part applies despite that choice.

(2)   For cases where the law applicable has not been chosen or the law of an EEA State is chosen, see Regulation (EC) No. 593/2008 of the European Parliament and of the Council of 17 June 2008 on the law applicable to contractual obligations.

75   Changes to other legislation

Schedule 4 (amendments consequential on this Part) has effect.

76   Interpretation of Part 2

(1)   In this Part—

'consumer contract' has the meaning given by section 61(3);

'consumer notice' has the meaning given by section 61(7);

'transparent' is to be construed in accordance with sections 64(3) and 68(2).

(2)   The following have the same meanings in this Part as they have in Part 1—

'trader' (see section 2(2));

'consumer' (see section 2(3));

'goods' (see section 2(8));

'digital content' (see section 2(9)).

(3)   Section 2(4) (trader who claims an individual is not a consumer must prove it) applies in relation to this Part as it applies in relation to Part 1.

. . .

SCHEDULE 2
CONSUMER CONTRACT TERMS WHICH MAY BE REGARDED AS UNFAIR

PART 1
LIST OF TERMS

1   A term which has the object or effect of excluding or limiting the trader's liability in the event of the death of or personal injury to the consumer resulting from an act or omission of the trader.

2   A term which has the object or effect of inappropriately excluding or limiting the legal rights of the consumer in relation to the trader or another party in the event of total or partial non-performance or inadequate performance by the trader

of any of the contractual obligations, including the option of offsetting a debt owed to the trader against any claim which the consumer may have against the trader.

3   A term which has the object or effect of making an agreement binding on the consumer in a case where the provision of services by the trader is subject to a condition whose realisation depends on the trader's will alone.

4   A term which has the object or effect of permitting the trader to retain sums paid by the consumer where the consumer decides not to conclude or perform the contract, without providing for the consumer to receive compensation of an equivalent amount from the trader where the trader is the party cancelling the contract.

5   A term which has the object or effect of requiring that, where the consumer decides not to conclude or perform the contract, the consumer must pay the trader a disproportionately high sum in compensation or for services which have not been supplied.

6   A term which has the object or effect of requiring a consumer who fails to fulfil his obligations under the contract to pay a disproportionately high sum in compensation.

7   A term which has the object or effect of authorising the trader to dissolve the contract on a discretionary basis where the same facility is not granted to the consumer, or permitting the trader to retain the sums paid for services not yet supplied by the trader where it is the trader who dissolves the contract.

8   A term which has the object or effect of enabling the trader to terminate a contract of indeterminate duration without reasonable notice except where there are serious grounds for doing so.

9   A term which has the object or effect of automatically extending a contract of fixed duration where the consumer does not indicate otherwise, when the deadline fixed for the consumer to express a desire not to extend the contract is unreasonably early.

10   A term which has the object or effect of irrevocably binding the consumer to terms with which the consumer has had no real opportunity of becoming acquainted before the conclusion of the contract.

11   A term which has the object or effect of enabling the trader to alter the terms of the contract unilaterally without a valid reason which is specified in the contract.

12   A term which has the object or effect of permitting the trader to determine the characteristics of the subject matter of the contract after the consumer has become bound by it.

13   A term which has the object or effect of enabling the trader to alter unilaterally without a valid reason any characteristics of the goods, digital content or services to be provided.

14   A term which has the object or effect of giving the trader the discretion to decide the price payable under the contract after the consumer has become bound by it, where no price or method of determining the price is agreed when the consumer becomes bound.

15   A term which has the object or effect of permitting a trader to increase the price of goods, digital content or services without giving the consumer the right to cancel the contract if the final price is too high in relation to the price agreed when the contract was concluded.

16   A term which has the object or effect of giving the trader the right to determine whether the goods, digital content or services supplied are in conformity with the contract, or giving the trader the exclusive right to interpret any term of the contract.

17   A term which has the object or effect of limiting the trader's obligation to respect commitments undertaken by the trader's agents or making the trader's commitments subject to compliance with a particular formality.

18   A term which has the object or effect of obliging the consumer to fulfil

all of the consumer's obligations where the trader does not perform the trader's obligations.

19   A term which has the object or effect of allowing the trader to transfer the trader's rights and obligations under the contract, where this may reduce the guarantees for the consumer, without the consumer's agreement.

20   A term which has the object or effect of excluding or hindering the consumer's right to take legal action or exercise any other legal remedy, in particular by—

(a)   requiring the consumer to take disputes exclusively to arbitration not covered by legal provisions,

(b)   unduly restricting the evidence available to the consumer, or

(c)   imposing on the consumer a burden of proof which, according to the applicable law, should lie with another party to the contract.

PART 2
SCOPE OF PART 1

Financial services

21   Paragraph 8 (cancellation without reasonable notice) does not include a term by which a supplier of financial services reserves the right to terminate unilaterally a contract of indeterminate duration without notice where there is a valid reason, if the supplier is required to inform the consumer of the cancellation immediately.

22   Paragraph 11 (variation of contract without valid reason) does not include a term by which a supplier of financial services reserves the right to alter the rate of interest payable by or due to the consumer, or the amount of other charges for financial services without notice where there is a valid reason, if—

(a)   the supplier is required to inform the consumer of the alteration at the earliest opportunity, and

(b)   the consumer is free to dissolve the contract immediately.

Contracts which last indefinitely

23   Paragraphs 11 (variation of contract without valid reason), 12 (determination of characteristics of goods etc after consumer bound) and 14 (determination of price after consumer bound) do not include a term under which a trader reserves the right to alter unilaterally the conditions of a contract of indeterminate duration if—

(a)   the trader is required to inform the consumer with reasonable notice, and

(b)   the consumer is free to dissolve the contract.

Sale of securities, foreign currency etc

24   Paragraphs 8 (cancellation without reasonable notice), 11 (variation of contract without valid reason), 14 (determination of price after consumer bound) and 15 (increase in price) do not apply to—

(a)   transactions in transferable securities, financial instruments and other products or services where the price is linked to fluctuations in a stock exchange quotation or index or a financial market rate that the trader does not control, and

(b)   contracts for the purchase or sale of foreign currency, traveller's cheques or international money orders denominated in foreign currency.

Price index clauses

25   Paragraphs 14 (determination of price after consumer bound) and 15 (increase in price) do not include a term which is a price-indexation clause (where otherwise lawful), if the method by which prices vary is explicitly described.

SCHEDULE 3
ENFORCEMENT OF THE LAW ON UNFAIR CONTRACT TERMS AND NOTICES

Application of Schedule

1   This Schedule applies to—
    (a)   a term of a consumer contract,
    (b)   a term proposed for use in a consumer contract,
    (c)   a term which a third party recommends for use in a consumer contract, or
    (d)   a consumer notice.

Consideration of complaints

2—(1)   A regulator may consider a complaint about a term or notice to which this Schedule applies (a 'relevant complaint').
(2)   If a regulator other than the CMA intends to consider a relevant complaint, it must notify the CMA that it intends to do so, and must then consider the complaint.
(3)   If a regulator considers a relevant complaint, but decides not to make an application under paragraph 3 in relation to the complaint, it must give reasons for its decision to the person who made the complaint.

Application for injunction or interdict

3—(1)   A regulator may apply for an injunction or (in Scotland) an interdict against a person if the regulator thinks that—
    (a)   the person is using, or proposing or recommending the use of, a term or notice to which this Schedule applies, and
    (b)   the term or notice falls within any one or more of sub-paragraphs (2), (3) or (5).
(2)   A term or notice falls within this sub-paragraph if it purports to exclude or restrict liability of the kind mentioned in—
    (a)   section 31 (exclusion of liability: goods contracts),
    (b)   section 47 (exclusion of liability: digital content contracts),
    (c)   section 57 (exclusion of liability: services contracts), or
    (d)   section 65(1) (business liability for death or personal injury resulting from negligence).
(3)   A term or notice falls within this sub-paragraph if it is unfair to any extent.
(4)   A term within paragraph 1(1)(b) or (c) (but not within paragraph 1(1)(a)) is to be treated for the purposes of section 62(4) and (5) (assessment of fairness) as if it were a term of a contract.
(5)   A term or notice falls within this sub-paragraph if it breaches section 68 (requirement for transparency).
(6)   A regulator may apply for an injunction or interdict under this paragraph in relation to a term or notice whether or not it has received a relevant complaint about the term or notice.

Notification of application

4—(1)   Before making an application under paragraph 3, a regulator other than the CMA must notify the CMA that it intends to do so.

(2)   The regulator may make the application only if—

(a)   the period of 14 days beginning with the day on which the regulator notified the CMA has ended, or

(b)   before the end of that period, the CMA agrees to the regulator making the application.

Determination of application

5—(1)   On an application for an injunction under paragraph 3, the court may grant an injunction on such conditions, and against such of the respondents, as it thinks appropriate.

(2)   On an application for an interdict under paragraph 3, the court may grant an interdict on such conditions, and against such of the defenders, as it thinks appropriate.

(3)   The injunction or interdict may include provision about—

(a)   a term or notice to which the application relates, or

(b)   any term of a consumer contract, or any consumer notice, of a similar kind or with a similar effect.

(4)   It is not a defence to an application under paragraph 3 to show that, because of a rule of law, a term to which the application relates is not, or could not be, an enforceable contract term.

(5)   If a regulator other than the CMA makes the application, it must notify the CMA of—

(a)   the outcome of the application, and

(b)   if an injunction or interdict is granted, the conditions on which, and the persons against whom, it is granted.

Undertakings

6—(1)   A regulator may accept an undertaking from a person against whom it has applied, or thinks it is entitled to apply, for an injunction or interdict under paragraph 3.

(2)   The undertaking may provide that the person will comply with the conditions that are agreed between the person and the regulator about the use of terms or notices, or terms or notices of a kind, specified in the undertaking.

(3)   If a regulator other than the CMA accepts an undertaking, it must notify the CMA of—

(a)   the conditions on which the undertaking is accepted, and

(b)   the person who gave it.

Publication, information and advice

7—(1)   The CMA must arrange the publication of details of—

(a)   any application it makes for an injunction or interdict under paragraph 3,

(b)   any injunction or interdict under this Schedule, and

(c)   any undertaking under this Schedule.

(2)   The CMA must respond to a request whether a term or notice, or one of a similar kind or with a similar effect, is or has been the subject of an injunction, interdict or undertaking under this Schedule.

(3)   Where the term or notice, or one of a similar kind or with a similar effect, is or has been the subject of an injunction or interdict under this Schedule, the CMA must give the person making the request a copy of the injunction or interdict.

(4)   Where the term or notice, or one of a similar kind or with a similar effect, is or has been the subject of an undertaking under this Schedule, the CMA must give the person making the request—

(a)   details of the undertaking, and

(b)   if the person giving the undertaking has agreed to amend the term or notice, a copy of the amendments.

(5)   The CMA may arrange the publication of advice and information about the provisions of this Part.

(6)   In this paragraph—

(a)   references to an injunction or interdict under this Schedule are to an injunction or interdict granted on an application by the CMA under paragraph 3 or notified to it under paragraph 5, and

(b)   references to an undertaking are to an undertaking given to the CMA under paragraph 6 or notified to it under that paragraph.

Meaning of 'regulator'

8—(1)   In this Schedule 'regulator' means—

(a)   the CMA,

(b)   the Department of Enterprise, Trade and Investment in Northern Ireland,

(c)   a local weights and measures authority in Great Britain,

(d)   the Financial Conduct Authority,

(e)   the Office of Communications,

(f)   the Information Commissioner,

(g)   the Gas and Electricity Markets Authority,

(h)   the Water Services Regulation Authority,

(i)   the Office of Rail Regulation,

(j)   the Northern Ireland Authority for Utility Regulation, or

(k)   the Consumers' Association.

(2)   The Secretary of State may by order made by statutory instrument amend sub-paragraph (1) so as to add, modify or remove an entry.

(3)   An order under sub-paragraph (2) may amend sub-paragraph (1) so as to add a body that is not a public authority only if the Secretary of State thinks that the body represents the interests of consumers (or consumers of a particular description).

(4)   The Secretary of State must publish (and may from time to time vary) other criteria to be applied by the Secretary of State in deciding whether to add an entry to, or remove an entry from, sub-paragraph (1).

(5)   An order under sub-paragraph (2) may make consequential amendments to this Schedule (including with the effect that any of its provisions apply differently, or do not apply, to a body added to sub-paragraph (1)).

(6)   An order under sub-paragraph (2) may contain transitional or transitory provision or savings.

(7)   No order may be made under sub-paragraph (2) unless a draft of the statutory instrument containing it has been laid before, and approved by a resolution of, each House of Parliament.

(8)   In this paragraph 'public authority' has the same meaning as in section 6 of the Human Rights Act 1998.

Other definitions

9   In this Schedule—

'the CMA' means the Competition and Markets Authority;

'injunction' includes an interim injunction;

'interdict' includes an interim interdict.

The Financial Conduct Authority

10   The functions of the Financial Conduct Authority under this Schedule are to be treated as functions of the Authority under the Financial Services and Markets Act 2000.

. . .

PART II
STATUTORY INSTRUMENTS

COMMERCIAL AGENTS (COUNCIL DIRECTIVE) REGULATIONS 1993
(SI 1993/3053)

PART I
GENERAL

1 Citation, commencement and applicable law

(1) These Regulations may be cited as the Commercial Agents (Council Directive) Regulations 1993 and shall come into force on 1st January 1994.

(2) These Regulations govern the relations between commercial agents and their principals and, subject to paragraph (3), apply in relation to the activities of commercial agents in Great Britain.

(3) Regulations 3 to 22 do not apply where the parties have agreed that the agency contract is to be governed by the law of another member State.

2 Interpretation, application and extent

(1) In these Regulations—

'commercial agent' means a self-employed intermediary who has continuing authority to negotiate the sale or purchase of goods on behalf of another person (the 'principal'), or to negotiate and conclude the sale or purchase of goods on behalf of and in the name of that principal; but shall be understood as not including in particular:

(i) a person who, in his capacity as an officer of a company or association, is empowered to enter into commitments binding on that company or association;

(ii) a partner who is lawfully authorised to enter into commitments binding on his partners;

(iii) a person who acts as an insolvency practitioner (as that expression is defined in section 388 of the Insolvency Act 1986) or the equivalent in any other jurisdiction;

'commission' means any part of the remuneration of a commercial agent which varies with the number or value of business transactions;

['EEA Agreement' means the Agreement on the European Economic Area signed at Oporto on 2nd May 1992 as adjusted by the Protocol signed at Brussels on 17th March 1993;

'member State' includes a State which is a contracting party to the EEA Agreement;]

'restraint of trade clause' means an agreement restricting the business activities of a commercial agent following termination of the agency contract.

(2) These Regulations do not apply to—

(a) commercial agents whose activities are unpaid;

(b) commercial agents when they operate on commodity exchanges or in the commodity market;

(c) the Crown Agents for Overseas Governments and Administrations, as set up under the Crown Agents Act 1979, or its subsidiaries.

(3) The provisions of the Schedule to these Regulations have effect for the pur-

pose of determining the persons whose activities as commercial agents are to be considered secondary.

(4) These Regulations shall not apply to the persons referred to in paragraph (3) above.

(5) These Regulations do not extend to Northern Ireland.

PART II
RIGHTS AND OBLIGATIONS

3 Duties of a commercial agent to his principal

(1) In performing his activities a commercial agent must look after the interests of his principal and act dutifully and in good faith.

(2) In particular, a commercial agent must—

(a) make proper efforts to negotiate and, where appropriate, conclude the transactions he is instructed to take care of;

(b) communicate to his principal all the necessary information available to him;

(c) comply with reasonable instructions given by his principal.

4 Duties of a principal to his commercial agent

(1) In his relations with his commercial agent a principal must act dutifully and in good faith.

(2) In particular, a principal must—

(a) provide his commercial agent with the necessary documentation relating to the goods concerned;

(b) obtain for his commercial agent the information necessary for the performance of the agency contract, and in particular notify his commercial agent within a reasonable period once he anticipates that the volume of commercial transactions will be significantly lower than that which the commercial agent could normally have expected.

(3) A principal shall, in addition, inform his commercial agent within a reasonable period of his acceptance or refusal of, and of any non-execution by him of, a commercial transaction which the commercial agent has procured for him.

5 Prohibition on derogation from regulations 3 and 4 and consequence of breach

(1) The parties may not derogate from regulations 3 and 4 above.

(2) The law applicable to the contract shall govern the consequence of breach of the rights and obligations under regulations 3 and 4 above.

PART III
REMUNERATION

6 Form and amount of remuneration in absence of agreement

(1) In the absence of any agreement as to remuneration between the parties, a commercial agent shall be entitled to the remuneration that commercial agents appointed for the goods forming the subject of his agency contract are customarily allowed in the place where he carries on his activities and, if there is no such customary practice, a commercial agent shall be entitled to reasonable remuneration taking into account all the aspects of the transaction.

(2) This regulation is without prejudice to the application of any enactment or rule of law concerning the level of remuneration.

(3) Where a commercial agent is not remunerated (wholly or in part) by commission, regulations 7 to 12 below shall not apply.

7 Entitlement to commission on transactions concluded during agency contract

(1) A commercial agent shall be entitled to commission on commercial transactions concluded during the period covered by the agency contract—

(a) where the transaction has been concluded as a result of his action; or

(b) where the transaction is concluded with a third party whom he has previously acquired as a customer for transactions of the same kind.

(2) A commercial agent shall also be entitled to commission on transactions concluded during the period covered by the agency contract where he has an exclusive right to a specific geographical area or to a specific group of customers and where the transaction has been entered into with a customer belonging to that area or group.

8 Entitlement to commission on transactions concluded after agency contract has terminated

Subject to regulation 9 below, a commercial agent shall be entitled to commission on commercial transactions concluded after the agency contract has terminated if—

(a) the transaction is mainly attributable to his efforts during the period covered by the agency contract and if the transaction was entered into within a reasonable period after that contract terminated; or

(b) in accordance with the conditions mentioned in regulation 7 above, the order of the third party reached the principal or the commercial agent before the agency contract terminated.

9 Apportionment of commission between new and previous commercial agents

(1) A commercial agent shall not be entitled to the commission referred to in regulation 7 above if that commission is payable, by virtue of regulation 8 above, to the previous commercial agent, unless it is equitable because of the circumstances for the commission to be shared between the commercial agents.

(2) The principal shall be liable for any sum due under paragraph (1) above to the person entitled to it in accordance with that paragraph, and any sum which the other commercial agent receives to which he is not entitled shall be refunded to the principal.

10 When commission due and date for payment

(1) Commission shall become due as soon as, and to the extent that, one of the following circumstances occurs:

(a) the principal has executed the transaction; or

(b) the principal should, according to his agreement with the third party, have executed the transaction; or

(c) the third party has executed the transaction.

(2) Commission shall become due at the latest when the third party has executed his part of the transaction or should have done so if the principal had executed his part of the transaction, as he should have.

(3) The commission shall be paid not later than on the last day of the month following the quarter in which it became due, and, for the purposes of these Regulations, unless otherwise agreed between the parties, the first quarter period shall run from the date the agency contract takes effect, and subsequent periods shall run from that date in the third month thereafter or the beginning of the fourth month, whichever is the sooner.

(4) Any agreement to derogate from paragraphs (2) and (3) above to the detriment of the commercial agent shall be void.

11 Extinction of right to commission

(1) The right to commission can be extinguished only if and to the extent that—

(a)   it is established that the contract between the third party and the principal will not be executed; and

(b)   that fact is due to a reason for which the principal is not to blame.

(2)   Any commission which the commercial agent has already received shall be refunded if the right to it is extinguished.

(3)   any agreement to derogate from paragraph (1) above to the detriment of the commercial agent shall be void.

12   Periodic supply of information as to commission due and right of inspection of principal's books

(1)   The principal shall supply his commercial agent with a statement of the commission due, not later than the last day of the month following the quarter in which the commission has become due, and such statement shall set out the main components used in calculating the amount of the commission.

(2)   A commercial agent shall be entitled to demand that he be provided with all the information (and in particular an extract from the books) which is available to his principal and which he needs in order to check the amount of the commission due to him.

(3)   Any agreement to derogate from paragraphs (1) and (2) above shall be void.

(4)   Nothing in this regulation shall remove or restrict the effect of, or prevent reliance upon, any enactment or rule of law which recognises the right of an agent to inspect the books of a principal.

PART IV
CONCLUSION AND TERMINATION OF THE AGENCY CONTRACT

13   Right to signed written statement of terms of agency contract

(1)   The commercial agent and principal shall each be entitled to receive from the other, on request, a signed written document setting out the terms of the agency contract including any terms subsequently agreed.

(2)   Any purported waiver of the right referred to in paragraph (1) above shall be void.

14   Conversion of agency contract after expiry of fixed period

An agency contract for a fixed period which continues to be performed by both parties after that period has expired shall be deemed to be converted into an agency contract for an indefinite period.

15   Minimum periods of notice for termination of agency contract

(1)   Where an agency contract is concluded for an indefinite period either party may terminate it by notice.

(2)   The period of notice shall be—

(a)   1 month for the first year of the contract;

(b)   2 months for the second year commenced;

(c)   3 months for the third year commenced and for the subsequent years;

and the parties may not agree on any shorter periods of notice.

(3)   If the parties agree on longer periods than those laid down in paragraph (2) above, the period of notice to be observed by the principal must not be shorter than that to be observed by the commercial agent.

(4)   Unless otherwise agreed by the parties, the end of the period of notice must coincide with the end of a calendar month.

(5)   The provisions of this regulation shall also apply to an agency contract for a fixed period where it is converted under regulation 14 above into an agency contract for an indefinite period subject to the proviso that the earlier fixed period must be taken into account in the calculation of the period of notice.

16   Savings with regard to immediate termination
These Regulations shall not affect the application of any enactment or rule of law which provides for the immediate termination of the agency contract—
(a)   because of the failure of one party to carry out all or part of his obligations under that contract; or
(b)   where exceptional circumstances arise.

17   Entitlement of commercial agent to indemnity or compensation on termination of agency contract
(1)   This regulation has effect for the purpose of ensuring that the commercial agent is, after termination of the agency contract, indemnified in accordance with paragraphs (3) to (5) below or compensated for damage in accordance with paragraphs (6) and (7) below.
(2)   Except where the agency [contract] otherwise provides, the commercial agent shall be entitled to be compensated rather than indemnified.
(3)   Subject to paragraph (9) and to regulation 18 below, the commercial agent shall be entitled to an indemnity if and to the extent that—
(a)   he has brought the principal new customers or has significantly increased the volume of business with existing customers and the principal continues to derive substantial benefits from the business with such customers; and
(b)   the payment of this indemnity is equitable having regard to all the circumstances and, in particular, the commission lost by the commercial agent on the business transacted with such customers.
(4)   The amount of the indemnity shall not exceed a figure equivalent to an indemnity for one year calculated from the commercial agent's average annual remuneration over the preceding five years and if the contract goes back less than five years the indemnity shall be calculated on the average for the period in question.
(5)   The grant of an indemnity as mentioned above shall not prevent the commercial agent from seeking damages.
(6)   Subject to paragraph (9) and to regulation 18 below, the commercial agent shall be entitled to compensation for the damage he suffers as a result of the termination of his relations with his principal.
(7)   For the purpose of these Regulations such damage shall be deemed to occur particularly when the termination takes place in either or both of the following circumstances, namely circumstances which—
(a)   deprive the commercial agent of the commission which proper performance of the agency contract would have procured for him whilst providing his principal with substantial benefits linked to the activities of the commercial agent; or
(b)   have not enabled the commercial agent to amortize the costs and expenses that he had incurred in the performance of the agency contract on the advice of his principal.
(8)   Entitlement to the indemnity or compensation for damage as provided for under paragraphs (2) to (7) above shall also arise where the agency contract is terminated as a result of the death of the commercial agent.
(9)   The commercial agent shall lose his entitlement to the indemnity or compensation for damage in the instances provided for in paragraphs (2) to (8) above if within one year following termination of his agency contract he has not notified his principal that he intends pursuing his entitlement.

18   Grounds for excluding payment of indemnity or compensation under regulation 17
The [indemnity or] compensation referred to in regulation 17 above shall not be payable to the commercial agent where—
(a)   the principal has terminated the agency contract because of default attribu-

table to the commercial agent which would justify immediate termination of the agency contract pursuant to regulation 16 above; or

(b)   the commercial agent has himself terminated the agency contract, unless such termination is justified—

(i)   by circumstances attributable to the principal, or

(ii)   on grounds of the age, infirmity or illness of the commercial agent in consequence of which he cannot reasonably be required to continue his activities; or

(c)   the commercial agent, with the agreement of his principal, assigns his rights and duties under the agency contract to another person.

19   Prohibition on derogation from regulations 17 and 18
The parties may not derogate from regulations 17 and 18 to the detriment of the commercial agent before the agency contract expires.

20   Restraint of trade clauses
(1)   A restraint of trade clause shall be valid only if and to the extent that—

(a)   it is concluded in writing; and

(b)   it relates to the geographical area or the group of customers and the geographical area entrusted to the commercial agent and to the kind of goods covered by his agency under the contract.

(2)   A restraint of trade clause shall be valid for not more than two years after termination of the agency contract.

(3)   Nothing in this regulation shall affect any enactment or rule of law which imposes other restrictions on the validity or enforceability of restraint of trade clauses or which enables a court to reduce the obligations on the parties resulting from such clauses.

PART V
MISCELLANEOUS AND SUPPLEMENTAL

21   Disclosure of information
Nothing in these Regulations shall require information to be given where such disclosure would be contrary to public policy.

22   Service of notice etc
(1)   Any notice, statement or other document to be given or supplied to a commercial agent or to be given or supplied to the principal under these Regulations may be so given or supplied:

(a)   by delivering it to him;

(b)   by leaving it at his proper address addressed to him by name;

(c)   by sending it by post to him addressed either to his registered address or to the address of his registered or principal office;

or by any other means provided for in the agency contract.

(2)   Any such notice, statement or document may—

(a)   in the case of a body corporate, be given or served on the secretary or clerk of that body;

(b)   in the case of a partnership, be given to or served on any partner or on any person having the control or management of the partnership business.

23   Transitional provisions
(1)   Notwithstanding any provision in an agency contract made before 1st January 1994, these Regulations shall apply to that contract after that date and, accordingly any provision which is inconsistent with these Regulations shall have effect subject to them.

(2)   Nothing in these Regulations shall affect the rights and liabilities of a commercial agent or a principal which have accrued before 1st January 1994.

Regulation 2(3)   THE SCHEDULE

1 The activities of a person as a commercial agent are to be considered secondary where it may reasonably be taken that the primary purpose of the arrangement with his principal is other than as set out in paragraph 2 below.

2 An arrangement falls within this paragraph if—

(a) the business of the principal is the sale, or as the case may be purchase, of goods of a particular kind; and

(b) the goods concerned are such that—

(i) transactions are normally individually negotiated and concluded on a commercial basis, and

(ii) procuring a transaction on one occasion is likely to lead to further transactions in those goods with that customer on future occasions, or to transactions in those goods with other customers in the same geographical area or among the same group of customers, and

that accordingly it is in the commercial interests of the principal in developing the market in those goods to appoint a representative to such customers with a view to the representative devoting effort, skill and expenditure from his own resources to that end.

3 The following are indications that an arrangement falls within paragraph 2 above, and the absence of any of them is an indication to the contrary—

(a) the principal is the manufacturer, importer or distributor of the goods;

(b) the goods are specifically identified with the principal in the market in question rather than, or to a greater extent than, with any other person;

(c) the agent devotes substantially the whole of his time to representative activities (whether for one principal or for a number of principals whose interests are not conflicting);

(d) the goods are not normally available in the market in question other than by means of the agent;

(e) the arrangement is described as one of commercial agency.

4 The following are indications that an arrangement does not fall within paragraph 2 above—

(a) promotional material is supplied direct to potential customers;

(b) persons are granted agencies without reference to existing agents in a particular area or in relation to a particular group;

(c) customers normally select the goods for themselves and merely place their orders through the agent.

5 The activities of the following categories of persons are presumed, unless the contrary is established, not to fall within paragraph 2 above—

Mail order catalogue agents for consumer goods.

Consumer credit agents.

PROVISION AND USE OF WORK EQUIPMENT REGULATIONS 1998
(SI 1998/2306)

2 Interpretation

(1) In these Regulations, unless the context otherwise requires—

'the 1974 Act' means the Health and Safety at Work etc Act 1974;

'employer' except in regulation 3(2) and (3) includes a person to whom the requirements imposed by the Regulations apply by virtue of regulation 3(3)(a) and (b);

'essential requirements' means requirements described in regulation 10(1);

'the Executive' means the Health and Safety Executive;

'inspection' in relation to an inspection under paragraph (1) or (2) of regulation 6—

(a)   means such visual or more rigorous inspection by a competent person as is appropriate for the purpose described in the paragraph;

(b)   where it is appropriate to carry out testing for the purpose, includes testing the nature and extent of which are appropriate for the purpose;

'power press' means a press or press brake for the working of metal by means of tools, or for die proving, which is power driven and which embodies a flywheel and clutch;

'thorough examination' in relation to a thorough examination under paragraph (1), (2), (3) or (4) of regulation 32—

(a)   means a thorough examination by a competent person;

(b)   includes testing the nature and extent of which are appropriate for the purpose described in the paragraph;

'use' in relation to work equipment means any activity involving work equipment and includes starting, stopping, programming, setting, transporting, repairing, modifying, maintaining, servicing and cleaning;

'work equipment' means any machinery, appliance, apparatus, tool or installation for use at work (whether exclusively or not);

and related expressions shall be construed accordingly.

4   Suitability of work equipment

(1)   Every employer shall ensure that work equipment is so constructed or adapted as to be suitable for the purpose for which it is used or provided.

(2)   In selecting work equipment, every employer shall have regard to the working conditions and to the risks to the health and safety of persons which exist in the premises or undertaking in which that work equipment is to be used and any additional risk posed by the use of that work equipment.

(3)   Every employer shall ensure that work equipment is used only for operations for which, and under conditions for which, it is suitable.

(4)   In this regulation 'suitable' [—

(a)   subject to subparagraph (b), means suitable in any respect which it is reasonably foreseeable will affect the health or safety of any person; . . .]

5   Maintenance

(1)   Every employer shall ensure that work equipment is maintained in an efficient state, in efficient working order and in good repair.

(2)   Every employer shall ensure that where any machinery has a maintenance log, the log is kept up to date.

6   Inspection

(1)   Every employer shall ensure that, where the safety of work equipment depends on the installation conditions, it is inspected—

(a)   after installation and before being put into service for the first time; or

(b)   after assembly at a new site or in a new location,

to ensure that it has been installed correctly and is safe to operate.

(2)   Every employer shall ensure that work equipment exposed to conditions causing deterioration which is liable to result in dangerous situations is inspected—

(a)   at suitable intervals; and

(b)   each time that exceptional circumstances which are liable to jeopardise the safety of the work equipment have occurred,

to ensure that health and safety conditions are maintained and that any deterioration can be detected and remedied in good time.

(3)   Every employer shall ensure that the result of an inspection made under this regulation is recorded and kept until the next inspection under this regulation is recorded.

(4)   Every employer shall ensure that no work equipment—

(a)   leaves his undertaking; or

(b)   if obtained from the undertaking of another person, is used in his under-taking, unless it is accompanied by physical evidence that the last inspection required to be carried out under this regulation has been carried out.

7   Specific risks

(1)   Where the use of work equipment is likely to involve a specific risk to health or safety, every employer shall ensure that—

(a)   the use of that work equipment is restricted to those persons given the task of using it; and

(b)   repairs, modifications, maintenance or servicing of that work equipment is restricted to those persons who have been specifically designated to perform operations of that description (whether or not also authorised to perform other operations).

(2)   The employer shall ensure that the persons designated for the purposes of sub-paragraph (b) of paragraph (1) have received adequate training related to any operations in respect of which they have been so designated.

8   Information and instructions

(1)   Every employer shall ensure that all persons who use work equipment have available to them adequate health and safety information and, where appro-priate, written instructions pertaining to the use of the work equipment.

(2)   Every employer shall ensure that any of his employees who supervises or manages the use of work equipment has available to him adequate health and safety information and, where appropriate, written instructions pertaining to the use of the work equipment.

(3)   Without prejudice to the generality of paragraph (1) or (2), the information and instructions required by either of those paragraphs shall include information and, where appropriate, written instructions on—

(a)   the conditions in which and the methods by which the work equipment may be used;

(b)   foreseeable abnormal situations and the action to be taken if such a situa-tion were to occur; and

(c)   any conclusions to be drawn from experience in using the work equip-ment.

(4)   Information and instructions required by this regulation shall be readily comprehensive to those concerned.

9   Training

(1)   Every employer shall ensure that all persons who use work equipment have received adequate training for purposes of health and safety, including train-ing in the methods which may be adopted when using the work equipment, any risks which such use may entail and precautions to be taken.

(2)   Every employer shall ensure that any of his employees who supervises or manages the use of work equipment has received adequate training for purposes of health and safety, including training in the methods which may be adopted when using the work equipment, any risks which such use may entail and pre-cautions to be taken.

10   Conformity with Community requirements

[(1)   Every employer shall ensure that an item of work equipment conforms at all times with any essential requirements, other than requirements which, at the time of its being first supplied or put into service in any place in which these Regulations apply, did not apply to work equipment of its type.

(2)   In this regulation 'essential requirements', in relation to an item of work equipment, means requirements relating to the design and construction of work equipment of its type in any of the instruments listed in Schedule 1 (being instru-ments which give effect to Community directives concerning the safety of products)].

(3)   This regulation applies to items of work equipment provided for use in the premises or undertaking of the employer for the first time after 31 December 1992.

11   Dangerous parts of machinery

(1)   Every employer shall ensure that measures are taken in accordance with paragraph (2) which are effective—

(a)   to prevent access to any dangerous part of machinery or to any rotating stock-bar; or

(b)   to stop the movement of any dangerous part of machinery or rotating stock-bar before any part of a person enters a danger zone.

[(2)   The measures required by paragraph (1) shall consist of—

(a)   the provision of fixed guards enclosing every dangerous part or rotating stock-bar where and to the extent that it is practicable to do so, but where or to the extent that it is not, then

(b)   the provision of other guards or protection devices where and to the extent that it is practicable to do so, but where or to the extent that it is not, then

(c)   the provision of jigs, holders, push-sticks or similar protection appliances used in conjunction with the machinery where and to the extent that it is practicable to do so, and the provision of such information, instruction, training and supervision as is necessary.]

(3)   All guards and protection devices provided under sub-paragraphs (a) or (b) of paragraph (2) shall—

(a)   be suitable for the purpose for which they are provided;

(b)   be of good construction, sound material and adequate strength;

(c)   be maintained in an efficient state, in efficient working order and in good repair;

(d)   not give rise to any increased risk to health or safety;

(e)   not be easily bypassed or disabled;

(f)   be situated at sufficient distance from the danger zone;

(g)   not unduly restrict the view of the operating cycle of the machinery, where such a view is necessary;

(h)   be so constructed or adapted that they allow operations necessary to fit or replace parts and for maintenance work, restricting access so that it is allowed only to the area where the work is to be carried out and, if possible, without having to dismantle the guard or protection device.

(4)   All protection appliances provided under sub-paragraph (c) of paragraph (2) shall comply with sub-paragraphs (a) to (d) and (g) of paragraph (3).

(5)   In this regulation—

'danger zone' means any zone in or around machinery in which a person is exposed to a risk to health or safety from contact with a dangerous part of machinery or a rotating stock-bar;

'stock-bar' means any part of a stock-bar which projects beyond the head-stock of a lathe.

12   Protection against specified hazards

(1)   Every employer shall take measures to ensure that the exposure of a person using work equipment to any risk to his health or safety from any hazard specified in paragraph (3) is either prevented, or, where that is not reasonably practicable, adequately controlled.

(2)   The measures required by paragraph (1) shall—

(a)   be measures other than the provision of personal protective equipment or of information, instruction, training and supervision, so far as is reasonably practicable; and

(b)   include, where appropriate, measures to minimise the effects of the hazard as well as to reduce the likelihood of the hazard occurring.

(3)   The hazards referred to in paragraph (1) are—

(a)   any article or substance falling or being ejected from work equipment;

(b)   rupture or disintegration of parts of work equipment;

(c)   work equipment catching fire or overheating;

(d)   the unintended or premature discharge of any article or of any gas, dust, liquid, vapour or other substance which, in each case, is produced, used or stored in the work equipment;

(e)   the unintended or premature explosion of the work equipment or any article or substance produced, used or stored in it.

(4)   For the purposes of this regulation 'adequately' means adequately having regard only to the nature of the hazard and the nature and degree of exposure to the risk.

(5)   This regulation shall not apply where any of the following Regulations apply in respect of any risk to a person's health or safety for which such Regulations require measures to be taken to prevent or control such risk, namely—

(a)   the Ionising Radiations Regulations 1985;

(b)   [the Control of Asbestos at Work Regulations 2012];

(c)   the Control of Substances Hazardous to Health Regulations 1994;

(d)   [the Control of Noise at Work Regulations 2005];

[. . .]

(f)   the Control of Lead at Work Regulations 1998 [;

(g)   the Control of Vibration at Work Regulations 2005.]

13   High or very low temperature

Every employer shall ensure that work equipment, parts of work equipment and any article or substance produced, used or stored in work equipment which, in each case, is at a high or very low temperature shall have protection where appropriate so as to prevent injury to any person by burn, scald or sear.

14   Controls for starting or making a significant change in operating conditions

(1)   Every employer shall ensure that, where appropriate, work equipment is provided with one or more controls for the purposes of—

(a)   starting the work equipment (including re-starting after a stoppage for any reason); or

(b)   controlling any change in the speed, pressure or other operating conditions of the work equipment where such conditions after the change result in risk to health and safety which is greater than or of a different nature from such risks before the change.

(2)   Subject to paragraph (3), every employer shall ensure that, where a control is required by paragraph (1), it shall not be possible to perform any operation mentioned in sub-paragraph (a) or (b) of that paragraph except by a deliberate action on such control.

(3)   Paragraph (1) shall not apply to re-starting or changing operating conditions as a result of the normal operating cycle of an automatic device.

15   Stop controls

(1)   Every employer shall ensure that, where appropriate, work equipment is provided with one or more readily accessible controls the operation of which will bring the work equipment to a safe condition in a safe manner.

(2)   Any control required by paragraph (1) shall bring the work equipment to a complete stop where necessary for reasons of health and safety.

(3)   Any control required by paragraph (1) shall, if necessary for reasons of health and safety, switch off all sources of energy after stopping the functioning of the work equipment.

(4)   Any control required by paragraph (1) shall operate in priority to any control which starts or changes the operating conditions of the work equipment.

16 Emergency stop controls

(1) Every employer shall ensure that, where appropriate, work equipment is provided with one or more readily accessible emergency stop controls unless it is not necessary by reason of the nature of the hazards and the time taken for the work equipment to come to a complete stop as a result of the action of any control provided by virtue of regulation 15(1).

(2) Any control required by paragraph (1) shall operate in priority to any control required by regulation 15(1).

17 Controls

(1) Every employer shall ensure that all controls for work equipment are clearly visible and identifiable, including by appropriate marking where necessary.

(2) Except where necessary, the employer shall ensure that no control for work equipment is in a position where any person operating the control is exposed to a risk to his health or safety.

(3) Every employer shall ensure where appropriate—

(a) that, so far as is reasonably practicable, the operator of any control is able to ensure from the position of that control that no person is in a place where he would be exposed to any risk to his health or safety as a result of the operation of that control, but where or to the extent that it is not reasonably practicable;

(b) that, so far as is reasonably practicable, systems of work are effective to ensure that, when work equipment is about to start, no person is in a place where he would be exposed to a risk to his health or safety as a result of the work equipment starting, but where neither of these is reasonably practicable;

(c) that an audible, visible or other suitable warning is given by virtue of regulation 24 whenever work equipment is about to start,

(4) Every employer shall take appropriate measures to ensure that any person who is in a place where he would be exposed to a risk to his health or safety as a result of the starting or stopping of work equipment has sufficient time and suitable means to avoid that risk.

18 Control systems

(1) Every employer shall ensure, so far as is reasonably practicable, that all control systems of work equipment—

(a) are safe; and

(b) are chosen making due allowance for the failures, faults and constraints to be expected in the planned circumstances of use.

(2) Without prejudice to the generality of paragraph (1), a control system shall not be safe unless—

(a) its operation does not create any increased risk to health or safety;

(b) it ensures, so far as is reasonably practicable, that any fault in or damage to any part of the control system or the loss of supply of any source of energy used by the work equipment cannot result in additional or increased risk to health or safety;

(c) it does not impede the operation of any control required by regulation 15 or 16.

19 Isolation from sources of energy

(1) Every employer shall ensure that where appropriate work equipment is provided with suitable means to isolate it from all its sources of energy.

(2) Without prejudice to the generality of paragraph (1), the means mentioned in that paragraph shall not be suitable unless they are clearly identifiable and readily accessible.

(3) Every employer shall take appropriate measures to ensure that re-connection of any energy source to work equipment does not expose any person using the work equipment to any risk to his health or safety.

20   Stability
Every employer shall ensure that work equipment or any part of work equipment is stabilised by clamping or otherwise where necessary for purposes of health or safety.

21   Lighting
Every employer shall ensure that suitable and sufficient lighting, which takes account of the operations to be carried out, is provided at any place where a person uses work equipment.

22   Maintenance operations
Every employer shall take appropriate measures to ensure that work equipment is so constructed or adapted that, so far as is reasonably practicable, maintenance operations which involve a risk to health or safety can be carried out while the work equipment is shut down, or in other cases—
(a)   maintenance operations can be carried out without exposing the person carrying them out to a risk to his health or safety; or
(b)   appropriate measures can be taken for the protection of any person carrying out maintenance operations which involve a risk to his health or safety.

23   Markings
Every employer shall ensure that work equipment is marked in a clearly visible manner with any marking appropriate for reasons of health and safety.

24   Warnings
(1)   Every employer shall ensure that work equipment incorporates any warnings or warning devices which are appropriate for reasons of health and safety.
(2)   Without prejudice to the generality of paragraph (1), warnings given by warning devices on work equipment shall not be appropriate unless they are unambiguous, easily perceived and easily understood.

EMPLOYERS' LIABILITY (COMPULSORY INSURANCE)
REGULATIONS 1998
(SI 1998/2573)

1   Citation, commencement and interpretation

. . .
(2)   In these Regulations—
'the 1969 Act' means the Employers' Liability (Compulsory Insurance) Act 1969;
. . .

2   Prohibition of certain conditions in policies of insurance
(1)   For the purposes of the 1969 Act, there is prohibited in any contract of insurance any condition which provides (in whatever terms) that no liability (either generally or in respect of a particular claim) shall arise under the policy, or that any such liability so arising shall cease, if—
(a)   some specified thing is done or omitted to be done after the happening of the event giving rise to a claim under the policy,
(b)   the policy holder does not take reasonable care to protect his employees against the risk of bodily injury or disease in the course of their employment;
(c)   the policy holder fails to comply with the requirements of any enactment for the protection of employees against the risk of bodily injury or disease in the course of their employment; or

(d)   the policy holder does not keep specified records or fails to provide the insurer with or make available to him information from such records.

(2)   For the purposes of the 1969 Act there is also prohibited in a policy of insurance any condition which requires—

(a)   a relevant employee to pay; or

(b)   an insured employer to pay the relevant employee,

the first amount of any claim or any aggregation of claims.

(3)   Paragraphs (1) and (2) above do not prohibit for the purposes of the 1969 Act a condition in a policy of insurance which requires the employer to pay or contribute any sum to the insurer in respect of the satisfaction of any claim made under the contract of insurance by a relevant employee or any costs and expenses incurred in relation to any such claim.

3   Limit of amount of compulsory insurance

(1)   Subject to paragraph (2) below, the amount for which an employer is required by the 1969 Act to insure and maintain insurance in respect of relevant employees under one or more policies of insurance shall be, or shall in aggregate be not less than £5 million in respect of—

(a)   a claim relating to any one or more of those employees arising out of any one occurrence; and

(b)   any costs and expenses incurred in relation to any such claim.

ELECTRONIC SIGNATURES REGULATIONS 2002
(SI 2002/318)

1   Citation and commencement

These Regulations may be cited as the Electronic Signatures Regulations 2002 and shall come into force on 8th March 2002.

2   Interpretation

In these Regulations—

'advanced electronic signature' means an electronic signature—

(a)   which is uniquely linked to the signatory,

(b)   which is capable of identifying the signatory,

(c)   which is created using means that the signatory can maintain under his sole control, and

(d)   which is linked to the data to which it relates in such a manner that any subsequent change of the data is detectable;

'certificate' means an electronic attestation which links signature-verification data to a person and confirms the identity of that person;

'certification-service-provider' means a person who issues certificates or provides other services related to electronic signatures;

'Directive' means Directive 1999/93/EC of the European Parliament and of the Council on a Community framework for electronic signatures;

'electronic signature' means data in electronic form which are attached to or logically associated with other electronic data and which serve as a method of authentication;

'qualified certificate' means a certificate which meets the requirements in Schedule 1 and is provided by a certification-service-provider who fulfils the requirements in Schedule 2;

'signatory' means a person who holds a signature-creation device and acts either on his own behalf or on behalf of the person he represents;

'signature-creation data' means unique data (including, but not limited to, codes or private cryptographic keys) which are used by the signatory to create an electronic signature;

'signature-creation device' means configured software or hardware used to implement the signature-creation data;

'signature-vertification data' means data (including, but not limited to, codes or public cryptographic keys) which are used for the purpose of verifying an electronic signature;

'signature-vertification device' means configured software or hardware used to implement the signature-verification data;

'voluntary accreditation' means any permission, setting out rights and obligations specific to the provision of certification services, to be granted upon request by the certification-service-provider concerned by the person charged with the elaboration of, and supervision of compliance with, such rights and obligations, where the certification-service-provider is not entitled to exercise the rights stemming from the permission until he has received the decision of that person.

3   Supervision of certification-service-providers

(1)   It shall be the duty of the Secretary of State to keep under review the carrying on of activities of certification-service-providers who are established in the United Kingdom and who issue qualified certificates to the public and the persons by whom they are carried on with a view to her becoming aware of the identity of those persons and the circumstances relating to the carrying on of those activities.

(2)   It shall also be the duty of the Secretary of State to establish and maintain a register of certification-service-providers who are established in the United Kingdom and who issue qualified certificates to the public.

(3)   The Secretary of State shall record in the register the names and addresses of those certification-service-providers of whom she is aware who are established in the United Kingdom and who issue qualified certificates to the public.

(4)   The Secretary of State shall publish the register in such manner as she considers appropriate.

(5)   The Secretary of State shall have regard to evidence becoming available to her with respect to any course of conduct of a certification-service-provider who is established in the United Kingdom and who issues qualified certificates to the public and which appears to her to be conduct detrimental to the interests of those persons who use or rely on those certificates with a view to making any of this evidence as she considers expedient available to the public in such manner as she considers appropriate.

4   Liability of certification-service-providers

(1)   Where—

(a)   a certification-service-provider either—

(i)   issues a certificate as a qualified certificate to the public, or

(ii)   guarantees a qualified certificate to the public,

(b)   a person reasonably relies on that certificate for any of the following matters—

(i)   the accuracy of any of the information contained in the qualified certificate at the time of issue,

(ii)   the inclusion in the qualified certificate of all the details referred to in Schedule 1,

(iii)   the holding by the signatory identified in the qualified certificate at the time of its issue of the signature-creation data corresponding to the signature-verification data given or identified in the certificate, or

(iv)   the ability of the signature-creation data and the signature-verification data to be used in a complementary manner in cases where the certification-service-provider generates them both,

(c)   that person suffers loss as a result of such reliance, and

(d)   the certification-service-provider would be liable in damages in respect of any extent of the loss—

    (i) had a duty of care existed between him and the person referred to in sub-paragraph (b) above, and

    (ii) had the certification-service-provider been negligent,

then that certification-service-provider shall be so liable to the same extent notwithstanding that there is no proof that the certification-service-provider was negligent unless the certification-service-provider proves that he was not negligent.

(2) For the purposes of the certification-service-provider's liability under paragraph (1) above there shall be a duty of care between that certification-service-provider and the person referred to in paragraph (1)(b) above.

(3) Where—

    (a) a certification-service-provider issues a certificate as a qualified certificate to the public,

    (b) a person reasonably relies on that certificate,

    (c) that person suffers loss as a result of any failure by the certification-service-provider to register revocation of the certificate, and

    (d) the certification-service-provider would be liable in damages in respect of any extent of the loss—

    (i) had a duty of care existed between him and the person referred to in sub-paragraph (b) above, and

    (ii) had the certification-service-provider been negligent,

then that certification-service-provider shall be so liable to the same extent notwithstanding that there is no proof that the certification-service-provider was negligent unless the certification-service-provider proves that he was not negligent.

(4) For the purposes of the certification-service-provider's liability under paragraph (3) above there shall be a duty of care between that certification-service-provider and the person referred to in paragraph (3)(b) above.

5 Data Protection

(1) A certification-service-provider who issues a certificate to the public and to whom this paragraph applies in accordance with paragraph (6) below—

    (a) shall not obtain personal data for the purpose of issuing or maintaining that certificate otherwise than directly from the data subject or after the explicit consent of the data subject, and

    (b) shall not process the personal data referred to in sub-paragraph (a) above—

    (i) to a greater extent than is necessary for the purpose of issuing or maintaining that certificate, or

    (ii) to a greater extent than is necessary for any other purpose to which the data subject has explicitly consented,

unless the processing is necessary for compliance with any legal obligation, to which the certification-service-provider is subject, other than an obligation imposed by contract.

(2) The obligation to comply with paragraph (1) above shall be a duty owed to any data subject who may be affected by a contravention of paragraph (1).

(3) Where a duty is owed by virtue of paragraph (2) above to any data subject, any breach of that duty which causes that data subject to sustain loss or damage shall be actionable by him.

(4) Compliance with paragraph (1) above shall also be enforceable by civil proceedings brought by the Crown for an injunction or for an interdict or for any other appropriate relief or remedy.

(5) Paragraph (4) above shall not prejudice any right that a data subject may have by virtue of paragraph (3) above to bring civil proceedings for the contravention or apprehended contravention of paragraph (1) above.

(6) Paragraph (1) above applies to a certification-service-provider in respect of personal data only if the certification-service-provider is established in the United Kingdom and the personal data are processed in the context of that establishment.

(7) For the purposes of paragraph (6) above, each of the following is to be treated as established in the United Kingdom—

(a) an individual who is ordinarily resident in the United Kingdom,

(b) a body incorporated under the law of, or in any part of, the United Kingdom,

(c) a partnership or other unincorporated association formed under the law of any part of the United Kingdom, and

(d) any person who does not fall within ssub-paragraph (a), (b) or (c) above but maintains in the United Kingdom—

(i) an office, branch or agency through which he carries on any activity, or

(ii) a regular practice.

(8) In this regulation—

'data subject' and 'personal data' and 'processing' shall have the same meanings as in section 1(1) of the Data Protection Act 1998, and

'obtain' shall bear the same interpretation as 'obtaining' in section 1(2) of the Data Protection Act 1998.

SCHEDULE 1   (Regulation 2)
(Annex I to the Directive)
REQUIREMENTS FOR QUALIFIED CERTIFICATES

Qualified certificates must contain:

(a) an indication that the certificate is issued as a qualified certificate;

(b) the identification of the certification-service-provider and the State in which it is established;

(c) the name of the signatory or a pseudonym, which shall be identified as such;

(d) provision for a specific attribute of the signatory to be included if relevant, depending on the purpose for which the certificate is intended;

(e) signature-verification data which correspond to signature-creation data under the control of the signatory;

(f) an indication of the beginning and end of the period of validity of the certificate;

(g) the identity code of the certificate;

(h) the advanced electronic signature of the certification-service-provider issuing it;

(i) limitations on the scope of use of the certificate, if applicable; and

(j) limits on the value of transactions for which the certificate can be used, if applicable.

SCHEDULE 2   (Regulation 2)
(Annex II to the Directive)
REQUIREMENTS FOR CERTIFICATION-SERVICE-PROVIDERS ISSUING
QUALIFIED CERTIFICATES

Certification-service-providers must:

(a) demonstrate the reliability necessary for providing certification services;

(b) ensure the operation of a prompt and secure directory and a secure and immediate revocation service;

(c) ensure that the date and time when a certificate is issued or revoked can be determined precisely;

(d) verify, by appropriate means in accordance with national law, the identity and, if applicable, any specific attributes of the person to which a qualified certificate is issued;

(e)   employ personnel who possess the expert knowledge, experience, and qualifications necessary for the services provided, in particular competence at managerial level, expertise in electronic signature technology and familiarity with proper security procedures; they must also apply administrative and management procedures which are adequate and correspond to recognised standards;

(f)   use trustworthy systems and products which are protected against modification and ensure the technical and cryptographic security of the process supported by them;

(g)   take measures against forgery of certificates, and, in cases where the certification-service-provider generates signature-creation data, guarantee confidentiality during the process of generating such data;

(h)   maintain sufficient financial resources to operate in conformity with the requirements laid down in the Directive, in particular to bear the risk of liability for damages, for example, by obtaining appropriate insurance;

(i)   record all relevant information concerning a qualified certificate for an appropriate period of time, in particular for the purpose of providing evidence of certification for the purposes of legal proceedings. Such recording may be done electronically;

(j)   not store or copy signature-creation data of the person to whom the certification-service-provider provided key management services;

(k)   before entering into a contractual relationship with a person seeking a certificate to support his electronic signature inform that person by a durable means of communication of the precise terms and conditions regarding the use of the certificate, including any limitations on its use, the existence of a voluntary accreditation scheme and procedures for complaints and dispute settlement. Such information, which may be transmitted electronically, must be in writing and in readily understandable language. Relevant parts of this information must also be made available on request to third parties relying on the certificate;

(l)   use trustworthy systems to store certificates in a verifiable form so that:
   – only authorised persons can make entries and changes,
   – information can be checked for authenticity,
   – certificates are publicly available for retrieval in only those cases for which the certificate-holder's consent has been obtained, and
   – any technical changes compromising these security requirements are apparent to the operator.

LATE PAYMENT OF COMMERCIAL DEBTS (SCOTLAND) REGULATIONS 2002
(SSI 2002/335)

3   Proceedings restraining use of grossly unfair terms

(1)   In this regulation—

(a)   'small and medium-sized enterprises' means those enterprises defined in Annex 1 to Commission Regulation (EC) No 70/2001 of 12th January 2001 on the application of Articles 87 and 88 of the EC Treaty to State aid to small and medium-sized enterprises;

(b)   'representative body' means an organisation established to represent the collective interests of small and medium-sized enterprises in general or in a particular sector or area.

(2)   This regulation applies where a person acting in the course of a business has written standard terms on which he or she enters (or intends to enter) as purchaser into contracts to which the Late Payment of Commercial Debts (Interest) Act 1998 applies which include a term purporting to oust or vary the right to statutory interest in relation to qualifying debts created by those contracts.

(3) If it appears to the Court of Session that in all or any circumstances the purported use of such a term in a relevant contract would be void under the Late Payment of Commercial Debts (Interest) Act 1998, the court on the application of a representative body may grant an interdict against that person prohibiting that person in those circumstances from using the offending term, on such terms as the court may think fit.

(4) Only a representative body may apply to the Court of Session under this regulation.

4 Saving for existing contracts
These Regulations do not affect contracts made before 7th August 2002.

LATE PAYMENT OF COMMERCIAL DEBTS (RATE OF INTEREST) (SCOTLAND) ORDER 2002
(SSI 2002/336)

1 Citation, commencement and extent
(1) This Order may be cited as the Late Payment of Commercial Debts (Rate of Interest) (Scotland) Order 2002 and shall come into force on 7th August 2002.

(2) This Order extends to Scotland only.

2 Revocation
The Late Payment of Commercial Debts (Rate of Interest) (No 2) Order 1998 is revoked.

3 Interpretation
In this Order, 'the official dealing rate' means the rate announced from time to time by the Monetary Policy Committee of the Bank of England ('the Bank') and for the time being in force as the official dealing rate, being the rate at which the Bank is willing to enter into transactions for providing short term liquidity in the money markets.

4 Rate of statutory interest
The rate of interest for the purposes of the Late Payment of Commercial Debts (Interest) Act 1998 shall be 8 per cent per annum over the official dealing rate in force on the 30th June (in respect of interest which starts to run between 1st July and 31st December) or the 31st December (in respect of interest which starts to run between 1st January and 30th June) immediately before the day on which statutory interest starts to run.

ELECTRONIC COMMERCE (EC DIRECTIVE) REGULATIONS 2002
(SI 2002/2013)

9 Information to be provided where contracts are concluded by electronic means
(1) Unless parties who are not consumers have agreed otherwise, where a contract is to be concluded by electronic means a service provider shall, prior to an order being placed by the recipient of a service, provide to that recipient in a clear, comprehensible and unambiguous manner the information set out in (a) to (d) below—

(a) the different technical steps to follow to conclude the contract;

(b) whether or not the concluded contract will be filed by the service provider and whether it will be accessible;

(c) the technical means for identifying and correcting input errors prior to the placing of the order; and

(d) the languages offered for the conclusion of the contract.

(2)   Unless parties who are not consumers have agreed otherwise, a service provider shall indicate which relevant codes of conduct he subscribes to and give information on how those codes can be consulted electronically.

(3)   Where the service provider provides terms and conditions applicable to the contract to the recipient, the service provider shall make them available to him in a way that allows him to store and reproduce them.

(4)   The requirements of paragraphs (1) and (2) above shall not apply to contracts concluded exclusively by exchange of electronic mail or by equivalent individual communications.

10   Other information requirements
Regulations 6, 7, 8 and 9(1) have effect in addition to any other information requirements in legislation giving effect to [EU] law.

11   Placing of the order
(1)   Unless parties who are not consumers have agreed otherwise, where the recipient of the service places his order through technological means, a service provider shall—

(a)   acknowledge receipt of the order to the recipient of the service without undue delay and by electronic means; and

(b)   make available to the recipient of the service appropriate, effective and accessible technical means allowing him to identify and correct input errors prior to the placing of the order.

(2)   For the purposes of paragraph (1)(a) above—

(a)   the order and the acknowledgement of receipt will be deemed to be received when the parties to whom they are addressed are able to access them; and

(b)   the acknowledgement of receipt may take the form of the provision of the service paid for where that service is an information society service.

(3)   The requirements of paragraph (1) above shall not apply to contracts concluded exclusively by exchange of electronic mail or by equivalent individual communications.

GENERAL PRODUCT SAFETY REGULATIONS 2005
(SI 2005/1803)

PART 1. GENERAL

1   Citation, commencement and revocation
(1)   These Regulations may be cited as the General Product Safety Regulations 2005 and shall come into force on 1st October 2005 with the exception of the reference to a civil partner in regulation 43(2) which shall come into force on 5th December 2005.

(2)   The General Product Safety Regulations 1994 are hereby revoked.

2   Interpretation
In these Regulations—

'the 1987 Act' means the Consumer Protection Act 1987;

'contravention' includes a failure to comply and cognate expressions shall be construed accordingly;

'dangerous product' means a product other than a safe product;

'distributor' means a professional in the supply chain whose activity does not affect the safety properties of a product;

'enforcement authority' means the Secretary of State, any other Minister of the Crown in charge of a government department, any such department and any authority or council mentioned in regulation 10;

['EU law'] includes a law in any part of the United Kingdom which implements [an EU] obligation [and does not include Regulation (EC) No 765/2008 of the European Parliament and the Council setting out the requirements for accreditation and market surveillance relating to the marketing of products and repealing Regulation (EEC) No 339/93];

'general safety requirement' means the requirement that only safe products should be placed on the market;

'the GPS Directive' means Directive 2001/95/EC of the European Parliament and of the Council of 3 December 2001 on general product safety;

'magistrates' court' in relation to Northern Ireland, means a court of summary jurisdiction;

'Member State' means a Member State, Norway, Iceland or Liechtenstein;

'notice' means a notice in writing;

'officer', in relation to an enforcement authority, means a person authorised in writing to assist the authority in carrying out its functions under or for the purposes of the enforcement of these Regulations and safety notices, except in relation to an enforcement authority which is a government department where it means an officer of that department;

'producer' means—

(a) the manufacturer of a product, when he is established in a Member State and any other person presenting himself as the manufacturer by affixing to the product his name, trade mark or other distinctive mark, or the person who reconditions the product;

(b) when the manufacturer is not established in a Member State—

(i) if he has a representative established in a Member State, the representative,

(ii) in any other case, the importer of the product from a state that is not a Member State into a Member State;

(c) other professionals in the supply chain, insofar as their activities may affect the safety properties of a product;

'product' means a product which is intended for consumers or likely, under reasonably foreseeable conditions, to be used by consumers even if not intended for them and which is supplied or made available, whether for consideration or not, in the course of a commercial activity and whether it is new, used or reconditioned and includes a product that is supplied or made available to consumers for their own use in the context of providing a service. 'Product' does not include equipment used by service providers themselves to supply a service to consumers, in particular equipment on which consumers ride or travel which is operated by a service provider;

'recall' means any measure aimed at achieving the return of a dangerous product that has already been supplied or made available to consumers;

'recall notice' means a notice under regulation 15;

'record' includes any book or document and any record in any form;

'requirement to mark' means a notice under regulation 12;

'requirement to warn' means a notice under regulation 13;

'safe product' means a product which, under normal or reasonably foreseeable conditions of use including duration and, where applicable, putting into service, installation and maintenance requirements, does not present any risk or only the minimum risks compatible with the product's use, considered to be acceptable and consistent with a high level of protection for the safety and health of persons. In determining the foregoing, the following shall be taken into account in particular—

(a) the characteristics of the product, including its composition, packaging, instructions for assembly and, where applicable, instructions for installation and maintenance,

(b)   the effect of the product on other products, where it is reasonably foreseeable that it will be used with other products,

(c)   the presentation of the product, the labelling, any warnings and instructions for its use and disposal and any other indication or information regarding the product, and

(d)   the categories of consumers at risk when using the product, in particular children and the elderly.

The feasibility of obtaining higher levels of safety or the availability of other products presenting a lesser degree of risk shall not constitute grounds for considering a product to be a dangerous product;

'safety notice' means a suspension notice, a requirement to mark, a requirement to warn, a withdrawal notice or a recall notice;

'serious risk' means a serious risk, including one the effects of which are not immediate, requiring rapid intervention;

'supply' in relation to a product includes making it available, in the context of providing a service, for use by consumers;

'suspension notice' means a notice under regulation 11;

'withdrawal' means any measure aimed at preventing the distribution, display or offer of a dangerous product to a consumer;

'withdrawal notice' means a notice under regulation 14.

3   Application

(1)   Each provision of these Regulations applies to a product in so far as there are no specific provisions with the same objective in rules of [EU] law governing the safety of the product other than the GPS Directive.

(2)   Where a product is subject to specific safety requirements imposed by rules of [EU] law other than the GPS Directive, these Regulations shall apply only to the aspects and risks or category of risks not covered by those requirements. This means that:

(a)   the definition of 'safe product' and 'dangerous product' in regulation 2 and regulations 5 and 6 shall not apply to such a product in so far as concerns the risks or category of risks covered by the specific rules, and

(b)   the remainder of these Regulations shall apply except where there are specific provisions governing the aspects covered by those regulations with the same objective.

4   These Regulations do not apply to a second-hand product supplied as a product to be repaired or reconditioned prior to being used, provided the supplier clearly informs the person to whom he supplies the product to that effect.

PART 2. OBLIGATIONS OF PRODUCERS AND DISTRIBUTORS

5   General safety requirement

(1)   No producer shall place a product on the market unless the product is a safe product.

(2)   No producer shall offer or agree to place a product on the market or expose or possess a product for placing on the market unless the product is a safe product.

(3)   No producer shall offer or agree to supply a product or expose or possess a product for supply unless the product is a safe product.

(4)   No producer shall supply a product unless the product is a safe product.

6   Presumption of conformity

(1)   Where, in the absence of specific provisions in rules of [EU] law governing the safety of a product, the product conforms to the specific rules of the law of part of the United Kingdom laying down the health and safety requirements

which the product must satisfy in order to be marketed in the United Kingdom, the product shall be deemed safe so far as concerns the aspects covered by such rules.

(2) Where a product conforms to a voluntary national standard of the United Kingdom giving effect to a European standard the reference of which has been published in the Official Journal of the European Union in accordance with Article 4 of the GPS Directive, the product shall be presumed to be a safe product so far as concerns the risks and categories of risk covered by that national standard. The Secretary of State shall publish the reference number of such national standards in such manner as he considers appropriate.

(3) In circumstances other than those referred to in paragraphs (1) and (2), the conformity of a product to the general safety requirement shall be assessed taking into account—

(a) any voluntary national standard of the United Kingdom giving effect to a European standard, other than one referred to in paragraph (2),

(b) other national standards drawn up in the United Kingdom,

(c) recommendations of the European Commission setting guidelines on product safety assessment,

(d) product safety codes of good practice in the sector concerned,

(e) the state of the art and technology, and

(f) reasonable consumer expectations concerning safety.

(4) Conformity of a product with the criteria designed to ensure the general safety requirement is complied with, in particular the provisions mentioned in paragraphs (1) to (3), shall not bar an enforcement authority from exercising its powers under these Regulations in relation to that product where there is evidence that, despite such conformity, it is dangerous.

7 Other obligations of producers

(1) Within the limits of his activities, a producer shall provide consumers with the relevant information to enable them—

(a) to assess the risks inherent in a product throughout the normal or reasonably foreseeable period of its use, where such risks are not immediately obvious without adequate warnings, and

(b) to take precautions against those risks.

(2) The presence of warnings does not exempt any person from compliance with the other requirements of these Regulations.

(3) Within the limits of his activities, a producer shall adopt measures commensurate with the characteristics of the products which he supplies to enable him to—

(a) be informed of the risks which the products might pose, and

(b) take appropriate action including, where necessary to avoid such risks, withdrawal, adequately and effectively warning consumers as to the risks or, as a last resort, recall.

(4) The measures referred to in paragraph (3) include—

(a) except where it is not reasonable to do so, an indication by means of the product or its packaging of—

(i) the name and address of the producer, and

(ii) the product reference or where applicable the batch of products to which it belongs; and

(b) where and to the extent that it is reasonable to do so—

(i) sample testing of marketed products,

(ii) investigating and if necessary keeping a register of complaints concerning the safety of the product, and

(iii) keeping distributors informed of the results of such monitoring where a product presents a risk or may present a risk.

8   Obligations of distributors

(1)   A distributor shall act with due care in order to help ensure compliance with the applicable safety requirements and in particular he—

(a)   shall not expose or possess for supply or offer or agree to supply, or supply, a product to any person which he knows or should have presumed, on the basis of the information in his possession and as a professional, is a dangerous product; and

(b)   shall, within the limits of his activities, participate in monitoring the safety of a product placed on the market, in particular by—

(i)   passing on information on the risks posed by the product,

(ii)   keeping the documentation necessary for tracing the origin of the product,

(iii)   producing the documentation necessary for tracing the origin of the product, and (iv) cooperating in action taken by a producer or an enforcement authority to avoid the risks.

(2)   Within the limits of his activities, a distributor shall take measures enabling him to co-operate efficiently in the action referred to in paragraph (1)(b)(iii).

9   Obligations of producers and distributors

(1)   Subject to paragraph (2), where a producer or a distributor knows that a product he has placed on the market or supplied poses risks to the consumer that are incompatible with the general safety requirement, he shall forthwith notify an enforcement authority in writing of that information and—

(a)   the action taken to prevent risk to the consumer; and

(b)   where the product is being or has been marketed or otherwise supplied to consumers outside the United Kingdom, of the identity of each Member State in which, to the best of his knowledge, it is being or has been so marketed or supplied.

(2)   Paragraph (1) shall not apply—

(a)   in the case of a second-hand product supplied as an antique or as a product to be repaired or reconditioned prior to being used, provided the supplier clearly informed the person to whom he supplied the product to that effect,

(b)   in conditions concerning isolated circumstances or products.

(3)   In the event of a serious risk the notification under paragraph (1) shall include the following—

(a)   information enabling a precise identification of the product or batch of products in question,

(b)   a full description of the risks that the product presents,

(c)   all available information relevant for tracing the product, and

(d)   a description of the action undertaken to prevent risks to the consumer.

(4)   Within the limits of his activities, a person who is a producer or a distributor shall co-operate with an enforcement authority (at the enforcement authority's request) in action taken to avoid the risks posed by a product which he supplies or has supplied. Every enforcement authority shall maintain procedures for such co-operation, including procedures for dialogue with the producers and distributors concerned on issues related to product safety.

PART 3. ENFORCEMENT

10   Enforcement

(1)   It shall be the duty of every authority to which paragraph (4) applies to enforce within its area these Regulations and safety notices.

(2)   An authority in England or Wales to which paragraph (4) applies shall have the power to investigate and prosecute for an alleged contravention of any provision imposed by or under these Regulations which was committed outside its area in any part of England and Wales.

(3)   A district council in Northern Ireland shall have the power to investigate and prosecute for an alleged contravention of any provision imposed by or under these Regulations which was committed outside its area in any part of Northern Ireland.

(4)   The authorities to which this paragraph applies are:

(a)   in England, a county council, district council, London Borough Council, the Common Council of the City of London in its capacity as a local authority and the Council of the Isles of Scilly,

(b)   in Wales, a county council or a county borough council,

(c)   in Scotland, a council constituted under section 2 of the Local Government etc (Scotland) Act 1994,

(d)   in Northern Ireland any district council.

(5)   An enforcement authority shall in enforcing these Regulations act in a manner proportionate to the seriousness of the risk and shall take due account of the precautionary principle. In this context, it shall encourage and promote voluntary action by producers and distributors. Notwithstanding the foregoing, an enforcement authority may take any action under these Regulations urgently and without first encouraging and promoting voluntary action if a product poses a serious risk.

11   Suspension notices

(1)   Where an enforcement authority has reasonable grounds for suspecting that a requirement of these Regulations has been contravened in relation to a product, the authority may, for the period needed to organise appropriate safety evaluations, checks and controls, serve a notice ('a suspension notice') prohibiting the person on whom it is served from doing any of the following things without the consent of the authority, that is to say—

(a)   placing the product on the market, offering to place it on the market, agreeing to place it on the market or exposing it for placing on the market, or

(b)   supplying the product, offering to supply it, agreeing to supply it or exposing it for supply.

(2)   A suspension notice served by an enforcement authority in relation to a product may require the person on whom it is served to keep the authority informed of the whereabouts of any such product in which he has an interest.

(3)   A consent given by the enforcement authority for the purposes of paragraph (1) may impose such conditions on the doing of anything for which the consent is required as the authority considers appropriate.

12   Requirements to mark

(1)   Where an enforcement authority has reasonable grounds for believing that a product is a dangerous product in that it could pose risks in certain conditions, the authority may serve a notice ('a requirement to mark') requiring the person on whom the notice is served at his own expense to undertake either or both of the following, as specified in the notice—

(a)   to ensure that the product is marked in accordance with requirements specified in the notice with warnings as to the risks it may present,

(b)   to make the marketing of the product subject to prior conditions as specified in the notice so as to ensure the product is a safe product.

(2)   The requirements referred to in paragraph (1)(a) shall be such as to ensure that the product is marked with a warning which is suitable, clearly worded and easily comprehensible.

13   Requirements to warn

Where an enforcement authority has reasonable grounds for believing that a product is a dangerous product in that it could pose risks for certain persons, the authority may serve a notice ('a requirement to warn') requiring the person on whom the notice is served at his own expense to undertake one or more of the following, as specified in the notice—

(a)   where and to the extent it is practicable to do so, to ensure that any person who could be subject to such risks and who has been supplied with the product be given warning of the risks in good time and in a form specified in the notice,

(b)   to publish a warning of the risks in such form and manner as is likely to bring those risks to the attention of any such person,

(c)   to ensure that the product carries a warning of the risks in a form specified in the notice.

14   Withdrawal notices

(1)   Where an enforcement authority has reasonable grounds for believing that a product is a dangerous product, the authority may serve a notice ('a withdrawal notice') prohibiting the person on whom it is served from doing any of the following things without the consent of the authority, that is to say—

(a)   placing the product on the market, offering to place it on the market, agreeing to place it on the market or exposing it for placing on the market, or

(b)   supplying the product, offering to supply it, agreeing to supply it or exposing it for supply.

(2)   A withdrawal notice may require the person on whom it is served to take action to alert consumers to the risks that the product presents.

(3)   In relation to a product that is already on the market, a withdrawal notice may only be served by an enforcement authority where the action being undertaken by the producer or the distributor concerned in fulfilment of his obligations under these Regulations is unsatisfactory or insufficient to prevent the risks concerned to the health and safety of persons.

(4)   Paragraph (3) shall not apply in the case of a product posing a serious risk requiring, in the view of the enforcement authority, urgent action.

(5)   A withdrawal notice served by an enforcement authority in relation to a product may require the person on whom it is served to keep the authority informed of the whereabouts of any such product in which he has an interest.

(6)   A consent given by the enforcement authority for the purposes of paragraph (1) may impose such conditions on the doing of anything for which the consent is required as the authority considers appropriate.

15   Recall notices

(1)   Subject to paragraph (4), where an enforcement authority has reasonable grounds for believing that a product is a dangerous product and that it has already been supplied or made available to consumers, the authority may serve a notice ('a recall notice') requiring the person on whom it is served to use his reasonable endeavours to organise the return of the product from consumers to that person or to such other person as is specified in the notice.

(2)   A recall notice may require—

(a)   the recall to be effected in accordance with a code of practice applicable to the product concerned, or

(b)   the recipient of the recall notice to—

(i)   contact consumers who have purchased the product in order to inform them of the recall, where and to the extent it is practicable to do so,

(ii)   publish a notice in such form and such manner as is likely to bring to the attention of purchasers of the product the risk the product poses and the fact of the recall, or

(iii)   make arrangements for the collection or return of the product from consumers who have purchased it or for its disposal,

and may impose such additional requirements on the recipient of the notice as are reasonable and practicable with a view to achieving the return of the product from consumers to the person specified in the notice or its disposal.

(3) In determining what requirements to include in a recall notice, the enforcement authority shall take into consideration the need to encourage distributors, users and consumers to contribute to its implementation.

(4) A recall notice may only be issued by an enforcement authority where—

(a) other action which it may require under these Regulations would not suffice to prevent the risks concerned to the health and safety of persons,

(b) the action being undertaken by the producer or the distributor concerned in fulfilment of his obligations under these Regulations is unsatisfactory or insufficient to prevent the risks concerned to the health and safety of persons, and

(c) the authority has given not less than [ten] days' notice to the person on whom the recall notice is to be served of its intention to serve such a notice and where that person has before the expiry of that period by notice required the authority to seek the advice of such person as the Institute determines on the questions of—

(i) whether the product is a dangerous product,

(ii) whether the issue of a recall notice is proportionate to the seriousness of the risk,

and the authority has taken account of such advice.

(5) Paragraphs (4)(b) and (c) shall not apply in the case of a product posing a serious risk requiring, in the view of the enforcement authority, urgent action.

(6) Where a person requires an enforcement authority to seek advice as referred to in paragraph (4)(c), that person shall be responsible for the fees, costs and expenses of the Institute and of the person appointed by the Institute to advise the authority.

(7) In paragraphs 4(c) and (6) 'the Institute' means the charitable organisation with registered number 803725 and known as the Chartered Institute of Arbitrators.

(8) A recall notice served by an enforcement authority in relation to a product may require the person on whom it is served to keep the authority informed of the whereabouts of any such product to which the recall notice relates, so far as he is able to do so.

(9) Where the conditions in paragraph (1) for serving a recall notice are satisfied and either the enforcement authority has been unable to identify any person on whom to serve a recall notice, or the person on whom such a notice has been served has failed to comply with it, then the authority may itself take such action as could have been required by a recall notice.

(10) Where—

(a) an authority has complied with the requirements of paragraph (4); and

(b) the authority has exercised its powers under paragraph (9) to take action following the failure of the person on whom the recall notice has been served to comply with that notice,

then the authority may recover from the person on whom the notice was served summarily as a civil debt, any costs or expenses reasonably incurred by it in undertaking the action referred to in sub-paragraph (b).

(11) A civil debt recoverable under the preceding paragraph may be recovered—

(a) in England and Wales by way of complaint (as mentioned in section 58 of the Magistrates' Courts Act 1980,

(b) in Northern Ireland in proceedings under Article 62 of the Magistrates' Courts (Northern Ireland) Order 1981.

16 Supplementary provisions relating to safety notices

(1) Whenever feasible, prior to serving a safety notice the authority shall give an opportunity to the person on whom the notice is to be served to submit his

views to the authority. Where, due to the urgency of the situation, this is not feasible the person shall be given an opportunity to submit his views to the authority after service of the notice.

(2)   A safety notice served by an enforcement authority in respect of a product shall—

(a)   describe the product in a manner sufficient to identify it;

(b)   state the reasons on which the notice is based;

(c)   indicate the rights available to the recipient of the notice under these Regulations and (where applicable) the time limits applying to their exercise; and

(d)   in the case of a suspension notice, state the period of time for which it applies.

(3)   A safety notice shall have effect throughout the United Kingdom.

(4)   Where an enforcement authority serves a suspension notice in respect of a product, the authority shall be liable to pay compensation to a person having an interest in the product in respect of any loss or damage suffered by reason of the notice if—

(a)   there has been no contravention of any requirement of these Regulations in relation to the product; and

(b)   the exercise by the authority of the power to serve the suspension notice was not attributable to any neglect or default by that person.

(5)   Where an enforcement authority serves a withdrawal notice in respect of a product, the authority shall be liable to pay compensation to a person having an interest in the product in respect of any loss or damage suffered by reason of the notice if—

(a)   the product was not a dangerous product; and

(b)   the exercise by the authority of the power to serve the withdrawal notice was not attributable to any neglect or default by that person.

(6)   Where an enforcement authority serves a recall notice in respect of a product, the authority shall be liable to pay compensation to the person on whom the notice was served in respect of any loss or damage suffered by reason of the notice if—

(a)   the product was not a dangerous product; and

(b)   the exercise by the authority of the power to serve the recall notice was not attributable to any neglect or default by that person.

(7)   An enforcement authority may vary or revoke a safety notice which it has served provided that the notice is not made more restrictive for the person on whom it is served or more onerous for that person to comply with.

(8)   Wherever feasible prior to varying a safety notice the authority shall give an opportunity to the person on whom the original notice was served to submit his views to the authority.

17   Appeals against safety notices

(1)   A person on whom a safety notice has been served and a person having an interest in a product in respect of which a safety notice (other than a recall notice) has been served may, before the end of the period of 21 days beginning with the day on which the notice was served, apply for an order to vary or set aside the terms of the notice.

(2)   On an application under paragraph (1) the court or the sheriff, as the case may be, shall make an order setting aside the notice only if satisfied that—

(a)   in the case of a suspension notice, there has been no contravention in relation to the product of any requirement of these Regulations,

(b)   in the case of a requirement to mark or a requirement to warn, the product is not a dangerous product,

(c)   in the case of a withdrawal notice—

(i)   the product is not a dangerous product, or

(ii)   where applicable, regulation 14(3) has not been complied with by the enforcement authority concerned,

(d)   in the case of a recall notice—

(i)   the product is not a dangerous product, or

(ii)   regulation 15(4) has not been complied with,

(e)   in any case, the serving of the safety notice concerned was not proportionate to the seriousness of the risk.

(3)   On an application concerning the period of time specified in a suspension notice as the period for which it applies, the court or the sheriff, as the case may be, may reduce the period to such period as it considers sufficient for organising appropriate safety evaluations, checks and controls.

(4)   On an application to vary the terms of a notice, the court or the sheriff, as the case may be, may vary the requirements specified in the notice as it considers appropriate.

(5)   A person on whom a recall notice has been served and who proposes to make an application under paragraph (1) in relation to the notice may, before the end of the period of seven days beginning with the day on which the notice was served, apply to the court or the sheriff for an order suspending the effect of the notice and the court or the sheriff may, in any case where it considers it appropriate to do so, make an order suspending the effect of the notice.

(6)   If the court or the sheriff makes an order suspending the effect of a recall notice under paragraph (5) in the absence of the enforcement authority, the enforcement authority may apply for the revocation of such order.

(7)   An order under paragraph (5) shall take effect from the time it is made until—

(a)   it is revoked under paragraph (6),

(b)   where no application is made under paragraph (1) in respect of the recall notice within the time specified in that paragraph, the expiration of that time,

(c)   where such an application is made but is withdrawn or dismissed for want of prosecution, the date of dismissal or withdrawal of the application, or

(d)   where such an application is made and is not withdrawn or dismissed for want of prosecution, the determination of the application.

(8)   Subject to paragraph (6), in Scotland the sheriff's decision under paragraph (5) shall be final.

(9)   An application under this regulation may be made—

(a)   by way of complaint to any magistrates' court in which proceedings have been brought in England and Wales or Northern Ireland—

(i)   in respect of a contravention in relation to the product of a requirement imposed by or under these Regulations; or

(ii)   for the forfeiture of the product under regulation 18;

(b)   where no such proceedings have been brought, by way of complaint to any magistrates' court; or

(c)   in Scotland, by summary application to the sheriff.

(10)   A person aggrieved by an order made pursuant to an application under paragraph (1) by a magistrates' court in England, Wales or Northern Ireland, or by a decision of such a court not to make such an order, may appeal against that order or decision—

(a)   in England and Wales, to the Crown Court;

(b)   in Northern Ireland, to the county court.

[18   *Does not apply to Scotland*]

19   Forfeiture: Scotland

(1)   In Scotland a sheriff may make an order for forfeiture of a product on the grounds that the product is a dangerous product—

(a)   on an application by a procurator-fiscal made in the manner specified in section 134 of the Criminal Procedure (Scotland) Act 1995, or

(b) where a person is convicted of any offence in respect of a contravention in relation to the product of a requirement imposed by or under these Regulations, in addition to any other penalty which the sheriff may impose.

(2) The procurator-fiscal making an application under paragraph (1)(a) shall serve on any person appearing to him to be the owner of, or otherwise to have an interest in, the product to which the application relates a copy of the application, together with a notice giving him the opportunity to appear at the hearing of the application to show cause why the product should not be forfeited.

(3) Service under paragraph (2) shall be carried out, and such service may be proved, in the manner specified for citation of an accused in summary proceedings under the Criminal Procedure (Scotland) Act 1995.

(4) A person upon whom notice is served under paragraph (2) and any other person claiming to be the owner of, or otherwise to have an interest in, the product to which the application relates shall be entitled to appear at the hearing of the application to show cause why the product should not be forfeited.

(5) The sheriff shall not make an order following an application under paragraph (1)(a)—

(a) if any person on whom notice is served under paragraph (2) does not appear, unless service of the notice on that person is proved; or

(b) if no notice under paragraph (2) has been served, unless the sheriff is satisfied that in the circumstances it was reasonable not to serve notice on any person.

(6) The sheriff may make an order under this regulation only if he is satisfied that the product is a dangerous product.

(7) Where an order for the forfeiture of a product is made following an application by the procurator-fiscal under paragraph (1)(a), any person who appeared, or was entitled to appear to show cause why the product should not be forfeited may, within twenty-one days of the making of the order, appeal to the High Court by Bill of Suspension on the ground of an alleged miscarriage of justice; and section 182(5)(a) to (e) of the Criminal Procedure (Scotland) Act 1995 shall apply to an appeal under this paragraph as it applies to a stated case under Part X of that Act.

(8) An order following an application under paragraph (1)(a) shall not take effect—

(a) until the end of the period of twenty-one days beginning with the day after the day on which the order is made; or

(b) if an appeal is made under paragraph (7) within that period, until the appeal is determined or abandoned.

(9) An order under paragraph (1)(b) shall not take effect—

(a) until the end of the period within which an appeal against the order could be brought under the Criminal Procedure (Scotland) Act 1995; or

(b) if an appeal is made within that period, until the appeal is determined or abandoned.

(10) Subject to paragraph (11), a product forfeited under this regulation shall be destroyed in accordance with such directions as the sheriff may give.

(11) If he thinks fit, the sheriff may direct that the product be released to such person as he may specify, on condition that that person does not supply the product to any other person otherwise than as mentioned in paragraph (11) of regulation 18.

20 Offences

(1) A person who contravenes regulations 5 or 8(1)(a) shall be guilty of an offence and liable on conviction on indictment to imprisonment for a term not exceeding 12 months or to a fine not exceeding £20,000 or to both, or on summary conviction to imprisonment for a term not exceeding three months or to a fine not exceeding the statutory maximum or to both.

(2) A person who contravenes regulation 7(1), 7(3) (by failing to take any of the

measures specified in regulation 7(4)), 8(1)(b)(i), (ii) or (iii) or 9(1) shall be guilty of an offence and liable on summary conviction to imprisonment for a term not exceeding three months or to a fine not exceeding level 5 on the standard scale or to both.

(3) A producer or distributor who does not give notice to an enforcement authority under regulation 9(1) in respect of a product he has placed on the market or supplied commits an offence where it is proved that he ought to have known that the product poses risks to consumers that are incompatible with the general safety requirement and he shall be liable on summary conviction to imprisonment for a term not exceeding three months or to a fine not exceeding level 5 on the standard scale or to both.

(4) A person who contravenes a safety notice shall be guilty of an offence and liable on conviction on indictment to imprisonment for a term not exceeding 12 months or to a fine not exceeding £20,000 or to both, or on summary conviction to imprisonment for a term not exceeding three months or to a fine not exceeding the statutory maximum or to both.

21 Test purchases

(1) An enforcement authority shall have power to organise appropriate checks on the safety properties of a product, on an adequate scale, up to the final stage of use or consumption and for that purpose may make a purchase of a product or authorise an officer of the authority to make a purchase of a product.

(2) Where a product purchased under paragraph (1) is submitted to a test and the test leads to—

(a) the bringing of proceedings for an offence in respect of a contravention in relation to the product of any requirement imposed by or under these Regulations or for the forfeiture of the product under regulation 18 or 19, or

(b) the serving of a safety notice in respect of the product, and

(c) the authority is requested to do so and it is practicable for the authority to comply with the request,

then the authority shall allow the person from whom the product was purchased, a person who is a party to the proceedings, on whom the notice was served or who has an interest in the product to which the notice relates, to have the product tested.

22 Powers of entry and search etc

(1) An officer of an enforcement authority may at any reasonable hour and on production, if required, of his credentials exercise any of the powers conferred by the following provisions of this regulation.

(2) The officer may, for the purposes of ascertaining whether there has been a contravention of a requirement imposed by or under these Regulations, enter any premises other than premises occupied only as a person's residence and inspect any record or product.

(3) The officer may, for the purpose of ascertaining whether there has been a contravention of a requirement imposed by or under these Regulations, examine any procedure (including any arrangements for carrying out a test) connected with the production of a product.

(4) If the officer has reasonable grounds for suspecting that the product has not been placed on the market or supplied in the United Kingdom since it was manufactured or imported he may for the purpose of ascertaining whether there has been a contravention in relation to the product of a requirement imposed by or under these Regulations—

(a) require a person carrying on a commercial activity, or employed in connection with a commercial activity, to supply all necessary information relating to the activity, including by the production of records,

(b) require any record which is stored in an electronic form and is accessible from the premises to be produced in a form—

      (i)   in which it can be taken away, and

      (ii) in which it is visible and legible.

    (c)   for the purpose of ascertaining (by testing or otherwise) whether there has been any such contravention, seize and detain samples of the product,

    (d)   take copies of, or of an entry in, any records produced by virtue of sub-paragraph (a).

(5) If the officer has reasonable grounds for suspecting that there has been a contravention in relation to a product of a requirement imposed by or under these Regulations, he may—

    (a)   for the purpose of ascertaining whether there has been any such contravention, require a person carrying on a commercial activity, or employed in connection with a commercial activity, to supply all necessary information relating to the activity, including by the production of records,

    (b)   for the purpose of ascertaining whether there has been any such contravention, require any record which is stored in an electronic form and is accessible from the premises to be produced in a form—

      (i)   in which it can be taken away, and

      (ii) in which it is visible and legible,

    (c)   for the purpose of ascertaining (by testing or otherwise) whether there has been any such contravention, seize and detain samples of the product,

    (d)   take copies of, or of an entry in, any records produced by virtue of sub-paragraph (a).

(6) The officer may seize and detain any products or records which he has reasonable grounds for believing may be required as evidence in proceedings for an offence in respect of a contravention of any requirement imposed by or under these Regulations.

(7) If and to the extent that it is reasonably necessary to do so to prevent a contravention of any requirement imposed by or under these Regulations, the officer may, for the purpose of exercising his power under paragraphs (4) to (6) to seize products or records—

    (a)   require any person having authority to do so to open any container or to open any vending machine; and

    (b)   himself open or break open any such container or machine where a requirement made under sub-paragraph (a) in relation to the container or machine has not been complied with.

23 Provisions supplemental to regulation 22 and search warrants etc

(1) An officer seizing any products or records shall, before he leaves the premises, provide to the person from whom they were seized a written notice—

    (a)   specifying the products (including the quantity thereof) and records seized,

    (b)   stating the reasons for their seizure, and

    (c)   explaining the right of appeal under regulation 25.

(2) References in paragraph (1) and regulation 25 to the person from whom something has been seized, in relation to a case in which the power of seizure was exercisable by reason of the product having been found on any premises, are references to the occupier of the premises at the time of the seizure.

(3) If a justice of the peace—

    (a)   is satisfied by written information on oath that there are reasonable grounds for believing either—

      (i)   that any products or records which an officer has power to inspect under regulation 22 are on any premises and that their inspection is likely to disclose evidence that there has been a contravention of any requirement imposed by or under these Regulations, or

(ii)   that such a contravention has taken place, is taking place or is about to take place on any premises, and

(b)   is also satisfied by such information either—

(i)   that admission to the premises has been or is likely to be refused and that notice of the intention to apply for a warrant under this paragraph has been given to the occupier, or

(ii)   that an application for admission, or the giving of such a notice, would defeat the object of the entry or that the premises are unoccupied or that the occupier is temporarily absent and it might defeat the object of the entry to await his return,

the justice may by warrant under his hand, which shall continue in force for a period of one month, authorise any officer of an enforcement authority to enter the premises, if need be by force.

(4)   An officer entering premises by virtue of regulation 22 or a warrant under paragraph (3) may take with him such other persons and equipment as may appear to him necessary.

(5)   On leaving any premises which a person is authorised to enter by a warrant under paragraph (3), that person shall, if the premises are unoccupied or the occupier is temporarily absent—

(a)   leave the premises as effectively secured against trespassers as he found them,

(b)   attach a notice such as is mentioned in paragraph (1) in a prominent place at the premises.

(6)   Where a product seized by an officer of an enforcement authority under regulation 22 or 23 is submitted to a test, the authority shall inform the person mentioned in paragraph (1) of the result of the test and, if—

(a)   proceedings are brought for an offence in respect of a contravention in relation to the product of any requirement imposed by or under these Regulations or for the forfeiture of the product under regulation 18 or 19; or

(b)   a safety notice is served in respect of the product; and

(c)   the authority is requested to do so and it is practicable for him to comply with the request,

then the authority shall allow a person who is a party to the proceedings or on whom the notice was served or who has an interest in the product to which the notice relates to have the product tested.

(7)   If a person who is not an officer of an enforcement authority purports to act as such under regulation 22 or under this regulation he shall be guilty of an offence and liable on summary conviction to a fine not exceeding level 5 on the standard scale.

(8)   In the application of this section to Scotland, the reference in paragraph (3) to a justice of the peace shall include a reference to a sheriff and the reference to written information on oath shall be construed as a reference to evidence on oath.

(9)   In the application of this section to Northern Ireland, the reference in paragraph (3) to a justice of the peace shall include a reference to a lay magistrate and the references to an information on oath shall be construed as a reference to a complaint on oath.

24   Obstruction of officers

(1)   A person who—

(a)   intentionally obstructs an officer of an enforcement authority who is acting in pursuance of any provision of regulation 22 or 23; or

(b)   intentionally fails to comply with a requirement made of him by an officer of an enforcement authority under any provision of those regulations; or

(c)   without reasonable cause fails to give an officer of an enforcement authority who is so acting any other assistance or information which the officer

may reasonably require of him for the purposes of the exercise of the officer's
functions under any provision of those regulations,
shall be guilty of an offence and liable on summary conviction to a fine not exceeding level 5 on the standard scale.

(2)   A person shall be guilty of an offence if, in giving any information which is
required by him by virtue of paragraph (1)(c)—

(a)   he makes a statement which he knows is false in a material particular; or

(b)   he recklessly makes a statement which is false in a material particular.

(3)   A person guilty of an offence under paragraph (2) shall be liable—

(a)   on conviction on indictment, to a fine;

(b)   on summary conviction, to a fine not exceeding the statutory maximum.

25   Appeals against detention of products and records

(1)   A person referred to in regulation 23(1) may apply for an order requiring
any product or record which is for the time being detained under regulation 22 or
23 by an enforcement authority or by an officer of such an authority to be released
to him or to another person.

(2)   An application under the preceding paragraph may be made—

(a)   to any magistrates' court in which proceedings have been brought in
England and Wales or Northern Ireland—

(i)   for an offence in respect of a contravention in relation to the product of
a requirement imposed by or under these Regulations, or

(ii)   for the forfeiture of the product under regulation 18,

(b)   where no such proceedings have been brought, by way of complaint to a
magistrates' court;

(c)   in Scotland, by summary application to the sheriff.

(3)   On an application under paragraph (1) to a magistrates' court or to the
sheriff, the court or the sheriff may make an order requiring a product or record to
be released only if the court or sheriff is satisfied—

(a)   that proceedings—

(i)   for an offence in respect of any contravention in relation to the product
or, in the case of a record, the product to which the record relates, of any
requirement imposed by or under these Regulations; or

(ii)   for the forfeiture of the product or, in the case of a record, the product
to which the record relates, under regulation 18 or 19,

have not been brought or, having been brought, have been concluded without
the product being forfeited; and

(b)   where no such proceedings have been brought, that more than six
months have elapsed since the product or records was seized.

(4)   In determining whether to make an order under this regulation requiring
the release of a product or record the court or sheriff shall take all the circumstances into account including the results of any tests on the product which have
been carried out by or on behalf of the enforcement authority and any statement
made by the enforcement authority to the court or sheriff as to its intention to
bring proceedings for an offence in respect of a contravention in relation to the
product of any requirement imposed by or under these Regulations.

(5)   Where—

(a)   more than 12 months have elapsed since a product or records were
seized and the enforcement authority has not commenced proceedings for an
offence in respect of a contravention in relation to the product (or, in the case of
records, the product to which the records relate) of any requirement imposed by
or under these Regulations or for the forfeiture of the product under regulation
18 or 19, or

(b)   an enforcement authority has brought proceedings for an offence as mentioned in sub-paragraph (a) and the proceedings were dismissed and all rights
of appeal have been exercised or the time for appealing has expired,

the authority shall be under a duty to return the product or records detained under regulation 22 or 23 to the person from whom they were seized.

(6) Where the authority is satisfied that some other person has a better right to a product or record than the person from whom it was seized, the authority shall, instead of the duty in paragraph (5), be under a duty to return it to that other person or, as the case may be, to the person appearing to the authority to have the best right to the product or record in question.

(7) Where different persons claim to be entitled to the return of a product or record that is required to be returned under paragraph (5), then it may be retained for as long as is reasonably necessary for the determination in accordance with paragraph (6) of the person to whom it must be returned.

(8) A person aggrieved by an order made under this regulation by a magistrates' court in England and Wales or Northern Ireland, or by a decision of such a court not to make such an order, may appeal against that order or decision—

    (a)   in England and Wales, to the Crown Court;

    (b)   in Northern Ireland, to the county court;

and an order so made may contain such provision as appears to the court to be appropriate for delaying the coming into force of the order pending the making and determination of any appeal (including any application under section 111 of the Magistrates' Courts Act 1980 or article 146 of the Magistrates' Courts (Northern Ireland) Order 1981 (statement of case)).

26 Compensation for seizure and detention

Where an officer of an enforcement authority exercises any power under regulation 22 or 23 to seize and detain a product, the enforcement authority shall be liable to pay compensation to any person having an interest in the product in respect of any loss or damage caused by reason of the exercise of the power if—

    (a)   there has been no contravention in relation to the product of any requirement imposed by or under these Regulations, and

    (b)   the exercise of the power is not attributable to any neglect or default by that person.

27 Recovery of expenses of enforcement

(1) This regulation shall apply where a court—

    (a)   convicts a person of an offence in respect of a contravention in relation to a product of any requirement imposed by or under these Regulations, or

    (b)   makes an order under regulation 18 or 19 for the forfeiture of a product.

(2) The court may (in addition to any other order it may make as to costs or expenses) order the person convicted or, as the case may be, any person having an interest in the product to reimburse an enforcement authority for any expenditure which has been or may be incurred by that authority—

    (a)   in connection with any seizure or detention of the product by or on behalf of the authority, or

    (b)   in connection with any compliance by the authority with directions given by the court for the purposes of any order for the forfeiture of the product.

28 Power of Secretary of State to obtain information

(1) If the Secretary of State considers that, for the purposes of deciding whether to serve a safety notice, or to vary or revoke a safety notice which he has already served, he requires information or a sample of a product he may serve on a person a notice requiring him—

    (a)   to furnish to the Secretary of State, within a period specified in the notice, such information as is specified;

    (b)   to produce such records as are specified in the notice at a time and place so specified (and to produce any such records which are stored in any electronic form in a form in which they are visible and legible) and to permit a person appointed by the Secretary of State for that purpose to take copies of the records at that time and place;

(c)   to produce such samples of a product as are specified in the notice at a time and place so specified.

(2)   A person shall be guilty of an offence if he—

(a)   fails, without reasonable cause, to comply with a notice served on him under paragraph (1); or

(b)   in purporting to comply with a requirement which by virtue of paragraph (1)(a) or (b) is contained in such a notice—

(i)   furnishes information or records which he knows are false in a material particular, or

(ii)   recklessly furnishes information or records which are false in a material particular.

(3)   A person guilty of an offence under paragraph (2) shall—

(a)   in the case of an offence under sub-paragraph (a) of that paragraph, be liable on summary conviction to a fine not exceeding level 5 on the standard scale; and

(b)   in the case of an offence under sub-paragraph (b) of that paragraph, be liable—

(i)   on conviction on indictment, to a fine;

(ii)   on summary conviction, to a fine not exceeding the statutory maximum.

29   Defence of due diligence

(1)   Subject to the following provisions of this regulation, in proceedings against a person for an offence under these Regulations it shall be a defence for that person to show that he took all reasonable steps and exercised all due diligence to avoid committing the offence.

(2)   Where in any proceedings against any person for such an offence the defence provided by paragraph (1) involves an allegation that the commission of the offence was due—

(a)   to the act or default of another, or

(b)   to reliance on information given by another,

that person shall not, without the leave of the court, be entitled to rely on the defence unless, not less than seven clear days before, in England, Wales and Northern Ireland, the hearing of the proceedings or, in Scotland, the trial diet, he has served a notice under paragraph (3) on the person bringing the proceedings.

(3)   A notice under this paragraph shall give such information identifying or assisting in the identification of the person who—

(a)   committed the act or default, or

(b)   gave the information,

as is in the possession of the person serving the notice at the time he serves it.

(4)   A person may not rely on the defence provided by paragraph (1) by reason of his reliance on information supplied by another, unless he shows that it was reasonable in all the circumstances to have relied on the information, having regard in particular—

(a)   to the steps which he took, and those which might reasonably have been taken, for the purpose of verifying the information; and

(b)   to whether he had any reason to disbelieve the information.

30   Defence in relation to antiques

(1)   This regulation shall apply in proceedings against any person for an offence under regulation 20(1) in respect of the supply, offer or agreement to supply or exposure or possession for supply of second hand products supplied as antiques.

(2)   It shall be a defence for that person to show that the terms on which he

supplied the product or agreed or offered to supply the product or, in the case of a product which he exposed or possessed for supply, the terms on which he intended to supply the product, contemplated the acquisition of an interest in the product by the person supplied or to be supplied.

(3)   Paragraph (2) applies only if the producer or distributor clearly informed the person to whom he supplied the product, or offered or agreed to supply the product or, in the case of a product which he exposed or possessed for supply, he intended to so inform that person, that the product is an antique.

31   Liability of person other than principal offender

(1)   Where the commission by a person of an offence under these Regulations is due to an act or default committed by some other person in the course of a commercial activity of his, the other person shall be guilty of the offence and may be proceeded against and punished by virtue of this paragraph whether or not proceedings are taken against the first-mentioned person.

(2)   Where a body corporate is guilty of an offence under these Regulations (including where it is so guilty by virtue of paragraph (1)) in respect of any act or default which is shown to have been committed with the consent or connivance of, or to be attributable to any neglect on the part of, any director, manager, secretary or other similar officer of the body corporate or any person who was purporting to act in any such capacity he, as well as the body corporate, shall be guilty of that offence and shall be liable to be proceeded against and punished accordingly.

(3)   Where the affairs of a body corporate are managed by its members, paragraph (2) shall apply in relation to the acts and defaults of a member in connection with his functions of management as if he were a director of the body corporate.

(4)   Where a Scottish partnership is guilty of an offence under these Regulations (including where it is so guilty by virtue of paragraph (1)) in respect of any act or default which is shown to have been committed with the consent or connivance of, or to be attributable to any neglect on the part of, a partner in the partnership, he, as well as the partnership, shall be guilty of that offence and shall be liable to be proceeded against and punished accordingly.

PART 4. MISCELLANEOUS

32   Reports

(1)   It shall be the duty of the Secretary of State to lay before each House of Parliament a report on the exercise during the period to which the report relates of the functions which are exercisable by enforcement authorities under these Regulations.

(2)   The first such report shall relate to the period beginning on the day on which these Regulations come into force and ending on 31 March 2008 and subsequent reports shall relate to a period of not more than five years beginning on the day after the day on which the period to which the previous report relates ends.

(3)   The Secretary of State may from time to time prepare and lay before each House of Parliament such other reports on the exercise of those functions as he considers appropriate.

(4)   The Secretary of State may direct an enforcement authority to report at such intervals as he may specify in the direction on the discharge by that authority of the functions exercisable by it under these Regulations.

(5)   A report under paragraph (4) shall be in such form and shall contain such particulars as are specified in the direction of the Secretary of State.

33   Duty to notify Secretary of State and Commission

(1)   An enforcement authority which has received a notification under regulation 9(1) shall immediately pass the same on to the Secretary of State, who shall

immediately pass it on to the competent authorities appointed for the purpose in the Member States where the product in question is or has been marketed or otherwise supplied to consumers.

(2) Where an enforcement authority takes a measure which restricts the placing on the market of a product, or requires its withdrawal or recall, it shall immediately notify the Secretary of State, specifying its reasons for taking the action. It shall also immediately notify the Secretary of State of any modification or lifting of such a measure.

(3) On receiving a notification under paragraph (2), or if he takes a measure which restricts the placing on the market of a product, or requires its withdrawal or recall, the Secretary of State shall (to the extent that such notification is not required under article 12 of the GPS Directive or any other [EU] legislation) immediately notify the European Commission of the measure taken, specifying the reasons for taking it. The Secretary of State shall also immediately notify the European Commission of any modification or lifting of such a measure. If the Secretary of State considers that the effects of the risk do not or cannot go beyond the territory of the United Kingdom, he shall notify the European Commission of the measure concerned insofar as it involves information likely to be of interest to Member States from the product safety standpoint, and in particular if it is in response to a new risk which has not yet been reported in other notifications.

(4) Where an enforcement authority adopts or decides to adopt, recommend or agree with producers and distributors, whether on a compulsory or voluntary basis, a measure or action to prevent, restrict or impose specific conditions on the possible marketing or use of a product (other than a pharmaceutical product) by reason of a serious risk, it shall immediately notify the Secretary of State. It shall also immediately notify the Secretary of State of any modification or withdrawal of any such measure or action.

(5) On receiving a notification under paragraph (4), or if he adopts or decides to adopt, recommend or agree with producers and distributors, whether on a compulsory or voluntary basis, a measure or action to prevent, restrict or impose specific conditions on the possible marketing or use of a product (other than a pharmaceutical product) by reason of a serious risk, the Secretary of State shall immediately notify the European Commission of it through the Community Rapid Information System, known as RAPEX. The Secretary of State shall also inform the European Commission without delay of any modification or withdrawal of any such measure or action.

(6) If the Secretary of State considers that the effects of the risk do not or cannot go beyond the territory of the United Kingdom, he shall notify the European Commission of the measures or action concerned insofar as they involve information likely to be of interest to Member States of the European Union from the product safety standpoint, and in particular if they are in response to a new risk which has not been reported in other notifications.

(7) Before deciding to adopt such a measure or take such an action as is referred to in paragraph (5), the Secretary of State may pass on to the European Commission any information in his possession regarding the existence of a serious risk. Where he does so, he must inform the European Commission, within 45 days of the day of passing the information to it, whether he confirms or modifies that information.

(8) Upon receipt of a notification from the European Commission under article 12(2) of the GPS Directive, the Secretary of State shall notify the Commission of the following—

(a) whether the product the subject of the notification has been marketed in the United Kingdom;

(b) what measure concerning the product the enforcement authorities in the United Kingdom may be adopting, stating the reasons, including any differing assessment of risk or any other special circumstance justifying the decision as to the measure, in particular lack of action or follow-up; and

(c)   any relevant supplementary information he has obtained on the risk involved, including the results of any test or analysis carried out.

(9)   The Secretary of State shall notify the European Commission without delay of any modification or withdrawal of any measures notified to it under paragraph (8)(b).

(10)   In this regulation—

(a)   references to a product excludes a second hand product supplied as an antique or as a product to be repaired or reconditioned prior to being used, provided the supplier clearly informs the person to whom he supplies the product to that effect;

(b)   'pharmaceutical product' means a product falling within Council Directive 2001/83/EC of the European Parliament and of the Council on the Community code relating to medicinal products for human use [as amended by Directive 2002/98/EC of the European Parliament and of the Council setting standards of quality and safety for the collection, testing, processing, storage and distribution of human blood and blood components, Commission Directive 2003/63/EC amending Directive 2001/83/EC on the Community code relating to medicinal products for human use, Directive 2004/24/EC of the European Parliament and of the Council amending, as regards traditional herbal medicinal products, Directive 2001/83/EC on the Community code relating to medicinal products for human use and Directive 2004/27/EC of the European Parliament and of the Council amending Directive 2001/83/EC on the Community code relating to medicinal products for human use].

34   Provisions supplemental to regulation 33

(1)   A notification under regulation 33(2) to (6), (8) or (9) to the Secretary of State or the Commission shall be in writing and shall provide all available details and at least the following information—

(a)   information enabling the product to be identified,

(b)   a description of the risk involved, including a summary of the results of any test or analysis and of their conclusions which are relevant to assessing the level of risk,

(c)   the nature and the duration of the measures or action taken or decided on, if applicable,

(d)   information on supply chains and distribution of the product, in particular on destination countries.

(2)   Where a measure notified to the Commission under regulation 33 seeks to limit the marketing or use of a chemical substance or preparation, the Secretary of State shall provide to the Commission as soon as possible either a summary or the references of the relevant data relating to the substance or preparation considered and to known and available substitutes, where such information is available. The Secretary of State shall also notify the Commission of the anticipated effects of the measure on consumer health and safety together with the assessment of the risk carried out in accordance with the general principles for the risk evaluation of chemical substances as referred to in article 10(4) of Council Regulation (EEC) No 793/93 of 23 March 1993 on the evaluation and control of the risks of existing substances, in the case of an existing substance, or in article 3(2) of Council Directive 67/548/EEC on the approximation of laws, regulations and administrative provisions relating to the classification, packaging and labelling of dangerous substances in the case of a new substance.

(3)   Where the Commission carries out an investigation under paragraph 5 of Annex II to the GPS Directive, the Secretary of State shall supply the Commission with such information as it requests, to the best of his ability.

35   Implementation of Commission decisions

(1)   This regulation applies where the Commission adopts a decision pursuant to article 13 of the GPS Directive.

(2)   The Secretary of State shall—

    (a)   take such action under these Regulations, or

    (b)   direct another enforcement authority to take such action under these Regulations, as is necessary to comply with the decision.

(3)   Where an enforcement authority serves a safety notice pursuant to paragraph (2), the following provisions of these Regulations shall not apply in relation to that notice, namely regulations 14(3), 15(4) to (6) and 16(1), 16(2)(c) and (d), 16(5) to (7) and 17.

(4)   Unless the Commission's decision provides otherwise, export from the Community of a dangerous product which is the subject of such a decision is prohibited with effect from the date the decision comes into force.

(5)   The enforcement of the prohibition in paragraph (4) shall be treated as an assigned matter within the meaning of section 1(1) of the Customs and Excise Management Act 1979.

(6)   The measures necessary to implement the decision shall be taken within 20 days, unless the decision specifies a different period.

(7)   The Secretary of State or, where the Secretary of State has directed another enforcement authority to take action under paragraph (2)(b), that enforcement authority shall, within one month, give the parties concerned an opportunity to submit their views and shall inform the Commission accordingly.

36   Market surveillance

In order to ensure a high level of consumer health and safety protection, enforcement authorities shall within the limits of their responsibility and to the extent of their ability undertake market surveillance of products employing appropriate means and procedures and co-operating with other enforcement authorities and competent authorities of other Member States which may include:

    (a)   establishment, periodical updating and implementation of sectoral surveillance programmes by categories of products or risks and the monitoring of surveillance activities, findings and results,

    (b)   follow-up and updating of scientific and technical knowledge concerning the safety of products,

    (c)   the periodical review and assessment of the functioning of the control activities and their effectiveness and, if necessary, revision of the surveillance approach and organisation put in place.

37   Complaints procedures

An enforcement authority shall maintain and publish a procedure by which complaints may be submitted by any person on product safety and on surveillance and control activities, which complaints shall be followed up as appropriate.

38   Co-operation between enforcement authorities

(1)   It shall be the duty of an enforcement authority to co-operate with other enforcement authorities in carrying out the functions conferred on them by these Regulations. In particular—

    (a)   enforcement authorities shall share their expertise and best practices with each other;

    (b)   enforcement authorities shall undertake collaborative working where they have a shared interest.

(2)   The Secretary of State shall inform the European Commission as to the arrangements for the enforcement of these Regulations, including which bodies are enforcement authorities.

39   Information

(1)   An enforcement authority shall in general make available to the public such

information as is available to it on the following matters relating to the risks to consumer health and safety posed by a product—

    (a)   the nature of the risk,

    (b)   the product identification,

and the measures taken in respect of the risk, without prejudice to the need not to disclose information for effective monitoring and investigation activities.

(2) Paragraph (1) shall not apply to any information obtained by an enforcement authority for the purposes of these Regulations which, by its nature, is covered by professional secrecy, unless the circumstances require such information to be made public in order to protect the health and safety of consumers.

(3) *[Amends Enterprise Act 2002 (Part 9 Restrictions on Disclosure of Information) (Amendment and Specification) Order 2003.]*

40 Service of documents

(1) A document required or authorised by virtue of these Regulations to be served on a person may be so served—

    (a)   on an individual by delivering it to him or by leaving it at his proper address or by sending it by post to him at that address;

    (b)   on a body corporate other than a limited liability partnership, by serving it in accordance with sub-paragraph (a) on the secretary of the body;

    (c)   on a limited liability partnership, by serving it in accordance with sub-paragraph (a) on a member of the partnership; or

    (d)   on a partnership, by serving it in accordance with sub-paragraph (a) on a partner or a person having the control or management of the partnership business;

    (e)   on any other person by leaving it at his proper address or by sending it by post to him at that address.

(2) For the purposes of paragraph (1), and for the purposes of section 7 of the Interpretation Act 1978 (which relates to the service of documents by post) in its application to that paragraph, the proper address of a person on whom a document is to be served by virtue of these Regulations shall be his last known address except that—

    (a)   in the case of a body corporate (other than a limited liability partnership) or its secretary, it shall be the address of the registered or principal office of the body;

    (b)   in the case of a limited liability partnership or a member of the partnership, it shall be the address of the registered or principal office of the partnership;

    (c)   in the case of a partnership or a partner or a person having the control or management of a partnership business, it shall be the address of the principal office of the partnership,

and for the purposes of this paragraph the principal officer of a company constituted under the law of a country or territory outside the United Kingdom or of a partnership carrying on business outside the United Kingdom is its principal office within the United Kingdom.

(3) A document required or authorised by virtue of these Regulations to be served on a person may also be served by transmitting the request by any means of electronic communication to an electronic address (which includes a fax number and an e-mail address) being an address which the person has held out as an address at which he or it can be contacted for the purposes of receiving such documents.

(4) A document transmitted by any means of electronic communication in accordance with the preceding paragraph is, unless the contrary is proved, deemed to be received on the business day after the notice was transmitted over a public electronic communications network.

41 Extension of time for bringing summary proceedings

(1) Notwithstanding section 127 of the Magistrates' Courts Act 1980 or article 19 of the Magistrates' Courts (Northern Ireland) Order 1981, in England, Wales and Northern Ireland a magistrates' court may try an information (in the case of England and Wales) or a complaint (in the case of Northern Ireland) in respect of an offence under these Regulations if (in the case of England and Wales) the information is laid or (in the case of Northern Ireland) the complaint is made within three years from the date of the offence or within one year from the discovery of the offence by the prosecutor whichever is the earlier.

(2) Notwithstanding section 136 of the Criminal Procedure (Scotland) Act 1995, in Scotland summary proceedings for an offence under these Regulations may be commenced within three years from the date of the offence or within one year from the discovery of the offence by the prosecutor whichever is the earlier.

(3) For the purposes of paragraph (2), section 136(3) of the Criminal Procedure (Scotland) Act 1995 shall apply as it applies for the purposes of that section.

42 Civil proceedings

These Regulations shall not be construed as conferring any right of action in civil proceedings in respect of any loss or damage suffered in consequence of a contravention of these Regulations.

43 Privileged information

(1) Nothing in these Regulations shall be taken as requiring a person to produce any records if he would be entitled to refuse to produce those records in any proceedings in any court on the grounds that they are the subject of legal professional privilege or, in Scotland, that they contain a confidential communication made by or to an advocate or solicitor in that capacity, or as authorising a person to take possession of any records which are in the possession of a person who would be so entitled.

(2) Nothing in these Regulations shall be construed as requiring a person to answer any question or give any information if to do so would incriminate that person or that person's spouse or civil partner.

44 Evidence in proceedings for offence relating to regulation 9(1)

(1) This regulation applies where a person has given a notification to an enforcement authority pursuant to regulation 9(1).

(2) No evidence relating to that statement may be adduced and no question relating to it may be asked by the prosecution in any criminal proceedings (other than proceedings in which that person is charged with an offence under regulation 20 for a contravention of regulation 9(1)), unless evidence relating to it is adduced, or a question relating to it is asked, in the proceedings by or on behalf of that person.

45 Transitional provisions

Where, in relation to a product, a suspension notice (within the meaning of the 1987 Act) has (by virtue of regulation 11(b) of the General Product Safety Regulations 1994) been served under section 14 of the 1987 Act and is in force immediately prior to the coming into force of these Regulations, it shall continue in force notwithstanding the revocation of the General Product Safety Regulations 1994 by these Regulations, and those Regulations shall continue to apply accordingly.

46–47 *[Amendment provisions]*

**BUSINESS PROTECTION FROM MISLEADING MARKETING
REGULATIONS 2008
(SI 2008/1276)**

PART 1
DEFINITIONS AND PROHIBITIONS

1 Citation and Commencement

These Regulations may be cited as the Business Protection from Misleading Marketing Regulations 2008 and shall come into force on 26th May 2008.

2 Interpretation

(1) In these Regulations—

'advertising' means any form of representation which is made in connection with a trade, business, craft or profession in order to promote the supply or transfer of a product and 'advertiser' shall be construed accordingly;

['CMA' means the Competition and Markets Authority;]

'code owner' means a trader or a body responsible for—

(a) the formulation and revision of a code of conduct; or

(b) monitoring compliance with the code by those who have undertaken to be bound by it;

'comparative advertising' means advertising which in any way, either explicitly or by implication, identifies a competitor or a product offered by a competitor;

'court', in relation to England and Wales and Northern Ireland, means a county court or the High Court, and, in relation to Scotland, the sheriff or the Court of Session;

['DETINI' means the Department of Enterprise, Trade and Investment in Northern Ireland;]

['enforcement authority' means the [CMA], every local weights and measures authority DETINI and GEMA;]

['GEMA' means the Gas and Electricity Markets Authority;]

'goods' includes ships, aircraft, animals, things attached to land and growing crops;

['local weights and measures authority' means a local weights and measures authority in Great Britain (within the meaning of section 69 of the Weights and Measures Act 1985);]

[. . .]

'premises' includes any place and any stall, vehicle, ship or aircraft;

'product' means any goods or services and includes immovable property, rights and obligations;

'ship' includes any boat and any other description of vessel used in navigation; and

'trader' means any person who is acting for purposes relating to his trade, craft, business or profession and anyone acting in the name of or on behalf of a trader.

(2) In the application of these Regulations to Scotland for references to an 'injunction' or an 'interim injunction' there shall be substituted references to an 'interdict' or an 'interim interdict' respectively.

3 Prohibition of advertising which misleads traders

(1) Advertising which is misleading is prohibited.

(2) Advertising is misleading which—

(a) in any way, including its presentation, deceives or is likely to deceive the traders to whom it is addressed or whom it reaches; and by reason of its deceptive nature, is likely to affect their economic behaviour; or

(b) for those reasons, injures or is likely to injure a competitor.

(3) In determining whether advertising is misleading, account shall be taken of all its features, and in particular of any information it contains concerning—

(a)   the characteristics of the product (as defined in paragraph (4));
(b)   the price or manner in which the price is calculated;
(c)   the conditions on which the product is supplied or provided; and
(d)   the nature, attributes and rights of the advertiser (as defined in paragraph (5)).
(4)   In paragraph (3)(a) the 'characteristics of the product' include—
(a)   availability of the product;
(b)   nature of the product;
(c)   execution of the product;
(d)   composition of the product;
(e)   method and date of manufacture of the product;
(f)   method and date of provision of the product;
(g)   fitness for purpose of the product;
(h)   uses of the product;
(i)   quantity of the product;
(j)   specification of the product;
(k)   geographical or commercial origin of the product;
(l)   results to be expected from use of the product; or
(m)   results and material features of tests or checks carried out on the product.
(5)   In paragraph (3)(d) the 'nature, attributes and rights' of the advertiser include the advertiser's—
(a)   identity;
(b)   assets;
(c)   qualifications;
(d)   ownership of industrial, commercial or intellectual property rights; or
(e)   awards and distinctions.

4   Comparative advertising
Comparative advertising shall, as far as the comparison is concerned, be permitted only when the following conditions are met—
(a)   it is not misleading under regulation 3;
(b)   it is not a misleading action under regulation 5 of the Consumer Protection from Unfair Trading Regulations 2008 or a misleading omission under regulation 6 of those Regulations;
(c)   it compares products meeting the same needs or intended for the same purpose;
(d)   it objectively compares one or more material, relevant, verifiable and representative features of those products, which may include price;
(e)   it does not create confusion among traders—
     (i)   between the advertiser and a competitor, or
     (ii)   between the trade marks, trade names, other distinguishing marks or products of the advertiser and those of a competitor;
(f)   it does not discredit or denigrate the trade marks, trade names, other distinguishing marks, products, activities, or circumstances of a competitor;
(g)   for products with designation of origin, it relates in each case to products with the same designation;
(h)   it does not take unfair advantage of the reputation of a trade mark, trade name or other distinguishing marks of a competitor or of the designation of origin of competing products;
(i)   it does not present products as imitations or replicas of products bearing a protected trade mark or trade name.

5   Promotion of misleading advertising and comparative advertising which is not permitted
A code owner shall not promote in a code of conduct—
(a)   advertising which is misleading under regulation 3; or
(b)   comparative advertising which is not permitted under regulation 4.

PART 2
OFFENCES

6 Misleading advertising

A trader is guilty of an offence if he engages in advertising which is misleading under regulation 3.

7 Penalty for offence under regulation 6

A person guilty of an offence under regulation 6 shall be liable—

(a) on summary conviction, to a fine not exceeding the statutory maximum; or

(b) on conviction on indictment, to a fine or imprisonment for a term not exceeding two years or both.

8 Offences committed by bodies of persons

(1) Where an offence under these Regulations committed by a body corporate is proved—

(a) to have been committed with the consent or connivance of an officer of the body, or

(b) to be attributable to any neglect on his part,

the officer as well as the body corporate is guilty of the offence and liable to be proceeded against and punished accordingly.

(2) In paragraph (1) a reference to an officer of a body corporate includes a reference to—

(a) a director, manager, secretary or other similar officer; and

(b) a person purporting to act as a director, manager, secretary or other similar officer.

(3) Where an offence under these Regulations committed by a Scottish partnership is proved—

(a) to have been committed with the consent or connivance of a partner, or

(b) to be attributable to any neglect on his part,

the partner as well as the partnership is guilty of the offence and liable to be proceeded against and punished accordingly.

(4) In paragraph (3) a reference to a partner includes a person purporting to act as a partner.

9 Offence due to the default of another person

(1) This regulation applies where a person 'X'—

(a) commits an offence under regulation 6, or

(b) would have committed an offence under regulation 6 but for a defence under regulation 11 or 12,

and the commission of the offence, or of what would have been an offence but for X being able to rely on a defence under regulations 11 or 12, is due to the act or default of some other person 'Y'.

(2) Where this regulation applies Y shall be guilty of the offence subject to regulations 11 and 12 whether or not Y is a trader and whether or not Y's act or default is advertising.

(3) Y may be charged with and convicted of the offence by virtue of paragraph (2) whether or not proceedings are taken against X.

10 Time limit for prosecution

(1) No proceedings for an offence under these Regulations shall be commenced after—

(a) the end of the period of three years beginning with the date of the commission of the offence; or

(b) the end of the period of one year beginning with the date of discovery of the offence by the prosecutor,

whichever is earlier.

(2)   For the purposes of paragraph (1)(b) a certificate signed by or on behalf of the prosecutor and stating the date on which the offence was discovered by him shall be conclusive evidence of that fact and a certificate stating that matter and purporting to be so signed shall be treated as so signed unless the contrary is proved.

(3)   Notwithstanding anything in section 127(1) of the Magistrates' Courts Act 1980, an information relating to an offence under these Regulations which is triable by a magistrates' court in England and Wales may be so tried if it is laid at any time before the end of the period of twelve months beginning with the date of the commission of the offence.

(4)   Notwithstanding anything in section 136 of the Criminal Procedure (Scotland) Act 1995 summary proceedings in Scotland for an offence under these Regulations may be commenced at any time before the end of the period of twelve months beginning with the date of the commission of the offence.

(5)   For the purposes of paragraph (4), section 136(3) of the Criminal Procedure (Scotland) Act 1995 shall apply as it applies for the purposes of that section.

(6)   Notwithstanding anything in Article 19(1) of the Magistrates' Courts (Northern Ireland) Order 1981 a complaint charging an offence under these Regulations which is triable by a magistrates' court in Northern Ireland may be so tried if it is made at any time before the end of the period of twelve months beginning with the date of the commission of the offence.

11   Due diligence defence

(1)   In any proceedings against a person for an offence under regulation 6 it is a defence for that person to prove—

(a)   that the commission of the offence was due to—
(i)   a mistake;
(ii)   reliance on information supplied to him by another person;
(iii)   the act or default of another person;
(iv)   an accident; or
(v)   another cause beyond his control; and

(b)   that he took all reasonable precautions and exercised all due diligence to avoid the commission of such an offence by himself or any person under his control.

(2)   A person shall not be entitled to rely on the defence provided by paragraph (1) by reason of the matters referred to in paragraph (ii) or (iii) of paragraph (1)(a) without the leave of the court unless—

(a)   he has served on the prosecutor a notice in writing giving such information identifying or assisting in the identification of that other person as was in his possession; and

(b)   the notice is served on the prosecutor at least seven clear days before the date of the hearing.

12   Innocent publication defence

In any proceedings against a person for an offence under regulation 6 committed by the publication of advertising it is a defence for that person to prove that—

(a)   he is a person whose business it is to publish or to arrange for the publication of advertising;

(b)   he received the advertising for publication in the ordinary course of business; and

(c)   he did not know and had no reason to suspect that its publication would amount to an offence under regulation 6.

PART 3
ENFORCEMENT

13   Duty and power to enforce

[(1)   It shall be the duty of every local weights and measures authority and DETINI to enforce these Regulations.

[(1A)   Each of the following may also enforce these Regulations—
    (a)   the [CMA];
    (b)   GEMA]
(2)   Where an enforcement authority is a local weights and measures authority the duty referred to in paragraph (1) shall apply to the enforcement of these Regulations within the authority's area.
(3)   Where the enforcement authority is the Department of Enterprise, Trade and Investment in Northern Ireland the duty referred to in paragraph (1) shall apply to the enforcement of these Regulations within Northern Ireland.
(4)   [In determining how to comply with paragraph (1), or as the case may be, paragraph (1A)] every enforcement authority shall have regard to the desirability of encouraging control of advertising which is misleading under regulation 3 and comparative advertising which is not permitted under regulation 4 by such established means as it considers appropriate having regard to all the circumstances of the particular case.
[(4A)   Nothing in this regulation shall authorise GEMA to bring proceedings for an offence.]
(5)   Nothing in this regulation shall authorise any enforcement authority to bring proceedings in Scotland for an offence.

14   Notice to [CMA] of intended prosecution
(1)   Where an enforcement authority is a local weights and measures authority in England and Wales it may bring proceedings for an offence under regulation 6 only if—
    (a)   it has notified the [CMA] of its intention to bring proceedings at least fourteen days before the date on which proceedings are brought; or
    (b)   the [CMA] consents to proceedings being brought in a shorter period.
(2)   The enforcement authority must also notify the [CMA] of the outcome of the proceedings after they are finally determined.
(3)   Such proceedings are not invalid by reason only of the failure to comply with this regulation.

15   Injunctions to secure compliance with the Regulations
(1)   This regulation applies where an enforcement authority considers that there has been or is likely to be a breach of regulation 3, 4 or 5.
(2)   Where this regulation applies an enforcement authority may, subject to paragraph (3), if it thinks it appropriate to do so, bring proceedings for an injunction (in which proceedings it may also apply for an interim injunction) against any person appearing to it to be concerned or likely to be concerned with the breach.
(3)   Where the enforcement authority is a local weights and measures authority in Great Britain [or GEMA] it may apply for an injunction only if—
    (a)   it has notified the [CMA] of its intention to apply for an injunction at least fourteen days before the date on which the application is made; or
    (b)   the [CMA] consents to the application for an injunction being made within a shorter period.
(4)   Proceedings referred to in paragraph (2) are not invalid by reason only of the failure to comply with paragraph (3).

16   Undertakings
Where an enforcement authority considers that there has been or is likely to be a breach of regulation 3, 4 or 5 it may accept from the person concerned or likely to be concerned with the breach an undertaking that he will comply with those regulations.

17   Co-ordination
(1)   If more than one local weights and measures authority in Great Britain is contemplating bringing proceedings under regulation 15 in any particular case, the

[CMA] may direct which enforcement authority is to bring the proceedings or decide that only it may do so.

(2)   Where the [CMA] directs that only it may bring such proceedings it may take into account whether compliance with regulation 3, 4 or 5 could be achieved by other means in deciding whether to bring proceedings.

18   Powers of the court

(1)   The court on an application by an enforcement authority may grant an injunction on such terms as it may think fit to secure compliance with regulation 3, 4 or 5.

(2)   Before granting an injunction the court shall have regard to all the interests involved and in particular the public interest.

(3)   An injunction may relate not only to particular advertising but to any advertising in similar terms or likely to convey a similar impression.

(4)   The court may also require any person against whom an injunction (other than an interim injunction) is granted to publish in such form and manner and to such extent as the court thinks appropriate for the purpose of eliminating any continuing effects of the advertising—

    (a)   the injunction; and

    (b)   a corrective statement.

(5)   In considering an application for an injunction the court may require the person named in the application to provide evidence as to the accuracy of any factual claim made as part of the advertising of that person if, taking into account the legitimate interests of that person and any other party to the proceedings, it appears appropriate in the circumstances.

(6)   If, having been required under paragraph (5) to provide evidence as to the accuracy of a factual claim, a person—

    (a)   fails to provide such evidence, or

    (b)   provides evidence as to the accuracy of the factual claim that the court considers inadequate,

the court may consider that the factual claim is inaccurate.

(7)   The court may grant an injunction even where there is no evidence of proof of actual loss or damage or of intention or negligence on the part of the advertiser.

19   Notifications of undertakings and orders to the [CMA]

An enforcement authority, other than the [CMA], shall notify the [CMA]—

    (a)   of any undertaking given to it under regulation 16;

    (b)   of the outcome of any application made by it under regulation 15 and the terms of any order made by the court; and

    (c)   of the outcome of any application made by it to enforce a previous order of the court.

20   Publication, information and advice

(1)   [The CMA] must arrange for the publication, in such form and manner as it considers appropriate, of—

    (a)   details of any undertaking or order notified to it under regulation 19;

    (b)   details of any undertaking given to it under regulation 16;

    (c)   details of any application made by it under regulation 15 and of the terms of any undertaking given to, or order made by, the court;

    (d)   details of any application made by it to enforce a previous order of the court.

(2)   [An enforcement authority] may arrange for the dissemination, in such form and manner as it considers appropriate, of such information and advice concerning the operation of these Regulations as appear to it to be expedient to give to the public and to all persons likely to be affected by these Regulations.

PART 4
INVESTIGATION POWERS

21   Powers of Enforcement Authorities to obtain information
(1)   For the purpose of determining whether to bring proceedings for an injunction under regulation 15, an enforcement authority may by notice in writing require a person to provide to it such information as may be specified or described in the notice or to produce to it any documents so specified or described.
(2)   A notice under paragraph (1) may—
  (a)   specify the way in which and the time within which it is to be complied with; and
  (b)   be varied or revoked by a subsequent notice.
(3)   Nothing in this regulation gives an enforcement authority any power to require another person to provide or produce any information or document which the other person would be entitled to refuse to provide or produce in proceedings in the High Court on the grounds of legal professional privilege or (in Scotland) in proceedings in the Court of Session on the grounds of confidentiality of communications.
(4)   In paragraph (3) 'communications' means—
  (a)   communications between a professional legal adviser and his client; or
  (b)   communications made in connection with or in contemplation of legal proceedings and for the purposes of those proceedings.
(5)   Nothing in this regulation shall be construed as requiring a person to provide information if to do so might incriminate him.
(6)   If a person does not comply with a notice under paragraph (1) the court may, on the application of an enforcement authority, make such order as the court thinks fit for requiring the default to be made good, and any such order may provide that all the costs or expenses of and incidental to the application shall be borne by the person in default or by any officers of a company or other association who are responsible for its default.

22   Power to make test purchases
An enforcement authority [, other than GEMA,] may or may authorise any of its officers on its behalf to—
  (a)   make a purchase of a product; or
  (b)   enter into an agreement to secure the provision of a product,
for the purposes of determining whether these Regulations are being complied with.

23   Power of entry and investigation, etc
(1)   A duly authorised officer of an enforcement authority [, other than GEMA,] may at all reasonable hours exercise the following powers—
  (a)   he may, for the purpose of ascertaining whether a breach of these Regulations has been committed, inspect any goods and enter any premises other than premises used only as a dwelling;
  (b)   if he has reasonable cause to suspect that a breach of these Regulations has been committed, he may, for the purpose of ascertaining whether it has been committed, require any trader to produce any documents relating to his trade, business, craft or profession and may take copies of, or of any entry in, any such document;
  (c)   if he has reasonable cause to believe that a breach of these Regulations has been committed, he may seize and detain any goods for the purpose of ascertaining, by testing or otherwise, whether the breach has been committed; and
  (d)   he may seize and detain goods or documents which he has reason to believe may be required as evidence in proceedings for a breach of these Regulations.

(2)   If and to the extent that it is reasonably necessary to do so to secure that the provisions of these Regulations are observed, the officer may for the purpose of exercising his powers under paragraphs (1)(c) and (d) to seize goods or documents—

(a)   require any person having authority to do so to break open any container or open any vending machine; and

(b)   himself open or break open any such container or open any vending machine where a requirement made under sub-paragraph (a) in relation to the container or vending machine has not been complied with.

(3)   An officer seizing any goods or documents in exercise of his powers under this regulation shall—

(a)   inform the person from whom they are seized; and

(b)   where goods are seized from a vending machine, inform—

(i)   the person whose name and address are stated on the vending machine as being the proprietor's, or

(ii)   if there is no such name or address stated on the vending machine, the occupier of the premises on which the machine stands or to which it is affixed,

that the goods or documents have been so seized.

(4)   In this regulation 'document' includes information recorded in any form.

(5)   The reference in paragraph (1)(b) to the production of documents is, in the case of a document which contains information recorded otherwise than in legible form, a reference to the production of a copy of the information in legible form.

(6)   An officer seeking to exercise a power under this regulation must produce evidence of his identity and authority to a person (if there is one) who appears to the officer to be the occupier of the premises.

(7)   Where an officer seizes goods or documents in exercise of a power under this regulation they may not be detained—

(a)   for a period of more than 3 months; or

(b)   where the goods or documents are reasonably required by the enforcement authority in connection with the enforcement of these Regulations, for longer than they are so required.

(8)   An officer entering any premises under this regulation may take with him such other persons and such equipment as may appear to him to be necessary.

(9)   Nothing in this regulation or in regulation 24 gives any power to an officer of an enforcement authority—

(a)   to require any person to produce, or

(b)   to seize from another person,

any document which the other person would be entitled to refuse to produce in proceedings in the High Court on the grounds of legal professional privilege or (in Scotland) in proceedings in the Court of Session on the grounds of confidentiality of communications.

(10)   In paragraph (9) 'communications' means—

(a)   communications between a professional legal adviser and his client; or

(b)   communications made in connection with or in contemplation of legal proceedings and for the purposes of those proceedings.

(11)   If any person who is not an officer of an enforcement authority purports to act as such under this regulation or regulation 24 he shall be guilty of an offence and liable on summary conviction to a fine not exceeding level 5 on the standard scale.

24   Power to enter premises with a warrant

(1)   If a justice of the peace by a written information on oath is satisfied—

(a)   that there are reasonable grounds for believing that Condition A or B is met, and

(b)   that Condition C, D or E is met,

the justice may by warrant under his hand authorise an officer of an enforcement authority [, other than GEMA,] to enter the premises at all reasonable times, if necessary by force.

(2)   Condition A is that there are on any premises goods or documents which a duly authorised officer of the enforcement authority has power under regulation 23(1) to inspect and that their inspection is likely to disclose evidence of a breach of these Regulations.

(3)   Condition B is that a breach of these Regulations has occurred, is occurring or is about to occur on any premises.

(4)   Condition C is that the admission to the premises has been or is likely to be refused and that notice of intention to apply for a warrant under this regulation has been given to the occupier.

(5)   Condition D is that an application for admission, or the giving of a notice of intention to apply for a warrant, would defeat the object of the entry.

(6)   Condition E is that the premises are unoccupied or that the occupier is absent and it might defeat the object of the entry to await his return.

(7)   A warrant under paragraph (1)—

(a)   ceases to have effect at the end of the period of one month beginning with the day it is issued;

(b)   must be produced for inspection to the person (if there is one) who appears to the officer to be the occupier of the premises.

(8)   An officer entering any premises under this regulation may take with him such other persons and such equipment as may appear to him to be necessary.

(9)   On leaving any premises which an officer is authorised to enter by warrant under this regulation the officer shall, if the premises are unoccupied or the occupier is temporarily absent, leave the premises as effectively secured against trespassers as he found them.

(10)   In its application to Scotland, this regulation has effect as if—

(a)   the references in paragraph (1) to a justice of the peace included references to a sheriff; and

(b)   the reference in paragraph (1) to information on oath were a reference to evidence on oath.

(11)   In its application to Northern Ireland, this regulation has effect as if the references in paragraph (1) to a justice of the peace were references to a lay magistrate.

25   Obstruction of authorised officers

(1)   Any person who—

(a)   intentionally obstructs an officer of an enforcement authority acting in pursuance of these Regulations;

(b)   intentionally fails to comply with any requirement properly made of him by such an officer under regulation 23; or

(c)   without reasonable cause fails to give such an officer any other assistance or information which he may reasonably require of him for the purpose of the performance of his functions under these Regulations,

is guilty of an offence and liable, on summary conviction, to a fine not exceeding level 5 on the standard scale.

(2)   Any person who, in giving any information which is required of him under paragraph (1)(c), makes any statement which he knows to be false in a material particular is guilty of an offence and liable—

(a)   on summary conviction, to a fine not exceeding the statutory maximum; or

(b)   on conviction on indictment, to a fine or imprisonment for a term not exceeding two years or both.

(3)   Nothing in this regulation shall be construed as requiring a person to answer any question or give any information if to do so might incriminate him.

(4) Paragraph (1)(a) does not apply in relation to the exercise by an enforcement authority of its power to require information under regulation 21.

26 Notice of test and intended proceedings

(1) Where goods purchased by an officer pursuant to regulation 22 are submitted to a test and the test leads to the institution of any proceedings for a breach of these Regulations the officer shall inform—

(a) the person from whom the goods were purchased; or

(b) where the goods were sold through a vending machine, the person mentioned in regulation 23(3)(b);

of the result of the test.

(2) Where goods seized by an officer pursuant to regulation 23 are submitted to a test then the officer shall inform the person mentioned in regulation 23(3) of the result of the test.

(3) Where, as a result of the test, proceedings for a breach of these Regulations are taken against any person, the officer shall allow him to have the goods tested on his behalf if it is reasonably practicable to do so.

27 Compensation

(1) Where an officer of an enforcement authority seizes and detains goods in exercise of the powers under regulation 23 the enforcement authority shall be liable to pay compensation to any person having an interest in the goods in respect of any loss or damage caused by reason of the exercise of the power if—

(a) there has been no breach of these Regulations in relation to the goods, and

(b) the exercise of that power is not attributable to any neglect or default by that person.

(2) Any disputed question as to the right to or the amount of any compensation payable under this provision shall be determined by arbitration or, in Scotland, by a single arbiter appointed, failing agreement between the parties, by the sheriff.

28 Crown

(1) The powers conferred by regulations 23 and 24 are not exercisable in relation to premises occupied by the Crown.

(2) The Crown is not criminally liable as a result of any provision of these Regulations.

(3) Paragraph (2) does not affect the application of any provision of these Regulations in relation to a person in the public service of the Crown.

29 Validity of agreements

An agreement shall not be void or unenforceable by reason only of a breach of these Regulations.

CONSUMER PROTECTION FROM UNFAIR TRADING REGULATIONS 2008
(SI 2008/1277)

PART 1
GENERAL

2 Interpretation

(1) In these Regulations—

'average consumer' shall be construed in accordance with paragraphs (2) to (6);

'business' includes [—

(a)] a trade, craft or profession [, and

(b) the activities of any government department or local or public authority;]

['the CMA' means the Competition and Markets Authority;]

'code of conduct' means an agreement or set of rules (which is not imposed by legal or administrative requirements), which defines the behaviour of traders who undertake to be bound by it in relation to one or more commercial practices or business sectors;

'code owner' means a trader or a body responsible for—

(a) the formulation and revision of a code of conduct; or

(b) monitoring compliance with the code by those who have undertaken to be bound by it;

'commercial practice' means any act, omission, course of conduct, representation or commercial communication (including advertising and marketing) by a trader, which is directly connected with the promotion, sale or supply of a product to or from consumers, whether occurring before, during or after a commercial transaction (if any) in relation to a product;

['consumer' means an individual acting for purposes that are wholly or mainly outside that individual's business;

'digital content' means data which are produced and supplied in digital form;]

['DETINI' means the Department of Enterprise, Trade and Investment in Northern Ireland;]

['enforcement authority' means the [CMA], every local weights and measures authority and DETINI;]

['goods' means any tangible moveable items, but that includes water, gas and electricity if and only if they are put up for sale in a limited volume or set quantity;]

'invitation to purchase' means a commercial communication which indicates characteristics of the product and the price in a way appropriate to the means of that commercial communication and thereby enables the consumer to make a purchase;

['local weights and measures authority' means a local weights and measures authority in Great Britain (within the meaning of section 69 of the Weights and Measures Act 1985);]

'materially distort the economic behaviour' means in relation to an average consumer, appreciably to impair the average consumer's ability to make an informed decision thereby causing him to take a transactional decision that he would not have taken otherwise;

[. . .]

'premises' includes any place and any stall, vehicle, ship or aircraft;

['product' means—

(a) goods,

(b) a service,

(c) digital content,

(d) immoveable property,

(e) rights or obligations, or

(f) a product of the kind mentioned in paragraphs (1A) and (1B), but the application of this definition to Part 4A is subject to regulations 27C and 27D;]

'professional diligence' means the standard of special skill and care which a trader may reasonably be expected to exercise towards consumers which is commensurate with either—

    (a)   honest market practice in the trader's field of activity, or

    (b)   the general principle of good faith in the trader's field of activity;

'ship' includes any boat and any other description of vessel used in navigation;

['trader'—

    (a)   means a person acting for purposes relating to that person's business, whether acting personally or through another person acting in the trader's name or on the trader's behalf, and

    (b)   except in Part 4A, includes a person acting in the name of or on behalf of a trader;]

'transactional decision' means any decision taken by a consumer, whether it is to act or to refrain from acting, concerning—

    (a)   whether, how and on what terms to purchase, make payment in whole or in part for, retain or dispose of a product; or

    (b)   whether, how and on what terms to exercise a contractual right in relation to a product.

[(but the application of this definition to regulations 5 and 7 as they apply for the purposes of Part 4A is subject to regulation 27B(2)).]

[(1A)   A trader ('T') who demands payment from a consumer ('C') in full or partial settlement of C's liabilities or purported liabilities to T is to be treated for the purposes of these Regulations as offering to supply a product to C.

(1B)   In such a case the product that T offers to supply comprises the full or partial settlement of those liabilities or purported liabilities.]

(2)   In determining the effect of a commercial practice on the average consumer where the practice reaches or is addressed to a consumer or consumers account shall be taken of the material characteristics of such an average consumer including his being reasonably well informed, reasonably observant and circumspect.

(3)   Paragraphs (4) and (5) set out the circumstances in which a reference to the average consumer shall be read as in addition referring to the average member of a particular group of consumers.

(4)   In determining the effect of a commercial practice on the average consumer where the practice is directed to a particular group of consumers, a reference to the average consumer shall be read as referring to the average member of that group.

(5)   In determining the effect of a commercial practice on the average consumer—

    (a)   where a clearly identifiable group of consumers is particularly vulnerable to the practice or the underlying product because of their mental or physical infirmity, age or credulity in a way which the trader could reasonably be expected to foresee, and

    (b)   where the practice is likely to materially distort the economic behaviour only of that group, a reference to the average consumer shall be read as referring to the average member of that group.

(6)   Paragraph (5) is without prejudice to the common and legitimate advertising practice of making exaggerated statements which are not meant to be taken literally.

PART 2
PROHIBITIONS

3   Prohibition of unfair commercial practices

(1)   Unfair commercial practices are prohibited.

(2)   Paragraphs (3) and (4) set out the circumstances when a commercial practice is unfair.

(3)   A commercial practice is unfair if—
    (a)   it contravenes the requirements of professional diligence; and
    (b)   it materially distorts or is likely to materially distort the economic be-
haviour of the average consumer with regard to the product.
(4)   A commercial practice is unfair if—
    (a)   it is a misleading action under the provisions of regulation 5;
    (b)   it is a misleading omission under the provisions of regulation 6;
    (c)   it is aggressive under the provisions of regulation 7; or
    (d)   it is listed in Schedule 1.

4   Prohibition of the promotion of unfair commercial practices

The promotion of any unfair commercial practice by a code owner in a code of
conduct is prohibited.

5   Misleading actions

(1)   A commercial practice is a misleading action if it satisfies the conditions in
either paragraph (2) or paragraph (3).
(2)   A commercial practice satisfies the conditions of this paragraph—
    (a)   if it contains false information and is therefore untruthful in relation to
any of the matters in paragraph (4) or if it or its overall presentation in any way
deceives or is likely to deceive the average consumer in relation to any of the
matters in that paragraph, even if the information is factually correct; and
    (b)   it causes or is likely to cause the average consumer to take a transactional
decision he would not have taken otherwise.
(3)   A commercial practice satisfies the conditions of this paragraph if—
    (a)   it concerns any marketing of a product (including comparative adver-
tising) which creates confusion with any products, trade marks, trade names or
other distinguishing marks of a competitor; or
    (b)   it concerns any failure by a trader to comply with a commitment con-
tained in a code of conduct which the trader has undertaken to comply with,
if—
        (i)   the trader indicates in a commercial practice that he is bound by that
code of conduct, and
        (ii)   the commitment is firm and capable of being verified and is not
aspirational, and it causes or is likely to cause the average consumer to take a
transactional decision he would not have taken otherwise, taking account of
its factual context and of all its features and circumstances.
(4)   The matters referred to in paragraph (2)(a) are—
    (a)   the existence or nature of the product;
    (b)   the main characteristics of the product (as defined in paragraph 5);
    (c)   the extent of the trader's commitments;
    (d)   the motives for the commercial practice;
    (e)   the nature of the sales process;
    (f)   any statement or symbol relating to direct or indirect sponsorship or
approval of the trader or the product;
    (g)   the price or the manner in which the price is calculated;
    (h)   the existence of a specific price advantage;
    (i)   the need for a service, part, replacement or repair;
    (j)   the nature, attributes and rights of the trader (as defined in paragraph 6);
    (k)   the consumer's rights or the risks he may face.
(5)   In paragraph (4)(b), the 'main characteristics of the product' include—
    (a)   availability of the product;
    (b)   benefits of the product;
    (c)   risks of the product;
    (d)   execution of the product;
    (e)   composition of the product;
    (f)   accessories of the product;

(g)   after-sale customer assistance concerning the product;
(h)   the handling of complaints about the product;
(i)   the method and date of manufacture of the product;
(j)   the method and date of provision of the product;
(k)   delivery of the product;
(l)   fitness for purpose of the product;
(m)   usage of the product;
(n)   quantity of the product;
(o)   specification of the product;
(p)   geographical or commercial origin of the product;
(q)   results to be expected from use of the product; and
(r)   results and material features of tests or checks carried out on the product.
(6)   In paragraph (4)(j), the 'nature, attributes and rights' as far as concern the trader include the trader's—
(a)   identity;
(b)   assets;
(c)   qualifications;
(d)   status;
(e)   approval;
(f)   affiliations or connections;
(g)   ownership of industrial, commercial or intellectual property rights; and
(h)   awards and distinctions.
(7)   In paragraph (4)(k) 'consumer's rights' include rights the consumer may have under Part 5A of the Sale of Goods Act 1979(5) or Part 1B of the Supply of Goods and Services Act 1982.

6   Misleading omissions

(1)   A commercial practice is a misleading omission if, in its factual context, taking account of the matters in paragraph (2)—
(a)   the commercial practice omits material information,
(b)   the commercial practice hides material information,
(c)   the commercial practice provides material information in a manner which is unclear, unintelligible, ambiguous or untimely, or
(d)   the commercial practice fails to identify its commercial intent, unless this is already apparent from the context, and as a result it causes or is likely to cause the average consumer to take a transactional decision he would not have taken otherwise.
(2)   The matters referred to in paragraph (1) are—
(a)   all the features and circumstances of the commercial practice;
(b)   the limitations of the medium used to communicate the commercial practice (including limitations of space or time); and
(c)   where the medium used to communicate the commercial practice imposes limitations of space or time, any measures taken by the trader to make the information available to consumers by other means.
(3)   In paragraph (1) 'material information' means—
(a)   the information which the average consumer needs, according to the context, to take an informed transactional decision; and
(b)   any information requirement which applies in relation to a commercial communication as a result of [an EU] obligation.
(4)   Where a commercial practice is an invitation to purchase, the following information will be material if not already apparent from the context in addition to any other information which is material information under paragraph (3)—
(a)   the main characteristics of the product, to the extent appropriate to the medium by which the invitation to purchase is communicated and the product;
(b)   the identity of the trader, such as his trading name, and the identity of any other trader on whose behalf the trader is acting;

(c)   the geographical address of the trader and the geographical address of any other trader on whose behalf the trader is acting;

(d)   either—

(i)   the price, including any taxes; or

(ii)   where the nature of the product is such that the price cannot reasonably be calculated in advance, the manner in which the price is calculated;

(e)   where appropriate, either—

(i)   all additional freight, delivery or postal charges; or

(ii)   where such charges cannot reasonably be calculated in advance, the fact that such charges may be payable;

(f)   the following matters where they depart from the requirements of professional diligence—

(i)   arrangements for payment,

(ii)   arrangements for delivery,

(iii)   arrangements for performance,

(iv)   complaint handling policy;

(g)   for products and transactions involving a right of withdrawal or cancellation, the existence of such a right.

7   Aggressive commercial practices

(1)   A commercial practice is aggressive if, in its factual context, taking account of all of its features and circumstances—

(a)   it significantly impairs or is likely significantly to impair the average consumer's freedom of choice or conduct in relation to the product concerned through the use of harassment, coercion or undue influence; and

(b)   it thereby causes or is likely to cause him to take a transactional decision he would not have taken otherwise.

(2)   In determining whether a commercial practice uses harassment, coercion or undue influence account shall be taken of—

(a)   its timing, location, nature or persistence;

(b)   the use of threatening or abusive language or behaviour;

(c)   the exploitation by the trader of any specific misfortune or circumstance of such gravity as to impair the consumer's judgment, of which the trader is aware, to influence the consumer's decision with regard to the product;

(d)   any onerous or disproportionate non-contractual barrier imposed by the trader where a consumer wishes to exercise rights under the contract, including rights to terminate a contract or to switch to another product or another trader; and

(e)   any threat to take any action which cannot legally be taken.

(3)   In this regulation—

(a)   'coercion' includes the use of physical force; and

(b)   'undue influence' means exploiting a position of power in relation to the consumer so as to apply pressure, even without using or threatening to use physical force, in a way which significantly limits the consumer's ability to make an informed decision.

PART 3

OFFENCES

8   Offences relating to unfair commercial practices

(1)   A trader is guilty of an offence if—

(a)   he knowingly or recklessly engages in a commercial practice which contravenes the requirements of professional diligence under regulation 3(3)(a); and

(b)   the practice materially distorts or is likely to materially distort the economic behaviour of the average consumer with regard to the product under regulation 3(3)(b).

(2)   For the purposes of paragraph (1)(a) a trader who engages in a commercial

practice without regard to whether the practice contravenes the requirements of professional diligence shall be deemed recklessly to engage in the practice, whether or not the trader has reason for believing that the practice might contravene those requirements.

9 A trader is guilty of an offence if he engages in a commercial practice which is a misleading action under regulation 5 otherwise than by reason of the commercial practice satisfying the condition in regulation 5(3)(b).

10 A trader is guilty of an offence if he engages in a commercial practice which is a misleading omission under regulation 6.

11 A trader is guilty of an offence if he engages in a commercial practice which is aggressive under regulation 7.

12 A trader is guilty of an offence if he engages in a commercial practice set out in any of paragraphs 1 to 10, 12 to 27 and 29 to 31 of Schedule 1.

13 Penalty for offences

A person guilty of an offence under regulation 8, 9, 10, 11 or 12 shall be liable—

(a) on summary conviction, to a fine not exceeding the statutory maximum; or

(b) on conviction on indictment, to a fine or imprisonment for a term not exceeding two years or both.

14 Time limit for prosecution

(1) No proceedings for an offence under these Reegulations shall be commenced after—

(a) the end of the period of three years beginning with the date of the commission of the offence, or

(b) the end of the period of one year beginning with the date of discovery of the offence by the prosecutor, whichever is earlier.

(2) For the purposes of paragraph (1)(b) a certificate signed by or on behalf of the prosecutor and stating the date on which the offence was discovered by him shall be conclusive evidence of that fact and a certificate stating that matter and purporting to be so signed shall be treated as so signed unless the contrary is proved.

(3) Notwithstanding anything in section 127(1) of the Magistrates' Courts Act 1980, an information relating to an offence under these Regulations which is triable by a magistrates' court in England and Wales may be so tried if it is laid at any time before the end of the period of twelve months beginning with the date of the commission of the offence.

(4) Notwithstanding anything in section 136 of the Criminal Procedure (Scotland) Act 1995 summary proceedings in Scotland for an offence under these Regulations may be commenced at any time before the end of the period of twelve months beginning with the date of the commission of the offence.

(5) For the purposes of paragraph (4), section 136(3) of the Criminal Procedure (Scotland) Act 1995 shall apply as it applies for the purposes of that subsection.

(6) Notwithstanding anything in Article 19(1) of the Magistrates' Courts (Northern Ireland) Order 1981 a complaint charging an offence under these Regulations which is triable by a magistrates' court in Northern Ireland may be so tried if it is made at any time before the end of the period of twelve months beginning with the date of the commission of the offence.

15 Offences committed by bodies of persons

(1) Where an offence under these Regulations committed by a body corporate is proved—

(a) to have been committed with the consent or connivance of an officer of the body, or

(b)   to be attributable to any neglect on his part, the officer as well as the body corporate is guilty of the offence and liable to be proceeded against and punished accordingly.

(2)   In paragraph (1) a reference to an officer of a body corporate includes a reference to—

(a)   a director, manager, secretary or other similar officer; and

(b)   a person purporting to act as a director, manager, secretary or other similar officer.

(3)   Where an offence under these Regulations committed by a Scottish partnership is proved—

(a)   to have been committed with the consent or connivance of a partner, or

(b)   to be attributable to any neglect on his part, the partner as well as the partnership is guilty of the offence and liable to be proceeded against and punished accordingly.

(4)   In paragraph (3) a reference to a partner includes a person purporting to act as a partner.

16   Offence due to the default of another person

(1)   This regulation applies where a person 'X'—

(a)   commits an offence under regulation 9, 10, 11 or 12, or

(b)   would have committed an offence under those regulations but for a defence under regulation 17 or 18, and the commission of the offence, or of what would have been an offence but for X being able to rely on a defence under regulation 17 or 18, is due to the act or default of some other person 'Y'.

(2)   Where this regulation applies Y is guilty of the offence, subject to regulations 17 and 18, whether or not Y is a trader and whether or not Y's act or default is a commercial practice.

(3)   Y may be charged with and convicted of the offence by virtue of paragraph (2) whether or not proceedings are taken against X.

17   Due diligence defence

(1)   In any proceedings against a person for an offence under regulation 9, 10, 11 or 12 it is a defence for that person to prove—

(a)   that the commission of the offence was due to—

(i)   a mistake;

(ii)   reliance on information supplied to him by another person;

(iii)   the act or default of another person;

(iv)   an accident; or

(v)   another cause beyond his control; and

(b)   that he took all reasonable precautions and exercised all due diligence to avoid the commission of such an offence by himself or any person under his control.

(2)   A person shall not be entitled to rely on the defence provided by paragraph (1) by reason of the matters referred to in paragraph (ii) or (iii) of paragraph (1)(a) without leave of the court unless—

(a)   he has served on the prosecutor a notice in writing giving such information identifying or assisting in the identification of that other person as was in his possession; and

(b)   the notice is served on the prosecutor at least seven clear days before the date of the hearing.

18   Innocent publication of advertisement defence

(1)   In any proceedings against a person for an offence under regulation 9, 10, 11 or 12 committed by the publication of an advertisement it shall be a defence for a person to prove that—

(a)   he is a person whose business it is to publish or to arrange for the publication of advertisements;

(b) he received the advertisement for publication in the ordinary course of business; and

(c) he did not know and had no reason to suspect that its publication would amount to an offence under the regulation to which the proceedings relate.

(2) In paragraph (1) 'advertisement' includes a catalogue, a circular and a price list.

PART 4
ENFORCEMENT

19 [Duty and power to enforce]

[(1) It shall be the duty of every local weights and measures authority and DETINI to enforce these Regulations other than Part 4A.]

(1A) The [CMA] may also enforce these Regulations.]

(2) Where the enforcement authority is a local weights and measures authority the duty referred to in paragraph (1) shall apply to the enforcement of these Regulations within the authority's area.

(3) Where the enforcement authority is [DETINI] the duty referred to in paragraph (1) shall apply to the enforcement of these Regulations within Northern Ireland.

(4) [In determining how to comply with paragraph (1), or as the case may be, paragraph (1A)] every enforcement authority shall have regard to the desirability of encouraging control of unfair commercial practices by such established means as it considers appropriate having regard to all the circumstances of the particular case.

(5) Nothing in this regulation shall authorise any enforcement authority to bring proceedings in Scotland for an offence.

20 Power to make test purchases

An enforcement authority may or may authorisse any of its officers on its behalf to—

(a) make a purchase of a product, or

(b) enter into an agreement to secure the provision of a product, for the purposes of determining whether these Regulations are being complied with.

21 Power of entry and investigation, etc

(1) A duly authorised officer of an enfoorcement authority may at all reasonable hours exercise the following powers—

(a) he may, for the purposes of ascertaining whether a breach of these Regulations has been committed, inspect any goods and enter any premises other than premises used only as a dwelling;

(b) if he has reasonable cause to suspect that a breach of these Regulations has been committed, he may, for the purpose of ascertaining whether it has been committed, require any trader to produce any documents relating to his business and may take copies of, or of any entry in, any such document;

(c) if he has reasonable cause to believe that a breach of these Regulations has been committed, he may seize and detain any goods for the purpose of ascertaining, by testing or otherwise, whether the breach has been committed; and

(d) he may seize and detain goods or documents which he has reason to believe may be required as evidence in proceedings for a breach of these Regulations.

(2) If and to the extent that it is reasonably necessary to secure that the provisions of these Regulations are observed, the officer may for the purpose of exercising his powers under paragraphs (1)(c) and (d) to seize goods or documents—

(a) require any person having authority to do so to break open any container or open any vending machine; and

(b) himself open or break open any such container or open any vending machine where a requirement made under sub-paragraph (a) in relation to the container or vending machine has not been complied with.

(3) An officer seizing any goods or documents in exercise of his powers under this regulation shall—

(a) inform the person from whom they are seized, and,

(b) where goods are seized from a vending machine, inform—

(i) the person whose name and address are stated on the machine as being the proprietor's; or

(ii) if there is no such name or address stated on the machine the occupier of the ppremises on which the machinestands or to which it is affixed, that the goods or documents have been so seized.

(4) In this regulation 'document' includes information recorded in any form.

(5) The reference in paragraph (1)(b) to the production of documents is, in the case of a document which contains information recorded otherwise than in legible form, a reference to the production of a copy of the information in legible form.

(6) An officer seeking to exercise a power under this regulation must produce evidence of his identity and authority to a person (if there is one) who appears to the officer to be the occupier of the premises.

(7) Where an officer seizes goods or documents in exercise of a power under this regulation they may not be detained—

(a) for a period of more than 3 months; or

(b) where the goods or documents are reasonably required by the enforcement authority in connection with the enforcement of these Regulations, for longer than they are so required.

(8) An officer entering any premises under this regulation may take with him such other persons and such equipment as may appear to him to be necessary.

(9) Nothing in this regulation or in regulation 22 gives any power to an officer of an enforcement authority—

(a) to require any person to produce, or

(b) to seize from another person, any document which the other person would be entitled to refuse to produce in proceedings in the High Court on the grounds of legal professional privilege or (in Scotland) in proceedings in the Court of Session on the grounds of confidentiality of communications.

(10) In paragraph (9) 'communications' means—

(a) communications between a professional legal adviser and his client; or

(b) communications made in connection with or in contemplation of legal proceedings and for the purposes of those proceedings.

(11) If any person who is not an officer of an enforcement authority purports to act as such under this regulation or under regulation 22 he shall be guilty of an offence and liable on summary conviction to a fine not exceeding level 5 on the standard scale.

22 Power to enter premises with a warrant

(1) If a justice of the peace by any wrritten information on oath is satisfied—

(a) that there are reasonable grounds for believing that Condition A or B is met, and

(b) that Condition C, D or E is met, the justice may by warrant under his hand authorise an officer of an enforcement authority to enter the premises at all reasonable times, if necessary by force.

(2) Condition A is that there are on any premises goods or documents which a duly authorised officer of the enforcement authority has power under regulation 21(1) to inspect and that their inspection is likely to disclose evidence of a breach of these Regulations.

(3) Condition B is that a breach of these Regulations has been, is being or is about to be committed on any premises.

(4)   Condition C is that the admission to the premises has been or is likely to be refused and that notice of intention to apply for a warrant under this regulation has been given to the occupier.

(5)   Condition D is that an application for admission, or the giving of a notice of intention to apply for a warrant, would defeat the object of the entry.

(6)   Condition E is that the premises are unoccupied or that the occupier is absent and it might defeat the object of the entry to await his return.

(7)   A warrant under paragraph (1)—

(a)   ceases to have effect at the end of the period of one month beginning with the day it is issued; (b) must be produced for inspection to the person (if there is one) who appears to the officer to be the occupier of the premises.

(8)   An officer entering any premises under this regulation may take with him such other persons and such equipment as may appear to him to be necessary.

(9)   On leaving any premises which an officer is authorised to enter by warrant under this regulation the officer shall, if the premises are unoccupied or the occupier is temporarily absent, leave the premises as effectively secured against trespassers as he found them.

(10)   In its application to Scotland, this regulation has effect as if—

(a)   the references in paragraph (1) to a justice of the peace included references to a sheriff; and

(b)   the reference in paragraph (1) to information on oath were a reference to evidence on oath.

(11)   In its application to Northern Ireland, this regulation has effect as if the references in paragraph (1) to a justice of the peace were references to a lay magistrate.

23   Obstruction of authorised officers

(1)   Any person who—

(a)   intentionally obstructs an officer of an enforcement authority acting in pursuance of these Regulations,

(b)   intentionally fails to comply with any requirement properly made of him by such an officer under regulation 21, or

(c)   without reasonable cause fails to give such an officer any other assistance or information which he may reasonably require of him for the purpose of the performance of his functions under these Regulations, is guilty of an offence and liable, on summary conviction, to a fine not exceeding level 5 on the standard scale.

(2)   Any person who, in giving any information which is required of him under paragraph (1)(c), makes any statement which he knows to be false in a material particular is guilty of an offence and liable—

(a)   on summary conviction, to a fine not exceeding the statutory maximum; or

(b)   on conviction on indictment, to a fine or imprisonment for a term not exceeding two years or both.

(3)   Nothing in this regulation shall be construed as requiring a person to answer any question or give any information if to do so might incriminate him.

24   Notice of test and intended proceedings

(1)   Where goods purchased by an officer pursuant to regulation 20 are submitted to a test and the test leads to the institution of any proceedings for a breach of these Regulations the officer shall inform—

(a)   the person from whom the goods were purchased, or

(b)   where the goods were sold through a vending machine, the person mentioned in regulation 21(3)(b), of the result of the test.

(2)   Where goods seized by an officer pursuant to regulation 21 are submitted

to a test then the officer shall inform the person mentioned in regulation 21(3) of the result of the test.

(3)   Where, as a result of the test, any proceedings in respect of a breach of these Regulations are taken against any person, the officer shall allow him to have the goods tested on his behalf if it is reasonably practicable to do so.

25   Compensation

(1)   Where an officer of an enforcement authority seizes and detains goods in exercise of the powers under regulation 21 the enforcement authority shall be liable to pay compensation to any person having an interest in the goods in respect of any loss or damage caused by reason of the exercise of the power if—

(a)   there has been no breach of these Regulations in relation to the goods, and

(b)   the exercise of that power is not attributable to any neglect or default by that person.

(2)   Any disputed question as to the right to or the amount of any compensation payable under this provision shall be determined by arbitration or, in Scotland, by a single arbiter appointed, failing agreement between the parties, by the sheriff.

26–27   *[Amend the Enterprise Act 2002]*

[PART 4A
CONSUMERS' RIGHTS TO REDRESS

27A   When does a consumer have a right to redress?

(1)   A consumer has a right to redress under this Part if—

(a)   the conditions in this regulation are met, and

(b)   the conditions (if any) in the following provisions of this Part for the availability of that right are met.

(2)   The first condition is that—

(a)   the consumer enters into a contract with a trader for the sale or supply of a product by the trader (a 'business to consumer contract'),

(b)   the consumer enters into a contract with a trader for the sale of goods to the trader (a 'consumer to business contract'), or

(c)   the consumer makes a payment to a trader for the supply of a product (a 'consumer payment').

(3)   Paragraph (2)(b) does not apply if, under the contract, the trader supplies or agrees to supply a product to the consumer as well as paying or agreeing to pay the consumer.

(4)   The second condition is that—

(a)   the trader engages in a prohibited practice in relation to the product, or

(b)   in a case where a consumer enters into a business to consumer contract for goods or digital content—

(i)   a producer engages in a prohibited practice in relation to the goods or digital content, and

(ii)   when the contract is entered into, the trader is aware of the commercial practice that constitutes the prohibited practice or could reasonably be expected to be aware of it.

(5)   In paragraph (4)(b) 'producer' means—

(a)   a manufacturer of the goods or digital content,

(b)   an importer of the goods or digital content into the European Economic Area, or

(c)   a person who purports to be a producer by placing the person's name, trade mark or other distinctive sign on the goods or using it in connection with the digital content, and includes a producer acting personally or through another person acting in the producer's name or on the producer's behalf.

(6)   The third condition is that the prohibited practice is a significant factor in the consumer's decision to enter into the contract or make the payment.

27B   What does 'prohibited practice' mean in this Part?

(1)   In this Part 'prohibited practice' means a commercial practice that—

(a)   is a misleading action under regulation 5, or

(b)   is aggressive under regulation 7.

(2)   Regulations 5 and 7 apply for the purposes of this Part as if for the definition of 'transactional decision' in regulation 2(1) there were substituted—

' "transactional decision" means any decision taken by a consumer to enter into a contract with a trader for the sale or supply of a product by the trader, or for the sale of goods to the trader, or to make a payment to a trader for the supply of a product.'.

27C   What immoveable property is covered by this Part?

(1)   In this Part 'product' does not include immoveable property other than a relevant lease.

(2)   In this regulation 'relevant lease' in relation to England and Wales means—

(a)   an assured tenancy within the meaning of Part 1 of the Housing Act 1988, or

(b)   a lease under which accommodation is let as holiday accommodation.

(3)   But none of the following are relevant leases for the purposes of paragraph (2)(a)—

(a)   a lease granted by—

(i)   a private registered provider of social housing, or

(ii)   a registered social landlord within the meaning of Part 1 of the Housing Act 1996;

(b)   a lease of a dwelling-house or part of a dwelling-house—

(i)   granted on payment of a premium calculated by reference to a percentage of the value of the dwelling-house or part or of the cost of providing it, or

(ii)   under which the lessee (or the lessee's personal representatives) will or may be entitled to a sum calculated by reference, directly or indirectly, to the value of the dwelling-house or part;

(c)   a lease granted to a person as a result of the exercise by a local housing authority within the meaning of the Housing Act 1996 of its functions under Part 7 (homelessness) of that Act.

(4)   In this regulation 'relevant lease' in relation to Scotland means—

(a)   an assured tenancy within the meaning of Part 2 of the Housing (Scotland) Act 1988, or

(b)   a lease under which accommodation is let as holiday accommodation.

(5)   In this regulation 'relevant lease' in relation to Northern Ireland means—

(a)   a private tenancy within the meaning of Article 3 of the Private Tenancies (Northern Ireland) Order 2006, or

(b)   a lease under which accommodation is let as holiday accommodation.

(6)   But neither of the following are relevant leases for the purposes of paragraph (5)(a)—

(a)   a lease of a dwelling-house or part of a dwelling-house—

(i)   granted on payment of a premium calculated by reference to a percentage of the value of the dwelling-house or part or of the cost of providing it, or

(ii)   under which the lessee (or the lessee's personal representatives) will or may be entitled to a sum calculated by reference, directly or indirectly, to the value of the dwelling-house or part;

(b)   a private tenancy resulting from the exercise by the Northern Ireland

Housing Executive of its functions under Part 2 (homelessness) of the Housing (Northern Ireland) Order 1988.

27D   What financial services are covered by this Part?
(1)   In this Part 'product' does not include a service provided in the course of carrying on a regulated activity within the meaning of section 22 of the Financial Services and Markets Act 2000, other than a service to which paragraph (2) applies.
(2)   This paragraph applies to a service consisting of the provision of credit under an agreement which is a restricted-use credit agreement within paragraph (a) or (b) of the definition of that term in article 60L(1) of the Financial Services and Markets Act 2000 (Regulated Activities) Order 2001.
(3)   But paragraph (2) does not apply to an agreement under which the obligation of the borrower to repay is secured by a legal or equitable mortgage on land (other than timeshare accommodation).
(4)   In paragraph (3)—
'mortgage' includes a charge and (in Scotland) a heritable security;
'timeshare accommodation' means overnight accommodation which is the subject of a timeshare contract within the meaning of the Timeshare, Holiday Products, Resale and Exchange Contracts Regulations 2010.
(5)   The fact that the supply of a product within regulation 2(1A) and (1B) may constitute an activity within article 39F (debt-collecting) of the Financial Services and Markets Act 2000 (Regulated Activities) Order 2001 does not prevent this Part from applying in relation to that supply.

27E   When does the right to unwind apply to a business to consumer contract?
(1)   A consumer has the right to unwind in respect of a business to consumer contract if the consumer indicates to the trader that the consumer rejects the product, and does so—
    (a)   within the relevant period, and
    (b)   at a time when the product is capable of being rejected.
(2)   An indication under paragraph (1) may be something that the consumer says or does, but it must be clear.
(3)   In paragraph (1)(a) 'the relevant period' means the period of 90 days beginning with the later of—
    (a)   the day on which the consumer enters into the contract, and
    (b)   the relevant day.
(4)   In this Part 'the relevant day' means the day on which—
    (a)   the goods are first delivered,
    (b)   the performance of the service begins,
    (c)   the digital content is first supplied,
    (d)   the lease begins, or
    (e)   the right is first exercisable,
(as the case may be).
(5)   But in the case of a mixed contract, 'the relevant day' means the latest of the days mentioned in paragraph (4) that is relevant to the contract.
(6)   In this Part 'mixed contract' means a contract relating to a product which consists of any two or more of goods, a service, digital content, immoveable property or rights.
(7)   For the purposes of this Part, where the consumer's access to digital content on a device requires its transmission to the device under arrangements initiated by the trader, the day on which the digital content is first provided is—
    (a)   the day on which it reaches the device, or
    (b)   if earlier, the day on which it reaches another trader chosen by the consumer to supply, under a contract with the consumer, a service by which digital content reaches the device.

(8)   For the purposes of paragraph (1)(b), a product remains capable of being rejected only if—

    (a)   the goods have not been fully consumed,

    (b)   the service has not been fully performed,

    (c)   the digital content has not been fully consumed,

    (d)   the lease has not expired, or

    (e)   the right has not been fully exercised,

(as the case may be).

(9)   For the purposes of paragraph (8)—

    (a)   goods have been fully consumed only if nothing is left of them, and

    (b)   digital content has been fully consumed only if the digital content was available to the consumer for a fixed period and that period has expired.

(10)   A consumer does not have the right to unwind in respect of a business to consumer contract if the consumer has exercised the right to a discount in respect of that contract and the same prohibited practice.

27F   How does the right to unwind work in the case of a business to consumer contract?

(1)   Where a consumer has the right to unwind in respect of a business to consumer contract—

    (a)   the contract comes to an end so that the consumer and the trader are released from their obligations under it,

    (b)   the trader has a duty to give the consumer a refund (subject as follows), and

    (c)   if the contract was wholly or partly for the sale or supply of goods the consumer must make the goods available for collection by the trader.

(2)   The consumer's entitlement to a refund works as follows.

(3)   To the extent that the consumer paid money under the contract, the consumer is entitled to receive back the same amount of money (but see paragraphs (7) to (10)).

(4)   To the extent that the consumer transferred anything else under the contract, the consumer is entitled to receive back the same amount of what the consumer transferred, unless paragraph (5) applies.

(5)   To the extent that the consumer transferred under the contract something for which the same amount of the same thing cannot be substituted—

    (a)   the consumer is entitled to receive back in its original state whatever the consumer transferred, or

    (b)   if it cannot be given back in its original state, the consumer is entitled to be paid its market price as at the time when the product was rejected.

(6)   There is no entitlement to a refund if none of paragraphs (3) to (5) applies.

(7)   The consumer's entitlement to receive back the same amount of money as the consumer paid is qualified by paragraphs (8) to (10) if—

    (a)   the contract was for the sale or supply of a product on a regular or continuous basis, and

    (b)   the period beginning with the relevant day and ending with the day on which the consumer rejected the product exceeds one month.

(8)   In that case the consumer is only entitled to receive back the amount (if any) found by deducting the market price, when the consumer rejected the product, of the product supplied up to that time from the amount the consumer paid for it.

(9)   But paragraph (8) does not apply if it is not appropriate to apply that deduction having regard to—

    (a)   the behaviour of the person who engaged in the prohibited practice, and

    (b)   the impact of the practice on the consumer.

(10)   Where the product supplied up to the time when the consumer rejected it consists wholly or partly of goods, their market price is only to be taken into account under paragraph (8) to the extent that they have been consumed.

27G How does the right to unwind work in the case of a consumer to business contract?

(1)   A consumer who has a right to redress in respect of a consumer to business contract has the right to unwind in respect of that contract.

(2)   Where paragraph (1) applies—

(a)   the consumer has the right to treat the contract as at an end so that the trader and the consumer are released from their obligations under it, and

(b)   the consumer has the right within paragraph (5) or (6).

(3)   To treat the contract as at an end, the consumer must indicate to the trader that the contract is ended.

(4)   An indication under paragraph (3) may be something that the consumer says or does, but it must be clear.

(5)   If the trader is able to return the goods to the consumer in the condition they were in when sold by the consumer—

(a)   the consumer has a right to the return of the goods, and

(b)   the consumer must repay to the trader the amount (if any) that the trader has paid for the goods.

(6)   If paragraph (5) does not apply, the consumer has a right to a payment from the trader of the amount (if any) by which the market price of the goods when the trader paid for them exceeds what the trader paid for them.

27H How does the right to unwind work if payments are demanded which are not due?

(1)   A consumer has the right to unwind in respect of a consumer payment for a product within regulation 2(1A) and (1B) if the consumer was not required to make all or part of the payment.

(2)   Where paragraph (1) applies, the consumer has the right to receive back from the trader—

(a)   the same amount of money as the consumer paid to the trader, or

(b)   in a case where the consumer was required to make part of the payment, an amount equal to the part of the payment the consumer was not required to make.

27I How does the right to a discount work?

(1)   A consumer has the right to a discount in respect of a business to consumer contract if—

(a)   the consumer has made one or more payments for the product to the trader or one or more payments under the contract have not been made, and

(b)   the consumer has not exercised the right to unwind in respect of the contract.

(2)   If the consumer has made one or more payments, the consumer has the right to receive back from the trader the relevant percentage of the payment or payments.

(3)   If one or more payments have not been made, the consumer has the right—

(a)   to reduce by the relevant percentage as many of those payments as is appropriate having regard to the seriousness of the prohibited practice, or

(b)   in a case within paragraph (6), to reduce all of those payments by the relevant percentage.

(4)   Subject to paragraph (6), the relevant percentage is as follows—

(a)   if the prohibited practice is more than minor, it is 25%,

(b)   if the prohibited practice is significant, it is 50%,

(c)   if the prohibited practice is serious, it is 75%, and

(d)   if the prohibited practice is very serious, it is 100%.

(5)   The seriousness of the prohibited practice is to be assessed by reference to—

(a)   the behaviour of the person who engaged in the practice,

(b)   the impact of the practice on the consumer, and

(c) the time that has elapsed since the prohibited practice took place.

(6) [Paragraph (4)] does not apply if—

(a) the amount payable for the product under the contract exceeds £5,000,

(b) the market price of the product, at the time that the consumer entered into the contract, is lower than the amount payable for it under the contract, and

(c) there is clear evidence of the difference between the market price of the product and the amount payable for it under the contract.

(7) In such a case, the relevant percentage is the percentage difference between the market price of the product and the amount payable for it under the contract.

(8) The application of this regulation does not affect any of the other rights and liabilities under the contract.

27J How does the right to damages work?

(1) Subject as follows, a consumer has the right to damages if the consumer—

(a) has incurred financial loss which the consumer would not have incurred if the prohibited practice in question had not taken place, or

(b) has suffered alarm, distress or physical inconvenience or discomfort which the consumer would not have suffered if the prohibited practice in question had not taken place.

(2) The right to damages is the right to be paid damages by the trader for the loss or the alarm, distress or physical inconvenience or discomfort in question.

(3) The right to be paid damages for financial loss does not include the right to be paid damages in respect of the difference between the market price of a product and the amount payable for it under a contract.

(4) The right to be paid damages under this regulation is a right to be paid only damages in respect of loss that was reasonably foreseeable at the time of the prohibited practice.

(5) A consumer does not have the right to damages if the trader proves that—

(a) the occurrence of the prohibited practice in question was due to—

(i) a mistake,

(ii) reliance on information supplied to the trader by another person,

(iii) the act or default of a person other than the trader,

(iv) an accident, or

(v) another cause beyond the trader's control, and

(b) the trader took all reasonable precautions and exercised all due diligence to avoid the occurrence of the prohibited practice.

27K How can a consumer enforce the rights to redress?

(1) A consumer with a right to redress under this Part may bring a claim in civil proceedings to enforce that right.

(2) In Scotland, proceedings to enforce the right to unwind may be brought before the sheriff or in the Court of Session.

(3) Paragraph (4) applies if in proceedings under this regulation the consumer establishes that the consumer has—

(a) the right to unwind,

(b) the right to a discount, or

(c) the right to damages.

(4) The court must make an order that gives effect to—

(a) that right, and

(b) any associated obligations of the consumer under this Part.

(5) The Limitation Act 1980 applies to a claim under this regulation in England and Wales as if it were an action founded on simple contract.

(6) The Limitation (Northern Ireland) Order 1989 applies to a claim under this regulation in Northern Ireland as if it were an action founded on simple contract.

27L How does this Part relate to the existing law?

(1) Nothing in this Part affects the ability of a consumer to make a claim under

a rule of law or equity, or under an enactment, in respect of conduct constituting a prohibited practice.

(2)   But a consumer may not—

(a)   make a claim to be compensated under a rule of law or equity, or under an enactment, in respect of such conduct if the consumer has been compensated under this Part in respect of the conduct, or

(b)   make a claim to be compensated under this Part in respect of such conduct if the consumer has been compensated under a rule of law or equity, or under an enactment, in respect of the conduct.

(3)   In this regulation 'enactment' includes—

(a)   an enactment contained in subordinate legislation within the meaning of the Interpretation Act 1978,

(b)   an enactment contained in, or in an instrument made under, a Measure or Act of the National Assembly for Wales,

(c)   an enactment contained in, or in an instrument made under, an Act of the Scottish Parliament, and

(d)   an enactment contained in, or in an instrument made under, Northern Ireland legislation.]

[[27M]   Inertia selling

(1)   This regulation applies where a trader engages in the unfair commercial practice described in paragraph 29 of Schedule 1 (inertia selling).

(2)   The consumer is exempted from any obligation to provide consideration for the products supplied by the trader.

(3)   The absence of a response from the consumer following the supply does not constitute consent to the provision of consideration for, or the return or safekeeping of, the products.

(4)   In the case of an unsolicited supply of goods, the consumer may, as between the consumer and the trader, use, deal with or dispose of the goods as if they were an unconditional gift to the consumer.]

PART 5
SUPPLEMENTARY

28   Crown

(1)   The powers conferred by regulations 21 aand 22 are not exercisable in relation to premises occupied by the Crown.

(2)   The Crown is not criminally liable as a result of any provision of these Regulations.

(3)   Paragraph (2) does not affect the application of any provision of these Regulations in relation to a person in the public service of the Crown.

29   Validity of agreements

[Except as provided by Part 4A,] an agreement shall not be void or unenforceablle by reason only of a breach of these Regulations.

. . .

SCHEDULE 1
COMMERCIAL PRACTICES WHICH ARE IN ALL CIRCUMSTANCES
CONSIDERED UNFAIR

1   Claiming to be a signatory to a code of conduct when the trader is not.

2   Displaying a trust mark, quality mark or equivalent without having obtained the necessary authorisation.

3   Claiming that a code of conduct has an endorsement from a public or other body which it does not have.

4 Claiming that a trader (including his commercial practices) or a product has been approved, endorsed or authorised by a public or private body when the trader, the commercial practices or the product have not or making such a claim without complying with the terms of the approval, endorsement or authorisation.

5 Making an invitation to purchase products at a specified price without disclosing the existence of any reasonable grounds the trader may have for believing that he will not be able to offer for supply, or to procure another trader to supply, those products or equivalent products at that price for a period that is, and in quantities that are, reasonable having regard to the product, the scale of advertising of the product and the price offered (bait advertising).

6 Making an invitation to purchase products at a specified price and then—
   (a)   refusing to show the advertised item to consumers,
   (b)   refusing to take orders for it or deliver it within a reasonable time, or
   (c)   demonstrating a defective sample of it, with the intention of promoting a different product (bait and switch).

7 Falsely stating that a product will only be available for a very limited time, or that it will only be available on particular terms for a very limited time, in order to elicit an immediate decision and deprive consumers of sufficient opportunity or time to make an informed choice.

8 Undertaking to provide after-sales service to consumers with whom the trader has communicated prior to a transaction in a language which is not an official language of the EEA State where the trader is located and then making such service available only in another language without clearly disclosing this to the consumer before the consumer is committed to the transaction.

9 Stating or otherwise creating the impression that a product can legally be sold when it cannot.

10 Presenting rights given to consumers in law as a distinctive feature of the trader's offer.

11 Using editorial content in the media to promote a product where a trader has paid for the promotion without making that clear in the content or by images or sounds clearly identifiable by the consumer (advertorial).

12 Making a materially inaccurate claim concerning the nature and extent of the risk to the personal security of the consumer or his family if the consumer does not purchase the product.

13 Promoting a product similar to a product made by a particular manufacturer in such a manner as deliberately to mislead the consumer into believing that the product is made by that same manufacturer when it is not.

14 Establishing, operating or promoting a pyramid promotional scheme where a consumer gives consideration for the opportunity to receive compensation that is derived primarily from the introduction of other consumers into the scheme rather than from the sale or consumption of products.

15 Claiming that the trader is about to cease trading or move premises when he is not.

16 Claiming that products are able to facilitate winning in games of chance.

17 Falsely claiming that a product is able to cure illnesses, dysfunction or malformations.

18 Passing on materially inaccurate information on market conditions or on the possibility of finding the product with the intention of inducing the consumer to acquire the product at conditions less favourable than normal market conditions.

19 Claiming in a commercial practice to offer a competition or prize promotion without awarding the prizes described or a reasonable equivalent.

20 Describing a product as 'gratis', 'free', 'without charge' or similar if the consumer has to pay anything other than the unavoidable cost of responding to the commercial practice and collecting or paying for delivery of the item.

21 Including in marketing material an invoice or similar document seeking

payment which gives the consumer the impression that he has already ordered the marketed product when he has not.

22   Falsely claiming or creating the impression that the trader is not acting for purposes relating to his trade, business, craft or profession, or falsely representing oneself as a consumer.

23   Creating the false impression that after-sales service in relation to a product is available in an EEA State other than the one in which the product is sold.

24   Creating the impression that the consumer cannot leave the premises until a contract is formed.

25   Conducting personal visits to the consumer's home ignoring the consumer's request to leave or not to return, except in circumstances and to the extent justified to enforce a contractual obligation.

26   Making persistent and unwanted solicitations by telephone, fax, e-mail or other remote media except in circumstances and to the extent justified to enforce a contractual obligation.

27   Requiring a consumer who wishes to claim on an insurance policy to produce documents which could not reasonably be considered relevant as to whether the claim was valid, or failing systematically to respond to pertinent correspondence, in order to dissuade a consumer from exercising his contractual rights.

28   Including in an advertisement a direct exhortation to children to buy advertised products or persuade their parents or other adults to buy advertised products for them.

29   Demanding immediate or deferred payment for or the return or safekeeping of products supplied by the trader, but not solicited by the consumer [. . .].

30   Explicitly informing a consumer that if he does not buy the product or service, the trader's job or livelihood will be in jeopardy.

31   Creating the false impression that the consumer has already won, will win, or will on doing a particular act win, a prize or other equivalent benefit, when in fact either—

(a)   there is no prize or other equivalent benefit, or

(b)   taking any action in relation to claiming the prize or other equivalent benefit is subject to the consumer paying money or incurring a cost.

CONSUMER RIGHTS (PAYMENT SURCHARGES) REGULATIONS 2012
(SI 2012/3110)

1   Citation and commencement

(1)   These Regulations may be cited as the Consumer Rights (Payment Surcharges) Regulations 2012 and come into force on 6th April 2013.

(2)   These Regulations apply in relation to contracts entered into on or after that date.

2   'Consumer' and 'trader'

In these Regulations—

'consumer' means an individual acting for purposes which are wholly or mainly outside that individual's trade, business, craft or profession;

['trader' means a person acting for purposes relating to that person's trade, business, craft or profession, whether acting personally or through another person acting in the trader's name or on the trader's behalf;]

3   Other definitions

In these Regulations—

['business' includes the activities of any government department or local or public authority;]

['CMA' means the Competitions and Markets Authority;]

'court' in relation to England and Wales and Northern Ireland means a county court or the High Court, and in relation to Scotland means the sheriff or the Court of Session;

'digital content' means data which are produced and supplied in digital form;

'district heating' means the supply of heat (in the form of steam or hot water or otherwise) from a central source of production through a transmission and distribution system to heat more than one building;

'goods' means any tangible movable items, but that includes water, gas and electricity if and only if they are put up for sale in a limited volume or a set quantity;

[. . .]

'sales contract' means a contract under which a trader transfers or agrees to transfer the ownership of goods to a consumer and the consumer pays or agrees to pay the price [, including any contract that has both goods and services as its object];

'service contract' means a contract, other than a sales contract, under which a trader supplies or agrees to supply a service to a consumer and the consumer pays or agrees to pay the price.

4 Excessive charges prohibited

A trader must not charge consumers, in respect of the use of a given means of payment, fees that exceed the cost borne by the trader for the use of that means.

5 Contracts where prohibition applies

(1) Regulation 4 applies only if the use is as a means for the consumer to make payments for the purposes of a contract with the trader, and only to the extent that that contract—

(a) is a sales or service contract, or a contract (other than a sales or service contract) for the supply of water, gas, electricity, district heating or digital content, and

(b) is not an excluded contract.

(2) An excluded contract is a contract—

(a) for social services, including social housing, childcare and support of families and persons permanently or temporarily in need, including long-term care;

(b) for health services provided, whether or not via healthcare facilities, by health professionals to patients to assess, maintain or restore their state of health, including the prescription, dispensation and provision of medicinal products and medical devices (and 'health professionals' has the meaning given by Article 3(f) of Directive 2011/24/EU of the European Parliament and of the Council on the application of patients' rights in cross-border healthcare);

(c) for gambling within the meaning of the Gambling Act 2005 (which includes gaming, betting and participating in a lottery);

(d) for services of a banking, credit, insurance, personal pension, investment or payment nature;

(e) for the creation of immovable property or of rights in immovable property;

(f) for rental of accommodation for residential purposes;

(g) for the construction of new buildings, or the construction of substantially new buildings by the conversion of existing buildings;

(h) which falls within the scope of Directive 2008/122/EC of the European Parliament and of the Council on the protection of consumers in respect of certain aspects of timeshare, long-term holiday product, resale and exchange contracts;

(i) for the supply of foodstuffs, beverages or other goods intended for current consumption in the household, and which are supplied by a trader on frequent and regular rounds to the consumer's home, residence or workplace;

(j) concluded by means of automatic vending machines or automated commercial premises;

(k)   concluded with a telecommunications operator through a public telephone for the use of the telephone;

(l)   concluded for the use of one single connection, by telephone, internet or fax, established by a consumer;

(m)   under which goods are sold by way of execution or otherwise by authority of law.

6   Temporary exemption for micro-businesses and new businesses

(1)   During the exemption period, regulation 4 does not apply if the trader is acting for purposes relating to the trader's business, and the business is—

(a)   an existing micro-business, or

(b)   a new business.

(2)   The Schedule defines those kinds of business, and the exemption period.

7   Complaints

(1)   It is the duty of an enforcement authority to consider any complaint made to it about a contravention of regulation 4, unless—

(a)   the complaint appears to the authority to be frivolous or vexatious; or

(b)   another enforcement authority has notified the [CMA] that it agrees to consider the complaint.

(2)   If an enforcement authority has notified the [CMA] as mentioned in paragraph (1)(b), that authority is under a duty to consider the complaint.

(3)   An enforcement authority which is under a duty to consider a complaint must—

(a)   decide whether or not to make an application under regulation 8, and

(b)   give reasons for its decision.

(4)   In deciding whether or not to make an application, an enforcement authority may, if it considers it appropriate to do so, have regard to any undertaking given to it or another enforcement authority by or on behalf of any person as to compliance with regulation 4 [and to any enforcement action taken under Part 8 of the Enterprise Act 2002].

(5)   The following are enforcement authorities for the purposes of these Regulations—

(a)   every local weights and measures authority in Great Britain (within the meaning of section 69 of the Weights and Measures Act 1985);

(b)   the Department of Enterprise, Trade and Investment in Northern Ireland.

8   Orders to secure compliance

(1)   An enforcement authority may apply for an injunction, or in Scotland an interdict or any other appropriate relief or remedy, against any person who appears to the authority to be responsible for a contravention of regulation 4.

(2)   The court on an application under this regulation may grant an injunction, interdict or order on such terms as it thinks fit to secure compliance with regulation 4.

9   Notification of undertakings and orders to the [CMA]

An enforcement authority must notify the [CMA]—

(a)   of any undertaking given to it by or on behalf of any person who appears to it to be responsible for a contravention of regulation 4;

(b)   of the outcome of any application made by it under regulation 8, and of the terms of any undertaking given to the court or of any order made by the court;

(c)   of the outcome of any application made by it to enforce a previous order of the court.

10   Consumer's right of redress

Where a trader charges a fee in contravention of regulation 4—

(a) any provision of a contract requiring the consumer to pay the fee is unenforceable to the extent of the excess charged, and

(b) the contract for the purposes of which the payment is made is to be treated as providing for the excess to be repaid to the consumer.

Regulation 6   SCHEDULE
MICRO-BUSINESSES AND NEW BUSINESSES

1 Micro-businesses

A micro-business is a business that has fewer than 10 employees (see paragraphs 7 to 9).

2 Existing micro-businesses

An existing micro-business is a business that was a micro-business immediately before 6th April 2013.

3 New businesses

(1) A new business is a business which a person, or a number of persons, ('P') begins to carry on during the period beginning with 6th April 2013 and ending with 12th June 2014.

(2) That is subject to sub-paragraphs (3), (4) and (6).

(3) A business ('Business 2') is not a new business if—

(a) P has, at any time during the period of 6 months ending immediately before the date on which P begins to carry on Business 2, carried on another business ('Business 1'), and

(b) Business 1 consisted of the activities of which Business 2 consists (or most of them),

unless Business 1 was itself a new business.

(4) A business is not a new business if—

(a) P begins to carry on the business on another person ceasing to carry on the activities of which it consists (or most of them), and

(b) P does so in consequence of arrangements involving P and the other person,

unless the activities, when carried on by that other person, were activities of a new business.

(5) For this purpose, P is to be taken to begin to carry on a business on another person ceasing to carry on such activities if—

(a) P begins to carry on the business otherwise than in partnership on such activities ceasing to be carried on by persons in partnership, or

(b) P is a number of persons in partnership who begin to carry on the business on such activities ceasing to be carried on—

(i) by a person, or a number of persons, otherwise than in partnership,

(ii) by persons in partnership who do not consist only of all the persons who constitute P, or

(iii) partly as mentioned in paragraph (i) and partly as mentioned in paragraph (ii).

(6) P is not to be regarded as beginning to carry on a business for the purposes of sub-paragraph (1) if—

(a) before P begins to carry on the business, P is a party to arrangements under which P may (at any time during the period beginning with 6th April 2013 and ending with 12th June 2014) carry on, as part of the business, activities carried on by any other person, and

(b) the business would have been prevented by sub-paragraph (3) from being a new business if—

(i) P had begun to carry on the activities when beginning to carry on the business, and

(ii) the other person had at that time ceased to carry them on.

(7) 'Arrangements' includes an agreement, understanding, scheme, transaction or series of transactions (whether or not legally enforceable).

4 The exemption period: existing micro-businesses

(1) This paragraph defines the exemption period in relation to an existing micro-business.

(2) The exemption period starts with 6th April 2013 and ends with—

(a) the day after a grace period in relation to the business ends, if the grace period is one in which the business grows (see paragraph 6), or

(b) (if sooner) 12th June 2014.

(3) The following are grace periods in relation to a business for the purposes of this paragraph—

(a) the 6-month period that starts with the first day after 6th April 2013 on which the business has 10 or more employees;

(b) the 6-month period that starts after the end of a grace period (the 'earlier grace period') that is not one in which the business grows, in accordance with sub-paragraph (4) or (5).

(4) If the business has 10 or more employees on the day after the end of the earlier grace period, the next grace period starts on that day.

(5) If the business has fewer than 10 employees on that day, the next grace period starts on the next day on which the business has 10 or more employees.

5 The exemption period: new businesses

(1) This paragraph defines the exemption period in relation to a new business.

(2) The exemption period starts with the date on which P begins to carry on the business and ends with—

(a) the date on which P ceases to carry on the business, or

(b) (if sooner) 12th June 2014.

(3) If P is the members of a partnership, or other unincorporated association, P is not to be taken for the purposes of sub-paragraph (2) to cease to carry on the business if—

(a) the members of the partnership or association change, or the partnership or association is dissolved, and

(b) after the change or dissolution, the business is carried on by at least one of the persons who constituted P.

6 Grace periods in which business grows

For the purposes of this Schedule, a grace period is one in which a business grows if A is greater than B, where—

A is the number of days in the grace period when the business has 10 or more employees, and

B is the number of days in the grace period when the business has fewer than 10 employees.

7 Number of employees of a business

For the purposes of this Schedule, the number of employees of a business is calculated as follows—

where TH is the total number of hours per week for which all the employees of the business are contracted to work.

8 Employees of a business

For the purposes of this Schedule, the employees of a business are the persons who are employed for the purposes of the business.

9 Employees

(1) In this Schedule, 'employee' means an individual who has entered into or works under a contract of employment.

(2) In sub-paragraph (1) 'contract of employment' means a contract of service, whether express or implied, and (if it is express) whether oral or in writing.

10 Franchises
For the purposes of this Schedule, a business that is carried on pursuant to a franchise agreement is treated as part of the business of the franchisor (and not as a separate business carried on by the franchisee).

CONSUMER CONTRACTS (INFORMATION, CANCELLATION AND ADDITIONAL CHARGES) REGULATIONS 2013
(SI 2013/3134)

PART 1
GENERAL

1 Citation and commencement
(1) These Regulations may be cited as the Consumer Contracts (Information, Cancellation and Additional Charges) Regulations 2013 and come into force on 13th June 2014.

(2) These Regulations apply in relation to contracts entered into on or after that date.

2 Regulations superseded
The following do not apply in relation to contracts entered into on or after 13th June 2014—

    (a) the Consumer Protection (Distance Selling) Regulations 2000;

    (b) the Cancellation of Contracts made in a Consumer's Home or Place of Work etc Regulations 2008.

3 Review
(1) The Secretary of State must before the end of each review period—

    (a) carry out a review of these Regulations,

    (b) set out the conclusions of the review in a report, and

    (c) publish the report.

(2) In carrying out the review, the Secretary of State must, so far as is reasonable, have regard to what is done in other member States to implement Directive 2011/83/EU of the European Parliament and of the Council of 25 October 2011 on consumer rights, amending Council Directive 93/13/EEC and Directive 1999/44/EC of the European Parliament and of the Council and repealing Council Directive 85/577/EC and Directive 97/7/EC of the European Parliament and of the Council.

(3) The report must in particular—

    (a) set out the objectives intended to be achieved by these Regulations,

    (b) assess the extent to which those objectives have been achieved, and

    (c) assess whether those objectives remain appropriate and, if so, the extent to which they could be achieved in a way that imposes less regulation.

(4) A review period is—

    (a) the period of 5 years beginning with the day on which these Regulations come into force, and

    (b) each successive period of 5 years.

4 'Consumer' and 'trader'
In these Regulations—

'consumer' means an individual acting for purposes which are wholly or mainly outside that individual's trade, business, craft or profession;

'trader' means a person acting for purposes relating to that person's trade, business, craft or profession, whether acting personally or through another person acting in the trader's name or on the trader's behalf.

5 Other definitions
In these Regulations—

'business' includes the activities of any government department or local or public authority;

'business premises' in relation to a trader means—

(a) any immovable retail premises where the activity of the trader is carried out on a permanent basis, or

(b) any movable retail premises where the activity of the trader is carried out on a usual basis;

'CMA' means the Competition and Markets Authority;

'commercial guarantee', in relation to a contract, means any undertaking by the trader or producer to the consumer (in addition to the trader's duty to supply goods that are in conformity with the contract) to reimburse the price paid or to replace, repair or service goods in any way if they do not meet the specifications or any other requirements not related to conformity set out in the guarantee statement or in the relevant advertising available at the time of the contract or before it is entered into;

'court'—

(a) in relation to England and Wales, means the county court or the High Court,

(b) in relation to Northern Ireland, means a county court or the High Court, and

(c) in relation to Scotland means the sheriff court or the Court of Session;

'delivery' means voluntary transfer of possession from one person to another;

'digital content' means data which are produced and supplied in digital form;

'distance contract' means a contract concluded between a trader and a consumer under an organised distance sales or service-provision scheme without the simultaneous physical presence of the trader and the consumer, with the exclusive use of one or more means of distance communication up to and including the time at which the contract is concluded;

'district heating' means the supply of heat (in the form of steam or hot water or otherwise) from a central source of production through a transmission and distribution system to heat more than one building;

'durable medium' means paper or email, or any other medium that—

(a) allows information to be addressed personally to the recipient,

(b) enables the recipient to store the information in a way accessible for future reference for a period that is long enough for the purposes of the information, and

(c) allows the unchanged reproduction of the information stored;

'functionality' in relation to digital content includes region coding, restrictions incorporated for the purposes of digital rights management, and other technical restrictions;

'goods' means any tangible moveable items, but that includes water, gas and electricity if and only if they are put up for sale in a limited volume or a set quantity;

'off-premises contract' means a contract between a trader and a consumer which is any of these—

(a) a contract concluded in the simultaneous physical presence of the trader and the consumer, in a place which is not the business premises of the trader;

(b) a contract for which an offer was made by the consumer in the simultaneous physical presence of the trader and the consumer, in a place which is not the business premises of the trader;

(c) a contract concluded on the business premises of the trader or through any means of distance communication immediately after the consumer was personally and individually addressed in a place which is not the business premises of the trader in the simultaneous physical presence of the trader and the consumer;

(d) a contract concluded during an excursion organised by the trader with the aim or effect of promoting and selling goods or services to the consumer;

'on-premises contract' means a contract between a trader and a consumer which is neither a distance contract nor an off-premises contract;

'public auction' means a method of sale where—

(a) goods or services are offered by a trader to consumers through a transparent, competitive bidding procedure run by an auctioneer,

(b) the consumers attend or are given the possibility to attend in person, and

(c) the successful bidder is bound to purchase the goods or services;

'sales contract' means a contract under which a trader transfers or agrees to transfer the ownership of goods to a consumer and the consumer pays or agrees to pay the price, including any contract that has both goods and services as its object;

'service' includes—

(a) the supply of water, gas or electricity if they are not put up for sale in a limited volume or a set quantity, and

(b) the supply of district heating;

'service contract' means a contract, other than a sales contract, under which a trader supplies or agrees to supply a service to a consumer and the consumer pays or agrees to pay the price.

6 Limits of application: general

(1) These Regulations do not apply to a contract, to the extent that it is—

(a) for—

(i) gambling within the meaning of the Gambling Act 2005 (which includes gaming, betting and participating in a lottery);

(ii) in relation to Northern Ireland, for betting, gaming or participating lawfully in a lottery within the meaning of the Betting, Gaming, Lotteries and Amusements (Northern Ireland) Order 1985; [or

(iii) participating in a lottery which forms part of the National Lottery within the meaning of the National Lottery etc Act 1993].

(b) for services of a banking, credit, insurance, personal pension, investment or payment nature;

(c) for the creation of immovable property or of rights in immovable property;

(d) for rental of accommodation for residential purposes;

(e) for the construction of new buildings, or the construction of substantially new buildings by the conversion of existing buildings;

(f) for the supply of foodstuffs, beverages or other goods intended for current consumption in the household and which are supplied by a trader on frequent and regular rounds to the consumer's home, residence or workplace;

(g) within the scope of Council Directive 90/314/EEC of 13 June 1990 on package travel, package holidays and package tours;

(h) within the scope of Directive 2008/122/EC of the European Parliament and of the Council on the protection of consumers in respect of certain aspects of timeshare, long-term holiday product, resale and exchange contracts.

(2) These Regulations do not apply to contracts—

(a) concluded by means of automatic vending machines or automated commercial premises;

(b) concluded with a telecommunications operator through a public telephone for the use of the telephone;

(c) concluded for the use of one single connection, by telephone, internet or fax, established by a consumer;

(d) under which goods are sold by way of execution or otherwise by authority of law.

(3)   Paragraph (1)(b) is subject to regulations 38(4) (ancillary contracts) and 40(3) (additional payments).

PART 2
INFORMATION REQUIREMENTS

Chapter 1
Provision of information

7   Application of Part 2
(1)   This Part applies to on-premises, off-premises and distance contracts, subject to paragraphs (2), (3) and (4) and regulation 6.
(2)   This Part does not apply to contracts to the extent that they are—
   (a)   for the supply of a medicinal product by administration by a prescriber, or under a prescription or directions given by a prescriber;
   (b)   for the supply of a product by a health care professional or a person included in a relevant list, under arrangements for the supply of services as part of the health service, where the product is one that, at least in some circumstances is available under such arrangements free or on prescription.
(3)   This Part, except for regulation 14(1) to (5), does not apply to contracts to the extent that they are for passenger transport services.
(4)   This Part does not apply to off-premises contracts under which the payment to be made by the consumer is not more than £42.
(5)   In paragraph (2)—
'health care professional' and 'prescriber' have the meaning given by regulation 2(1) of the National Health Service (Pharmaceutical and Local Pharmaceutical Services) Regulations 2013;
'health service' means—
   (a)   the health service as defined by section 275(1) of the National Health Service Act 2006(12) or section 206(1) of the National Health Service (Wales) Act 2006,
   (b)   the health service as defined by section 108(1) of the National Health Service (Scotland) Act 1978, or
   (c)   any of the health services under section 2(1)(a) of the Health and Social Care (Reform) Act (Northern Ireland) 2009;
'medicinal product' has the meaning given by regulation 2(1) of the Human Medicines Regulations 2012;
'relevant list' means—
   (d)   a relevant list for the purposes of the National Health Service (Pharmaceutical and Local Pharmaceutical Services) Regulations 2013, or
   (e)   a list maintained under those Regulations.

8   Making information etc available to a consumer
For the purposes of this Part, something is made available to a consumer only if the consumer can reasonably be expected to know how to access it.

9   Information to be provided before making an on-premises contract
(1)   Before the consumer is bound by an on-premises contract, the trader must give or make available to the consumer the information described in Schedule 1 in a clear and comprehensible manner, if that information is not already apparent from the context.
(2)   Paragraph (1) does not apply to a contract which involves a day-to-day transaction and is performed immediately at the time when the contract is entered into.
[(3)   If the contract is for the supply of digital content other than for a price paid by the consumer—

(a)   any information that the trader gives the consumer as required by this regulation is to be treated as included as a term of the contract, and

(b)   a change to any of that information, made before entering into the contract or later, is not effective unless expressly agreed between the consumer and the trader.]

[. . .]

10   Information to be provided before making an off-premises contract

(1)   Before the consumer is bound by an off-premises contract, the trader—

(a)   must give the consumer the information listed in Schedule 2 in a clear and comprehensible manner, and

(b)   if a right to cancel exists, must give the consumer a cancellation form as set out in part B of Schedule 3.

(2)   The information and any cancellation form must be given on paper or, if the consumer agrees, on another durable medium and must be legible.

(3)   The information referred to in paragraphs (l), (m) and (n) of Schedule 2 may be provided by means of the model instructions on cancellation set out in part A of Schedule 3; and a trader who has supplied those instructions to the consumer, correctly filled in, is to be treated as having complied with paragraph (1) in respect of those paragraphs.

(4)   If the trader has not complied with paragraph (1) in respect of paragraph (g), (h) or (m) of Schedule 2, the consumer is not to bear the charges or costs referred to in those paragraphs.

[(5)   If the contract is for the supply of digital content other than for a price paid by the consumer—

(a)   any information that the trader gives the consumer as required by this regulation is to be treated as included as a term of the contract, and

(b)   a change to any of that information, made before entering into the contract or later, is not effective unless expressly agreed between the consumer and the trader.]

[. . .]

(7)   This regulation is subject to regulation 11.

11   Provision of information in connection with repair or maintenance contracts

(1)   If the conditions in paragraphs (2), (3) and (4) are met, regulation 10(1) does not apply to an off-premises contract where—

(a)   the contract is a service contract,

(b)   the consumer has explicitly requested the trader to supply the service for the purpose of carrying out repairs or maintenance,

(c)   the obligations of the trader and the consumer under the contract are to be performed immediately, and

(d)   the payment to be made by the consumer is not more than £170.

(2)   The first condition is that, before the consumer is bound by the contract, the trader gives or makes available to the consumer on paper or, if the consumer expressly agrees, on another durable medium—

(a)   the information referred to in paragraphs (b) to (d), (f) and (g) of Schedule 2,

(b)   an estimate of the total price, where it cannot reasonably be calculated in advance, and

(c)   where a right to cancel exists, a cancellation form as set out in part B of Schedule 3.

(3)   The second condition is that, before the consumer is bound by the contract, the trader gives or makes available to the consumer the information referred to in paragraphs (a), (l) and (o) of Schedule 2, either on paper or another durable medium or otherwise if the consumer expressly agrees.

(4)   The third condition is that the confirmation of the contract provided in

accordance with regulation 12 contains the information required by regulation 10(1).

(5)   For the right to cancel where this regulation applies, see in particular—

(a)   regulation 28(1)(e) and (2) (cases where cancellation excluded: visit requested for urgent work);

(b)   regulation 36 (form of consumer's request, and consequences).

12   Provision of copy or confirmation of off-premises contracts

(1)   In the case of an off-premises contract, the trader must give the consumer—

(a)   a copy of the signed contract, or

(b)   confirmation of the contract.

(2)   The confirmation must include all the information referred to in Schedule 2 unless the trader has already provided that information to the consumer on a durable medium prior to the conclusion of the off-premises contract.

(3)   The copy or confirmation must be provided on paper or, if the consumer agrees, on another durable medium.

(4)   The copy or confirmation must be provided within a reasonable time after the conclusion of the contract, but in any event—

(a)   not later than the time of the delivery of any goods supplied under the contract, and

(b)   before performance begins of any service supplied under the contract.

(5)   If the contract is for the supply of digital content not on a tangible medium and the consumer has given the consent and acknowledgement referred to in regulation 37(1)(a) and (b), the copy or confirmation must include confirmation of the consent and acknowledgement.

13   Information to be provided before making a distance contract

(1)   Before the consumer is bound by a distance contract, the trader—

(a)   must give or make available to the consumer the information listed in Schedule 2 in a clear and comprehensible manner, and in a way appropriate to the means of distance communication used, and

(b)   if a right to cancel exists, must give or make available to the consumer a cancellation form as set out in part B of Schedule 3.

(2)   In so far as the information is provided on a durable medium, it must be legible.

(3)   The information referred to in paragraphs (l), (m) and (n) of Schedule 2 may be provided by means of the model instructions on cancellation set out in part A of Schedule 3; and a trader who has supplied those instructions to the consumer, correctly filled in, is to be treated as having complied with paragraph (1) in respect of those paragraphs.

(4)   Where a distance contract is concluded through a means of distance communication which allows limited space or time to display the information—

(a)   the information listed in paragraphs (a), (b), (f), (g), (h), (l) and (s) of Schedule 2 must be provided on that means of communication in accordance with paragraphs (1) and (2), but

(b)   the other information required by paragraph (1) may be provided in another appropriate way.

(5)   If the trader has not complied with paragraph (1) in respect of paragraph (g), (h) or (m) of Schedule 2, the consumer is not to bear the charges or costs referred to in those paragraphs.

[(6)   If the contract is for the supply of digital content other than for a price paid by the consumer—

(a)   any information that the trader gives the consumer as required by this regulation is to be treated as included as a term of the contract, and

(b)   a change to any of that information, made before entering into the contract or later, is not effective unless expressly agreed between the consumer and the trader.]

[. . .]

14 Requirements for distance contracts concluded by electronic means

(1) This regulation applies where a distance contract is concluded by electronic means.

(2) If the contract places the consumer under an obligation to pay, the trader must make the consumer aware in a clear and prominent manner, and directly before the consumer places the order, of the information listed in paragraphs (a), (f), (g), (h), (s) and (t) of Schedule 2.

(3) The trader must ensure that the consumer, when placing the order, explicitly acknowledges that the order implies an obligation to pay.

(4) If placing an order entails activating a button or a similar function, the trader must ensure that the button or similar function is labelled in an easily legible manner only with the words 'order with obligation to pay' or a corresponding unambiguous formulation indicating that placing the order entails an obligation to pay the trader.

(5) If the trader has not complied with paragraphs (3) and (4), the consumer is not bound by the contract or order.

(6) The trader must ensure that any trading website through which the contract is concluded indicates clearly and legibly, at the latest at the beginning of the ordering process, whether any delivery restrictions apply and which means of payment are accepted.

15 Telephone calls to conclude a distance contract

If the trader makes a telephone call to the consumer with a view to concluding a distance contract, the trader must, at the beginning of the conversation with the consumer, disclose—

(a) the trader's identity,

(b) where applicable, the identity of the person on whose behalf the trader makes the call, and

(c) the commercial purpose of the call.

16 Confirmation of distance contracts

(1) In the case of a distance contract the trader must give the consumer confirmation of the contract on a durable medium.

(2) The confirmation must include all the information referred to in Schedule 2 unless the trader has already provided that information to the consumer on a durable medium prior to the conclusion of the distance contract.

(3) If the contract is for the supply of digital content not on a tangible medium and the consumer has given the consent and acknowledgment referred to in regulation 37(1)(a) and (b), the confirmation must include confirmation of the consent and acknowledgement.

(4) The confirmation must be provided within a reasonable time after the conclusion of the contract, but in any event—

(a) not later than the time of delivery of any goods supplied under the contract, and

(b) before performance begins of any service supplied under the contract.

(5) For the purposes of paragraph (4), the confirmation is treated as provided as soon as the trader has sent it or done what is necessary to make it available to the consumer.

17 Burden of proof in relation to off-premises and distance contracts

(1) In case of dispute about the trader's compliance with any provision of regulations 10 to 16, it is for the trader to show that the provision was complied with.

(2) That does not apply to proceedings—

(a) for an offence under regulation 19, or

(b) relating to compliance with an injunction, interdict or order under regulation 45.

18   Effect on contract of failure to provide information

Every contract to which this Part applies is to be treated as including a term that the trader has complied with the provisions of—

(a)   regulations 9 to 14, and

(b)   regulation 16.

Chapter 2
Offences

19   Offence relating to the failure to give notice of the right to cancel

(1)   A trader is guilty of an offence if the trader enters into an off-premises contract to which regulation 10 applies but fails to give the consumer the information listed in paragraph (l), (m) or (n) of Schedule 2 in accordance with that regulation.

(2)   A person who is guilty of an offence under paragraph (1) is liable on summary conviction to a fine not exceeding level 5 on the standard scale.

20   Defence of due diligence

(1)   In any proceedings against a person (A) for an offence under regulation 19 it is a defence for A to prove—

(a)   that the commission of the offence was due to—

(i)   the act or default of another, or

(ii)   reliance on information given by another, and

(b)   that A took all reasonable precautions and exercised all due diligence to avoid the commission of such an offence by A or any person under A's control.

(2)   A person is not entitled to rely on the defence provided by paragraph (1) without leave of the court unless—

(a)   that person has served on the prosecutor a notice in writing giving such information as was in that person's possession identifying or assisting in the identification of the other person; and

(b)   the notice is served on the prosecutor not less than 7 days before the hearing of the proceedings or, in Scotland, 7 days before the intermediate diet or 14 days before the trial diet, whichever is earlier.

21   Liability of persons other than the principal offender

Where the commission by a person of an offence under regulation 19 is due to the act or default of another person, that other person is guilty of the offence and may be proceeded against and punished whether or not proceedings are taken against the first person.

22   Offences committed by bodies of persons

(1)   Where an offence under regulation 19 committed by a body corporate is proved—

(a)   to have been committed with the consent or connivance of an officer of the body corporate or

(b)   to be attributable to any neglect on the part of an officer of the body corporate,

the officer, as well as the body corporate, is guilty of the offence and liable to be proceeded against and punished accordingly.

(2)   In paragraph (1) a reference to an officer of a body corporate includes a reference to—

(a)   a director, manager, secretary or other similar officer; and

(b)   a person purporting to act as a director, manager, secretary or other similar officer.

(3)   Where an offence under regulation 19 committed in Scotland by a Scottish partnership is proved—

(a)   to have been committed with the consent or connivance of a partner, or

(b)   to be attributable to any neglect on the part of a partner, that partner, as well as the partnership shall be guilty of the offence and liable to be proceeded against and punished accordingly.

(4)   In paragraph (3) a reference to a partner includes a person purporting to act as a partner.

23   Duty to enforce

(1)   Subject to paragraphs (2) and (3)—

(a)   it is the duty of every weights and measures authority in Great Britain to enforce regulation 19 within its area; and

(b)   it is the duty of the Department of Enterprise, Trade and Investment in Northern Ireland to enforce regulation 19 within Northern Ireland.

(2)   No proceedings for an offence under regulation 19 may be instituted in England and Wales except by or on behalf of an enforcement authority.

(3)   Nothing in paragraph (1) authorises any weights and measures authority to bring proceedings in Scotland for an offence.

24   Powers of investigation

(1)   If a duly authorised officer of an enforcement authority has reasonable grounds for suspecting that an offence has been committed under regulation 19, the officer may require a person carrying on or employed in a business to produce any document relating to the business, and take copies of it or any entry in it for the purposes of ascertaining whether such an offence has been committed.

(2)   If the officer has reasonable grounds for believing that any documents may be required as evidence in proceedings for such an offence, the officer may seize and detain them and shall, if the officer does so, inform the person from whom they are seized.

(3)   In this regulation 'document' includes information recorded in any form.

(4)   The reference in paragraph (1) to production of documents is, in the case of a document which contains information recorded otherwise than in a legible form, a reference to the production of a copy of the information in a legible form.

(5)   An officer seeking to exercise a power under this regulation must do so only at a reasonable hour and on production of the officer's identification and authority.

(6)   Nothing in this regulation requires a person to produce or provide, or authorises a person to inspect or take possession of, anything in respect of which a claim to legal professional privilege (in Scotland, to confidentiality of communications) could be maintained in legal proceedings.

25   Obstruction of authorised officers

(1)   A person commits an offence if that person—

(a)   intentionally obstructs an officer of an enforcement authority acting in pursuance of functions under regulation 24;

(b)   fails without reasonable cause to comply with any requirement properly made by such an officer under regulation 24; or

(c)   fails without reasonable cause to give such an officer any other assistance or information which the officer may reasonably require for the purpose of the performance of functions under regulation 24.

(2)   A person giving any information which is required from that person under paragraph (1)(c) is guilty of an offence if, in doing so, the person makes any statement knowing it to be false in a material particular.

(3)   A person guilty of an offence under paragraph (1) or (2) is liable on summary conviction to a fine not exceeding level 3 on the standard scale.

26   Freedom from self-incrimination

Nothing in regulation 24 or 25 is to be construed as requiring a person to answer any question or give any information if to do so might incriminate that person.

PART 3
RIGHT TO CANCEL

27 Application of Part 3

(1) This Part applies to distance and off-premises contracts between a trader and a consumer, subject to paragraphs (2) and (3) and regulations 6 and 28.

(2) This Part does not apply to contracts to the extent that they are—

(a) for the supply of a medicinal product by administration by a prescriber, or under a prescription or directions given by a prescriber;

(b) for the supply of a product by a health care professional or a person included in a relevant list, under arrangements for the supply of services as part of the health service, where the product is one that, at least in some circumstances is available under such arrangements free or on prescription;

(c) for passenger transport services.

(3) This Part does not apply to off-premises contracts under which the payment to be made by the consumer is not more than £42.

(4) In paragraph (2)(a) and (b), expressions defined in regulation 7(5) have the meaning given there.

28 Limits of application: circumstances excluding cancellation

(1) This Part does not apply as regards the following—

(a) the supply of—

(i) goods, or

(ii) services, other than supply of water, gas, electricity or district heating,

for which the price is dependent on fluctuations in the financial market which cannot be controlled by the trader and which may occur within the cancellation period;

(b) the supply of goods that are made to the consumer's specifications or are clearly personalised;

(c) the supply of goods which are liable to deteriorate or expire rapidly;

(d) the supply of alcoholic beverages, where—

(i) their price has been agreed at the time of the conclusion of the sales contract,

(ii) delivery of them can only take place after 30 days, and

(iii) their value is dependent on fluctuations in the market which cannot be controlled by the trader;

(e) contracts where the consumer has specifically requested a visit from the trader for the purpose of carrying out urgent repairs or maintenance;

(f) the supply of a newspaper, periodical or magazine with the exception of subscription contracts for the supply of such publications;

(g) contracts concluded at a public auction;

(h) the supply of accommodation, transport of goods, vehicle rental services, catering or services related to leisure activities, if the contract provides for a specific date or period of performance.

(2) Sub-paragraph (e) of paragraph (1) does not prevent this Part applying to a contract for—

(a) services in addition to the urgent repairs or maintenance requested, or

(b) goods other than replacement parts necessarily used in making the repairs or carrying out the maintenance,

if the trader supplies them on the occasion of a visit such as is mentioned in that sub-paragraph.

(3) The rights conferred by this Part cease to be available in the following circumstances—

(a) in the case of a contract for the supply of sealed goods which are not suitable for return due to health protection or hygiene reasons, if they become unsealed after delivery;

(b) in the case of a contract for the supply of sealed audio or sealed video recordings or sealed computer software, if the goods become unsealed after delivery;

(c)   in the case of any sales contract, if the goods become mixed inseparably (according to their nature) with other items after delivery.

29   Right to cancel

(1)   The consumer may cancel a distance or off-premises contract at any time in the cancellation period without giving any reason, and without incurring any liability except under these provisions—

(a)   regulation 34(3) (where enhanced delivery chosen by consumer);

(b)   regulation 34(9) (where value of goods diminished by consumer handling);

(c)   regulation 35(5) (where goods returned by consumer);

(d)   regulation 36(4) (where consumer requests early supply of service).

(2)   The cancellation period begins when the contract is entered into and ends in accordance with regulation 30 or 31.

(3)   Paragraph (1) does not affect the consumer's right to withdraw an offer made by the consumer to enter into a distance or off-premises contract, at any time before the contract is entered into, without giving any reason and without incurring any liability.

30   Normal cancellation period

(1)   The cancellation period ends as follows, unless regulation 31 applies.

(2)   If the contract is—

(a)   a service contract, or

(b)   a contract for the supply of digital content which is not supplied on a tangible medium,

the cancellation period ends at the end of 14 days after the day on which the contract is entered into.

(3)   If the contract is a sales contract and none of paragraphs (4) to (6) applies, the cancellation period ends at the end of 14 days after the day on which the goods come into the physical possession of—

(a)   the consumer, or

(b)   a person, other than the carrier, identified by the consumer to take possession of them.

(4)   If the contract is a sales contract under which multiple goods are ordered by the consumer in one order but some are delivered on different days, the cancellation period ends at the end of 14 days after the day on which the last of the goods come into the physical possession of—

(a)   the consumer, or

(b)   a person, other than the carrier, identified by the consumer to take possession of them.

(5)   If the contract is a sales contract under which goods consisting of multiple lots or pieces of something are delivered on different days, the cancellation period ends at the end of 14 days after the day on which the last of the lots or pieces come into the physical possession of—

(a)   the consumer, or

(b)   a person, other than the carrier, identified by the consumer to take possession of them.

(6)   If the contract is a sales contract for regular delivery of goods during a defined period of more than one day, the cancellation period ends at the end of 14 days after the day on which the first of the goods come into the physical possession of—

(a)   the consumer, or

(b)   a person, other than the carrier, identified by the consumer to take possession of them.

31   Cancellation period extended for breach of information requirement

(1)   This regulation applies if the trader does not provide the consumer with the information on the right to cancel required by paragraph (l) of Schedule 2, in accordance with Part 2.

(2)   If the trader provides the consumer with that information in the period of 12 months beginning with the first day of the 14 days mentioned in regulation 30(2) to (6), but otherwise in accordance with Part 2, the cancellation period ends at the end of 14 days after the consumer receives the information.

(3)   Otherwise the cancellation period ends at the end of 12 months after the day on which it would have ended under regulation 30.

32   Exercise of the right to withdraw or cancel

(1)   To withdraw an offer to enter into a distance or off-premises contract, the consumer must inform the trader of the decision to withdraw it.

(2)   To cancel a contract under regulation 29(1), the consumer must inform the trader of the decision to cancel it.

(3)   To inform the trader under paragraph (2) the consumer may either—

(a)   use a form following the model cancellation form in part B of Schedule 3, or

(b)   make any other clear statement setting out the decision to cancel the contract.

(4)   If the trader gives the consumer the option of filling in and submitting such a form or other statement on the trader's website—

(a)   the consumer need not use it, but

(b)   if the consumer does, the trader must communicate to the consumer an acknowledgement of receipt of the cancellation on a durable medium without delay.

(5)   Where the consumer informs the trader under paragraph (2) by sending a communication, the consumer is to be treated as having cancelled the contract in the cancellation period if the communication is sent before the end of the period.

(6)   In case of dispute it is for the consumer to show that the contract was cancelled in the cancellation period in accordance with this regulation.

33   Effect of withdrawal or cancellation

(1)   If a contract is cancelled under regulation 29(1)—

(a)   the cancellation ends the obligations of the parties to perform the contract, and

(b)   regulations 34 to 38 apply.

(2)   Regulations 34 and 38 also apply if the consumer withdraws an offer to enter into a distance or off-premises contract.

34   Reimbursement by trader in the event of withdrawal or cancellation

(1)   The trader must reimburse all payments, other than payments for delivery, received from the consumer, subject to paragraph (10).

(2)   The trader must reimburse any payment for delivery received from the consumer, unless the consumer expressly chose a kind of delivery costing more than the least expensive common and generally acceptable kind of delivery offered by the trader.

(3)   In that case, the trader must reimburse any payment for delivery received from the consumer up to the amount the consumer would have paid if the consumer had chosen the least expensive common and generally acceptable kind of delivery offered by the trader.

(4)   Reimbursement must be without undue delay, and in any event not later than the time specified in paragraph (5) or (6).

(5)   If the contract is a sales contract and the trader has not offered to collect the goods, the time is the end of 14 days after—

(a)   the day on which the trader receives the goods back, or

(b)   if earlier, the day on which the consumer supplies evidence of having sent the goods back.

(6)   Otherwise, the time is the end of 14 days after the day on which the trader is informed of the consumer's decision to withdraw the offer or cancel the contract, in accordance with regulation [32].

(7)   The trader must make the reimbursement using the same means of payment as the consumer used for the initial transaction, unless the consumer has expressly agreed otherwise.

(8)   The trader must not impose any fee on the consumer in respect of the reimbursement.

(9)   If (in the case of a sales contract) the value of the goods is diminished by any amount as a result of handling of the goods by the consumer beyond what is necessary to establish the nature, characteristics and functioning of the goods, the trader may recover that amount from the consumer, up to the contract price.

(10)   An amount that may be recovered under paragraph (9)—

(a)   may be deducted from the amount to be reimbursed under paragraph (1);

(b)   otherwise, must be paid by the consumer to the trader.

(11)   Paragraph (9) does not apply if the trader has failed to provide the consumer with the information on the right to cancel required by paragraph (l) of Schedule 2, in accordance with Part 2.

(12)   For the purposes of paragraph (9) handling is beyond what is necessary to establish the nature, characteristics and functioning of the goods if, in particular, it goes beyond the sort of handling that might reasonably be allowed in a shop.

(13)   Where the provisions of this regulation apply to cancellation of a contract, the contract is to be treated as including those provisions as terms.

35   Return of goods in the event of cancellation

(1)   Where a sales contract is cancelled under regulation 29(1), it is the trader's responsibility to collect the goods if—

(a)   the trader has offered to collect them, or

(b)   in the case of an off-premises contract, the goods were delivered to the consumer's home when the contract was entered into and could not, by their nature, normally be returned by post.

(2)   If it is not the trader's responsibility under paragraph (1) to collect the goods, the consumer must—

(a)   send them back, or

(b)   hand them over to the trader or to a person authorised by the trader to receive them.

(3)   The address to which goods must be sent under paragraph (2)(a) is—

(a)   any address specified by the trader for sending the goods back;

(b)   if no address is specified for that purpose, any address specified by the trader for the consumer to contact the trader;

(c)   if no address is specified for either of those purposes, any place of business of the trader.

(4)   The consumer must send off the goods under paragraph (2)(a), or hand them over under paragraph (2)(b), without undue delay and in any event not later than 14 days after the day on which the consumer informs the trader as required by regulation 32(2).

(5)   The consumer must bear the direct cost of returning goods under paragraph (2), unless—

(a)   the trader has agreed to bear those costs, or

(b)   the trader failed to provide the consumer with the information about the consumer bearing those costs, required by paragraph (m) of Schedule 2, in accordance with Part 2.

(6)   The contract is to be treated as including a term that the trader must bear

the direct cost of the consumer returning goods under paragraph (2) where paragraph (5)(b) applies.

(7)   The consumer is not required to bear any other cost of returning goods under paragraph (2).

(8)   The consumer is not required to bear any cost of collecting goods under paragraph (1) [unless the trader has offered to collect the goods and the consumer has agreed to bear the costs of the trader doing so.]

36   Supply of service in cancellation period

(1)   The trader must not begin the supply of a service before the end of the cancellation period provided for in regulation 30(1) unless the consumer—

(a)   has made an express request, and

(b)   in the case of an off-premises contract, has made the request on a durable medium.

(2)   In the case of a service other than supply of water, gas, electricity or district heating, the consumer ceases to have the right to cancel a service contract under regulation 29(1) if the service has been fully performed, and performance of the service began—

(a)   after a request by the consumer in accordance with paragraph (1), and

(b)   with the acknowledgement that the consumer would lose that right once the contract had been fully performed by the trader.

(3)   Paragraphs (4) to (6) apply where a contract is cancelled under regulation 29(1) and a service has been supplied in the cancellation period.

(4)   Where the service is supplied in response to a request in accordance with paragraph (1), the consumer must (subject to paragraph (6)) pay to the trader an amount—

(a)   for the supply of the service for the period for which it is supplied, ending with the time when the trader is informed of the consumer's decision to cancel the contract, in accordance with regulation 32(2), and

(b)   which is in proportion to what has been supplied, in comparison with the full coverage of the contract.

(5)   The amount is to be calculated—

(a)   on the basis of the total price agreed in the contract, or

(b)   if the total price is excessive, on the basis of the market value of the service that has been supplied, calculated by comparing prices for equivalent services supplied by other traders.

(6)   The consumer bears no cost for supply of the service, in full or in part, in the cancellation period, if—

(a)   the trader has failed to provide the consumer with the information on the right to cancel required by paragraph (l) of Schedule 2, or the information on payment of that cost required by paragraph (n) of that Schedule, in accordance with Part 2, or

(b)   the service is not supplied in response to a request in accordance with paragraph (1).

37   Supply of digital content in cancellation period

(1)   Under a contract for the supply of digital content not on a tangible medium, the trader must not begin supply of the digital content before the end of the cancellation period provided for in regulation 30(1), unless—

(a)   the consumer has given express consent, and

(b)   the consumer has acknowledged that the right to cancel the contract under regulation 29(1) will be lost.

(2)   The consumer ceases to have the right to cancel such a contract under regulation 29(1) if, before the end of the cancellation period, supply of the digital content has begun after the consumer has given the consent and acknowledgement required by paragraph (1).

(3)   Paragraph (4) applies where a contract is cancelled under regulation 29(1)

and digital content has been supplied, not on a tangible medium, in the cancellation period.

(4)   The consumer bears no cost for supply of the digital content, in full or in part, in the cancellation period, if—

    (a)   the consumer has not given prior express consent to the beginning of the performance of the digital content before the end of the 14-day period referred to in regulation 30,

    (b)   the consumer gave that consent but did not acknowledge when giving it that the right to cancel would be lost, or

    (c)   the trader failed to provide confirmation required by regulation 12(5) or 16(3).

38 Effects of withdrawal or cancellation on ancillary contracts

(1)   If a consumer withdraws an offer to enter into a distance or off-premises contract, or cancels such a contract under regulation 29(1), any ancillary contracts are automatically terminated, without any costs for the consumer, other than any costs under these provisions—

    (a)   regulation 34(3) (where enhanced delivery chosen by consumer);

    (b)   regulation 34(9) (where value of goods diminished by consumer handling);

    (c)   regulation 35(5) (where goods returned by consumer);

    (d)   regulation 36(4) (where consumer requests early supply of service).

(2)   When a trader is informed by a consumer under regulation 32(1) or (2) of a decision to withdraw an offer or cancel a contract, the trader must inform any other trader with whom the consumer has an ancillary contract that is terminated by paragraph (1).

(3)   An 'ancillary contract', in relation to a distance or off-premises contract (the 'main contract'), means a contract by which the consumer acquires goods or services related to the main contract, where those goods or services are provided—

    (a)   by the trader, or

    (b)   by a third party on the basis of an arrangement between the third party and the trader.

(4)   Regulation 6(1)(b) (exclusion of financial services contracts) does not limit the contracts that are ancillary contracts for the purposes of this regulation.

PART 4
PROTECTION FROM INERTIA SELLING AND ADDITIONAL CHARGES

39 Inertia selling

Before regulation 28 of the Consumer Protection from Unfair Trading Regulations 2008 (and in Part 5 of those Regulations) insert—

'27A Inertia selling

(1)   This regulation applies where a trader engages in the unfair commercial practice described in paragraph 29 of Schedule 1 (inertia selling).

(2)   The consumer is exempted from any obligation to provide consideration for the products supplied by the trader.

(3)   The absence of a response from the consumer following the supply does not constitute consent to the provision of consideration for, or the return or safekeeping of, the products.

(4)   In the case of an unsolicited supply of goods, the consumer may, as between the consumer and the trader, use, deal with or dispose of the goods as if they were an unconditional gift to the consumer.'.

40 Additional payments under a contract

(1)   Under a contract between a trader and a consumer, no payment is payable in addition to the remuneration agreed for the trader's main obligation unless,

before the consumer became bound by the contract, the trader obtained the consumer's express consent.

(2)   There is no express consent (if there would otherwise be) for the purposes of this paragraph if consent is inferred from the consumer not changing a default option (such as a pre-ticked box on a website).

(3)   This regulation does not apply if the trader's main obligation is to supply services within regulation 6(1)(b), but in any other case it applies even if an additional payment is for such services.

(4)   Where a trader receives an additional payment which, under this regulation, is not payable under a contract, the contract is to be treated as providing for the trader to reimburse the payment to the consumer.

41   Help-line charges over basic rate

(1)   Where a trader operates a telephone line for the purpose of consumers contacting the trader by telephone in relation to contracts entered into with the trader, a consumer contacting the trader must not be bound to pay more than the basic rate.

(2)   If in those circumstances a consumer who contacts a trader in relation to a contract is bound to pay more than the basic rate, the contract is to be treated as providing for the trader to pay to the consumer any amount by which the charge paid by the consumer for the call is more than the basic rate.

[. . .]

PART 6
ENFORCEMENT

44   Complaints

(1)   It is the duty of an enforcement authority to consider any complaint made to it about a contravention of these Regulations, unless—

(a)   the complaint appears to the authority to be frivolous or vexatious, or

(b)   another enforcement authority has notified the CMA that it agrees to consider the complaint.

(2)   If an enforcement authority has notified the CMA as mentioned in paragraph (1)(b), that authority is under a duty to consider the complaint.

(3)   The following are enforcement authorities for the purposes of these Regulations—

(a)   every local weights and measures authority in Great Britain;

(b)   the Department of Enterprise, Trade and Investment in Northern Ireland.

45   Orders to secure compliance

(1)   An enforcement authority may apply for an injunction, or in Scotland an interdict or order of specific implement, against any person who appears to the authority to be responsible for a contravention of these Regulations.

(2)   The court on an application under this regulation may grant an injunction, interdict or order on such terms as it thinks fit to secure compliance with these Regulations.

46   Notification of undertakings and orders to the CMA

An enforcement authority must notify the CMA—

(a)   of any undertaking given to it by or on behalf of any person who appears to it to be responsible for a contravention of these Regulations;

(b)   of the outcome of any application made by it under regulation 45, and of the terms of any undertaking given to the court or of any order made by the court;

(c)   of the outcome of any application made by it to enforce a previous order of the court.

PART 7
CONSEQUENTIAL AMENDMENTS

47 Consequential amendments
Schedule 4 makes amendments that are consequential on these Regulations.

Regulation 9(1)   SCHEDULE 1
INFORMATION RELATING TO ON-PREMISES CONTRACTS

The information referred to in regulation 9(1) is—

(a)   the main characteristics of the [goods, services or digital content], to the extent appropriate to the medium of communication and to the [goods, services or digital content];

(b)   the identity of the trader (such as the trader's trading name), the geographical address at which the trader is established and the trader's telephone number;

(c)   the total price of the [goods, services or digital content] inclusive of taxes, or where the nature of the [goods, services or digital content] is such that the price cannot reasonably be calculated in advance, the manner in which the price is to be calculated;

(d)   where applicable, all additional delivery charges or, where those charges cannot reasonably be calculated in advance, the fact that such additional charges may be payable;

(e)   where applicable, the arrangements for payment, delivery, performance, and the time by which the trader undertakes to deliver the goods[, to perform the service or to supply the digital content];

(f)   where applicable, the trader's complaint handling policy;

(g)   in the case of a sales contract, a reminder that the trader is under a legal duty to supply goods that are in conformity with the contract;

(h)   where applicable, the existence and the conditions of after-sales services and commercial guarantees;

(i)   the duration of the contract, where applicable, or, if the contract is of indeterminate duration or is to be extended automatically, the conditions for terminating the contract;

(j)   where applicable, the functionality, including applicable technical protection measures, of digital content;

(k)   where applicable, any relevant compatibility of digital content with hardware and software that the trader is aware of or can reasonably be expected to have been aware of.

Regulations 10(1) and 13(1)   SCHEDULE 2
INFORMATION RELATING TO DISTANCE AND OFF-PREMISES
CONTRACTS

The information referred to in regulations 10(1) and 13(1) is (subject to the note at the end of this Schedule)—

(a)   the main characteristics of the [goods, services or digital content], to the extent appropriate to the medium of communication and to the [goods, services or digital content];

(b)   the identity of the trader (such as the trader's trading name);

(c)   the geographical address at which the trader is established and, where available, the trader's telephone number, fax number and e-mail address, to enable the consumer to contact the trader quickly and communicate efficiently;

(d)   where the trader is acting on behalf of another trader, the geographical address and identity of that other trader;

(e)   if different from the address provided in accordance with paragraph (c), the geographical address of the place of business of the trader, and, where the trader acts on behalf of another trader, the geographical address of the place of business of that other trader, where the consumer can address any complaints;

(f)   the total price of the [goods, services or digital content] inclusive of taxes, or where the nature of the [goods, services or digital content] is such that the price cannot reasonably be calculated in advance, the manner in which the price is to be calculated,

(g)   where applicable, all additional delivery charges and any other costs or, where those charges cannot reasonably be calculated in advance, the fact that such additional charges may be payable;

(h)   in the case of a contract of indeterminate duration or a contract containing a subscription, the total costs per billing period or (where such contracts are charged at a fixed rate) the total monthly costs;

(i)   the cost of using the means of distance communication for the conclusion of the contract where that cost is calculated other than at the basic rate;

(j)   the arrangements for payment, delivery, performance, and the time by which the trader undertakes to deliver the goods[, to perform the services or to supply the digital content];

(k)   where applicable, the trader's complaint handling policy;

(l)   where a right to cancel exists, the conditions, time limit and procedures for exercising that right in accordance with regulations 27 to 38;

(m)   where applicable, that the consumer will have to bear the cost of returning the goods in case of cancellation and, for distance contracts, if the goods, by their nature, cannot normally be returned by post, the cost of returning the goods;

(n)   that, if the consumer exercises the right to cancel after having made a request in accordance with regulation 36(1), the consumer is to be liable to pay the trader reasonable costs in accordance with regulation 36(4);

(o)   where under regulation 28, 36 or 37 there is no right to cancel or the right to cancel may be lost, the information that the consumer will not benefit from a right to cancel, or the circumstances under which the consumer loses the right to cancel;

(p)   in the case of a sales contract, a reminder that the trader is under a legal duty to supply goods that are in conformity with the contract;

(q)   where applicable, the existence and the conditions of after-sale customer assistance, after-sales services and commercial guarantees;

(r)   the existence of relevant codes of conduct, as defined in regulation 5(3)(b) of the Consumer Protection from Unfair Trading Regulations 2008, and how copies of them can be obtained, where applicable;

(s)   the duration of the contract, where applicable, or, if the contract is of indeterminate duration or is to be extended automatically, the conditions for terminating the contract;

(t)   where applicable, the minimum duration of the consumer's obligations under the contract;

(u)   where applicable, the existence and the conditions of deposits or other financial guarantees to be paid or provided by the consumer at the request of the trader;

(v)   where applicable, the functionality, including applicable technical protection measures, of digital content;

(w)   where applicable, any relevant compatibility of digital content with hardware and software that the trader is aware of or can reasonably be expected to have been aware of;

(x)   where applicable, the possibility of having recourse to an out-of-court complaint and redress mechanism, to which the trader is subject, and the methods for having access to it.

Note: In the case of a public auction, the information listed in paragraphs (b) to (e) may be replaced with the equivalent details for the auctioneer.

Regulations 10 and 13   SCHEDULE 3
INFORMATION ABOUT THE EXERCISE OF THE RIGHT TO CANCEL

A. Model instructions for cancellation

Right to cancel

You have the right to cancel this contract within 14 days without giving any reason.

The cancellation period will expire after 14 days from the day [See Note 1].

To exercise the right to cancel, you must inform us [See Note 2] of your decision to cancel this contract by a clear statement (eg a letter sent by post, fax or e-mail). You may use the attached model cancellation form, but it is not obligatory. [See Note 3]

To meet the cancellation deadline, it is sufficient for you to send your communication concerning your exercise of the right to cancel before the cancellation period has expired.

Effects of cancellation

If you cancel this contract, we will reimburse to you all payments received from you, including the costs of delivery (except for the supplementary costs arising if you chose a type of delivery other than the least expensive type of standard delivery offered by us).

We may make a deduction from the reimbursement for loss in value of any goods supplied, if the loss is the result of unnecessary handling by you.

We will make the reimbursement without undue delay, and not later than—
    (a)   14 days after the day we receive back from you any goods supplied, or
    (b)   (if earlier) 14 days after the day you provide evidence that you have returned the goods, or
    (c)   if there were no goods supplied, 14 days after the day on which we are informed about your decision to cancel this contract.

We will make the reimbursement using the same means of payment as you used for the initial transaction, unless you have expressly agreed otherwise; in any event, you will not incur any fees as a result of the reimbursement. [See Note 4].

[See Note 5]

[See Note 6]

Notes on instructions for completion:

1.   Insert one of the following texts between inverted commas:
    (a)   in the case of a service contract or a contract for the supply of digital content which is not supplied on a tangible medium: 'of the conclusion of the contract.';
    (b)   in the case of a sales contract: 'on which you acquire, or a third party other than the carrier and indicated by you acquires, physical possession of the goods.';
    (c)   in the case of a contract relating to multiple goods ordered by the consumer in one order and delivered separately: 'on which you acquire, or a

third party other than the carrier and indicated by you acquires, physical possession of the last good.';

(d)   in the case of a contract relating to delivery of a good consisting of
multiple lots or pieces: 'on which you acquire, or a third party other than the
carrier and indicated by you acquires, physical possession of the last lot or
piece.';

(e)   in the case of a contract for regular delivery of goods during a defined
period of time: 'on which you acquire, or a third party other than the carrier and
indicated by you acquires, physical possession of the first good.'.

2.   Insert your name, geographical address and, where available, your telephone
number, fax number and e-mail address.

3.   If you give the option to the consumer to electronically fill in and submit
information about the consumer's cancellation from the contract on your
website, insert the following: 'You can also electronically fill in and submit the
model cancellation form or any other clear statement on our website [insert
Internet address]. If you use this option, we will communicate to you an
acknowledgement of receipt of such a cancellation on a durable medium (eg by
e-mail) without delay.'.

4.   In the case of sales contracts in which you have not offered to collect the
goods in the event of cancellation insert the following: 'We may withhold
reimbursement until we have received the goods back or you have supplied
evidence of having sent back the goods, whichever is the earliest.'.

5.   If the consumer has received goods in connection with the contract

(a)   insert:

—'We will collect the goods.'; or,

—'You shall send back the goods or hand them over to us or ... [insert
the name and geographical address, where applicable, of the person
authorised by you to receive the goods], without undue delay and in any
event not later than 14 days from the day on which you communicate your
cancellation from this contract to us. The deadline is met if you send back
the goods before the period of 14 days has expired.'

(b)   insert:

—'We will bear the cost of returning the goods.';

—'You will have to bear the direct cost of returning the goods.';

—If, in a distance contract, you do not offer to bear the cost of returning
the goods and the goods, by their nature, cannot normally be returned by
post: 'You will have to bear the direct cost of returning the goods, ... EUR
[insert the amount].'; or if the cost of returning the goods cannot reasonably
be calculated in advance: 'You will have to bear the direct cost of returning
the goods. The cost is estimated at a maximum of approximately ... EUR
[insert the amount].'; or

—If, in an off-premises contract, the goods, by their nature, cannot
normally be returned by post and have been delivered to the consumer's
home at the time of the conclusion of the contract: 'We will collect the
goods at our own expense.'; and,

(c)   insert

—'You are only liable for any diminished value of the goods resulting
from the handling other than what is necessary to establish the nature,
characteristics and functioning of the goods.'

6. In the case of a service contract insert the following: 'If you requested to begin the performance of services during the cancellation period, you shall pay us an amount which is in proportion to what has been performed until you have communicated us your cancellation from this contract, in comparison with the full coverage of the contract.'.

B. Model cancellation form

To [here the trader's name, geographical address and, where available, fax number and e-mail address are to be inserted by the trader]:

I/We [*] hereby give notice that I/We [*] cancel my/our [*] contract of sale of the following goods [*]/for the supply of the following service [*],

Ordered on [*]/received on [*],

Name of consumer(s),

Address of consumer(s),

Signature of consumer(s) (only if this form is notified on paper),

Date

[*] Delete as appropriate.

PART III
EU MATERIALS

COUNCIL DIRECTIVE OF 25 JULY 1985
on the approximation of the laws, regulations and administrative provisions
of the Member States concerning liability for defective products
(85/374/EEC)

(amended by Directive 99/34/EC)

THE COUNCIL OF THE EUROPEAN COMMUNITIES,

. . .

HAS ADOPTED THIS DIRECTIVE:

Article 1
The producer shall be liable for damage caused by a defect in his product.

[Article 2
For the purpose of this Directive 'product' means all movables even if incorporated into another movable or into an immovable. 'Product' includes electricity.]

Article 3
1.   'Producer' means the manufacturer of a finished product, the producer of any raw material or the manufacturer of a component part and any person who, by putting his name, trade mark or other distinguishing feature on the product presents himself as its producer.

2.   Without prejudice to the liability of the producer, any person who imports into the Community a product for sale, hire, leasing or any form of distribution in the course of his business shall be deemed to be a producer within the meaning of this Directive and shall be responsible as a producer.

3.   Where the producer of the product cannot be identified, each supplier of the product shall be treated as its producer unless he informs the injured person, within a reasonable time, of the identity of the producer or of the person who supplied him with the product. The same shall apply, in the case of an imported product, if this product does not indicate the identity of the importer referred to in paragraph 2, even if the name of the producer is indicated.

Article 4
The injured person shall be required to prove the damage, the defect and the causal relationship between defect and damage.

Article 5
Where, as a result of the provisions of this Directive, two or more persons are liable for the same damage, they shall be liable jointly and severally, without prejudice to the provisions of national law concerning the rights of contribution or recourse.

Article 6
1.   A product is defective when it does not provide the safety which a person is entitled to expect, taking all circumstances into account, including:

(a)   the presentation of the product;

(b)   the use to which it could reasonably be expected that the product would be put;

(c)   the time when the product was put into circulation.

2.   A product shall not be considered defective for the sole reason that a better product is subsequently put into circulation.

Article 7

The producer shall not be liable as a result of this Directive if he proves:

(a)   that he did not put the product into circulation; or

(b)   that, having regard to the circumstances, it is probable that the defect which caused the damage did not exist at the time when the product was put into circulation by him or that this defect came into being afterwards; or

(c)   that the product was neither manufactured by him for sale or any form of distribution for economic purpose nor manufactured or distributed by him in the course of his business; or

(d)   that the defect is due to compliance of the product with mandatory regulations issued by the public authorities; or

(e)   that the state of scientific and technical knowledge at the time when he put the product into circulation was not such as to enable the existence of the defect to be discovered; or

(f)   in the case of a manufacturer of a component, that the defect is attributable to the design of the product in which the component has been fitted or to the instructions given by the manufacturer of the product.

Article 8

1.   Without prejudice to the provisions of national law concerning the right of contribution or recourse, the liability of the producer shall not be reduced when the damage is caused both by a defect in product and by the act or omission of a third party.

2.   The liability of the producer may be reduced or disallowed when, having regard to all the circumstances, the damage is caused both by a defect in the product and by the fault of the injured person or any person for whom the injured person is responsible.

Article 9

For the purpose of Article 1, 'damage' means:

(a)   damage caused by death or by personal injuries;

(b)   damage to, or destruction of, any item of property other than the defective product itself, with a lower threshold of 500 ECU, provided that the item of property:

(i)   is of a type ordinarily intended for private use or consumption, and

(ii)   was used by the injured person mainly for his own private use or consumption.

This Article shall be without prejudice to national provisions relating to non-material damage.

Article 10

1.   Member States shall provide in their legislation that a limitation period of three years shall apply to proceedings for the recovery of damages as provided for in this Directive. The limitation period shall begin to run from the day on which the plaintiff became aware, or should reasonably have become aware, of the damage, the defect and the identity of the producer.

2.   The laws of Member States regulating suspension or interruption of the limitation period shall not be affected by this Directive.

Article 11

Member States shall provide in their legislation that the rights conferred upon the injured person pursuant to this Directive shall be extinguished upon the expiry of a period of 10 years from the date on which the producer put into circulation the actual product which caused the damage, unless the injured person has in the meantime instituted proceedings against the producer.

Article 12
The liability of the producer arising from this Directive may not, in relation to the injured person, be limited or excluded by a provision limiting his liability or exempting him from liability.

Article 13
This Directive shall not affect any rights which an injured person may have according to the rules of the law of contractual or non-contractual liability or a special liability system existing at the moment when this Directive is notified.

Article 14
This Directive shall not apply to injury or damage arising from nuclear accidents and covered by international conventions ratified by the Member States.

Article 15
1. Each Member State may:
    (a)   [. . .]
    (b)   by way of derogation from Article 7(e), maintain or, subject to the procedure set out in paragraph 2 of this Article, provide in this legislation that the producer shall be liable even if he proves that the state of scientific and technical knowledge at the time when he put the product into circulation was not such as to enable the existence of a defect to be discovered.
2. A Member State wishing to introduce the measure specified in paragraph 1(b) shall communicate the text of the proposed measure to the Commission. The Commission shall inform the other Member States thereof.

The Member State concerned shall hold the proposed measure in abeyance for nine months after the Commission is informed and provided that in the meantime the Commission has not submitted to the Council a proposal amending this Directive on the relevant matter. However, if within three months of receiving the said information, the Commission does not advise the Member State concerned that it intends submitting such a proposal to the Council, the Member State may take the proposed measure immediately.

If the Commission does submit to the Council such a proposal amending this Directive within the aforementioned nine months, the Member State concerned shall hold the proposed measure in abeyance for a further period of 18 months from the date on which the proposal is submitted.
3. Ten years after the date of notification of this Directive, the Commission shall submit to the Council a report on the effect that rulings by the courts as to the application of Article 7(e) and of paragraph 1(b) of this Article have on consumer protection and the functioning of the common market. In the light of this report the Council, acting on a proposal from the Commission and pursuant to the terms of Article 100 of the Treaty, shall decide whether to repeal Article 7(e).

Article 16
1. Any Member State may provide that a producer's total liability for damage resulting from a death or personal injury and caused by identical items with the same defect shall be limited to an amount which may not be less than 70 million ECU.
2. Ten years after the date of notification of this Directive, the Commission shall submit to the Council a report on the effect on consumer protection and the functioning of the common market of the implementation of the financial limit on liability by those Member States which have used the option provided for in paragraph 1. In the light of this report the Council, acting on a proposal from the Com-

mission and pursuant to the terms of Article 100 of the Treaty, shall decide whether to repeal paragraph 1.

Article 17
This Directive shall not apply to products put into circulation before the date on which the provisions referred to in Article 19 enter into force.

Article 18
1. For the purposes of this Directive, the ECU shall be that defined by Regulation (EEC) No 3180/78, as amended by Regulation (EEC) No 2626/84. The equivalent in national currency shall initially be calculated at the rate obtaining on the date of adoption of this Directive.

2. Every five years the Council, acting on a proposal from the Commission, shall examine and, if need be, revise the amounts in this Directive, in the light of economic and monetary trends in the Community.

Article 19
1. Member States shall bring into force, not later than three years from the date of notification of this Directive, the laws, regulations and administrative provisions necessary to comply with this Directive. They shall forthwith inform the Commission thereof.

2. The procedure set out in Article 15(2) shall apply from the date of notification of this Directive.

Article 20
Member States shall communicate to the Commission the texts of the main provisions of national law which they subsequently adopt in the field governed by this Directive.

Article 21
Every five years the Commission shall present a report to the Council on the application of this Directive and, if necessary, shall submit appropriate proposals to it.

Article 22
This Directive is addressed to the Member States.

Done at Brussels, 25 July 1985.

COUNCIL DIRECTIVE NO 2000/31/EC OF 8 JUNE 2000
on certain legal aspects of information society services, in particular electronic commerce, in the internal market

THE EUROPEAN PARLIAMENT AND THE COUNCIL OF THE EUROPEAN UNION,

. . .

HAVE ADOPTED THIS DIRECTIVE:

CHAPTER I
GENERAL PROVISIONS

Article 1. Objective and scope
1. This Directive seeks to contribute to the proper functioning of the internal market by ensuring the free movement of information society services between the Member States.

2. This Directive approximates, to the extent necessary for the achievement of the objective set out in paragraph 1, certain national provisions on information

society services relating to the internal market, the establishment of service providers, commercial communications, electronic contracts, the liability of intermediaries, codes of conduct, out-of-court dispute settlements, court actions and cooperation between Member States.

3.   This Directive complements Community law applicable to information society services without prejudice to the level of protection for, in particular, public health and consumer interests, as established by Community acts and national legislation implementing them in so far as this does not restrict the freedom to provide information society services.

4.   This Directive does not establish additional rules on private international law nor does it deal with the jurisdiction of Courts.

5.   This Directive shall not apply to:

(a)   the field of taxation;

(b)   questions relating to information society services covered by Directives 95/46/EC and 97/66/EC;

(c)   questions relating to agreements or practices governed by cartel law;

(d)   the following activities of information society services:

– the activities of notaries or equivalent professions to the extent that they involve a direct and specific connection with the exercise of public authority,

– the representation of a client and defence of his interests before the courts,

– gambling activities which involve wagering a stake with monetary value in games of chance, including lotteries and betting transactions.

6.   This Directive does not affect measures taken at Community or national level, in the respect of Community law, in order to promote cultural and linguistic diversity and to ensure the defence of pluralism.

Article 2. Definitions

For the purpose of this Directive, the following terms shall bear the following meanings:

(a)   'information society services': services within the meaning of Article 1(2) of Directive 98/34/EC as amended by Directive 98/48/EC;

(b)   'service provider': any natural or legal person providing an information society service;

(c)   'established service provider': a service provider who effectively pursues an economic activity using a fixed establishment for an indefinite period. The presence and use of the technical means and technologies required to provide the service do not, in themselves, constitute an establishment of the provider;

(d)   'recipient of the service': any natural or legal person who, for professional ends or otherwise, uses an information society service, in particular for the purposes of seeking information or making it accessible;

(e)   'consumer': any natural person who is acting for purposes which are outside his or her trade, business or profession;

(f)   'commercial communication': any form of communication designed to promote, directly or indirectly, the goods, services or image of a company, organisation or person pursuing a commercial, industrial or craft activity or exercising a regulated profession. The following do not in themselves constitute commercial communications:

– information allowing direct access to the activity of the company, organisation or person, in particular a domain name or an electronic-mail address,

– communications relating to the goods, services or image of the company, organisation or person compiled in an independent manner, particularly when this is without financial consideration;

(g)   'regulated profession': any profession within the meaning of either Article 1(d) of Council Directive 89/48/EEC of 21 December 1988 on a general system for the recognition of higher-education diplomas awarded on completion of professional education and training of at least three-years' duration or of Article 1(f) of Council Directive 92/51/EEC of 18 June 1992 on a second general system for the recognition of professional education and training to supplement Directive 89/48/EEC;

(h) 'coordinated field': requirements laid down in Member States' legal systems applicable to information society service providers or information society services, regardless of whether they are of a general nature or specifically designed for them.

(i) The coordinated field concerns requirements with which the service provider has to comply in respect of:

– the taking up of the activity of an information society service, such as requirements concerning qualifications, authorisation or notification,

– the pursuit of the activity of an information society service, such as requirements concerning the behaviour of the service provider, requirements regarding the quality or content of the service including those applicable to advertising and contracts, or requirements concerning the liability of the service provider;

(ii) The coordinated field does not cover requirements such as:

– requirements applicable to goods as such,

– requirements applicable to the delivery of goods,

– requirements applicable to services not provided by electronic means.

Article 3. Internal market

1. Each Member State shall ensure that the information society services provided by a service provider established on its territory comply with the national provisions applicable in the Member State in question which fall within the coordinated field.

2. Member States may not, for reasons falling within the coordinated field, restrict the freedom to provide information society services from another Member State.

3. Paragraphs 1 and 2 shall not apply to the fields referred to in the Annex.

4. Member States may take measures to derogate from paragraph 2 in respect of a given information society service if the following conditions are fulfilled:

(a) the measures shall be:

(i) necessary for one of the following reasons:

– public policy, in particular the prevention, investigation, detection and prosecution of criminal offences, including the protection of minors and the fight against any incitement to hatred on grounds of race, sex, religion or nationality, and violations of human dignity concerning individual persons,

– the protection of public health,

– public security, including the safeguarding of national security and defence,

– the protection of consumers, including investors;

(ii) taken against a given information society service which prejudices the objectives referred to in point (i) or which presents a serious and grave risk of prejudice to those objectives;

(iii) proportionate to those objectives;

(b) before taking the measures in question and without prejudice to court proceedings, including preliminary proceedings and acts carried out in the framework of a criminal investigation, the Member State has:

– asked the Member State referred to in paragraph 1 to take measures and the latter did not take such measures, or they were inadequate,

– notified the Commission and the Member State referred to in paragraph 1 of its intention to take such measures.

5. Member States may, in the case of urgency, derogate from the conditions stipulated in paragraph 4(b). Where this is the case, the measures shall be notified

in the shortest possible time to the Commission and to the Member State referred to in paragraph 1, indicating the reasons for which the Member State considers that there is urgency.

6. Without prejudice to the Member State's possibility of proceeding with the measures in question, the Commission shall examine the compatibility of the notified measures with Community law in the shortest possible time; where it comes to the conclusion that the measure is incompatible with Community law, the Commission shall ask the Member State in question to refrain from taking any proposed measures or urgently to put an end to the measures in question.

CHAPTER II
PRINCIPLES

Section 1: Establishment and information requirements

Article 4. Principle excluding prior authorisation

1. Member States shall ensure that the taking up and pursuit of the activity of an information society service provider may not be made subject to prior authorisation or any other requirement having equivalent effect.

2. Paragraph 1 shall be without prejudice to authorisation schemes which are not specifically and exclusively targeted at information society services, or which are covered by Directive 97/13/EC of the European Parliament and of the Council of 10 April 1997 on a common framework for general authorisations and individual licences in the field of telecommunications services.

Article 5. General information to be provided

1. In addition to other information requirements established by Community law, Member States shall ensure that the service provider shall render easily, directly and permanently accessible to the recipients of the service and competent authorities, at least the following information:

    (a) the name of the service provider;

    (b) the geographic address at which the service provider is established;

    (c) the details of the service provider, including his electronic mail address, which allow him to be contacted rapidly and communicated with in a direct and effective manner;

    (d) where the service provider is registered in a trade or similar public register, the trade register in which the service provider is entered and his registration number, or equivalent means of identification in that register;

    (e) where the activity is subject to an authorisation scheme, the particulars of the relevant supervisory authority;

    (f) as concerns the regulated professions:

    – any professional body or similar institution with which the service provider is registered,

    – the professional title and the Member State where it has been granted,

    – a reference to the applicable professional rules in the Member State of establishment and the means to access them;

    (g) where the service provider undertakes an activity that is subject to VAT, the identification number referred to in Article 22(1) of the sixth Council Directive 77/388/EEC of 17 May 1977 on the harmonisation of the laws of the Member States relating to turnover taxes—Common system of value added tax: uniform basis of assessment.

2. In addition to other information requirements established by Community law, Member States shall at least ensure that, where information society services refer to prices, these are to be indicated clearly and unambiguously and, in particular, must indicate whether they are inclusive of tax and delivery costs.

Section 2: Commercial communications

Article 6. Information to be provided

In addition to other information requirements established by Community law, Member States shall ensure that commercial communications which are part of, or constitute, an information society service comply at least with the following conditions:

(a) the commercial communication shall be clearly identifiable as such;

(b) the natural or legal person on whose behalf the commercial communication is made shall be clearly identifiable;

(c) promotional offers, such as discounts, premiums and gifts, where permitted in the Member State where the service provider is established, shall be clearly identifiable as such, and the conditions which are to be met to qualify for them shall be easily accessible and be presented clearly and unambiguously;

(d) promotional competitions or games, where permitted in the Member State where the service provider is established, shall be clearly identifiable as such, and the conditions for participation shall be easily accessible and be presented clearly and unambiguously.

Article 7. Unsolicited commercial communication

1. In addition to other requirements established by Community law, Member States which permit unsolicited commercial communication by electronic mail shall ensure that such commercial communication by a service provider established in their territory shall be identifiable clearly and unambiguously as such as soon as it is received by the recipient.

2. Without prejudice to Directive 97/7/EC and Directive 97/66/EC, Member States shall take measures to ensure that service providers undertaking unsolicited commercial communications by electronic mail consult regularly and respect the opt-out registers in which natural persons not wishing to receive such commercial communications can register themselves.

Article 8. Regulated professions

1. Member States shall ensure that the use of commercial communications which are part of, or constitute, an information society service provided by a member of a regulated profession is permitted subject to compliance with the professional rules regarding, in particular, the independence, dignity and honour of the profession, professional secrecy and fairness towards clients and other members of the profession.

2. Without prejudice to the autonomy of professional bodies and associations, Member States and the Commission shall encourage professional associations and bodies to establish codes of conduct at Community level in order to determine the types of information that can be given for the purposes of commercial communication in conformity with the rules referred to in paragraph 1.

3. When drawing up proposals for Community initiatives which may become necessary to ensure the proper functioning of the Internal Market with regard to the information referred to in paragraph 2, the Commission shall take due account of codes of conduct applicable at Community level and shall act in close cooperation with the relevant professional associations and bodies.

4. This Directive shall apply in addition to Community Directives concerning access to, and the exercise of, activities of the regulated professions.

Section 3: Contracts concluded by electronic means

Article 9. Treatment of contracts

1. Member States shall ensure that their legal system allows contracts to be concluded by electronic means. Member States shall in particular ensure that the

legal requirements applicable to the contractual process neither create obstacles for the use of electronic contracts nor result in such contracts being deprived of legal effectiveness and validity on account of their having been made by electronic means.

2. Member States may lay down that paragraph 1 shall not apply to all or certain contracts falling into one of the following categories:

(a) contracts that create or transfer rights in real estate, except for rental rights;

(b) contracts requiring by law the involvement of courts, public authorities or professions exercising public authority;

(c) contracts of suretyship granted and on collateral securities furnished by persons acting for purposes outside their trade, business or profession;

(d) contracts governed by family law or by the law of succession.

3. Member States shall indicate to the Commission the categories referred to in paragraph 2 to which they do not apply paragraph 1. Member States shall submit to the Commission every five years a report on the application of paragraph 2 explaining the reasons why they consider it necessary to maintain the category referred to in paragraph 2(b) to which they do not apply paragraph 1.

Article 10. Information to be provided

1. In addition to other information requirements established by Community law, Member States shall ensure, except when otherwise agreed by parties who are not consumers, that at least the following information is given by the service provider clearly, comprehensibly and unambiguously and prior to the order being placed by the recipient of the service:

(a) the different technical steps to follow to conclude the contract;

(b) whether or not the concluded contract will be filed by the service provider and whether it will be accessible;

(c) the technical means for identifying and correcting input errors prior to the placing of the order;

(d) the languages offered for the conclusion of the contract.

2. Member States shall ensure that, except when otherwise agreed by parties who are not consumers, the service provider indicates any relevant codes of conduct to which he subscribes and information on how those codes can be consulted electronically.

3. Contract terms and general conditions provided to the recipient must be made available in a way that allows him to store and reproduce them.

4. Paragraphs 1 and 2 shall not apply to contracts concluded exclusively by exchange of electronic mail or by equivalent individual communications.

Article 11. Placing of the order

1. Member States shall ensure, except when otherwise agreed by parties who are not consumers, that in cases where the recipient of the service places his order through technological means, the following principles apply:

– the service provider has to acknowledge the receipt of the recipient's order without undue delay and by electronic means,

– the order and the acknowledgement of receipt are deemed to be received when the parties to whom they are addressed are able to access them.

2. Member States shall ensure that, except when otherwise agreed by parties who are not consumers, the service provider makes available to the recipient of the service appropriate, effective and accessible technical means allowing him to identify and correct input errors, prior to the placing of the order.

3. Paragraph 1, first indent, and paragraph 2 shall not apply to contracts concluded exclusively by exchange of electronic mail or by equivalent individual communications.

Section 4: Liability of intermediary service providers

Article 12. 'Mere conduit'

1. Where an information society service is provided that consists of the transmission in a communication network of information provided by a recipient of the service, or the provision of access to a communication network, Member States shall ensure that the service provider is not liable for the information transmitted, on condition that the provider:

  (a) does not initiate the transmission;

  (b) does not select the receiver of the transmission; and

  (c) does not select or modify the information contained in the transmission.

2. The acts of transmission and of provision of access referred to in paragraph 1 include the automatic, intermediate and transient storage of the information transmitted in so far as this takes place for the sole purpose of carrying out the transmission in the communication network, and provided that the information is not stored for any period longer than is reasonably necessary for the transmission.

3. This Article shall not affect the possibility for a court or administrative authority, in accordance with Member States' legal systems, of requiring the service provider to terminate or prevent an infringement.

Article 13. 'Caching'

1. Where an information society service is provided that consists of the transmission in a communication network of information provided by a recipient of the service, Member States shall ensure that the service provider is not liable for the automatic, intermediate and temporary storage of that information, performed for the sole purpose of making more efficient the information's onward transmission to other recipients of the service upon their request, on condition that:

  (a) the provider does not modify the information;

  (b) the provider complies with conditions on access to the information;

  (c) the provider complies with rules regarding the updating of the information, specified in a manner widely recognised and used by industry;

  (d) the provider does not interfere with the lawful use of technology, widely recognised and used by industry, to obtain data on the use of the information; and

  (e) the provider acts expeditiously to remove or to disable access to the information it has stored upon obtaining actual knowledge of the fact that the information at the initial source of the transmission has been removed from the network, or access to it has been disabled, or that a court or an administrative authority has ordered such removal or disablement.

2. This Article shall not affect the possibility for a court or administrative authority, in accordance with Member States' legal systems, of requiring the service provider to terminate or prevent an infringement.

Article 14. Hosting

1. Where an information society service is provided that consists of the storage of information provided by a recipient of the service, Member States shall ensure that the service provider is not liable for the information stored at the request of a recipient of the service, on condition that:

  (a) the provider does not have actual knowledge of illegal activity or information and, as regards claims for damages, is not aware of facts or circumstances from which the illegal activity or information is apparent; or

  (b) the provider, upon obtaining such knowledge or awareness, acts expeditiously to remove or to disable access to the information.

2. Paragraph 1 shall not apply when the recipient of the service is acting under the authority or the control of the provider.

3. This Article shall not affect the possibility for a court or administrative authority, in accordance with Member States' legal systems, of requiring the ser-

vice provider to terminate or prevent an infringement, nor does it affect the possibility for Member States of establishing procedures governing the removal or disabling of access to information.

Article 15. No general obligation to monitor

1. Member States shall not impose a general obligation on providers, when providing the services covered by Articles 12, 13 and 14, to monitor the information which they transmit or store, nor a general obligation actively to seek facts or circumstances indicating illegal activity.

2. Member States may establish obligations for information society service providers promptly to inform the competent public authorities of alleged illegal activities undertaken or information provided by recipients of their service or obligations to communicate to the competent authorities, at their request, information enabling the identification of recipients of their service with whom they have storage agreements.

CHAPTER III
IMPLEMENTATION

Article 16. Codes of conduct

1. Member States and the Commission shall encourage:

   (a) the drawing up of codes of conduct at Community level, by trade, professional and consumer associations or organisations, designed to contribute to the proper implementation of Articles 5 to 15;

   (b) the voluntary transmission of draft codes of conduct at national or Community level to the Commission;

   (c) the accessibility of these codes of conduct in the Community languages by electronic means;

   (d) the communication to the Member States and the Commission, by trade, professional and consumer associations or organisations, of their assessment of the application of their codes of conduct and their impact upon practices, habits or customs relating to electronic commerce;

   (e) the drawing up of codes of conduct regarding the protection of minors and human dignity.

2. Member States and the Commission shall encourage the involvement of associations or organisations representing consumers in the drafting and implementation of codes of conduct affecting their interests and drawn up in accordance with paragraph 1(a). Where appropriate, to take account of their specific needs, associations representing the visually impaired and disabled should be consulted.

Article 17. Out-of-court dispute settlement

1. Member States shall ensure that, in the event of disagreement between an information society service provider and the recipient of the service, their legislation does not hamper the use of out-of-court schemes, available under national law, for dispute settlement, including appropriate electronic means.

2. Member States shall encourage bodies responsible for the out-of-court settlement of, in particular, consumer disputes to operate in a way which provides adequate procedural guarantees for the parties concerned.

3. Member States shall encourage bodies responsible for out-of-court dispute settlement to inform the Commission of the significant decisions they take regarding information society services and to transmit any other information on the practices, usages or customs relating to electronic commerce.

Article 18. Court actions

1. Member States shall ensure that court actions available under national law concerning information society services' activities allow for the rapid adoption of measures, including interim measures, designed to terminate any alleged infringement and to prevent any further impairment of the interests involved.

2.   The Annex to Directive 98/27/EC shall be supplemented as follows:

'11. Directive 2000/31/EC of the European Parliament and of the Council of 8
June 2000 on certain legal aspects on information society services, in particular
electronic commerce, in the internal market (Directive on electronic commerce) (OJ
L 178, 17.7.2000, p 1).'

Article 19. Cooperation

1.   Member States shall have adequate means of supervision and investigation
necessary to implement this Directive effectively and shall ensure that service providers supply them with the requisite information.

2.   Member States shall cooperate with other Member States; they shall, to that
end, appoint one or several contact points, whose details they shall communicate
to the other Member States and to the Commission.

3.   Member States shall, as quickly as possible, and in conformity with national
law, provide the assistance and information requested by other Member States or
by the Commission, including by appropriate electronic means.

4.   Member States shall establish contact points which shall be accessible at least
by electronic means and from which recipients and service providers may:

(a)   obtain general information on contractual rights and obligations as well
as on the complaint and redress mechanisms available in the event of disputes,
including practical aspects involved in the use of such mechanisms;

(b)   obtain the details of authorities, associations or organisations from which
they may obtain further information or practical assistance.

5.   Member States shall encourage the communication to the Commission of
any significant administrative or judicial decisions taken in their territory regarding disputes relating to information society services and practices, usages and customs relating to electronic commerce. The Commission shall communicate these
decisions to the other Member States.

Article 20. Sanctions

Member States shall determine the sanctions applicable to infringements of
national provisions adopted pursuant to this Directive and shall take all measures
necessary to ensure that they are enforced. The sanctions they provide for shall be
effective, proportionate and dissuasive.

CHAPTER IV
FINAL PROVISIONS

Article 21. Re-examination

1.   Before 17 July 2003, and thereafter every two years, the Commission shall
submit to the European Parliament, the Council and the Economic and Social
Committee a report on the application of this Directive, accompanied, where
necessary, by proposals for adapting it to legal, technical and economic developments in the field of information society services, in particular with respect to
crime prevention, the protection of minors, consumer protection and to the proper
functioning of the internal market.

2.   In examining the need for an adaptation of this Directive, the report shall in
particular analyse the need for proposals concerning the liability of providers of
hyperlinks and location tool services, 'notice and take down' procedures and the
attribution of liability following the taking down of content. The report shall also
analyse the need for additional conditions for the exemption from liability, provided for in Articles 12 and 13, in the light of technical developments, and the
possibility of applying the internal market principles to unsolicited commercial
communications by electronic mail.

Article 22. Transposition

1.   Member States shall bring into force the laws, regulations and administrative

provisions necessary to comply with this Directive before 17 January 2002. They shall forthwith inform the Commission thereof.

2. When Member States adopt the measures referred to in paragraph 1, these shall contain a reference to this Directive or shall be accompanied by such reference at the time of their official publication. The methods of making such reference shall be laid down by Member States.

Article 23. Entry into force
This Directive shall enter into force on the day of its publication in the Official Journal of the European Communities.

Article 24. Addressees
This Directive is addressed to the Member States.

Done at Luxemburg, 8 June 2000.

COUNCIL DIRECTIVE NO 2011/83/EU OF 25 OCTOBER ON CONSUMER RIGHTS

Official Journal L 304, 22/11/2011 pp 64–88

THE EUROPEAN PARLIAMENT AND THE COUNCIL OF THE EUROPEAN UNION,

Having regard to the Treaty on the Functioning of the European Union, and in particular Article 114 thereof,
  Having regard to the proposal from the European Commission,
  Having regard to the opinion of the European Economic and Social Committee,
  Having regard to the opinion of the Committee of the Regions,
  Acting in accordance with the ordinary legislative procedure,

HAVE ADOPTED THIS DIRECTIVE:

CHAPTER I
SUBJECT MATTER, DEFINITIONS AND SCOPE

Article 1. Subject matter
The purpose of this Directive is, through the achievement of a high level of consumer protection, to contribute to the proper functioning of the internal market by approximating certain aspects of the laws, regulations and administrative provisions of the Member States concerning contracts concluded between consumers and traders.

Article 2. Definitions
For the purpose of this Directive, the following definitions shall apply:
  (1) 'consumer' means any natural person who, in contracts covered by this Directive, is acting for purposes which are outside his trade, business, craft or profession;
  (2) 'trader' means any natural person or any legal person, irrespective of whether privately or publicly owned, who is acting, including through any other person acting in his name or on his behalf, for purposes relating to his trade, business, craft or profession in relation to contracts covered by this Directive;
  (3) 'goods' means any tangible movable items, with the exception of items sold by way of execution or otherwise by authority of law; water, gas and electricity shall be considered as goods within the meaning of this Directive where they are put up for sale in a limited volume or a set quantity;

(4) 'goods made to the consumer's specifications' means non-prefabricated goods made on the basis of an individual choice of or decision by the consumer;

(5) 'sales contract' means any contract under which the trader transfers or undertakes to transfer the ownership of goods to the consumer and the consumer pays or undertakes to pay the price thereof, including any contract having as its object both goods and services;

(6) 'service contract' means any contract other than a sales contract under which the trader supplies or undertakes to supply a service to the consumer and the consumer pays or undertakes to pay the price thereof;

(7) 'distance contract' means any contract concluded between the trader and the consumer under an organised distance sales or service-provision scheme without the simultaneous physical presence of the trader and the consumer, with the exclusive use of one or more means of distance communication up to and including the time at which the contract is concluded;

(8) 'off-premises contract' means any contract between the trader and the consumer:

(a)   concluded in the simultaneous physical presence of the trader and the consumer, in a place which is not the business premises of the trader;

(b)   for which an offer was made by the consumer in the same circumstances as referred to in point (a);

(c)   concluded on the business premises of the trader or through any means of distance communication immediately after the consumer was personally and individually addressed in a place which is not the business premises of the trader in the simultaneous physical presence of the trader and the consumer; or

(d)   concluded during an excursion organised by the trader with the aim or effect of promoting and selling goods or services to the consumer;

(9) 'business premises' means:

(a)   any immovable retail premises where the trader carries out his activity on a permanent basis; or

(b)   any movable retail premises where the trader carries out his activity on a usual basis;

(10) 'durable medium' means any instrument which enables the consumer or the trader to store information addressed personally to him in a way accessible for future reference for a period of time adequate for the purposes of the information and which allows the unchanged reproduction of the information stored;

(11) 'digital content' means data which are produced and supplied in digital form;

(12) 'financial service' means any service of a banking, credit, insurance, personal pension, investment or payment nature;

(13) 'public auction' means a method of sale where goods or services are offered by the trader to consumers, who attend or are given the possibility to attend the auction in person, through a transparent, competitive bidding procedure run by an auctioneer and where the successful bidder is bound to purchase the goods or services;

(14) 'commercial guarantee' means any undertaking by the trader or a producer (the guarantor) to the consumer, in addition to his legal obligation relating to the guarantee of conformity, to reimburse the price paid or to replace, repair or service goods in any way if they do not meet the specifications or any other requirements not related to conformity set out in the guarantee statement or in the relevant advertising available at the time of, or before the conclusion of the contract;

(15) 'ancillary contract' means a contract by which the consumer acquires goods or services related to a distance contract or an off-premises contract and where those goods are supplied or those services are provided by the trader or by a third party on the basis of an arrangement between that third party and the trader.

Article 3. Scope

1. This Directive shall apply, under the conditions and to the extent set out in its provisions, to any contract concluded between a trader and a consumer. It shall also apply to contracts for the supply of water, gas, electricity or district heating, including by public providers, to the extent that these commodities are provided on a contractual basis.

2. If any provision of this Directive conflicts with a provision of another Union act governing specific sectors, the provision of that other Union act shall prevail and shall apply to those specific sectors.

3. This Directive shall not apply to contracts:

(a) for social services, including social housing, childcare and support of families and persons permanently or temporarily in need, including long-term care;

(b) for healthcare as defined in point (a) of Article 3 of Directive 2011/24/EU, whether or not they are provided via healthcare facilities;

(c) for gambling, which involves wagering a stake with pecuniary value in games of chance, including lotteries, casino games and betting transactions;

(d) for financial services;

(e) for the creation, acquisition or transfer of immovable property or of rights in immovable property;

(f) for the construction of new buildings, the substantial conversion of existing buildings and for rental of accommodation for residential purposes;

(g) which fall within the scope of Council Directive 90/314/EEC of 13 June 1990 on package travel, package holidays and package tours;

(h) which fall within the scope of Directive 2008/122/EC of the European Parliament and of the Council of 14 January 2009 on the protection of consumers in respect of certain aspects of timeshare, long-term holiday product, resale and exchange contracts;

(i) which, in accordance with the laws of Member States, are established by a public office-holder who has a statutory obligation to be independent and impartial and who must ensure, by providing comprehensive legal information, that the consumer only concludes the contract on the basis of careful legal consideration and with knowledge of its legal scope;

(j) for the supply of foodstuffs, beverages or other goods intended for current consumption in the household, and which are physically supplied by a trader on frequent and regular rounds to the consumer's home, residence or workplace;

(k) for passenger transport services, with the exception of Article 8(2) and Articles 19 and 22;

(l) concluded by means of automatic vending machines or automated commercial premises;

(m) concluded with telecommunications operators through public payphones for their use or concluded for the use of one single connection by telephone, Internet or fax established by a consumer.

4. Member States may decide not to apply this Directive or not to maintain or introduce corresponding national provisions to off-premises contracts for which the payment to be made by the consumer does not exceed EUR 50. Member States may define a lower value in their national legislation.

5. This Directive shall not affect national general contract law such as the rules on the validity, formation or effect of a contract, in so far as general contract law aspects are not regulated in this Directive.

6. This Directive shall not prevent traders from offering consumers contractual arrangements which go beyond the protection provided for in this Directive.

Article 4. Level of harmonisation

Member States shall not maintain or introduce, in their national law, provisions diverging from those laid down in this Directive, including more or less stringent provisions to ensure a different level of consumer protection, unless otherwise provided for in this Directive.

CHAPTER II
CONSUMER INFORMATION FOR CONTRACTS OTHER THAN DISTANCE OR OFF-PREMISES CONTRACTS

Article 5. Information requirements for contracts other than distance or off-premises contracts

1. Before the consumer is bound by a contract other than a distance or an off-premises contract, or any corresponding offer, the trader shall provide the consumer with the following information in a clear and comprehensible manner, if that information is not already apparent from the context:

(a) the main characteristics of the goods or services, to the extent appropriate to the medium and to the goods or services;

(b) the identity of the trader, such as his trading name, the geographical address at which he is established and his telephone number;

(c) the total price of the goods or services inclusive of taxes, or where the nature of the goods or services is such that the price cannot reasonably be calculated in advance, the manner in which the price is to be calculated, as well as, where applicable, all additional freight, delivery or postal charges or, where those charges cannot reasonably be calculated in advance, the fact that such additional charges may be payable;

(d) where applicable, the arrangements for payment, delivery, performance, the time by which the trader undertakes to deliver the goods or to perform the service, and the trader's complaint handling policy;

(e) in addition to a reminder of the existence of a legal guarantee of conformity for goods, the existence and the conditions of after-sales services and commercial guarantees, where applicable;

(f) the duration of the contract, where applicable, or, if the contract is of indeterminate duration or is to be extended automatically, the conditions for terminating the contract;

(g) where applicable, the functionality, including applicable technical protection measures, of digital content;

(h) where applicable, any relevant interoperability of digital content with hardware and software that the trader is aware of or can reasonably be expected to have been aware of.

2. Paragraph 1 shall also apply to contracts for the supply of water, gas or electricity, where they are not put up for sale in a limited volume or set quantity, of district heating or of digital content which is not supplied on a tangible medium.

3. Member States shall not be required to apply paragraph 1 to contracts which involve day-to-day transactions and which are performed immediately at the time of their conclusion.

4. Member States may adopt or maintain additional pre-contractual information requirements for contracts to which this Article applies.

CHAPTER III
CONSUMER INFORMATION AND RIGHT OF WITHDRAWAL FOR DISTANCE AND OFF-PREMISES CONTRACTS

Article 6. Information requirements for distance and off-premises contracts

1. Before the consumer is bound by a distance or off-premises contract, or any corresponding offer, the trader shall provide the consumer with the following information in a clear and comprehensible manner:

(a) the main characteristics of the goods or services, to the extent appropriate to the medium and to the goods or services;

(b)   the identity of the trader, such as his trading name;

(c)   the geographical address at which the trader is established and the trader's telephone number, fax number and e-mail address, where available, to enable the consumer to contact the trader quickly and communicate with him efficiently and, where applicable, the geographical address and identity of the trader on whose behalf he is acting;

(d)   if different from the address provided in accordance with point (c), the geographical address of the place of business of the trader, and, where applicable, that of the trader on whose behalf he is acting, where the consumer can address any complaints;

(e)   the total price of the goods or services inclusive of taxes, or where the nature of the goods or services is such that the price cannot reasonably be calculated in advance, the manner in which the price is to be calculated, as well as, where applicable, all additional freight, delivery or postal charges and any other costs or, where those charges cannot reasonably be calculated in advance, the fact that such additional charges may be payable. In the case of a contract of indeterminate duration or a contract containing a subscription, the total price shall include the total costs per billing period. Where such contracts are charged at a fixed rate, the total price shall also mean the total monthly costs. Where the total costs cannot be reasonably calculated in advance, the manner in which the price is to be calculated shall be provided;

(f)   the cost of using the means of distance communication for the conclusion of the contract where that cost is calculated other than at the basic rate;

(g)   the arrangements for payment, delivery, performance, the time by which the trader undertakes to deliver the goods or to perform the services and, where applicable, the trader's complaint handling policy;

(h)   where a right of withdrawal exists, the conditions, time limit and procedures for exercising that right in accordance with Article 11(1), as well as the model withdrawal form set out in Annex I(B);

(i)   where applicable, that the consumer will have to bear the cost of returning the goods in case of withdrawal and, for distance contracts, if the goods, by their nature, cannot normally be returned by post, the cost of returning the goods;

(j)   that, if the consumer exercises the right of withdrawal after having made a request in accordance with Article 7(3) or Article 8(8), the consumer shall be liable to pay the trader reasonable costs in accordance with Article 14(3);

(k)   where a right of withdrawal is not provided for in accordance with Article 16, the information that the consumer will not benefit from a right of withdrawal or, where applicable, the circumstances under which the consumer loses his right of withdrawal;

(l)   a reminder of the existence of a legal guarantee of conformity for goods;

(m)   where applicable, the existence and the conditions of after sale customer assistance, after-sales services and commercial guarantees;

(n)   the existence of relevant codes of conduct, as defined in point (f) of Article 2 of Directive 2005/29/EC, and how copies of them can be obtained, where applicable;

(o)   the duration of the contract, where applicable, or, if the contract is of indeterminate duration or is to be extended automatically, the conditions for terminating the contract;

(p)   where applicable, the minimum duration of the consumer's obligations under the contract;

(q)   where applicable, the existence and the conditions of deposits or other financial guarantees to be paid or provided by the consumer at the request of the trader;

(r)   where applicable, the functionality, including applicable technical protection measures, of digital content;

(s)   where applicable, any relevant interoperability of digital content with hardware and software that the trader is aware of or can reasonably be expected to have been aware of;

(t)   where applicable, the possibility of having recourse to an out-of-court complaint and redress mechanism, to which the trader is subject, and the methods for having access to it.

2.   Paragraph 1 shall also apply to contracts for the supply of water, gas or electricity, where they are not put up for sale in a limited volume or set quantity, of district heating or of digital content which is not supplied on a tangible medium.

3.   In the case of a public auction, the information referred to in points (b), (c) and (d) of paragraph 1 may be replaced by the equivalent details for the auctioneer.

4.   The information referred to in points (h), (i) and (j) of paragraph 1 may be provided by means of the model instructions on withdrawal set out in Annex I(A). The trader shall have fulfilled the information requirements laid down in points (h), (i) and (j) of paragraph 1 if he has supplied these instructions to the consumer, correctly filled in.

5.   The information referred to in paragraph 1 shall form an integral part of the distance or off-premises contract and shall not be altered unless the contracting parties expressly agree otherwise.

6.   If the trader has not complied with the information requirements on additional charges or other costs as referred to in point (e) of paragraph 1, or on the costs of returning the goods as referred to in point (i) of paragraph 1, the consumer shall not bear those charges or costs.

7.   Member States may maintain or introduce in their national law language requirements regarding the contractual information, so as to ensure that such information is easily understood by the consumer.

8.   The information requirements laid down in this Directive are in addition to information requirements contained in Directive 2006/123/EC and Directive 2000/31/EC and do not prevent Member States from imposing additional information requirements in accordance with those Directives.

Without prejudice to the first subparagraph, if a provision of Directive 2006/123/EC or Directive 2000/31/EC on the content and the manner in which the information is to be provided conflicts with a provision of this Directive, the provision of this Directive shall prevail.

9.   As regards compliance with the information requirements laid down in this Chapter, the burden of proof shall be on the trader.

Article 7. Formal requirements for off-premises contracts

1.   With respect to off-premises contracts, the trader shall give the information provided for in Article 6(1) to the consumer on paper or, if the consumer agrees, on another durable medium. That information shall be legible and in plain, intelligible language.

2.   The trader shall provide the consumer with a copy of the signed contract or the confirmation of the contract on paper or, if the consumer agrees, on another durable medium, including, where applicable, the confirmation of the consumer's prior express consent and acknowledgement in accordance with point (m) of Article 16.

3.   Where a consumer wants the performance of services or the supply of water, gas or electricity, where they are not put up for sale in a limited volume or set quantity, or of district heating to begin during the withdrawal period provided for in Article 9(2), the trader shall require that the consumer makes such an express request on a durable medium.

4.   With respect to off-premises contracts where the consumer has explicitly requested the services of the trader for the purpose of carrying out repairs or maintenance for which the trader and the consumer immediately perform their

contractual obligations and where the payment to be made by the consumer does not exceed EUR 200:

(a)   the trader shall provide the consumer with the information referred to in points (b) and (c) of Article 6(1) and information about the price or the manner in which the price is to be calculated together with an estimate of the total price, on paper or, if the consumer agrees, on another durable medium. The trader shall provide the information referred to in points (a), (h) and (k) of Article 6(1), but may choose not to provide it on paper or another durable medium if the consumer expressly agrees;

(b)   the confirmation of the contract provided in accordance with paragraph 2 of this Article shall contain the information provided for in Article 6(1).

Member States may decide not to apply this paragraph.

5.   Member States shall not impose any further formal pre-contractual information requirements for the fulfilment of the information obligations laid down in this Directive.

Article 8. Formal requirements for distance contracts

1.   With respect to distance contracts, the trader shall give the information provided for in Article 6(1) or make that information available to the consumer in a way appropriate to the means of distance communication used in plain and intelligible language. In so far as that information is provided on a durable medium, it shall be legible.

2.   If a distance contract to be concluded by electronic means places the consumer under an obligation to pay, the trader shall make the consumer aware in a clear and prominent manner, and directly before the consumer places his order, of the information provided for in points (a), (e), (o) and (p) of Article 6(1).

The trader shall ensure that the consumer, when placing his order, explicitly acknowledges that the order implies an obligation to pay. If placing an order entails activating a button or a similar function, the button or similar function shall be labelled in an easily legible manner only with the words 'order with obligation to pay' or a corresponding unambiguous formulation indicating that placing the order entails an obligation to pay the trader. If the trader has not complied with this subparagraph, the consumer shall not be bound by the contract or order.

3.   Trading websites shall indicate clearly and legibly at the latest at the beginning of the ordering process whether any delivery restrictions apply and which means of payment are accepted.

4.   If the contract is concluded through a means of distance communication which allows limited space or time to display the information, the trader shall provide, on that particular means prior to the conclusion of such a contract, at least the pre-contractual information regarding the main characteristics of the goods or services, the identity of the trader, the total price, the right of withdrawal, the duration of the contract and, if the contract is of indeterminate duration, the conditions for terminating the contract, as referred to in points (a), (b), (e), (h) and (o) of Article 6(1). The other information referred to in Article 6(1) shall be provided by the trader to the consumer in an appropriate way in accordance with paragraph 1 of this Article.

5.   Without prejudice to paragraph 4, if the trader makes a telephone call to the consumer with a view to concluding a distance contract, he shall, at the beginning of the conversation with the consumer, disclose his identity and, where applicable, the identity of the person on whose behalf he makes that call, and the commercial purpose of the call.

6.   Where a distance contract is to be concluded by telephone, Member States may provide that the trader has to confirm the offer to the consumer who is bound only once he has signed the offer or has sent his written consent. Member States may also provide that such confirmations have to be made on a durable medium.

7.   The trader shall provide the consumer with the confirmation of the contract

concluded, on a durable medium within a reasonable time after the conclusion of the distance contract, and at the latest at the time of the delivery of the goods or before the performance of the service begins. That confirmation shall include:

(a)   all the information referred to in Article 6(1) unless the trader has already provided that information to the consumer on a durable medium prior to the conclusion of the distance contract; and

(b)   where applicable, the confirmation of the consumer's prior express consent and acknowledgment in accordance with point (m) of Article 16.

8.   Where a consumer wants the performance of services, or the supply of water, gas or electricity, where they are not put up for sale in a limited volume or set quantity, or of district heating, to begin during the withdrawal period provided for in Article 9(2), the trader shall require that the consumer make an express request.

9.   This Article shall be without prejudice to the provisions on the conclusion of e-contracts and the placing of e-orders set out in Articles 9 and 11 of Directive 2000/31/EC.

10.   Member States shall not impose any further formal pre-contractual information requirements for the fulfilment of the information obligations laid down in this Directive.

Article 9. Right of withdrawal

1.   Save where the exceptions provided for in Article 16 apply, the consumer shall have a period of 14 days to withdraw from a distance or off-premises contract, without giving any reason, and without incurring any costs other than those provided for in Article 13(2) and Article 14.

2.   Without prejudice to Article 10, the withdrawal period referred to in paragraph 1 of this Article shall expire after 14 days from:

(a)   in the case of service contracts, the day of the conclusion of the contract;

(b)   in the case of sales contracts, the day on which the consumer or a third party other than the carrier and indicated by the consumer acquires physical possession of the goods or:

(i)   in the case of multiple goods ordered by the consumer in one order and delivered separately, the day on which the consumer or a third party other than the carrier and indicated by the consumer acquires physical possession of the last good;

(ii)   in the case of delivery of a good consisting of multiple lots or pieces, the day on which the consumer or a third party other than the carrier and indicated by the consumer acquires physical possession of the last lot or piece;

(iii)   in the case of contracts for regular delivery of goods during defined period of time, the day on which the consumer or a third party other than the carrier and indicated by the consumer acquires physical possession of the first good;

(c)   in the case of contracts for the supply of water, gas or electricity, where they are not put up for sale in a limited volume or set quantity, of district heating or of digital content which is not supplied on a tangible medium, the day of the conclusion of the contract.

3.   The Member States shall not prohibit the contracting parties from performing their contractual obligations during the withdrawal period. Nevertheless, in the case of off-premises contracts, Member States may maintain existing national legislation prohibiting the trader from collecting the payment from the consumer during the given period after the conclusion of the contract.

Article 10. Omission of information on the right of withdrawal

1.   If the trader has not provided the consumer with the information on the right of withdrawal as required by point (h) of Article 6(1), the withdrawal period shall expire 12 months from the end of the initial withdrawal period, as determined in accordance with Article 9(2).

2. If the trader has provided the consumer with the information provided for in paragraph 1 of this Article within 12 months from the day referred to in Article 9(2), the withdrawal period shall expire 14 days after the day upon which the consumer receives that information.

Article 11. Exercise of the right of withdrawal

1. Before the expiry of the withdrawal period, the consumer shall inform the trader of his decision to withdraw from the contract. For this purpose, the consumer may either:

(a) use the model withdrawal form as set out in Annex I(B); or

(b) make any other unequivocal statement setting out his decision to withdraw from the contract.

Member States shall not provide for any formal requirements applicable to the model withdrawal form other than those set out in Annex I(B).

2. The consumer shall have exercised his right of withdrawal within the withdrawal period referred to in Article 9(2) and Article 10 if the communication concerning the exercise of the right of withdrawal is sent by the consumer before that period has expired.

3. The trader may, in addition to the possibilities referred to in paragraph 1, give the option to the consumer to electronically fill in and submit either the model withdrawal form set out in Annex I(B) or any other unequivocal statement on the trader's website. In those cases the trader shall communicate to the consumer an acknowledgement of receipt of such a withdrawal on a durable medium without delay.

4. The burden of proof of exercising the right of withdrawal in accordance with this Article shall be on the consumer.

Article 12. Effects of withdrawal

The exercise of the right of withdrawal shall terminate the obligations of the parties:

(a) to perform the distance or off-premises contract; or

(b) to conclude the distance or off-premises contract, in cases where an offer was made by the consumer.

Article 13. Obligations of the trader in the event of withdrawal

1. The trader shall reimburse all payments received from the consumer, including, if applicable, the costs of delivery without undue delay and in any event not later than 14 days from the day on which he is informed of the consumer's decision to withdraw from the contract in accordance with Article 11.

The trader shall carry out the reimbursement referred to in the first subparagraph using the same means of payment as the consumer used for the initial transaction, unless the consumer has expressly agreed otherwise and provided that the consumer does not incur any fees as a result of such reimbursement.

2. Notwithstanding paragraph 1, the trader shall not be required to reimburse the supplementary costs, if the consumer has expressly opted for a type of delivery other than the least expensive type of standard delivery offered by the trader.

3. Unless the trader has offered to collect the goods himself, with regard to sales contracts, the trader may withhold the reimbursement until he has received the goods back, or until the consumer has supplied evidence of having sent back the goods, whichever is the earliest.

Article 14. Obligations of the consumer in the event of withdrawal

1. Unless the trader has offered to collect the goods himself, the consumer shall send back the goods or hand them over to the trader or to a person authorised by the trader to receive the goods, without undue delay and in any event not later than 14 days from the day on which he has communicated his decision to withdraw from the contract to the trader in accordance with Article 11. The deadline

shall be met if the consumer sends back the goods before the period of 14 days has expired.

The consumer shall only bear the direct cost of returning the goods unless the trader has agreed to bear them or the trader failed to inform the consumer that the consumer has to bear them.

In the case of off-premises contracts where the goods have been delivered to the consumer's home at the time of the conclusion of the contract, the trader shall at his own expense collect the goods if, by their nature, those goods cannot normally be returned by post.

2. The consumer shall only be liable for any diminished value of the goods resulting from the handling of the goods other than what is necessary to establish the nature, characteristics and functioning of the goods. The consumer shall in any event not be liable for diminished value of the goods where the trader has failed to provide notice of the right of withdrawal in accordance with point (h) of Article 6(1).

3. Where a consumer exercises the right of withdrawal after having made a request in accordance with Article 7(3) or Article 8(8), the consumer shall pay to the trader an amount which is in proportion to what has been provided until the time the consumer has informed the trader of the exercise of the right of withdrawal, in comparison with the full coverage of the contract. The proportionate amount to be paid by the consumer to the trader shall be calculated on the basis of the total price agreed in the contract. If the total price is excessive, the proportionate amount shall be calculated on the basis of the market value of what has been provided.

4. The consumer shall bear no cost for:

(a) the performance of services or the supply of water, gas or electricity, where they are not put up for sale in a limited volume or set quantity, or of district heating, in full or in part, during the withdrawal period, where:

(i) the trader has failed to provide information in accordance with points (h) or (j) of Article 6(1); or

(ii) the consumer has not expressly requested performance to begin during the withdrawal period in accordance with Article 7(3) and Article 8(8); or

(b) the supply, in full or in part, of digital content which is not supplied on a tangible medium where:

(i) the consumer has not given his prior express consent to the beginning of the performance before the end of the 14-day period referred to in Article 9;

(ii) the consumer has not acknowledged that he loses his right of withdrawal when giving his consent; or

(iii) the trader has failed to provide confirmation in accordance with Article 7(2) or Article 8(7).

5. Except as provided for in Article 13(2) and in this Article, the consumer shall not incur any liability as a consequence of the exercise of the right of withdrawal.

Article 15. Effects of the exercise of the right of withdrawal on ancillary contracts

1. Without prejudice to Article 15 of Directive 2008/48/EC of the European Parliament and of the Council of 23 April 2008 on credit agreements for consumers, if the consumer exercises his right of withdrawal from a distance or an off-premises contract in accordance with Articles 9 to 14 of this Directive, any ancillary contracts shall be automatically terminated, without any costs for the consumer, except as provided for in Article 13(2) and in Article 14 of this Directive.

2. The Member States shall lay down detailed rules on the termination of such contracts.

Article 16. Exceptions from the right of withdrawal

Member States shall not provide for the right of withdrawal set out in Articles 9 to 15 in respect of distance and off-premises contracts as regards the following:

(a)   service contracts after the service has been fully performed if the performance has begun with the consumer's prior express consent, and with the acknowledgement that he will lose his right of withdrawal once the contract has been fully performed by the trader;

(b)   the supply of goods or services for which the price is dependent on fluctuations in the financial market which cannot be controlled by the trader and which may occur within the withdrawal period;

(c)   the supply of goods made to the consumer's specifications or clearly personalised;

(d)   the supply of goods which are liable to deteriorate or expire rapidly;

(e)   the supply of sealed goods which are not suitable for return due to health protection or hygiene reasons and were unsealed after delivery;

(f)   the supply of goods which are, after delivery, according to their nature, inseparably mixed with other items;

(g)   the supply of alcoholic beverages, the price of which has been agreed upon at the time of the conclusion of the sales contract, the delivery of which can only take place after 30 days and the actual value of which is dependent on fluctuations in the market which cannot be controlled by the trader;

(h)   contracts where the consumer has specifically requested a visit from the trader for the purpose of carrying out urgent repairs or maintenance. If, on the occasion of such visit, the trader provides services in addition to those specifically requested by the consumer or goods other than replacement parts necessarily used in carrying out the maintenance or in making the repairs, the right of withdrawal shall apply to those additional services or goods;

(i)   the supply of sealed audio or sealed video recordings or sealed computer software which were unsealed after delivery;

(j)   the supply of a newspaper, periodical or magazine with the exception of subscription contracts for the supply of such publications;

(k)   contracts concluded at a public auction;

(l)   the provision of accommodation other than for residential purpose, transport of goods, car rental services, catering or services related to leisure activities if the contract provides for a specific date or period of performance;

(m)   the supply of digital content which is not supplied on a tangible medium if the performance has begun with the consumer's prior express consent and his acknowledgment that he thereby loses his right of withdrawal.

CHAPTER IV
OTHER CONSUMER RIGHTS

Article 17. Scope

1.   Articles 18 and 20 shall apply to sales contracts. Those Articles shall not apply to contracts for the supply of water, gas or electricity, where they are not put up for sale in a limited volume or set quantity, of district heating or the supply of digital content which is not supplied on a tangible medium.

2.   Articles 19, 21 and 22 shall apply to sales and service contracts and to contracts for the supply of water, gas, electricity, district heating or digital content.

Article 18. Delivery

1.   Unless the parties have agreed otherwise on the time of delivery, the trader shall deliver the goods by transferring the physical possession or control of the goods to the consumer without undue delay, but not later than 30 days from the conclusion of the contract.

2.   Where the trader has failed to fulfil his obligation to deliver the goods at the time agreed upon with the consumer or within the time limit set out in paragraph 1, the consumer shall call upon him to make the delivery within an additional period of time appropriate to the circumstances. If the trader fails to deliver the

goods within that additional period of time, the consumer shall be entitled to terminate the contract.

The first subparagraph shall not be applicable to sales contracts where the trader has refused to deliver the goods or where delivery within the agreed delivery period is essential taking into account all the circumstances attending the conclusion of the contract or where the consumer informs the trader, prior to the conclusion of the contract, that delivery by or on a specified date is essential. In those cases, if the trader fails to deliver the goods at the time agreed upon with the consumer or within the time limit set out in paragraph 1, the consumer shall be entitled to terminate the contract immediately.

3. Upon termination of the contract, the trader shall, without undue delay, reimburse all sums paid under the contract.

4. In addition to the termination of the contract in accordance with paragraph 2, the consumer may have recourse to other remedies provided for by national law.

Article 19. Fees for the use of means of payment
Member States shall prohibit traders from charging consumers, in respect of the use of a given means of payment, fees that exceed the cost borne by the trader for the use of such means.

Article 20. Passing of risk
In contracts where the trader dispatches the goods to the consumer, the risk of loss of or damage to the goods shall pass to the consumer when he or a third party indicated by the consumer and other than the carrier has acquired the physical possession of the goods. However, the risk shall pass to the consumer upon delivery to the carrier if the carrier was commissioned by the consumer to carry the goods and that choice was not offered by the trader, without prejudice to the rights of the consumer against the carrier.

Article 21. Communication by telephone
Member States shall ensure that where the trader operates a telephone line for the purpose of contacting him by telephone in relation to the contract concluded, the consumer, when contacting the trader is not bound to pay more than the basic rate. The first subparagraph shall be without prejudice to the right of telecommunication services providers to charge for such calls.

Article 22. Additional payments
Before the consumer is bound by the contract or offer, the trader shall seek the express consent of the consumer to any extra payment in addition to the remuneration agreed upon for the trader's main contractual obligation. If the trader has not obtained the consumer's express consent but has inferred it by using default options which the consumer is required to reject in order to avoid the additional payment, the consumer shall be entitled to reimbursement of this payment.

. . .

Article 27. Inertia selling
The consumer shall be exempted from the obligation to provide any consideration in cases of unsolicited supply of goods, water, gas, electricity, district heating or digital content or unsolicited provision of services, prohibited by Article 5(5) and point 29 of Annex I to Directive 2005/29/EC. In such cases, the absence of a response from the consumer following such an unsolicited supply or provision shall not constitute consent.

. . .

Done at Strasbourg, 25 October 2011.

PART IV
CODES

DRAFT RULES ON UNJUSTIFIED ENRICHMENT
(SLC Discussion Paper No 99 (1996), Appendix)

1 General principle
A person who has been enriched at the expense of another person is bound, if the enrichment is unjustified, to redress the enrichment.

2 Enrichment
(1) A person is enriched if he acquires an economic benefit.

(2) A person acquires an economic benefit if his net worth is increased or is prevented from being decreased, and accordingly a person may be enriched, among other ways, by
  (a) acquiring money or other property
  (b) having value added to property
  (c) being freed, in whole or in part, from an obligation, or
  (d) being saved from a loss or expenditure

(3) A person is treated as acquiring an economic benefit under a void contract, or under a voidable contract which has been reduced, rescinded or otherwise set aside, or under a contract which has been terminated by frustration or rescission for breach or by some other means (apart from full performance) or under any other transaction or purported transaction which does not provide legal cause for the acquisition, if he would have acquired an economic benefit but for the fact that he gave consideration, and accordingly in such circumstances both parties to the transaction or purported transaction may be regarded as being enriched.

3 At the expense of another person
(1) The enrichment of one person is at the expense of another person if it is the direct result of
  (a) a payment, grant, transfer, incurring of liability, or rendering of services by the other person
    (i) to the enriched person
    (ii) in fulfilment of an obligation of the enriched person
    (iii) in adding value to the enriched person's property, or
    (iv) in acquiring some other economic benefit for the enriched person, or
  (b) in any case not covered by paragraph (a), an interference with the patrimonial rights of the other person otherwise than by the operation of natural forces.

(2) A person interferes with the patrimonial rights of another person if, among other things, he
  (a) extinguishes those rights or acts in such a way that they are extinguished
  (b) disposes or purports to dispose of property belonging to that other person
  (c) uses property which that other person has the right to use to the exclusion of the interferer, or
  (d) actively intercepts a benefit due to the other person

but a person does not interfere with the patrimonial rights of another person merely because he breaches a contract between himself and the other person.

(3)   A person who claims redress or any unjustified enrichment resulting from an interference with his patrimonial rights is treated for the purpose of any claims by or against third parties as thereby ratifying the interference.

(4)   A person who purchases property in good faith from someone who is not the owner of the property is not treated as being enriched at the expense of the owner or of any former owner by reason only of any economic benefit derived by him from the purchase of the property; and the same rule applies to any other acquirer, in good faith and for value, of the right, or of what purports to be the right, to deal with the property or rights of another, and to anyone deriving title from such a purchaser or acquirer.

(5)   Where a person (E) has been enriched indirectly as a result of performance by another person (C) under a contract between C and a third party (T), E's enrichment is not regarded as being at the expense of C, even if C is unable to recover under his contract with T.

(6)   This rule is subject to rule 8 (which deals with certain exceptional cases where redress is due for indirect enrichment).

4   Unjustified

An enrichment is unjustified unless it is justified under rules 5 or 6.

5   Enrichment justified by legal cause

(1)   An enrichment is justified if the enriched person is entitled to it by virtue of
   (a)   an enactment
   (b)   a rule of law
   (c)   a court decree
   (d)   a contract (whether or not the person claiming redress is a party) or unilateral voluntary obligation
   (e)   a will or trust
   (f)   a gift, or
   (g)   some other legal cause.

(2)   The reference to an enactment or rule of law in rule 5(1) is to an enactment or rule of law which confers rights directly and not to an enactment or rule of law in so far as it operates indirectly by regulating the effects of court decrees, contracts, wills, trusts, gifts or other legal causes.

(3)   A purported or apparent legal cause does not justify an enrichment if it is void or if, being voidable, it has been reduced, rescinded or otherwise set aside.

(4)   An acquisition of property is not a justified enrichment merely because legal title to the property has been acquired.

6   Enrichment justified by public policy

(1)   An enrichment is justified if it is the result of
   (a)   work or expenditure which was undertaken or incurred by the other person for his own benefit, or for the benefit of a third party or the public at large, which has incidentally conferred a benefit on the enriched person, and which was undertaken or incurred when the person knew or could reasonably have been expected to know that there would be a benefit to the enriched person and accepted, or could reasonably be supposed to have accepted, the risk that the enriched person would not pay for the benefit
   (b)   the voluntary and deliberate conferring by the other person of a benefit on the enriched person, in the knowledge that it is not due and in acceptance of the risk that the enriched person may choose not to pay or do anything in return
   (c)   a voluntary performance by the other person of an obligation which has prescribed, even if he erroneously believed that the obligation was still due, provided that any due counter-performance has been given
   (d)   a voluntary performance by the other person of an obligation which is

invalid for some formal reason only, even if he erroneously believed that the obligation was valid, provided that any due counter-performance has been given or if there is some other consideration of public policy which requires it to be regarded as justified.

(2) For the purpose of rule 6(1)(a) 'benefit', in relation to a person who has done work or provided services in tendering for a contract or in the anticipation of obtaining a contract, includes the benefit to the person of having, or improving, the chance of obtaining the contract.

7 Exceptions to rules 5 and 6

(1) Rule 5(1)(b) does not apply in so far as the enrichment is the result of any rule of law on the acquisition of property by accession or specification, or any analogous rule whereby one person may acquire another's property when it becomes attached to or mixed with his own.

(2) Rule 5(1)(d) does not apply in so far as the contract or obligation,

(a) is unenforceable because of an enactment or rule of law (whether or not it is also illegal), unless allowing redress for the enrichment would contravene the policy underlying the enactment or rule of law,

(b) has been terminated by rescission or frustration or some other means (apart from full performance) and the contract or obligation does not, expressly or impliedly, exclude redress in respect of the benefit in question.

(3) For the purpose of rule 7(2)(b) a contract which provides for performance in several parts or stages is presumed, unless the contract indicates the contrary, to exclude redress in so far as performance by one party under, and substantially in accordance with, the contract has been met by performance by the other party under, and substantially in accordance with, the contract.

(4) Rule 5(1)(f) does not apply where the gift

(a) was made in error, whether of fact or law, or

(b) was subject to a condition, which has been met, that it would be returned.

(5) Rule 6(1)(a) and (b) do not apply where the other person has, in circumstances where it was reasonable to do so,

(a) paid a monetary debt due by the enriched person

(b) fulfilled an alimentary obligation due by the enriched person

(c) incurred expenditure or performed services necessary for preserving the life, health or welfare of the enriched person, or

(d) incurred expenditure or performed services urgently necessary for preserving the property of the enriched person or preventing it from being dangerous.

8 Redress for indirect enrichment

(1)(a) Where a person (E) has acquired money or money's worth from a third party (T) by disposing or purporting to dispose of property belonging to another person (C), or by otherwise interfering with C's patrimonial rights, or by disposing of property acquired by him from C under a transaction voidable at C's instance, E's enrichment is treated, notwithstanding anything in the preceding rules, as being at the expense of C and as not being justified by any contract between himself and T.

(b) Paragraph (a) does not apply if E was a purchaser in good faith of the property in question, or had otherwise acquired, in good faith and for value, the right, or what purported to be the right, to deal with the property or rights in question, or had derived title from such a purchaser or acquirer.

(2) Where a person (T) has been enriched at the expense of another person (C) and T has transferred to another person (E) any benefit arising out of the enrichment then, notwithstanding anything in the preceding rules, E is taken to be enriched at the expense of C and neither the transfer by T to E, nor any voluntary obligation underlying the transfer, justifies the enrichment if

(a)   T's enrichment at the expense of C was unjustified or was justified only by a transaction voidable at C's instance

(b)   C is unable to recover from T, or cannot reasonably be expected to attempt to recover from T, and

(c)   the acquisition by E from T was not in good faith and for value.

(3)   Where a person (E) has been enriched by receiving a benefit from a trust estate or from the estate of a deceased person, the fact that E's enrichment is the result of a transfer from a trustee or executor does not prevent him from being liable to make redress to

(a)   a creditor of the estate to the extent that the creditor, because of the transfer to the beneficiary, has been unable to recover from the trustee or executor, or

(b)   a person (the true beneficiary) who is legally entitled to the benefit in question.

(4)   Where a debtor pays the wrong person, that person is enriched at the expense of the true creditor in so far as the payment extinguishes the liability of the debtor to the true creditor.

(5)   Nothing in these rules affects any procedural rule designed to avoid duplication of proceedings.

9   Redress due

(1)   The redress due by an enriched person under these rules is such transfer of property or payment of money, or both, as is required to redress the enriched person's unjustified enrichment at the expense of the claimant.

(2)   The redress due is assessed in accordance with the rules in the schedule in any case where those rules are applicable.

(3)   Where the enriched person has been enriched at the expense of the claimant in more than one way, the rules in the schedule apply cumulatively unless there would be double redress in respect of the same enrichment.

(4)   This rule is subject to the provisions of rule 10.

10   Court's powers to refuse or modify award

(1)   Where, in an action for unjustified enrichment, it appears to the court that each party is bound to make redress to the other, the court may

(a)   refuse to grant decree against the defender until satisfied that the pursuer has made, or will make, the redress due by him, or

(b)   where both obligations are to pay money, set off one entitlement against the other and grant decree for the difference.

(2)   Where, in an action for unjustified enrichment based on the passive receipt of a benefit by the enriched person, it appears to the court

(a)   that the enriched person had no reasonable opportunity to refuse the benefit

(b)   that the enriched person would have refused the benefit if he had had such an opportunity

(c)   that the enriched person cannot, or cannot reasonably be expected to, convert the value of the benefit into money or money's worth, and

(d)   that it would be inequitable to make a full award

the court may refuse or modify the award accordingly.

(3)   Where, in an action for unjustified enrichment based on the defender's acquisition of the pursuer's property by accession or specification or any analogous rule, it appears to the court that the pursuer has acted in good faith and that, having regard to the respective values of the properties involved, the conduct of the parties and all other relevant factors, the most appropriate and equitable solution would be for the defender to be ordered to sell to the pursuer such property at such a price as would enable the pursuer to regain his property without prejudice to the defender, the court may grant decree accordingly.

(4)   Notwithstanding anything in the preceding rules, a court deciding an

action for unjustified enrichment may refuse to make an award, or may make a reduced award, or may grant decree subject to conditions, if it considers

(a)   that the person enriched, where he did not know, and could not reasonably be expected to know, that redress was due, changed his position (whether by spending money, disposing of property, consuming property or its fruits, abandoning rights, failing to exercise rights in time, or otherwise) in reliance on his enrichment, and it would for that reason be inequitable to make a full award or grant decree unconditionally

(b)   that the claimant was so culpable or negligent in causing the unjustified enrichment that it would be inequitable or contrary to public policy to make a full award or grant decree unconditionally

(c)   that the claimant would be unjustly enriched if a full award were made or if decree were granted unconditionally, or

(d)   that, for any other reason, it would be inequitable or contrary to public policy to make a full award or grant decree unconditionally.

11   Bars to proceedings

(1)(a)   An action for unjustified enrichment cannot be brought under these rules if there is, or was,

(i)   a special statutory or contractual procedure for dealing with the situation giving rise to the enrichment or

(ii)   another legal remedy for the enrichment

and if the claimant could reasonably have been expected to use that procedure or remedy.

(b)   Paragraph (a) does not apply if the enactment or contract providing the other procedure or remedy indicates expressly or impliedly that it is intended to be in addition to any remedy available under the general law on unjustified enrichment.

(c)   The availability of damages for loss does not preclude an action for redress of unjustified enrichment but, without prejudice to his right to claim damages for any consequential or other loss, the claimant cannot claim both redress of the other party's unjustified enrichment and damages for his corresponding loss.

(2)(a)   A person who, before a court decision in proceedings to which he was not a party, has made a payment or transfer which was apparently due under the law as it was commonly supposed to be at that time cannot bring an action for unjustified enrichment in respect of that payment or transfer on the ground that the decision has shown that the law was not as it was commonly supposed to be and that the payment or transfer was accordingly not in fact due.

(b)   In the preceding paragraph, 'decision' in any case where a decision is affirmed or restored on appeal means the decision so affirmed or restored and not the decision affirming or restoring it.

(3)   The bars mentioned in this rule are in addition to any bar resulting from the operation of the general law on personal bar.

12   Areas of law not affected

(1)   These rules replace the existing Scottish common law on unjustified enrichment, including

(a)   the common law on restitution in so far as it is part of the law on unjustified enrichment

(b)   the common law on repetition and recompense, and

(c)   the *condictio indebiti*; the *condictio causa data causa non secuta*; the *condictio ob turpem vel iniustam causam*; the *condictio ob non causam*; the *condictio sine causa*; the *actio in quantum locupletior factus est*; and the *actio de in rem verso* in so far as they form part of the existing law.

(2)   Nothing in these rules affects

(a)   any enacted law

(b)   the law on rights of relief of cautioners and co-obligants

(c)   the law on subrogation of insurers or those who have paid an indemnity

(d)   the law derived from the case of *Walker v Milne* (whereby loss suffered or expenditure incurred in the expectation of a contract may in certain circumstances be recovered)

(e)   the law on the rights of a defrauded person as against the creditors of the person who defrauded him

(f)   the law on the recovery by a person of the possession or control of his own property or of any other property to the possession or control of which he is entitled

(g)   the law on the special obligations of those in a fiduciary position

(h)   the law on general average or salvage

(i)   the law on *negotiorum gestio*.

13   Interpretation

(1)   In these rules, and in the schedule where applicable,

(a)   'court decree' includes the decision of any tribunal, quasi-judicial body or arbiter having jurisdiction

(b)   'enactment' includes subordinate legislation

(c)   'gift' includes a gratuitous waiver, renunciation or discharge of a right

(d)   'he' means he, she or it; 'him' means him, her or it; and 'his' means his, hers or its

(e)   'patrimonial rights' include rights flowing from the ownership of property, rights to protect confidential information and other rights having an economic value but do not include purely personal rights, such as the rights to life, liberty, bodily integrity or reputation, and

(f)   'property' means property of any kind, corporeal or incorporeal, heritable or moveable.

(2)   Any reference in these rules to a contract which has been terminated by rescission or frustration includes a reference to a contract which has been substantially terminated by rescission or frustration and a reference to a severable part of a contract which has been terminated by rescission or frustration.

SCHEDULE. REDRESS DUE

PART I

E acquires benefit directly from C

1.   This part of the schedule applies where the enriched person (E) has been enriched by acquiring a benefit directly from the claimant (C).

2(1)   Where the unjustified enrichment resulted from the acquisition of money by E from C, the redress due by E to C is the amount acquired, with interest from the time of acquisition.

(2)   Where the unjustified enrichment resulted from the acquisition of other property by E from C, the redress due by E to C is

(a)   if the property is corporeal and can be returned in substantially the same condition as it was in at the time of the acquisition, the return of the property in that condition along with a sum of money to take account of any benefit derived by E from the ownership, use or possession of the property and interest on that sum where appropriate

(b)   if the property is corporeal and cannot be returned in substantially the same condition as it was in at the time of the acquisition, the amount which it would have been reasonable to expect E to pay C for the property at the time of its acquisition by E, with interest on that amount from the time of acquisition

(c)   if the property is incorporeal, the return of the property where possible and, whether or not return is possible, a sum of money to take account of any benefit derived by E from the ownership of the property and interest on that sum where appropriate.

3. Where the unjustified enrichment resulted from the addition of value by C to E's property, the redress due by E to C is the amount which it would have been reasonable to expect E to pay C for his work or expenditure in adding that value, or the amount of value added (at the time when the addition was made), if less, with interest where appropriate.

4. Where the unjustified enrichment resulted from the discharge or reduction of any liability of E by means of a payment by C, the redress due by E to C is the amount paid, with interest from the date of payment.

5. Where the unjustified enrichment resulted from E's being saved a loss or expenditure by receiving C's services, the redress due by E to C is the amount which it would have been reasonable to expect E to pay for those services, or the amount of loss or expenditure saved, if less, with interest where appropriate.

6(1) Where the unjustified enrichment resulted from E's being saved a loss or expenditure by using or possessing C's property, the redress due by E to C is the amount which it would have been reasonable to expect E to pay for that use or possession, or the amount of loss or expenditure saved, if less, with interest where appropriate.

(2) Where the unjustified enrichment resulted from E's being saved a loss or expenditure by consuming C's property, the redress due by E to C is the amount which it would have been reasonable to expect E to pay for the property at the time of consumption, or the amount of loss or expenditure saved, if less, with interest where appropriate.

(3) Where the unjustified enrichment resulted from E's being saved a loss or expenditure by interfering with C's patrimonial rights in any other way, the redress due by E to C is the amount which it would have been reasonable to expect E to pay C, at the time of the interference, for permission to interfere with those rights in that way in the circumstances, or the amount of loss or expenditure saved, if less, with interest where appropriate.

7. Where the unjustified enrichment resulted from the acquisition of any other benefit by E from C, the redress due by E to C is the amount which it would have been reasonable to expect E to pay C for the benefit at the time or acquisition, or the amount of E's actual enrichment, if less, with interest where appropriate.

PART II

E acquires benefit from T at indirect expense of C

8. This part of the schedule applies where the enriched person (E) has been enriched indirectly at the expense of the claimant (C).

9. Where E has enriched himself by using or disposing of C's property, or otherwise interfering with C's patrimonial rights, in order to obtain money or money's worth from a third party (T) the redress due by E to C is the amount which it would have been reasonable for E to pay C at the time of the use, disposal or interference for permission to use or dispose of C's property or to interfere with his rights in that way, or the amount of E's actual enrichment attributable to the use, disposal or interference, if less, with interest where appropriate.

10. Where E has been indirectly enriched at the expense of C as a result of the transfer of a benefit from a third party (T) in the circumstances covered by rule 8(2) (transfer of benefit arising from unjustified enrichment to person taking otherwise than in good faith and for value) T is treated as if he had been acting as E's agent and accordingly the redress due by E to C is the same, and is due on the same conditions, as it would have been if E had acquired the benefit directly from C.

11.   Where E has been indirectly enriched at the expense of C in the circumstances covered by rule 8(3) (transfers from trusts or executries) the redress due by E to C is

(1)   where C is a creditor claiming under rule 8(3)(a) the amount of the debt due to C out of the estate or the amount of E's enrichment out of the estate, whichever is the less, with interest where appropriate

(2)   where C is a true beneficiary claiming under rule 8(3)(b), and the benefit due to him out of the estate and received by E was a special legacy, the transfer of the subject matter of the legacy along with a sum to take account of any benefit derived by E from its use or possession or, if the subject matter of the legacy cannot be transferred in substantially the same condition as it was in when acquired by E, an amount representing its value when acquired by E, with interest from that date

(3)   where C is a true beneficiary claiming under rule 8(3)(b), and the benefit due to him out of the estate and received by E was not a special legacy, the amount of the benefit due to C out of the estate or the amount of E's unjustified enrichment out of the estate, whichever is the less, with interest where appropriate.

PART III

General

12.   Any reference in this schedule to the return of property includes a reference to a return by reconveyance or by any other means by which ownership can be restored to the other person.

13.   For the purposes of paragraph 2(2) corporeal property acquired by the enriched person by accession or specification, or any analogous rule whereby one person may acquire another's property when it becomes attached to or mixed with his own, is treated as property which cannot be returned in substantially the same condition as it was in at the time of acquisition.

14.   Where property is to be returned or transferred to the claimant by the enriched person under these rules, the expenses of the return or transfer are to be borne

(1)   by the claimant if the enrichment was in good faith, or

(2)   by the enriched person if the enrichment was in bad faith unless a court dealing with the claim orders otherwise.

15.   In assessing what it would have been reasonable for E to pay C for any interference with C's rights or for permission to interfere with those rights regard may be had to any factors which would have made C reluctant or unwilling to permit the interference.

UNIDROIT PRINCIPLES FOR INTERNATIONAL COMMERCIAL CONTRACTS 2010*

PREAMBLE

(Purpose of the Principles)
These Principles set forth general rules for international commercial contracts.

They shall be applied when the parties have agreed that their contract be governed by them.†)

They may be applied when the parties have agreed that their contract be governed by general principles of law, the *lex mercatoria* or the like.

They may be applied when the parties have not chosen any law to govern their contract.

They may be used to interpret or supplement international uniform law instruments.

They may be used to interpret or supplement domestic law.

They may serve as a model for national and international legislators.

CHAPTER 1. GENERAL PROVISIONS

Article 1.1   Freedom of contract
The parties are free to enter into a contract and to determine its content.

Article 1.2   No form required
Nothing in these Principles requires a contract, statement or any other act to be made in or evidenced by a particular form. It may be proved by any means, including witnesses.

Article 1.3   Binding character of contract
A contract validly entered into is binding upon the parties. It can only be modified or terminated in accordance with its terms or by agreement or as otherwise provided in these Principles.

Article 1.4   Mandatory rules
Nothing in these Principles shall restrict the application of mandatory rules, whether of national, international or supranational origin, which are applicable in accordance with the relevant rules of private international law.

Article 1.5   Exclusion or modification by the parties
The parties may exclude the application of these Principles or derogate from or vary the effect of any of their provisions, except as otherwise provided in the Principles.

---

*The reader is reminded that the complete version of the Unidroit Principles contains not only the black-letter rules reproduced hereunder, but also detailed comments on each article and, where appropriate, illustrations. The complete version can be obtained from Unidroit (see http://www.unidroit.org). For international case law relating to the Unidroit Principles see the Unilex database at http://www.unilex.info.

† Parties wishing to provide that their agreement be governed by the Principles might use the following words, adding any desired exceptions or modifications: 'This contract shall be governed by the Unidroit Principles (2010) [except as to Articles . . .]'.

Parties wishing to provide in addition for the application of the law of a particular jurisdiction might use the following words: 'This contract shall be governed by the Unidroit Principles (2010) [except as to Articles . . .]', supplemented when necessary by the law of [jurisdiction X].

Article 1.6 Interpretation and supplementation of the Principles

(1) In the interpretation of these Principles, regard is to be had to their international character and to their purposes including the need to promote uniformity in their application.

(2) Issues within the scope of these Principles but not expressly settled by them are as far as possible to be settled in accordance with their underlying general principles.

Article 1.7 Good faith and fair dealing

(1) Each party must act in accordance with good faith and fair dealing in international trade.

(2) The parties may not exclude or limit this duty.

Article 1.8 Inconsistent behaviour

A party cannot act inconsistently with an understanding it has caused the other party to have and upon which that other party reasonably has acted in reliance to its detriment.

Article 1.9 Usages and practices

(1) The parties are bound by any usage to which they have agreed and by any practices which they have established between themselves.

(2) The parties are bound by a usage that is widely known to and regularly observed in international trade by parties in the particular trade concerned except where the application of such a usage would be unreasonable.

Article 1.10 Notice

(1) Where notice is required it may be given by any means appropriate to the circumstances.

(2) A notice is effective when it reaches the person to whom it is given.

(3) For the purpose of paragraph (2) a notice 'reaches' a person when given to that person orally or delivered at that person's place of business or mailing address.

(4) For the purpose of this article 'notice' includes a declaration, demand, request or any other communication of intention.

Article 1.11 Definitions

In these Principles

– 'court' includes an arbitral tribunal;

– where a party has more than one place of business the relevant 'place of business' is that which has the closest relationship to the contract and its performance, having regard to the circumstances known to or contemplated by the parties at any time before or at the conclusion of the contract;

– 'obligor' refers to the party who is to perform an obligation and 'obligee' refers to the party who is entitled to performance of that obligation.

– 'writing' means any mode of communication that preserves a record of the information contained therein and is capable of being reproduced in tangible form.

Article 1.12 Computation of time set by parties

(1) Official holidays or non-business days occurring during a period set by parties for an act to be performed are included in calculating the period.

(2) However, if the last day of the period is an official holiday or a non-business day at the place of business of the party to perform the act, the period is extended until the first business day which follows, unless the circumstances indicate otherwise.

(3) The relevant time zone is that of the place of business of the party setting the time, unless the circumstances indicate otherwise.

CHAPTER 2 — FORMATION AND AUTHORITY OF AGENTS

Section 1: Formation

Article 2.1.1   Manner of formation
A contract may be concluded either by the acceptance of an offer or by conduct of the parties that is sufficient to show agreement.

Article 2.1.2   Definition of offer
A proposal for concluding a contract constitutes an offer if it is sufficiently definite and indicates the intention of the offeror to be bound in case of acceptance.

Article 2.1.3   Withdrawal of offer
(1)   An offer becomes effective when it reaches the offeree.

(2)   An offer, even if it is irrevocable, may be withdrawn if the withdrawal reaches the offeree before or at the same time as the offer.

Article 2.1.4   Revocation of offer
(1)   Until a contract is concluded an offer may be revoked if the revocation reaches the offeree before it has dispatched an acceptance.

(2)   However, an offer cannot be revoked

(a)   if it indicates, whether by stating a fixed time for acceptance or otherwise, that it is irrevocable; or

(b)   if it was reasonable for the offeree to rely on the offer as being irrevocable and the offeree has acted in reliance on the offer.

Article 2.1.5   Rejection of offer
An offer is terminated when a rejection reaches the offeror.

Article 2.1.6   Mode of acceptance
(1)   A statement made by or other conduct of the offeree indicating assent to an offer is an acceptance. Silence or inactivity does not in itself amount to acceptance.

(2)   An acceptance of an offer becomes effective when the indication of assent reaches the offeror.

(3)   However, if, by virtue of the offer or as a result of practices which the parties have established between themselves or of usage, the offeree may indicate assent by performing an act without notice to the offeror, the acceptance is effective when the act is performed.

Article 2.1.7   Time of acceptance
An offer must be accepted within the time the offeror has fixed or, if no time is fixed, within a reasonable time having regard to the circumstances, including the rapidity of the means of communication employed by the offeror. An oral offer must be accepted immediately unless the circumstances indicate otherwise.

Article 2.1.8   Acceptance within a fixed period of time
A period of acceptance fixed by the offeror begins to run from the time that the offer is dispatched. A time indicated in the offer is deemed to be the time of dispatch unless the circumstances indicate otherwise.

Article 2.1.9   Late acceptance. Delay in transmission
(1)   A late acceptance is nevertheless effective as an acceptance if without undue delay the offeror so informs the offeree or gives notice to that effect.

(2)   If a communication containing a late acceptance shows that it has been sent in such circumstances that if its transmission had been normal it would have reached the offeror in due time, the late acceptance is effective as an acceptance unless, without undue delay, the offeror informs the offeree that it considers the offer as having lapsed.

Article 2.1.10   Withdrawal of acceptance
An acceptance may be withdrawn if the withdrawal reaches the offeror before or at the same time as the acceptance would have become effective.

Article 2.1.11   Modified acceptance
(1)   A reply to an offer which purports to be an acceptance but contains additions, limitations or other modifications is a rejection of the offer and constitutes a counter-offer.

(2)   However, a reply to an offer which purports to be an acceptance but contains additional or different terms which do not materially alter the terms of the offer constitutes an acceptance, unless the offeror, without undue delay, objects to the discrepancy. If the offeror does not object, the terms of the contract are the terms of the offer with the modifications contained in the acceptance.

Article 2.1.12   Writings in confirmation
If a writing which is sent within a reasonable time after the conclusion of the contract and which purports to be a confirmation of the contract contains additional or different terms, such terms become part of the contract, unless they materially alter the contract or the recipient, without undue delay, objects to the discrepancy.

Article 2.1.13   Conclusion of contract dependent on agreement on specific matters or in particular form
Where in the course of negotiations one of the parties insists that the contract is not concluded until there is agreement on specific matters or in a particular form, no contract is concluded before agreement is reached on those matters or in that form.

Article 2.1.14   Contract with terms deliberately left open
(1)   If the parties intend to conclude a contract, the fact that they intentionally leave a term to be agreed upon in further negotiations or to be determined by a third person does not prevent a contract from coming into existence.

(2)   The existence of the contract is not affected by the fact that subsequently
    (a)   the parties reach no agreement on the term; or
    (b)   the third person does not determine the term,
provided that there is an alternative means of rendering the term definite that is reasonable in the circumstances, having regard to the intention of the parties.

Article 2.1.15   Negotiations in bad faith
(1)   A party is free to negotiate and is not liable for failure to reach an agreement.

(2)   However, a party who negotiates or breaks off negotiations in bad faith is liable for the losses caused to the other party.

(3)   It is bad faith, in particular, for a party to enter into or continue negotiations when intending not to reach an agreement with the other party.

Article 2.1.16   Duty of confidentiality
Where information is given as confidential by one party in the course of negotiations, the other party is under a duty not to disclose that information or to use it improperly for its own purposes, whether or not a contract is subsequently concluded. Where appropriate, the remedy for breach of that duty may include compensation based on the benefit received by the other party.

Article 2.1.17   Merger clauses
A contract in writing which contains a clause indicating that the writing completely embodies the terms on which the parties have agreed cannot be contradicted or supplemented by evidence of prior statements or agreements. However, such statements or agreements may be used to interpret the writing.

Article 2.1.18   Modification in a particular form
A contract in writing which contains a clause requiring any modification or termi-

nation by agreement to be in a particular form may not be otherwise modified or terminated. However, a party may be precluded by its conduct from asserting such a clause to the extent that the other party has reasonably acted in reliance on that conduct.

Article 2.1.19   Contracting under standard terms

(1)   Where one party or both parties use standard terms in concluding a contract, the general rules on formation apply, subject to Articles 2.1.20–2.1.22.

(2)   Standard terms are provisions which are prepared in advance for general and repeated use by one party and which are actually used without negotiation with the other party.

Article 2.1.20   Surprising terms

(1)   No term contained in standard terms which is of such a character that the other party could not reasonably have expected it, is effective unless it has been expressly accepted by that party.

(2)   In determining whether a term is of such a character regard shall be had to its content, language and presentation.

Article 2.1.21   Conflict between standard terms and non-standard terms

In case of conflict between a standard term and a term which is not a standard term the latter prevails.

Article 2.1.22   Battle of forms

Where both parties use standard terms and reach agreement except on those terms, a contract is concluded on the basis of the agreed terms and of any standard terms which are common in substance unless one party clearly indicates in advance, or later and without undue delay informs the other party, that it does not intend to be bound by such a contract.

Section 2: Authority of Agents

Article 2.2.1   Scope of the Section

(1)   This Section governs the authority of a person ('the agent'), to affect the legal relations of another person ('the principal'), by or with respect to a contract with a third party, whether the agent acts in its own name or in that of the principal.

(2)   It governs only the relations between the principal or the agent on the one hand, and the third party on the other.

(3)   It does not govern an agent's authority conferred by law or the authority of an agent appointed by a public or judicial authority.

Article 2.2.2   Establishment and scope of the authority of the agent

(1)   The principal's grant of authority to an agent may be express or implied.

(2)   The agent has authority to perform all acts necessary in the circumstances to achieve the purposes for which the authority was granted.

Article 2.2.3   Agency disclosed

(1)   Where an agent acts within the scope of its authority and the third party knew or ought to have known that the agent was acting as an agent, the acts of the agent shall directly affect the legal relations between the principal and the third party and no legal relation is created between the agent and the third party.

(2)   However, the acts of the agent shall affect only the relations between the agent and the third party, where the agent with the consent of the principal undertakes to become the party to the contract.

Article 2.2.4   Agency undisclosed

(1)   Where an agent acts within the scope of its authority and the third party neither knew nor ought to have known that the agent was acting as an agent, the

acts of the agent shall affect only the relations between the agent and the third party.

(2)   However, where such an agent, when contracting with the third party on behalf of a business, represents itself to be the owner of that business, the third party, upon discovery of the real owner of the business, may exercise also against the latter the rights it has against the agent.

Article 2.2.5   Agent acting without or exceeding its authority

(1)   Where an agent acts without authority or exceeds its authority, its acts do not affect the legal relations between the principal and the third party.

(2)   However, where the principal causes the third party reasonably to believe that the agent has authority to act on behalf of the principal and that the agent is acting within the scope of that authority, the principal may not invoke against the third party the lack of authority of the agent.

Article 2.2.6   Liability of agent acting without or exceeding its authority

(1)   An agent that acts without authority or exceeds its authority is, failing ratification by the principal, liable for damages that will place the third party in the same position as if the agent had acted with authority and not exceeded its authority.

(2)   However, the agent is not liable if the third party knew or ought to have known that the agent had no authority or was exceeding its authority.

Article 2.2.7   Conflict of interests

(1)   If a contract concluded by an agent involves the agent in a conflict of interests with the principal of which the third party knew or ought to have known, the principal may avoid the contract. The right to avoid is subject to Articles 3.2.9 and 3.2.11 to 3.2.15.

(2)   However, the principal may not avoid the contract
  (a)   if the principal had consented to, or knew or ought to have known of, the agent's involvement in the conflict of interests; or
  (b)   if the agent had disclosed the conflict of interests to the principal and the latter had not objected within a reasonable time.

Article 2.2.8   Sub-agency

An agent has implied authority to appoint a sub-agent to perform acts which it is not reasonable to expect the agent to perform itself. The rules of this Section apply to the sub-agency.

Article 2.2.9   Ratification

(1)   An act by an agent that acts without authority or exceeds its authority may be ratified by the principal. On ratification the act produces the same effects as if it had initially been carried out with authority.

(2)   The third party may by notice to the principal specify a reasonable period of time for ratification. If the principal does not ratify within that period of time it can no longer do so.

(3)   If, at the time of the agent's act, the third party neither knew nor ought to have known of the lack of authority, it may, at any time before ratification, by notice to the principal indicate its refusal to become bound by a ratification.

Article 2.2.10   Termination of authority

(1)   Termination of authority is not effective in relation to the third party unless the third party knew or ought to have known of it.

(2)   Notwithstanding the termination of its authority, an agent remains authorised to perform the acts that are necessary to prevent harm to the principal's interests.

CHAPTER 3 — VALIDITY

Section 1: General Provisions

Article 3.1.1   Matters not covered
This Chapter does not deal with lack of capacity.

Article 3.1.2   Validity of mere agreement
A contract is concluded, modified or terminated by the mere agreement of the parties, without any further requirement.

Article 3.1.3   Initial impossibility
(1)   The mere fact that at the time of the conclusion of the contract the performance of the obligation assumed was impossible does not affect the validity of the contract.

(2)   The mere fact that at the time of the conclusion of the contract a party was not entitled to dispose of the assets to which the contract relates does not affect the validity of the contract.

Article 3.1.4   Mandatory character of the provision
The provisions on fraud, threat, gross disparity and illegality contained in this Chapter are mandatory.

Section 2: Grounds for Avoidance

Article 3.2.1   Definition of mistake
Mistake is an erroneous assumption relating to facts or to law existing when the contract was concluded.

Article 3.2.2   Relevant mistake
(1)   A party may only avoid the contract for mistake if, when the contract was concluded, the mistake was of such importance that a reasonable person in the same situation as the party in error would only have concluded the contract on materially different terms or would not have concluded it at all if the true state of affairs had been known, and

(a)   the other party made the same mistake, or caused the mistake, or knew or ought to have known of the mistake and it was contrary to reasonable commercial standards of fair dealing to leave the mistaken party in error; or

(b)   the other party had not at the time of avoidance reasonably acted in reliance on the contract.

(2)   However, a party may not avoid the contract if
(a)   it was grossly negligent in committing the mistake; or

(b)   the mistake relates to a matter in regard to which the risk of mistake was assumed or, having regard to the circumstances, should be borne by the mistaken party.

Article 3.2.3   Error in expression or transmission
An error occurring in the expression or transmission of a declaration is considered to be a mistake of the person from whom the declaration emanated.

Article 3.2.4   Remedies for non-performance
A party is not entitled to avoid the contract on the ground of mistake if the circumstances on which that party relies afford, or could have afforded, a remedy for non-performance.

Article 3.2.5   Fraud
A party may avoid the contract when it has been led to conclude the contract by the other party's fraudulent representation, including language or practices, or fraudulent non-disclosure of circumstances which, according to reasonable commercial standards of fair dealing, the latter party should have disclosed.

Article 3.2.6 Threat

A party may avoid the contract when it has been led to conclude the contract by the other party's unjustified threat which, having regard to the circumstances, is so imminent and serious as to leave the first party no reasonable alternative. In particular, a threat is unjustified if the act or omission with which a party has been threatened is wrongful in itself, or it is wrongful to use it as a means to obtain the conclusion of the contract.

Article 3.2.7 Gross disparity

(1) A party may avoid the contract or an individual term of it if, at the time of the conclusion of the contract, the contract or term unjustifiably gave the other party an excessive advantage. Regard is to be had, among other factors, to

(a) the fact that the other party has taken unfair advantage of the first party's dependence, economic distress or urgent needs, or of its improvidence, ignorance, inexperience or lack of bargaining skill, and

(b) the nature and purpose of the contract.

(2) Upon the request of the party entitled to avoidance, a court may adapt the contract or term in order to make it accord with reasonable commercial standards of fair dealing.

(3) A court may also adapt the contract or term upon the request of the party receiving notice of avoidance, provided that that party informs the other party of its request promptly after receiving such notice and before the other party has reasonably acted in reliance on it. The provisions of Article 3.2.10(2) apply accordingly.

Article 3.2.8 Third persons

(1) Where fraud, threat, gross disparity or a party's mistake is imputable to, or is known or ought to be known by, a third person for whose acts the other party is responsible, the contract may be avoided under the same conditions as if the behaviour or knowledge had been that of the party itself.

(2) Where fraud, threat or gross disparity is imputable to a third person for whose acts the other party is not responsible, the contract may be avoided if that party knew or ought to have known of the fraud, threat or disparity, or has not at the time of avoidance reasonably acted in reliance on the contract.

Article 3.2.9 Confirmation

If the party entitled to avoid the contract expressly or impliedly confirms the contract after the period of time for giving notice of avoidance has begun to run, avoidance of the contract is excluded.

Article 3.2.10 Loss of right to avoid

(1) If a party is entitled to avoid the contract for mistake but the other party declares itself willing to perform or performs the contract as it was understood by the party entitled to avoidance, the contract is considered to have been concluded as the latter party understood it. The other party must make such a declaration or render such performance promptly after having been informed of the manner in which the party entitled to avoidance had understood the contract and before that party has reasonably acted in reliance on a notice of avoidance.

(2) After such a declaration or performance the right to avoidance is lost and any earlier notice of avoidance is ineffective.

Article 3.2.11 Notice of avoidance

The right of a party to avoid the contract is exercised by notice to the other party.

Article 3.2.12 Time limits

(1) Notice of avoidance shall be given within a reasonable time, having regard to the circumstances, after the avoiding party knew or could not have been unaware of the relevant facts or became capable of acting freely.

(2) Where an individual term of the contract may be avoided by a party under

Article 3.2.7, the period of time for giving notice of avoidance begins to run when that term is asserted by the other party.

Article 3.2.13 Partial avoidance

Where a ground of avoidance affects only individual terms of the contract, the effect of avoidance is limited to those terms unless, having regard to the circumstances, it is unreasonable to uphold the remaining contract.

Article 3.2.14 Retroactive effect of avoidance

Avoidance takes effect retroactively.

Article 3.2.15 Restitution

(1) On avoidance either party may claim restitution of whatever it has supplied under the contract, or the part of it avoided, provided that the party concurrently makes restitution of whatever it has received under the contract, or the part of it avoided.

(2) If restitution in kind is not possible or appropriate, an allowance has to be made in money whenever reasonable.

(3) The recipient of the performance does not have to make an allowance in money if the impossibility to make restitution in kind is attributable to the other party.

(4) Compensation may be claimed for expenses reasonably required to preserve or maintain the performance received.

Article 3.2.16 Damages

Irrespective of whether or not the contract has been avoided, the party who knew or ought to have known of the ground for avoidance is liable for damages so as to put the other party in the same position in which it would have been if it had not concluded the contract.

Article 3.2.17 Unilateral declarations

The provisions of this Chapter apply with appropriate adaptations to any communication of intention addressed by one party to the other.

Section 3: Illegality

Article 3.3.1 Contracts infringing mandatory rules

(1) Where a contract infringes a mandatory rule, whether of national, international or supranational origin, applicable under Article 1.4 of these Principles, the effects of that infringement upon the contract are the effects, if any, expressly prescribed by that mandatory rule.

(2) Where the mandatory rule does not expressly prescribe the effects of an infringement upon a contract, the parties have the right to exercise such remedies under the contract as in the circumstances are reasonable.

(3) In determining what is reasonable regard is to be had in particular to:

  (a) the purpose of the rule which has been infringed;
  (b) the category of persons for whose protection the rule exists;
  (c) any sanction that may be imposed under the rule infringed;
  (d) the seriousness of the infringement;
  (e) whether one or both parties knew or ought to have known of the infringement;
  (f) whether the performance of the contract necessitates the infringement; and
  (g) the parties' reasonable expectations.

Article 3.3.2 Restitution

(1) Where there has been performance under a contract infringing a mandatory rule under Article 3.3.1, restitution may be granted where this would be reasonable in the circumstances.

(2) In determining what is reasonable, regard is to be had, with the appropriate adaptations, to the criteria referred to in Article 3.3.1(3).

(3) If restitution is granted, the rules set out in Article 3.2.15 apply with appropriate adaptations.

CHAPTER 4 — INTERPRETATION

Article 4.1 Intention of the parties
(1) A contract shall be interpreted according to the common intention of the parties.

(2) If such an intention cannot be established, the contract shall be interpreted according to the meaning that reasonable persons of the same kind as the parties would give to it in the same circumstances.

Article 4.2 Interpretation of statements and other conduct
(1) The statements and other conduct of a party shall be interpreted according to that party's intention if the other party knew or could not have been unaware of that intention.

(2) If the preceding paragraph is not applicable, such statements and other conduct shall be interpreted according to the meaning that a reasonable person of the same kind as the other party would give to it in the same circumstances.

Article 4.3 Relevant circumstances
In applying Articles 4.1 and 4.2, regard shall be had to all the circumstances, including
  (a) preliminary negotiations between the parties;
  (b) practices which the parties have established between themselves;
  (c) the conduct of the parties subsequent to the conclusion of the contract;
  (d) the nature and purpose of the contract;
  (e) the meaning commonly given to terms and expressions in the trade concerned;
  (f) usages.

Article 4.4 Reference to contract or statement as a whole
Terms and expressions shall be interpreted in the light of the whole contract or statement in which they appear.

Article 4.5 All terms to be given effect
Contract terms shall be interpreted so as to give effect to all the terms rather than to deprive some of them of effect.

Article 4.6 Contra proferentem rule
If contract terms supplied by one party are unclear, an interpretation against that party is preferred.

Article 4.7 Linguistic discrepancies
Where a contract is drawn up in two or more language versions which are equally authoritative there is, in case of discrepancy between the versions, a preference for the interpretation according to a version in which the contract was originally drawn up.

Article 4.8 Supplying an omitted term
(1) Where the parties to a contract have not agreed with respect to a term which is important for a determination of their rights and duties, a term which is appropriate in the circumstances shall be supplied.

(2) In determining what is an appropriate term regard shall be had, among other factors, to
  (a) the intention of the parties;
  (b) the nature and purpose of the contract;
  (c) good faith and fair dealing;
  (d) reasonableness.

CHAPTER 5 — CONTENT AND THIRD PARTY RIGHTS

Section 1: Content

Article 5.1.1   Express and implied obligations
The contractual obligations of the parties may be express or implied.

Article 5.1.2   Implied obligations
Implied obligations stem from
    (a)   the nature and purpose of the contract;
    (b)   practices established between the parties and usages;
    (c)   good faith and fair dealing;
    (d)   reasonableness.

Article 5.1.3   Co-operation between the parties
Each party shall co-operate with the other party when such co-operation may reasonably be expected for the performance of that party's obligations.

Article 5.1.4   Duty to achieve a specific result. Duty of best efforts
(1)   To the extent that an obligation of a party involves a duty to achieve a specific result, that party is bound to achieve that result.
(2)   To the extent that an obligation of a party involves a duty of best efforts in the performance of an activity, that party is bound to make such efforts as would be made by a reasonable person of the same kind in the same circumstances.

Article 5.1.5   Determination of kind of duty involved
In determining the extent to which an obligation of a party involves a duty of best efforts in the performance of an activity or a duty to achieve a specific result, regard shall be had, among other factors, to
    (a)   the way in which the obligation is expressed in the contract;
    (b)   the contractual price and other terms of the contract;
    (c)   the degree of risk normally involved in achieving the expected result;
    (d)   the ability of the other party to influence the performance of the obligation.

Article 5.1.6   Determination of quality of performance
Where the quality of performance is neither fixed by, nor determinable from, the contract a party is bound to render a performance of a quality that is reasonable and not less than average in the circumstances.

Article 5.1.7   Price determination
(1)   Where a contract does not fix or make provision for determining the price, the parties are considered, in the absence of any indication to the contrary, to have made reference to the price generally charged at the time of the conclusion of the contract for such performance in comparable circumstances in the trade concerned or, if no such price is available, to a reasonable price.
(2)   Where the price is to be determined by one party and that determination is manifestly unreasonable, a reasonable price shall be substituted notwithstanding any contract term to the contrary.
(3)   Where the price is to be fixed by a third person, and that person cannot or will not do so, the price shall be a reasonable price.
(4)   Where the price is to be fixed by reference to factors which do not exist or have ceased to exist or to be accessible, the nearest equivalent factor shall be treated as a substitute.

Article 5.1.8   Contract for an indefinite period
A contract for an indefinite period may be ended by either party by giving notice a reasonable time in advance.

Article 5.1.9   Release by agreement

(1)   An obligee may release its right by agreement with the obligor.

(2)   An offer to release a right gratuitously shall be deemed accepted if the obligor does not reject the offer without delay after having become aware of it.

Section 2: Third Party Rights

Article 5.2.1   Contracts in favour of third parties

(1)   The parties (the 'promisor' and the 'promisee') may confer by express or implied agreement a right on a third party (the 'beneficiary').

(2)   The existence and content of the beneficiary's right against the promisor are determined by the agreement of the parties and are subject to any conditions or other limitations under the agreement.

Article 5.2.2   Third party identifiable

The beneficiary must be identifiable with adequate certainty by the contract but need not be in existence at the time the contract is made.

Article 5.2.3   Exclusion and limitation clauses

The conferment of rights in the beneficiary includes the right to invoke a clause in the contract which excludes or limits the liability of the beneficiary.

Article 5.2.4   Defences

The promisor may assert against the beneficiary all defences which the promisor could assert against the promisee.

Article 5.2.5   Revocation

The parties may modify or revoke the rights conferred by the contract on the beneficiary until the beneficiary has accepted them or reasonably acted in reliance on them.

Article 5.2.6   Renunciation

The beneficiary may renounce a right conferred on it.

Section 3: Conditions

Article 5.3.1   Types of condition

A contract or a contractual obligation may be made conditional upon the occurrence of a future uncertain event, so that the contract or the contractual obligation only takes effect if the event occurs (suspensive condition) or comes to an end if the event occurs (resolutive condition).

Article 5.3.2   Effect of conditions

Unless the parties otherwise agree:

(a)   the relevant contract or contractual obligation takes effect upon fulfilment of a suspensive condition;

(b)   the relevant contract or contractual obligation comes to an end upon fulfilment of a resolutive condition.

Article 5.3.3   Interference with conditions

(1)   If fulfilment of a condition is prevented by a party, contrary to the duty of good faith and fair dealing or the duty of co-operation, that party may not rely on the non-fulfilment of the condition.

(2)   If fulfilment of a condition is brought about by a party, contrary to the duty of good faith and fair dealing or the duty of co-operation, that party may not rely on the fulfilment of the condition

Article 5.3.4   Duty to preserve rights

Pending fulfilment of a condition, a party may not, contrary to the duty to act in accordance with good faith and fair dealing, act so as to prejudice the other party's rights in case of fulfilment of the condition.

Article 5.3.5   Restitution in case of fulfilment of a resolutive condition
(1)   On fulfilment of a resolutive condition, the rules on restitution set out in Articles 7.3.6 and 7.3.7 apply with appropriate adaptations.

(2)   If the parties have agreed that the resolutive condition is to operate retroactively, the rules on restitution set out in Article 3.2.15 apply with appropriate adaptations.

CHAPTER 6 — PERFORMANCE

Section 1: Performance in General

Article 6.1.1   Time of performance
A party must perform its obligations:

(a)   if a time is fixed by or determinable from the contract, at that time;

(b)   if a period of time is fixed by or determinable from the contract, at any time within that period unless circumstances indicate that the other party is to choose a time;

(c)   in any other case, within a reasonable time after the conclusion of the contract.

Article 6.1.2   Performance at one time or in instalments
In cases under Article 6.1.1(b) or (c), a party must perform its obligations at one time if that performance can be rendered at one time and the circumstances do not indicate otherwise.

Article 6.1.3   Partial performance
(1)   The obligee may reject an offer to perform in part at the time performance is due, whether or not such offer is coupled with an assurance as to the balance of the performance, unless the obligee has no legitimate interest in so doing.

(2)   Additional expenses caused to the obligee by partial performance are to be borne by the obligor without prejudice to any other remedy.

Article 6.1.4   Order of performance
(1)   To the extent that the performances of the parties can be rendered simultaneously, the parties are bound to render them simultaneously unless the circumstances indicate otherwise.

(2)   To the extent that the performance of only one party requires a period of time, that party is bound to render its performance first, unless the circumstances indicate otherwise.

Article 6.1.5   Earlier performance
(1)   The obligee may reject an earlier performance unless it has no legitimate interest in so doing.

(2)   Acceptance by a party of an earlier performance does not affect the time for the performance of its own obligations if that time has been fixed irrespective of the performance of the other party's obligations.

(3)   Additional expenses caused to the obligee by earlier performance are to be borne by the obligor, without prejudice to any other remedy.

Article 6.1.6   Place of performance
(1)   If the place of performance is neither fixed by, nor determinable from, the contract, a party is to perform:

(a)   a monetary obligation, at the obligee's place of business;

(b)   any other obligation, at its own place of business.

(2)   A party must bear any increase in the expenses incidental to performance which is caused by a change in its place of business subsequent to the conclusion of the contract.

Article 6.1.7   Payment by cheque or other instrument

(1)   Payment may be made in any form used in the ordinary course of business at the place for payment.

(2)   However, an obligee who accepts, either by virtue of paragraph (1) or voluntarily, a cheque, any other order to pay or a promise to pay, is presumed to do so only on condition that it will be honoured.

Article 6.1.8   Payment by funds transfer

(1)   Unless the obligee has indicated a particular account, payment may be made by a transfer to any of the financial institutions in which the obligee has made it known that it has an account.

(2)   In case of payment by a transfer the obligation of the obligor is discharged when the transfer to the obligee's financial institution becomes effective.

Article 6.1.9   Currency of payment

(1)   If a monetary obligation is expressed in a currency other than that of the place for payment, it may be paid by the obligor in the currency of the place for payment unless

 (a)   that currency is not freely convertible; or

 (b)   the parties have agreed that payment should be made only in the currency in which the monetary obligation is expressed.

(2)   If it is impossible for the obligor to make payment in the currency in which the monetary obligation is expressed, the obligee may require payment in the currency of the place for payment, even in the case referred to in paragraph (1)(b).

(3)   Payment in the currency of the place for payment is to be made according to the applicable rate of exchange prevailing there when payment is due.

(4)   However, if the obligor has not paid at the time when payment is due, the obligee may require payment according to the applicable rate of exchange prevailing either when payment is due or at the time of actual payment.

Article 6.1.10   Currency not expressed

Where a monetary obligation is not expressed in a particular currency, payment must be made in the currency of the place where payment is to be made.

Article 6.1.11   Costs of performance

Each party shall bear the costs of performance of its obligations.

Article 6.1.12   Imputation of payments

(1)   An obligor owing several monetary obligations to the same obligee may specify at the time of payment the debt to which it intends the payment to be applied. However, the payment discharges first any expenses, then interest due and finally the principal.

(2)   If the obligor makes no such specification, the obligee may, within a reasonable time after payment, declare to the obligor the obligation to which it imputes the payment, provided that the obligation is due and undisputed.

(3)   In the absence of imputation under paragraphs (1) or (2), payment is imputed to that obligation which satisfies one of the following criteria in the order indicated:

 (a)   an obligation which is due or which is the first to fall due;

 (b)   the obligation for which the obligee has least security;

 (c)   the obligation which is the most burdensome for the obligor;

 (d)   the obligation which has arisen first.

If none of the preceding criteria applies, payment is imputed to all the obligations proportionally.

Article 6.1.13   Imputation of non-monetary obligations

Article 6.1.12 applies with appropriate adaptations to the imputation of performance of non-monetary obligations.

Article 6.1.14 Application for public permission

Where the law of a State requires a public permission affecting the validity of the contract or its performance and neither that law nor the circumstances indicate otherwise

(a) if only one party has its place of business in that State, that party shall take the measures necessary to obtain the permission;

(b) in any other case the party whose performance requires permission shall take the necessary measures.

Article 6.1.15 Procedure in applying for permission

(1) The party required to take the measures necessary to obtain the permission shall do so without undue delay and shall bear any expenses incurred.

(2) That party shall whenever appropriate give the other party notice of the grant or refusal of such permission without undue delay.

Article 6.1.16 Permission neither granted nor refused

(1) If, notwithstanding the fact that the party responsible has taken all measures required, permission is neither granted nor refused within an agreed period or, where no period has been agreed, within a reasonable time from the conclusion of the contract, either party is entitled to terminate the contract.

(2) Where the permission affects some terms only, paragraph (1) does not apply if, having regard to the circumstances, it is reasonable to uphold the remaining contract even if the permission is refused.

Article 6.1.17 Permission refused

(1) The refusal of a permission affecting the validity of the contract renders the contract void. If the refusal affects the validity of some terms only, only such terms are void if, having regard to the circumstances, it is reasonable to uphold the remaining contract.

(2) Where the refusal of a permission renders the performance of the contract impossible in whole or in part, the rules on non-performance apply.

Section 2: Hardship

Article 6.2.1 Contract to be observed

Where the performance of a contract becomes more onerous for one of the parties, that party is nevertheless bound to perform its obligations subject to the following provisions on hardship.

Article 6.2.2 Definition of hardship

There is hardship where the occurrence of events fundamentally alters the equilibrium of the contract either because the cost of a party's performance has increased or because the value of the performance a party receives has diminished, and

(a) the events occur or become known to the disadvantaged party after the conclusion of the contract;

(b) the events could not reasonably have been taken into account by the disadvantaged party at the time of the conclusion of the contract;

(c) the events are beyond the control of the disadvantaged party; and

(d) the risk of the events was not assumed by the disadvantaged party.

Article 6.2.3 Effects of hardship

(1) In case of hardship the disadvantaged party is entitled to request renegotiations. The request shall be made without undue delay and shall indicate the grounds on which it is based.

(2) The request for renegotiation does not in itself entitle the disadvantaged party to withhold performance.

(3) Upon failure to reach agreement within a reasonable time either party may resort to the court.

(4) If the court finds hardship it may, if reasonable,
    (a) terminate the contract at a date and on terms to be fixed, or
    (b) adapt the contract with a view to restoring its equilibrium.

CHAPTER 7 — NON-PERFORMANCE

Section 1: Non-Performance in General

Article 7.1.1   Non-performance defined
Non-performance is failure by a party to perform any of its obligations under the contract, including defective performance or late performance.

Article 7.1.2   Interference by the other party
A party may not rely on the non-performance of the other party to the extent that such non-performance was caused by the first party's act or omission or by another event for which the first party bears the risk.

Article 7.1.3   Withholding performance
(1) Where the parties are to perform simultaneously, either party may withhold performance until the other party tenders its performance.

(2) Where the parties are to perform consecutively, the party that is to perform later may withhold its performance until the first party has performed.

Article 7.1.4   Cure by non-performing party
(1) The non-performing party may, at its own expense, cure any non-performance, provided that
    (a) without undue delay, it gives notice indicating the proposed manner and timing of the cure;
    (b) cure is appropriate in the circumstances;
    (c) the aggrieved party has no legitimate interest in refusing cure; and
    (d) cure is effected promptly.

(2) The right to cure is not precluded by notice of termination.

(3) Upon effective notice of cure, rights of the aggrieved party that are inconsistent with the non-performing party's performance are suspended until the time for cure has expired.

(4) The aggrieved party may withhold performance pending cure.

(5) Notwithstanding cure, the aggrieved party retains the right to claim damages for delay as well as for any harm caused or not prevented by the cure.

Article 7.1.5   Additional period for performance
(1) In a case of non-performance the aggrieved party may by notice to the other party allow an additional period of time for performance.

(2) During the additional period the aggrieved party may withhold performance of its own reciprocal obligations and may claim damages but may not resort to any other remedy. If it receives notice from the other party that the latter will not perform within that period, or if upon expiry of that period due performance has not been made, the aggrieved party may resort to any of the remedies that may be available under this Chapter.

(3) Where in a case of delay in performance which is not fundamental the aggrieved party has given notice allowing an additional period of time of reasonable length, it may terminate the contract at the end of that period. If the additional period allowed is not of reasonable length it shall be extended to a reasonable length. The aggrieved party may in its notice provide that if the other party fails to perform within the period allowed by the notice the contract shall automatically terminate.

(4) Paragraph (3) does not apply where the obligation which has not been performed is only a minor part of the contractual obligation of the non-performing party.

Article 7.1.6   Exemption clauses

A clause which limits or excludes one party's liability for non-performance or which permits one party to render performance substantially different from what the other party reasonably expected may not be invoked if it would be grossly unfair to do so, having regard to the purpose of the contract.

Article 7.1.7   Force majeure

(1)   Non-performance by a party is excused if that party proves that the non-performance was due to an impediment beyond its control and that it could not reasonably be expected to have taken the impediment into account at the time of the conclusion of the contract or to have avoided or overcome it or its consequences.

(2)   When the impediment is only temporary, the excuse shall have effect for such period as is reasonable having regard to the effect of the impediment on the performance of the contract.

(3)   The party who fails to perform must give notice to the other party of the impediment and its effect on its ability to perform. If the notice is not received by the other party within a reasonable time after the party who fails to perform knew or ought to have known of the impediment, it is liable for damages resulting from such non-receipt.

(4)   Nothing in this article prevents a party from exercising a right to terminate the contract or to withhold performance or request interest on money due.

Section 2: Right to Performance

Article 7.2.1   Performance of monetary obligation

Where a party who is obliged to pay money does not do so, the other party may require payment.

Article 7.2.2   Performance of non-monetary obligation

Where a party who owes an obligation other than one to pay money does not perform, the other party may require performance, unless

(a)   performance is impossible in law or in fact;

(b)   performance or, where relevant, enforcement is unreasonably burdensome or expensive;

(c)   the party entitled to performance may reasonably obtain performance from another source;

(d)   performance is of an exclusively personal character; or

(e)   the party entitled to performance does not require performance within a reasonable time after it has, or ought to have, become aware of the non-performance.

Article 7.2.3   Repair and replacement of defective performance

The right to performance includes in appropriate cases the right to require repair, replacement, or other cure of defective performance. The provisions of Articles 7.2.1 and 7.2.2 apply accordingly.

Article 7.2.4   Judicial penalty

(1)   Where the court orders a party to perform, it may also direct that this party pay a penalty if it does not comply with the order.

(2)   The penalty shall be paid to the aggrieved party unless mandatory provisions of the law of the forum provide otherwise. Payment of the penalty to the aggrieved party does not exclude any claim for damages.

Article 7.2.5   Change of remedy

(1)   An aggrieved party who has required performance of a non-monetary obligation and who has not received performance within a period fixed or otherwise within a reasonable period of time may invoke any other remedy.

(2)   Where the decision of a court for performance of a non-monetary obligation cannot be enforced, the aggrieved party may invoke any other remedy.

Section 3: Termination

Article 7.3.1   Right to terminate the contract

(1)   A party may terminate the contract where the failure of the other party to perform an obligation under the contract amounts to a fundamental non-performance.

(2)   In determining whether a failure to perform an obligation amounts to a fundamental non-performance regard shall be had, in particular, to whether

(a)   the non-performance substantially deprives the aggrieved party of what it was entitled to expect under the contract unless the other party did not foresee and could not reasonably have foreseen such result;

(b)   strict compliance with the obligation which has not been performed is of essence under the contract;

(c)   the non-performance is intentional or reckless;

(d)   the non-performance gives the aggrieved party reason to believe that it cannot rely on the other party's future performance;

(e)   the non-performing party will suffer disproportionate loss as a result of the preparation or performance if the contract is terminated.

(3)   In the case of delay the aggrieved party may also terminate the contract if the other party fails to perform before the time allowed it under Article 7.1.5 has expired.

Article 7.3.2   Notice of termination

(1)   The right of a party to terminate the contract is exercised by notice to the other party.

(2)   If performance has been offered late or otherwise does not conform to the contract the aggrieved party will lose its right to terminate the contract unless it gives notice to the other party within a reasonable time after it has or ought to have become aware of the offer or of the non-conforming performance.

Article 7.3.3   Anticipatory non-performance

Where prior to the date for performance by one of the parties it is clear that there will be a fundamental non-performance by that party, the other party may terminate the contract.

Article 7.3.4   Adequate assurance of due performance

A party who reasonably believes that there will be a fundamental non-performance by the other party may demand adequate assurance of due performance and may meanwhile withhold its own performance. Where this assurance is not provided within a reasonable time the party demanding it may terminate the contract.

Article 7.3.5   Effects of termination in general

(1)   Termination of the contract releases both parties from their obligation to effect and to receive future performance.

(2)   Termination does not preclude a claim for damages for non-performance.

(3)   Termination does not affect any provision in the contract for the settlement of disputes or any other term of the contract which is to operate even after termination.

Article 7.3.6   Restitution with respect to contracts to be performed at one time

(1)   On termination of a contract to be performed at one time either party may claim restitution of whatever it has supplied under the contract, provided that such party concurrently makes restitution of whatever it has received under the contract.

(2)   If restitution in kind is not possible or appropriate, an allowance has to be made in money whenever reasonable.

(3)   The recipient of the performance does not have to make an allowance in money if the impossibility to make restitution in kind is attributable to the other party.

(4)   Compensation may be claimed for expenses reasonably required to preserve or maintain the performance received.

Article 7.3.7   Restitution with respect to contracts to be performed over a period of time

(1)   On termination of a contract to be performed over a period of time restitution can only be claimed for the period after termination has taken effect, provided the contract is divisible.

(2)   As far as restitution has to be made, the provisions of Article 7.3.6 apply.

Section 4: Damages

Article 7.4.1   Right to damages

Any non-performance gives the aggrieved party a right to damages either exclusively or in conjunction with any other remedies except where the non-performance is excused under these Principles.

Article 7.4.2   Full compensation

(1)   The aggrieved party is entitled to full compensation for harm sustained as a result of the non-performance. Such harm includes both any loss which it suffered and any gain of which it was deprived, taking into account any gain to the aggrieved party resulting from its avoidance of cost or harm.

(2)   Such harm may be non-pecuniary and includes, for instance, physical suffering or emotional distress.

Article 7.4.3   Certainty of harm

(1)   Compensation is due only for harm, including future harm, that is established with a reasonable degree of certainty.

(2)   Compensation may be due for the loss of a chance in proportion to the probability of its occurrence.

(3)   Where the amount of damages cannot be established with a sufficient degree of certainty, the assessment is at the discretion of the court.

Article 7.4.4   Foreseeability of harm

The non-performing party is liable only for harm which it foresaw or could reasonably have foreseen at the time of the conclusion of the contract as being likely to result from its non-performance.

Article 7.4.5   Proof in harm in case of replacement transaction

Where the aggrieved party has terminated the contract and has made a replacement transaction within a reasonable time and in a reasonable manner it may recover the difference between the contract price and the price of the replacement transaction as well as damages for any further harm.

Article 7.4.6   Proof of harm by current price

(1)   Where the aggrieved party has terminated the contract and has not made a replacement transaction but there is a current price for the performance contracted for, it may recover the difference between the contract price and the price current at the time the contract is terminated as well as damages for any further harm.

(2)   Current price is the price generally charged for goods delivered or services rendered in comparable circumstances at the place where the contract should have been performed or, if there is no current price at that place, the current price at such other place that appears reasonable to take as a reference.

Article 7.4.7   Harm due in part to aggrieved party

Where the harm is due in part to an act or omission of the aggrieved party or to another event for which that party bears the risk, the amount of damages shall be reduced to the extent that these factors have contributed to the harm, having regard to the conduct of each of the parties.

Article 7.4.8 Mitigation of harm

(1) The non-performing party is not liable for harm suffered by the aggrieved party to the extent that the harm could have been reduced by the latter party's taking reasonable steps.

(2) The aggrieved party is entitled to recover any expenses reasonably incurred in attempting to reduce the harm.

Article 7.4.9 Interest for failure to pay money

(1) If a party does not pay a sum of money when it falls due the aggrieved party is entitled to interest upon that sum from the time when payment is due to the time of payment whether or not the non-payment is excused.

(2) The rate of interest shall be the average bank short-term lending rate to prime borrowers prevailing for the currency of payment at the place for payment, or where no such rate exists at that place, then the same rate in the State of the currency of payment. In the absence of such a rate at either place the rate of interest shall be the appropriate rate fixed by the law of the State of the currency of payment.

(3) The aggrieved party is entitled to additional damages if the non-payment caused it a greater harm.

Article 7.4.10 Interest on damages

Unless otherwise agreed, interest on damages for non-performance of non-monetary obligations accrues as from the time of non-performance.

Article 7.4.11 Manner of monetary redress

(1) Damages are to be paid in a lump sum. However, they may be payable in instalments where the nature of the harm makes this appropriate.

(2) Damages to be paid in instalments may be indexed.

Article 7.4.12 Currency in which to assess damages

Damages are to be assessed either in the currency in which the monetary obligation was expressed or in the currency in which the harm was suffered, whichever is more appropriate.

Article 7.4.13 Agreed payment for non-performance

(1) Where the contract provides that a party who does not perform is to pay a specified sum to the aggrieved party for such non-performance, the aggrieved party is entitled to that sum irrespective of its actual harm.

(2) However, notwithstanding any agreement to the contrary the specified sum may be reduced to a reasonable amount where it is grossly excessive in relation to the harm resulting from the non-performance and to the other circumstances.

CHAPTER 8 — SET-OFF

Article 8.1 Conditions of set-off

(1) Where two parties owe each other money or other performances of the same kind, either of them ('the first party') may set off its obligation against that of its obligee ('the other party') if at the time of set-off,

(a) the first party is entitled to perform its obligation;

(b) the other party's obligation is ascertained as to its existence and amount and performance is due.

(2) If the obligations of both parties arise from the same contract, the first party may also set off its obligation against an obligation of the other party which is not ascertained as to its existence or to its amount.

Article 8.2 Foreign currency set-off

Where the obligations are to pay money in different currencies, the right of set-off may be exercised, provided that both currencies are freely convertible and the parties have not agreed that the first party shall pay only in a specified currency.

Article 8.3   Set-off by notice
The right of set-off is exercised by notice to the other party.

Article 8.4   Content of notice
(1)   The notice must specify the obligations to which it relates.

(2)   If the notice does not specify the obligation against which set-off is exercised, the other party may, within a reasonable time, declare to the first party the obligation to which set-off relates. If no such declaration is made, the set-off will relate to all the obligations proportionally.

Article 8.5   Effect of set-off
(1)   Set-off discharges the obligations.

(2)   If obligations differ in amount, set-off discharges the obligations up to the amount of the lesser obligation.

(3)   Set-off takes effect as from the time of notice.

CHAPTER 9 — ASSIGNMENT OF RIGHTS, TRANSFER OF OBLIGATIONS, ASSIGNMENT OF CONTRACTS

Section 1: Assignment of rights

Article 9.1.1   Definitions
'Assignment of a right' means the transfer by agreement from one person (the 'assignor') to another person (the 'assignee'), including transfer by way of security, of the assignor's right to payment of a monetary sum or other performance from a third person ('the obligor').

Article 9.1.2   Exclusions
This Section does not apply to transfers made under the special rules governing the transfers:

(a)   of instruments such as negotiable instruments, documents of title or financial instruments, or

(b)   of rights in the course of transferring a business.

Article 9.1.3   Assignability of non-monetary rights
A right to non-monetary performance may be assigned only if the assignment does not render the obligation significantly more burdensome.

Article 9.1.4   Partial assignment
(1)   A right to the payment of a monetary sum may be assigned partially.

(2)   A right to other performance may be assigned partially only if it is divisible, and the assignment does not render the obligation significantly more burdensome.

Article 9.1.5   Future rights
A future right is deemed to be transferred at the time of the agreement, provided the right, when it comes into existence, can be identified as the right to which the assignment relates.

Article 9.1.6   Rights assigned without individual specification
A number of rights may be assigned without individual specification, provided such rights can be identified as rights to which the assignment relates at the time of the assignment or when they come into existence.

Article 9.1.7   Agreement between assignor and assignee sufficient
(1)   A right is assigned by mere agreement between the assignor and the assignee, without notice to the obligor.

(2)   The consent of the obligor is not required unless the obligation in the circumstances is of an essentially personal character.

Article 9.1.8   Obligor's additional costs
The obligor has a right to be compensated by the assignor or the assignee for any additional costs caused by the assignment.

Article 9.1.9   Non-assignment clauses
(1)   The assignment of a right to the payment of a monetary sum is effective notwithstanding an agreement between the assignor and the obligor limiting or prohibiting such an assignment. However, the assignor may be liable to the obligor for breach of contract.

(2)   The assignment of a right to other performance is ineffective if it is contrary to an agreement between the assignor and the obligor limiting or prohibiting the assignment. Nevertheless, the assignment is effective if the assignee, at the time of the assignment, neither knew nor ought to have known of the agreement. The assignor may then be liable to the obligor for breach of contract.

Article 9.1.10   Notice to the obligor
(1)   Until the obligor receives a notice of the assignment from either the assignor or the assignee, it is discharged by paying the assignor.

(2)   After the obligor receives such a notice, it is discharged only by paying the assignee.

Article 9.1.11   Successive assignments
If the same right has been assigned by the same assignor to two or more successive assignees, the obligor is discharged by paying according to the order in which the notices were received.

Article 9.1.12   Adequate proof of assignment
(1)   If notice of the assignment is given by the assignee, the obligor may request the assignee to provide within a reasonable time adequate proof that the assignment has been made.

(2)   Until adequate proof is provided, the obligor may withhold payment.

(3)   Unless adequate proof is provided, notice is not effective.

(4)   Adequate proof includes, but is not limited to, any writing emanating from the assignor and indicating that the assignment has taken place.

Article 9.1.13   Defences and rights of set-off
(1)   The obligor may assert against the assignee all defences that the obligor could assert against the assignor.

(2)   The obligor may exercise against the assignee any right of set-off available to the obligor against the assignor up to the time notice of assignment was received.

Article 9.1.14   Rights related to the right assigned
The assignment of a right transfers to the assignee:

(a)   all the assignor's rights to payment or other performance under the contract in respect of the right assigned, and

(b)   all rights securing performance of the right assigned.

Article 9.1.15   Undertakings of the assignor
The assignor undertakes towards the assignee, except as otherwise disclosed to the assignee, that:

(a)   the assigned right exists at the time of the assignment, unless the right is a future right;

(b)   the assignor is entitled to assign the right;

(c)   the right has not been previously assigned to another assignee, and it is free from any right or claim from a third party;

(d)   the obligor does not have any defences;

(e)   neither the obligor nor the assignor has given notice of set-off concerning the assigned right and will not give any such notice;

(f)   the assignor will reimburse the assignee for any payment received from the obligor before notice of the assignment was given.

Section 2: Transfer of obligations

Article 9.2.1   Modes of transfer
An obligation to pay money or render other performance may be transferred from one person (the 'original obligor') to another person (the 'new obligor') either
(a)   by an agreement between the original obligor and the new obligor subject to Article 9.2.3, or
(b)   by an agreement between the obligee and the new obligor, by which the new obligor assumes the obligation.

Article 9.2.2   Exclusion
This Section does not apply to transfers of obligations made under the special rules governing transfers of obligations in the course of transferring a business.

Article 9.2.3   Requirement of obligee's consent to transfer
The transfer of an obligation by an agreement between the original obligor and the new obligor requires the consent of the obligee.

Article 9.2.4   Advance consent of obligee
(1)   The obligee may give its consent in advance.
(2)   If the obligee has given its consent in advance, the transfer of the obligation becomes effective when a notice of the transfer is given to the obligee or when the obligee acknowledges it.

Article 9.2.5   Discharge of original obligor
(1)   The obligee may discharge the original obligor.
(2)   The obligee may also retain the original obligor as an obligor in case the new obligor does not perform properly.
(3)   Otherwise the original obligor and the new obligor are jointly and severally liable.

Article 9.2.6   Third party performance
(1)   Without the obligee's consent, the obligor may contract with another person that this person will perform the obligation in place of the obligor, unless the obligation in the circumstances has an essentially personal character.
(2)   The obligee retains its claim against the obligor.

Article 9.2.7   Defences and rights of set-off
(1)   The new obligor may assert against the obligee all defences which the original obligor could assert against the obligee.
(2)   The new obligor may not exercise against the obligee any right of set-off available to the original obligor against the obligee.

Article 9.2.8   Rights related to the obligation transferred
(1)   The obligee may assert against the new obligor all its rights to payment or other performance under the contract in respect of the obligation transferred.
(2)   If the original obligor is discharged under Article 9.2.5(1), a security granted by any person other than the new obligor for the performance of the obligation is discharged, unless that other person agrees that it should continue to be available to the obligee.
(3)   Discharge of the original obligor also extends to any security of the original obligor given to the obligee for the performance of the obligation, unless the security is over an asset which is transferred as part of a transaction between the original obligor and the new obligor.

Section 3: Assignment of contracts

Article 9.3.1 Definitions

'Assignment of a contract' means the transfer by agreement from one person (the 'assignor') to another person (the 'assignee') of the assignor's rights and obligations arising out of a contract with another person (the 'other party').

Article 9.3.2 Exclusion

This Section does not apply to the assignment of contracts made under the special rules governing transfers of contracts in the course of transferring a business.

Article 9.3.3 Requirement of consent of the other party

The assignment of a contract requires the consent of the other party.

Article 9.3.4 Advance consent of the other party

(1) The other party may give its consent in advance.

(2) If the other party has given its consent in advance, the assignment of the contract becomes effective when a notice of the assignment is given to the other party or when the other party acknowledges it.

Article 9.3.5 Discharge of the assignor

(1) The other party may discharge the assignor.

(2) The other party may also retain the assignor as an obligor in case the assignee does not perform properly.

(3) Otherwise the assignor and the assignee are jointly and severally liable.

Article 9.3.6 Defences and rights of set-off

(1) To the extent that the assignment of a contract involves an assignment of rights, Article 9.1.13 applies accordingly.

(2) To the extent that the assignment of a contract involves a transfer of obligations, Article 9.2.7 applies accordingly.

Article 9.3.7 Rights transferred with the contract

(1) To the extent that the assignment of a contract involves an assignment of rights, Article 9.1.14 applies accordingly.

(2) To the extent that the assignment of a contract involves a transfer of obligations, Article 9.2.8 applies accordingly.

CHAPTER 10 — LIMITATION PERIODS

Article 10.1 Scope of the Chapter

(1) The exercise of rights governed by the Principles is barred by the expiration of a period of time, referred to as 'limitation period', according to the rules of this Chapter.

(2) This Chapter does not govern the time within which one party is required under the Principles, as a condition for the acquisition or exercise of its right, to give notice to the other party or to perform any act other than the institution of legal proceedings.

Article 10.2 Limitation periods

(1) The general limitation period is three years beginning on the day after the day the obligee knows or ought to know the facts as a result of which the obligee's right can be exercised.

(2) In any event, the maximum limitation period is ten years beginning on the day after the day the right can be exercised.

Article 10.3 Modification of limitation periods by the parties

(1) The parties may modify the limitation periods.

(2) However they may not

(a) shorten the general limitation period to less than one year;

(b)   shorten the maximum limitation period to less than four years;

(c)   extend the maximum limitation period to more than fifteen years.

Article 10.4   New limitation period by acknowledgement

(1)   Where the obligor before the expiration of the general limitation period acknowledges the right of the obligee, a new general limitation period begins on the day after the day of the acknowledgement.

(2)   The maximum limitation period does not begin to run again, but may be exceeded by the beginning of a new general limitation period under Article 10.2(1).

Article 10.5   Suspension by judicial proceedings

(1)   The running of the limitation period is suspended

(a)   when the obligee performs any act, by commencing judicial proceedings or in judicial proceedings already instituted, that is recognised by the law of the court as asserting the obligee's right against the obligor;

(b)   in the case of the obligor's insolvency when the obligee has asserted its rights in the insolvency proceedings; or

(c)   in the case of proceedings for dissolution of the entity which is the obligor when the obligee has asserted its rights in the dissolution proceedings.

(2)   Suspension lasts until a final decision has been issued or until the proceedings have been otherwise terminated.

Article 10.6   Suspension by arbitral proceedings

(1)   The running of the limitation period is suspended when the obligee performs any act, by commencing arbitral proceedings or in arbitral proceedings already instituted, that is recognised by the law of the arbitral tribunal as asserting the obligee's right against the obligor. In the absence of regulations for arbitral proceedings or provisions determining the exact date of the commencement of arbitral proceedings, the proceedings are deemed to commence on the date on which a request that the right in dispute should be adjudicated reaches the obligor.

(2)   Suspension lasts until a binding decision has been issued or until the proceedings have been otherwise terminated.

Article 10.7   Alternative dispute resolution

The provisions of Articles 10.5 and 10.6 apply with appropriate modifications to other proceedings whereby the parties request a third person to assist them in their attempt to reach an amicable settlement of their dispute.

Article 10.8   Suspension in case of force majeure, death or incapacity

(1)   Where the obligee has been prevented by an impediment that is beyond its control and that it could neither avoid nor overcome, from causing a limitation period to cease to run under the preceding Articles, the general limitation period is suspended so as not to expire before one year after the relevant impediment has ceased to exist.

(2)   Where the impediment consists of the incapacity or death of the obligee or obligor, suspension ceases when a representative for the incapacitated or deceased party or its estate has been appointed or a successor has inherited the respective party's position. The additional one-year period under paragraph (1) applies accordingly.

Article 10.9   Effects of expiration of limitation period

(1)   The expiration of the limitation period does not extinguish the right.

(2)   For the expiration of the limitation period to have effect, the obligor must assert it as a defence.

(3)   A right may still be relied on as a defence even though the expiration of the limitation period for that right has been asserted.

Article 10.10   Right of set-off
The obligee may exercise the right of set-off until the obligor has asserted the expiration of the limitation period.

Article 10.11   Restitution
Where there has been performance in order to discharge an obligation, there is no right of restitution merely because the limitation period has expired.

CHAPTER 11—PLURALITY OF OBLIGORS AND OF OBLIGEES

Section 1: Plurality of Obligors

Article 11.1.1   Definitions
When several obligors are bound by the same obligation towards an obligee:
    (a)   the obligations are joint and several when each obligor is bound for the whole obligation;
    (b)   the obligations are separate when each obligor is bound only for its share.

Article 11.1.2   Presumption of joint and several obligations
When several obligors are bound by the same obligation towards an obligee, they are presumed to be jointly and severally bound, unless the circumstances indicate otherwise.

Article 11.1.3   Obligee's rights against joint and several obligors
When obligors are jointly and severally bound, the obligee may require performance from any one of them, until full performance has been received.

Article 11.1.4   Availability of defences and rights of set-off
A joint and several obligor against whom a claim is made by the obligee may assert all the defences and rights of set-off that are personal to it or that are common to all the co-obligors, but may not assert defences or rights of set-off that are personal to one or several of the other co-obligors.

Article 11.1.5   Effect of performance or set-off
Performance or set-off by a joint and several obligor or set-off by the obligee against one joint and several obligor discharges the other obligors in relation to the obligee to the extent of the performance or set-off.

Article 11.1.6   Effect of release or settlement
    (1)   Release of one joint and several obligor, or settlement with one joint and several obligor, discharges all the other obligors for the share of the released or settling obligor, unless the circumstances indicate otherwise.
    (2)   When the other obligors are discharged for the share of the released obligor, they no longer have a contributory claim against the released obligor under Article 11.1.10.

Article 11.1.7   Effect of expiration or suspension of limitation period
    (1)   Expiration of the limitation period of the obligee's rights against one joint and several obligor does not affect:
    (a)   the obligations to the obligee of the other joint and several obligors; or
    (b)   the rights of recourse between the joint and several obligors under Article 11.1.10.
    (2)   If the obligee initiates proceedings under Articles 10.5, 10.6 or 10.7 against one joint and several obligor, the running of the limitation period is also suspended against the other joint and several obligors.

Article 11.1.8   Effect of judgment
    (1)   A decision by a court as to the liability to the obligee of one joint and several obligor does not affect:

(a)   the obligations to the obligee of the other joint and several obligors; or

(b)   the rights of recourse between the joint and several obligors under Article 11.1.10.

(2)   However, the other joint and several obligors may rely on such a decision, except if it was based on grounds personal to the obligor concerned. In such a case, the rights of recourse between the joint and several obligors under Article 11.1.10 are affected accordingly.

Article 11.1.9   Apportionment among joint and several obligors

As among themselves, joint and several obligors are bound in equal shares, unless the circumstances indicate otherwise.

Article 11.1.10   Extent of contributory claim

A joint and several obligor who has performed more than its share may claim the excess from any of the other obligors to the extent of each obligor's unperformed share.

Article 11.1.11   Rights of the obligee

(1)   A joint and several obligor to whom Article 11.1.10 applies may also exercise the rights of the obligee, including all rights securing their performance, to recover the excess from all or any of the other obligors to the extent of each obligor's unperformed share.

(2)   An obligee who has not received full performance retains its rights against the co-obligors to the extent of the unperformed part, with precedence over co-obligors exercising contributory claims.

Article 11.1.12   Defences in contributory claims

A joint and several obligor against whom a claim is made by the co-obligor who has performed the obligation:

(a)   may raise any common defences and rights of set-off that were available to be asserted by the co-obligor against the obligee;

(b)   may assert defences which are personal to itself;

(c)   may not assert defences and rights of set-off which are personal to one or several of the other co-obligors.

Article 11.1.13   Inability to recover

If a joint and several obligor who has performed more than that obligor's share is unable, despite all reasonable efforts, to recover contribution from another joint and several obligor, the share of the others, including the one who has performed, is increased proportionally.

Section 2: Plurality of Obligees

Article 11.2.1   Definitions

When several obligees can claim performance of the same obligation from an obligor:

(a)   the claims are separate when each obligee can only claim its share;

(b)   the claims are joint and several when each obligee can claim the whole performance;

(c)   the claims are joint when all obligees have to claim performance together.

Article 11.2.2   Effects of joint and several claims

Full performance of an obligation in favour of one of the joint and several obligees discharges the obligor towards the other obligees.

Article 11.2.3   Availability of defences against joint and several obligees

(1)   The obligor may assert against any of the joint and several obligees all the defences and rights of set-off that are personal to its relationship to that obligee or that it can assert against all the co-obligees, but may not assert defences and rights

of set-off that are personal to its relationship to one or several of the other co-obligees.

(2) The provisions of Articles 11.1.5, 11.1.6, 11.1.7 and 11.1.8 apply, with appropriate adaptations, to joint and several claims.

Article 11.2.4 Allocation between joint and several obligees

(1) As among themselves, joint and several obligees are entitled to equal shares, unless the circumstances indicate otherwise.

(2) An obligee who has received more than its share must transfer the excess to the other obligees to the extent of their respective shares.

INDEX OF MATERIALS